COMPLETE MOTORING
ATLAS
OF AUSTRALIA

GW00417745

Contents

Touring Australia	iv
Quick find guide	x
Australia-wide distance chart	xii
Tasmania distance chart	xiv
Inter-city route maps	xv

NEW SOUTH WALES xviii

Key map	3
Sydney	4

MAPS

Central Sydney	5
Metro Sydney & Surrounds	6
New South Wales	12
City & town centres	21
Albury, Armidale, Ballina, Batemans Bay	21
Bathurst, Berrima, Bowral, Broken Hill	22
Byron Bay, Cessnock, Coffs Harbour, Cooma	23
Cootamundra, Dubbo, Forster–Tuncurry, Gosford	24
Goulburn, Grafton, Griffith, Katoomba	25
Lismore, Maitland, Mudgee, Newcastle	26
Nowra, Orange, Port Macquarie, Queanbeyan	27
Singleton, Tamworth, Taree, Tweed Heads	28
Ulladulla, Wagga Wagga, Wollongong, Yass	29

AUSTRALIAN CAPITAL TERRITORY 30

Australian Capital Territory map	31
Canberra	32

MAPS

Central Canberra	33
Metro Canberra	34

VICTORIA 36

Key map	39
Melbourne	40

MAPS

Central Melbourne	41
Metro Melbourne & Surrounds	42
Victoria	48
City & town centres	59
Bairnsdale, Ballarat, Benalla, Bendigo	59
Castlemaine, Colac, Geelong, Hamilton	60
Horsham, Lakes Entrance, Mildura, Morwell	61
Portland, Sale, Shepparton, Stawell	62
Traralgon, Wangaratta, Warrnambool, Wodonga	63

SOUTH AUSTRALIA   64

Key map   65
Adelaide   66

MAPS

Central Adelaide   67
Metro Adelaide & Surrounds   68
South Australia   72
City & town centres   84

  Mount Gambier, Murray Bridge,
  Port Augusta, Port Lincoln   84
  Port Pirie, Renmark, Victor Harbor,
  Whyalla   85

WESTERN AUSTRALIA   86

Key map   87
Perth   88

MAPS

Central Perth   89
Metro Perth & Surrounds   90
Western Australia   94
City & town centres   104

  Albany, Augusta, Broome,
  Bunbury   104
  Busselton, Carnarvon, Collie,
  Esperance   105
  Fremantle, Geraldton, Kalgoorlie,
  Kununurra   106
  Mandurah, Norseman, Northam,
  Port Hedland   107

NORTHERN TERRITORY   108

Key map   109
Darwin   110

MAPS

Central Darwin   111
Metro Darwin & Surrounds   112
Northern Territory   116
City & town centres   122

  Alice Springs, Kakadu National Park,
  Katherine, Palmerston   122
  Tennant Creek, Kata Tjuta (The Olgas),
  Uluru (Ayers Rock),
  Yulara (Ayers Rock Resort)   123

QUEENSLAND   124

Key map   127
Brisbane   128

MAPS

Central Brisbane   129
Metro Brisbane & Surrounds   130
Queensland   136
City & town centres   148

  Airlie Beach, Bundaberg, Cairns,
  Gladstone   148
  Gympie, Hervey Bay, Mackay,
  Maroochydore   149
  Maryborough, Mount Isa,
  Noosa Heads, Rockhampton   150
  Surfers Paradise, Toowoomba,
  Townsville, Warwick   151

TASMANIA   152

Key map   153
Hobart   154

MAPS

Central Hobart   155
Metro Hobart & Surrounds   156
Tasmania   160
City & town centres   164

  Bicheno, Burnie, Devonport,
  George Town   164
  Huonville, Launceston,
  Port Arthur, Queenstown   165
  Richmond, Strahan, Swansea,
  Ulverstone   166

Planning your trip   167
Motoring hints   168
Motoring survival   169

INDEX   170

Touring Australia

GEOGRAPHY

Australia is immense, diverse and intensely beautiful. The mainland stretches roughly 3300 kilometres from north to south and 4000 kilometres from east to west, with 8222 islands lying just off the coast. The landscape ranges from monsoonal wetlands in the north, tropical rainforests and coral reefs in the north-east, red deserts and salt lakes in the central outback to temperate forests, coastal plains and mountain ranges (some with winter snowfields) in the south-east. In the south-west, the sandstone cliffs of the vast Nullarbor Plain drop into the Great Australian Bight, where southern right whales calve and rest.

Some of the world's great deserts are in Australia, broken by spectacular rocky ranges and outcrops that stand high in the surrounding flatness. The desert landscape holds many surprises: hot springs, the overnight appearance of wildflowers after rain, and the arrival of masses of birds at large ephemeral lakes.

Tourism Australia has identified 16 outstanding Australian National Landscapes, each is a stunning example of nature at its best. Among them are the Australian Alps, rising from northern Victoria through to southern New South Wales; Australia's Coastal Wilderness stretching from East Gippsland in Victoria to southern New South Wales; Australia's Green Cauldron deep in northern New South Wales; Australia's Red Centre encompassing much of southern Northern Territory, spreading through the Flinders Ranges and eastern South Australia; the Great Ocean Road winding along Victoria's south coast; the Greater Blue Mountains in New South Wales; The Kimberley in north-west Western Australia; Kakadu National Park in the Northern Territory; Kangaroo Island off the South Australian coast; and the Ningaloo Coast and Shark Bay area in Western Australia.

In addition to this, Australia has 19 listings on the World Heritage List, some of which are made up of multiple areas. These listings include outstanding sites of natural beauty, such as Uluru–Kata Tjuta National Park, the Great Barrier Reef and the Tasmanian Wilderness, and cultural treasures such as the Sydney Opera House, the Royal Exhibition Building and Carlton Gardens in Melbourne, and 11 convict sites across Australia.

There are more than 10,000 listings in the National Reserve System (Australia's network of protected areas), including national parks, Indigenous protected areas and conservation reserves, covering more than 17 per cent of the continent. Protection of special areas continues offshore, with marine protected areas covering 3.1 million square kilometres. So, wherever you travel, whether on land or water, you will encounter many of Australia's wonders and treasures.

Touring large parts of this incredible country usually requires time and planning, but the rewards are substantial for well-prepared travellers with a sense of adventure. Australia's capital cities are linked by sealed highways which are suitable for all vehicles. Rural areas, or 'the bush', can be accessed from networks of roads, although four-wheel drive vehicles may be necessary in some areas.

CLIMATE

Australia's diverse environments reflect its varying climate. Depending on where and when you travel, the climate can change dramatically. Generally, it is hottest in December and January. In the midwinter months of July and August the Australian alps are covered in snow and nights in the desert can fall well below freezing; even in summer, desert nights can be cold.

About 40 per cent of the country lies north of the Tropic of Capricorn, experiencing tropical weather with very high humidity and monsoonal deluges during the wet season (November–April). The dry season (May–October) is warm to hot, but not wet.

South of the Tropic of Capricorn, the climate becomes more temperate and major population centres such as Sydney, Brisbane and Perth generally have mild winters. The seasons are not usually as defined as they are in some Northern Hemisphere areas, except in highland regions.

The island of Tasmania, in the south, is on average the coldest and wettest state. The best times to visit are during spring and summer.

NATIVE ANIMALS

Australia's geographical isolation is believed to be the main reason for the existence of so many animal species not found elsewhere. Nearly half of the mammal species found here are marsupials, a group with pouches for their suckling young. The most commonly found marsupials are kangaroos, wallabies, koalas, wombats and possums. There are a host of others that are less

Lamington National Park, Queensland

well known, such as dunnarts, bandicoots, gliders, quokkas and the carnivorous Tasmanian devil.

Since many of Australia's native animals are shy night-time creatures, the nocturnal houses at zoos and animal parks provide the best opportunities to see them.

There are more than 860 bird species in Australia; kookaburras, colourful rosellas and the noisy cockatoos are among the best known. Some have adapted well to urban life and are frequently seen in local parks.

Australia's largest birds are the flightless emus and cassowaries. Shaggy brown emus, slightly smaller than an ostrich, can sometimes be spotted when driving on country roads. The colourful cassowaries are endangered and live in northern Queensland rainforests. Drive carefully if you see signs warning that cassowaries are around and if you see one when on foot give it plenty of room as they have been known to attack with sharp claws if they feel threatened.

DANGEROUS CREATURES

Visitors sometimes express concern about Australia's poisonous and dangerous creatures. However, the number of people injured or killed by native animals is quite small, so try not to let fear of these creatures affect your enjoyment of Australia. The risk is minimal if precautions are taken; do not antagonise, hurt or try to kill any wildlife, and, as much as possible, give potentially dangerous animals a wide berth.

Australia has about 140 species of land snakes including the most poisonous land snakes in the world. Many

Incomparable Australia

▶ *the world's smallest continent and largest island*

▶ *the only country to govern a whole continent and its outlying islands*

▶ *averages less than three people per square kilometre*

▶ *the world's lowest and flattest continent with an average elevation of only 330 metres*

▶ *the sixth largest country in the world after Russia, Canada, China, USA and Brazil*

▶ *the Great Dividing Range is the fifth longest mountain range in the world*

▶ *the world's oldest fossilised life forms, about 3.4 billion years old, were found in Western Australia*

WORLD RECORDS

▶ *Uluru (Ayers Rock), Northern Territory, largest monolith*

▶ *Great Barrier Reef, Queensland, longest coral reef*

▶ *Nullarbor Plain, South Australia–Western Australia, largest flat bedrock surface*

▶ *Simpson Desert, South Australia / Northern Territory / Queensland, largest sand ridge desert*

▶ *Mount Augustus, Western Australia, largest exposed rocky outcrop*

are highly venomous but they are nearly all shy and will slither away or stay still if they feel the vibrations of a human approaching. Long trousers, thick socks and stout shoes are recommended when walking in the bush.

Some Australian spiders are also venomous, including the Sydney funnel-web and the distinctive red-back. Since effective antivenene was created, deaths from these creatures are now almost non-existent.

Generally, if someone is bitten by a venomous snake or spider, first-aid treatment is a compression bandage, keeping the patient or limb still and seeking urgent medical attention. The exception to using this treatment is for a red-back spider bite: do not bandage the bite but apply ice instead and use painkillers while seeking urgent medical attention. Try to identify or remember details of the creature, as it could help with identifying the appropriate antivenene.

The waters off northern Queensland and the northern coastline harbour box jellyfish. These particularly dangerous creatures keep swimmers out of the ocean in the summer months. Beaches are usually signposted with stinger warning signs. The box jellyfish has long, fine, stinging tentacles that drift some way from the creature and wrap themselves around a victim causing severe pain, paralysis and sometimes death. Paddling in just a few centimetres of water in these areas is extremely dangerous.

The tiny, clear Irukandji jellyfish are found in similar areas, are almost as poisonous and cause excruciating pain. Even outside of the normal 'stinger season' (October–May) it is advisable to swim in stinger suits or wetsuits or stick to swimming on beaches with stinger nets because jellyfish can be present in tropical waters year-round.

Also in northern areas, beware of saltwater crocodiles or 'salties'. They can grow up to 6 metres long, making them the world's largest living reptiles. They are found in both saltwater and freshwater rivers, creeks, estuaries and gorges, and can be aggressive. Salties can lie still and hidden in the water, but they move with astonishing speed. Extreme caution must be taken when near the water in these parts.

Wasps, bees, ants and mosquitoes are found throughout Australia. Whilst not generally harmful (except to people with allergies), their sting will cause minor pain and discomfort. Ticks can also be a problem in Australia, especially if found on small children. A reliable way to remove a tick is by using tweezers, removing the whole body. Antihistamine may be helpful for insect bites and stings.

NATIVE PLANTS

Australia's potpourri of native plants includes about 18,000 species of flowering plants, about 500 species of ferns, conifers and cycads, as well as hundreds of thousands of species of mosses, algae, lichens and fungi.

The most prevalent tree type is the eucalyptus or gum. There are more than 700 eucalyptus species and they are found in almost every environment in the country – from gums eking out a living in the harshest deserts, to the snow gums glistening in the alps. They also count among their ranks some of the tallest trees in the world – the mountain ashes of Victoria and Tasmania that can grow to 100 metres. Some eucalypts, such as ash, box, mahogany, stringybark, ironbark, peppermint, lemon-scented and mallee, are named for their timber type.

Many of the forests that covered large sections of New South Wales and Queensland were logged by early settlers for timber and to clear land for pasture. What remains is mostly restricted to small protected pockets.

Staghorns, elkhorns, orchids and bird's nest ferns grow in the treetops of the rainforest canopies. Below, the rainforest floors are green worlds of dampness: dripping leaves, wet ground and decaying logs covered with mosses, lichens and fungi.

Alpine regions provide a completely different floral environment. On the lower slopes, savannah woodlands dominate with an understorey rich in herbaceous plants including dandelions, buttercups and orchids. In the higher, colder woodlands are the manna gum and black sally, with stunted snow gums near the snowline.

Across much of Australia, native grasses and spinifex dominate broad swathes of the land. Spinifex is tough and often as sharp as needles. It is highly flammable, and lightning strikes in spinifex country will often start huge outback fires that in turn rejuvenate the land. Many of Australia's native plant species have evolved with fire and need fire or smoke to regenerate or reseed.

Australia's wildflowers are distinctively beautiful. They include banksias, boronias, bottlebrushes, billy buttons, Christmas bushes, Sturt's desert peas, everlasting daisies, grevilleas, orchids, kangaroo-paw, waratahs and wattles. Some parts of Australia are well known for their spring and summer wildflower displays. The south-west of Western Australia,

Streeters Jetty, Broome, Western Australia

the Flinders Ranges of South Australia and the Grampians of Victoria are particularly famous for their spectacular displays.

HISTORY

For some 50,000 years or so before European settlement, Australia was inhabited by hundreds of Aboriginal and Torres Strait Islander tribes, and the histories of the continent and its landscapes were told and recorded by these Indigenous people. The stories varied between different tribes. None were written down, rather they were spoken (in hundreds of different languages), sung, danced, painted on bark, rocks or inside caves or sculpted on the ground.

There are no accurate figures for the Indigenous population before European settlement but estimates range from 300,000 to over 1 million.

The northern shores were visited by Asian sailors and traders for hundreds of years before Dutchman Willem Jansz landed on Australian soil near the Wenlock River in Queensland in 1606. The most notable voyage by the Dutch was that of Abel Tasman, who sailed around Tasmania and to New Zealand in 1642. The first Englishman to land was William Dampier, a buccaneer who came ashore in 1688, in the vicinity of the Western Australian town that is now named after him.

In 1770 Captain James Cook became the first European to navigate the south-eastern coastline. He wrote a favourable report about the land he named New South Wales. This was remembered when the British parliament needed somewhere to establish a new penal colony, to relieve the overcrowded British prisons. In 1788, the 11 ships of the First Fleet, carrying a motley collection of sailors, soldiers and convicts, under the command of Captain Arthur Phillip, sailed into Sydney Harbour.

The first few years were very difficult for the little settlement, with starvation always threatening until farms could be established in the unfamiliar land. The Aboriginal population also suffered greatly, subjected to murder, rape, the devastating introduction of diseases for which they had no immunity, and ultimately the dispossession of their land.

The Second Fleet arrived in 1790. A year later the arrival of the Third Fleet increased the British population to 4000.

For the first 20 years, the spread of settlement was slow. Sydney was established and there were small penal settlements at Norfolk Island and Hobart. Expansion inland was restricted until the formidable barrier of the Blue Mountains, west of Sydney, was crossed by Europeans in 1813.

This feat began a tide of exploration and movement of people across the land to take up vast rural holdings where they introduced cattle, sheep and crops such as wheat. Explorers whose names have gone down in history and folklore, such as Charles Sturt, Ludwig Leichhardt, Augustus Gregory, and Burke and Wills, made incredible journeys across this uncharted country.

Australia's geographical shape wasn't confirmed until Matthew Flinders made his circumnavigation in 1803. Flinders was also the first person to use the name 'Australia' in his three-volume work *Voyage to Terra Australis*.

Initially, the whole landmass, except Western Australia (which was created as an independent colony in 1829), was known as New South Wales. This huge entity was gradually reduced as the settlements established at Hobart, Brisbane, Adelaide and Melbourne became colonies in their own right.

In 1851, gold was discovered near Orange in New South Wales. This was the first of many discoveries of gold and other sought-after metals during the second half of the century. As miners rushed to the diggings, the population boom opened up Australia. Wealth from the mines helped to build inland cities and, when the gold rushes were over, many of the miners stayed, turning to farming and other trades.

GOVERNMENT

Australia's political stability has helped it rank as the ninth most peaceful country in the world in the Global Peace Index, published by the Institute for Economics and Peace. However, it is also considered by some to be one of the most over-governed nations in the world, with a complex three-tiered system of government – federal, state and local – which evolved from when the country was a collection of six self-governing colonies.

Although first discussed 50 years before, it was not until 1 January 1901 that the Commonwealth of Australia finally came into being. Rivalry between Sydney and Melbourne (which to some extent survives today) led to a new national capital being built in the specially created Australian Capital Territory. This had to be established 'no less than 100 miles from Sydney'. In 1911 land was acquired by the Commonwealth Government in the Brindabella Ranges, 290 kilometres (180 miles) south-west of Sydney, and a competition was launched for the design of a new capital city, Canberra.

The first Parliament House building was completed in 1927, and was situated among grazing sheep. Although it was only intended as a temporary home for the Parliament, it was used for 60 years until a more permanent one was completed in 1988.

As the nation's capital, Canberra is the site of national monuments and institutions, many of them attractively placed around the shores of Lake Burley Griffin.

THE PEOPLE

In the years before World War II, non-Indigenous Australians were primarily of English, Scottish or Irish descent, a mix of free settlers and descendants of the convicts. There was also a minority of people from countries such as China, who had made their way to Australia as prospectors during the 19th-century gold rushes, or as refugees.

The post-war immigration scheme, with the theme 'populate or perish', changed the ethnic mix, bringing in thousands of refugees from Italy, Greece, Yugoslavia, Germany and other parts of war-torn Europe; a second wave of refugees and migrants came from Asia during the Vietnam War in the 1960s and 1970s. Immigration continues to play an important role in Australia, making up about 50 per cent of the country's annual population growth.

Australia today is a diverse, truly multicultural society. More than 28 per cent of Australians are foreign-born and more than 40 per cent are of mixed cultural origin. Of the more than 300 languages spoken among Australians, English is the most popular followed by Mandarin, Italian, Arabic, Cantonese and Greek.

This rich cultural heritage is reflected in Australia's food and festivals. Australia is also a religiously diverse community, encompassing Aboriginal traditions as well as Christian, Muslim, Jewish, Sikh, Hindu and Buddhist faiths.

ECONOMY

Mining and agriculture remain important to the Australian economy. The mining industry is Australia's largest export earner, with mining exports accounting for nearly 50 per cent of the annual value of total exports of goods and services in recent years. Australia is among the world's largest producers of coal, gold, silver, nickel, lead and uranium.

Australia has more than 135,000 farms that are dedicated to producing agricultural products including wool, meat, milk, wheat, rice, fruit and vegetables. Australian farmers produce more than 90 per cent of Australia's food supply, and some 60 per cent of total agricultural production.

Tourism is a significant industry that generates more than $80 billion a year.

Cape Byron Lighthouse, Byron Bay, New South Wales

MAP SYMBOLS

Metro Maps

━━ M31 ━━	Freeway with National Highway Route Marker
━━ M7 ━━	Tollway with Motorway Route Marker
━ 1 ━ A1 ━ 1 ━	Highway, sealed, with National Highway Route Marker
-------------	Highway, unsealed
━ C141 ━ 26 ━	Arterial road, sealed, with State Route Marker
·············	Arterial road, unsealed
———————	Collector road, sealed
--------------	Collector road, unsealed
———————	Local road
▼ 12 ▼	Total kilometres between two points
———————	Railway
SYDNEY	State capital city
ROSEVILLE	Suburb
✛	Landing ground
▲	Hill, mountain or peak

Capital City & Town Maps

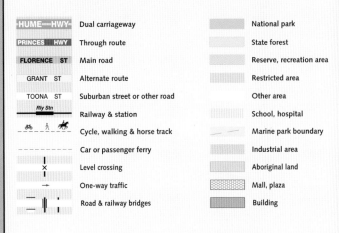

HUME HWY	Dual carriageway			National park
PRINCES HWY	Through route			State forest
FLORENCE ST	Main road			Reserve, recreation area
GRANT ST	Alternate route			Restricted area
TOONA ST	Suburban street or other road			Other area
Rly Stn	Railway & station			School, hospital
	Cycle, walking & horse track			Marine park boundary
	Car or passenger ferry			Industrial area
	Level crossing			Aboriginal land
	One-way traffic			Mall, plaza
	Road & railway bridges			Building

M3	Motorway Route Marker
1 A1	National Highway Marker
94 A10	State Highway Marker
1	Metroad Route Marker
5 2	Tourist Route Marker

◉	Aboriginal community	🏛	Library
✈	Airport		Lighthouse
✴	Ambulance station	※ ※	Lookout, 360° & 180°
	Boat ramp		Masonic lodge
	Bowling club	▲	Monument
▲	Camping ground		Motel
	Caravan park	⚘	Picnic area
P	Car park	★	Place of interest
∩	Cave		Place of worship
	College - private		Playground
	College - public	★	Police station
Cncl Off ■	Council office	✉	Post office
	Court house	**30**	Road distance city centre
▽	Drive-in	⁖	Ruins
✉	Express Post		School - private
F	Fire station		School - public
	Forest recreation area	✛	Scouts
♣	Girl Guides		Service station
St Lucia	Golf course	🛒	Shopping centre
H	Hall		Speed camera - fixed
	Highway exit	SES	State Emergency Service
✚	Hospital		Swimming pool
	Hotel	☎	Telephone
Tungatinah	Hydro-electric power station		Toilets
	Visitor information	ⓦ	Weighbridge
	Kindergarten		Winery
✛	Landing ground		

State Maps

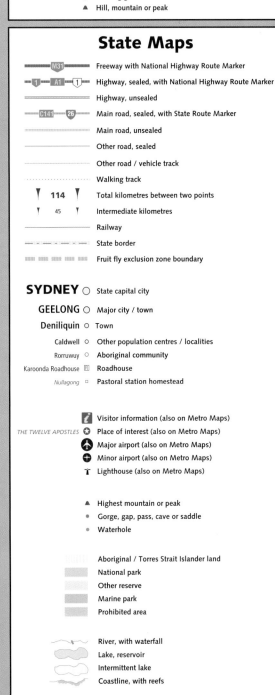

━━ M31 ━━	Freeway with National Highway Route Marker
━ 1 ━ A1 ━ 1 ━	Highway, sealed, with National Highway Route Marker
———————	Highway, unsealed
━ C141 ━ 26 ━	Main road, sealed, with State Route Marker
·············	Main road, unsealed
———————	Other road, sealed
·············	Other road / vehicle track
·············	Walking track
▼ 114 ▼	Total kilometres between two points
▼ 45 ▼	Intermediate kilometres
———————	Railway
— — —	State border
▦ ▦ ▦	Fruit fly exclusion zone boundary
SYDNEY ○	State capital city
GEELONG ○	Major city / town
Deniliquin ○	Town
Caldwell ○	Other population centres / localities
Rorruwuy ○	Aboriginal community
Karoonda Roadhouse 🅷	Roadhouse
Nullagong □	Pastoral station homestead
	Visitor information (also on Metro Maps)
THE TWELVE APOSTLES ✪	Place of interest (also on Metro Maps)
✈	Major airport (also on Metro Maps)
⊕	Minor airport (also on Metro Maps)
	Lighthouse (also on Metro Maps)
▲	Highest mountain or peak
•	Gorge, gap, pass, cave or saddle
•	Waterhole
	Aboriginal / Torres Strait Islander land
	National park
	Other reserve
	Marine park
	Prohibited area
	River, with waterfall
	Lake, reservoir
	Intermittent lake
	Coastline, with reefs

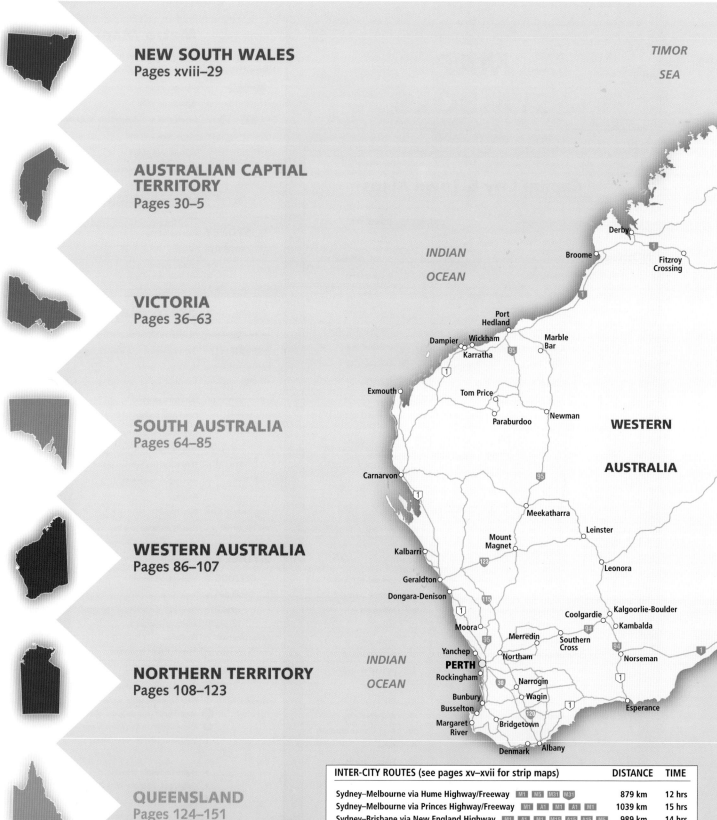

NEW SOUTH WALES
Pages xviii–29

AUSTRALIAN CAPTIAL TERRITORY
Pages 30–5

VICTORIA
Pages 36–63

SOUTH AUSTRALIA
Pages 64–85

WESTERN AUSTRALIA
Pages 86–107

NORTHERN TERRITORY
Pages 108–123

QUEENSLAND
Pages 124–151

TASMANIA
Pages 152–166

TIMOR SEA

INDIAN OCEAN

Derby
Broome
Fitzroy Crossing

Port Hedland
Dampier Wickham Marble Bar
Karratha

Exmouth
Tom Price
Paraburdoo Newman

WESTERN AUSTRALIA

Carnarvon

Meekatharra
Leinster

Kalbarri
Mount Magnet
Leonora

Geraldton
Dongara-Denison
Coolgardie Kalgoorlie-Boulder
Moora Merredin Kambalda
Southern Cross
Yanchep Northam
Norseman
PERTH
Rockingham Narrogin
Bunbury Wagin
Busselton Esperance
Margaret River Bridgetown
Denmark Albany

INDIAN OCEAN

INTER-CITY ROUTES (see pages xv–xvii for strip maps)	DISTANCE	TIME
Sydney–Melbourne via Hume Highway/Freeway M1 M5 M31 M31	879 km	12 hrs
Sydney–Melbourne via Princes Highway/Freeway M1 A1 M1 A1 M1	1039 km	15 hrs
Sydney–Brisbane via New England Highway M1 A1 M1 A15 A15 M5	989 km	14 hrs
Melbourne–Adelaide via Western & Dukes highways M8 A8 M1 A1	729 km	8 hrs
Melbourne–Adelaide via Princes Highway M1 A1 B1 M1 A1	911 km	11 hrs
Melbourne–Brisbane via Newell Highway M1 M39 A39 A39 A2 M5	1676 km	20 hrs
Darwin–Adelaide via Stuart Highway 1 87 A87 A1	3026 km	31 hrs
Adelaide–Perth via Eyre & Great Eastern highways A1 1 94	2700 km	32 hrs
Adelaide–Sydney via Sturt & Hume highways A20 A20 M31 M5 M1	1415 km	19 hrs
Perth–Darwin via Great Northern Highway 95 1	4032 km	46 hrs
Sydney–Brisbane via Pacific Highway M1 A1 M1 A1 M1	936 km	14 hrs
Brisbane–Darwin via Warrego Highway M5 A2 66 87 1	3406 km	39 hrs
Brisbane–Cairns via Bruce Highway M1 A1	1703 km	20 hrs
Hobart–Launceston via Midland Highway 1	197 km	3 hrs
Hobart–Devonport via Midland & Bass highways 1 B52 1	279 km	4 hrs

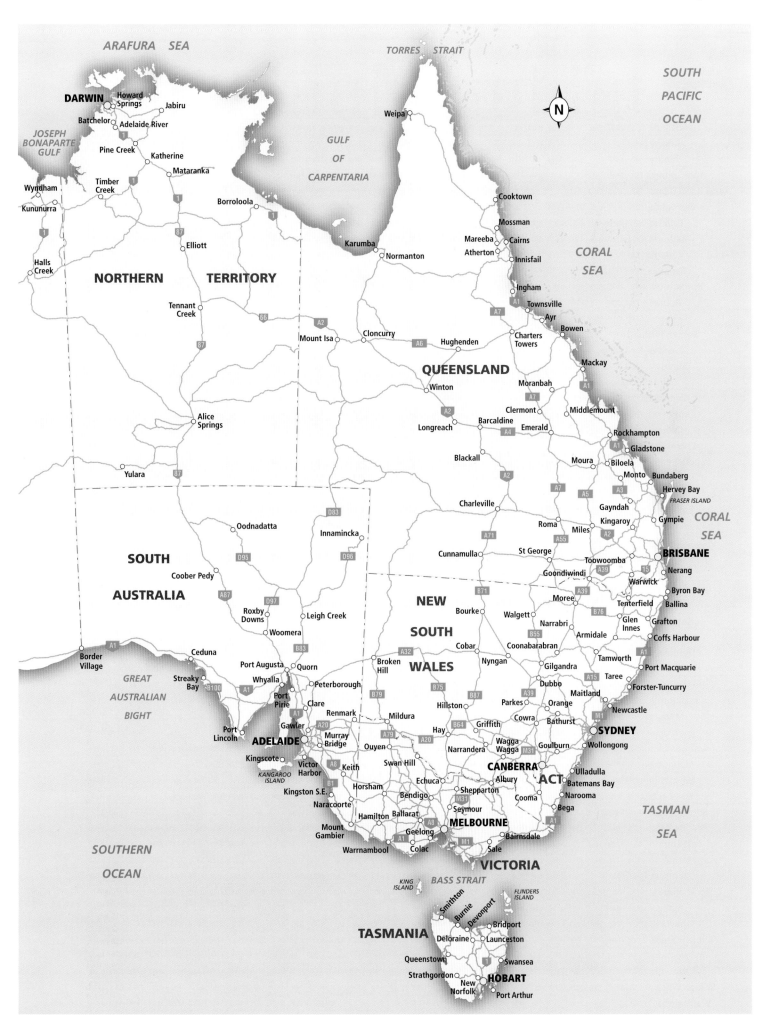

0 100 200 300 400 500 km

ARAFURA SEA

SOUTH

PACIFIC

OCEAN

TORRES STRAIT

DARWIN
Howard Springs
Batchelor
Adelaide River
Jabiru

JOSEPH
BONAPARTE
GULF

Pine Creek

Katherine

Mataranka

Wyndham

Timber
Creek

Kununurra

Halls
Creek

Elliott

GULF
OF
CARPENTARIA

Weipa

Cooktown
Mossman
Mareeba Cairns
Atherton Innisfail

CORAL
SEA

Borroloola

NORTHERN   TERRITORY

Tennant
Creek

Karumba

Normanton

Ingham
Townsville
Ayr
Bowen

Mount Isa   Cloncurry

Hughenden

Charters
Towers

Mackay

QUEENSLAND

Winton

Moranbah

Alice
Springs

Longreach

Barcaldine

Clermont

Middlemount

Emerald

Rockhampton
Gladstone

Yulara

Blackall

Moura
Biloela
Monto
Bundaberg
Hervey Bay
FRASER ISLAND

Oodnadatta

Innamincka

Charleville

Gayndah
Kingaroy   Gympie

CORAL
SEA

SOUTH

AUSTRALIA

Cunnamulla

Roma Miles

St George

Coober Pedy

Toowoomba

BRISBANE
Nerang

Goondiwindi
Warwick
Byron Bay
Ballina

Roxby
Downs

Leigh Creek

Moree

Tenterfield

NEW

Bourke

Walgett

Narrabri

Glen
Innes

Grafton

Woomera

SOUTH

Coonabarabran

Armidale

Coffs Harbour

Ceduna

Broken
Hill

Cobar

Nyngan

Gilgandra

Tamworth

Taree

Port Macquarie

Border
Village

Streaky
Bay

Port Augusta
Quorn

WALES

Coonamble

Dubbo

Maitland

Forster-Tuncurry

Whyalla

Peterborough

Hillston

Parkes

Orange

Newcastle

Port
Pirie
Clare

Renmark

Mildura

Hay

Griffith

Cowra

Bathurst

SYDNEY

GREAT

AUSTRALIAN

BIGHT

Port
Lincoln

Gawler

Murray
Bridge

Ouyen

Narrandera

Wagga
Wagga

Goulburn

Wollongong

ADELAIDE

Kingscote

Victor
Harbor

Keith

Swan Hill

CANBERRA

Ulladulla

KANGAROO
ISLAND

Kingston S.E.

Horsham

Echuca

Shepparton

Albury

ACT

Batemans Bay

Cooma

Narooma

Naracoorte

Bendigo

Seymour

Bega

TASMAN

Hamilton

Ballarat

SEA

Mount
Gambier

Geelong

MELBOURNE

SOUTHERN

Warrnambool

Colac

Sale

Bairnsdale

OCEAN

VICTORIA

KING
ISLAND

BASS STRAIT

FLINDERS
ISLAND

Smithton
Burnie
Devonport
Bridport

TASMANIA

Deloraine

Launceston

Queenstown

Swansea

Strathgordon

New
Norfolk

HOBART

Port Arthur

Approximate Distances AUSTRALIA	Adelaide	Albany	Albury	Alice Springs	Ayers Rock/Yulara	Bairnsdale	Ballarat	Bathurst	Bega	Bendigo	Bordertown	Bourke	Brisbane	Broken Hill	Broome	Bunbury	Cairns	Canberra	Carnarvon	Ceduna	Charleville	Coober Pedy	Darwin	Dubbo	Esperance	Eucla	Geelong	Geraldton
Adelaide		2662	965	1537	1578	1010	625	1198	1338	640	274	1129	2048	514	4268	2887	3207	1197	3568	772	1582	847	3026	1194	2183	1267	711	3086
Albany	2662		3487	3585	3626	3672	3287	3720	4000	3302	2936	3388	4310	2773	2626	335	5466	3719	1300	1890	3841	2895	4428	3526	479	1395	3373	818
Albury	965	3487		2362	2403	336	412	466	427	313	679	779	1407	865	5093	3712	2764	348	4393	1597	1232	1672	3851	553	3008	2092	382	3911
Alice Springs	1537	3585	2362		443	2547	2162	2595	2875	2177	1811	2263	2979	1648	2731	3810	2376	2594	4114	1695	2320	690	1489	2401	3106	2190	2248	4009
Ayers Rock/Yulara	1578	3626	2403	443		2588	2203	2636	2916	2218	1852	2304	3226	1689	3174	3851	2819	2635	4532	1736	2763	731	1932	2442	3147	2231	2289	4050
Bairnsdale	1010	3672	336	2547	2588		388	802	328	423	736	1115	1743	1119	5278	3897	3100	455	4578	1782	1568	1857	4036	863	3193	2277	349	4096
Ballarat	625	3287	412	2162	2203	388		878	716	124	351	996	1747	754	4893	3512	3104	760	4193	1397	1449	1472	3651	893	2808	1892	86	3711
Bathurst	1198	3720	466	2595	2636	802	878		531	779	1180	569	1000	958	5011	3945	2416	309	4626	1830	1022	1905	3769	205	3241	2325	848	4144
Bega	1338	4000	427	2875	2916	328	716	531		751	1064	994	1399	1447	5436	4225	2910	222	4906	2110	1447	2185	4364	630	3521	2605	677	4424
Bendigo	640	3302	313	2177	2218	423	124	779	751		366	872	1623	696	4908	3527	2980	661	4208	1412	1325	1487	3666	769	2823	1907	210	3726
Bordertown	274	2936	679	1811	1852	736	351	1180	1064	366		1138	1922	788	4542	3161	3257	1071	3842	1046	1591	1121	3300	1068	2457	1541	437	3360
Bourke	1129	3388	779	2263	2304	1115	996	569	994	872	1138		922	615	4442	3613	2078	772	4294	1498	453	1573	3200	364	2909	1993	1082	3812
Brisbane	2048	4310	1407	2979	3226	1743	1747	1000	1399	1623	1922	922		1537	4648	4535	1703	1241	5216	2420	742	2495	3406	854	3831	2915	1745	4734
Broken Hill	514	2773	865	1648	1689	1119	754	958	1447	696	788	615	1537		4379	2998	2693	1097	3679	883	1068	958	3137	753	2294	1378	840	3197
Broome	4268	2626	5093	2731	3174	5278	4893	5011	5436	4908	4542	4442	4648	4379		2417	4045	5214	1451	3750	3989	3421	1870	4806	2745	3255	4979	1921
Bunbury	2887	335	3712	3810	3851	3897	3512	3945	4225	3527	3161	3613	4535	2998	2417		5691	3944	1091	2115	4066	3120	4219	3751	664	1620	3598	609
Cairns	3207	5466	2764	2376	2819	3100	3104	2416	2910	2980	3257	2078	1703	2693	4045	5691		2619	5428	3576	1625	3066	2803	2211	4987	4071	3102	5890
Canberra	1197	3719	348	2594	2635	455	760	309	222	661	1071	772	1241	1097	5214	3944	2619		4625	1829	1225	1904	3972	408	3240	2324	730	4143
Carnarvon	3568	1300	4393	4114	4532	4578	4193	4626	4906	4208	3842	4294	5216	3679	1451	1091	5428	4625		2796	4747	3801	3253	4432	1628	2301	4279	482
Ceduna	772	1890	1597	1695	1736	1782	1397	1830	2110	1412	1046	1498	2420	883	3750	2115	3576	1829	2796		1951	1005	3184	1636	1411	495	1483	2314
Charleville	1582	3841	1232	2320	2763	1568	1449	1022	1447	1325	1591	453	742	1068	3989	4066	1625	1225	4747	1951		2026	2747	817	3362	2446	1500	4265
Coober Pedy	847	2895	1672	690	731	1857	1472	1905	2185	1487	1121	1573	2495	958	3421	3120	3066	1904	3801	1005	2026		2179	1711	2416	1500	1558	3319
Darwin	3026	4428	3851	1489	1932	4036	3651	3769	4364	3666	3300	3200	3406	3137	1870	4219	2803	3972	3253	3184	2747	2179		3564	4547	3679	3737	3723
Dubbo	1194	3526	553	2401	2442	863	893	205	630	769	1068	364	854	753	4806	3751	2211	408	4432	1636	817	1711	3564		3047	2131	891	3950
Esperance	2183	479	3008	3106	3147	3193	2808	3241	3521	2823	2457	2909	3831	2294	2745	664	4987	3240	1628	1411	3362	2416	4547	3047		916	2894	1160
Eucla	1267	1395	2092	2190	2231	2277	1892	2325	2605	1907	1541	1993	2915	1378	3255	1620	4071	2324	2301	495	2446	1500	3679	2131	916		1978	1819
Geelong	711	3373	382	2248	2289	349	86	848	677	210	437	1082	1745	840	4979	3598	3102	730	4279	1483	1500	1558	3737	891	2894	1978		3797
Geraldton	3086	818	3911	4009	4050	4096	3711	4144	4424	3726	3360	3812	4734	3197	1921	609	5890	4143	482	2314	4265	3319	3723	3950	1160	1819	3797	
Grafton	1845	4177	1184	3052	3093	1397	1544	825	1069	1420	1719	808	330	1404	4975	4402	2033	911	5083	2287	1069	2362	3733	651	3698	2782	1542	4601
Horsham	433	3095	531	1970	2011	577	192	997	905	218	159	1067	1841	599	4701	3320	3145	879	4001	1205	1520	1280	3459	987	2616	1700	278	3519
Kalgoorlie–Boulder	2184	886	3009	3107	3148	3194	2809	3242	3522	2824	2458	2910	3832	2295	2338	779	4988	3241	1460	1412	3363	2417	4140	3048	407	917	2895	978
Katherine	2712	4114	3537	1175	1618	3722	3337	3455	3880	3352	2986	2886	3092	2823	1556	3905	2489	3658	2939	2870	2433	1865	314	3250	4233	3365	3423	3409
Kununurra	3224	3602	4049	1687	2130	4234	3849	3967	4392	3864	3498	3398	3604	3335	1044	3393	3001	4170	2427	3382	2945	2377	826	3762	3721	3877	3935	2897
Longreach	2098	4357	1748	1804	2247	2084	1965	1538	1963	1841	2107	969	1175	1584	3473	4582	1109	1741	4856	2467	516	2494	2231	1333	3878	2962	2016	4781
Mackay	2670	4932	2029	2451	2894	2365	2369	1681	2106	2245	2544	1544	968	2159	4120	5157	735	1884	5503	3042	1091	3141	2878	1476	4453	3537	2367	5356
Meekatharra	3055	1159	3880	3978	4019	4065	3680	4113	4393	3695	3329	3781	4703	3166	1467	950	5444	4112	627	2283	4234	3288	3269	3919	1278	1788	3766	541
Melbourne	733	3395	313	2270	2311	277	111	779	605	146	459	978	1676	842	5001	3620	3033	661	4301	1505	1431	1580	3759	822	2916	2000	72	3819
Mildura	394	2916	571	1791	1832	825	460	804	956	402	417	870	1654	294	4522	3141	2948	803	3822	1026	1323	1101	3280	800	2437	1521	546	3340
Moree	1567	3829	926	2704	2745	1262	1294	578	1003	1141	1482	441	481	1056	4608	4054	1838	781	4735	1939	702	2014	3366	373	3350	2434	1264	4253
Mount Gambier	452	3114	721	1989	2030	697	309	1187	1025	433	186	1324	2098	856	4720	3339	3402	1069	4020	1224	1777	1299	3478	1244	2635	1719	365	3538
Mount Isa	2706	4754	2383	1169	1612	2719	2600	2173	2598	2476	2742	1604	1810	2219	2838	4979	1207	2736	4221	2864	1151	1859	1596	1968	4275	3359	2651	4691
Newcastle	1553	3930	704	2805	2846	917	1116	338	589	1017	1427	768	821	1157	5111	4155	2341	431	4836	2040	1205	2115	3869	404	3451	2535	1086	4354
Perth	2700	410	3525	3623	3664	3710	3325	3758	4038	3340	2974	3426	4348	2811	2230	187	5504	3757	904	1928	3879	2933	4032	3564	738	1433	3411	422
Port Augusta	307	2355	1132	1230	1271	1317	932	1365	1645	947	581	1033	1955	418	3961	2580	3111	1364	3261	465	1486	540	2719	1171	1876	960	1018	2779
Port Hedland	3921	2025	4746	3264	3707	5100	4546	4979	5259	4561	4195	4647	5181	4032	601	1816	4578	4978	850	3149	4522	3954	2403	4785	2144	2654	4632	1320
Port Lincoln	647	2289	1472	1570	1611	1657	1272	1705	1985	1287	921	1373	2295	758	4149	2514	3451	1704	3195	399	1826	880	3059	1511	1751	894	1358	2713
Port Macquarie	1804	4136	942	3011	3052	1155	1354	565	827	1255	1665	859	584	1363	5150	4361	2287	669	5042	2246	1244	2321	3908	610	3657	2741	1324	4560
Renmark	250	2772	715	1647	1688	969	604	948	1100	546	269	1014	1798	438	4378	2997	3092	947	3678	882	1467	957	3136	944	2293	1377	690	3196
Rockhampton	2336	4598	1695	2486	2929	2031	2035	1347	1772	1911	2210	1210	634	1825	4155	4823	1069	1550	5504	2708	831	3176	2913	1142	4119	3203	2033	5022
Sydney	1414	3936	565	2811	2852	759	977	211	431	878	1288	780	966	1169	5222	4161	2479	292	4842	2046	1233	2121	3980	416	3457	2541	947	4360
Tamworth	1534	3866	893	2741	2782	1186	1233	457	858	1109	1408	589	573	1093	4880	4091	2110	700	4772	1965	974	2051	3638	340	3387	2471	1231	4290
Tennant Creek	2043	4091	2868	531	949	3053	2668	2836	3261	2683	2317	2267	2473	2154	2225	4316	1870	3039	3608	2201	1814	1196	983	2631	3612	2696	2754	4078
Toowoomba	1921	4183	1280	2852	3099	1616	1620	956	1357	1496	1795	795	127	1410	4521	4408	1705	1199	5089	2293	615	2368	3279	727	3704	2788	1618	4607
Townsville	2862	5121	2419	2061	2504	2755	2759	2071	2496	2635	2871	1733	1358	2348	3730	5346	345	2274	5113	3231	1280	2751	2488	1866	4642	3726	2757	5545
Wagga Wagga	948	3470	145	2345	2386	481	550	321	402	426	822	711	1262	848	5076	3695	2619	249	4376	1580	1164	1655	3834	408	2991	2075	527	3894
Warrnambool	649	3311	567	2186	2227	534	174	1052	862	298	383	1170	1933	829	4917	3536	3278	987	4217	1421	1623	1496	3675	1067	2832	1916	185	3735

Distances on this chart have been calculated over main roads and do not necessarily reflect the shortest route between towns.
Refer to page xiv for a distance chart of Tasmania.

Approximate Distances AUSTRALIA

	Grafton	Horsham	Kalgoorlie–Boulder	Katherine	Kununurra	Longreach	Mackay	Meekatharra	Melbourne	Mildura	Moree	Mount Gambier	Mount Isa	Newcastle	Perth	Port Augusta	Port Hedland	Port Lincoln	Port Macquarie	Renmark	Rockhampton	Sydney	Tamworth	Tennant Creek	Toowoomba	Townsville	Wagga Wagga	Warrnambool
Adelaide	1845	433	2184	2712	3224	2098	2670	3055	733	394	1567	452	2706	1553	2700	307	3921	647	1804	250	2336	1414	1534	2043	1921	2862	948	649
Albany	4177	3095	886	4114	3602	4357	4932	1159	3395	2916	3829	3114	4754	3930	410	2355	2025	2289	4136	2772	4598	3936	3866	4091	4183	5121	3470	3311
Albury	1184	531	3009	3537	4049	1748	2029	3880	313	571	926	721	2383	704	3525	1132	4746	1472	942	715	1695	565	893	2868	1280	2419	145	567
Alice Springs	3052	1970	3107	1175	1687	1804	2451	3978	2270	1791	2704	1989	1169	2805	3623	1230	3264	1570	3011	1647	2486	2811	2741	531	2852	2061	2345	2186
Ayers Rock/Yulara	3093	2011	3148	1618	2130	2247	2894	4019	2311	1832	2745	2030	1612	2846	3664	1271	3707	1611	3052	1688	2929	2852	2782	949	3099	2504	2386	2227
Bairnsdale	1397	577	3194	3722	4234	2084	2365	4065	277	825	1262	697	2719	917	3710	1317	5100	1657	1155	969	2031	759	1186	3053	1616	2755	481	534
Ballarat	1544	192	2809	3337	3849	1965	2369	3680	111	460	1294	309	2600	1116	3325	932	4546	1272	1354	604	2035	977	1233	2668	1620	2759	550	174
Bathurst	825	997	3242	3455	3967	1538	1681	4113	779	804	578	1187	2173	338	3758	1365	4979	1705	565	948	1347	211	457	2836	956	2071	321	1052
Bega	1069	905	3522	3880	4392	1963	2106	4393	605	956	1003	1025	2598	589	4038	1645	5259	1985	827	1100	1772	431	858	3261	1357	2496	402	862
Bendigo	1420	218	2824	3352	3864	1841	2245	3695	146	402	1141	433	2476	1017	3340	947	4561	1287	1255	546	1911	878	1109	2683	1496	2635	426	298
Bordertown	1719	159	2458	2986	3498	2107	2544	3329	459	417	1482	186	2742	1427	2974	581	4195	921	1665	269	2210	1288	1408	2317	1795	2871	822	383
Bourke	808	1067	2910	2886	3398	969	1544	3781	978	870	441	1324	1604	768	3426	1033	4647	1373	859	1014	1210	780	589	2267	795	1733	711	1170
Brisbane	330	1841	3832	3092	3604	1175	968	4703	1676	1654	481	2098	1810	821	4348	1955	5181	2295	584	1798	634	966	573	2473	127	1358	1262	1933
Broken Hill	1404	599	2295	2823	3335	1584	2159	3166	842	294	1056	856	2219	1157	2811	418	4032	758	1363	438	1825	1169	1093	2154	1410	2348	848	829
Broome	4975	4701	2338	1556	1044	3473	4120	1467	5001	4522	4608	4720	2838	5111	2230	3961	601	4149	5150	4378	4155	5222	4880	2225	4521	3730	5076	4917
Bunbury	4402	3320	779	3905	3393	4582	5157	950	3620	3141	4054	3339	4979	4155	187	2580	1816	2514	4361	2997	4823	4161	4091	4316	4408	5346	3695	3536
Cairns	2033	3145	4988	2489	3001	1109	735	5444	3033	2948	1838	3402	1207	2341	5504	3111	4578	3451	2287	3092	1069	2479	2110	1870	1705	345	2619	3278
Canberra	911	879	3241	3658	4170	1741	1884	4112	661	803	781	1069	2736	431	3757	1364	4978	1704	669	947	1550	292	700	3039	1199	2274	249	987
Carnarvon	5083	4001	1460	2939	2427	4856	5503	627	4301	3822	4735	4020	4221	4836	904	3261	850	3195	5042	3678	5504	4842	4772	3608	5089	5113	4376	4217
Ceduna	2287	1205	1412	2870	3382	2467	3042	2283	1505	1026	1939	1224	2864	2040	1928	465	3149	399	2246	882	2708	2046	1965	2201	2293	3231	1580	1421
Charleville	1069	1520	3363	2433	2945	516	1091	4234	1431	1323	702	1777	1151	1205	3879	1486	4522	1826	1244	1467	831	1233	974	1814	615	1280	1164	1623
Coober Pedy	2362	1280	2417	1865	2377	2494	3141	3288	1580	1101	2014	1299	1859	2115	2933	540	3954	880	2321	957	3176	2121	2051	1196	2368	2751	1655	1496
Darwin	3733	3459	4140	314	826	2231	2878	3269	3759	3280	3366	3478	1596	3869	4032	2719	2403	3059	3908	3136	2913	3980	3638	983	3279	2488	3834	3675
Dubbo	651	987	3048	3250	3762	1333	1476	3919	822	800	373	1244	1968	404	3564	1171	4785	1511	610	944	1142	416	340	2631	727	1866	408	1067
Esperance	3698	2616	407	4233	3721	3878	4453	1278	2916	2437	3350	2635	4275	3451	738	1876	2144	1751	3657	2293	4119	3457	3387	3612	3704	4642	2991	2832
Eucla	2782	1700	917	3365	3877	2962	3537	1788	2000	1521	2434	1719	3359	2535	1433	960	2654	894	2741	1377	3203	2541	2471	2696	2788	3726	2075	1916
Geelong	1542	278	2895	3423	3935	2016	2367	3766	72	546	1264	365	2651	1086	3411	1018	4632	1358	1324	690	2033	947	1231	2754	1618	2757	527	185
Geraldton	4601	3519	978	3409	2897	4781	5356	541	3819	3340	4253	3538	4691	4354	422	2779	1320	2713	4560	3196	5022	4360	4290	4078	4607	5545	3894	3735
Grafton		1638	3699	3419	3931	1502	1298	4570	1473	1451	367	1895	2137	491	4215	1822	5436	2162	254	1595	964	638	311	2800	431	1688	1059	1718
Horsham	1638		2451	3145	3657	2036	2463	3322	300	305	1360	257	2671	1235	3133	740	4188	1080	1462	428	2129	1096	1327	2476	1714	2800	644	230
Kalgoorlie–Boulder	3699	2451		3826	3314	3879	4454	871	2917	2438	3351	2636	4276	3452	582	1877	1737	1811	3658	2294	4120	3458	3388	3613	3705	4643	2992	2833
Katherine	3419	3145	3826		512	1917	2564	2955	3445	2966	3052	3164	1282	3556	3718	2405	2089	2745	3594	2822	2599	3666	3324	669	2965	2174	3520	3361
Kununurra	3931	3657	3314	512		2429	3076	2443	3957	3478	3564	3676	1794	4067	3206	2917	1577	3257	4106	3334	3111	4178	3836	1181	3477	2686	4032	3873
Longreach	1502	2036	3879	1917	2429		791	4750	1947	1839	1135	2293	635	1638	4395	2002	4006	2342	1677	1983	682	1749	1407	1298	1048	764	1680	2139
Mackay	1298	2463	4454	2564	3076	791		5325	2298	2276	1103	2720	1282	1606	4970	2577	4653	2917	1552	2420	334	1744	1375	1945	970	390	1884	2543
Meekatharra	4570	3322	871	2955	2443	4750	5325		3788	3309	4222	3507	4237	4323	763	2748	866	2682	4529	3165	5524	4329	4259	3624	4576	5129	3863	3704
Melbourne	1473	300	2917	3445	3957	1947	2298	3788		548	1195	420	2582	1017	3433	1040	4823	1380	1255	692	1964	878	1162	2776	1549	2688	458	257
Mildura	1451	305	2438	2966	3478	1839	2276	3309	548		1173	562	2474	1159	2954	561	4175	901	1397	144	1942	1020	1140	2297	1527	2603	554	535
Moree	367	1360	3351	3052	3564	1135	1103	4222	1195	1173		1627	1770	503	3867	1474	5088	1814	542	1317	769	641	272	2433	354	1493	781	1449
Mount Gambier	1895	257	2636	3164	3676	2293	2720	3507	420	562	1627		2928	1425	3152	759	4373	1099	1663	455	2386	1286	1584	2495	1971	3057	901	197
Mount Isa	2137	2671	4276	1282	1794	635	1282	4237	2582	2474	1770	2928		2273	4792	2399	3371	2739	2312	2618	1317	2384	2042	663	1683	892	2315	2774
Newcastle	491	1235	3452	3556	4067	1638	1606	4323	1017	1159	503	1425	2273		3968	1575	5189	1915	249	1303	1272	158	289	2936	788	1996	605	1271
Perth	4215	3133	582	3718	3206	4395	4970	763	3433	2954	3867	3152	4792	3968		2393	1629	2327	4174	2810	4636	3974	3904	4129	4221	5159	3508	3349
Port Augusta	1822	740	1877	2405	2917	2002	2577	2748	1040	561	1474	759	2399	1575	2393		3614	340	1781	417	2243	1581	1511	1736	1828	2766	1115	956
Port Hedland	5436	4188	1737	2089	1577	4006	4653	866	4823	4175	5088	4373	3371	5189	1629	3614		3548	5395	4031	4688	5195	5125	2758	5054	4263	4729	4570
Port Lincoln	2162	1080	1811	2745	3257	2342	2917	2682	1380	901	1814	1099	2739	1915	2327	340	3548		2121	757	2583	1921	1851	2076	2168	3106	1455	1296
Port Macquarie	254	1462	3658	3594	4106	1677	1552	4529	1255	1397	542	1663	2312	249	4174	1781	5395	2121		1541	1218	396	270	2975	630	1942	843	1509
Renmark	1595	428	2294	2822	3334	1983	2420	3165	692	144	1317	455	2618	1303	2810	417	4031	757	1541		2086	1164	1284	2153	1671	2747	698	652
Rockhampton	964	2129	4120	2599	3111	682	334	5524	1964	1942	769	2386	1317	1272	4636	2243	4688	2583	1218	2086		1410	1041	1980	636	724	1550	2209
Sydney	638	1096	3458	3666	4178	1749	1744	4329	878	1020	641	1286	2384	158	3974	1581	5195	1921	396	1164	1410		427	3047	926	2134	466	1132
Tamworth	311	1327	3388	3324	3836	1407	1375	4259	1162	1140	272	1584	2042	289	3904	1511	5125	1851	270	1284	1041	427		2705	499	1765	748	1407
Tennant Creek	2800	2476	3613	669	1181	1298	1945	3624	2776	2297	2433	2495	663	2936	4129	1736	2758	2076	2975	2153	1980	3047	2705		2346	1555	2851	2692
Toowoomba	431	1714	3705	2965	3477	1048	970	4576	1549	1527	354	1971	1683	788	4221	1828	5054	2168	630	1671	636	926	499	2346		1360	1135	1794
Townsville	1688	2800	4643	2174	2686	764	390	5129	2688	2603	1493	3057	892	1996	5159	2766	4263	3106	1942	2747	724	2134	1765	1555	1360		2274	2933
Wagga Wagga	1059	644	2992	3520	4032	1680	1884	3863	458	554	781	901	2315	605	3508	1115	4729	1455	843	698	1550	466	748	2851	1135	2274		724
Warrnambool	1718	230	2833	3361	3873	2139	2543	3704	257	535	1449	197	2774	1271	3349	956	4570	1296	1509	652	2209	1132	1407	2692	1794	2933	724	

Approximate Distances TASMANIA	Burnie	Campbell Town	Deloraine	Devonport	Geeveston	George Town	Hobart	Launceston	New Norfolk	Oatlands	Port Arthur	Queenstown	Richmond	Rosebery	St Helens	St Marys	Scottsdale	Smithton	Sorell	Strahan	Swansea	Ulverstone
Burnie		200	101	50	391	204	333	152	328	247	432	163	304	110	300	263	222	88	318	185	267	28
Campbell Town	200		99	150	191	119	133	67	128	47	232	304	104	357	122	85	137	288	118	344	67	172
Deloraine	101	99		51	290	103	232	51	227	146	331	207	203	211	199	162	121	189	217	247	166	73
Devonport	50	150	51		341	154	283	102	278	197	382	213	254	160	250	213	172	138	268	235	217	22
Geeveston	391	191	290	341		310	58	258	95	144	157	308	85	361	313	276	328	479	84	348	197	363
George Town	204	119	103	154	310		252	52	247	166	351	310	223	314	182	182	83	292	237	350	186	176
Hobart	333	133	232	283	58	252		200	37	86	99	250	27	303	265	228	270	421	26	290	139	305
Launceston	152	67	51	102	258	52	200		195	114	299	258	171	262	167	130	70	240	185	298	134	124
New Norfolk	328	128	227	278	95	247	37	195		81	136	213	64	266	250	213	265	416	63	253	176	300
Oatlands	247	47	146	197	144	166	86	114	81		175	257	57	310	169	132	184	335	71	297	125	219
Port Arthur	432	232	331	382	157	351	99	299	136	175		349	87	402	312	275	369	520	73	389	186	404
Queenstown	163	304	207	213	308	310	250	258	213	257	349		277	53	426	389	328	253	276	40	389	191
Richmond	304	104	203	254	85	223	27	171	64	57	87	277		330	226	189	241	392	14	317	123	276
Rosebery	110	357	211	160	361	314	303	262	266	310	402	53	330		410	373	332	222	329	75	442	138
St Helens	300	122	199	250	313	182	265	167	250	169	312	426	226	410		37	99	388	240	466	126	272
St Marys	263	85	162	213	276	182	228	130	213	132	275	389	189	373	37		136	351	203	429	89	235
Scottsdale	222	137	121	172	328	83	270	70	265	184	369	328	241	332	99	136		310	255	368	204	194
Smithton	88	288	189	138	479	292	421	240	416	335	520	253	392	222	388	351	310		406	275	355	116
Sorell	318	118	217	268	84	237	26	185	63	71	73	276	14	329	240	203	255	406		316	113	290
Strahan	185	344	247	235	348	350	290	298	253	297	389	40	317	75	466	429	368	275	316		429	213
Swansea	267	67	166	217	197	186	139	134	176	125	186	389	123	442	126	89	204	355	113	429		239
Ulverstone	28	172	73	22	363	176	305	124	300	219	404	191	276	138	272	235	194	116	290	213	239	

Distances on this chart have been calculated over main roads and do not necessarily reflect the shortest route between towns.

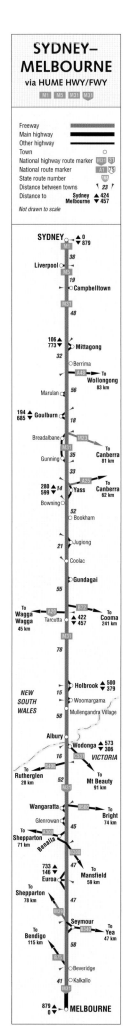

SYDNEY– MELBOURNE
via HUME HWY/FWY
M1 M5 M31 M31

Freeway	━━━
Main highway	━━━
Other highway	──
Town	○
National highway route marker	M31 31
National route marker	75
State route number	168
Distance between towns	◥ 23 ◢
Distance to	Sydney ▲ 424 / Melbourne ▼ 457

Not drawn to scale

SYDNEY ▲ 0 / ▼ 879
38
Liverpool
19
Campbelltown
48
106▲ 773▼ Mittagong
32
Berrima
To Wollongong 83 km
Marulan 56
194▲ 685▼ Goulburn
18
Breadalbane
Gunning 35
33
280▲ 599▼ 14 Yass
Bowning
To Canberra 81 km
Canberra 62 km
52
Bookham
21
Jugiong
Coolac
Gundagai
55
To Wagga Wagga 45 km Tarcutta 422▲ 457▼ Cooma 241 km
78
Holbrook 500▲ 379▼
15
Woomargama
58 Mullengandra Village
Albury
Wodonga 573▲ 306▼
16
To Rutherglen 28 km 52 Mt Beauty 91 km
Wangaratta To Bright 74 km
Glenrowan 45
To Shepparton 71 km Benalla
733▲ 146▼ 47 Euroa Mansfield 59 km
Shepparton 78 km
47
Seymour To Yea 47 km
Bendigo 115 km 58
Beveridge
41 Kalkallo
879▲ 0▼ MELBOURNE

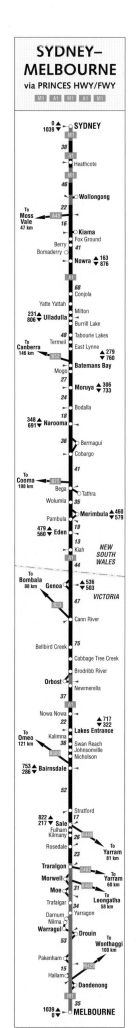

SYDNEY– MELBOURNE
via PRINCES HWY/FWY
M1 A1 M1 A1 M1

0▲ 1039▼ SYDNEY
38
Heathcote
46
Wollongong
22
To Moss Vale 47 km 16 Kiama / Fox Ground
Berry 41
Bomaderry Nowra 163▲ 876▼
68
Conjola
Yatte Yattah Milton
231▲ 806▼ Ulladulla Burrill Lake
Tabourie Lakes
48
Termeil East Lynne
To Canberra 146 km Batemans Bay 279▲ 760▼
Mogo 27
Moruya 306▲ 733▼
24
Bodalla
348▲ 691▼ Narooma 18
36
Bermagui
Cobargo
41
To Cooma 108 km Bega
Wolumla 35
Pambula Merimbula 460▲ 579▼
479▲ 560▼ Eden 19
13
Kiah 44
To Bombala 88 km Genoa 536▲ 503▼
47
Cann River
75
Bellbird Creek
Cabbage Tree Creek
Brodribb River
Orbost Newmerella
37
Nowa Nowa
22
To Omeo 121 km Kalimna Lakes Entrance 717▲ 322▼
36 Swan Reach / Johnsonville / Nicholson
753▲ 286▼ Bairnsdale
52
Stratford
822▲ 217▼ Sale 17
Fulham / Kilmany 26
Rosedale 23
Traralgon To Yarram 81 km
Morwell To Yarram 60 km
Moe 31 Leongatha 58 km
Trafalgar 34
Darnum / Nilma / Yarragon
Warragul Drouin To Wonthaggi 100 km
53
Pakenham 15
Hallam Dandenong
M1
1039▲ 0▼ MELBOURNE

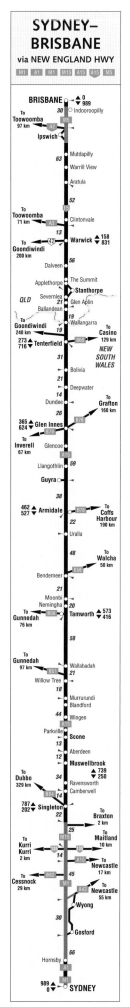

SYDNEY– BRISBANE
via NEW ENGLAND HWY
M1 A1 M1 M15 A15 A15 M5

BRISBANE ▲ 0 / ▼ 989
30 Indooroopilly
To Toowoomba 97 km Ipswich
63
Mutdapilly
Warrill View
Aratula
52
To Toowoomba 71 km Clintonvale
15
13 Warwick 158▲ 831▼
To Goondiwindi 200 km 56
Dalveen
Applethorpe The Summit
Severnlea Stanthorpe
21 Glen Aplin
Ballandean 19
To Goondiwindi 240 km Wallangarra
273▲ 716▼ Tenterfield 19 Casino 129 km
31 B60
Bolivia
21
Deepwater
14
365▲ 624▼ Glen Innes Dundee 26 Grafton 160 km
Glencoe
Inverell 67 km 59 Llangothlin
Guyra
38
462▲ 527▼ Armidale To Coffs Harbour 190 km
22
Uralla
48 Walcha 50 km
Bendemeer
21
Moonbi / Nemingha 20
Tamworth 573▲ 416▼
To Gunnedah 76 km 58
To Gunnedah 97 km Wallabadah
21
Willow Tree
18
Murrurundi / Blandford
44 Wingen
Parkville Scone
13
Aberdeen 12
Muswellbrook ▲ 739 / ▼ 250
To Dubbo 329 km 34
787▲ 202▼ Singleton 22 To Braxton 2 km
25 To Maitland 10 km
To Kurri Kurri 2 km 14 To Newcastle 17 km
Cessnock 29 km 45 To Newcastle 55 km
Wyong
30
Gosford
66
Hornsby
989▲ 0▼ SYDNEY

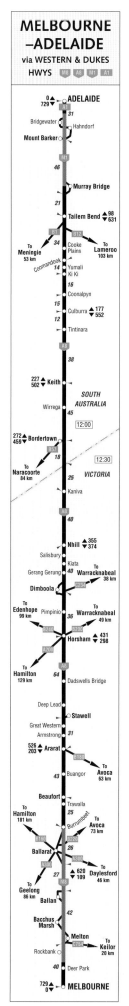

MELBOURNE –ADELAIDE
via WESTERN & DUKES HWYS
M8 A8 M1 A1

0▲ 729▼ ADELAIDE
Bridgewater Hahndorf
Mount Barker
46
Murray Bridge
21
Tailem Bend 98▲ 631▼
To Meningie 53 km 34 Cooke Plains To Lameroo 103 km
Coomandook 14 Yumali / Ki Ki
16
15 Coonalpyn
12 Culburra 177▲ 552▼
Tintinara
38
227▲ 502▼ Keith
Wirrega 45 SOUTH AUSTRALIA
12:00
272▲ 459▼ Bordertown
18
To Naracoorte 84 km 12:30 VICTORIA
Kaniva
A8 40
Nhill 355▲ 374▼
Salisbury Kiata
Gerang Gerung 40 Warracknabeal 38 km
Dimboola C234
Edenhope 99 km Pimpinio 36 Warracknabeal 49 km
B240 B200
Horsham 431▲ 298▼
A200
To Hamilton 129 km 64 Dadswells Bridge
Deep Lead
Stawell
Great Western
Armstrong 31
526▲ 203▼ Ararat
To Hamilton 181 km 43 Buangor To Avoca 63 km
Beaufort
Trawalla 25
Burrumbeet To Avoca 73 km
Ballarat 26
27
620▲ 109▼ To Daylesford 46 km
Geelong 86 km Ballan
Bacchus Marsh 42
Melton
Rockbank To Keilor 20 km
40 Deer Park
729▲ 0▼ MELBOURNE

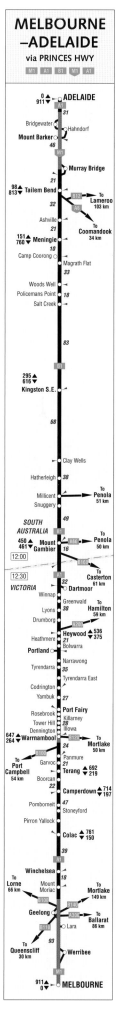

MELBOURNE –ADELAIDE
via PRINCES HWY
M1 A1 B1 M1 A1

0▲ 911▼ ADELAIDE
31
Bridgewater Hahndorf
Mount Barker
46
Murray Bridge
21
98▲ 813▼ Tailem Bend To Lameroo 103 km
32
Ashville To Coomandook 34 km
21
151▲ 760▼ Meningie 10
Camp Coorong Magrath Flat
33
Woods Well
Policemans Point 18
Salt Creek
83
295▲ 616▼ Kingston S.E.
68
Clay Wells
Hatherleigh 38
To Penola 51 km
Millicent Snuggery
49 To Penola 50 km
450▲ 461▼ Mount Gambier To Casterton 61 km
16 A66
12:00 32 Dartmoor
12:30 VICTORIA Winnap Greenvale To Hamilton 59 km
Lyons 38
Drumborg A200
Heathmere Heywood 536▲ 375▼
Portland 21 Bolwarra
Tyrendarra Narrawong 35
Codrington Tyrendarra East
Yambuk 27
Rosebrook Port Fairy
Tower Hill Killarney 28
647▲ 264▼ Warrnambool Dennington / Illowa
To Mortlake 50 km
Port Campbell 54 km 24 Panmure / Garvoc
21 Terang 692▲ 219▼
Boorcan 22
Camperdown 714▲ 197▼
Pomborneit 47
Pirron Yallock Stoneyford
Colac 761▲ 150▼
39
Winchelsea
18
To Lorne 66 km Mount Moriac To Mortlake 149 km
Geelong B140
93 To Ballarat 86 km
Lara
Queenscliff 30 km Werribee
911▲ 0▼ MELBOURNE

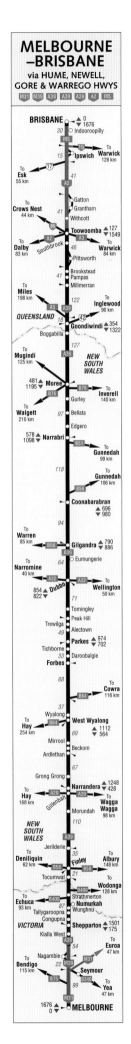

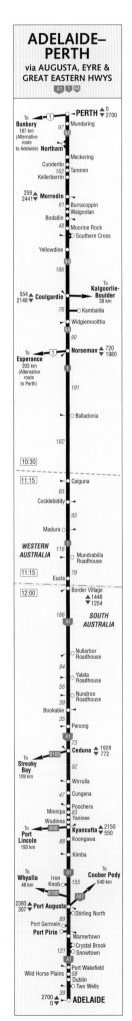

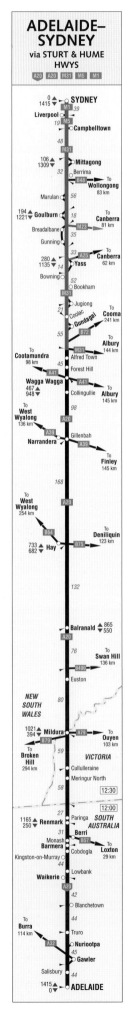

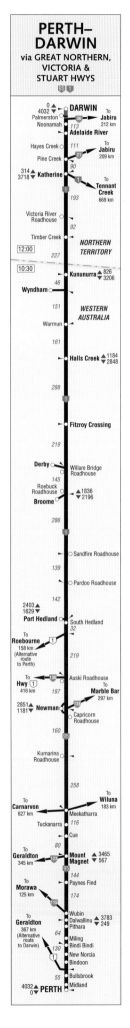

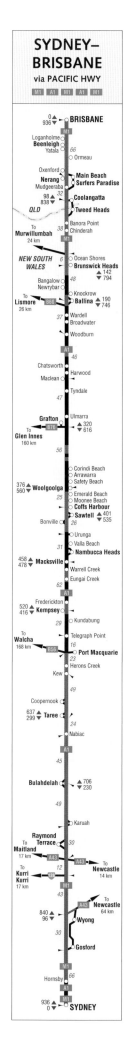

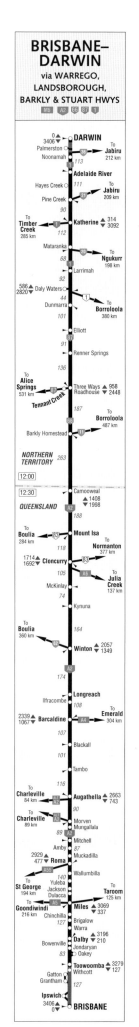

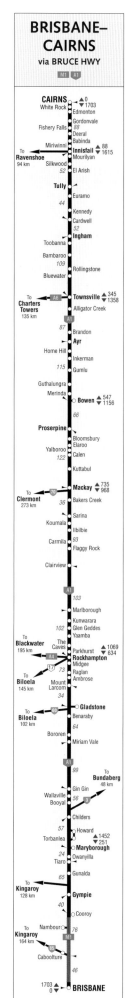

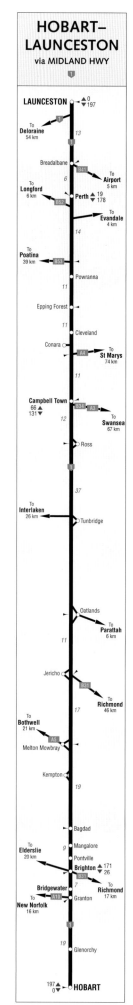

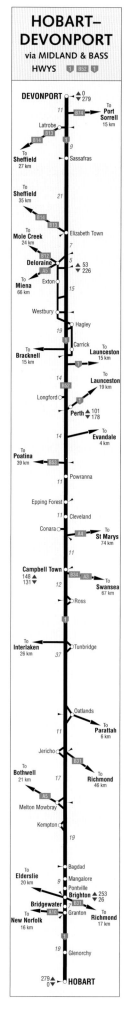

NEW SOUTH WALES

The oldest state in Australia, New South Wales is a prime example of the diversity of the continent's landscape and climate. From the Snowy Mountains in the south to the beaches of the east coast, there is something for everyone.

New South Wales also offers a huge range of activities that cater for all levels of fitness and interest. Spend a few days skiing in the Snowy Mountains region, close to the Victorian border where you'll find Mount Kosciuszko, Australia's highest peak or explore the magnificent gorges and waterfalls of the Blue Mountains. Take a tour of the Hunter Valley, home to some of the best wineries in Australia or discover hidden rainforests in the state's north-east. You can fish in some of the country's most secluded spots; sail or cruise the bays of Sydney Harbour, watch whales and dolphins off the coast, visit the country's oldest townships or just let a saltwater waves wash you ashore onto one of the state's golden beaches.

Located in the south-east of the country, New South Wales is more than three times the size of Great Britain and nearly twice as large as California. It boasts the largest population of any state or territory in Australia, with around 7.6 million people. The climate varies from subtropical temperatures in the north and along parts of the coast, to the dry, desert-like conditions of the far west, and the snowfalls of the southern alps.

Throughout New South Wales there are many reminders of a rich historical and cultural heritage. Aboriginal middens, rock art and artefacts found in caves and national parks all over the state are testimony to the long Indigenous history of the area. Lake Mungo, in Mungo National Park, was the site of the discovery of Mungo Man and Woman: the preserved remains of two ancient Aboriginal people, estimated to be around 40,000 years old.

European settlement, despite its relatively shorter history, has had a profound impact on the land. Initially, it was the solution to overcrowded British prisons after the American War of Independence spelt the end of British penal settlements in North America. Later, the discovery of gold saw the beginning of the Australian gold-rush era. The relics of penal settlements and goldmining towns, heritage-listed buildings and the present-day built environment are testament to the tremendous changes that have taken place since Captain Arthur Phillip raised the British flag at Sydney Cove in 1788.

Sydney, the state capital, has the largest population of any city in the country and is widely accepted as the business and financial capital of Australia. Built around the largest natural harbour in the world, Sydney is a beautiful and sophisticated city with a uniquely welcoming and cosmopolitan atmosphere.

The Farm Beach, Illawarra

Places of interest

	MAP REF			MAP REF	
Abercrombie Caves	12	G6	Menindee Lakes	18	D11
Age of Fishes Museum, Canowindra	12	F5	Moree Artesian Aquatic Centre (MAAC)	14	G4
Australian Reptile Park	13	K5	Mungo National Park	16	G4
Bald Rock National Park	15	L3	Murramarang National Park	20	F6
Barrington Tops National Park	13	L1	Myall Lakes National Park	13	N3
Blue Mountains National Park	10	E4	Port Stephens	13	M3
Bondi Beach	9	N5	The Rocks, Sydney	5	D4
Cape Byron	15	O3	Royal National Park	9	I9
Central Tilba	20	E8	Shear Outback, Hay	17	J7
Cowra Japanese Garden	12	F6	Siding Spring Observatory	14	D9
CSIRO Parkes Radio Telescope	12	E3	Sofala and Hill End	12	H4
Dorrigo National Park	15	M8	Taronga Western Plains Zoo, Dubbo	12	F1
Eden Killer Whale Museum	20	E10	Taronga Zoo, Sydney	7	M11
The Great Lakes, Forster	13	N2	The Three Sisters, Katoomba	10	D6
Hunter Valley wineries	13	L3	Timbertown, Wauchope	15	L11
The International Cricket Hall of Fame	20	G2	Trial Bay Gaol, South West Rocks	15	M9
Jenolan Caves	10	A6	Warrumbungle National Park	14	D9
Kiama Blowhole	20	H3	Wellington Caves & Phosphate Mine	12	G2
Kosciuszko National Park	20	A7	Wollumbin National Park	15	O2
Lake Macquarie	13	L4	Wombeyan Caves	20	F2
Maitland and Morpeth	13	L3			

INFORMATION CENTRE

Level 1, cnr Argyle and Playfair sts,
The Rocks; (02) 8273 0000 or 1800 067 676
www.visitnsw.com
www.sydney.com

Walls of China, Mungo National Park

MAPS

NEW SOUTH WALES and AUSTRALIAN CAPITAL TERRITORY

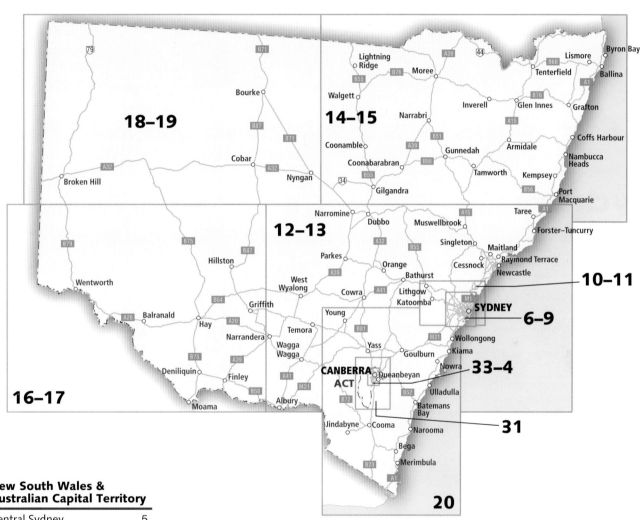

New South Wales & Australian Capital Territory

Central Sydney	5
Metro Sydney, North	6–7
Metro Sydney, South	8–9
Sydney & Surrounds	10–11
Central-eastern New South Wales	12–13
North-eastern New South Wales	14–15
South-western New South Wales	16–17
North-western New South Wales	18–19
South-eastern New South Wales	20
Australian Capital Territory	31
Central Canberra	33
Metro Canberra	34

INTER-CITY ROUTES		DISTANCE
Sydney–Melbourne via Hume Hwy/Fwy	M1 M5 M31 M31	879 km
Sydney–Melbourne via Princes Hwy/Fwy	M1 A1 M1 A1 M1	1039 km
Sydney–Brisbane via New England Hwy	M1 A1 M1 A43 A15 A15 M5	989 km
Sydney–Brisbane via Pacific Hwy	M1 A1 M1 A1 M1	936 km
Sydney–Adelaide via Hume & Sturt hwys	M1 M5 M31 A20 A20	1415 km

Circular Quay

Sydney

Sydney Cove, now known as Circular Quay, was where Captain Arthur Phillip proclaimed the colony of New South Wales on 26 January 1788. First Fleet convicts laboured to clear the site around Sydney Cove that was later to become the City of Sydney. The Rocks is an integral part of Sydney's history, and the sandstone buildings and winding lanes built by the convicts in this area are still in use today.

Sydney is a cosmopolitan city that offers a huge variety of attractions for visitors. The magnificent natural harbour defines the city, and sightseeing and getting around Sydney's CBD is easy. Sydney's major icons, the Sydney Harbour Bridge and Sydney Opera House, are located on the harbour's shores, along with Circular Quay, the Rocks, Darling Harbour, Cockle Bay and the Royal Botanic Gardens – all of which are popular attractions for visitors and locals alike.

Sydney's surburbia extends to the Hawkesbury River in the north, the Blue Mountains in the west and Royal National Park in the south. Historic suburbs that reflect early colonial times include Richmond, Windsor and Parramatta. A string of easily accessible family and surf beaches runs all the way from Palm Beach to Manly, north of the harbour, and from world-famous Bondi to Cronulla in the south.

Places of interest

	MAP REF			MAP REF
Anzac War Memorial	5 E8	Museum of Contemporary Art	5 D4
Archibald Fountain	5 E7	Museum of Sydney	5 E5
Art Gallery of New South Wales	5 F6	National Trust Centre	5 C4
Australian Museum	5 E8	Powerhouse Museum	5 B9
Australian National Maritime Museum	5 B6	Queen Victoria Building	5 D7
Cadman's Cottage	5 D4	Royal Botanic Gardens	5 F5
Chinatown	5 C8	St Mary's Cathedral	5 E7
Chinese Garden of Friendship	5 C8	SEA LIFE Sydney Aquarium	5 C6
Circular Quay	5 E4	The Star Casino	5 A6
Customs House	5 E5	State Library of New South Wales	5 E6
Darling Harbour	5 B5	Sydney Harbour Bridge	5 E2
Fort Denison	5 H3	Sydney Observatory	5 C4
Hyde Park	5 E7	Sydney Opera House	5 F3
Justice & Police Museum	5 E5	Sydney Tower	5 D7
Martin Place	5 E6	Sydney Town Hall	5 D7

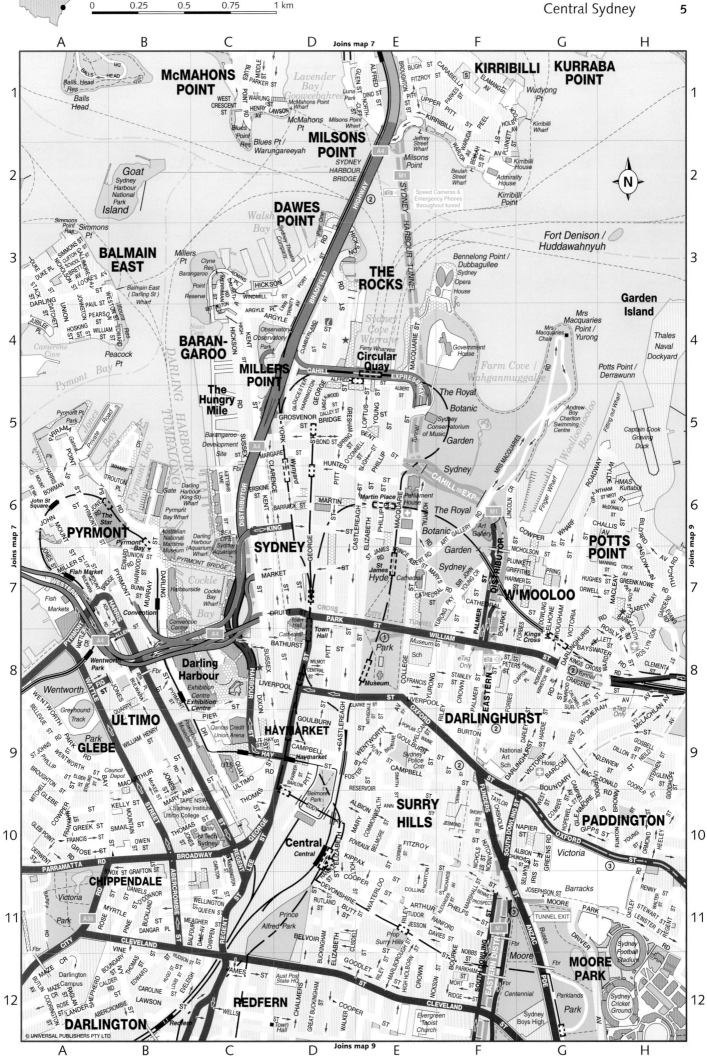

NSW

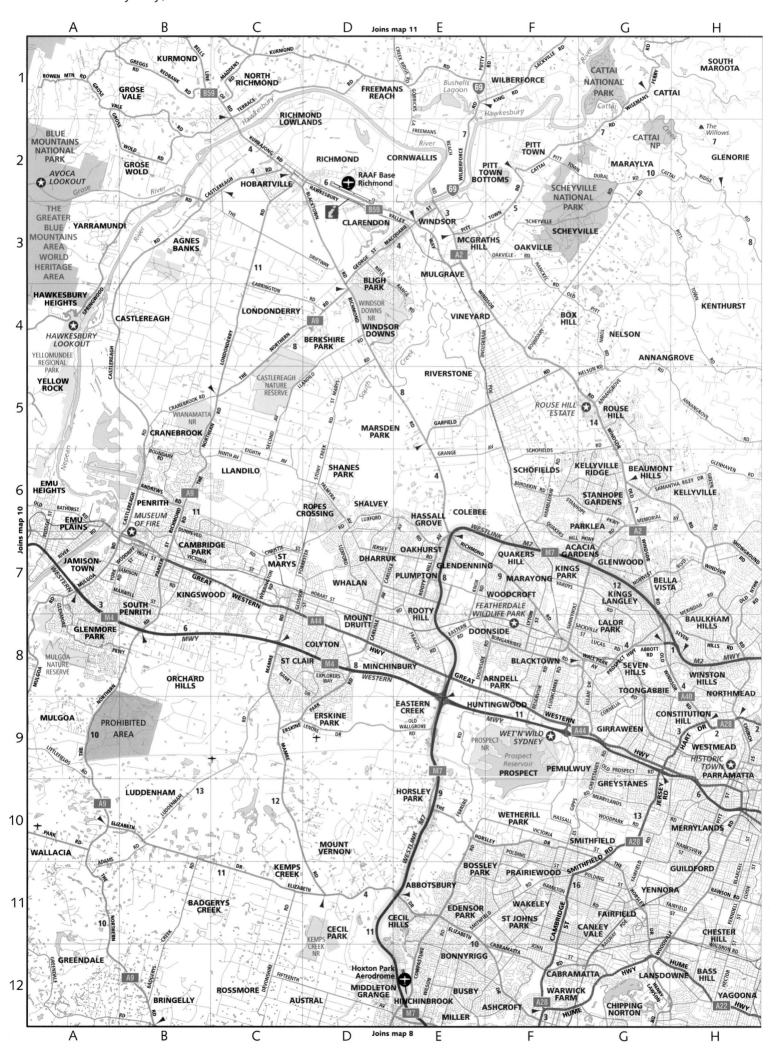

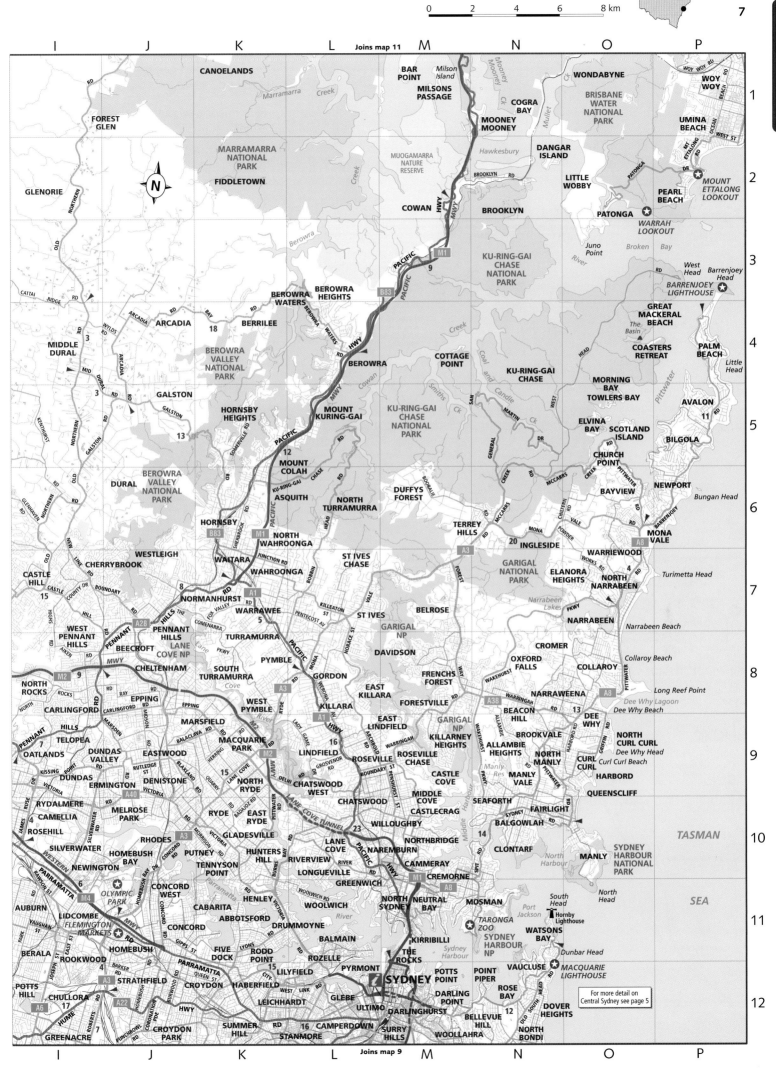

NSW

0 2 4 6 8 km

Joins map 11

I   J   K   L   M   N   O   P

CANOELANDS

BAR POINT
Milson Island
MILSONS PASSAGE
WONDABYNE
WOY WOY
WOY WOY BEACH

FOREST GLEN
Marramarra Creek
MOONEY MOONEY
COGRA BAY
BRISBANE WATER NATIONAL PARK
UMINA BEACH

MARRAMARRA NATIONAL PARK
FIDDLETOWN
Hawkesbury
DANGAR ISLAND
MT ETTALONG
MOUNT ETTALONG LOOKOUT

GLENORIE
MUOGAMARRA NATURE RESERVE
BROOKLYN RD
LITTLE WOBBY
PATONGA
PEARL BEACH

COWAN
BROOKLYN
WARRAH LOOKOUT

PACIFIC
M1
9
KU-RING-GAI CHASE NATIONAL PARK
Juno Point
Broken Bay
West Head
Barrenjoey Head
BARRENJOEY LIGHTHOUSE

BEROWRA WATERS
BEROWRA HEIGHTS
B83
GREAT MACKERAL BEACH

ARCADIA
18
BERRILEE
BEROWRA VALLEY NATIONAL PARK
The Basin
COASTERS RETREAT
PALM BEACH
Little Head

MIDDLE DURAL
3
GALSTON
BEROWRA
COTTAGE POINT
KU-RING-GAI CHASE
MORNING BAY
TOWLERS BAY
AVALON
11

3
13
HORNSBY HEIGHTS
MOUNT KURING-GAI
KU-RING-GAI CHASE NATIONAL PARK
ELVINA BAY
SCOTLAND ISLAND
BILGOLA

DURAL
BEROWRA VALLEY NATIONAL PARK
12
MOUNT COLAH
DUFFYS FOREST
CHURCH POINT
BAYVIEW
NEWPORT
Bungan Head

ASQUITH
NORTH TURRAMURRA
TERREY HILLS
20
INGLESIDE
MONA VALE
A8

CASTLE HILL
CHERRYBROOK
WESTLEIGH
HORNSBY
B83
NORTH WAHROONGA
ST IVES CHASE
A3
GARIGAL NATIONAL PARK
ELANORA HEIGHTS
NORTH NARRABEEN
WARRIEWOOD
Turimetta Head

15
WEST PENNANT HILLS
WAITARA
M1
WAHROONGA
BELROSE
NARRABEEN
Narrabeen Lakes
Narrabeen Beach

8
NORMANHURST
A1
WARRAWEE
5
ST IVES
GARIGAL NP
CROMER
Collaroy Beach
COLLAROY

NORTH ROCKS
A28
PENNANT HILLS
LANE COVE NP
TURRAMURRA
PYMBLE
GORDON
DAVIDSON
OXFORD FALLS
NARRAWEENA
A8
Long Reef Point

M2
9
BEECROFT
CHELTENHAM
SOUTH TURRAMURRA
A3
EAST KILLARA
FRENCHS FOREST
FORESTVILLE
BEACON HILL
DEE WHY
Dee Why Beach

WEST PYMBLE
A1
KILLARA
EAST LINDFIELD
KILLARNEY HEIGHTS
ALLAMBIE HEIGHTS
13
NORTH CURL CURL
Dee Why Head

CARLINGFORD
EPPING
MARSFIELD
A1
LINDFIELD
ROSEVILLE CHASE
CASTLE COVE
NORTH MANLY
CURL CURL
Curl Curl Beach

TELOPEA
MACQUARIE PARK
LANE COVE
ROSEVILLE
MANLY VALE
HARBORD

OATLANDS
DUNDAS VALLEY
EASTWOOD
M2
NORTH RYDE
CHATSWOOD WEST
Manly Res
SEAFORTH
QUEENSCLIFF

DUNDAS
ERMINGTON
DENISTONE
15
EAST RYDE
CHATSWOOD
MIDDLE COVE
CASTLECRAG
BALGOWLAH
FAIRLIGHT

A40
RYDE
WILLOUGHBY
14
CLONTARF
MANLY
SYDNEY HARBOUR NATIONAL PARK
TASMAN

RYDALMERE
MELROSE PARK
GLADESVILLE
LANE COVE TUNNEL
23
NORTHBRIDGE
North Harbour

CAMELLIA
RHODES
A3
PUTNEY
HUNTERS HILL
RIVERVIEW
NAREMBURN
CAMMERAY
SEA

ROSEHILL
SILVERWATER
HOMEBUSH BAY
CONCORD WEST
LONGUEVILLE
M1
CREMORNE
10

PARRAMATTA
NEWINGTON
6
HENLEY
WOOLWICH
GREENWICH
NORTH SYDNEY
NEUTRAL BAY
MOSMAN
South Head
North Head
SYDNEY HARBOUR NP

AUBURN
M4
OLYMPIC PARK
CABARITA
ABBOTSFORD
DRUMMOYNE
Port Jackson
TARONGA ZOO
WATSONS BAY

LIDCOMBE
FLEMINGTON MARKETS
CONCORD
BALMAIN
KIRRIBILLI
SYDNEY HARBOUR NP
Hornby Lighthouse

BERALA
ROOKWOOD
FIVE DOCK
RODD POINT
ROZELLE
THE ROCKS
NORTH SYDNEY
VAUCLUSE
MACQUARIE LIGHTHOUSE

HOMEBUSH
PARRAMATTA
LILYFIELD
PYRMONT
SYDNEY
POTTS POINT
POINT PIPER
ROSE BAY

POTTS HILL
STRATHFIELD
A3
CROYDON
HABERFIELD
GLEBE
ULTIMO
DARLING POINT
BELLEVUE HILL
DOVER HEIGHTS

CHULLORA
17
A22
LEICHHARDT
DARLINGHURST
SURRY HILLS
WOOLLAHRA
NORTH BONDI
12

GREENACRE
A6
HUME
CROYDON PARK
SUMMER HILL
16
CAMPERDOWN
STANMORE

Joins map 9

For more detail on Central Sydney see page 5

I   J   K   L   M   N   O   P

1
2
3
4
5
6
7
8
9
10
11
12

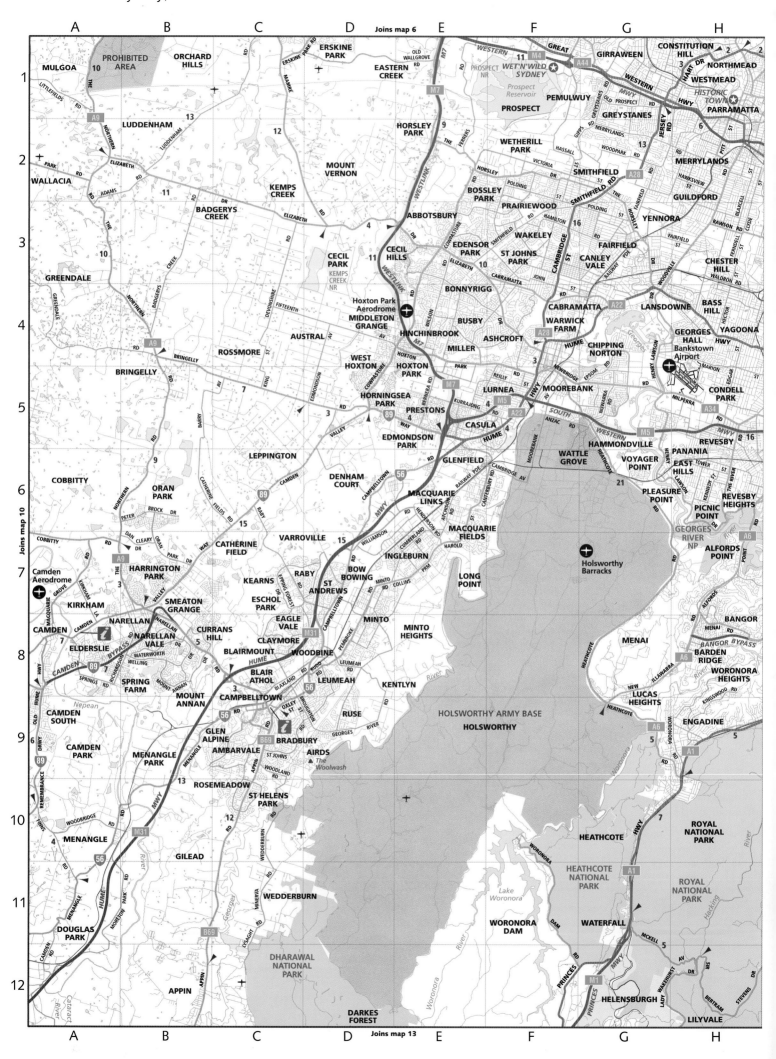

Joins map 6
Joins map 10
Joins map 13

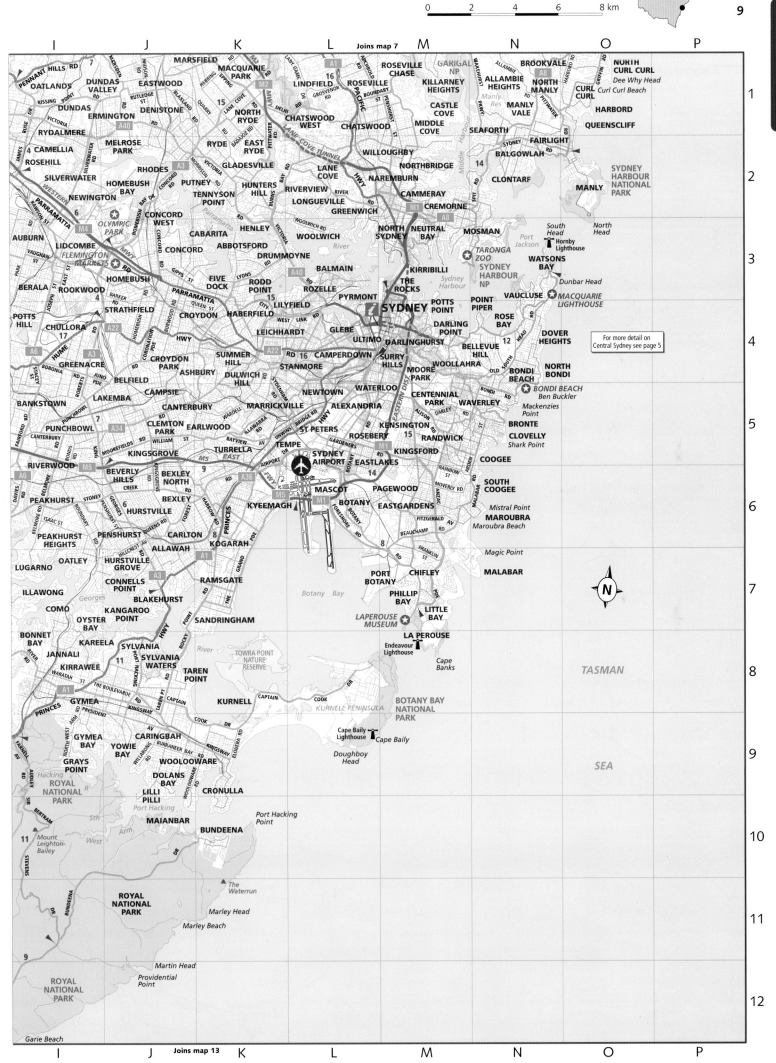

NSW

0 2 4 6 8 km

Joins map 7

I J K L M N O P

1

PENNANT HILLS RD
OATLANDS
DUNDAS VALLEY
EASTWOOD
MARSFIELD
MACQUARIE PARK
LINDFIELD
ROSEVILLE CHASE
GARIGAL NP
KILLARNEY HEIGHTS
ALLAMBIE HEIGHTS
BROOKVALE
NORTH CURL CURL
Dee Why Head
DUNDAS
KISSING POINT
DENISTONE
EPPING
NORTH RYDE
ROSEVILLE
PACIFIC
CASTLE COVE
ALLAMBIE HEIGHTS
NORTH MANLY
CURL CURL
Curl Curl Beach
ERMINGTON
VICTORIA
RYDE
EAST RYDE
CHATSWOOD WEST
CHATSWOOD
MIDDLE COVE
MANLY VALE
HARBORD
RYDALMERE
MELROSE PARK
GLADESVILLE
WILLOUGHBY
SEAFORTH
FAIRLIGHT
QUEENSCLIFF
CAMELLIA
ROSEHILL
RHODES
PUTNEY
LANE COVE
NORTHBRIDGE
BALGOWLAH
SILVERWATER
HOMEBUSH BAY
TENNYSON POINT
HUNTERS HILL
RIVERVIEW
NAREMBURN
CLONTARF

2

NEWINGTON
PARRAMATTA
CONCORD WEST
LONGUEVILLE
GREENWICH
CAMMERAY
MANLY
SYDNEY HARBOUR NATIONAL PARK
OLYMPIC PARK
CABARITA
HENLEY
WOOLWICH
NORTH SYDNEY
NEUTRAL BAY
CREMORNE
AUBURN
LIDCOMBE
CONCORD
ABBOTSFORD
DRUMMOYNE
MOSMAN
South Head
North Head
FLEMINGTON MARKETS
HOMEBUSH
BALMAIN
KIRRIBILLI
TARONGA ZOO
Port Jackson
Hornby Lighthouse

3

BERALA
ROOKWOOD
FIVE DOCK
RODD POINT
ROZELLE
THE ROCKS
POTTS POINT
SYDNEY HARBOUR NP
WATSONS BAY
Dunbar Head
POTTS HILL
STRATHFIELD
PYRMONT
SYDNEY
POINT PIPER
VAUCLUSE
MACQUARIE LIGHTHOUSE
CHULLORA
CROYDON
HABERFIELD
LILYFIELD
DARLING POINT
ROSE BAY
HUME
GREENACRE
SUMMER HILL
LEICHHARDT
GLEBE
ULTIMO
DARLINGHURST
BELLEVUE HILL
DOVER HEIGHTS
For more detail on Central Sydney see page 5

4

BELFIELD
CROYDON PARK
ASHBURY
DULWICH HILL
STANMORE
CAMPERDOWN
SURRY HILLS
MOORE PARK
WOOLLAHRA
NORTH BONDI
CAMPSIE
MARRICKVILLE
NEWTOWN
WATERLOO
CENTENNIAL PARK
WAVERLEY
BONDI BEACH
BANKSTOWN
LAKEMBA
CANTERBURY
ALEXANDRIA
KENSINGTON
BONDI BEACH
Ben Buckler
Mackenzies Point

5

PUNCHBOWL
CLEMTON PARK
EARLWOOD
ST PETERS
ROSEBERY
RANDWICK
BRONTE
CLOVELLY
Shark Point
RIVERWOOD
KINGSGROVE
TURRELLA
TEMPE EAST
KINGSFORD
COOGEE
BEVERLY HILLS
BEXLEY NORTH
SYDNEY AIRPORT
EASTLAKES
SOUTH COOGEE
PEAKHURST
BEXLEY
MASCOT
PAGEWOOD
Mistral Point

6

HURSTVILLE
KYEEMAGH
BOTANY
EASTGARDENS
MAROUBRA
Maroubra Beach
PEAKHURST HEIGHTS
PENSHURST
CARLTON
KOGARAH
Magic Point
LUGARNO
OATLEY
HURSTVILLE GROVE
ALLAWAH
PORT BOTANY
CHIFLEY
MALABAR

7

CONNELLS POINT
RAMSGATE
PHILLIP BAY
LITTLE BAY
ILLAWONG
COMO
BLAKEHURST
Botany Bay
LAPEROUSE MUSEUM
BONNET BAY
KANGAROO POINT
SANDRINGHAM
LA PEROUSE
Endeavour Lighthouse
Cape Banks

8

OYSTER BAY
KAREELA
SYLVANIA
TAREN POINT
TASMAN
JANNALI
KIRRAWEE
SYLVANIA WATERS
TOWRA POINT NATURE RESERVE
GYMEA
KURNELL
KURNELL PENINSULA
BOTANY BAY NATIONAL PARK

9

GYMEA BAY
CARINGBAH
WOOLOOWARE
Cape Baily Lighthouse
Cape Baily
Doughboy Head
SEA
GRAYS POINT
YOWIE BAY
DOLANS BAY
CRONULLA
LILLI PILLI
ROYAL NATIONAL PARK

10

MAIANBAR
BUNDEENA
Port Hacking Point
Mount Leighton-Bailey

11

ROYAL NATIONAL PARK
The Waterrun
Marley Head
Marley Beach

12

ROYAL NATIONAL PARK
Martin Head
Providential Point
Garie Beach

Joins map 13

I J K L M N O P

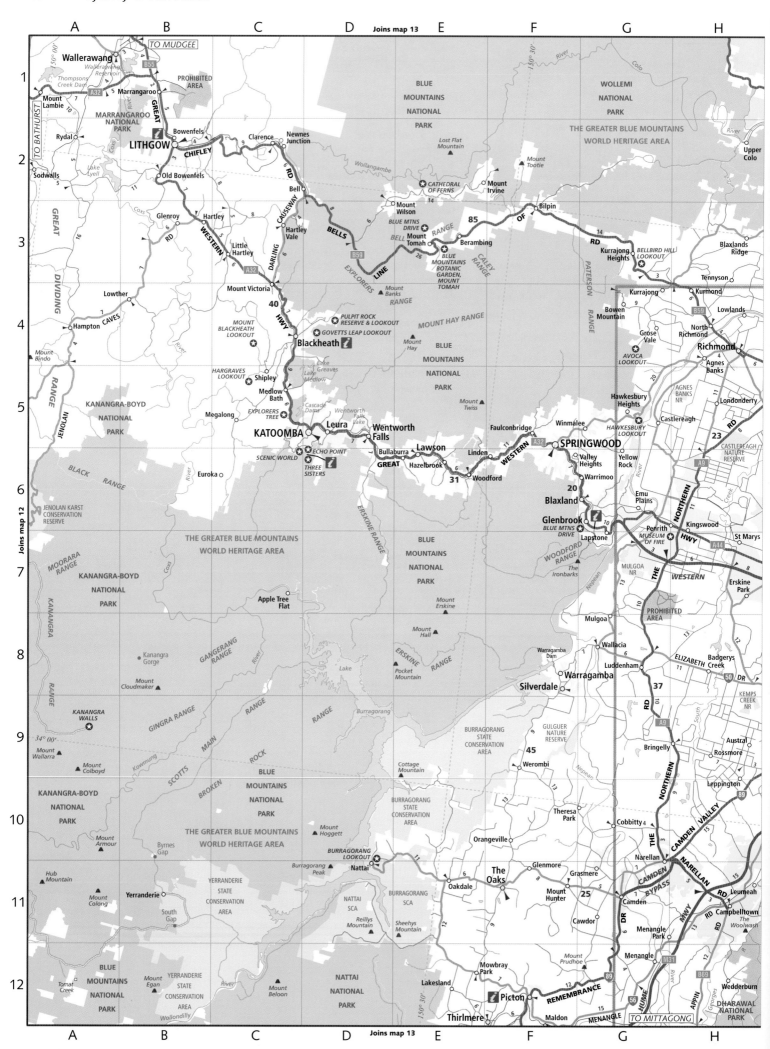

Joins map 13

| | A | B | C | D | E | F | G | H |

0 5 10 15 20 km

I J K L M N O P

TO NEWCASTLE
Gorokan
Wyong Creek
Wyong
Tuggerawong
Tacoma
Rocky Point
Central Mangrove
Fowlers Lookout
Mardi Dam
Tuggerah
Upper Mangrove
Mangrove Mountain
Peats Ridge
Palm Grove
Palm Dale
Fountaindale
The Entrance North
Berkeley Vale
The Entrance
Long Jetty
THE SHELL MUSEUM
Mangrove Creek
JILLIBY STATE CONSERVATION AREA
BRISBANE WATER
Somersby
Niagara Park
Ourimbah
Lisarow
Tumbi Umbi
Toowoon Bay
Shelly Beach
Bateau Bay
CRACKNECK POINT LOOKOUT
Webbs Creek
YENGO NATIONAL PARK
Mooney Mooney Upper Dam
Narara
Wyoming
Holgate
KEN DUNCAN GALLERY
Bateau Bay
Colo Heights
Wisemans Ferry
Leets Vale
Laughtondale
DHARUG NATIONAL PARK
Mount Olive
Lower Mangrove
AUSTRALIAN REPTILE PARK
Calga
Belltrees
HENRY KENDALL COTTAGE
Gosford
Kariong
Point Clare
GOSFORD CITY ARTS CENTRE
Erina
Matcham
Wamberal
WYRRABALONG NP
Wamberal Point
PUTTY
Central Colo
Colo
WOLLEMI NATIONAL PARK
Sackville North
Maroota
Gunderman
Spencer
Mount White
POPRAN NP
Mount Kariong
BULGANDRY ABORIGINAL ENGRAVINGS
Tascott
Koolewong
Green Point
Yattalunga
Kincumber
Terrigal
THE SKILLION
COAST
East Kurrajong
Glossodia
Freemans Reach
Ebenezer
SACKVILLE
WISEMANS
MARRAMARRA
POPRAN NATIONAL PARK
BRISBANE
Saratoga
Woy Woy
Davistown
Empire Bay
Avoca Beach
Copacabana
Wilberforce
Cattai
CATTAI NP
Forest Glen
Milson Island
MUOGAMARRA NATURE RESERVE
Mooney Mooney
WATER
Ettalong Beach
Umina
Tudibaring Head
Mourawaring Point
CENTRAL
Pitt Town
SCHEYVILLE NP
Maraylya
Glenorie
NATIONAL PARK
Brooklyn
Dangar Island
Patonga
Pearl Beach
Lion Island
BOUDDI NP
Bombi Point
THE MAITLAND WRECK
Clarendon
WINDSOR
McGraths Hill
Scheyville
Nelson
Berowra Waters
Berowra Heights
Cowan
Long Island
Broken Bay
June Point
West Head
Barrenjoey Head
WINDSOR DOWNS NR
Vineyard
Middle Dural
Arcadia
BEROWRA VALLEY RP
Berowra
KU-RING-GAI CHASE NATIONAL PARK
The Basin
Palm Beach
Little Head
RICHMOND
Riverstone
ROUSE HILL RP
Schofields
Kenthurst
Annangrove
Galston
Hornsby Heights
Mount Kuring-Gai
Bobbin Head
Duffys Forest
Church Point
Avalon
Bangalley Head
Quakers Hill
WESTLINK
OLD WINDSOR
Round Corner
Dural
Glenhaven
Castle Hill
BEROWRA VALLEY RP
Mount Colah
Asquith
Hornsby
Terrey Hills
Bayview
Ingleside
Newport
Mona Vale
Bungan Head
Mount Druitt
Rooty Hill
Doonside
HILLS
Baulkham Hills
Normanhurst
Warrawee
GARIGAL NP
St Ives
Davidson
Belrose
Elanora Heights
Turimetta Head
GREAT
Eastern Creek
WESTERN
Blacktown
Pennant Hills
LANE COVE
Pymble
Killara
GARIGAL NATIONAL PARK
Frenchs Forest
Narraweena
Narrabeen Beach
Collaroy Plateau
Collaroy Beach
Northmead
Carlingford
Epping
Eastwood
NP
Brookvale
Dee Why Beach
Long Reef Point
Pendle Hill
Wentworthville
Parramatta
Meadowbank
Ryde
Chatswood
Manly
Dee Why Head
Curl Curl Beach
Horsley Park
Cecil Park
Merrylands
Granville
Rhodes
Lane Cove
Balgowlah
Middle Harbour
SYDNEY HARBOUR NP
TASMAN
Guildford
Auburn
Concord
North Sydney
Mosman
North Head
Yennora
Lidcombe
Drummoyne
SYDNEY
Kings Cross
South Head
Hornby Lighthouse
Villawood
Cabramatta
Regents Park
Birrong
Croydon
Edgecliff
Bondi Junction
North Bondi
Dunbar Head
ELIZABETH
WESTLINK
Warwick Farm
HUME
Bankstown
Summer Hill
Marrickville
Newtown
Redfern
Waverley
Randwick
Ben Buckler
SEA
Liverpool
Belmore
Canterbury
Tempe
Mascot
Kingsford
Shark Point
WAY
Casula
SOUTH
East Hills
Revesby
Wiley Park
Beverly Hills
Banksia
Arncliffe
SYDNEY AIRPORT
Botany
Mistral Point
Macquarie Fields
Sandy Point
GEORGES RIVER NP
Penshurst
Hurstville
Kogarah
Maroubra Beach
Magic Point
For more detail on Metro Sydney see pages 6–9
Minto
Oatley
Illawong
Como
Georges River
Botany Bay
HOLSWORTHY ARMY BASE
Menai
Woronora
Sutherland
Miranda
Caringbah
Kurnell
Cape Banks
KAMAY BOTANY BAY NATIONAL PARK
Kentlyn
Lucas Heights
Kirrawee
Loftus
TOWRA POINT NR
KURNELL PENINSULA
Cape Baily
Doughboy Head
Yarrawarrah
Engadine
Wooloware
Cronulla
Port Hacking
Woronora Dam
Heathcote
Mount Leighton-Bailey
Maianbar
Bundeena
Port Hacking Point
HEATHCOTE NP
PRINCES
Waterfall
Lake Woronora
ROYAL NATIONAL PARK
The Waterrun
Marley Head
Marley Beach
Providential Head
Boy Martin Point

TO SHELLHARBOUR

I J K L M N O P

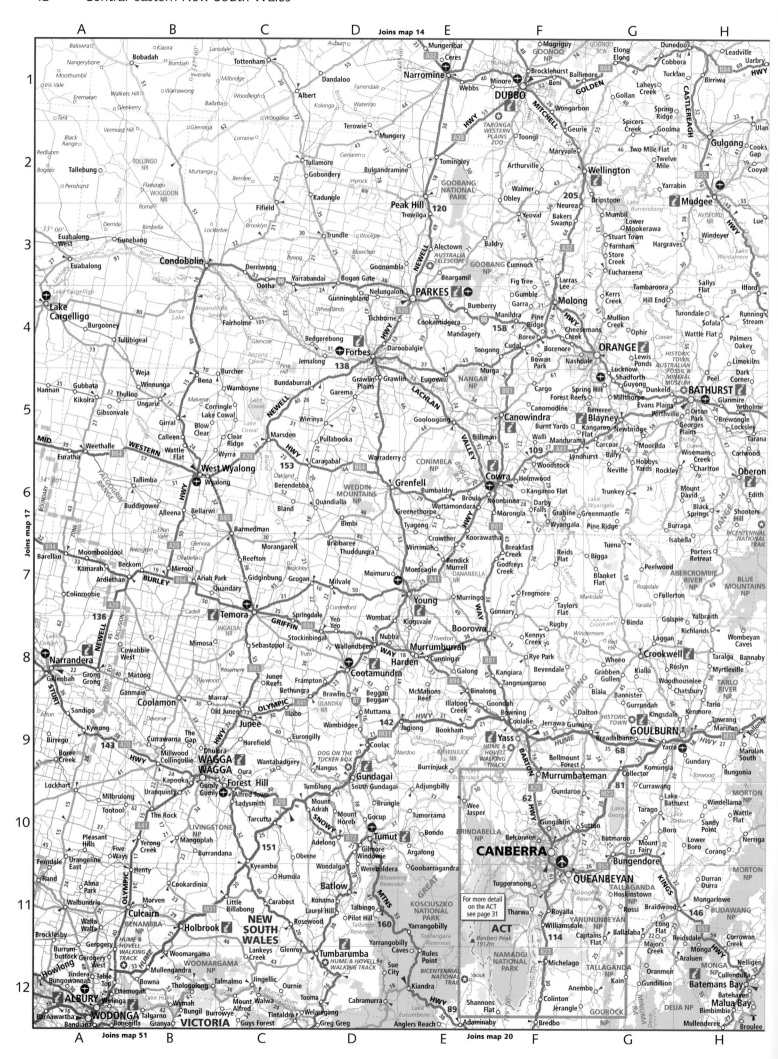

0 20 40 60 80 100 km

Joins map 15

I J K L M N O P

1 2 3 4 5 6 7 8 9 10 11 12

153° 00'
32° 00'
33° 00'
34° 00'
35° 00'
151° 00'
152° 00'

TASMAN SEA

N

For more detail on Sydney & Surrounds see pages 8–9

Towns and places

Cassilis, Borambil, Collaroy, Turill, Merriwa, Bow, GOLDEN, Wollar, Bylong, Gungal, Wappinguy, Manobalai, Wybong, Kerrabee, Sandy Hollow, Baerami, Upper Bylong, Denman, Martindale, Breakfast Creek, Rylstone, Olinda, Kandos, Clandulla, Capertee, GARDENS OF STONE NP, Newnes, Ben Bullen, Glen Alice, Glen Davis, Cullen Bullen, Portland, Wallerawang, Marrangaroo, LITHGOW, Clarence, Mount Lambie, Hartley, Glenroy, Lowther, Hampton, Medlow Bath, Blackheath, Leura, Lawson, KATOOMBA, Wentworth Falls, Jenolan Caves, Glenbrook, BLUE MTNS NP, KANANGRA-BOYD NP, Yerranderie, Nattai, Oakdale, The Oaks, Picton, Thirlmere, Long Flat, NATTAI NP, Buxton, Bargo, Hilltop, High Range, BANGADILLY NP, Colo Vale, Yanderra, Yerrinbool, Mittagong, Berrima, Sutton Forest, Bowral, Moss Vale, Avondale, Exeter, Penrose, Burrawang, Robertson, Wingello, Bundanoon, BUDDEROO NP, Kangaroo Valley, Berry, Cambewarra, Bomaderry, NOWRA, Nowra Hill, Apple Tree Flat, Yalwal, MORTON NP, Falls Creek, Sassafras, Twelve Mile Conjola, MORTON NP, Yatte Yattah, Milton, Kings Point, Ulladulla, Burrill Lake, Tabourie Lake, Termeil, Bawley Point, Kioloa, MURRAMARANG NP, Pebbly Beach, Durras, Beagle Bay

Karns Springs, Wingen, TOWARRI NP, Bunnan, Parkville, Gundy, Scone, Belltrees, Moonan Flat, Ellerston, WOKO NP, Bretti, Bobin, Killabakh, Johns River, Laurieton, CROWDY BAY NP, Crowdy Head, Coopernook, Moorland, Wyoming, Marlee, Lansdowne, Wingham, TAREE, Harrington, Manning Point, Old Bar, Wallabi Point, Diamond Beach, Hallidays Point, Bunyah, Wang Wauk, Nabiac, FORSTER-TUNCURRY, Bennetts Head, Cape Hawke, Green Point, Tiona, Elizabeth Beach, Blueys Beach, Smiths Lake, Bungwahl, Seal Rocks, Sugarloaf Point, MYALL LAKES NP, Bombah Broadwater, Tamboy, Broughton Island, Bulahdelah, Coomba, Pacific Palms, Willina, Wootton, Markwell, Rosenthal, Booral, Stroud Road, Stroud, Upper Myall, Coolongolook, Weismantels, Wards River, Bandon Grove, Craven, Krambach, Stratford, Gloucester, Belbora, Burrell Creek, Rainbow Flat, Tinonee, Purfleet, Mount George, Bundook, Copeland, Barrington, Rawdon Vale, Upper Bowman, BARRINGTON TOPS NP, BICENTENNIAL NATIONAL TRAIL, Rookhurst, Salisbury, Eccleston, Lostock, Halton, Bendolba, Dungog, Wallaroo, Marshdale, Main Creek, Limeburners Creek, Tea Gardens, Hawks Nest, Nelson Bay, Shoal Bay, TOMAREE NP, Anna Bay, Port Stephens, Karuah, Lemon Tree Passage, PACIFIC HWY, Beresfield, RAYMOND TERRACE, Hexham, Morpeth, MAITLAND, Kurri Kurri, CESSNOCK, Bellbird, Millfield, Ellalong, Wollombi, WATAGANS NP, Paynes Crossing, Bucketty, Murrays Run, Toronto, Rathmines, Swansea, NEWCASTLE, Stockton Bight, TILLIGERRY HABITAT, Mannering Park, Catherine Hill Bay, Lake Munmorah, Morisset, Wyee, Coranbong, Doyalson, Toukley, Norah Head, Wyong, Tuggerah, The Entrance, Long Jetty, Terrigal, Gosford, Kincumber, Woy Woy, Umina, Barrenjoey Head, Palm Beach, CENTRAL COAST, Kulnura, Central Mangrove, Peats Ridge, Ourimbah, Mount White, Mangrove Creek, Mangrove Mountain, St Albans, Upper Macdonald, Colo Heights, Wisemans Ferry, Central Colo, Upper Colo, Maroota, Bilpin, Freemans Reach, Wilberforce, WINDSOR, Galston, Cowan, Newport, Mona Vale, Frenchs Forest, Manly, Hornsby, Blacktown, Parramatta, Cabramatta, Liverpool, SYDNEY, Randwick, Botany, Kurnell, Cronulla, Bundeena, ROYAL NP, Waterfall, Heathcote, Menangle, Campbelltown, Camden, Narellan, Cobbitty, Austral, Orangeville, Werombi, Wallacia, Mulgoa, Badgerys Creek, Penrith, Springwood, Blaxland, Richmond, Silverdale, Warragamba, Appin, Helensburgh, Wilton, Stanwell Park, Scarborough, WOLLONGONG, Port Kembla, Windang, Shellharbour, Bass Point, Jamberoo, KIAMA, Gerringong, Shoalhaven Heads, Greenwell Point, Culburra, Callala Bay, Currarong, Vincentia, Huskisson, JERVIS BAY NP, JERVIS BAY MP, Point Perpendicular, JBT, St Georges Basin, Sussex Inlet, Swanhaven, CONJOLA NP, BOODEREE NP, Lake Conjola, Bendalong

Merriwa, Aberdeen, MUSWELLBROOK, McCullys Gap, Castle Rock, Roxburgh, Mangoola, Hollydeen, WOLLEMI NATIONAL PARK, Jerrys Plains, Warkworth, Mount Thorley, Bulga, North Rothbury, Belford, Branxton, SINGLETON, Fordwich, Broke, Howes Valley, Putty, YENGO NATIONAL PARK, Boree, Colo, GONDWANA RAINFORESTS OF AUSTRALIA WORLD HERITAGE AREA, Davis Creek, Dangarfield, Ravensworth, Hebden, Ravensworth, Camberwell, Glendon Brook, East Gresford, Gresford, Trevallyn, Vacy, Paterson, Lochinvar, Rothbury, Seaham, Glen Oak, Clarence Town, Booral, Dawsons Hill, Lake St Clair, Mirannie, St Clair, Bandon Grove, HUNTER VALLEY WINERIES, GLENBAWN, Lake Glenbawn, Wollemi, Macdonald River, DHARUG NP, Kurrajong Heights, Central Colo, Mount Wilson, Mount Victoria, Kurrajong, BLUE MTNS NP

390, B84, 41, 44, 67, 55, 58, NP, 53, 37, 36, 40, 109, NEW ENGLAND HWY, B84, HUME, 42, 69, 162, 54, 22, 32, 55, 100, 111, 99, 90, 137, 83, 79, 68, 48, 74, 150, 62, 64, 14, PRINCES HWY, PACIFIC HWY, ILLAWARRA HWY, PRINCES HWY

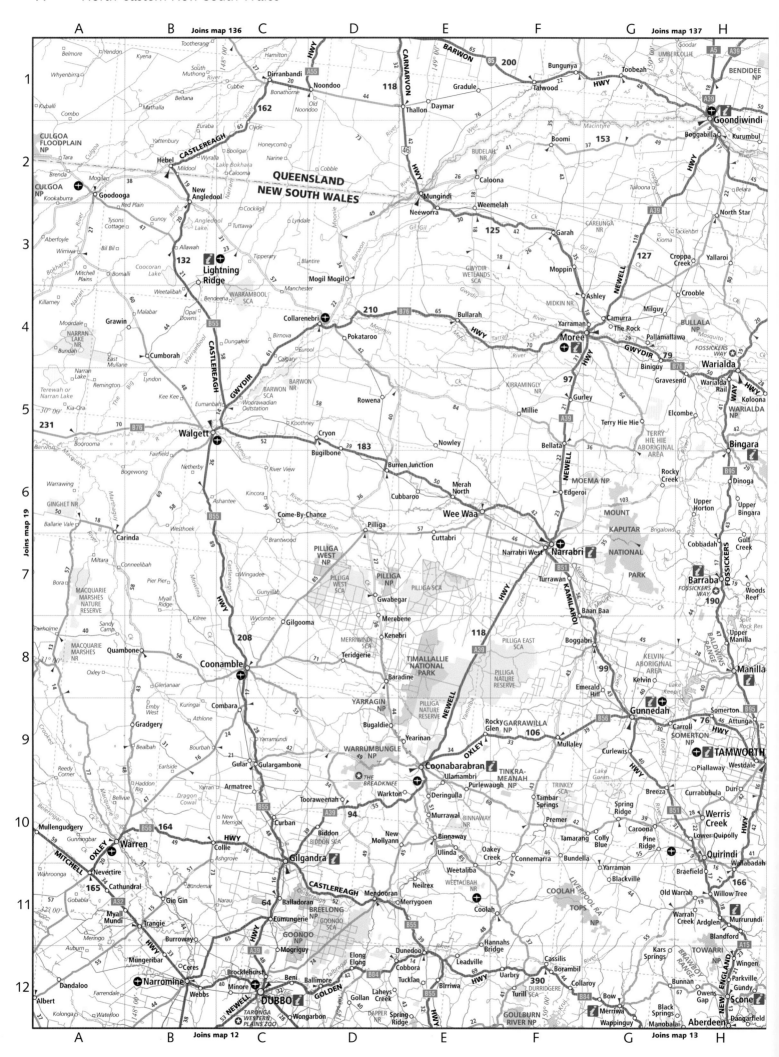

0 20 40 60 80 100 km

For more detail on Brisbane & Surrounds, South see page 135

QUEENSLAND

NEW SOUTH WALES

CORAL SEA

TASMAN SEA

GOLD COAST

Whetstone, Inglewood, Yelarbon, Karara, Greymare, Pratten, Thanes Creek, Cunningham, Berat, Goomburra, Clintonvale, Willowvale, Freestone, Yangan, Boonah, Mount Alford, Kooralbyn, Tamrookum, Maroon, Helensvale, Paradise Point, Labrador, Main Beach, Surfers Paradise, Broadbeach, Burleigh Heads, Palm Beach

WARWICK, Tannymorel, Killarney, Braeside, Legume, Woodenbong, Lamington, Hillview, Kerry, Josephville, Laravale, Rathdowney, NERANG, Mudgeeraba, Numinbah Valley, Natural Bridge, Springbrook, Currumbin, Terranora, Coolangatta, Tweed Heads

Pozieres, Amiens, Cottonvale, Thulimbah, The Summit, Applethorpe, Cannon Creek, Lower Acacia Creek, Wylie Creek, Urbenville, Mulli Mulli, Woodenbong, Cougal, Tumbulgum, Condong, Bogangar, Hastings Point, Pottsville, Billinudgel, Ocean Shores

STANTHORPE, Severnlea, Liston, Amosfield, Tooloom, Toonumba, Old Bonalbo, Kyogle, Cawongla, Nimbin, The Channel, Dunoon, Mullumbimby, Brunswick Heads

Fletcher, Glen Aplin, Eukey, Ballandean, Wallangarra, Boonoo Boonoo, Bonalbo, Ettrick, Georgica, Modanville, Goolmangar, Bangalow, Clunes, Bexhill, Byron Bay, Cape Byron, Suffolk Park, CAPE BYRON LIGHTHOUSE, WATEGO BEACH, WHALES

Mingoola, Clifton, Tenterfield, Sandy Hill, Drake, Tabulam, Mallanganee, Casino, LISMORE, Wollongbar, Alphadale, Knockrow, Lennox Head

Graman, Bonshaw, Limevale, Smithfield, Yetman, BRUXNER, Rocky Dam, Coolatai, Wallangra, Red Rock, Ashford, The Gulf, Torrington, Sandy Flat, Bolivia, Leeville, Tatham, Coraki, Meerschaum Vale, Wardell, Empire Vale, BALLINA

Delungra, Bukkulla, Emmaville, Deepwater, Woodville, Dundee, Baryulgil, Coombell, Wyan, Rappville, Woodburn, New Italy, Tabbimoble, Evans Head, Goanna Headland

Inverell, Gilgai, Brodies Plains, Elsmore, Stonehenge, Glen Innes, Red Range, Cangai, Apple Tree Flat, Coaldale, Whiporie, Lawrence Road, Chatsworth, Harwood, Palmers Island, Iluka, Yamba, Angourie

Stanborough, Tingha, Matheson, Sapphire, Glencoe, Jackadgery, Copmanhurst, Seelands, Cowper, Tyndale, Brooms Head, Shelley Beach Head

Black Springs, Stannifer, Ben Lomond, Llangothlin, Newton Boyd, Dalmorton, Eatonville, Waterview Heights, Junction Hill, Ulmarra, Tucabia, Sandon Bluffs

Bundarra, Wandsworth, Guyra, Black Mountain, Marengo, Clouds Creek, Obx Creek, Coutts Crossing, GRAFTON, Pillar Valley, Minnie Water, Wooli, North Solitary Island

Kingstown, Brushgrove, Rocky River, Dundurrabin, Billys Creek, Nymboida, Towallum, Glenreagh, Corindi, Red Rock, Corindi Beach, Arrawarra, Mullaway, Woolgoolga

ARMIDALE, Wollomombi, Ebor, Darkwood, Dorrigo, Bonville, Korora, COFFS HARBOUR, SAWTELL

Uralla, Dangarsleigh, Hillgrove, Jeogla, Thora, Bellingen, Raleigh, Mylestom, Urunga

Watsons Creek, Kentucky, Wollun, Lower Creek, Bowraville, Valla Beach, Hyland Park

Bendemeer, Woolbrook, Walcha Road, Walcha, Comara, Taylors Arm, Macksville, Scotts Head, Nambucca Heads

Kootingal, Moonbi, Nemingha, Calala, Dungowan, Woolomin, Niangala, Brackendale, Tia, Bellbrook, Warrell Creek, Eungai Creek, Stuarts Point, South West Rocks, Smoky Cape

Moona Plains, Willawarrin, Collombatti, Clybucca, Jerseyville, Kinchela, Gladstone, Korogoro Point

Yarrowitch, Green Hill, Kempsey, Smithtown, Frederickton, Hat Head, HAT HEAD NP

Mount Seaview, Birdwood, Rollands Plains, Kundabung, Crescent Head, Racecourse Head

Nowendoc, Cooplacurripa, Ellenborough, Long Flat, Beechwood, Pembroke, Telegraph Point, Point Plomer, LIMEBURNERS CREEK NP

Barry, Upper Bowman, Rookhurst, Bagnoo, Byabarra, Comboyne, Wauchope, PORT MACQUARIE, Nobby Head, Tacking Point, LAKE INNES NR

Ellerston, Moonan Flat, Belltrees, Rawdon Vale, Copeland, Barrington, Gloucester, Wingham, TAREE, Herons Creek, Kendall, Kew, Lake Cathie, Bonny Hills, North Haven, Laurieton, CROWDY BAY NP, Diamond Head

Bobin, Killabakh, Lorne, Johns River, Lansdowne, Moorland, Coopernook, Harrington, Manning Point, Old Bar, Crowdy Head

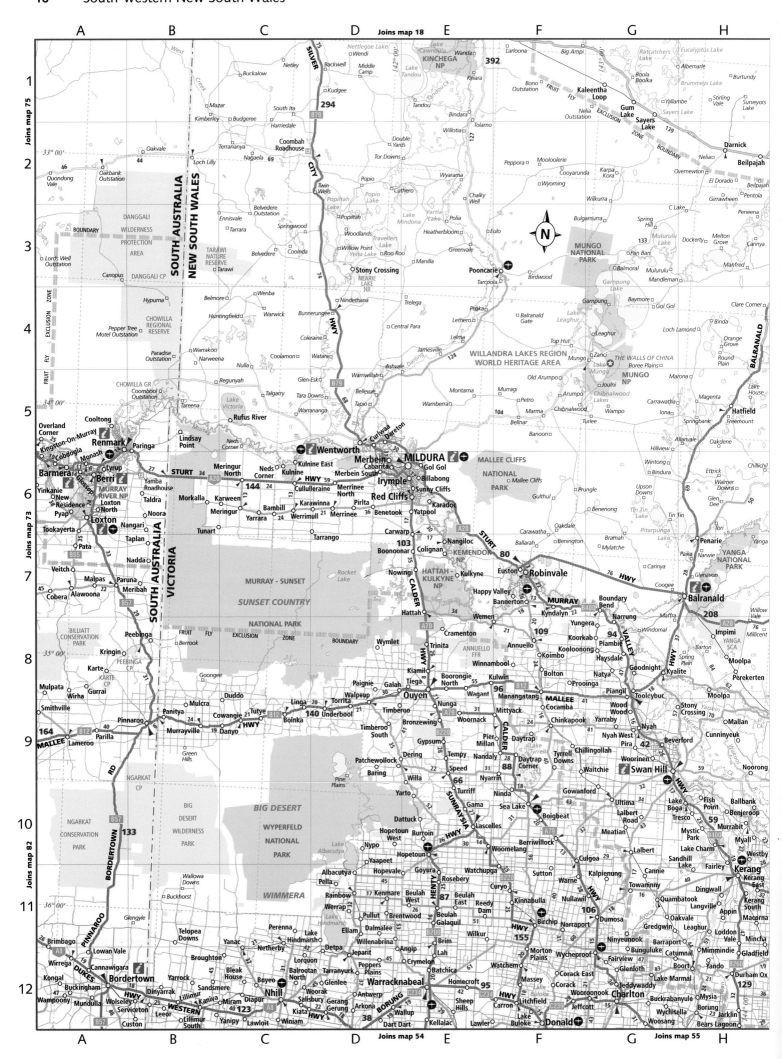

Joins map 18
Joins map 75
Joins map 73
Joins map 82

0 20 40 60 80 100 km

Joins map 19

I J K L M N O P

COBB HWY

Manara
Marfield
Boingadah
Berangaban
Tasman
Yallock
W-Tree
Red Tank
Karwarn
Warbraccan
Bedooba
Balowra
Kiaora
Lansdale
Bobadah
Bombah
Milbridge
Tottenham

Rose Hill
Gypsum Palace
Bonuna
Kajuligah
Wing Ding
Ashleigh Downs
Irymple
Stanifords
GILGUNNIA RANGE
Gilgunnia
Iris Vale
Nangerybone
Walkers Hill
Inveralla
Warrawong

Bonton
Canally
IVANHOE RD
Moolah
Coombie
Yathong
YATHONG NATURE RESERVE
Eremaran
Glenkerry
Vermont Hill
Murtanga
Ballatta
Woodleigh
Lorraine

Quamby
Orana
Morning Side
Tiarra
Marlow
Mintinery
Glenlea
FRUIT
Mawonga
Vivigani
FLY
Mount Hope
Nombiginni
Yara
Pine Ridge
Black Range
Redluom
Tara
Penshurst
Palistan
Flamingo
WOGGOON NR
Roma
Berrilee
Wongala

Kilfera
Abbotsford
Oxford
Conoble
Irish Lords
Kalamunda
Roto
Matakana
Mylone
BROKEN RANGE
KIDMAN WAY
Illewong
Crowie
Derrida
Bimbella
Brooklyn

Moornanyah Lake
Ivandale
Waiko
Trida
Conoble Lake
Murrumbong
NOMBINNIE SCA
NOMBINNIE NR
ROUND HILL NR
Euabalong West
Euabalong
Gunebang
Condobolin
Derriwong
Oota

Bellevue
Barneys Lake
Strathavon
Thollolobby
Willandra
Mulga
NOMBINNIE EXCLUSION NATURE RESERVE
Lowlands
Lake Cargelligo
Burgooney
Fairholme
Glencoe

Mossgiel
208
Moangul
Clearview
WILLANDRA NATIONAL PARK
Moolbong
Ballatherie
Willandra Ck
Tullibigeal
Nerang Cowal
Burcher

Alma Lake
Stanbridge
Yandembah
Vieta
99
Lake Ballyrogan
Weja
Winnunga
Bena
Wamboyne

COBB HWY
Clare Calpa
Yarto
Naradhan
Hannan
Gubbata
Thulloo
Ungarie
Lake Cowal
Corringle

Murrungrung
Culpataro
Ravensfield
Toms Lake
Merungle
HILLSTON
Cowl Cowl
Kikoira
Gibsonvale
Girral
Blow Clear
Clear Lake Cowal

Yamba
Mutherumbung
Alma
LACHLAN VALLEY SCA
KIDMAN
Merriwagga
BOUNDARY
Erigolia
Weethalle
Calleen
Wyrra
Marsden

Merritop
Curragh
Natue
Booligal
LACHLAN VALLEY NP
254
Rankins Springs
Euratha
HWY
Wattle Flat
Clear Ridge

Merrowie
Woorandara
Gunbar
Goolgowi
COCOPARA NR
Tallimba
West Wyalong
Wyalong

Glen Alvie Box
Oxley
One Tree
Tarana
Belaly
Wyoming
Berngame
Tabbita
COCOPARA NP
YALGOGRIN RANGE
Buddigower
Alleena
Bellarwi
Barmedman

Itta Lake
Nullagong
MID WESTERN HWY
Days
Yeadon
Barren Box Swamp
Beelbangera
Yenda
Binya
Barellan
Moombooldool
Reefton
Gidginbung

Toopunful
LACHLAN VALLEY SCA
Darcoola
Bagomba
Tharbogang
GRIFFITH
Hanwood
Yoogali
BURLEY GRIFFIN WAY
Kamarah
Beckom
Mirrool
Ariah Park
Quandary

Maude
LACHLAN VALLEY NP
Carrathool
Bringagee
RIVERINA WINERIES
Murrami
Ardlethan
Colinroobie
NEWELL HWY
Temora

Torry Plain
Hay
Willbriggie
Darlington Point
Whitton
Wamoon
Leeton
Yanco
Mimosa
Sebastopol

Braemar
Glenhope
Wahwoon
STURT HWY
168
Gum Creek
Waddi
Tuegan
Lake Coolah
Cowabbie West
Marrar
Old Junee

STURT HWY
Elginbah
Oolambeyan
Eurolie
OOLAMBEYAN NATIONAL PARK
Singorimbah
Clifford Downs
Coleambally
Narrandera
Gillenbah
Grong Grong
Matong
136
Ganmain
Coolamon
Junee Reefs

Moulamein
Inverness
Warwillah
Booabula East
Wargam
Golden Bays
Cuddell
Corobimilla
Morundah
Oak Vale
Birrego
Kywong
Currawarna
Junee
Harefield

Dhuragoon
Niemur
Wanganella
123
Willurah
Barabo
182
Coonong
Bundure
Emu Plains
Boree Creek
143
The Gap
Millwood
Collingullie
WAGGA WAGGA
Oura

Burraboi
Werai
Redbank
Conargo
Yanco
Widgiewa
Lake Urana
Urana
Lake Cullival
Lockhart
Kapooka
Uranquinty
Gumly Gumly
Forest Hill
Alfred Town

Wakool
Yallook
Dahwilly
Forest Creek
Mayrung
Jerilderie
Urana
Milbrulong
Tootool
The Rock
Ladysmith

Barham
Koondrook
Caldwell
Logie Brae
Blighty
Myall Plains
RIVERINA HWY
Oaklands
Ferndale
Rand
Pleasant Hills
Yerong Creek
LIVINGSTONE NP
Mangoplah
Burrandana
Kyeamba

Cohuna
GUNBOWER NP
Bunnaloo
Mathoura
NEW SOUTH WALES
74
MURRAY VALLEY NP
Finley
Berrigan
217
Sangar
Daysdale
Coreen
Walbundrie
Alma Park
Urangeline East
Five Ways
Henty
Cookardinia
Little Billabong
151

Leitchville
Gunbower
Womboota
Picnic Point
Tocumwal
Savenake
Rennie
HWY
Lowesdale
Brocklesby
Walla Walla
Morven
Culcain
M31
Carabost

Pyramid Hill
Bald Rock
Torrumbarry
Moira
BARMAH NP
96
Bearii
Koonoomoo
Barooga
Mulwala
Buraja
Balldale
Gerogery
BENAMBRA NP
HUME & HOVELL WALKING TRACK
Holbrook

Terrick Terrick
Sylvaterre
Barnes
Barmah
106
Waaia
Katunga
Yarrawonga
Lake Mulwala
Corowa
Wahgunyah
Gerogery West
Howlong
Jindera
Woomargama
WOOMARGAMA NP
Lankeys Creek

ECHUCA
Moama
Nathalia
Picola
Numurkah
Katamatite
128
Bundalong
Rutherglen
Barnawartha
Table Top
Bowna
Thologolong
Jingellic

VICTORIA
Kotta
Prairie
Lockington
Bamawm
HISTORIC TOWN
Tongala
MURRAY VALLEY
Kotupna
Wyuna
Kaarimba
Wunghnu
Telford
Esmond
Wilby
Tungamah
Youanmite
Marungi
Bunbartha
RUTHERGLEN WINERIES
Peechelba
Chiltern
ALBURY
WODONGA
Barnawartha
68
Talgarno
Granya
Burrowye
MOUNT LAWSON SP
Walwa

Joins map 50   Joins map 51

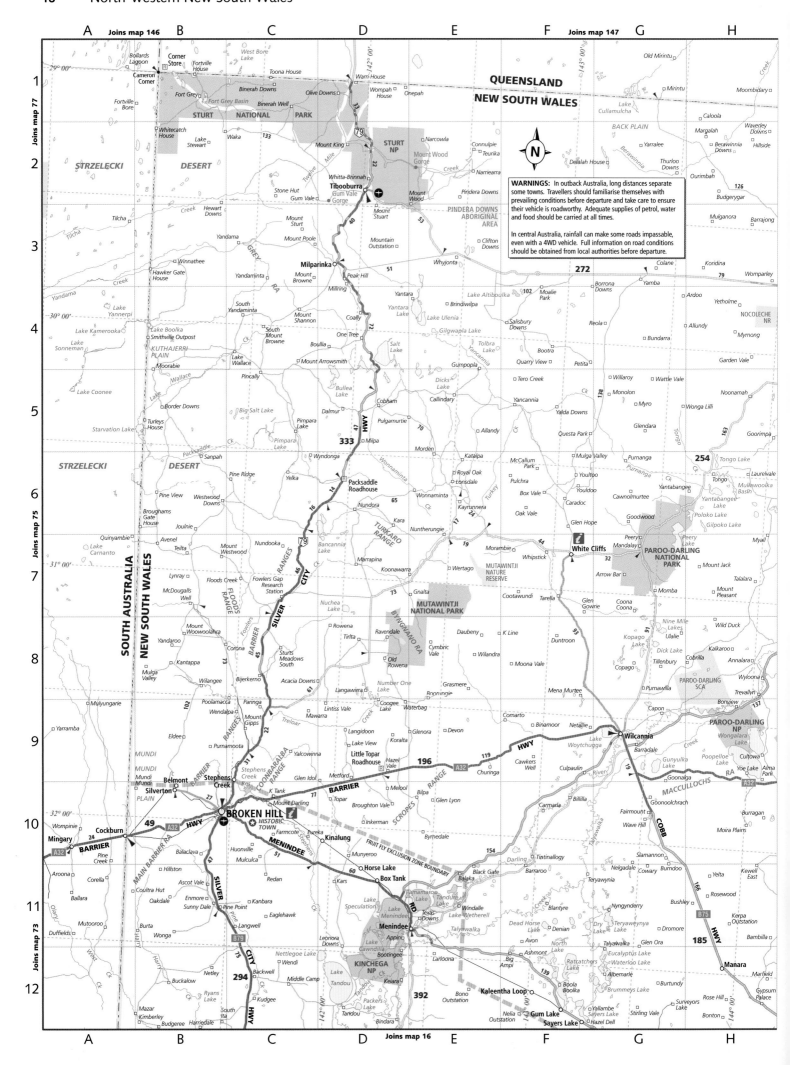

WARNINGS: In outback Australia, long distances separate some towns. Travellers should familiarise themselves with prevailing conditions before departure and take care to ensure their vehicle is roadworthy. Adequate supplies of petrol, water and food should be carried at all times.

In central Australia, rainfall can make some roads impassable, even with a 4WD vehicle. Full information on road conditions should be obtained from local authorities before departure.

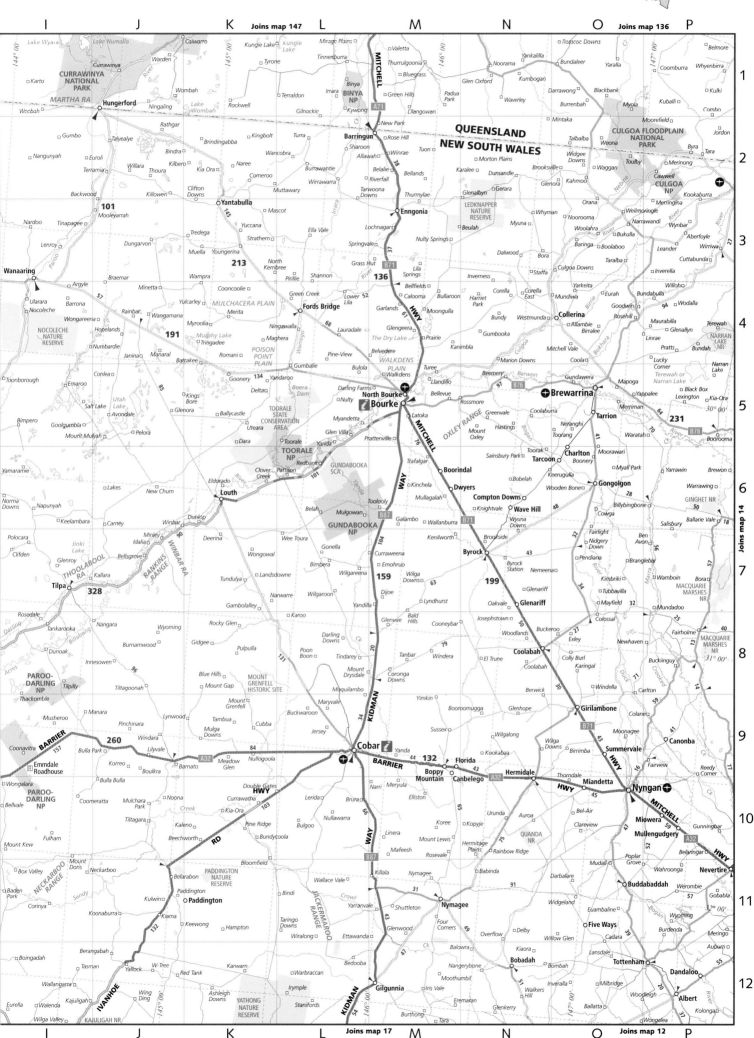

0 20 40 60 80 100 km

Joins map 147
Joins map 136
Joins map 14
Joins map 17
Joins map 12

QUEENSLAND
NEW SOUTH WALES

CURRAWINYA
NATIONAL
PARK

MARTHA RA

Hungerford

Wanaaring

CULGOA FLOODPLAIN
NATIONAL PARK

CULGOA
NP

LEDKNAPPER
NATURE
RESERVE

NARRAN
LAKE
NR

NOCOLECHE
NATURE
RESERVE

Yantabulla

Fords Bridge

MULCHACERA PLAIN

Enngonia

Collerina

Brewarrina

MITCHELL

Tarrion

POISON
POINT
PLAIN

WALKDENS
PLAIN

North Bourke
Bourke

Tarcoon
Charlton

Gongolgon

TOORALE
STATE
CONSERVATION
AREA

TOORALE
NP

OXLEY RANGE

Mount
Oxley

Boorindal
Dwyers

GINGHET NR

Louth

GUNDABOOKA
SCA

GUNDABOOKA
NP

Compton Downs
Wave Hill

Byrock

MACQUARIE
MARSHES
NR

THOOLABOOL
RA

WINBAR RA

RANKINS RANGE

Glenariff

Coolabah

MACQUARIE
MARSHES
NR

Tilpa

Girilambone

Summervale

PAROO-
DARLING NP

Canonba

Cobar

Nyngan

Miowera
Mullengudgery

Nevertire

PAROO-
DARLING
NP

Emmdale
Roadhouse

BARRIER

Boppy
Mountain
Canbelego

Florida
Hermidale
Miandetta

NECKARBOO
RANGE

PADDINGTON
NATURE
RESERVE

QUANDA
NR

Paddington

Buddabaddah

JACKERMAROO
RANGE

Nymagee

Five Ways

Bobadah

Tottenham

Dandaloo

IVANHOE

KIDMAN

Gilgunnia

YATHONG
NATURE
RESERVE

Albert

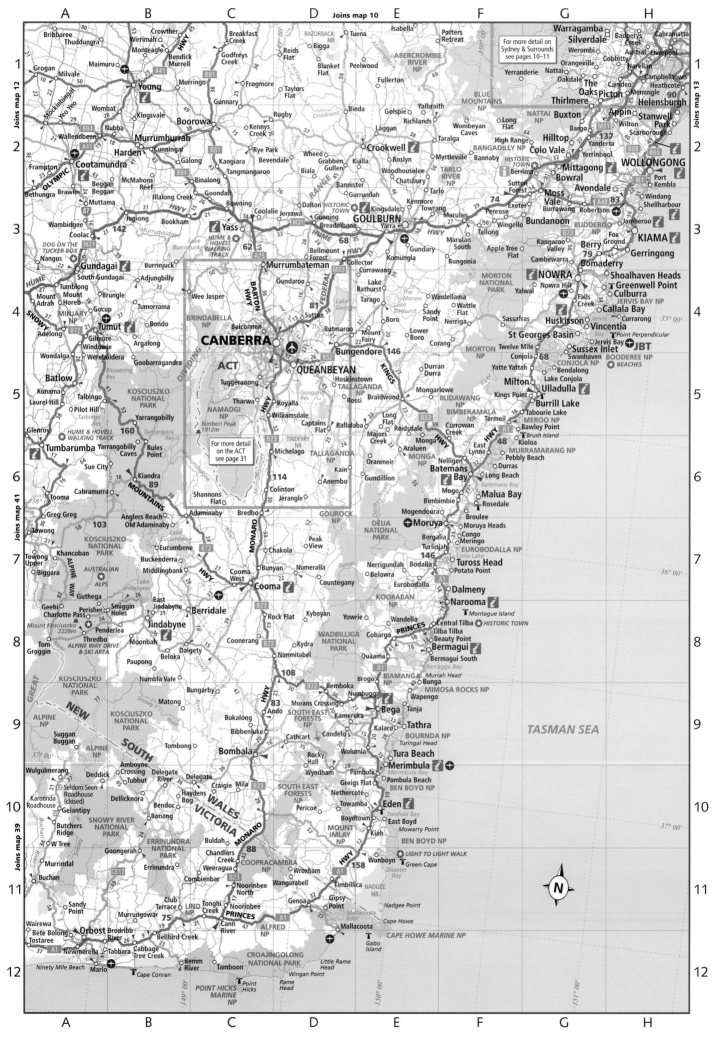

NSW

ALBURY *page 12 A12*

Railway Pl
Cnr Smollett and Young sts, Albury
1300 252 879
www.visitalburywodonga.com.au

ARMIDALE *page 15 J8*

82 Marsh St
(02) 6770 3888
www.armidaletourism.com.au

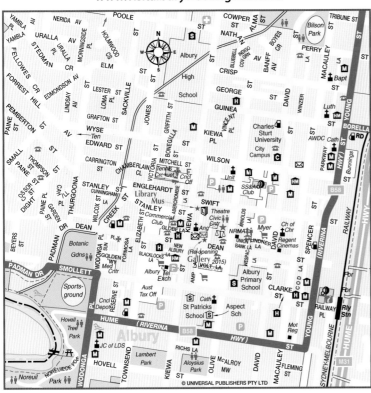

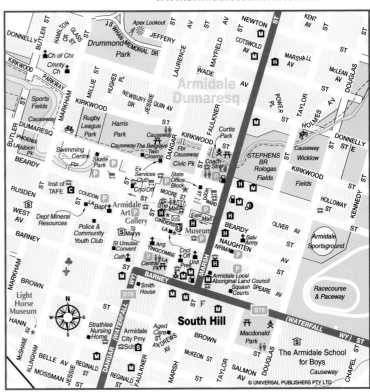

BALLINA *page 15 O4*

Cnr River St and Las Balsas Plaza
(02) 6686 3484 or 1800 777 666
www.discoverballina.com

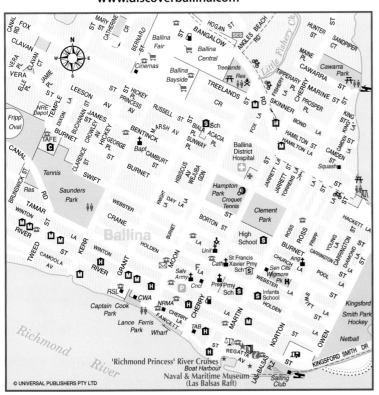

BATEMANS BAY *page 20 F6*

Cnr Princes Hwy and Beach Rd
(02) 4472 6900 or 1800 802 528
www.eurobodalla.com.au

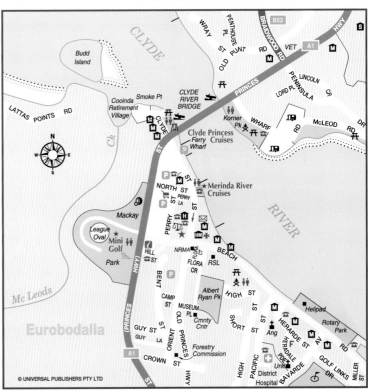

BATHURST *page 12 H5*

i 1 Kendall Ave
(02) 6332 1444 or 1800 681 000
www.bathurstregion.com.au

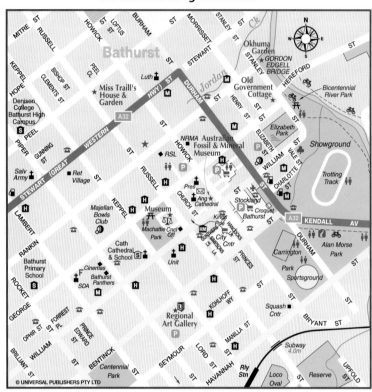

BERRIMA *page 13 I8*

i Berrima Court House
Cnr Argyle and Wilshire sts
(02) 4877 1505
www.southern-highlands.com.au or
www.berrimavillage.com.au

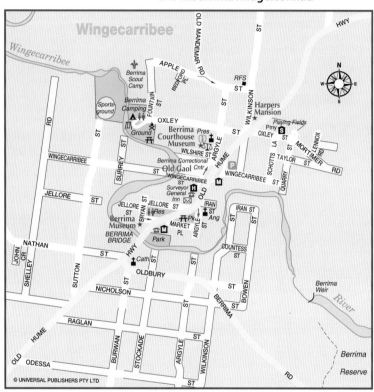

BOWRAL *page 13 I8*

i 62–70 Main St, Mittagong
(02) 4871 2888 or 1300 657 559
www.southern-highlands.com.au

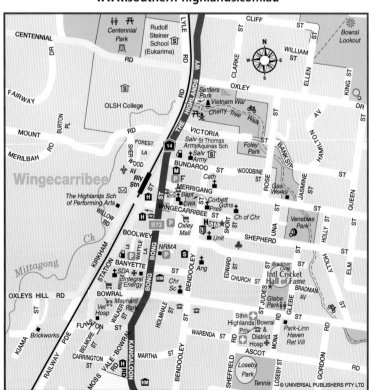

BROKEN HILL *page 18 B10*

i Cnr Blende and Bromide sts
(08) 8080 3560
www.brokenhillaustralia.com.au

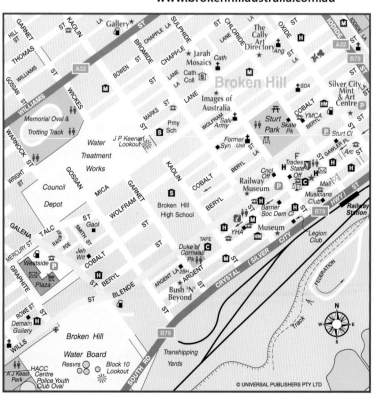

BYRON BAY *page 15 O3*

80 Jonson St
(02) 6680 8558
www.visitbyronbay.com

Byron
Bay

Coffs
Harbour

Cessnock

Cooma

CESSNOCK *page 13 L4*

455 Wine Country Dr, Pokolbin
(02) 4993 6700 or 1300 6948 6837
www.huntervalleyvisitorcentre.com.au

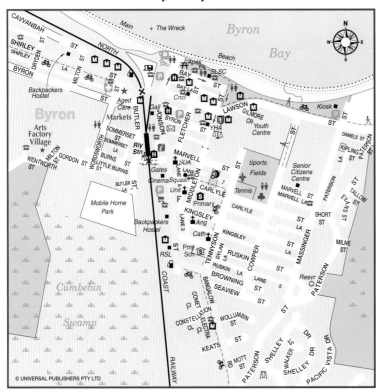

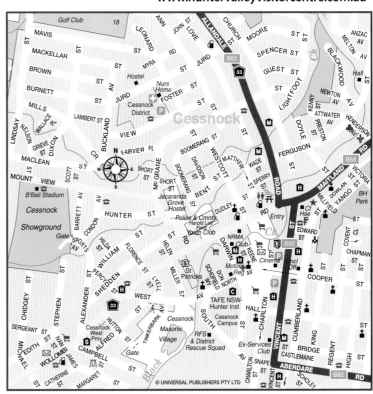

COFFS HARBOUR *page 15 N8*

Big Banana
351 Pacific Hwy
(02) 6648 4990
www.coffscoast.com.au

COOMA *page 20 C7*

119 Sharp St
(02) 6455 1742 or 1800 636 525
www.visitcooma.com.au

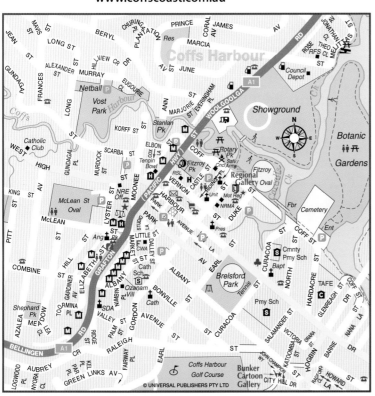

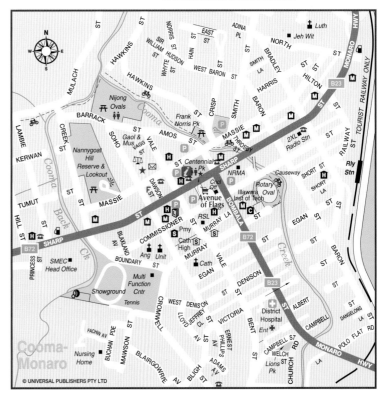

COOTAMUNDRA *page 12 D8*

Arts Centre Cootamundra
18–20 Wallendoon St
(02) 6942 4212
www.cootamundra.nsw.gov.au

DUBBO *page 12 F1*

22 Macquarie St
(02) 6801 4450
www.dubbo.com.au

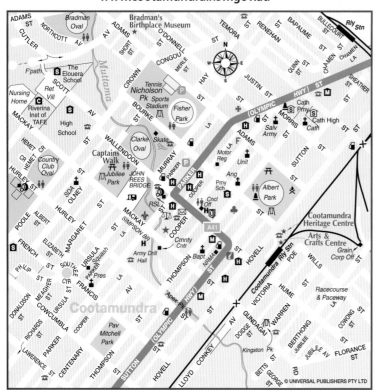

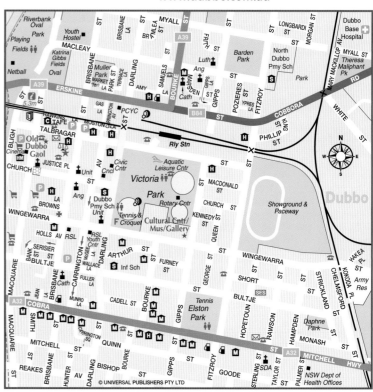

FORSTER–TUNCURRY *page 13 O2*

12 Little St, Forster
1800 802 692
www.greatlakes.org.au

GOSFORD *page 11 O3*

200 Mann St
(02) 4343 4444
www.visitcentralcoast.com.au

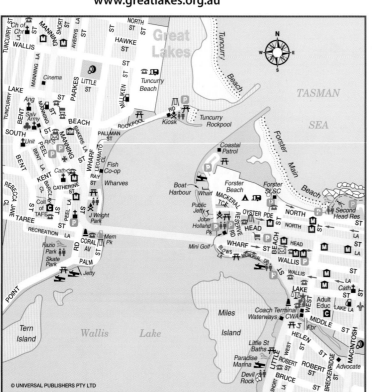

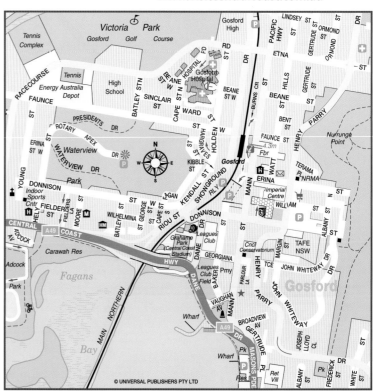

GOULBURN *page 12 H9*

201 Sloane St
(02) 4823 4492 or 1800 353 646
www.goulburnaustralia.com.au

GRAFTON *page 15 M6*

Cnr Pacific Hwy and Spring St,
South Grafton
(02) 6643 0800
www.clarencetourism.com

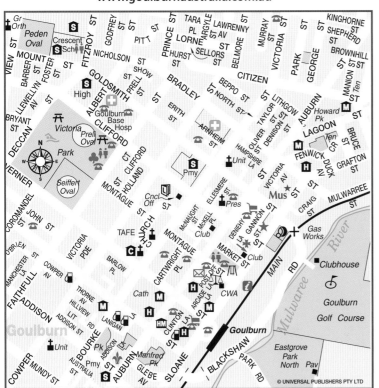

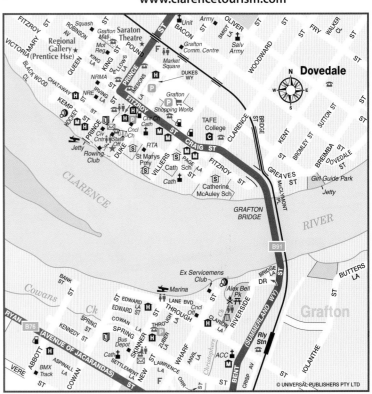

GRIFFITH *page 17 M7*

Cnr Banna and Jondaryan aves
(02) 6962 8400 or 1800 681 141
www.visitgriffith.com.au

KATOOMBA *page 10 D5*

Echo Point Rd
1300 653 408
www.bluemountainscitytourism.com.au

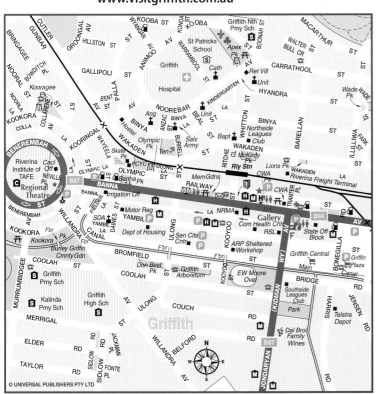

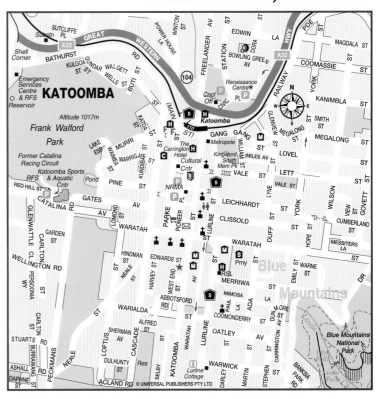

LISMORE *page 15 O3*

i Cnr Ballina Rd and Molesworth St
(02) 6626 0100 or 1300 369 795
www.visitlismore.com.au

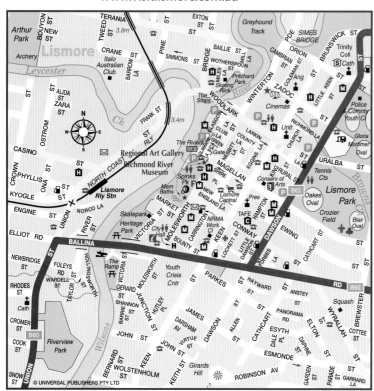

MAITLAND *page 13 L3*

i Cnr New England Hwy and High St
(02) 4931 2800
www.mymaitland.com.au

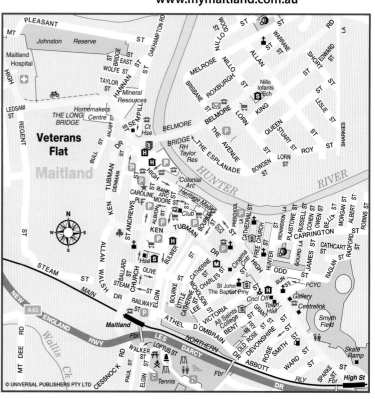

MUDGEE *page 12 H2*

i 84 Market St
(02) 6372 1020 or 1800 816 304
www.visitmudgeeregion.com.au

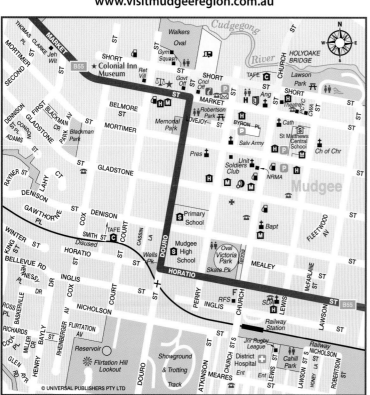

NEWCASTLE *page 13 M4*

i 3 Honeysuckle Dr
(02) 4929 2588
www.visitnewcastle.com.au

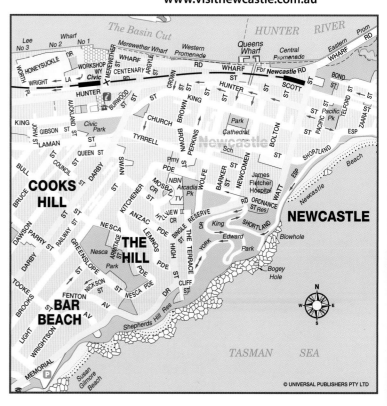

NSW

NOWRA *page 20 G4*

i **Bridge Rd**
(02) 4421 0778 or 1300 662 808
www.shoalhaven.com.au

ORANGE *page 12 G4*

i **149 Byng St**
(02) 6393 8225 or 1800 069 466
www.visitorange.com.au

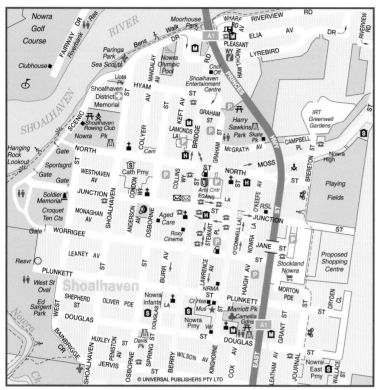

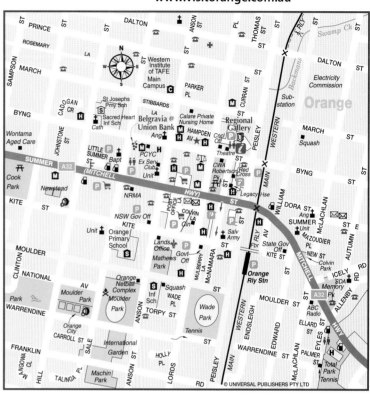

PORT MACQUARIE *page 15 M11*

i **Cnr Clarence and Hay sts**
(02) 6581 8000 or 1300 303 155
www.portmacquarieinfo.com.au

QUEANBEYAN *page 12 F11*

i **1 Farrer Pl**
(02) 6285 6307
www.visitqueanbeyan.com.au

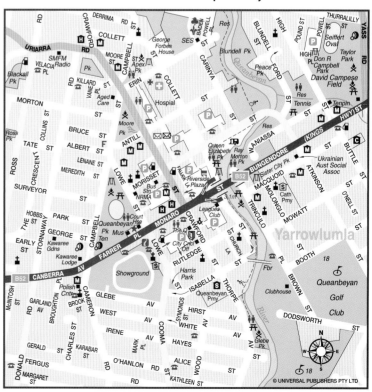

SINGLETON *page 13 K3*

Town Head Park
New England Hwy
(02) 6571 5888 or 1800 449 888
www.visitsingleton.com

TAMWORTH *page 14 H9*

The Big Golden Guitar
2 The Ringers Rd
(02) 6767 5300
www.destinationtamworth.com.au

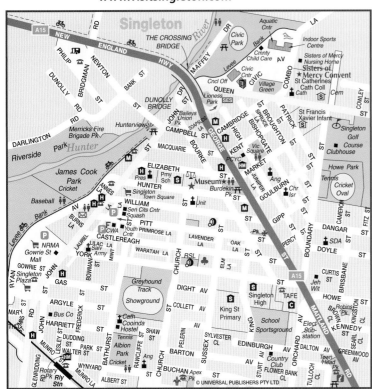

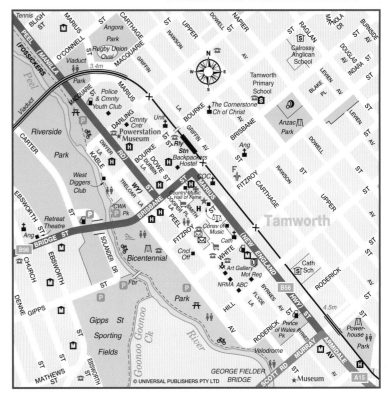

TAREE *page 13 N1*

21 Manning River Dr, Taree North
(02) 6592 5444 or 1800 182 733
www.manningvalley.info

TWEED HEADS *page 15 O1*

Cnr Wharf and Bay sts
(07) 5536 6737 or 1800 674 414
www.destinationtweed.com.au

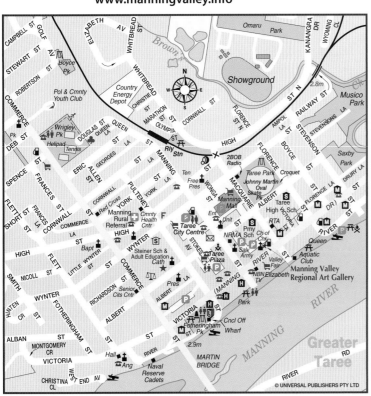

ULLADULLA *page 13 I11*

i Civic Centre
Princes Hwy
(02) 4444 8819 or 1300 662 808
www.shoalhavenholidays.com.au

Wagga
Wagga   Yass   Wollongong

Ulladulla

WAGGA WAGGA *page 12 B9*

i 183 Tarcutta St
(02) 6926 9621 or 1300 100 122
www.waggawaggaaustralia.com.au

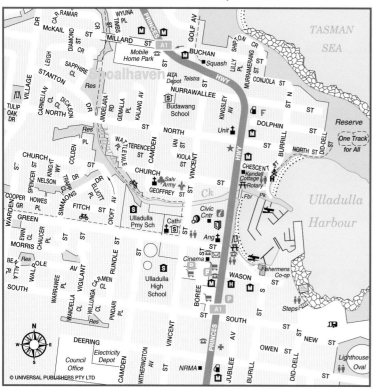

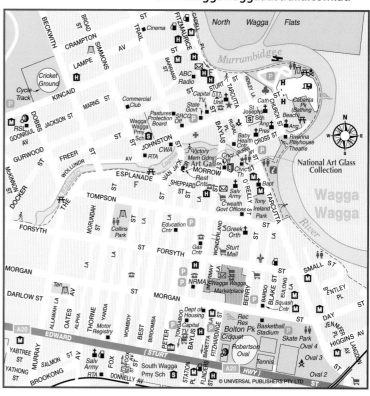

WOLLONGONG *page 13 J8*

i 93 Crown St
(02) 4267 5910 or 1800 240 737
www.visitwollongong.com.au

YASS *page 12 F9*

i 259 Comur St
(02) 6226 2557 or 1300 886 014
www.yassvalley.com.au

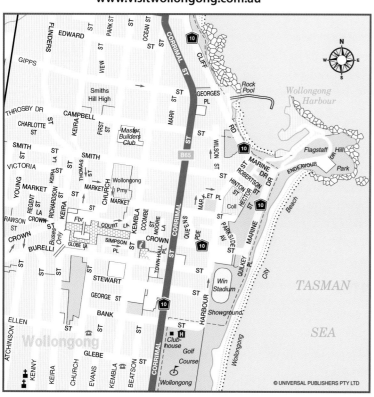

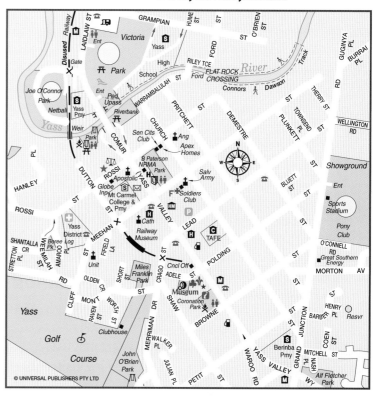

Corin Dam, Tidbinbilla

AUSTRALIAN CAPITAL TERRITORY

The Australian Capital Territory encompasses only 0.03 per cent of the entire continent, yet is the political centre of the nation and is rich with history and fine examples of modern architecture, art and culture.

The Australian Capital Territory – completely surrounded by New South Wales – is bordered by farmland, bushland, and national parks; almost half of its area is covered by the mountains and valleys of Namadgi National Park.

In 1908, the area of the Australian Capital Territory was selected as the site for the future national capital to appease bitter interstate rivalry between New South Wales and Victoria. The planning and creation of Canberra (Australia's only inland capital city) was the physical compromise between Sydney and Melbourne.

Today, the Australian Capital Territory is a place where politics and Australian history come face-to-face with architecture, art and design, and cutting-edge advancements in science and sport. Rounded-off with colourful festivals, cool-climate wineries and top-class dining and bars, the Australian Capital Territory offers a diverse range of activities and sights to suit every taste – from nature and science lovers to history and culture buffs.

Take a stroll through the Australian National Botanical Gardens or the National Arboretum, hike up Mount Ainslie, explore Namadgi National Park or cycle around Lake Burley Griffin. Visit Australia's only combined zoo and aquarium, venture back in time at the National Dinosaur museum or explore science at Questacon, the CSIRO Discovery Centre and the Deep Space Communication Complex. Admire art works from all over the world at one of the many museums and galleries, and delve into history at the Australian National Museum. Pay your respect at the Australian War Memorial, and create your own dollar coin at the Royal Mint – the Australian Capital Territory offers a host of interesting attractions for all ages.

INFORMATION CENTRE

Canberra and Region Visitor Centre
330 Northbourne Ave, Dickson;
(02) 6205 0044 or 1300 554 114
www.visitcanberra.com.au

Places of interest

	MAP REF	
Canberra Deep Space Communication		
Complex	34	A9
Corin Forest	31	B7
Molonglo Gorge	31	F5
Namadgi National Park	31	D8
Tidbinbilla Nature Reserve	31	C6

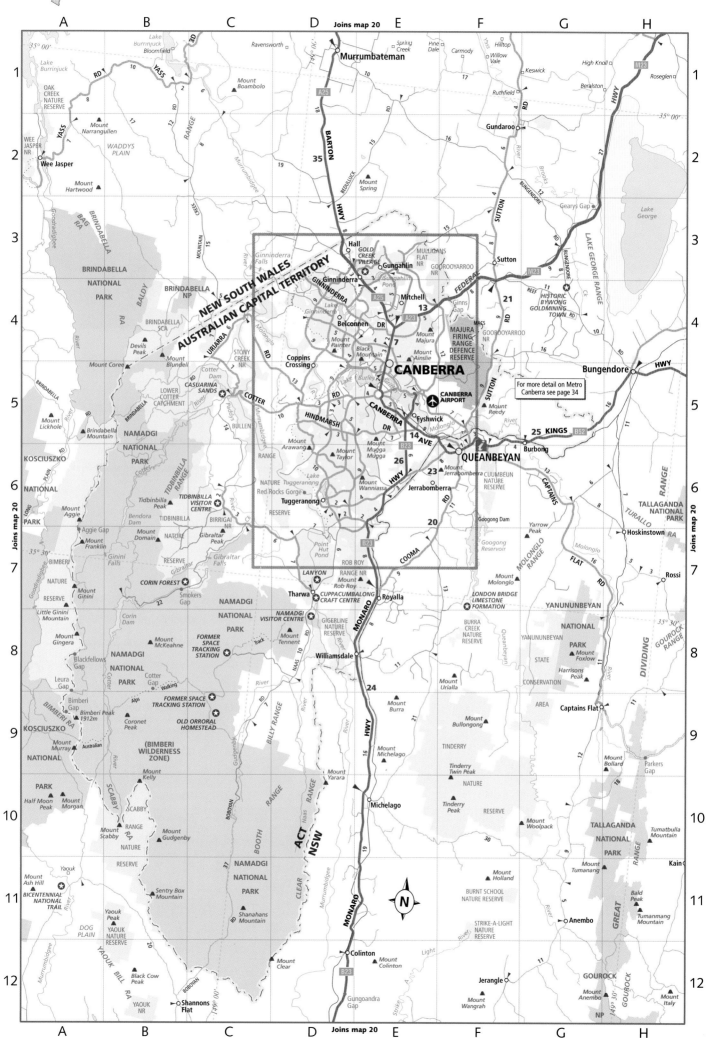

0 5 10 15 20 km

A B C D E F G H

Joins map 20

Murrumbateman

Ravensworth
Spring Creek
Pine Dale
Carmody
Willow Vale
Hilltop
High Knoll
Roseglen
Keswick
Beralston
Ruthfield

Lake Burrinjuck
Lake Burrinjuck
Bloomfield
Mount Boambolo

OAK CREEK NATURE RESERVE

YASS
RD

Gundaroo

35° 00'

WEE JASPER NR
Wee Jasper

Mount Narrangullen

YASS

Mount Hartwood

WADDYS PLAIN

RANGE

Gearys Gap

Lake George

BRINDABELLA
BAG RA

Sutton

LAKE GEORGE RANGE

BRINDABELLA
NATIONAL
PARK

BALDY RA

BRINDABELLA NP

BRINDABELLA SCA

NEW SOUTH WALES
AUSTRALIAN CAPITAL TERRITORY

Ginninderra Falls

Hall
GOLD CREEK VILLAGE
Gungahlin

MULLIGANS FLAT NR
GOOROOYARROO NR

21

HISTORIC BYWONG GOLDMINING TOWN

Devils Peak
Mount Coree
Mount Blundell

URIARRA
STONY CREEK NR

Ginninderra
Lake Ginninderra

Mitchell
13

Mount Painter
Black Mountain
Belconnen

Mount Ainslie
Mount Majura
Mount Majura

MAJURA FIRING RANGE DEFENCE RESERVE

GOOROOYARROO NR

CASUARINA SANDS
LOWER COTTER CATCHMENT

Cotter Dam

Coppins Crossing

CANBERRA

Bungendore
HWY

Mount Lickhole
Brindabella Mountain

NAMADGI
NATIONAL
PARK

BULLEN

COTTER RD

CANBERRA AIRPORT
Fyshwick

25 KINGS
Burbong

KOSCIUSZKO
NATIONAL
NATIONAL

HINDMARSH DR

Mount Reedy

CUUMBEUN NATURE RESERVE

TALLAGANDA NATIONAL PARK

Mount Aggie
Tidbinbilla Peak
TIDBINBILLA VISITOR CENTRE

TIDBINBILLA RANGE

Mount Arawang
Mount Taylor

14 AVE
Mount Mugga Mugga
26

QUEANBEYAN
Mount Jerrabomberra
23
Jerrabomberra

TURALLO RANGE

Mount Franklin
Aggie Gap
Bendora Dam

Mount Domain
TIDBINBILLA
BIRRIGAI NR

Gibraltar Peak

Lake Tuggeranong
Red Rocks Gorge
RESERVE

Mount Wanniassa

20

Googong Dam
Googong Reservoir

Yarrow Peak

MOLONGLO RANGE

Hoskinstown

BIMBERI
NATURE
RESERVE

Ginini Falls
Little Ginini Mountain

Mount Ginini

Gibraltar Falls

Tuggeranong

Point Hut Pond

ROB ROY

London Bridge Limestone Formation

FLAT RD

Rossi

YANUNUNBEYAN

Mount Gingera
CORIN FOREST

Corin Dam

NAMADGI
NATIONAL
PARK

LANYON
RANGE NR
Mount Rob Roy

Tharwa
CUPPACUMBALONG CRAFT CENTRE
Royalla

BURRA CREEK NATURE RESERVE

NATIONAL
PARK

GOUROCK RANGE

Blackfellows Gap
Mount McKeahnie

FORMER SPACE TRACKING STATION

NAMADGI VISITOR CENTRE
GIGERLINE NATURE RESERVE
Mount Tennent

MONARO HWY

YANUNUNBEYAN

Mount Foxlow

DIVIDING

Leura Gap
Cotter Gap

Williamsdale

STATE
CONSERVATION

Harrisons Peak

BIMBERI RA
KOSCIUSZKO
Bimberi Gap
Bimberi Peak 1912m
Coronet Peak
OLD ORRORAL HOMESTEAD
FORMER SPACE TRACKING STATION

24

Mount Uriala

AREA
Captains Flat

Mount Murray
Australian
NATIONAL
PARK

(BIMBERI WILDERNESS ZONE)

Mount Kelly
SCABBY RANGE

BILLY RANGE

Mount Burra
21

Mount Bullongong

TINDERRY

Mount Bollard
Parkers Gap

Half Moon Peak
Mount Morgan
Mount Scabby
SCABBY RANGE NATURE
Mount Gudgenby

Mount Yarara

Mount Michelago
Tinderry Twin Peak

TINDERRY
NATURE

Mount Woolpack

TALLAGANDA
NATIONAL
PARK

Tumatbulla Mountain

Mount Ash Hill
Yaouk
BICENTENNIAL NATIONAL TRAIL

Yaouk Peak
YAOUK NATURE RESERVE

Mount Kelly

NAMADGI
NATIONAL
PARK

Michelago
Tinderry Peak
RESERVE

Mount Tumanang
Kain

DOG PLAIN
YAOUK BILL RA
YAOUK NR

Black Cow Peak

Sentry Box Mountain
Shanahans Mountain

ACT
NSW
BOOTH RANGE
CLEAR RANGE
NAAS RANGE

Mount Holland
BURNT SCHOOL NATURE RESERVE
STRIKE-A-LIGHT NATURE RESERVE

Anembo

GREAT

Bald Peak
Tumanmang Mountain

N

Colinton
B23
Gungoandra Gap

Mount Colinton
Mount Clear

Jerangle

Mount Wangrah

GOUROCK
Mount Anembo
NP
Mount Italy

Joins map 20

A B C D E F G H

For more detail on Metro Canberra see page 34

Canberra

In 1820, the first European settlers called the area that is now known as Canberra the Limestone Plains. In 1824, Joshua Moore established a 2500 hectare property beside the Murrumbidgee River, naming it 'Canberry'. It is thought that Moore derived the term from the Aboriginal word for meeting place, kamberra, and that the city's name, Canberra, is based on this Aboriginal origin.

Sydney merchant Robert Campbell took up 10,000 hectares of land in the Canberra region in 1825, establishing the first part of the Duntroon Estate. After selecting the area as the site for the nation's capital in 1908, the Commonwealth Government acquired the land surrounding Duntroon in 1911 and began construction of public buildings in 1913.

Canberra was developed based on the design of American architect Walter Burley Griffin and his wife, Marion Mahony Griffin. It is one of the world's best planned cities, with Lake Burley Griffin as its centrepiece. The lake was created in 1963–4 by the damming of the Molonglo River, a tributary of the Murrumbidgee River. The lake is popular for activities such as rowing, sailing and fishing. Ferry cruises and a self-guided walking or cycling tour are a perfect way to take in the important public buildings, landmarks and memorials along its 40.5-kilometre shoreline.

A special time to visit Canberra is during Floriade, the city's annual spring flower festival celebrated in Commonwealth Park in September–October.

Places of interest

	MAP REF			MAP REF
Anzac Parade	33 H4		Lanyon Historic Homestead	34 C12
Australian Institute of Sport	34 E4		Mount Ainslie Lookout	34 F5
Australian National Botanic Gardens	33 A1		Mugga-Mugga Cottage	34 F8
Australian National University	33 C3		Museum of Australian Democracy at	
Australian War Memorial	34 F5		Old Parliament House	33 E8
Blundell's Cottage	33 H6		National Arboretum Canberra	34 C5
Calthorpes' House	34 E7		National Carillon	33 H7
Canberra Theatre Centre	33 F3		National Film and Sound Archive	33 D3
Captain Cook Memorial Water Jet	33 F6		National Gallery of Australia	33 G8
Casino Canberra	33 F3		National Library of Australia	33 E7
City Hill Lookout	33 E3		National Museum of Australia	33 D6
Commonwealth Park	33 F5		National Portrait Gallery	33 F8
CSIRO Discovery Centre	33 C1		National Zoo & Aquarium	34 C6
Gold Creek Village/Ginninderra Village:			Parliament House	33 D10
Australian Reptile Centre, Cockington			Questacon – the National Science and	
Green, National Dinosaur Museum	34 D2		Technology Centre	33 F7
Gorman House Arts Centre	33 G2		Royal Australian Mint	34 D7
High Court of Australia	33 G7		Telstra Tower (Black Mountain Tower)	34 D5
Lake Burley Griffin	34 E6			

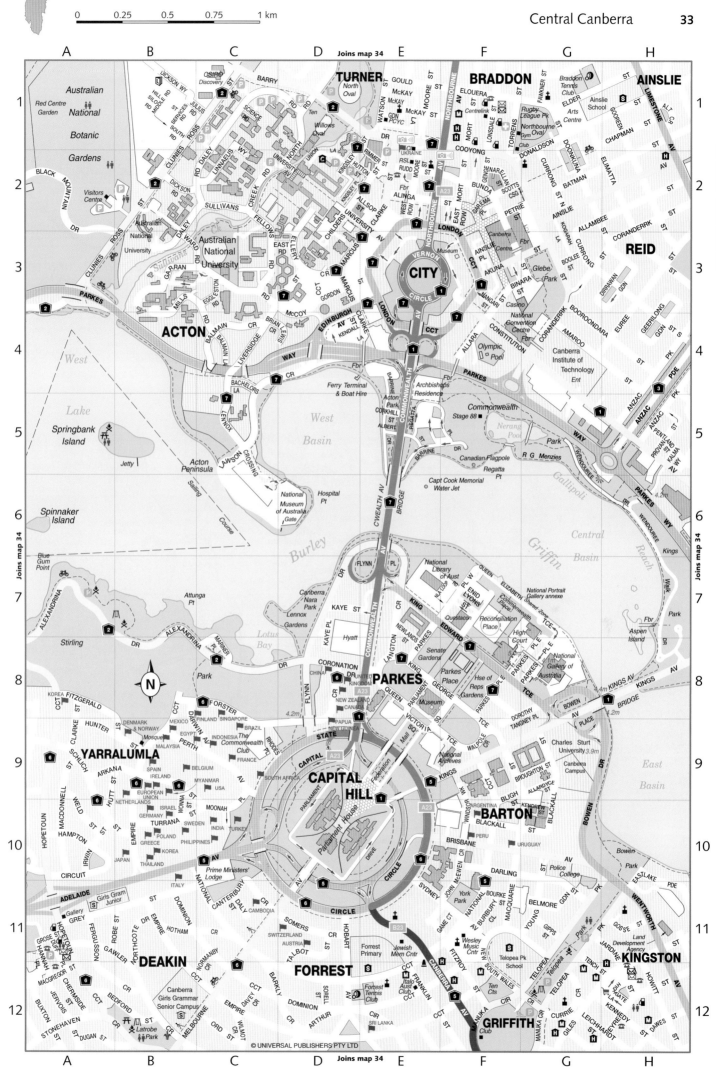

ACT

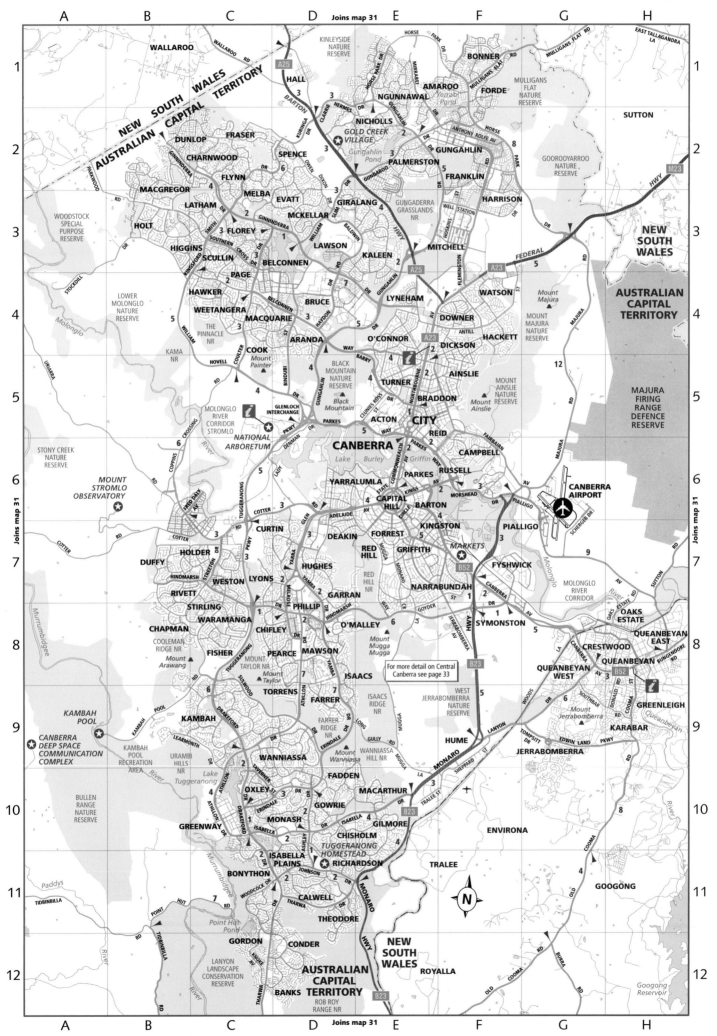

0 1 2 3 4 5 km

A B C D **Joins map 31** E F G H

WALLAROO

NEW SOUTH WALES

AUSTRALIAN CAPITAL TERRITORY

HALL

KINLEYSIDE NATURE RESERVE

BONNER

AMAROO
FORDE

MULLIGANS FLAT RD

MULLIGANS FLAT NATURE RESERVE

SUTTON

DUNLOP
FRASER
CHARNWOOD
SPENCE

NGUNNAWAL

NICHOLLS
GOLD CREEK VILLAGE

PALMERSTON

GUNGAHLIN
FRANKLIN

GOOROOYARROO NATURE RESERVE

NEW SOUTH WALES

MACGREGOR
FLYNN
MELBA
EVATT

LATHAM
MELBA
MCKELLAR
GIRALANG

HARRISON

MITCHELL

HOLT
FLOREY
BELCONNEN
LAWSON
KALEEN

WATSON

AUSTRALIAN CAPITAL TERRITORY

HIGGINS
SCULLIN
PAGE

HAWKER
WEETANGERA
MACQUARIE
BRUCE
ARANDA

LYNEHAM

DOWNER
DICKSON
HACKETT

MOUNT MAJURA

MOUNT MAJURA NATURE RESERVE

MAJURA FIRING RANGE DEFENCE RESERVE

LOWER MOLONGLO NATURE RESERVE

THE PINNACLE NR

COOK

O'CONNOR

12

WOODSTOCK SPECIAL PURPOSE RESERVE

Molonglo

KAMA NR

Mount Painter

BLACK MOUNTAIN NATURE RESERVE

TURNER

AINSLIE

MOUNT AINSLIE NATURE RESERVE

Mount Ainslie

URIARRA

MOLONGLO RIVER CORRIDOR STROMLO

GLENLOCH INTERCHANGE

NATIONAL ARBORETUM

Black Mountain

ACTON

BRADDON

CITY

REID

STONY CREEK NATURE RESERVE

MOUNT STROMLO OBSERVATORY

CANBERRA

Lake Burley Griffin

YARRALUMLA

PARKES

CAMPBELL

RUSSELL

CANBERRA AIRPORT

CURTIN

CAPITAL HILL
BARTON

MORSHEAD

PIALLIGO

HOLDER
DUFFY

DEAKIN

FORREST
GRIFFITH

KINGSTON

MARKETS

FYSHWICK

SYMONSTON

OAKS ESTATE

WESTON
LYONS

HUGHES
RED HILL

GARRAN

NARRABUNDAH

Molonglo

MOLONGLO RIVER CORRIDOR

RIVETT
STIRLING
WARAMANGA
PHILLIP
CHIFLEY

O'MALLEY

QUEANBEYAN EAST

CRESTWOOD

CHAPMAN

FISHER

PEARCE
MAWSON

Mount Mugga Mugga

QUEANBEYAN WEST

QUEANBEYAN

COOLEMAN RIDGE NR

Mount Arawang

MOUNT TAYLOR NR
Mount Taylor

TORRENS

ISAACS

For more detail on Central Canberra see page 33

WEST JERRABOMBERRA NATURE RESERVE

Mount Jerrabomberra

GREENLEIGH

KAMBAH POOL

CANBERRA DEEP SPACE COMMUNICATION COMPLEX

KAMBAH POOL RECREATION AREA

KAMBAH

FARRER

ISAACS RIDGE NR

KARABAR

URAMBI HILLS NR

Lake Tuggeranong

FARRER RIDGE NR

Mount Wanniassa
WANNIASSA HILL NR

HUME

JERRABOMBERRA

BULLEN RANGE NATURE RESERVE

WANNIASSA

FADDEN

ENVIRONA

OXLEY
GREENWAY
MONASH

MACARTHUR
GOWRIE
GILMORE

CHISHOLM
TUGGERANONG HOMESTEAD

ISABELLA PLAINS
RICHARDSON

TRALEE

BONYTHON

CALWELL

THEODORE

GOOGONG

Paddys

TIDBINBILLA

Point Hut Pond

GORDON
CONDER

BANKS

LANYON LANDSCAPE CONSERVATION RESERVE

AUSTRALIAN CAPITAL TERRITORY

ROB ROY RANGE NR

NEW SOUTH WALES

ROYALLA

N

Googong Reservoir

Tulips during the Floriade Festival

VICTORIA

In a country full of mind-numbing distances, nothing seems far away in Victoria and there is a huge array of natural, cultural and historic areas just waiting to be discovered.

Victoria packs a lot within its borders. The Murray River stretches along the northern border with New South Wales and is a delightful destination. The southern coastline is spectacular and varied, encompassing the Great Ocean Road to the west and Wilsons Promontory and the Gippsland Lakes area to the east. Victoria's magnificent High Country, boasting the beautiful peaks of Mount Buller and Mount Hotham, offers much to explore, and the Goldfields districts, including the towns of Ballarat and Bendigo, are testimony to an exciting episode in the state's history. Tranquil lakes, an amazing selection of national parks, cool forests and fertile countryside await, and visitors will feel welcome in the cities, towns and villages along the way.

Covering 227,416 square kilometres of the south-eastern corner of Australia, Victoria is a relatively compact state – the second smallest after Tasmania. The state's mostly temperate climate has four distinct seasons, each with its own attractions, making Victoria a destination to visit and explore at any time of the year.

Victoria's manageable size and efficient road system make travelling within the state easy and comfortable. Transport options are excellent: coaches, trains and planes carry visitors into and around Victoria, and for those who want to explore independently, touring by car is convenient. Most places in the state can be reached within a day's drive of the capital city, Melbourne. In a half-hour drive from Melbourne you could be taking in mist-laden mountain ranges and fern gullies; in an hour you could be lying on a sandy beach in a sheltered bay, or surfing the rugged Southern Ocean; in around four hours you could be standing on the edge of an immense desert that stretches away into Australia's centre.

The discerning traveller will find plenty to enjoy in Victoria. Wine-lovers can select from over 800 wineries across 21 wine regions, ranging from the Grampians in the south-west to Rutherglen in the north-east. Fresh produce is also a specialty throughout the state, with specific gourmet focal points like the Milawa Gourmet Region and Gippsland Gourmet Country.

Melbourne, the state's capital, is a vibrant city. Its calendar is full of events and festivals including the Melbourne Food & Wine Festival, the Melbourne International Comedy Festival and the Melbourne Festival. It is also the nation's sporting capital, hosting major sporting events including the Australian Open tennis championships and the Melbourne Cup horserace.

Houseboat on the Murray at sunrise

Places of interest

	MAP REF			MAP REF	
Alexandra Timber Tramway	47	N1	Mornington Peninsula	44, 46, 47	
Alpine National Park	49	J1	Mount Buffalo National Park	51	J9
Beechworth	51	J7	Murray River	50, 51, 52, 53, 55	
Buchan Caves	58	A10	Otway Fly Treetop Adventures	46	A11
Central Deborah Gold Mine, Bendigo	50	A9	Phillip Island Penguin Parade	47	J11
Croajingolong National Park	58	G11	Pioneer Settlement, Swan Hill	55	L2
Dandenong Ranges National Park	43	P10	Port Campbell National Park	57	J10
Flagstaff Hill Maritime Village,			Port of Echuca Discovery Centre	50	C5
Warrnambool	56	G8	Portland Maritime Discovery Centre	56	D8
Gippsland Heritage Park, Moe	47	P9	Puffing Billy Steam Train	43	O12
Gippsland Lakes	49	N6	Rutherglen wineries	51	I6
Glenrowan	50	H8	Sovereign Hill, Ballarat	46	D3
Golden Dragon Museum, Bendigo	50	A9	Surf World Museum, Torquay	46	F9
Grampians National Park	56	H2	Tarra–Bulga National Park	49	I8
Great Ocean Road	46	E10	Tower Hill Wildlife Reserve	56	G8
Gum San Chinese Heritage Centre,			Victorian Goldfields Railway	55	N11
Ararat	57	I2	Werribee Open Range Zoo	46	H6
Hanging Rock	46	H2	William Ricketts Sanctuary,		
Healesville Sanctuary	47	M5	Mt Dandenong	43	O9
Lake Eildon	47	O1	Wilsons Promontory	48	H11
Milawa Gourmet Region	51	I8			

INFORMATION CENTRE

Melbourne Visitor Centre
Federation Square, 2 Swanston St,
Melbourne; (03) 9658 9658
www.visitvictoria.com
www.visitmelbourne.com

The Great Ocean Road

MAPS

VICTORIA

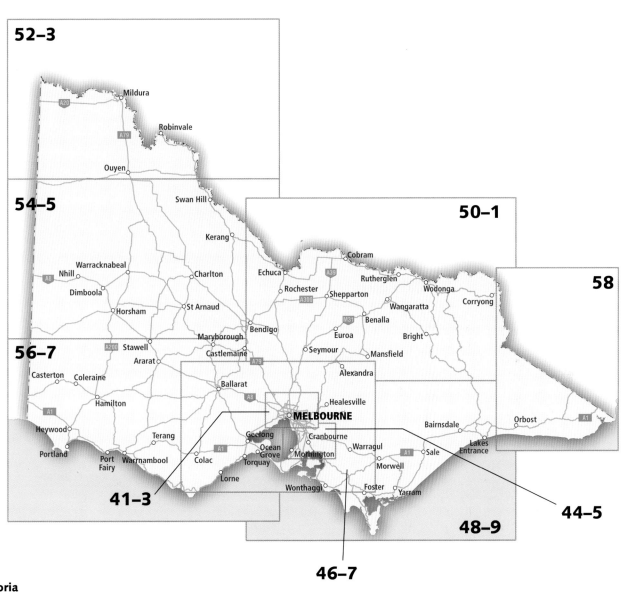

52–3

54–5

50–1

58

56–7

41–3

44–5

48–9

46–7

Victoria

Central Melbourne	41
Metro Melbourne, North	42–3
Metro Melbourne, South	44–5
Melbourne & Surrounds	46–7
Southern Central Victoria	48–9
Northern Central Victoria	50–1
North-western Victoria	52–3
Central-western Victoria	54–5
South-western Victoria	56–7
Eastern Victoria	58

INTER-CITY ROUTES	DISTANCE
Melbourne–Sydney via Hume Hwy/Fwy M31 M31 M5 M1	879 km
Melbourne–Sydney via Princes Hwy/Fwy M1 A1 M1 A1 M1	1039 km
Melbourne–Adelaide via Western & Dukes hwys M8 A8 M1 A1	729 km
Melbourne–Adelaide via Princes Hwy M1 A1 B1 M1 A1	911 km
Melbourne–Brisbane via Newell Hwy M31 M39 A39 A39 A2 M5	1676 km

Royal Exhibition Building

Melbourne

Melbourne, the capital of Victoria, is a culturally sophisticated city with a decidedly European feel. Grand buildings and a vibrant network of laneways invite visitors to explore theatres, art galleries and boutique shops. But sport is also intrinsic to the Melbourne identity, and watching an AFL footy match at the MCG is a must.

The discovery of gold in Victoria in 1851 made Melbourne a wealthy city, reflected in its impressive buildings, wide streets and boulevards and beautiful public gardens.

Today, Melbourne is renowned for its fine dining and love of sport. Foodie hubs are scattered throughout the city, offering a multicultural smorgasbord of quality produce. Melbourne also hosts many major sporting events including the Australian Open tennis championships, the Formula 1 Australian Grand Prix and the Melbourne Cup horserace.

Shopping is another highlight in Melbourne. Many of the city's major stores and unique boutiques can be found on the streets running west from Swanston Street. Brunswick Street in the suburb of Fitzroy is also known for its vibrant and eclectic shops, as well as its fine restaurants.

Happily, Melbourne's many attractions can be visited by travelling on its famous trams. With their old-world charm, they are one of the most unique public transport systems in Australia.

Places of interest

	MAP REF		MAP REF
Albert Park	41 E12	Melbourne Museum	41 F2
The Arts Centre	41 F7	Melbourne and Olympic Parks	41 H8
Australian Centre for Contemporary Art	41 E8	Melbourne Zoo	42 G7
Australian Centre for the Moving Image	41 F6	National Gallery of Victoria	41 F7
		Old Melbourne Gaol	41 E3
Carlton Gardens	41 F2	Old Treasury Building	41 G5
Champions: Thoroughbred Racing Gallery	41 H6	Parliament House	41 G4
		Polly Woodside, Maritime Museum	41 C8
Chinatown	41 E4	Queen Victoria Market	41 C3
Chinese Museum	41 E4	Royal Botanic Gardens Melbourne	41 H9
Crown Entertainment Complex	41 D7	Royal Exhibition Building	41 F2
Eureka Skydeck	41 E7	SEALIFE Melbourne Aquarium	41 D7
Federation Square	41 F6	Sidney Myer Music Bowl	41 F7
Fitzroy Gardens	41 H4	Southgate	41 E7
Immigration Museum	41 D6	State Library of Victoria	41 E4
Melbourne Cricket Ground (MCG) and National Sports Museum	41 H6		

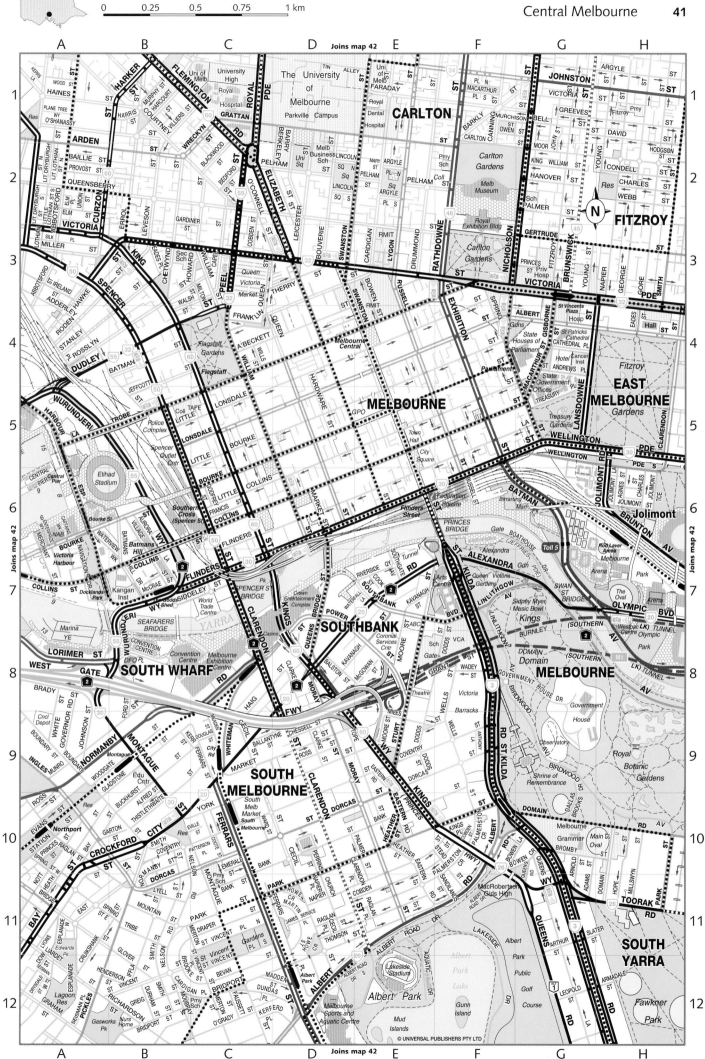

© UNIVERSAL PUBLISHERS PTY LTD

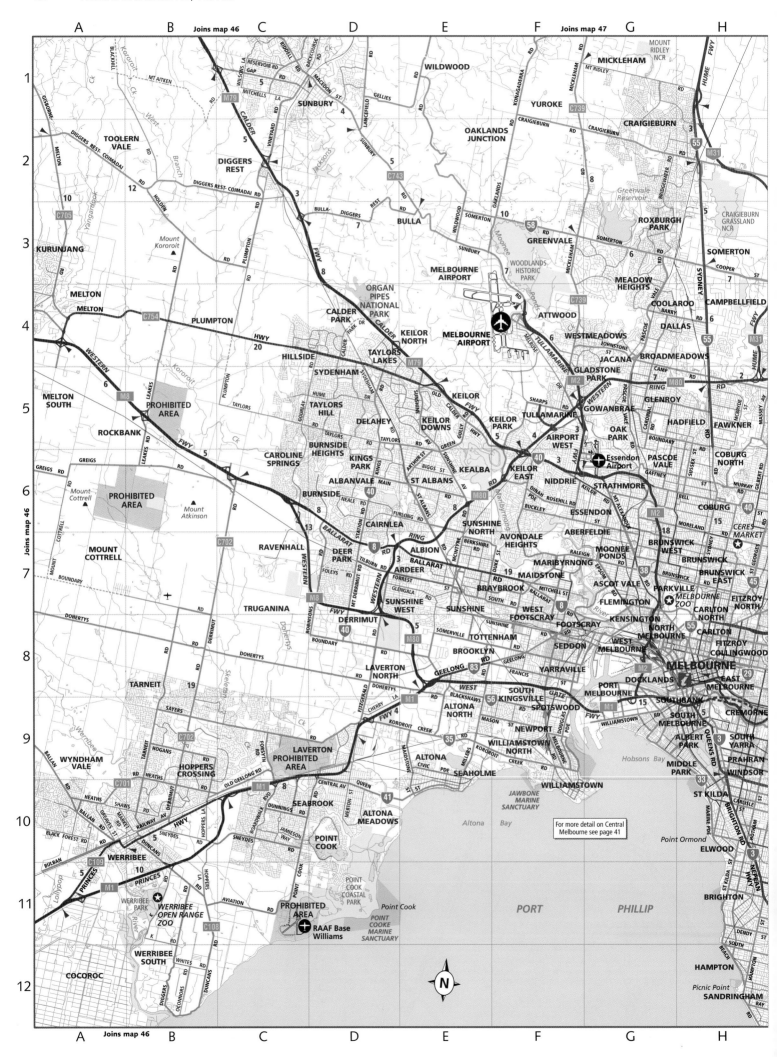

Joins map 46
Joins map 47
Joins map 46
Joins map 46

For more detail on Central Melbourne see page 41

VIC

0 2 4 6 8 km

Joins map 47

Joins map 44

Joins map 45

Joins map 47

I J K L M N O P

1 2 3 4 5 6 7 8 9 10 11 12

DONNYBROOK
WOODSTOCK
YAN YEAN
KINGLAKE NATIONAL PARK
Mount Sugarloaf
STRATHEWEN
KINGLAKE NATIONAL PARK
HEALESVILLE-KINGLAKE

WOLLERT
MERNDA
ARTHURS CREEK
St ANDREWS
KINGLAKE
Mount Beggary
KINGLAKE NATIONAL PARK

CRAIGIEBURN
DOREEN
NUTFIELD
COTTLES BRIDGE
SMITHS GULLY
KINGLAKE NATIONAL PARK
STEELS CREEK

EPPING
SOUTH MORANG
YARRAMBAT
HURSTBRIDGE
PANTON HILL
WATSONS CREEK
CHRISTMAS HILLS
WARRANDYTE-KINGLAKE NATURE CONSERVATION RESERVE

LALOR
MILL PARK
PLENTY
DIAMOND CREEK
WATTLE GLEN
KANGAROO GROUND
YARRA GLEN
YARRA VALLEY WINERIES

THOMASTOWN
PLENTY GORGE PARKLANDS
SAINT HELENA
BEND OF ISLANDS
YERING
YERING BUSHLAND RESERVE

BUNDOORA
WATSONIA NORTH
GREENSBOROUGH
BRIAR HILL
ELTHAM NORTH
RESEARCH
WONGA PARK
COLDSTREAM

RESERVOIR
WATSONIA
MACLEOD
YALLAMBIE
MONTMORENCY
ELTHAM
NORTH WARRANDYTE
WARRANDYTE STATE PARK
CHIRNSIDE PARK

KINGSBURY
PRESTON
HEIDELBERG WEST
ROSANNA
VIEWBANK
LOWER PLENTY
HEIDE MUSEUM OF MODERN ART
YARRA VALLEY PARKLANDS
WARRANDYTE
LILYDALE

BELLFIELD
HEIDELBERG HEIGHTS
HEIDELBERG
WARRANDYTE SOUTH
CROYDON NORTH

THORNBURY
IVANHOE
EAGLEMONT
TEMPLESTOWE
WARRANWOOD
CROYDON HILLS

NORTHCOTE
IVANHOE EAST
BULLEEN
TEMPLESTOWE LOWER
PARK ORCHARDS
CROYDON

ALPHINGTON
FAIRFIELD
DONCASTER
DONVALE
RINGWOOD NORTH
MOOROOLBARK
MOUNT EVELYN

KEW
KEW EAST
BALWYN NORTH
DONCASTER EAST
MITCHAM
RINGWOOD
CROYDON SOUTH
KILSYTH
MONTROSE

RICHMOND
BALWYN
MONT ALBERT NORTH
BOX HILL NORTH
BLACKBURN NORTH
NUNAWADING
RINGWOOD EAST
BAYSWATER NORTH
KILSYTH SOUTH
KALORAMA

HAWTHORN
CANTERBURY
SURREY HILLS
BOX HILL
BLACKBURN
HEATHMONT
MOUNT DANDENONG
DANDENONG RANGES NATIONAL PARK

TOORAK
KOOYONG
CAMBERWELL
BOX HILL SOUTH
BLACKBURN SOUTH
FOREST HILL
VERMONT
WANTIRNA
BORONIA
THE BASIN
MOUNT DANDENONG
OLINDA

ARMADALE
GLEN IRIS
BURWOOD
VERMONT SOUTH
HEATHMONT
MOUNTAIN
BAYSWATER
DANDENONG RANGES DRIVE
Silvan Reservoir

MALVERN
ASHBURTON
BURWOOD EAST
WANTIRNA SOUTH
SASSAFRAS

CAULFIELD NORTH
MALVERN EAST
ASHWOOD
GLEN WAVERLEY
WANTIRNA SOUTH
FERNY CREEK

CAULFIELD
CHADSTONE
MOUNT WAVERLEY
DANDENONG VALLEY PARKLANDS
KNOXFIELD
TREMONT
SHERBROOKE

CAULFIELD SOUTH
CARNEGIE
MURRUMBEENA
SCORESBY
FERNTREE GULLY
THE PATCH

ORMOND
OAKLEIGH
OAKLEIGH EAST
NOTTING HILL
WHEELERS HILL
SHERBROOKE

McKINNON
BENTLEIGH EAST
HUNTINGDALE
UPPER FERNTREE GULLY
TECOMA
KALLISTA

BENTLEIGH
CLAYTON
MULGRAVE
ROWVILLE
UPWEY
DANDENONG RANGES NP
BELGRAVE

MOORABBIN
OAKLEIGH SOUTH
CLAYTON SOUTH
SPRINGVALE
CHURCHILL NATIONAL PARK
LYSTERFIELD
BELGRAVE HEIGHTS
SELBY

HIGHETT
HEATHERTON
CLARINDA
ROWVILLE
LYSTERFIELD PARK
Mount Morton
BELGRAVE SOUTH
MENZIES CREEK

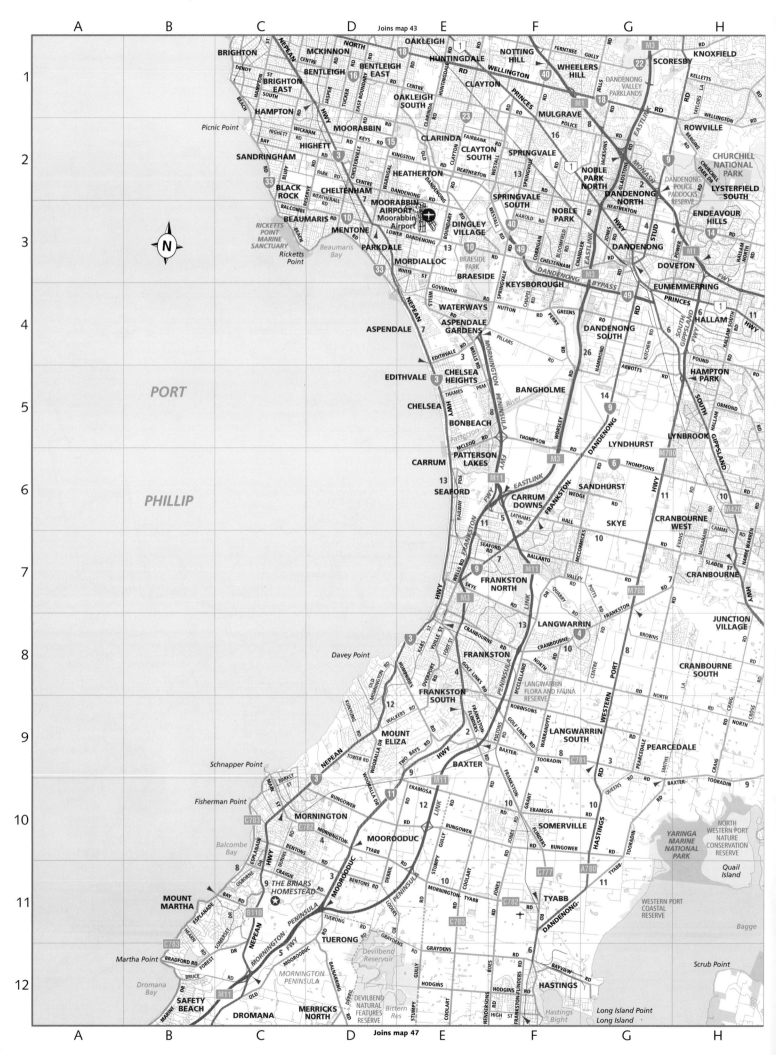

Joins map 43

Joins map 47

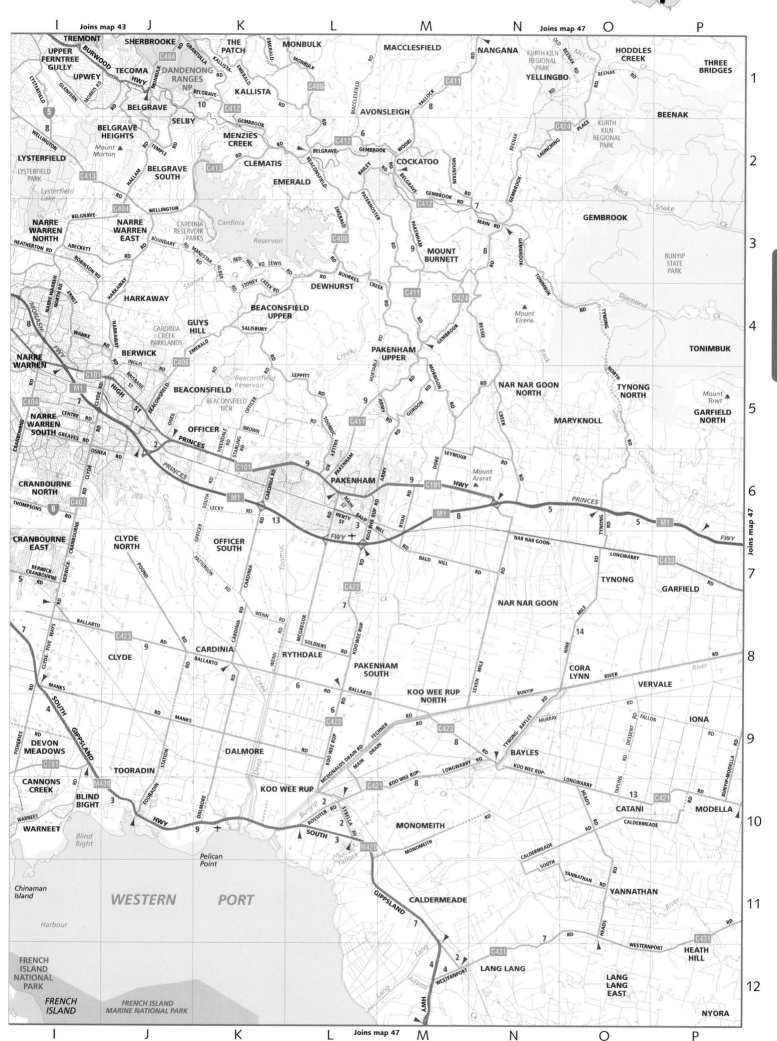

VIC

0 2 4 6 8 km

I J K L M N O P

TREMONT
UPPER FERNTREE GULLY
BURWOOD
SHERBROOKE
THE PATCH
MONBULK
MACCLESFIELD
NANGANA
KURTH KILN REGIONAL PARK
HODDLES CREEK
THREE BRIDGES
TECOMA
UPWEY
DANDENONG RANGES NP
KALLISTA
MONBULK
YELLINGBO
BEENAK
BELGRAVE
SELBY
BELGRAVE HEIGHTS
MENZIES CREEK
Mount Morton
KALLISTA
AVONSLEIGH
KURTH KILN REGIONAL PARK
LYSTERFIELD
LYSTERFIELD PARK
BELGRAVE SOUTH
CLEMATIS
BELGRAVE
GEMBROOK
COCKATOO
GEMBROOK
Lysterfield Lake
EMERALD
Cardinia Reservoir
MOUNT BURNETT
NARRE WARREN NORTH
NARRE WARREN EAST
CARDINIA RESERVOIR PARKS
DEWHURST
Mount Eirene
GEMBROOK
HARKAWAY
BEACONSFIELD UPPER
PAKENHAM UPPER
NAR NAR GOON NORTH
TONIMBUK
GUYS HILL
CARDINIA CREEK PARKLANDS
SALISBURY
TYNONG NORTH
GARFIELD NORTH
Mount Towt
BERWICK
NARRE WARREN
BEACONSFIELD
Beaconsfield Reservoir
BEACONSFIELD NCR
OFFICER
MARYKNOLL
Mount Ararat
NARRE WARREN SOUTH
PRINCES
PAKENHAM
PRINCES
CRANBOURNE NORTH
FWY
PAKENHAM
NAR NAR GOON
TYNONG
GARFIELD
CRANBOURNE EAST
BERWICK-CRANBOURNE RD
CLYDE NORTH
OFFICER SOUTH
CORA LYNN
VERVALE
CLYDE
CARDINIA
RYTHDALE
PAKENHAM SOUTH
KOO WEE RUP NORTH
IONA
DEVON MEADOWS
DALMORE
BAYLES
CATANI
MODELLA
TOORADIN
KOO WEE RUP
CANNONS CREEK
BLIND BIGHT
WARNEET
KOO WEE RUP SOUTH
MONOMEITH
YANNATHAN
Chinaman Island
WESTERN PORT
CALDERMEADE
Harbour
LANG LANG
HEATH HILL
Pelican Point
Blind Bight
FRENCH ISLAND NATIONAL PARK
FRENCH ISLAND MARINE NATIONAL PARK
FRENCH ISLAND
LANG LANG EAST
NYORA
GIPPSLAND
BUNYIP STATE PARK

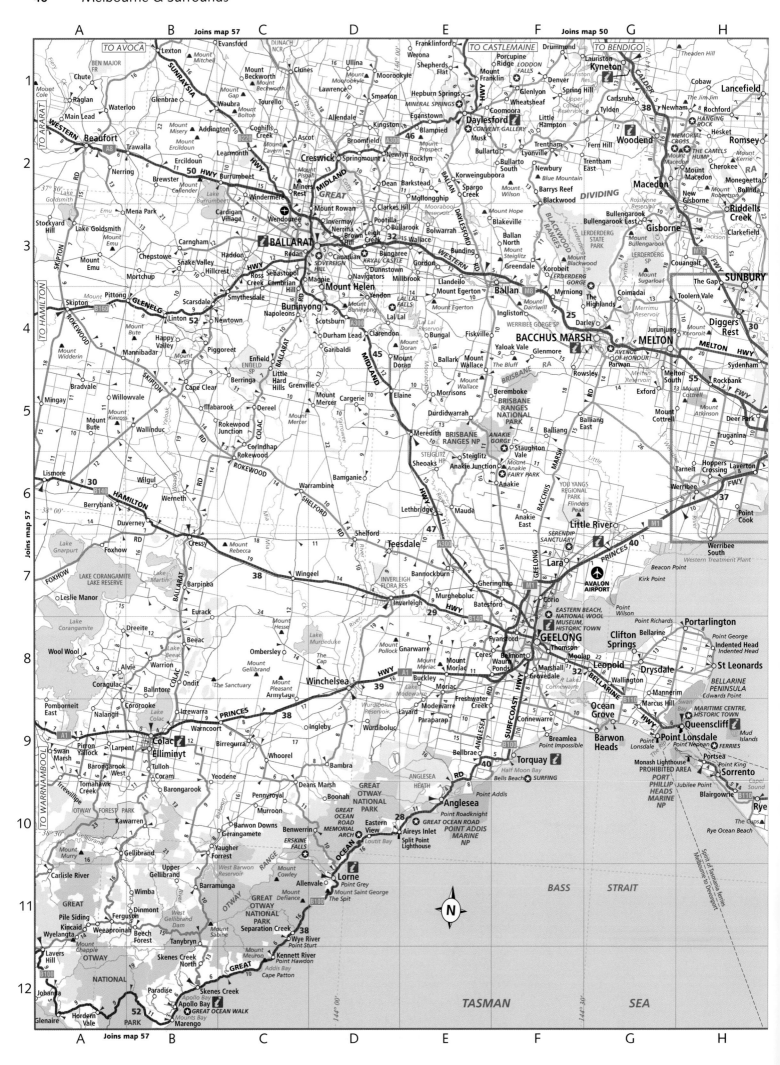

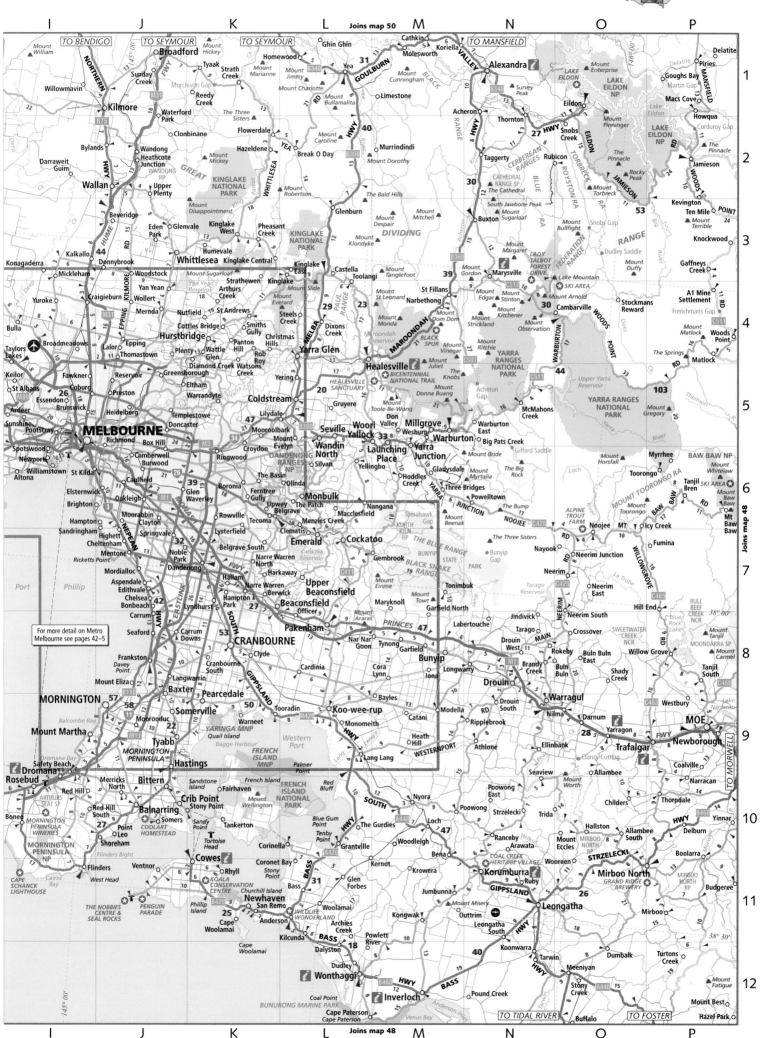

VIC

Joins map 50

47

Joins map 57

A   B   C   D   E   F   G   H

1   2   3   4   5   6   7   8   9   10   11   12

Malmsbury
Lauriston
Drummond
Denver
Kyneton
Spring Hill
Little Hampton
Tylden   Carlsruhe
Fern Hill
Woodend
Trentham
Newbury
Barrys Reef
Macedon
Blackwood
Bullengarook
Bullengarook East
Greendale
Korobeit
Myrniong
BACCHUS MARSH
111
The Highlands
Darley
Coimadai
Toolern Vale
The Gap
Glenmore
Rowsley
Parwan
Exford
Balliang
Balliang East
LERDERDERG STATE PARK
BRISBANE RANGES NP
Cobaw
Newham
Hesket   Rochford
Cherokee   Kerrie
Mount Macedon
Barringo
New Gisborne
Gisborne
Riddells Creek
Clarkefield
Couangalt
66
SUNBURY
Diggers Rest
Jurunjung
MELTON
Melton South
Rockbank
Mount Cottrell
Deer Park
Truganina
Tarneit
Werribee
Hoppers Crossing
Little River
Lara
72
YOU YANGS RP
Corio
Point Wilson
GEELONG
Belmont
Leopold
Marshall
Connewarre
Breamlea
Barwon Heads
Ocean Grove
Clifton Springs
Drysdale
Wallington
Mannerim
Marcus Hill
Portarlington
Point George
Indented Head
Bellarine
St Leonards
BELLARINE PENINSULA
Queenscliff
Point Lonsdale
Portsea
Point Nepean
Sorrento
Blairgowrie
Rosebud
Rye
Boneo
Dromana
Safety Beach
Merricks North
Red Hill
Somers
Point Leo
Shoreham
Balnarring
Flinders
West Head
Cape Schanck
The Nobbies
Seal Rocks
MORNINGTON PENINSULA NATIONAL PARK
MORNINGTON PENINSULA
MORNINGTON
Mount Martha
Mount Eliza
101
Baxter
Pearcedale
Somerville
Mooroduc
Tyabb
Hastings
Bittern
Crib Point
Stony Point
Tankerton
Cowes
Ventnor
Newhaven
San Remo
Rhyll
Cape Woolamai
Phillip Island
Kilcunda
Dalyston
Dudley
Wonthaggi
BUNURONG MARINE PARK
Cape Paterson
Inverloch
Pound Creek
Venus Bay
Tarwin Lower
Tarwin Meadows
Waratah North
Waratah Bay
Arch Rock
Walkerville South
Cape Liptrap
Grinder Point
Fish Creek
Hoddle
90
Foster
Tidal River
Norman Point
Oberon Bay
Dannevig Island
Great Glennie Island
Oberon Point
South West Point
Anser Island
Kanowna Island
WILSONS PROMONTORY MARINE PARK
WILSONS PROMONTORY NATIONAL PARK
WILSONS PROMONTORY, COASTAL WALKS
WILSONS PROMONTORY MNP
Shellback Island
Tongue Point
Norman Island
Sandy Point
Walkerville
Duck Point
Yanakie
CORNER INLET MARINE & COASTAL PARK
CORNER INLET MNP
Bell Point
Barry Point
Port Welshpool
Port Franklin
Agnes
Tgora   Welshpool
Woorarra
Ryton
Budgeree East
Budgeree
Mirboo
Dumbalk
Turtons Creek
Meeniyan
Stony Creek
Buffalo
Koonwarra
Tarwin
Leongatha South
Leongatha
Korumburra
GIPPSLAND HWY
BASS HWY
Anderson
Archies Creek
Powlett River
Woolamai
Kongwak
Outtrim
Ruby
Jumbunna
Kernot
Glen Forbes
Bass
Corinella
Coronet Bay
Grantville
The Gurdies
Woodleigh
Loch
82
Nyora
Poowong
Poowong East
Lang Lang
Koo Wee Rup
Monomeith
Caldermeade
Bayles
Cora Lynn
Garfield
Tynong
Nar Nar Goon
Longwarry
Drouin
Drouin West
Drouin South
Warragul
88
Nilma
Darnum
Yarragon
Trafalgar
MOE
Newborough
Coalville
MORWELL
Churchill
Hazelwood
MORWELL NP
Yinnar
Delburn
Boolarra
Mirboo North
58
Hallston
Arawata
Strzelecki
Mount Eccles
Childers
Thorpdale
Narracan
Seaview
Allambee South
Wooreen
Ranceby
Bena
Krowera
Kardella
Ellinbank
Buln Buln
Buln Buln East
Shady Creek
Tanjil South
Willow Grove
Rokeby
Crossover
Labertouche
Jindivick
Drouin
PRINCES
Neerim South
Neerim East
Neerim Junction
Neerim
Nayook
Noojee
Tonimbuk
Maryknoll
Garfield North
Tarago
Tarago Reservoir
BUNYIP STATE PARK
Gembrook
Cockatoo
Emerald
Upper Beaconsfield
Beaconsfield
Officer
Berwick
Pakenham
CRANBOURNE
Clyde
Cardinia
Cranbourne South
Tooradin
Warneet
Western Port
FRENCH ISLAND NP
French Island
Tortoise Head
Swan Bay
61
Narre Warren
Lynbrook
Lyndhurst
Hampton Park
Dandenong
Springvale
Noble Park
Keysborough
Carrum Downs
Seaford
Frankston
Carrum
Chelsea
Aspendale
Edithvale
Mordialloc
Ricketts Point
Mentone
Cheltenham
Sandringham
Moorabbin
Oakleigh
Glen Waverley
Mount Eliza
44
Clayton
3
Brighton
Elsternwick
St Kilda
Caulfield
Port Phillip
Western Treatment Plant
Werribee South
Point Cook
Altona
Williamstown
Footscray
MELBOURNE
Richmond
Box Hill
Doncaster
Ringwood
Boronia
Ferntree Gully
Belgrave
Lysterfield
Monbulk
Macclesfield
Nangana
Hoddles Creek
Gladysdale
Three Bridges
Powelltown
KURTH KILN RP
DANDENONG RANGES NP
Olinda
Montrose
Lilydale
Seville
Wandin North
Woori Yallock
Yarra Junction
Warburton
Millgrove
Launching Place
Coldstream
Yering
Yarra Glen
Healesville
YARRA RANGES NP
YARRA RANGES NATIONAL PARK
McMahons Creek
Upper Yarra Reservoir
Cambarville
Marysville
Narbethong
St Fillans
Toolangi
Castella
Kinglake
Kinglake Central
Kinglake West
Glenvale
KINGLAKE NATIONAL PARK
Pheasant Creek
St Andrews
Smiths Gully
Hurstbridge
Diamond Creek
Research
Eltham
Greensborough
Templestowe
Warrandyte
Wonga Park
Dixons Creek
Glenburn
Break O Day
Murrindindi
Taggerty
Rubicon
Buxton
CATHEDRAL RANGE STATE PARK
Acheron
Thornton
Eildon
Snobs Creek
LAKE EILDON
LAKE EILDON NP
Jamieson
Kevington
Ten Mile
Howqua
Macs Cove
Goughs Bay
Piries
Merrijig
Delatite
C320
19
Woods Point
Matlock
Jericho
Red Jacket
Violet Town
Aberfeldy
Myrrhee
Toorongo
Tanjil Bren
Mt Baw Baw
BAW BAW NATIONAL PARK
Icy Creek
Fumina
Parkers Corner
Tyers Junction
Erica
C425
C466
Tanjil South
Moondarra
MOONDARRA STATE PARK
BULL BEEF CREEK NCR
Blue Rock Lake
Westbury
Yallourn North
Gaffneys Creek
A1 Mine
Stockmans Reward
Knockwood
C511
Marysville
Alexandra
Koriella
Cathkin
Molesworth
Yea
Homewood
Ghin Ghin
Kerrisdale
Strath Creek
Reedy Creek
Flowerdale
Hazeldene
Clonbinane
Wandong
Heathcote Junction
Upper Plenty
Beveridge
Wallan
Kilmore
58
Willowmavin
Lancefield
Romsey
Darraweit Guim
Monegeetta
Bolinda
Clarkefield
Kalkallo
Donnybrook
Woodstock
Wollert
Epping
Mernda
Yan Yean
Arthurs Creek
Strathewen
Whittlesea
Humevale
Glenburn
Limestone
GOULBURN VALLEY HWY
MELBA HWY
MAROONDAH HWY
B360
B340
B300
109
Yarrambat
Diamond Creek
Nutfield
Thomastown
Broadmeadows
Fawkner
Preston
Brunswick
Essendon
Keilor
St Albans
Sydenham
Keilor
Broadmeadows
Craigieburn
41
Bulla
Mickleham
Craigieburn
Roxburgh Park
High Camp
Broadford
Tyaak
Waterford Park
Bylands
Wallan
Heathcote Junction
175
M31
M79
M80
M8
M1
M3
Strath Creek
BASS STRAIT
TASMAN SEA

For more detail on Melbourne & Surrounds see pages 46-7

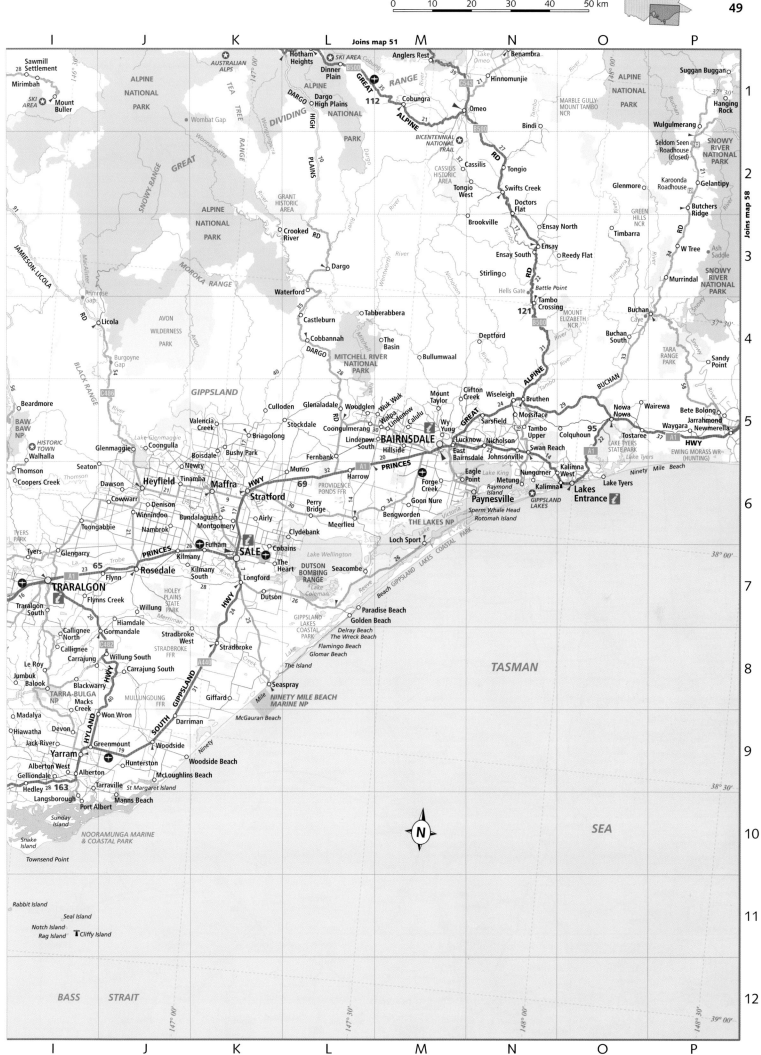

0 10 20 30 40 50 km

VIC

Sawmill Settlement
Mirimbah
SKI AREA
Mount Buller

ALPINE NATIONAL PARK

AUSTRALIAN ALPS

Wombat Gap

GREAT DIVIDING RANGE

DARGO HIGH PLAINS

Hotham Heights
Dinner Plain
SKI AREA
112
Cobungra

ALPINE NATIONAL PARK

Dargo High Plains

Anglers Rest

ALPINE RANGE

Benambra

Hinnmunjie

Omeo

Suggan Buggan

Alpine National Park

Hanging Rock

Wulgulmerang

Snowy River National Park

Bindi

Seldom Seen Roadhouse (closed)

Gelantipy

Glenmore

Karoonda Roadhouse

Butchers Ridge

Timbarra

W Tree

Ash Saddle

SNOWY RIVER NATIONAL PARK

SNOWY RANGE

GREAT DIVIDING RANGE

WONNANGATTA RANGE

TEA TREE RANGE

Crooked River

ALPINE NATIONAL PARK

GRANT HISTORIC AREA

BICENTENNIAL NATIONAL TRAIL

CASSILIS HISTORIC AREA

Cassilis
Tongio West
Tongio
Swifts Creek
Doctors Flat
Brookville

Ensay North
Ensay
Reedy Flat

Ensay South

Stirling

MARBLE GULLY-MOUNT TAMBO NCR

GREEN HILLS NCR

Dargo
Waterford

JAMIESON-LICOLA RD

Licola

MOROKA RANGE

AVON WILDERNESS PARK

Castleburn
Cobbannah

DARGO

MITCHELL RIVER NATIONAL PARK

Tabberabbera
The Basin

Hells Gate
121
Tambo Crossing

MOUNT ELIZABETH NCR

Buchan
Buchan Cave

Murrindal

Buchan South

BUCHAN

TARA RANGE PARK

Sandy Point

BLACK RANGE

Burgoyne Gap

GIPPSLAND

Culloden
Glenaladale
Woodglen
Stockdale

Deptford

Bullumwaal

Mount Taylor
Clifton Creek
Wiseleigh
Bruthen
Mossiface

Nowa Nowa
Wairewa

Bete Bolong
Jarrahmond
Newmerella

Beardmore

BAW BAW NP

Thomson
Coopers Creek

HISTORIC TOWN Walhalla

Seaton
Glenmaggie
Coongulla

Briagolong
Boisdale
Bushy Park

Valencia Creek

Newry

Wuk Wuk
Walpa
Lindenow
Calulu

Lindenow South

BAIRNSDALE

Wy Yung
Sarsfield
GREAT ALPINE RD

Tambo Upper

Colquhoun

Waygara
Tostaree
95
Lake Tyers

A1 HWY

EWING MORASS WR (HUNTING)

Dawson
Heyfield
Tinamba
Maffra

Denison
Winnindoo
Nambrok

Fernbank
Munro
Stratford

Cowwarr

Coongulmerang

Hillside
Harrow
69
PRINCES HWY

Lucknow
Nicholson
East Bairnsdale
Johnsonville
Swan Reach

Eagle Point
Metung
Nungurner
Kalimna West
Kalimna

Lakes Entrance

LAKE TYERS STATE PARK

Ninety Mile Beach

Toongabbie
Glenmaggie

Tyers
TYERS PARK

Glengarry
65
PRINCES

Rosedale
Flynn
Flynns Creek

TRARALGON
Traralgon South

Kilmany
Fulham
SALE
Cobains
The Heart

Longford
Dutson

Perry Bridge
Airly
Clydebank

Meerlieu
Bengworden
Goon Nure

Forge Creek

Sperm Whale Head
Rotomah Island

THE LAKES NP

Loch Sport

Seacombe

DUTSON BOMBING RANGE

GIPPSLAND LAKES COASTAL PARK

Providence Ponds FFR

HOLEY PLAINS STATE PARK

Callignee North
Callignee
Carrajung
Le Roy
Jumbuk
Balook

Hiamdale
Gormandale
Willung
Willung South
Carrajung South

Stradbroke West
Stradbroke

GIPPSLAND HWY

A440

Paradise Beach
Golden Beach

Delray Beach
The Wreck Beach
Flamingo Beach
Glomar Beach

The Island

TASMAN

Madalya
Hiawatha
Jack River

TARRA-BULGA NP
Macks Creek

Devon
Won Wron
Greenmount

Darriman
Woodside

Giffard
Seaspray

McGauran Beach

NINETY MILE BEACH MARINE NP

SEA

HYLAND HWY

SOUTH GIPPSLAND

Yarram
Alberton West
Gelliondale
Hedley 28 163
Langsborough

Alberton
Tarraville
St Margaret Island

Hunterston
McLoughlins Beach

Woodside Beach

Manns Beach
Port Albert

Sunday Island

NOORAMUNGA MARINE & COASTAL PARK

Snake Island

Townsend Point

Rabbit Island

Seal Island

Notch Island
Rag Island
Cliffy Island

N

BASS STRAIT

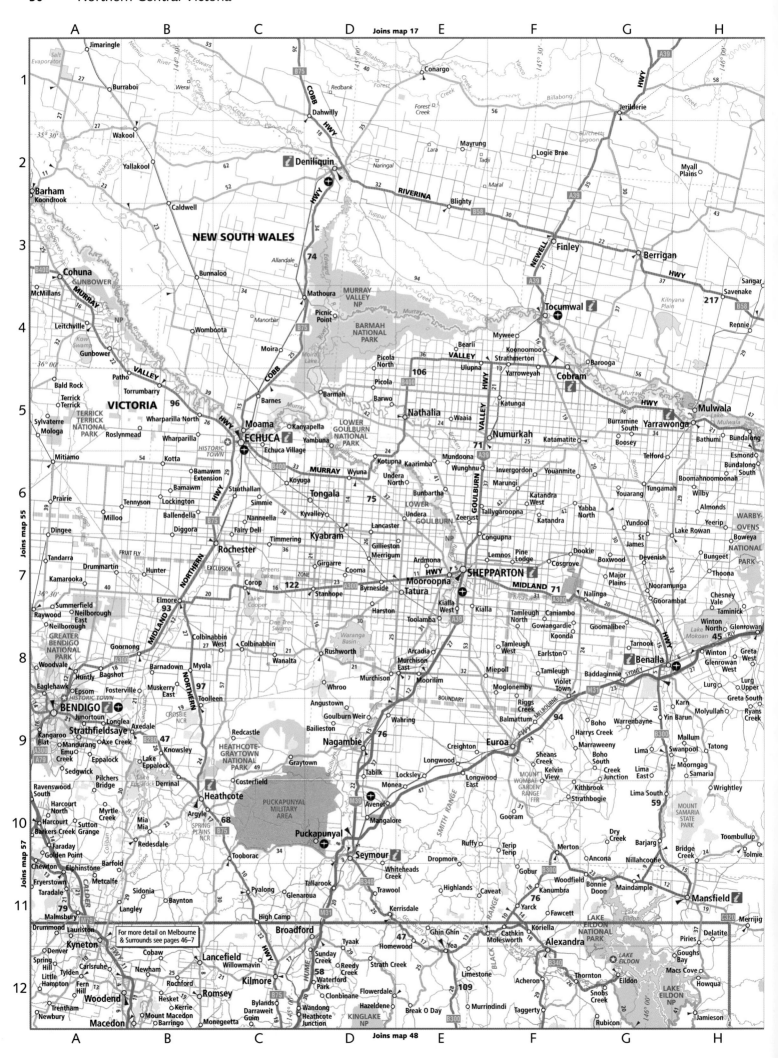

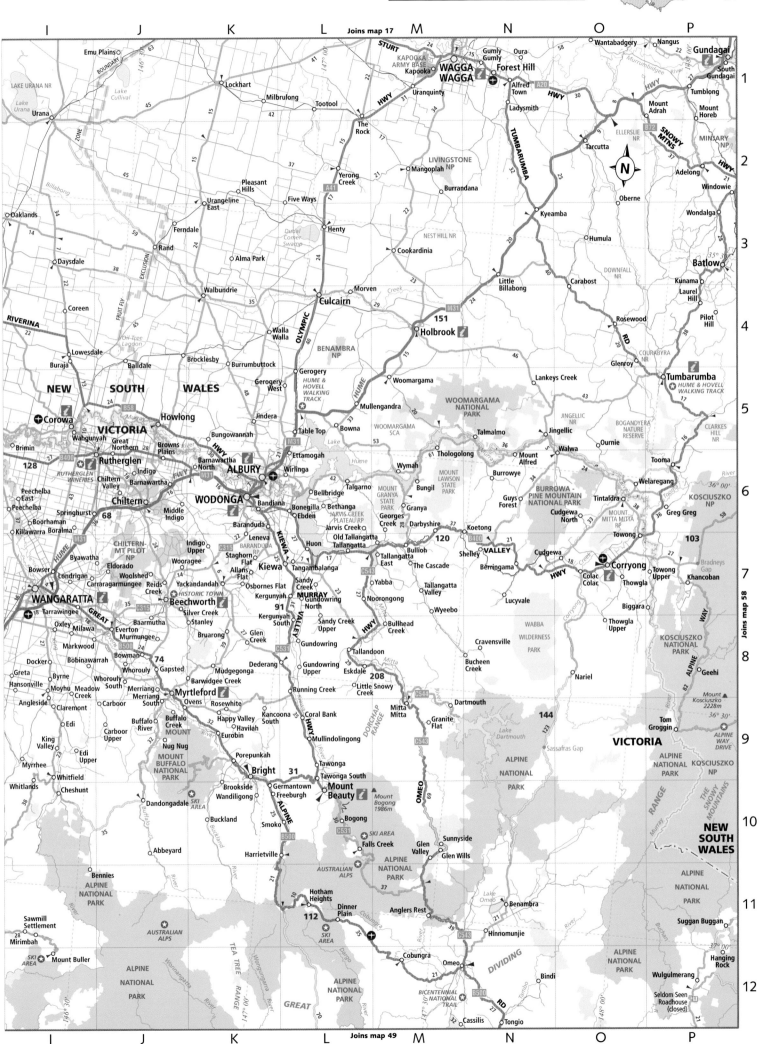

VIC

Joins map 58

1
2
3
4
5
6
7
8
9
10
11
12

I   J   K   L   M   N   O   P

0   10   20   30   40   50 km

NEW SOUTH WALES

VICTORIA

Gundagai
South Gundagai
Tumbling
Mount Horeb
Mount Adrah
Adelong
Windowie
Wondalga
Batlow
Kunama
Laurel Hill
Pilot Hill
Tumbarumba
HUME & HOVELL WALKING TRACK

Wantabadgery
Nangus
Oura
Gumly Gumly
Forest Hill
WAGGA WAGGA
Kapooka
KAPOOKA ARMY BASE
Uranquinty
Alfred Town
Ladysmith
Tarcutta
ELLERSLIE NR
Oberne
Kyeamba
Humula
Little Billabong
Carabost
DOWNFALL NR
Rosewood
Glenroy
COURABYRA NR
BOGANDYERA NATURE RESERVE
JINGELLIC NR
CLARKES HILL NR
KOSCIUSZKO NP
Lockhart
Milbrulong
Tootool
The Rock
Yerong Creek
Mangoplah
LIVINGSTONE NP
Burrandana
Cookardinia
NEST HILL NR
Pleasant Hills
Urangeline East
Five Ways
Henty
Morven
Culcairn
Holbrook
Woomargama
WOOMARGAMA NATIONAL PARK
WOOMARGAMA SCA
Lankeys Creek
Talmalmo
Jingellic
Ournie
Tooma
CLARKES HILL NR
Walla Walla
BENAMBRA NP
Gerogery
Gerogery West
HUME & HOVELL WALKING TRACK
Mullengandra
Wymah
Mount Lawson STATE PARK
Burrowye
Guys Forest
BURROWA - PINE MOUNTAIN NATIONAL PARK
Cudgewa North
MOUNT MITTA MITTA RP
Towong
Greg Greg
Walbundrie
Oaklands
Ferndale
Rand
Alma Park
Daysdale
Coreen
Lowesdale
Buraja
Balldale
Brocklesby
Burrumbuttock
Bowna
Table Top
Jindera
Ettamogah
Wirlinga
ALBURY
Bellbridge
Talgarno
Bethanga
Ebden
Bonegilla
Granya
Georges Creek
Darbyshire
Koetong
Shelley
Berringama
Cudgewa
VALLEY
Corryong
Colac Colac
Thowgla
Towong Upper
Biggara
Thowgla Upper
KOSCIUSZKO NATIONAL PARK
Khancoban
Geehi
Mount Kosciuszko 2228m
Tom Groggin
Corowa
Howlong
Wahgunyah
Great Northern
Browns Plains
Barnawartha North
Rutherglen
RUTHERGLEN WINERIES
Indigo
Chiltern Valley
Barnawartha
Chiltern
Middle Indigo
WODONGA
Bandiana
Baranduda
Leneva
Huon
Old Tallangatta
Tallangatta
Bullioh
The Cascade
Tallangatta Valley
Wyeebo
Lucyvale
Cravensville
WABBA WILDERNESS PARK
Nariel
Bucheen Creek
Springhurst
Byawatha
Eldorado
Woolshed
CHILTERN- MT PILOT NP
Indigo Upper
BARANDUDA RP
Staghorn Flat
Wooragee
Kiewa
Tangambalanga
Tallangatta East
Yabba
Noorongong
Bullhead Creek
WANGARATTA
Tarrawingee
Londrigan
Carraragarmungee
Reids Creek
HISTORIC TOWN
Beechworth
Silver Creek
Stanley
Allans Flat
Osbornes Flat
Kergunyah
MURRAY
Gundowring North
Sandy Creek Upper
Tallandoon
Eskdale
Little Snowy Creek
Dartmouth
Oxley
Milawa
Everton
Murmungee
Bruarong
Glen Creek
Gundowring
Gundowring Upper
Running Creek
Mitta Mitta
Granite Flat
LAKE Dartmouth
Sassafras Gap
ALPINE NATIONAL PARK
Markwood
Bowman
Whorouly
Gapsted
Mudgegonga
Barwidgee Creek
Dederang
Coral Bank
Mullindolingong
DORCHAP RANGE
Docker
Bobinawarrah
Whorouly South
Merriang
Merriang South
Myrtleford
Ovens
Rosewhite
Kancoona South
Happy Valley
Havilah
Greta
Byrne
Moyhu
Meadow Creek
Carboor
Buffalo River
Carboor Upper
Buffalo Creek
MOUNT
Eurobin
Tawonga
Tawonga South
VICTORIA
Hansonville
Angleside
Claremont
Edi
King Valley
Edi Upper
Nug Nug
MOUNT BUFFALO NATIONAL PARK
Porepunkah
Bright
Germantown
Freeburgh
Mount Beauty
Mount Bogong 1986m
Benambra
Myrrhee
Whitfield
Cheshunt
Whitlands
Brookside
Wandiligong
Bogong
Sunnyside
Glen Valley
Glen Wills
ALPINE NATIONAL PARK
NEW SOUTH WALES
Dandongadale
SKI AREA
Buckland
Smoko
Falls Creek
SKI AREA
Harrietville
AUSTRALIAN ALPS
Bennies
ALPINE NATIONAL PARK
AUSTRALIAN ALPS
Hotham Heights
Dinner Plain
SKI AREA
Anglers Rest
Hinnomunjie
LAKE Omeo
Sawmill Settlement
Mirimbah
SKI AREA
Mount Buller
ALPINE NATIONAL PARK
Cobungra
Omeo
Bindi
ALPINE NATIONAL PARK
Suggan Buggan
Wulgulmerang
Hanging Rock
Seldom Seen Roadhouse (closed)
Cobungra
Cassilis
Tongio
GREAT DIVIDING RANGE
BICENTENNIAL NATIONAL TRAIL
THE SNOWY MOUNTAINS
ALPINE WAY DRIVE
RANGE
TEA TREE RANGE

Joins map 16

A B C D E F G H

1

DANGGALI WILDERNESS AREA
TARAWI NATURE RESERVE
Springwood
Heatherbloom
Aston
Greenvale
Belvedere
Cooinda
Willow Point
Yelta Lake
Nialia Lake
Roo Roo
Travellers Lake
Manilla
Windamingle
Stony Crossing
Wyndham
Nearie Lake
NEARIE LAKE NATURE RESERVE

33° 30'
Canopus
Tarawi
DANGGALI CP

2
Hypurna
Belmore
Sunshine
Wenba
Warwick
Huntingfield
Bunnerungee
Nindethana
Warrawenia Lake
Milkengay
Lake Milkengay
Waukeroo
Trelega

SILVER CITY

3
Pepper Tree Motel Outstation
NEW SOUTH WALES
Warrakoo
Bellsgrove
Coleraine
Toora
Quambi
Coolamon
Central Para
Studley
Camboon
Jamesville
Burtundy
Darling River
124

B79

4
SOUTH AUSTRALIA
Paradise Outstation
Narweena
Regunyah
Nulla
Glen-Esk
Wilton
Allanvale
Talgarry
Warnwillah
Dunvegan
Garston
Balcatherine
Ashvale
Wamberra

34° 00'
Coombool Outstation
Nelwood
Bunyip Reach
Tareena
Tara Downs
Tooperoopna
Orchard Bend
Avoca
Bellevue
Tapio
Milpara

HWY
89

5
Cooltong
MURRAY RIVER NP
Renmark
Paringa
Lindsay Point
Rufus River
Neds Corner
Lake Wallawalla
Moorna
River
MURRAY-SUNSET NATIONAL PARK
Wentworth
Dareton
Curlwaa
Yelta
Fletchers Lake
Mourquong Saltwater Disposal Basin
30

Murray River
COOLTONG CP
Monash
14

6
Glossop
Lyrup
STURT
Yamba Roadhouse
Meringur North
144
Neds Corner
Kulnine East
Kulnine
Cullulleraine
Merrinee North
Sandlewood Park
Merbein West
Birdwoodton
Merbein South
Merbein
Cabarita
MILDURA
Irymple
Buronga
Gol Gol
Nicholls Point
Trentham Cliffs
Billabong
MALLEE CLIFFS NATIONAL PARK
Berri
Winkie
24
34
A20
13
VICTORIA
13
59
HWY
Koorlong
Cardross
Red Cliffs
Sunny Cliffs
Monak
A20

7
MURRAY RIVER NATIONAL PARK
Pyap
Loxton North
Loxton
Taldra
Taparoo
Morkalla
Karween
Meringur
Yarrara
YARRARA FFR
Bambill
Werrimull
Karawinna
Merrinee
Pirlta
36
Benetook
Thurla
Yatpool
Karadoc
STURT

24
Noora
COPI PLAINS
Tunart
Pinemont
Redcourts
Kurnwill
Tarrango
CALLAGHAN PLAIN
Carwarp
17
Nangiloc
KEMENDOK NP

34° 30'
Tookayerta
B55
Pata
Nangari
21
24
Boonoonar
Colignan
35

8
Veitch
Taplan
Nadda
COPI PLAINS
RAAK PLAIN
Rocket Lake
Nowingi
Kulkyne
PARUNA
35
29
Malpas
Paruna
Meribah
SUNSET COUNTRY
CALDER
103
HATTAH-KULKYNE NATIONAL PARK
Alawoona
RD

9
BILLIATT WILDERNESS AREA
MURRAY-SUNSET NATIONAL PARK
ONE TREE PLAIN
Hattah
HATTAH-KULKYNE NP
Cramenton
B57
Peebinga
FRUIT FLY EXCLUSION ZONE BOUNDARY
35° 00'
Berrook

10
Karte
Kringin
PEEBINGA CP
Goongee
Wymlet
Trinita
26
Kiamil
ANNUELLO FLORA AND FAUNA RESERVE
Gurrai
KARTE CP
8

11
Mulcra
Duddo
KOONDA FR
Paignie
Galah
Tiega
Ouyen
Boorongie North
Wagant
55
Panitya
140
Linga
20
Underbool
Walpeup
Timberoo
Boorongie
Nunga
HWY
31
Parilla
Pinnaroo
6
24
Murrayville
19
Danyo
Cowangie
Tutye
Boinka
21
Torrita
TIMBEROO FFR
Boulka
A79
Woornack
MALLEE
MURRAYVILLE FFR
B12
B12
Timberoo South
Bronzewing
B220

12
40
Green Hills
WYPERFELD NATIONAL PARK
WIRRENGREN PLAIN
Pine Plains
BIG DESERT
35
Timberoo South
BRONZEWING FLORA AND FAUNA RESERVE
Dering
Patchewollock
Baring
41
Gypsum
Tempy
22
Speed
SUNRAYSIA HWY
NGARKAT CP
BIG DESERT WILDERNESS PARK
141° 00'
141° 30'
142° 00'

Joins map 49
Joins map 54
Joins map 73

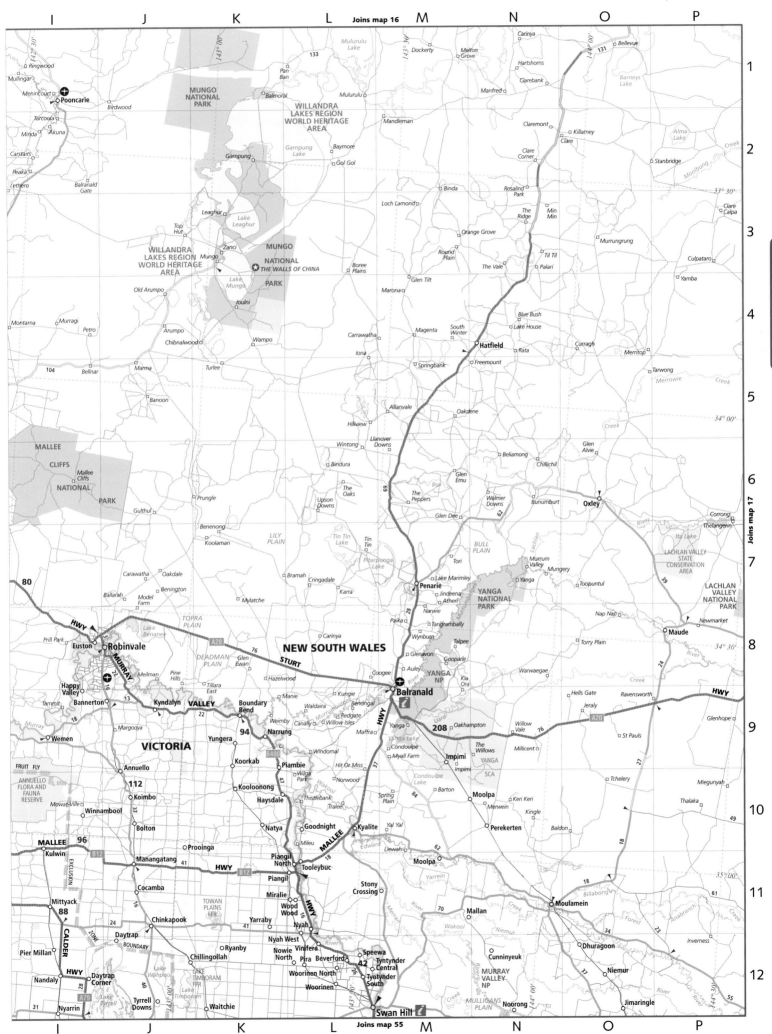

0 10 20 30 40 50 km

VIC

I J K L M N O P

1
2
3
4
5
6
7
8
9
10
11
12

Joins map 17

NEW SOUTH WALES

VICTORIA

Pooncarie
Menincourt
Ringwood
Mullingar
Tarcoola
Akuna
Minda
Carstairs
Peaka
Lethero
Birdwood
Balranald Gate

MUNGO NATIONAL PARK

133
Pan Ban
Balmoral
Mulurulu Lake
Mulurulu
Gol Gol

WILLANDRA LAKES REGION WORLD HERITAGE AREA

Garnpung
Garnpung Lake
Baymore
Mandleman

Carinya
Dockerty
Melton Grove
Hartshorns
Clarebank
Bellevue
131
Barneys Lake
Alma Lake
Moolbong Creek

WILLANDRA LAKES REGION WORLD HERITAGE AREA

Leaghur
Top Hut
Zanci
Mungo
Lake Leaghur
Lake Mungo

MUNGO NATIONAL THE WALLS OF CHINA PARK

Old Arumpo
Arumpo
Chibnalwood
Joulni

Montarna
Murragi
Petro
Marma
Wampo
Turlee

104
Bellnar
Banoon

MALLEE CLIFFS NATIONAL PARK
Mallee Cliffs

Prungle
Gulthul

Koolaman
Benenong

Carrawatha
Oakdale
Benington
Ballarah
Model Farm
Mylatche

80

Prill Park
HWY
Euston
Robinvale
Happy Valley
Bannerton
Tammit
Wemen
Meilman
Pine Hills
Tillara East
Margooya

18

Koorkab
Narrung
Boundary Bend
94
Weimby
Waldaira
Manie
Canally
Willow Isles
Benongal
Kungie
Maffra
Coogee

Glen Tilt
Marona

Hillview
Wintong
Llanover Downs

Bindura

The Oaks
Upson Downs
LILY PLAIN
Tin Tin Lake
Tin Tin
Pitarponga Lake

Bramah
Cringadale
Karra

Lake Marimley
Penarie
Jindeena
Atheri
Narwie
Paika

YANGA NATIONAL PARK

Tori
Murrum Valley
Mungery
Yanga

BULL PLAIN

Toopuntul

39

LACHLAN VALLEY STATE CONSERVATION AREA

Corrong
Thelangerin

LACHLAN VALLEY NATIONAL PARK

Newmarket
Maude

24

Hells Gate
Jeraly
Ravensworth
Glenhope
HWY
A20

St Pauls
Willow Vale
76

Tchelery
Miegunyah
Thalaka

Keri Keri
Kingle
Merwein

49

27

Balranald
208
Yanga
Oakhampton

Impimi
Moolpa

Barton
Moolpa

Perekerten
Baldon

18

Moulamein
Billabong

Mallan
Cunninyeuk

70
Wakool River
Niemur River

Dhuragoon
Niemur
Jimaringle

34

23

Inverness

61

31

Noorong

MULLIGANS PLAIN

55

TOPRA PLAIN
Lake Benanee
DEADMAN PLAIN
Glen Ewan
Hazelwood
STURT
MURRAY
Kyndalyn
VALLEY
13
22

Yungera
Koorkab
Piambie
Wilga Park
Kooloonong
Thistlebank
Tralee
Haysdale
47

Annuello
112
Koimbo
Winnambool
Bolton
Prooinga

112

ANNUELLO FLORA AND FAUNA RESERVE
FRUIT FLY

Mowat-Ville
31

MALLEE
96
Kulwin
Manangatang
41
HWY
B12
Cocamba

B12

Mittyack
88
Chinkapook
Daytrap
Ryanby

CALDER
HWY
Pier Millan
Nandaly
Daytrap Corner
28
Nyarrin
31
Tyrrell Downs
Waitchie
Chillingollah

LAKE TIMBORAM FFR
Lake Timboram
Lake Wahpool

TOWAN PLAINS FFR

Natya
Goodnight
Mileu
Kyalite
Yal Yal
MALLEE
Edward River
Liewah
62
Stony Crossing
Yarrein

Windomal
Hit Or Miss
Norwood
Spring Plain
Condoulpe
Myall Farm
Condoulpe Lake
YANGA SCA
Millicent
The Willows

84

Piangil North
Tooleybuc
Piangil
Miralie
Wood Wood
Nyah
HWY
16
Yarraby
Nyah West
Nowie North
Pira
Vinifera
Beverford
42
Speewa
Tyntynder Central
Tyntynder South
Woorinen North
Woorinen

Swan Hill

143° 00'
142° 30'
141° 30'
144° 00'
144° 30'
33° 30'
34° 00'
34° 30'
35° 00'

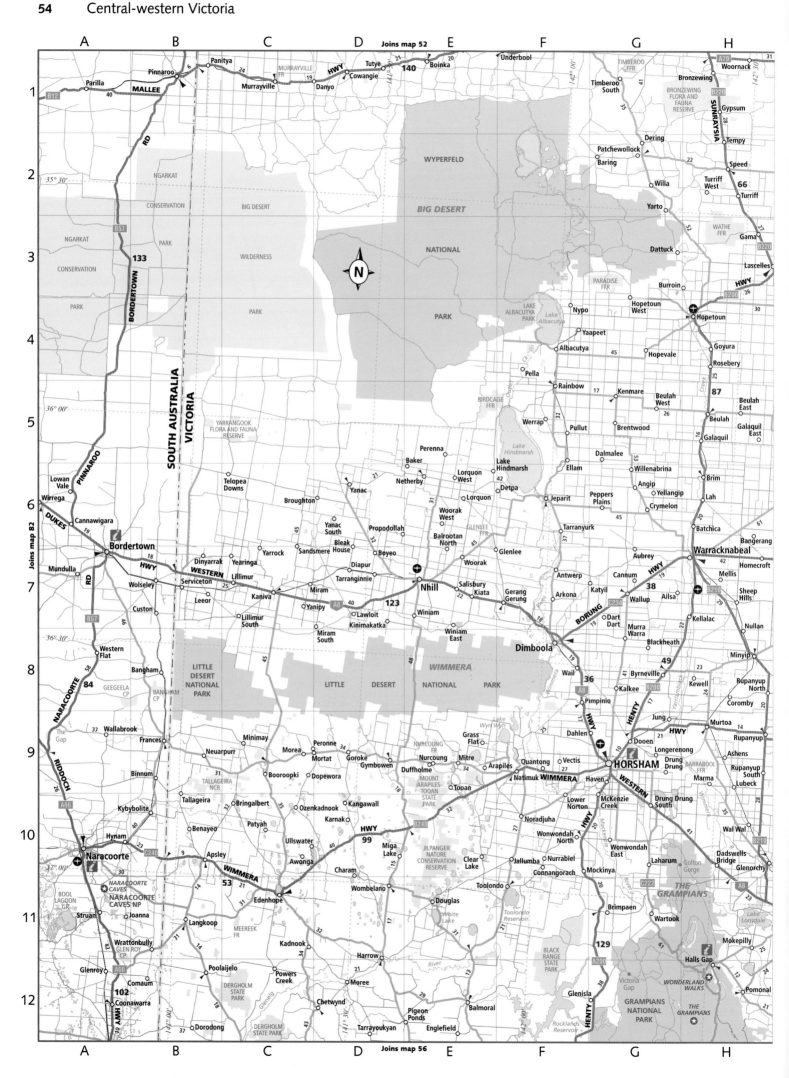

Joins map 52

Joins map 82

Joins map 56

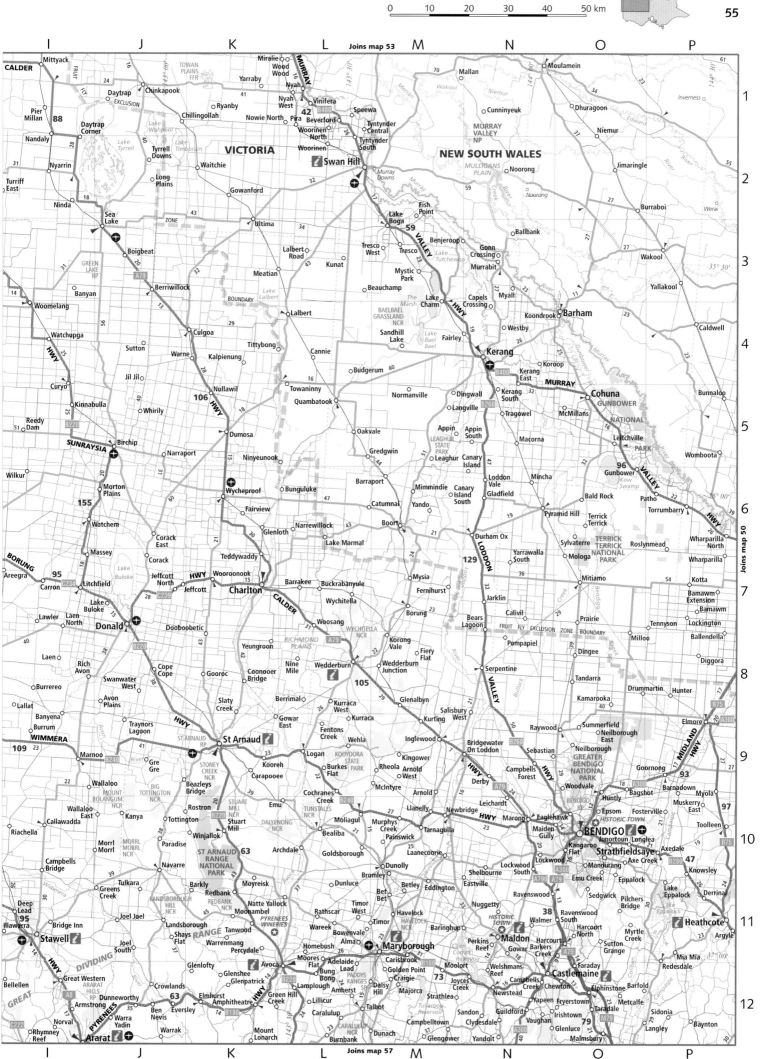

Joins map 50

0 10 20 30 40 50 km

VICTORIA

NEW SOUTH WALES

MURRAY VALLEY NP

MULLIGANS PLAIN

CALDER

I J K L M N O P

1
2
3
4
5
6
7
8
9
10
11
12

Mittyack
Miralie
Wood Wood
Yarraby
Mallan
Moulamein
Inverness

Pier Millan
88
Daytrap Corner
Chinkapook
Ryanby
Nowie North
Nyah
Nyah West
Vinifera
Speewa
42
B400
Cunninyeuk
Dhuragoon
Niemur

Nandaly
Daytrap EXCLUSION
Chillingollah
Pira
Beverford
Woorinen North
Tyntynder Central
Noorong
Jimaringle

Turriff East
Nyarrin
Tyrrell Downs
Long Plains
Waitchie
Woorinen
Tyntynder South
Murray Downs
Swan Hill
Noorong
Burraboi
Werai

Ninda
Sea Lake
Boigbeat
Gowanford
Lake Boga
59
Fish Point
Ballbank
Wakool
Yallakool

Woomelang
Banyan
Berriwillock
Ultima
Lalbert Road
Tresco West
Tresco
Benjeroop
Gonn Crossing
Murrabit
Koondrook
Barham
Caldwell

Watchupga
Sutton
Culgoa
Meatian
Kunat
Mystic Park
Beauchamp
Lake Charm
Capels Crossing
Myall
Westby

Curyo
Jil Jil
Warne
Kalpienung
Tittybong
Cannie
Normanville
Sandhill Lake
Fairley
Kerang
Kerang East
Koroop
Cohuna

Kinnabulla
Whirily
Nullawil
Budgerum
Towaninny
Quambatook
Dingwall
Langville
Kerang South
Tragowel
McMillans
Bunnaloo

Reedy Dam
Birchip
Narraport
Dumosa
Ninyeunook
Oakvale
Gredgwin
Appin
Appin South
Leaghur
Canary Island
Macorna
Bald Rock
Leitchville
96
Womboota

Wilkur
Morton Plains
Wycheproof
Bunguluke
Barraport
Catumnal
Yando
Mimmindie
Canary Island South
Loddon Vale
Gladfield
Mincha
Gunbower
Patho
Torrumbarry

Areegra
95
Watchem
Fairview
Glenloth
Narrewillock
Boort
Durham Ox
Yarrawalla South
Sylvaterre
Mologa
Roslynmead
Wharparilla North
Wharparilla

Carron
Litchfield
Lake Buloke
Massey
Corack East
Corack
Teddywaddy
Barrakee
Buckrabanyule
Wychitella
Mysia
Fernihurst
Borung
129
Jarklin
Calivil
Mitiamo
Kotta
Bamawm Extension
Bamawm
Ballendella

Lawler
Laen North
Rich Avon
Jeffcott North
Jeffcott
Wooroonook
Charlton
Woosang
Korong Vale
Fiery Flat
Bears Lagoon
Pompapiel
Dingee
Milloo
Tennyson
Lockington
Diggora

Donald
Dooboobetic
Yeungroon
Nine Mile
Wedderburn
Wedderburn Junction
Serpentine
Tandarra
Drummartin
Hunter

Laen
Swanwater West
Avon Plains
Cope Cope
Gooroc
Coonooer Bridge
Slaty Creek
Berrimal
Glenalbyn
Salisbury West
Raywood
Summerfield
Neilborough East
Kamarooka
Elmore

Burreo
Banyena
Traynors Lagoon
Gowar East
Kurraca West
Kurraca
Wehla
Kurting
Inglewood
Bridgewater On Loddon
Sebastian
Neilborough
Woodvale
Goornong
93
Barnadown
Myola
97

Lallat
Marnoo
St Arnaud
Logan
Fentons Creek
Rheola
Arnold West
Kingower
Derby
Campbells Forest
Huntly
Bagshot
Muskerry East
Toolleen

Wallaloo
Gre Gre
Kooreh
Burkes Flat
McIntyre
Arnold
Leichardt
Marong
Eaglehawk
Epsom
Fosterville

Wallaloo East
Beazleys Bridge
Rostron
Carapooee
Cochranes Creek
Moliagul
Llanelly
Newbridge
BENDIGO
Junortoun
Longlea
Axedale

Callawadda
Kanya
Tottington
Stuart Mill
Emu
Murphys Creek
Painswick
Tarnagulla
Maiden Gully
Kangaroo Flat
Strathfieldsaye
Axe Creek
47

Riachella
Morrl Morrl
Paradise
Winjallok
Archdale
Goldsborough
Bealiba
Dunolly
Laanecoorie
Lockwood
Lockwood South
Mandurang
Emu Creek
Eppalock
Knowsley

Campbells Bridge
Navarre
63
Barkly
Redbank
Moyreisk
Dunluce
Bromley
Betley
Eddington
Eastville
Shelbourne
Ravenswood
Sedgwick
Pilchers Bridge
Lake Eppalock
Derrinal

Deep Lead
Tulkara
Greens Creek
Landsborough
Shays Flat
Natte Yallock
Moonambel
Rathscar
Timor West
Havelock
Baringhup
Nuggetty
Ravenswood South
Walmer
38
Maldon
Harcourt
Sutton Grange
Heathcote

Stawell
95
Bridge Inn
Illawarra
Joel Joel
Warrenmang
Tanwood
Wareek
Bowenvale
Alma
Perkins Reef
Barkers Creek
Harcourt North
Myrtle Creek
Argyle

Bellellen
Great Western
Glenlofty
Avoca
Moores Flat
Homebush
Carisbrook
Maryborough
Moolort
Welshmans Reef
Campbells Creek
Castlemaine
Mia Mia

Dunneworthy
63
Elmhurst
Amphitheatre
Green Hill Creek
Bung Bong
Adelaide Lead
Lamplough
Amherst
Golden Point
Craigie
Daisy Hill
Joyces Creek
73
Chewton
Elphinstone
Redesdale

Armstrong
Ben Nevis
Eversley
Lillicur
Majorca
Strathlea
Newstead
Yapeen
Fryerstown
Taradale
Sidonia

Rhymney Reef
Norval
Warra Yadin
Crowlands
Glenpatrick
Warrak
Percydale
Mount Lonarch
Caralulup
Talbot
Campbelltown
Dunach
Burnbank
Glengower
Yandoit
Sandon
Clydesdale
Vaughan
Guildford
Irishtown
79
Glenluce
Metcalfe
Langley
Baynton

Ararat

PYRENEES
GREAT DIVIDING RANGE
BORUNG HWY
WIMMERA HWY
SUNRAYSIA HWY
CALDER HWY
MIDLAND HWY
LODDON VALLEY
MURRAY VALLEY HWY

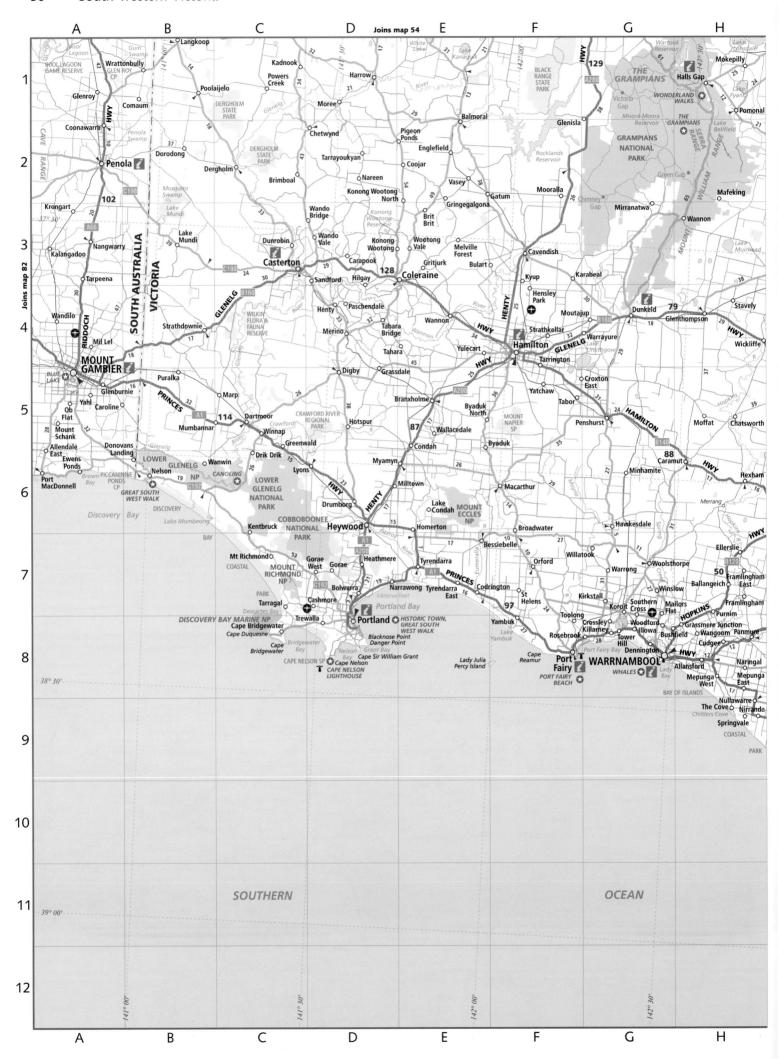

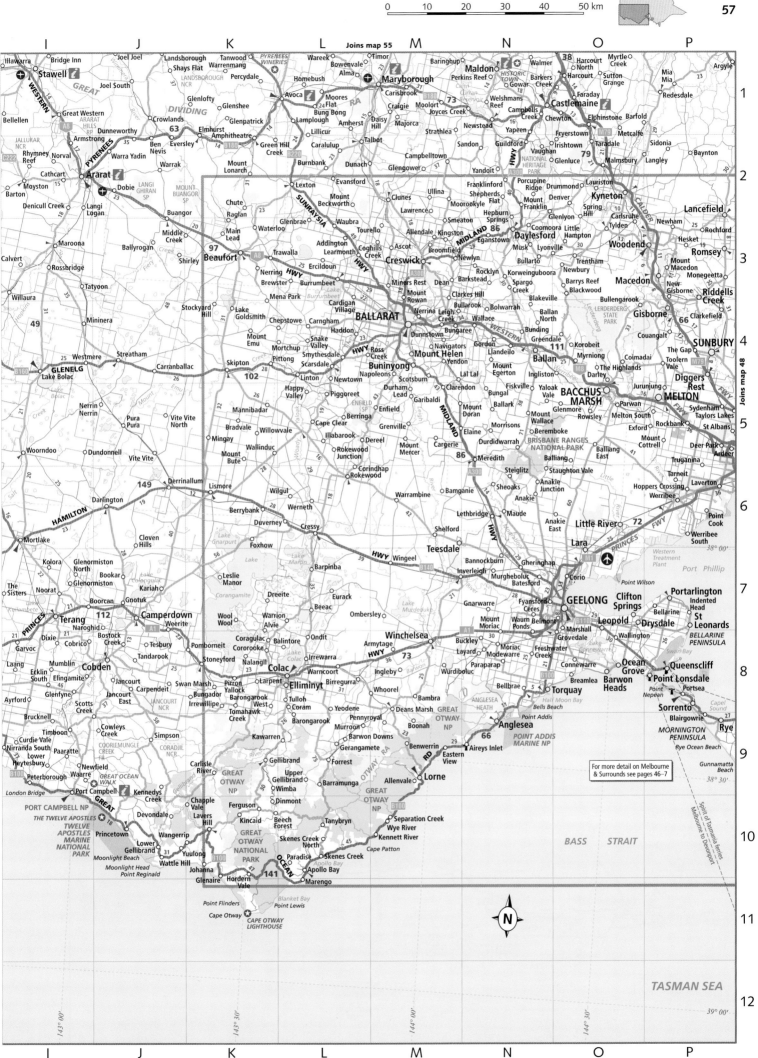

VIC

0   10   20   30   40   50 km

Joins map 55

Joins map 48

I

Illawarra · Bridge Inn · Joel Joel · Landsborough · Tanwood · Timor · Wareek · Bowenvale · Baringhup · Walmer · 38 · Harcourt · Myrtle Creek · Mia Mia · Argyle

Stawell · GREAT · Shays Flat · Warrenmang · Alma · Maldon · HISTORIC TOWN · Perkins Reef · Harcourt North · Harcourt · Sutton Grange · Mia Mia · Redesdale

Percydale · Homebush · Maryborough · Carisbrook · Gowar · Barkers Creek · Castlemaine

WESTERN · GREAT · Glenlofty · Glenshee · Avoca · Moores Flat · Craigie · Moolort · Joyces Creek · Welshmans Reef · Campbells Creek · Chewton · Elphinstone · Barfold

Bellellen · Great Western · Crowlands · 63 · Glenpatrick · Bung Bong · Lamplough · Amherst · Majorca · Strathlea · Newstead · Yapeen · Fryerstown · Taradale · Metcalfe · Sidonia

DIVIDING · Dunneworthy · Elmhurst · Lillicur · Talbot · Campbelltown · Sandon · Guildford · Irishtown · Vaughan · Glenlue · Malmsbury · Langley

Rhymney Reef · Norval · Warra Yadin · Eversley · Green Hill Creek · Caralulup · Burnbank · Dunach · Glengower · 37 · Yandoit · NATIONAL HERITAGE PARK · 79 · Baynton

Armstrong · Ben Nevis · Warrak · Lexton · Evansford · Ullina · Franklinford · Porcupine Ridge · Drummond · Lauriston · Langley

Ararat · Dobie · Langi Ghiran SP · Chute · Raglan · Mount Beckworth · Clunes · Lawrence · Smeaton · Mooroolyke · Mount Franklin · Denver · Kyneton · Lancefield

Moyston · Denicull Creek · Langi Logan · Buangor · Waterloo · Glenbrae · Waubra · Tourello · Allendale · Kingston · Hepburn Springs · Glenlyon · Spring Hill · Carlsruhe · Tylden · Newham · Rochford

Barton · Middle Creek · Ballyrogan · Main Lead · Trawalla · Ercildoun · Creswick · Musk · Lyonville · Daylesford · Coomoora · Little Hampton · Woodend · Hesket · Monegeetta

Maroona · Beaufort · Shirley · Nerring · Brewster · Burrumbeet · Miners Rest · Dean · Barkstead · Rocklyn · Korweinguboora · Spargo Creek · Trentham · Newbury · Mount Macedon · Romsey

Rossbridge · Stockyard Hill · Lake Goldsmith · Chepstowe · Carngham · Mount Rowan · Clarkes Hill · Shepherds Flat · Barrys Reef · Blackwood · Bullengarook · New Gisborne · Riddells Creek

Tatyoon · Mininera · Chepstowe · Haddon · Nerrina · Leigh Creek · Bullarook · Bolwarrah · Ballan North · Greendale · Gisborne · Clarkefield

Willaura · Westmere · Streatham · Carranballac · Skipton · Snake Valley · Smythesdale · Dunnstown · Bungaree · Gordon · Wallace · Ballan · Bunding · Korobeit · Couangalt · 66 · SUNBURY

Calvert · Mount Emu · Mortchup · Pittong · Scarsdale · Buninyong · Napoleons · Yendon · Llandeilo · Myrniong · Coimadai · The Gap · Toolern Vale · Diggers Rest

Westmere · Linton · Newtown · Durham Lead · Scotsburn · Lal Lal · Mount Egerton · Ingliston · The Highlands · Darley · Jurunjung · MELTON

GLENELG · Lake Bolac · Happy Valley · Piggoreet · Garibaldi · Clarendon · Fiskville · Yaloak Vale · BACCHUS MARSH · Rowsley · Melton South · Exford · Sydenham · Taylors Lakes · St Albans

Nerrin Nerrin · Pura Pura · Vite Vite North · Mannibadar · Berringa · Enfield · Bungal · Mount Doran · Glenmore · Parwan · Mount Cottrell · Rockbank · Deer Park · Ardeer

Woorndoo · Dundonnell · Vite Vite · Bradvale · Willowvale · Illabarook · Dereel · Grenville · Elaine · Morrisons · Mount Wallace · Beremboke · Mount Cottrell · Truganina

149 · Mingay · Wallinduc · Rokewood Junction · Mount Mercer · Cargerie · Durdidwarrah · BRISBANE RANGES NATIONAL PARK · Balliang · Tarneit · Laverton

Darlington · Derrinallum · Wilgul · Rokewood · Corindhap · 86 · Meredith · Steiglitz · Staughton Vale · Balliang East · Hoppers Crossing · Werribee

HAMILTON · Berrybank · Werneth · Warrambine · Bamganie · Sheoaks · Anakie Junction · Point Cook

Mortlake · Cloven Hills · Duverney · Cressy · Lethbridge · Maude · Anakie · Anakie East · Little River · 72 · Werribee South

Kolora · Glenormiston North · Foxhow · Shelford · Anakie · Teesdale · Lara · 38° 00'

The Sisters · Noorat · Bookar · Glenormiston · Leslie Manor · Barpinba · Wingeel · Bannockburn · Gheringhap · Corio · Point Wilson · Port Phillip

Boorcan · Gnotuk · Kariah · Dreeite · Beeac · Eurack · Inverleigh · Murghebolluc · Batesford · Western Treatment Plant

Terang · 112 · Camperdown · Weerite · Wool Wool · Warrion · Ombersley · Gnarwarre · Fyansford · Ceres · GEELONG · Clifton Springs · Portarlington · Indented Head

Dixie · Naroghid · Coragulac · Balintore · Ondit · Winchelsea · Buckley · Mount Moriac · Belmont · Marshall · Leopold · Bellarine · St Leonards

Garvoc · Bostock Creek · Tesbury · Pomborneit · Cororooke · Irrewarra · Armytage · Layard · Modewarre · Waurn Ponds · Grovedale · Drysdale · Wallington · BELLARINE PENINSULA

Mumblin · Cobrico · Tandarook · Nalangil · Larpent · Colac · Winchelsea · 73 · Paraparap · Freshwater Creek · Conneware · Ocean Grove · Queenscliff

Laang · Ecklin South · Stoneyford · Pirron Yallock · Elliminyt · Birregurra · Ingleby · Wurdiboluc · Breamlea · Barwon Heads · Point Lonsdale

Cobden · Jancourt · Swan Marsh · Warncoort · Whoorel · Bambra · Bellbrae · Torquay · Point Nepean · Portsea

Glenfyne · Jancourt East · Carpendeit · Bungador · Barongarook West · Tulloh · Coram · Yeodene · Deans Marsh · GREAT OTWAY NP · Bells Beach · Sorrento

Ayrford · Scotts Creek · Irrewillipe · Tomahawk Creek · Barongarook · Pennyroyal · Murroon · Boonah · Anglesea · Point Addis · Blairgowrie · Rye

Brucknell · Cowleys Creek · Simpson · Kawarren · Gerangamete · Barwon Downs · Benwerrin · 66 · POINT ADDIS MARINE NP · MORNINGTON PENINSULA · Rye Ocean Beach

Timboon · Curdie Vale · Paaratte · Newfield · Gellibrand · Forrest · Eastern View · Aireys Inlet · 29

Nirranda South · Lower Heytesbury · Peterborough · Carlisle River · GREAT OTWAY NP · Upper Gellibrand · Wimba · Barramunga · Allenvale · Lorne · For more detail on Melbourne & Surrounds see pages 46–7 · Gunnamatta Beach

London Bridge · Port Campbell · Kennedys Creek · Chapple Vale · Lavers Hill · Ferguson · Kincaid · Dinmont · Beech Forest · Tanybryn · Separation Creek · Wye River · 38° 30'

PORT CAMPBELL NP · THE TWELVE APOSTLES · Devondale · GREAT OCEAN WALK · GREAT OTWAY NATIONAL PARK · Skenes Creek North · Kennett River · Cape Patton

TWELVE APOSTLES MARINE NATIONAL PARK · Princetown · Wangerrip · 18 · Lower Gellibrand · Yuulong · Paradise · Skenes Creek · Apollo Bay · BASS STRAIT

Moonlight Beach · Wattle Hill · Johanna · 31 · 141 · Hordern Vale · Apollo Bay · Marengo · Spirit of Tasmania ferries Melbourne to Devonport

Moonlight Head · Point Reginald · Glenaire · OCEAN · Point Flinders · Point Lewis · Blanket Bay

Cape Otway · CAPE OTWAY LIGHTHOUSE · **N** · TASMAN SEA · 39° 00'

143° 00' · 143° 30' · 144° 00' · 144° 30'

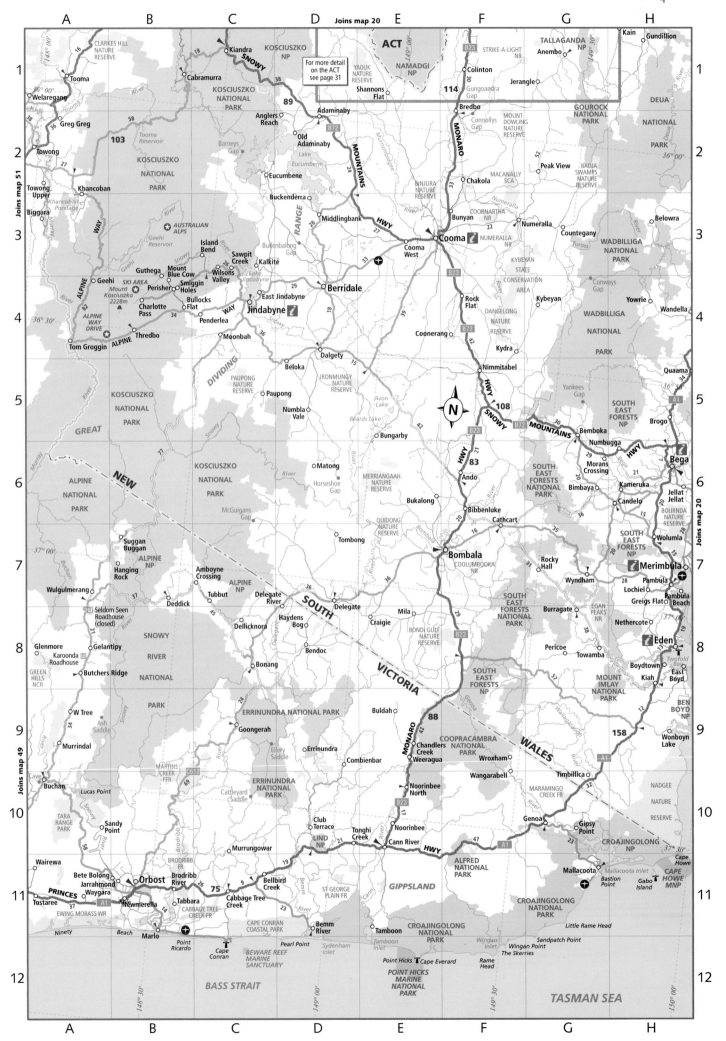

0 10 20 30 40 50 km

Joins map 20

Joins map 51

Joins map 49

Joins map 20

ACT

For more detail
on the ACT
see page 31

A B C D E F G H

1 2 3 4 5 6 7 8 9 10 11 12

KOSCIUSZKO NATIONAL PARK

KOSCIUSZKO NATIONAL PARK

CLARKES HILL NATURE RESERVE

Tooma
Welaregang
Greg Greg
Towong
Towong Upper
Biggara
Khancoban

Kiandra
Cabramurra

Adaminaby
Anglers Reach
Old Adaminaby
Eucumbene
Buckenderra

Shannons Flat
YAOUK NATURE RESERVE
NAMADGI NP

Colinton
Jerangle
Kain
Gundillion

TALLAGANDA NP
STRIKE-A-LIGHT NR
Anembo

GOUROCK NATIONAL PARK

DEUA NATIONAL PARK

Middlingbank

Cooma
Cooma West

Bredbo
Connollys Gap
MOUNT DOWLING NATURE RESERVE
Bunyan

Chakola
MACANALLY SCA
Peak View

BADJA SWAMPS NATURE RESERVE
Belowra

AUSTRALIAN ALPS
Geehi Reservoir

Island Bend
Guthega
Mount Blue Cow
Perisher
Smiggin Holes
Wilsons Valley
Sawpit Creek
Kalkite

East Jindabyne
Berridale

Numeralla
Countegany
Kybeyan

WADBILLIGA NATIONAL PARK

Geehi
Mount Kosciuszko 2228m
Bullocks Flat
Charlotte Pass
Penderlea
Jindabyne
Moonbah

Rock Flat
Kydra

Conways Gap
Yowrie
Wandella

Tom Groggin
Thredbo

Beloka
Dalgety
Coonerang
Nimmitabel

Quaama

Paupong
Numbla Vale

SOUTH EAST FORESTS NP
Brogo

GREAT
DIVIDING
Matong
Bungarby

Bemboka
Numbugga
Morans Crossing
Bega

NEW
ALPINE NATIONAL PARK
KOSCIUSZKO NATIONAL PARK

Horseshoe Gap
McGuigans Gap
Bukalong
Ando
Bibbenluke
Cathcart

SOUTH EAST FORESTS NATIONAL PARK
Bimbaya
Kameruka
Candelo
Jellat Jellat
Wolumla

Suggan Buggan
Hanging Rock
Wulgulmerang

Amboyne Crossing
Tubbut
Deddick

Tombong
Bombala
COOLUMBOOKA NR

Rocky Hall
Wyndham

BOURNDA NATURE RESERVE
Merimbula
Pambula
Lochiel
Greigs Flat
Pambula Beach

Seldom Seen Roadhouse (closed)
Dellicknora
Bonang

ALPINE NP
Delegate River
Haydens Bog
Bendoc

Delegate
Craigie
Mila

SOUTH EAST FORESTS NATIONAL PARK
Burragate
EGAN PEAKS NR
Nethercote

Glenmore
Karoonda Roadhouse
Gelantipy
Butchers Ridge

SNOWY RIVER NATIONAL PARK
Goongerah

Pericoe
Towamba
Eden
Boydtown
Kiah
East Boyd

GREEN HILLS NCR
W Tree
Murrindal

ERRINUNDRA NATIONAL PARK
Errinundra
Combienbar

Buldah
Chandlers Creek
Weeragua
Wroxham
Wangarabell

BEN BOYD NP
MOUNT IMLAY NATIONAL PARK

SOUTH EAST FORESTS NP

Ash Saddle
Ellery Saddle
Cattleyard Saddle

Timbillica
Wonboyn Lake

Buchan
Lucas Point
Sandy Point

ERRINUNDRA NATIONAL PARK
MARTINS CREEK FFR

Club Terrace
Noorinbee North
Noorinbee

Genoa
Gipsy Point

NADGEE NATURE RESERVE

TARA RANGE PARK
Wairewa

Murrungowar
Tonghi Creek
Cann River
LIND NP

ALFRED NATIONAL PARK

CROAJINGOLONG NP

Bete Bolong
Jarrahmond
Waygara
Orbost
Brodribb River
Bellbird Creek
Cabbage Tree Creek

Mallacoota
Bastion Point
Gabo Island

Cape Howe
CAPE HOWE MNP

Tostaree
Newmerella
Tabbara
CABBAGE TREE CREEK FR

Bemm River

GIPPSLAND

CROAJINGOLONG NATIONAL PARK

Marlo
Point Ricardo
Cape Conran

Pearl Point
BEWARE REEF MARINE SANCTUARY

ST GEORGE PLAIN FR

Tamboon
CROAJINGOLONG NATIONAL PARK

Sandpatch Point
Wingan Point
The Skerries

CAPE CONRAN COASTAL PARK
Bemm River

POINT HICKS MARINE NATIONAL PARK
Point Hicks
Cape Everard

Little Rame Head
Rame Head

BASS STRAIT

TASMAN SEA

PRINCES HWY
ALPINE WAY
MONARO HWY
SNOWY MOUNTAINS HWY
SOUTH

VICTORIA
WALES

BAIRNSDALE *page 49 M5*

240 Main St
(03) 5152 3444 or 1800 637 060
www.discovereastgippsland.com.au

BALLARAT *page 46 D3*

Town Hall
225 Sturt St
(03) 5337 4337 or 1800 446 633
www.visitballarat.com.au

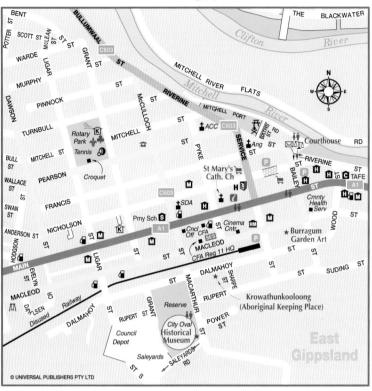

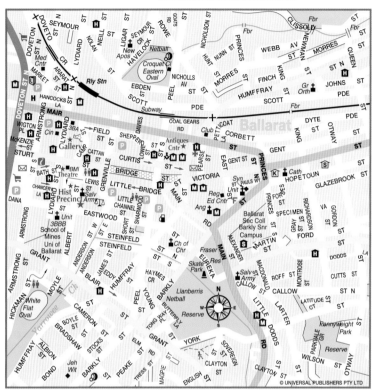

VIC

BENALLA *page 50 G8*

14 Mair St
(03) 5762 1749
www.benalla.vic.gov.au

BENDIGO *page 50 A9*

51–67 Pall Mall
(03) 5434 6060 or 1800 813 153
www.bendigotourism.com.au

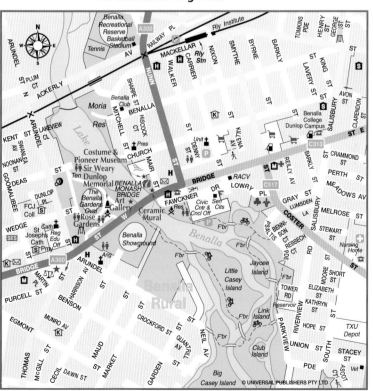

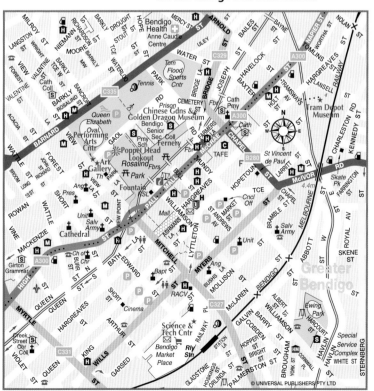

CASTLEMAINE *page 55 N12*

Historic Market Building
44 Mostyn St
(03) 5471 1795 or 1800 171 888
www.maldoncastlemaine.com.au

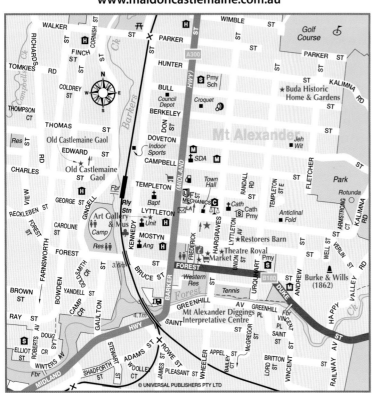

COLAC *page 46 B9*

Cnr Murray and Queen sts
1300 689 297
www.visitotways.com

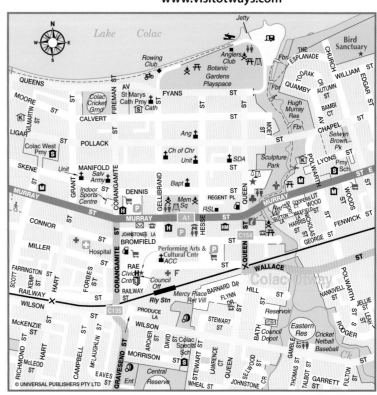

GEELONG *page 46 F8*

26 Moorabool St
(03) 5222 2900 or 1800 755 611
vwww.visitgeelongbellarine.com.au

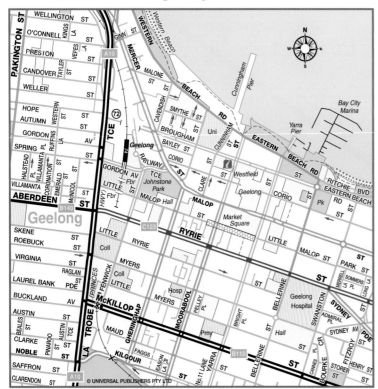

HAMILTON *page 56 F4*

Cnr Lonsdale and Thompson sts
1800 807 056
www.visitgreaterhamilton.com.au

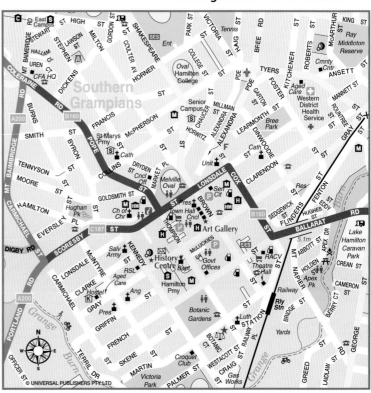

HORSHAM *page 54 G9*

20 O'Callaghans Pde
(03) 5382 1832 or 1800 633 218
www.visithorsham.com.au

LAKES ENTRANCE *page 49 O6*

2 Marine Pde
(03) 5155 1966 or 1800 637 060
www.discovereastgippsland.com.au

VIC

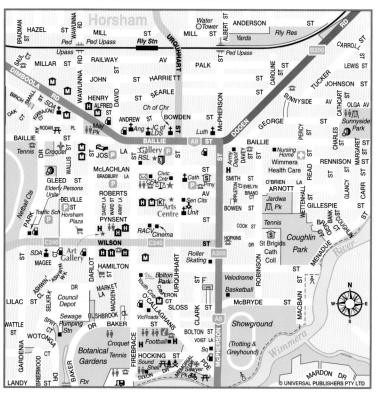

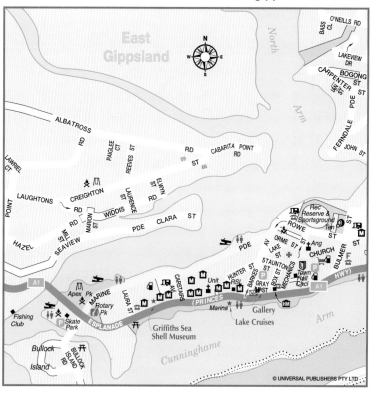

MILDURA *page 52 G6*

180–190 Deakin Ave
(03) 5018 8380 or 1800 039 043
www.visitmildura.com.au

MORWELL *page 48 H7*

The Old Church
Princes Hwy, Traralgon
1800 621 409
www.visitlatrobevalley.com

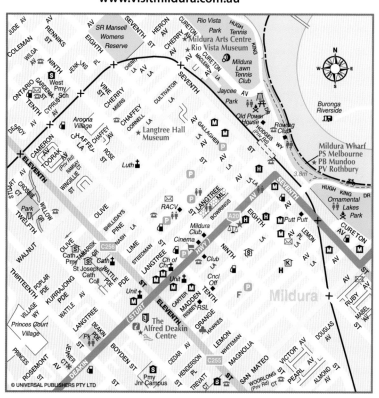

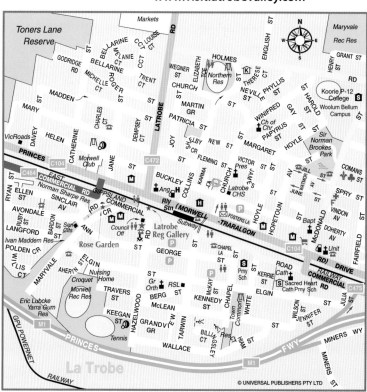

PORTLAND *page 56 D8*

 Lee Breakwater Rd
(03) 5522 2130 or 1800 035 567
www.visitportland.com.au

SALE *page 49 K7*

Wellington Visitor Information Centre
8 Foster St (Princes Hwy)
(03) 5144 1108 or 1800 677 520
www.tourismwellington.com.au

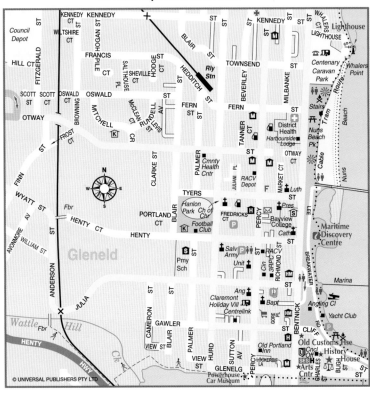

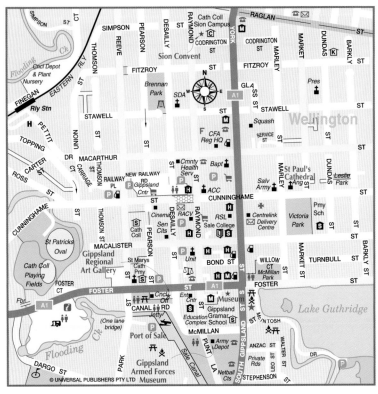

SHEPPARTON *page 50 E7*

33 Nixon St
1800 808 839
www.discovershepparton.com.au

STAWELL *page 55 I11*

6 Main St
(03) 5358 2314 or 1800 330 080
www.visitgrampians.com.au

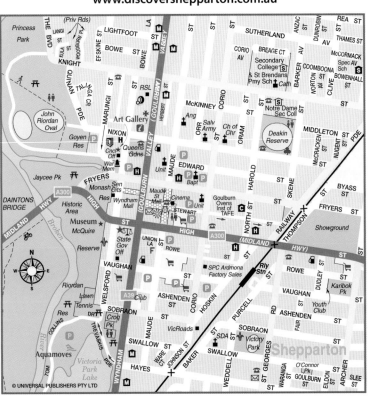

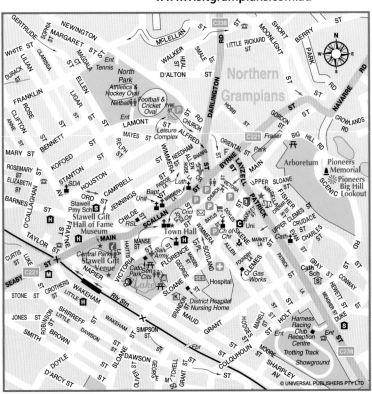

TRARALGON *page 49 I7*

The Old Church
Princes Hwy
1800 621 409
www.visitlatrobecity.com.au

WANGARATTA *page 51 I7*

100 Murphy St
(03) 5721 5711 or 1800 801 065
www.visitwangaratta.com.au

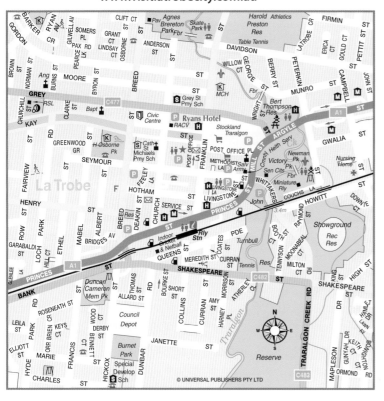

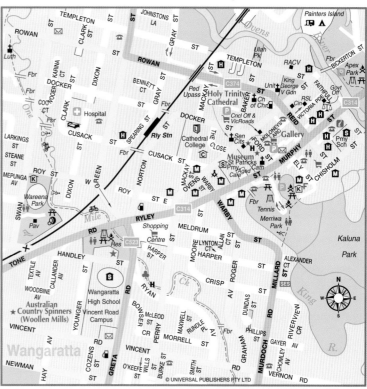

VIC

WARRNAMBOOL *page 56 G8*

89 Merri St
(03) 5559 4620 or 1800 637 725
www.visitwarrnambool.com.au

WODONGA *page 51 K6*

69–73 Hovell St
1300 796 222
www.visitalburywodonga.com

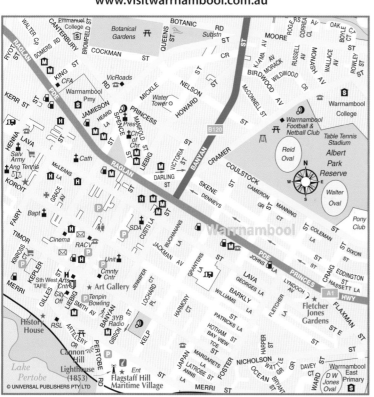

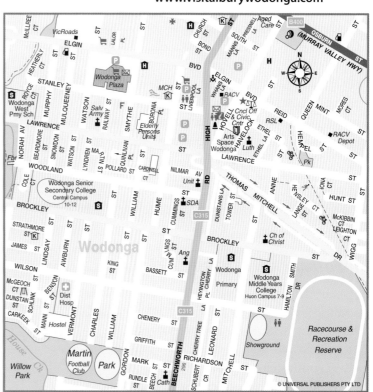

Barossa Valley vineyards

SOUTH AUSTRALIA

Although it's Australia's driest state, one of South Australia's many attractions is its extensive 3816-kilometre coastline, offering scenic driving and walking routes along its many indentations and offshore islands.

South Australia's north and west is dominated by a near-desert environment where immense plains, rugged mountains and dry lakes entice many visitors; the beautiful Flinders Ranges National Park, is among the top attractions. The southern gulf lands, including the Eyre, Yorke and Fleurieu peninsulas, are fringed by quiet beaches, fishing towns and the Mount Lofty Ranges.

For travellers, South Australia is the perfect place to get off the beaten track. The outback begins just an hour or two up the road from Adelaide, the state's capital. Touring by car is easy, with links from Adelaide to the Barrier, Sturt, Ouyen, Dukes and Princes highways heading to the eastern states; the Stuart Highway, crossing the continent to Darwin; and the Eyre Highway, traversing the Nullarbor Plain to Western Australia.

INFORMATION CENTRE

Adelaide Visitor Information Centre
9 James Pl, off Rundle Mall,
Adelaide; (08) 8203 7611 or 1300 764 227 or
1300 588 140
www.southaustralia.com
www.adelaidecitycouncil.com

Places of interest

	MAP REF			MAP REF
Australian Arid Lands Botanic Garden	72 H2		Lake Eyre	76 E8
The Barossa Goldfields	70 D6		Lincoln National Park	72 D9
Barossa Valley wineries	70 F4		Loxton Historical Village	82 G1
Belair National Park	70 C9		McLaren Vale wineries	69 C10
Birdsville Track	76, 77		Mount Lofty summit and	
Blue Lake, Mount Gambier	86 G12		Botanic Garden	69 G3
Bunda Cliffs, Nullarbor Plain	80 C7		Murphy's Haystacks	72 A3
Clare Valley wineries	73 J6		Naracoorte Caves	82 G9
Cleland Wildlife Park	69 G3		National Motor Museum, Birdwood	82 C2
Coober Pedy opal mines	76 A10		Pichi Richi Railway, Quorn	73 I7
Coonawarra wineries	82 G10		Remarkable Rocks, Kangaroo Island	72 F12
Copper Triangle: Kadina, Monta and			South Australian Maritime Museum	68 B9
Wallaroo Mines Historic Area	72 H6		South Australian Whale Centre,	
Flinders Ranges National Park	75 I6		Victor Harbor	71 F9
Granite Island	71 F3		SteamRanger Heritage Railway,	
Hahndorf	71 H3		Mount Barker–Victor Harbor	71 F9
Hallett Cove Conservation Park	71 E3		Wadlata Outback Centre, Port Augusta	72 H2
Koppio Smithy Museum	72 D7		Wilpena Pound	75 I6

MAPS

SOUTH AUSTRALIA

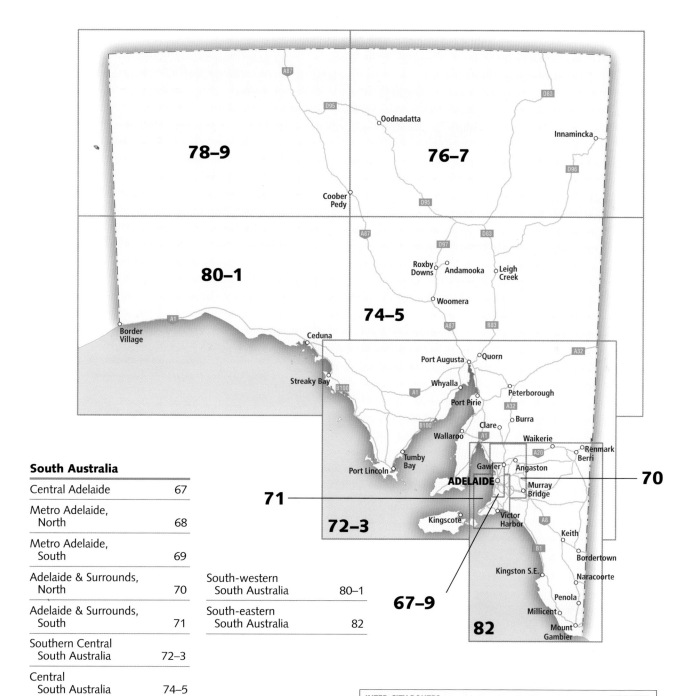

South Australia

Central Adelaide	67
Metro Adelaide, North	68
Metro Adelaide, South	69
Adelaide & Surrounds, North	70
Adelaide & Surrounds, South	71
Southern Central South Australia	72–3
Central South Australia	74–5
North-eastern South Australia	76–7
North-western South Australia	78–9

South-western South Australia	80–1
South-eastern South Australia	82

INTER-CITY ROUTES	DISTANCE
Adelaide–Darwin via Stuart Hwy	3026 km
Adelaide–Perth via Eyre & Great Eastern hwys	2700 km
Adelaide–Sydney via Sturt & Hume hwys	1415 km
Adelaide–Melbourne via Dukes & Western hwys	729 km
Adelaide–Melbourne via Princes Hwy	911 km

South Australian Museum

Adelaide

South Australia's capital city, Adelaide, was named after the wife of King William IV. This well-planned city of gardens, historic buildings and churches lies on a narrow coastal plain between the Mount Lofty Ranges and the waters of Gulf St Vincent.

As envisioned by Colonel William Light, Surveyor-General for the new colony from 1836, the city centre is surrounded by open parklands, which separate the CBD from the suburbs.

The tree-lined boulevard of North Terrace contains so many fine colonial buildings and places of interest that it is not uncommon to see groups of people on organised history walks. At the western end of the street is Holy Trinity Church, the oldest church in the state. Nearby are the two oldest buildings remaining in Adelaide: the Regency-style Government House, started in 1838 and not completed until 1878; and Adelaide Gaol, opened in 1841 and last used in 1988.

Adelaide is known for its cafe culture, restaurants and wines. The city has a multicultural population and this is reflected in the city's markets and restaurants.

Adelaide is also well known for its festivals, including the legendary Adelaide Festival, the Adelaide Fringe Festival and the Adelaide Film Festival.

Places of interest

	MAP REF		MAP REF
Adelaide Botanic Garden	67 G6	Light's Vision	67 C4
Adelaide Central Market		Lion Arts Centre	67 C7
and Chinatown	67 D9	Migration Museum	67 E6
Adelaide Convention Centre	67 D6	National Wine Centre of Australia	67 H6
Adelaide Festival Centre	67 D6	Parliament House	67 D6
Adelaide Gaol	67 A6	Rundle Mall	67 E7
Adelaide Himeji Garden	67 G10	SKYCITY Adelaide Casino	67 D6
Adelaide Town Hall	67 E8	South Australian Museum	67 E6
Adelaide Zoo	67 F4	State Library of South Australia	67 E6
Art Gallery of South Australia	67 F6	Tandanya, National Aboriginal	
Ayers House Museum	67 G7	Cultural Institute	67 G7
Elder Park and Rotunda	67 D6	Torrens Lake	67 C6
Glenelg Tram	68 D11	University of South Australia	67 F6
Government House	67 E6	Victoria Park	67 H10
International Rose Garden	67 G5	Victoria Square	67 E8

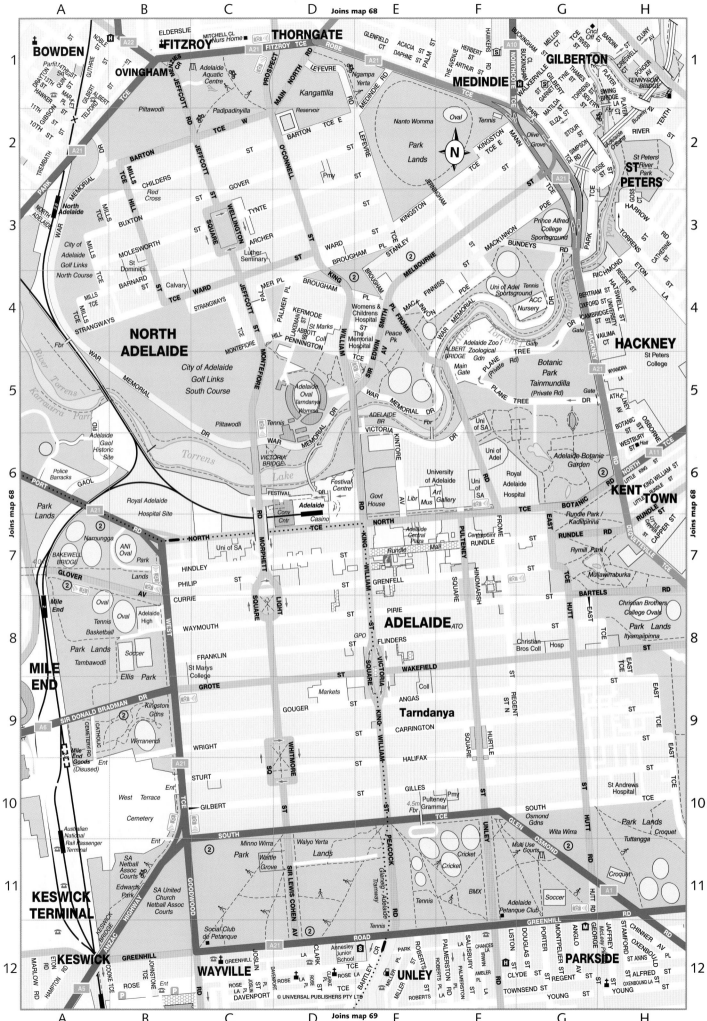

0   0.25   0.5   0.75   1 km

A   B   C   D   E   F   G   H

BOWDEN
OVINGHAM
FITZROY
THORNGATE
MEDINDIE
GILBERTON
ST PETERS
NORTH ADELAIDE
HACKNEY
KENT TOWN
MILE END
ADELAIDE *ATO*
Tarndanya
KESWICK TERMINAL
KESWICK
WAYVILLE
UNLEY
PARKSIDE

© UNIVERSAL PUBLISHERS PTY LTD

SA

0   2   4   6   8 km

Joins map 70

MIDDLE BEACH

Salt

PORT GAWLER
PORT GAWLER CONSERVATION PARK

TWO WELLS

LEWISTON

REEVES PLAINS

WARD BELT

GAWLER BELT

HEWETT
STURT HWY
WILLASTON
GAWLER HISTORIC TOWN
GAWLER WEST
GAWLER SOUTH
EVANSTON
EVANSTON PARK
EVANSTON GARDENS
EVANSTON SOUTH
BIBARINGA

BUCHFELDE
GAWLER RIVER
HILLIER

ANGLE VALE
MUNNO PARA DOWNS
MUNNO PARA WEST
MUNNO PARA
KUDLA
ULEYBURY

BUCKLAND PARK

VIRGINIA

PENFIELD GARDENS
MACDONALD PARK
ANDREWS FARM
SMITHFIELD PLAINS
SMITHFIELD
BLAKEVIEW
CRAIGMORE
ONE TREE HILL

WATERLOO CORNER

PENFIELD
Edinburgh Aerodrome
EDINBURGH RAAF BASE DEFENCE RESERVE
EDINBURGH

DAVOREN PARK
ELIZABETH NORTH
ELIZABETH WEST
ELIZABETH DOWNS
ELIZABETH PARK
ELIZABETH
ELIZABETH GROVE
ELIZABETH SOUTH
ELIZABETH EAST
HILLBANK

GULF ST VINCENT

DIREK
BURTON
SALISBURY NORTH
PARALOWIE
SALISBURY
SALISBURY PARK
SALISBURY HEIGHTS
GREENWITH

BOLIVAR
SALISBURY DOWNS
PARAFIELD GARDENS
BRAHMA LODGE
SALISBURY EAST
COBBLER CREEK REGIONAL PARK
GOLDEN GROVE

Point Grey
Pelican Point
OUTER HARBOR
NORTH HAVEN
OSBORNE
TORRENS ISLAND CP
Torrens Island
Garden Island

SALISBURY SOUTH
GREEN FIELDS
Parafield Airport
PARAFIELD
GULFVIEW HEIGHTS
WYNN VALE
YATALA VALE
UPPER HERMITAGE

TAPEROO
LARGS NORTH
LARGS BAY
SEMAPHORE

GLOBE DERBY PARK
DRY CREEK
MAWSON LAKES
POORAKA
CAVAN
PARA HILLS WEST
PARA HILLS
MODBURY HEIGHTS
REDWOOD PARK
FAIRVIEW PARK
BANKSIA PARK
LOWER HERMITAGE

SOUTH AUSTRALIAN MARITIME MUSEUM
GILLMAN
PORT RIVER
SALISBURY
INGLE FARM
PARA VISTA
MODBURY NORTH
MODBURY
ST AGNES
TEA TREE GULLY
HOUGHTON

SEMAPHORE SOUTH
Point Malcolm
GLANVILLE
BIRKENHEAD
PORT ADELAIDE
OTTOWAY
WINGFIELD
GEPPS CROSS
WALKLEY HEIGHTS
VALLEY VIEW
GILLES PLAINS
HOPE VALLEY
VISTA
ANSTEY HILL REGIONAL PARK
PARACOMBE

SEMAPHORE PARK
ANGLE PARK
KILBURN
CLEARVIEW
OAKDEN
HOLDEN HILL
HIGHBURY

WEST LAKES SHORE
ROSEWATER
ATHOL PARK
ENFIELD
NORTHGATE
WINDSOR GARDENS
DERNANCOURT
ATHELSTONE
CASTAMBUL

WEST LAKES
ROYAL PARK
CHELTENHAM
ALBERT PARK
FERRYDEN PARK
REGENCY PARK
BLAIR ATHOL
GREENACRES
KLEMZIG
PARADISE
BLACK HILL CONSERVATION PARK

TENNYSON
WOODVILLE
CROYDON PARK
BROADVIEW
CAMPBELLTOWN
NEWTON

SEATON
WOODVILLE SOUTH
WEST CROYDON
R.M. WILLIAMS OUTBACK HERITAGE MUSEUM
COLLINSWOOD
PROSPECT
FELIXSTOW
HECTORVILLE
ROSTREVOR
MONTACUTE

GRANGE
FINDON
BROMPTON
MEDINDIE
MARDEN
PAYNEHAM
MORIALTA CONSERVATION PARK

HENLEY BEACH
FULHAM GARDENS
FLINDERS PARK
WELLAND
HINDMARSH
NORTH ADELAIDE
ST PETERS
TRANMERE
MAGILL
WOODFORDE

KIDMAN PARK
THEBARTON
HACKNEY
KENSINGTON GARDENS
AULDANA
TERINGIE
NORTON SUMMIT

HENLEY BEACH SOUTH
FULHAM
LOCKLEYS
TORRENSVILLE
MILE END
NORWOOD
LEABROOK
WATTLE PARK
PENFOLDS MAGILL ESTATE
SKYE
MARBLE HILL

WEST BEACH
ADELAIDE AIRPORT
RICHMOND
ADELAIDE
DULWICH
GLENSIDE
BURNSIDE
STONYFELL
HORSNELL GULLY CP
GILES CP
ASHTON
BASKET RANGE

WAYVILLE
PARKSIDE
Joins map 69

For more detail on Central Adelaide see page 67

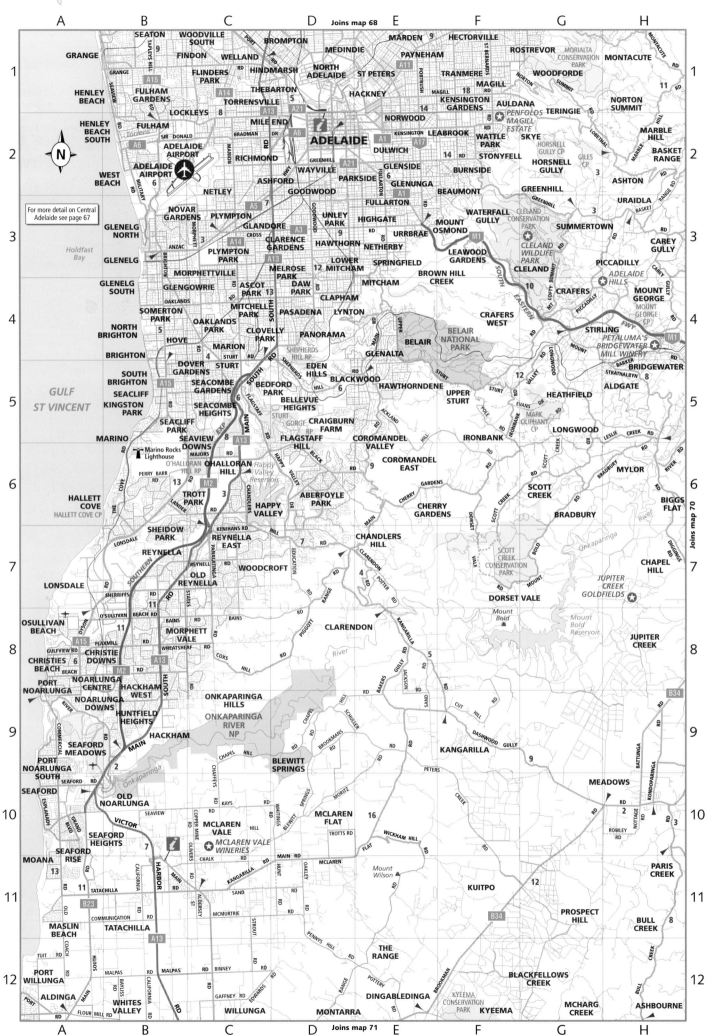

0 2 4 6 8 km

A B C D E F G H

GRANGE

SEATON
WOODVILLE
SOUTH
BROMPTON
FINDON
WELLAND
MEDINDIE
MARDEN
HECTORVILLE
PAYNEHAM
ROSTREVOR
MORIALTA
CONSERVATION
PARK
WOODFORDE
MONTACUTE

HENLEY
BEACH
FULHAM
GARDENS
FLINDERS
PARK
HINDMARSH
THEBARTON
NORTH
ADELAIDE
ST PETERS
HACKNEY
TRANMERE
MAGILL
KENSINGTON
GARDENS
AULDANA
PENFOLDS
MAGILL
ESTATE
TERINGIE

NORTON
SUMMIT

MARBLE
HILL

HENLEY
BEACH
SOUTH
FULHAM
LOCKLEYS
TORRENSVILLE
MILE END
NORWOOD
LEABROOK
WATTLE
PARK
SKYE
HORSNELL
GULLY CP
STONYFELL
HORSNELL
GULLY
ASHTON
BASKET
RANGE

WEST
BEACH
ADELAIDE
AIRPORT
RICHMOND
BRADMAN
ADELAIDE
DULWICH
BURNSIDE
GREENHILL
URAIDLA

ADELAIDE
AIRPORT
ASHFORD
WAYVILLE
PARKSIDE
GLENSIDE
GLENUNGA
BEAUMONT
WATERFALL
GULLY
CLELAND
CONSERVATION
PARK
SUMMERTOWN
CAREY
GULLY

For more detail on Central
Adelaide see page 67
NETLEY
GOODWOOD
NOVAR
GARDENS
PLYMPTON
GLANDORE
UNLEY
PARK
HIGHGATE
FULLARTON
URRBRAE
MOUNT
OSMOND
LEAWOOD
GARDENS
CLELAND
WILDLIFE
PARK
CLELAND
PICCADILLY

GLENELG
NORTH
PLYMPTON
PARK
CLARENCE
GARDENS
HAWTHORN
NETHERBY
SPRINGFIELD
ADELAIDE
HILLS
MOUNT
GEORGE

GLENELG
MORPHETTVILLE
MELROSE
PARK
LOWER
MITCHAM
MITCHAM
BROWN HILL
CREEK
CRAFERS
STIRLING
PETALUMA'S
BRIDGEWATER
MILL WINERY

GLENELG
SOUTH
GLENGOWRIE
ASCOT
PARK
DAW
PARK
CLAPHAM
CRAFERS
WEST
BRIDGEWATER

SOMERTON
PARK
OAKLANDS
PARK
MITCHELL
PARK
PASADENA
LYNTON
BELAIR
NATIONAL
PARK
BELAIR
GLENALTA
HEATHFIELD
ALDGATE

NORTH
BRIGHTON
HOVE
MARION
CLOVELLY
PARK
PANORAMA
SHEPHERDS
HILL RP
EDEN
HILLS
LONGWOOD

BRIGHTON
DOVER
GARDENS
STURT
SEACOMBE
GARDENS
BEDFORD
PARK
BLACKWOOD
HAWTHORNDENE
IRONBANK

GULF
ST VINCENT
SOUTH
BRIGHTON
SEACLIFF
KINGSTON
PARK
SEACOMBE
HEIGHTS
BELLEVUE
HEIGHTS
CRAIGBURN
FARM
UPPER
STURT
MARK
OLIPHANT
CP

MARINO
SEACLIFF
PARK
SEAVIEW
DOWNS
FLAGSTAFF
HILL
COROMANDEL
VALLEY
MYLOR

Marino Rocks
Lighthouse
O'HALLORAN
HILL
HAPPY
VALLEY
RESERVOIR
COROMANDEL
EAST
SCOTT
CREEK
BIGGS
FLAT

HALLETT
COVE
HALLETT COVE CP
TROTT
PARK
HAPPY
VALLEY
ABERFOYLE
PARK
CHERRY
GARDENS
BRADBURY

SHEIDOW
PARK
REYNELLA
EAST
CHANDLERS
HILL
CHAPEL
HILL

REYNELLA
WOODCROFT
SCOTT
CREEK
CONSERVATION
PARK

LONSDALE
OLD
REYNELLA
CLARENDON
DORSET VALE
JUPITER
CREEK
GOLDFIELDS

OSULLIVAN
BEACH
MORPHETT
VALE
JUPITER
CREEK

CHRISTIES
BEACH
CHRISTIE
DOWNS
KANGARILLA

PORT
NOARLUNGA
NOARLUNGA
CENTRE
HACKHAM
WEST
ONKAPARINGA
HILLS
MEADOWS

NOARLUNGA
DOWNS
HUNTFIELD
HEIGHTS
HACKHAM
ONKAPARINGA
RIVER
NP
KANGARILLA

SEAFORD
MEADOWS
BLEWITT
SPRINGS

PORT
NOARLUNGA
SOUTH
OLD
NOARLUNGA
MCLAREN
FLAT
PARIS
CREEK

SEAFORD
SEAFORD
HEIGHTS
MCLAREN
VALE
KUITPO
BULL
CREEK

MOANA
SEAFORD
RISE
MCLAREN VALE
WINERIES
PROSPECT
HILL

PORT
WILLUNGA
TATACHILLA
THE
RANGE
BLACKFELLOWS
CREEK

MASLIN
BEACH
WILLUNGA
DINGABLEDINGA
KYEEMA
CONSERVATION
PARK
KYEEMA
MCHARG
CREEK
ASHBOURNE

ALDINGA
WHITES
VALLEY
MONTARRA

0 5 10 15 20 km

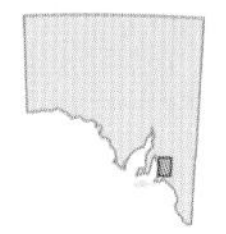

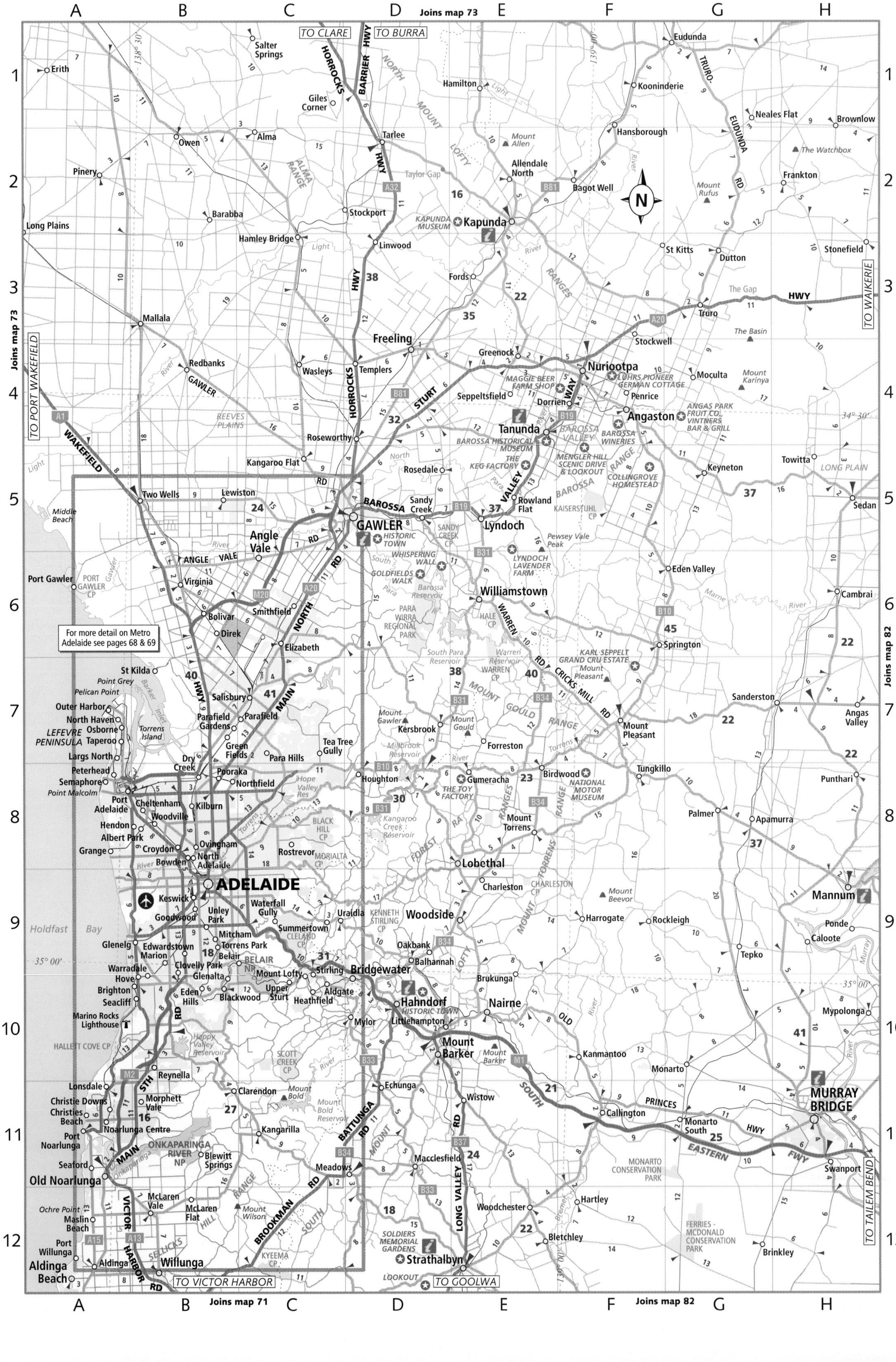

Joins map 73

TO CLARE
TO BURRA

N

Grid columns: A B C D E F G H
Grid rows: 1–12

TO PORT WAKEFIELD
TO WAKERIE

Erith
Salter Springs
Giles Corner
Hamilton
Eudunda
Kooninderie
The Watchbox
Pinery
Owen
Alma
Tarlee
Mount Allen
Hansborough
Neales Flat
Brownlow
Long Plains
Barabba
Stockport
Allendale North
Bagot Well
Mount Rufus
Frankton
Hamley Bridge
Linwood
KAPUNDA MUSEUM
Kapunda
St Kitts
Dutton
Stonefield
Mallala
Fords
Truro
The Gap
HWY
Redbanks
Wasleys
Templers
Greenock
Nuriootpa
Stockwell
Moculta
Freeling
MAGGIE BEER FARM SHOP
LUHRS PIONEER GERMAN COTTAGE
Mount Karinya
Roseworthy
Seppeltsfield
Dorrien
Penrice
ANGAS PARK FRUIT CO
VINTNERS BAR & GRILL
Kangaroo Flat
Tanunda
Angaston
BAROSSA HISTORICAL MUSEUM
THE KEG FACTORY
MENGLER HILL SCENIC DRIVE & LOOKOUT
Keyneton
Towitta
Two Wells
Lewiston
Rosedale
BAROSSA WINERIES
COLLINGROVE HOMESTEAD
Sedan
Sandy Creek
Rowland Flat
Port Gawler
PORT GAWLER CP
Angle Vale
GAWLER HISTORIC TOWN
Lyndoch
KAISERSTUHL CP
Pewsey Vale Peak
Eden Valley
Middle Beach
ANGLE VALE RD
Virginia
WHISPERING WALL
LYNDOCH LAVENDER FARM
Cambrai
St Kilda
Point Grey
Pelican Point
Smithfield
Bolivar
Direk
Elizabeth
GOLDFIELDS WALK
Barossa Reservoir
Williamstown
HALE CP
Springton
Outer Harbor
North Haven
Osborne
Taperoo
LEFEVRE PENINSULA
Salisbury
PARA WIRRA REGIONAL PARK
South Para Reservoir
Warren Reservoir
WARREN CP
KARL SEPPELT GRAND CRU ESTATE
Mount Pleasant
Sanderston
Largs North
Peterhead
Semaphore
Point Malcolm
Parafield Gardens
Parafield
Tea Tree Gully
Mount Gawler
Kersbrook
Mount Gould
Millbrook Reservoir
Forreston
Mount Pleasant
Tungkillo
Angas Valley
Punthari
Dry Creek
Green Fields
Para Hills
Houghton
Gumeracha
THE TOY FACTORY
Birdwood
NATIONAL MOTOR MUSEUM
Palmer
Apamurra
Port Adelaide
Cheltenham
Woodville
Kilburn
Pooraka
Northfield
Kangaroo Creek Reservoir
BLACK HILL CP
Mount Torrens
Mannum
Hendon
Albert Park
Ovingham
Rostrevor
MORIALTA CP
Lobethal
Grange
Croydon
Bowden
North Adelaide
Charleston
CHARLESTON CP
Mount Beevor
ADELAIDE
Keswick
Waterfall Gully
Uraidla
KENNETH STIRLING CP
Woodside
Harrogate
Rockleigh
Ponde
Caloote
Goodwood
Unley Park
Summertown
CLELAND CP
Glenelg
Mitcham
Torrens Park
Belair
Oakbank
Balhannah
Tepko
Edwardstown
Marion
BELAIR NP
Mount Lofty
Stirling
Bridgewater
Brukunga
Warradale
Hove
Clovelly Park
Glenalta
Upper Sturt
Aldgate
Hahndorf
Nairne
Mypolonga
Brighton
Seacliff
Eden Hills
Blackwood
Heathfield
HAHNDORF HISTORIC TOWN
Littlehampton
Marino Rocks Lighthouse
Mylor
Mount Barker
Mount Barker
HALLETT COVE CP
Happy Valley Reservoir
SCOTT CREEK CP
Kanmantoo
Lonsdale
Reynella
Mount Bold
Echunga
MURRAY BRIDGE
Christie Downs
Morphett Vale
Clarendon
Mount Bold Reservoir
Wistow
Callington
Monarto
Christies Beach
Noarlunga Centre
Kangarilla
Monarto South
Port Noarlunga
ONKAPARINGA RIVER NP
Blewitt Springs
Macclesfield
MONARTO CONSERVATION PARK
Seaford
Meadows
PRINCES HWY
Old Noarlunga
McLaren Vale
Mount Wilson
Woodchester
Hartley
FERRIES-MCDONALD CONSERVATION PARK
Brinkley
Ochre Point
McLaren Flat
KYEEMA CP
SOLDIERS MEMORIAL GARDENS
Bletchley
Swanport
Maslin Beach
Port Willunga
Willunga
Strathalbyn
Aldinga
Aldinga Beach
BROOKMAN
LOOKOUT

TO VICTOR HARBOR
TO GOOLWA
TO TAILEM BEND

Joins map 73
Joins map 71
Joins map 82
Joins map 82

For more detail on Metro Adelaide see pages 68 & 69

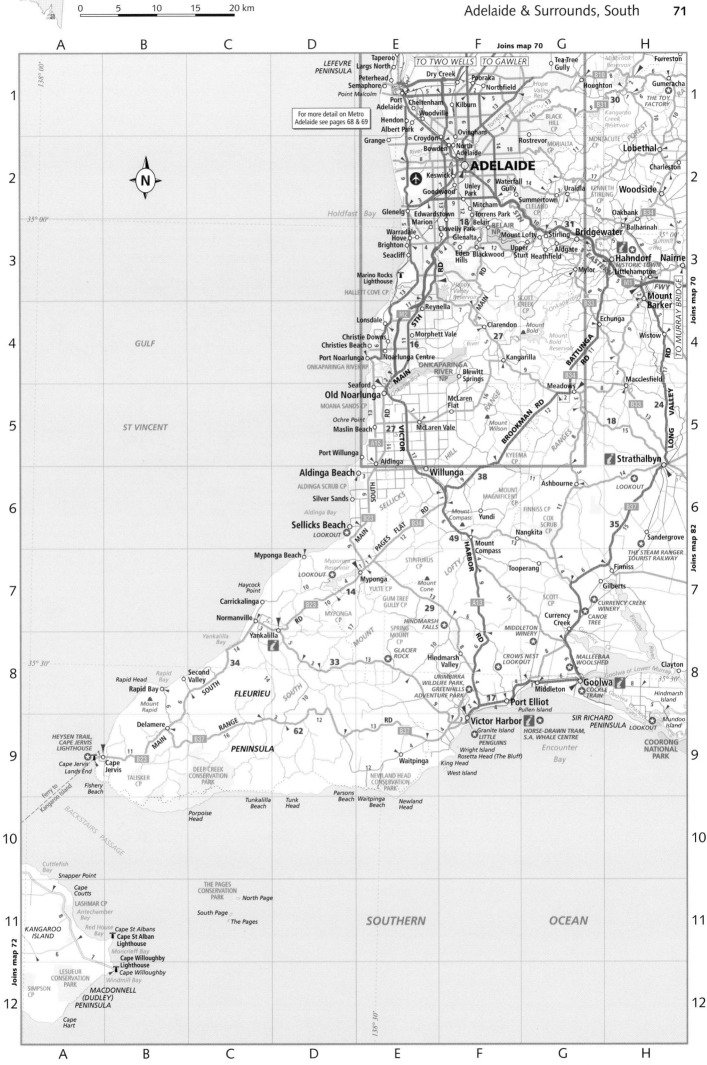

ADELAIDE

LEFEVRE PENINSULA

TO TWO WELLS   TO GAWLER

For more detail on Metro Adelaide see pages 68 & 69

138° 00'

35° 00'

GULF
ST VINCENT

Holdfast Bay

Taperoo
Largs North
Peterhead
Semaphore
Point Malcolm
Port Adelaide
Hendon
Albert Park
Grange
Croydon
Cheltenham
Kilburn
Woodville
Ovingham
Bowden
North Adelaide
Dry Creek
Poraka
Northfield

Tea Tree Gully
Houghton
Rostrevor

Millbrook Reservoir
Forreston
Gumeracha
THE TOY FACTORY

Hope Valley Res
BLACK HILL CP
MONTACUTE CP
Lobethal
Charleston

Keswick
Goodwood
Unley Park
Waterfall Gully
Mitcham
Torrens Park
Edwardstown
Marion
Glenelg
Belair
Clovelly Park
Glenalta
Warradale
Hove
Brighton
Eden Hills
Seacliff
Blackwood
Upper Sturt
Summertown
CLELAND CP
Uraidla
Stirling
Mount Lofty
Aldgate
Heathfield
Mylor
Bridgewater
Hahndorf HISTORIC TOWN
Littlehampton
Nairne
Balhannah
Oakbank
Woodside
KENNETH STIRLING CP

Marino Rocks Lighthouse
HALLETT COVE CP
Reynella
Lonsdale
Christie Downs
Christies Beach
Port Noarlunga
Noarlunga Centre
Morphett Vale
Clarendon
Kangarilla
Mount Bold
Mount Bold Reservoir
Echunga
Mount Barker
Wistow
Macclesfield

ONKAPARINGA RIVER RP
Seaford
Old Noarlunga
ONKAPARINGA RIVER NP
MOANA SANDS CP
Ochre Point
Maslin Beach
Blewitt Springs
McLaren Flat
McLaren Vale
Mount Wilson
Meadows
Strathalbyn
LONG VALLEY RD

Port Willunga
Aldinga
Willunga
KYEEMA CP
Ashbourne
LOOKOUT

Aldinga Beach
ALDINGA SCRUB CP
Silver Sands
Aldinga Bay
Sellicks Beach
LOOKOUT
Mount Compass
Yundi
Nangkita
COX SCRUB CP
FINNISS CP
Sandergrove
THE STEAM RANGER TOURIST RAILWAY

Myponga Beach
Myponga Reservoir
LOOKOUT
Myponga
YULTE CP
GUM TREE GULLY CP
MYPONGA CP
Mount Cone
Mount Compass
Tooperang
Finniss
Gilberts
CURRENCY CREEK WINERY
CANOE TREE

Haycock Point
Carrickalinga
Normanville
Yankalilla
Yankalilla Bay

HINDMARSH FALLS
SPRING MOUNT CP
Hindmarsh Valley
GLACIER ROCK
Currency Creek
MIDDLETON WINERY
CROWS NEST LOOKOUT
MALLEEBAA WOOLSHED
Clayton

Rapid Head
Rapid Bay
Rapid Bay
Mount Rapid
Second Valley
Delamere
FLEURIEU
SOUTH
MAIN
RANGE
PENINSULA
SOUTH
MOUNT LOFTY
URIMBIRRA WILDLIFE PARK, GREENHILLS ADVENTURE PARK
Middleton
Port Elliot
Pullen Island
Goolwa
COCKLE TRAIN
Hindmarsh Island
Mundoo Island
LOOKOUT

HEYSEN TRAIL, CAPE JERVIS LIGHTHOUSE
Cape Jervis
Lands End
Fishery Beach
Ferry to Kangaroo Island
BACKSTAIRS PASSAGE
TALISKER CP
DEEP CREEK CONSERVATION PARK
Waitpinga
Victor Harbor
Granite Island LITTLE PENGUINS
Wright Island
Rosetta Head (The Bluff)
King Head
West Island
HORSE-DRAWN TRAM, S.A. WHALE CENTRE
SIR RICHARD PENINSULA
Encounter Bay
COORONG NATIONAL PARK

35° 30'
Porpoise Head
Tunkalilla Beach
Tunk Head
Parsons Beach
Waitpinga Beach
Newland Head
NEWLAND HEAD CONSERVATION PARK

Cuttlefish Bay
Snapper Point
Cape Coutts
LASHMAR CP
Antechamber Bay
Red House Bay
Cape St Albans
Cape St Alban Lighthouse
Moncrieff Bay
Cape Willoughby Lighthouse
Cape Willoughby
Windmill Bay
THE PAGES CONSERVATION PARK
North Page
South Page
The Pages

SOUTHERN   **OCEAN**

KANGAROO ISLAND
LESUEUR CONSERVATION PARK
SIMPSON CP
MACDONNELL (DUDLEY) PENINSULA
Cape Hart

138° 30'

Joins map 70
Joins map 82
Joins map 72

SA

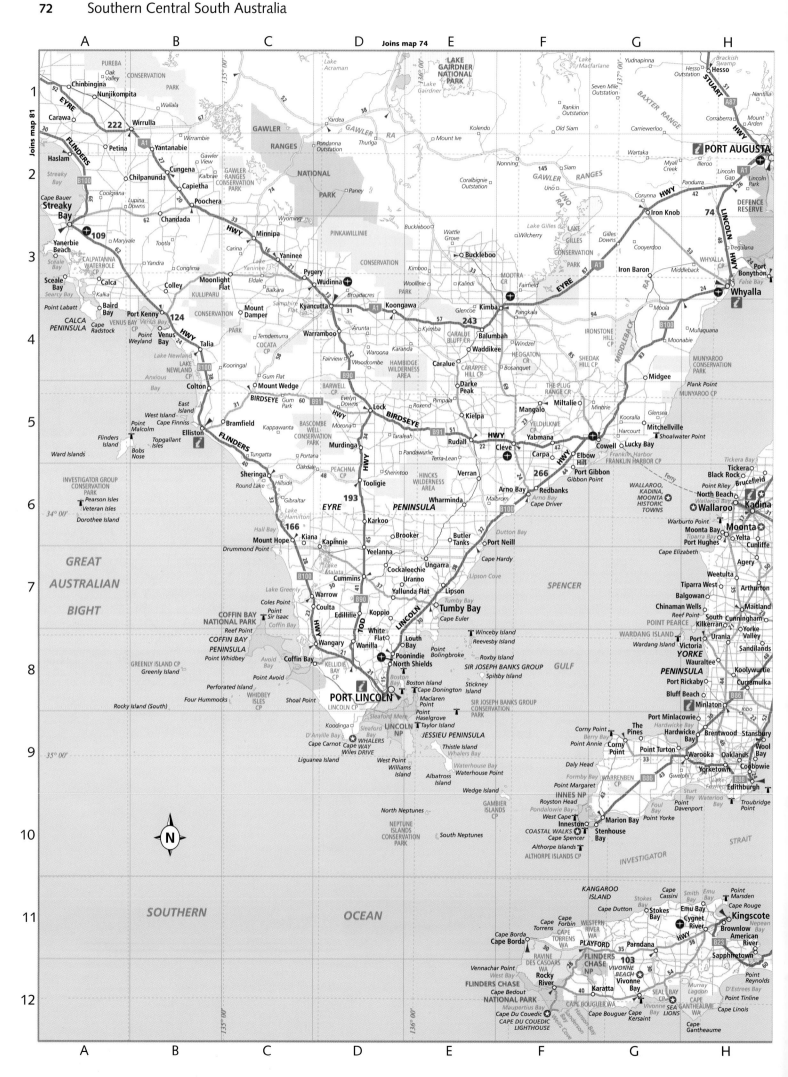

Joins map 74

Joins map 81

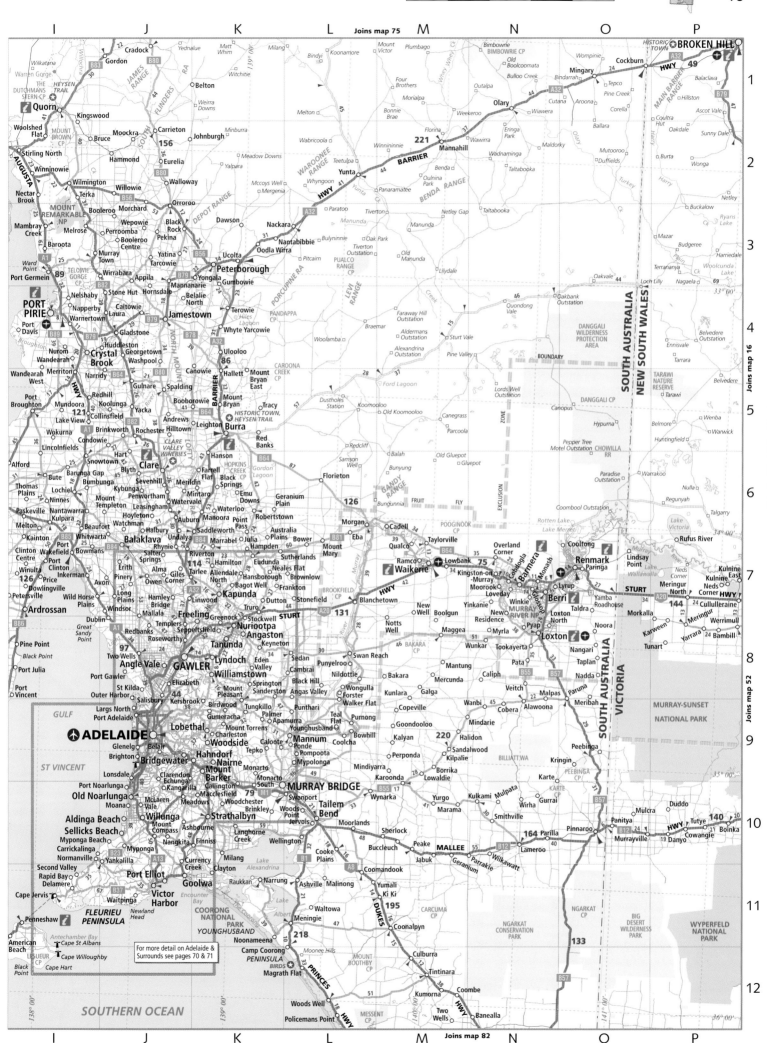

SA

0   20   40   60   80   100 km

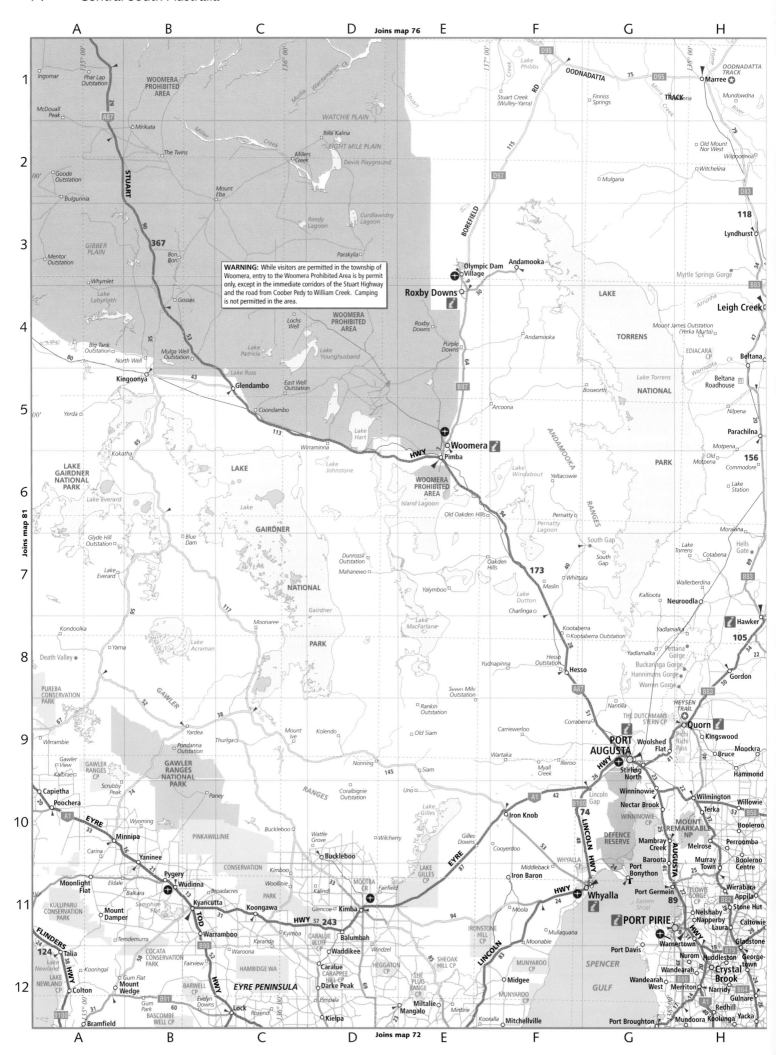

Joins map 76

Joins map 81

Joins map 72

WARNING: While visitors are permitted in the township of Woomera, entry to the Woomera Prohibited Area is by permit only, except in the immediate corridors of the Stuart Highway and the road from Coober Pedy to William Creek. Camping is not permitted in the area.

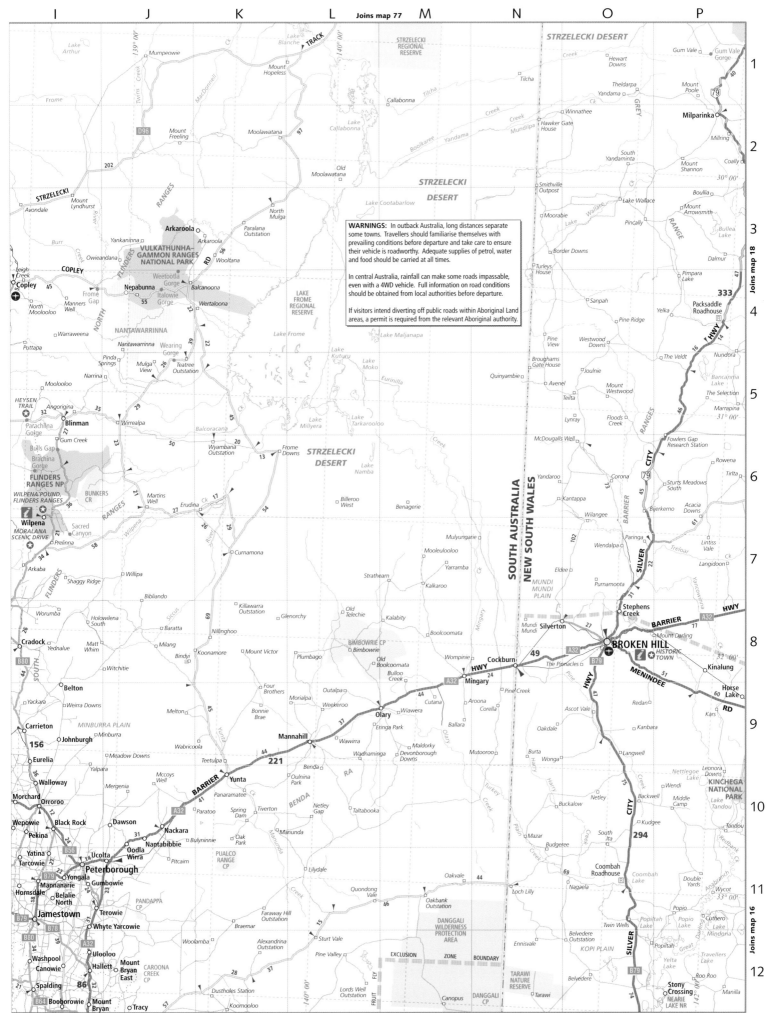

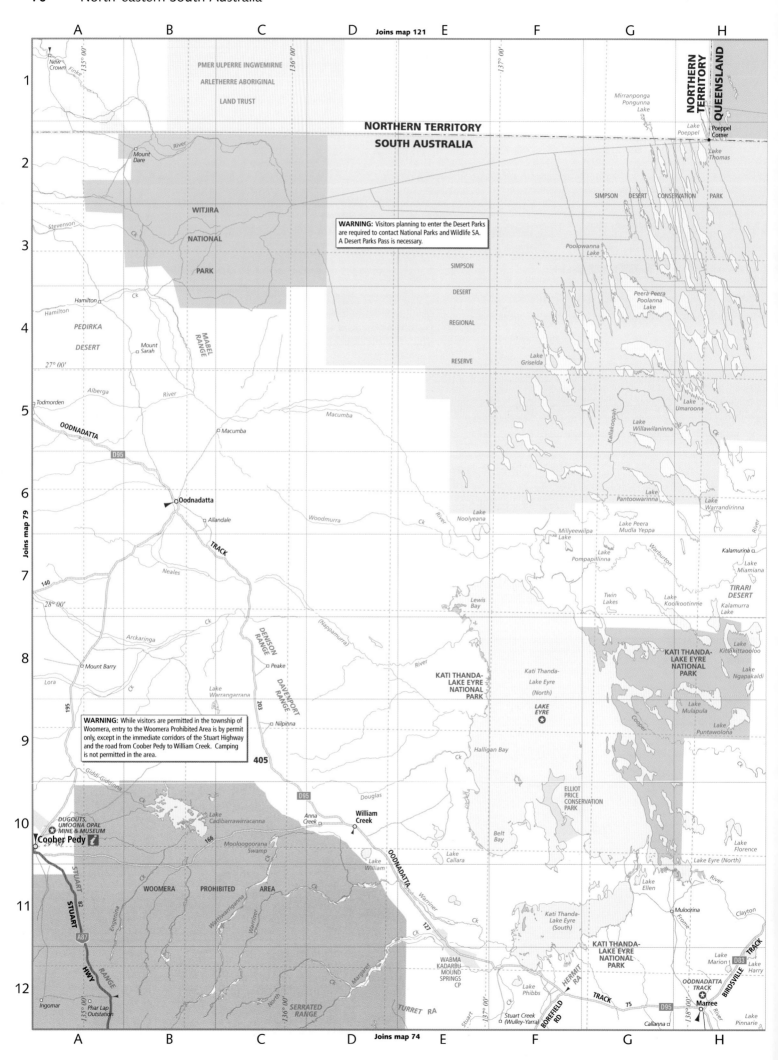

Joins map 121

NORTHERN TERRITORY

SOUTH AUSTRALIA

PMER ULPERRE INGWEMIRNE

ARLETHERRE ABORIGINAL

LAND TRUST

New Crown
Finke

Mount Dare

Stevenson

WITJIRA

NATIONAL

PARK

Hamilton
Ck

Hamilton

PEDIRKA

DESERT

Mount Sarah

MABEL RANGE

27° 00'

Alberga
River

Todmorden

OODNADATTA

D95

Macumba

Macumba

Oodnadatta

Allandale

TRACK

Neales

140

28° 00'

Arckaringa

Ck

Mount Barry

Lora

Ck

DENISON RANGE

Peake

Lake Warrangarrana

DAVENPORT RANGE

195

203

Nilpinna

405

WARNING: While visitors are permitted in the township of Woomera, entry to the Woomera Prohibited Area is by permit only, except in the immediate corridors of the Stuart Highway and the road from Coober Pedy to William Creek. Camping is not permitted in the area.

Giddi-Giddinna

DUGOUTS, UMOONA OPAL MINE & MUSEUM

Coober Pedy

166

Lake Cadibarrawirracanna

Mooloogoorana Swamp

Lake William

D95

Anna Creek

Douglas

William Creek

WOOMERA   PROHIBITED   AREA

Wattiwarrganna

Warriner

STUART

82

STUART

A87

HWY

RANGE

Engenina

Ingomar

Phar Lap Outstation

136° 00'

SERRATED RANGE

TURRET RA

WARNING: Visitors planning to enter the Desert Parks are required to contact National Parks and Wildlife SA. A Desert Parks Pass is necessary.

SIMPSON

DESERT

REGIONAL

RESERVE

Lake Griselda

Macumba

Woodmurra

Ck

River

Lewis Bay

Lake Noolyeana

KATI THANDA-LAKE EYRE NATIONAL PARK

Kati Thanda-Lake Eyre (North)

LAKE EYRE

Halligan Bay

Ck

Douglas

OODNADATTA

Belt Bay

Lake Callara

Warriner

127

Lake William

ELLIOT PRICE CONSERVATION PARK

Kati Thanda-Lake Eyre (South)

WABMA KADARBU MOUND SPRINGS CP

BOREFIELD RD

Stuart Creek (Wulley-Yarra)

Lake Phibbs

137° 00'

Stuart

Ck

HERMIT RA

TRACK

75

137° 00'

SIMPSON   DESERT   CONSERVATION   PARK

Mirranponga Pongunna Lake

Lake Poeppel

Poolowanna Lake

Peera Peera Poolanna Lake

Lake Umaroona

Kallakoopah

Lake Willawilaninna

Lake Pantoowarinna

Millyeewilpa Lake

Lake Peera Mudla Yeppa

Lake Pompapillinna

Twin Lakes

Lake Koolkootinne

Warburton

KATI THANDA-LAKE EYRE NATIONAL PARK

Lake Mulapula

Cooper

Lake Puntawolona

Lake Florence

Lake Eyre (North)

Lake Ellen

Muloorina

Frome

KATI THANDA-LAKE EYRE NATIONAL PARK

Clayton

Lake Marion

D83

Lake Harry

OODNADATTA TRACK

BIRDSVILLE TRACK

Marree

D95

Callanna

River

Lake Pinnarie

NORTHERN TERRITORY

QUEENSLAND

Poeppel Corner

Lake Thomas

Kalamurina

Lake Miamiana

TIRARI DESERT

Kalamurra Lake

Lake Kittaooloo

Lake Ngapakaldi

138° 00'

Joins map 74

0 20 40 60 80 100 km

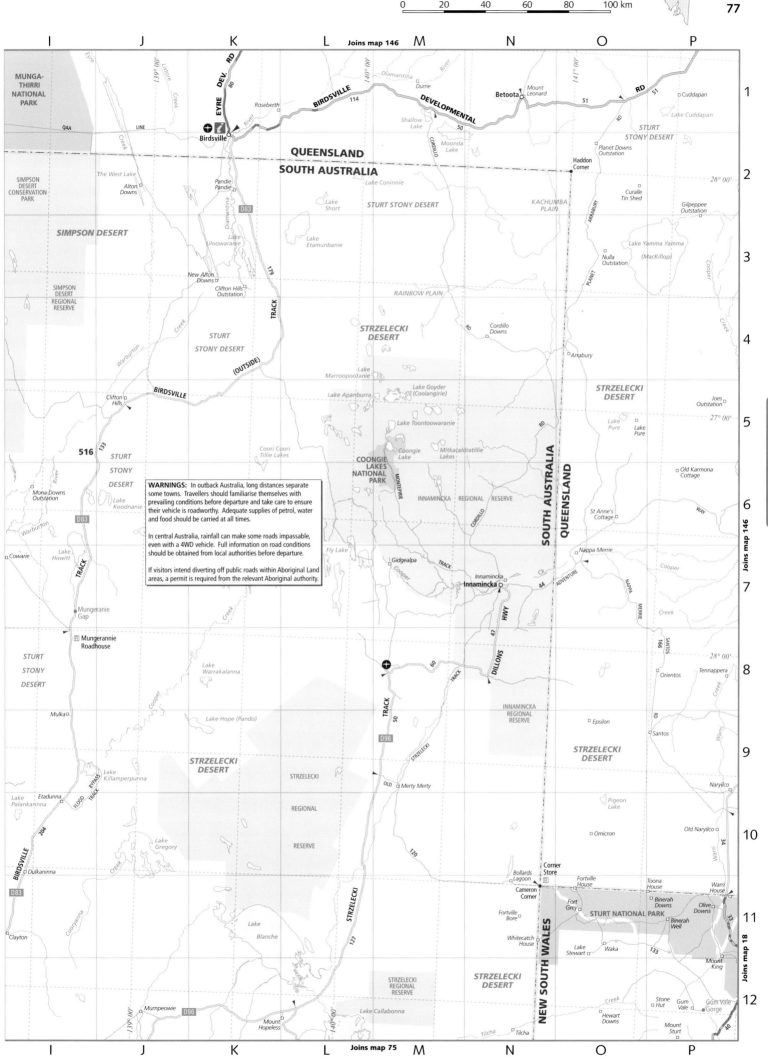

I J K L M N O P

SA

MUNGA-THIRRI NATIONAL PARK

QAA

LINE

SIMPSON DESERT CONSERVATION PARK

The West Lake

Alton Downs

SIMPSON DESERT

SIMPSON DESERT REGIONAL RESERVE

Eyre

Listure Creek

Creek

EYRE DEV. RD

BIRDSVILLE

Roseberth

Birdsville

Pandie Pandie

D83

Lake Uloowaranie

Diamantina

New Alton Downs

Clifton Hills Outstation

179

TRACK

Warburton

Creek

STURT STONY DESERT

(OUTSIDE)

BIRDSVILLE

Clifton Hills

516

133

STURT STONY DESERT

Mona Downs Outstation

River

D83

Warburton

Lake Koodnanie

Lake Howitt

Cowarie

TRACK

Mungeranie Gap

Mungerannie Roadhouse

STURT STONY DESERT

Mulka

Cooper

Lake Warrakalanna

Lake Hope (Pando)

STRZELECKI DESERT

BYPASS TRACK

FLOOD TRACK

Lake Killamperpunna

Lake Palankarinna

Etadunna

204

BIRDSVILLE

D83

Dulkaninna

Clayton

Lake Gregory

Cooryanna Creek

Lake Blanche

Murnpeowie

D96

Mount Hopeless

DEVELOPMENTAL

114

Diamantina

River

Durrie

Shallow Lake

Lake Short

Lake Coninnie

Lake Etamunbanie

STURT STONY DESERT

RAINBOW PLAIN

STRZELECKI DESERT

Lake Marroopootanie

Lake Apanburra

Lake Goyder (Coolangirie)

Lake Toontoowaranie

Coori Coori Tillie Lakes

Coongie Lake

Mitkacaldratillie Lakes

COONGIE LAKES NATIONAL PARK

MONTEPIRE

INNAMINCKA REGIONAL RESERVE

Fly Lake

Gidgealpa

Cooper

Creek

TRACK

Innamincka

Innamincka

47

DILLONS HWY

60

TRACK

50

D96

TRACK

STRZELECKI

OLD

Merty Merty

STRZELECKI REGIONAL RESERVE

120

STRZELECKI

127

Lake Callabonna

STRZELECKI REGIONAL RESERVE

Tilcha

Tilcha Creek

WARNINGS: In outback Australia, long distances separate some towns. Travellers should familiarise themselves with prevailing conditions before departure and take care to ensure their vehicle is roadworthy. Adequate supplies of petrol, water and food should be carried at all times.

In central Australia, rainfall can make some roads impassable, even with a 4WD vehicle. Full information on road conditions should be obtained from local authorities before departure.

If visitors intend diverting off public roads within Aboriginal Land areas, a permit is required from the relevant Aboriginal authority.

QUEENSLAND
SOUTH AUSTRALIA

Betoota

Mount Leonard

50

CORDILLO

Moonda Lake

Haddon Corner

Planet Downs Outstation

KACHUMBA PLAIN

ARRABURY

PLANET

Nulla Outstation

RD

Cordillo Downs

Artabury

CORDILLO

RD

St Anne's Cottage

Nappa Merrie

44

ADVENTURE

Ck

NAPPA

MERRIE

Creek

SOUTH AUSTRALIA
QUEENSLAND

INNAMINCKA REGIONAL RESERVE

Epsilon

Santos

Pigeon Lake

Omicron

Bollards Lagoon

Corner Store

Cameron Corner

Fortville House

Fortville Bore

Fort Grey

Whitecatch House

NEW SOUTH WALES

Lake Stewart

Waka

STRZELECKI DESERT

Hewart Downs

Mount Sturt

51

Cuddapan

Lake Cuddapan

STURT STONY DESERT

Curalle Tin Shed

Gilpeppee Outstation

Lake Yamma Yamma (MacKillop)

Cooper

Creek

STRZELECKI DESERT

Joes Outstation

Lake Pure

Lake Pure

Old Karmona Cottage

WAY

166

SANTOS

Tennappera

Orientos

RD

Warri Creek

STRZELECKI DESERT

Naryilco

Old Naryilco

Toona House

Warri House

Binerah Downs

Olive Downs

Binerah Well

STURT NATIONAL PARK

133

34

Warri River

32

Mount King

Stone Hut

Gum Vale

Gum Vale Gorge

Mount King

40

Joins map 146

Joins map 18

I J K L M N O P

1 2 3 4 5 6 7 8 9 10 11 12

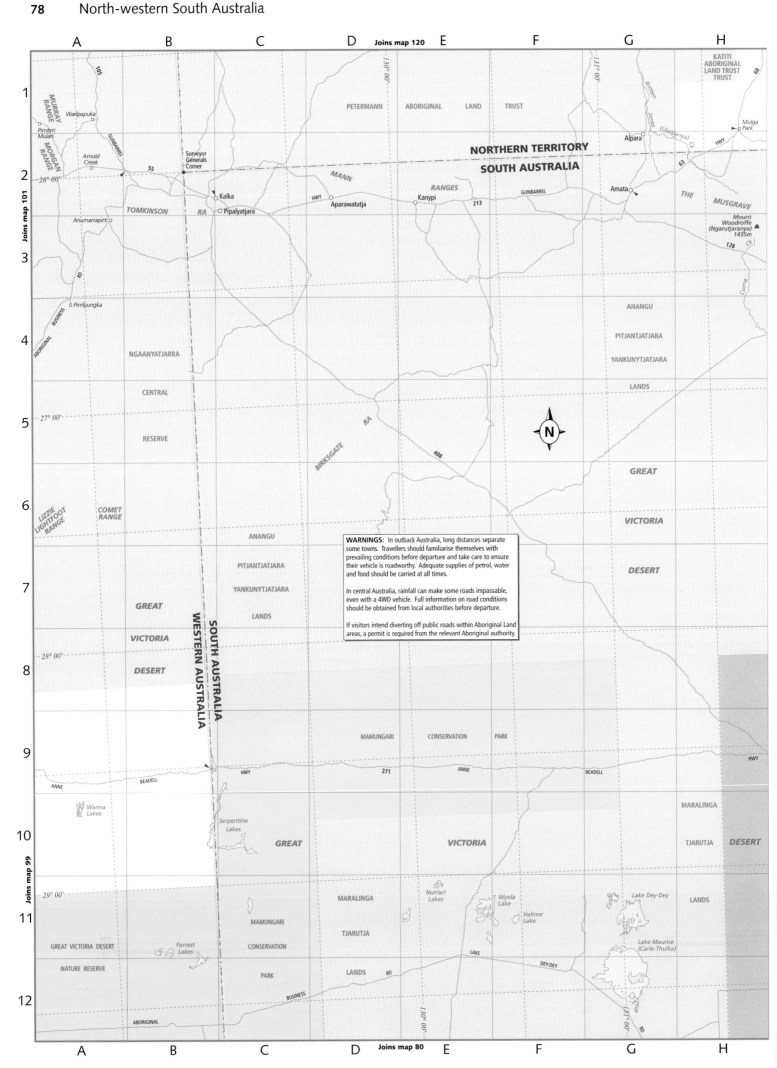

Joins map 120
Joins map 101
Joins map 99
Joins map 80

A   B   C   D   E   F   G   H

1

2

3

4

5

6

7

8

9

10

11

12

KATITI
ABORIGINAL
LAND TRUST
TRUST

68

PETERMANN   ABORIGINAL   LAND   TRUST

131° 00'

130° 00'

105

MURRAY RANGE

Warlpapuka

Pirntirri Mulan

MORGAN RANGE

Arnold Creek

GUNBARREL

55

26° 00'

Surveyor Generals Corner

Kalka

Pipalyatjara

Anumarrapirti

TOMKINSON   RA

HWY

Aparawatatja

MANN

RANGES

Kanypi

213

GUNBARREL

NORTHERN TERRITORY

SOUTH AUSTRALIA

Alpara

Britten

Jones (Ulaianjanya) CK

HWY

63

Amata

THE   MUSGRAVE

Mount Woodroffe (Ngarutjaranya) 1435m

128

Currie CK

Mulga Park

RD

BUSINESS

Pirrilyungka

NGAANYATJARRA

CENTRAL

RESERVE

27° 00'

BIRKSGATE   RA

408

ANANGU

PITJANTJATJARA

YANKUNYTJATJARA

LANDS

N

GREAT

VICTORIA

DESERT

LIZZIE LIGHTFOOT RANGE

COMET RANGE

ANANGU

PITJANTJATJARA

YANKUNYTJATJARA

LANDS

GREAT

VICTORIA

28° 00'

DESERT

SOUTH AUSTRALIA

WESTERN AUSTRALIA

WARNINGS: In outback Australia, long distances separate some towns. Travellers should familiarise themselves with prevailing conditions before departure and take care to ensure their vehicle is roadworthy. Adequate supplies of petrol, water and food should be carried at all times.

In central Australia, rainfall can make some roads impassable, even with a 4WD vehicle. Full information on road conditions should be obtained from local authorities before departure.

If visitors intend diverting off public roads within Aboriginal Land areas, a permit is required from the relevant Aboriginal authority.

MAMUNGARI   CONSERVATION   PARK

HWY

ANNE

BEADELL

271

ANNE

BEADELL

HWY

Wanna Lakes

Serpentine Lakes

GREAT

VICTORIA

MARALINGA

TJARUTJA

DESERT

29° 00'

Nurrari Lakes

Wyola Lake

Halinor Lake

Lake Dey-Dey

LANDS

MARALINGA

TJARUTJA

MAMUNGARI

CONSERVATION

Forrest Lakes

Lake Maurice (Carle-Thulka)

GREAT VICTORIA DESERT

NATURE RESERVE

PARK

LANDS

RD

LAKE

DEY-DEY

BUSINESS

ABORIGINAL

130° 00'

131° 00'

RD

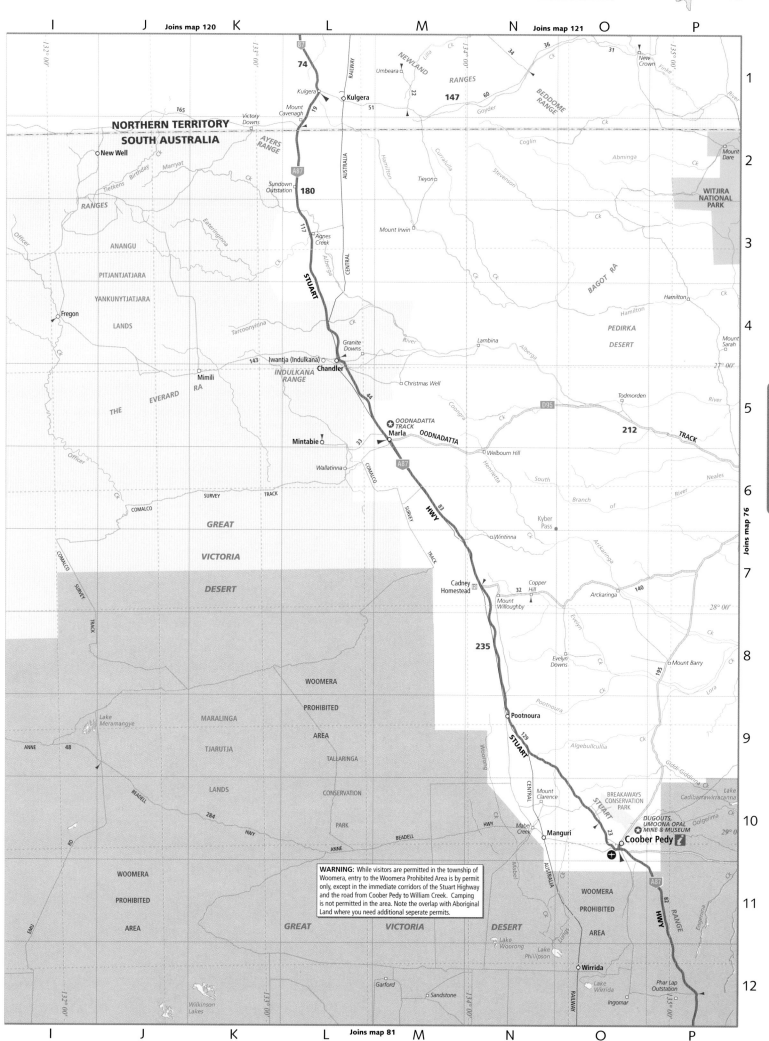

Joins map 120
Joins map 121
Joins map 76
Joins map 81

SA

0   20   40   60   80   100 km

NORTHERN TERRITORY
SOUTH AUSTRALIA

WITJIRA NATIONAL PARK

New Well

RANGES

ANANGU

PITJANTJATJARA

YANKUNYTJATJARA

LANDS

Fregon

Mimili

THE EVERARD RA

INDULKANA RANGE

Iwantja (Indulkana)

Chandler

Mintabie

Marla

OODNADATTA TRACK

OODNADATTA

STUART HWY

GREAT

VICTORIA

DESERT

WOOMERA

PROHIBITED

AREA

MARALINGA

TJARUTJA

LANDS

TALLARINGA

CONSERVATION

PARK

BEADELL HWY

ANNE

WOOMERA

PROHIBITED

AREA

GREAT VICTORIA DESERT

Garford

Sandstone

Wilkinson Lakes

Kulgera

Mount Cavenagh

Victory Downs

AYERS RANGE

Sundown Outstation

Agnes Creek

Granite Downs

Christmas Well

Wallatinna

Cadney Homestead

Mount Willoughby

Pootnoura

Manguri

Mabel Creek

STUART

Mount Clarence

Lake Woorong

Lake Phillipson

Wirrida

Lake Wirrida

Ingomar

RAILWAY

Umbeara

Tieyon

Mount Irwin

NEWLAND RANGES

BEDDOME RANGE

New Crown

Abminga

Mount Dare

Coglin

Stevenson

BAGOT RA

PEDIRKA DESERT

Hamilton

Mount Sarah

Lambina

Welbourn Hill

Todmorden

South Branch of

Kyber Pass

Wintinna

Copper Hill

Arckaringa

Evelyn Downs

Mount Barry

Algebullcullia

BREAKAWAYS CONSERVATION PARK

Cadibarrawirracanna

Lake

Oolgelima

Coober Pedy

DUGOUTS, UMOONA OPAL MINE & MUSEUM

WOOMERA

PROHIBITED

AREA

RANGE

STUART HWY

Phar Lap Outstation

WARNING: While visitors are permitted in the township of Woomera, entry to the Woomera Prohibited Area is by permit only, except in the immediate corridors of the Stuart Highway and the road from Coober Pedy to William Creek. Camping is not permitted in the area. Note the overlap with Aboriginal Land where you need additional seperate permits.

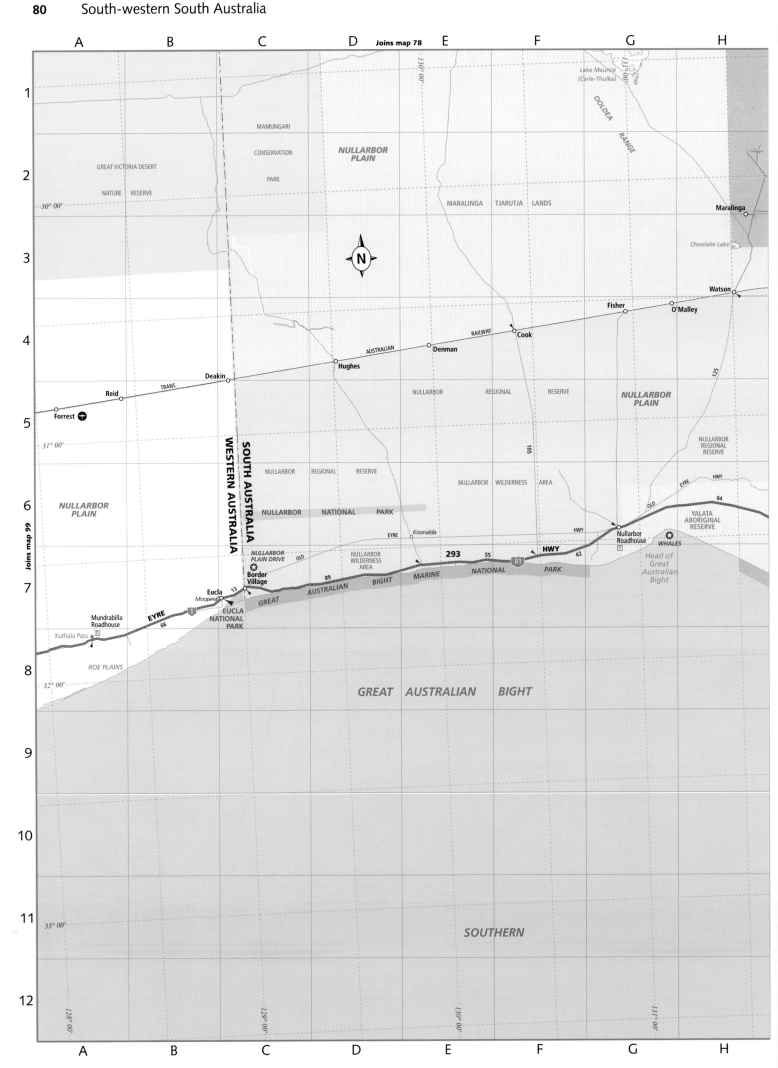

Joins map 78

Joins map 99

A B C D E F G H

Lake Maurice
(Carle-Thulka)

OOLDEA RANGE

MAMUNGARI

CONSERVATION

PARK

NULLARBOR PLAIN

GREAT VICTORIA DESERT

NATURE RESERVE

MARALINGA TJARUTJA LANDS

Maralinga

Choolalie Lake

–30° 00'

Watson

Fisher

O'Malley

Cook

RAILWAY

Denman

AUSTRALIAN

Hughes

125

Reid

Deakin

TRANS

Forrest

NULLARBOR REGIONAL RESERVE

NULLARBOR PLAIN

–31° 00'

WESTERN AUSTRALIA

SOUTH AUSTRALIA

NULLARBOR REGIONAL RESERVE

NULLARBOR PLAIN

NULLARBOR WILDERNESS AREA

NULLARBOR REGIONAL RESERVE

105

NULLARBOR NATIONAL PARK

EYRE HWY

94

Koonalda

OLD EYRE HWY

YALATA ABORIGINAL RESERVE

Nullarbor Roadhouse

NULLARBOR
PLAIN DRIVE

NULLARBOR
WILDERNESS
AREA

293

55

A1

HWY

41

WHALES

Head of
Great
Australian
Bight

OLD

Border
Village

Eucla

Moopina

89

GREAT AUSTRALIAN BIGHT MARINE NATIONAL PARK

13

EUCLA
NATIONAL
PARK

Mundrabilla
Roadhouse

EYRE

66

Kuthala Pass

ROE PLAINS

–32° 00'

GREAT AUSTRALIAN BIGHT

–33° 00'

SOUTHERN

–128° 00'

–129° 00'

–130° 00'

–131° 00'

A B C D E F G H

1 2 3 4 5 6 7 8 9 10 11 12

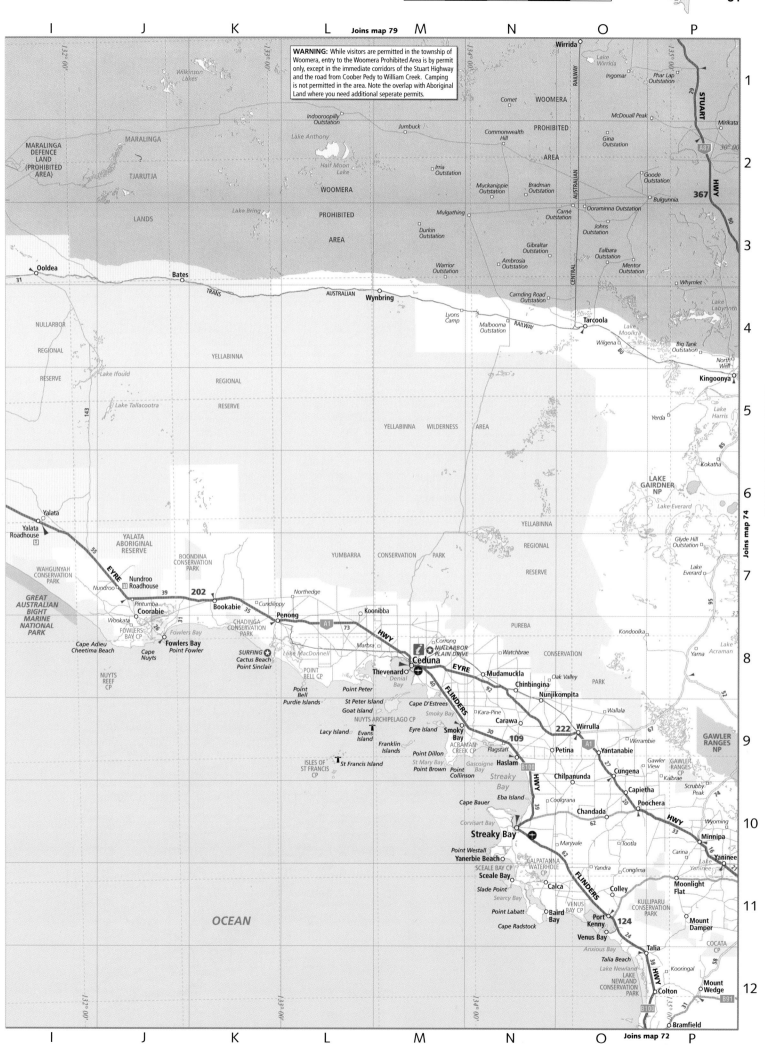

WARNING: While visitors are permitted in the township of Woomera, entry to the Woomera Prohibited Area is by permit only, except in the immediate corridors of the Stuart Highway and the road from Coober Pedy to William Creek. Camping is not permitted in the area. Note the overlap with Aboriginal Land where you need additional seperate permits.

I J K L M N O P

1 2 3 4 5 6 7 8 9 10 11 12

SA

Wirrida
Lake Wirrida
Ingomar
Phar Lap Outstation
Mirikata
STUART
29
A87
Comet
WOOMERA
McDouall Peak
Indooroopilly Outstation
Jumbuck
PROHIBITED
Commonwealth Hill
Gina Outstation
Lake Anthony
Half Moon Lake
WOOMERA
Irria Outstation
AREA
Goode Outstation
Bulgunnia
367
HWY
90
Lake Bring
PROHIBITED
Muckanippie Outstation
Bradman Outstation
Oraminna Outstation
Mulgathing
Carne Outstation
Johns Outstation
Ealbara Outstation
LANDS
AREA
Durkin Outstation
Gibraltar Outstation
Mentor Outstation
Warrior Outstation
Ambrosia Outstation
Whymlet
Ooldea
Bates
TRANS
AUSTRALIAN
Wynbring
Carnding Road Outstation
Tarcoola
Lake Labyrinth
31
Lyons Camp
Malbooma Outstation
RAILWAY
Lake Moolkra
80
Big Tank Outstation
North Well
Kingoonya
NULLARBOR
REGIONAL
YELLABINNA
Lake Ifould
REGIONAL
Yerda
Lake Harris
143
Lake Tallacootra
RESERVE
RESERVE
YELLABINNA WILDERNESS AREA
85
Kokatha
LAKE GAIRDNER NP
Lake Everard
Yalata
YELLABINNA
Glyde Hill Outstation
Yalata Roadhouse
YALATA ABORIGINAL RESERVE
BOONDINA CONSERVATION PARK
YUMBARRA CONSERVATION PARK
REGIONAL
Lake Everard
55
EYRE
Nundroo Roadhouse
39
202
Northedge
RESERVE
95
WAHGUNYAH CONSERVATION PARK
Nundroo
Pintumba
Coorabie
31
Bookabie
35
Cundilippy
Penong
Koonibba
PUREBA
Kondoolka
Lake Acraman
GREAT AUSTRALIAN BIGHT MARINE NATIONAL PARK
Wookata
FOWLERS BAY CP
26
Fowlers Bay
CHADINGA CONSERVATION PARK
A1
73
Marbra
HWY
Corrong
NULLARBOR PLAIN DRIVE
Watchbrae
CONSERVATION
Yarna
Lake Acraman
Cape Adieu
Cheetima Beach
Cape Nuyts
Fowlers Bay
Point Fowler
SURFING
Cactus Beach
Point Sinclair
Lake MacDonnell
Ceduna
EYRE
Mudamuckla
Oak Valley
PARK
NUYTS REEF CP
POINT BELL CP
Thevenard
Denial Bay
40
FLINDERS
Chinbingina
Wallala
GAWLER RANGES NP
Point Bell
Point Peter
St Peter Island
Cape D'Estrees
92
Nunjikompita
Purdie Islands
Goat Island
Smoky Bay
Kara-Pine
Carawa
NUYTS ARCHIPELAGO CP
Eyre Island
Smoky Bay
30
222
Wirrulla
Wirrambie
Lacy Island
Evans Island
Franklin Islands
Point Dillon
109
Flagstaff
Petina
A1
Yantanabie
Gawler View
GAWLER RANGES CP
Kalbrae
ISLES OF ST FRANCIS CP
St Francis Island
St Mary Bay
Point Brown
Gascoigne Bay
ACRAMAN CREEK CP
Haslam
B100
Chilpanunda
Cungena
27
Scrubby Peak
Point Collinson
Streaky Bay
Capietha
74
Cape Bauer
Eba Island
39
Coolgrana
Chandada
62
Poochera
33
HWY
Wyoming
Corvisart Bay
Streaky Bay
Maryvale
Tootla
Carina
16
Minnipa
Yaninee
Point Westall
Yanerbie Beach
CALPATANNA WATERHOLE CP
Yandra
Conglima
67
Moonlight Flat
21
Yaninee
SCEALE BAY CP
Sceale Bay
Calca
FLINDERS
Colley
KULLIPARU CONSERVATION PARK
Mount Damper
OCEAN
Slade Point
Searcy Bay
VENUS BAY CP
Port Kenny
124
COCATA CP
Point Labatt
Baird Bay
Venus Bay
24
Cape Radstock
Anxious Bay
Talia
85
Talia Beach
Lake Newland
Kooringal
Mount Wedge
LAKE NEWLAND CONSERVATION PARK
38
HWY
31
B91
B100
Colton
Bramfield

I J K L M N O P

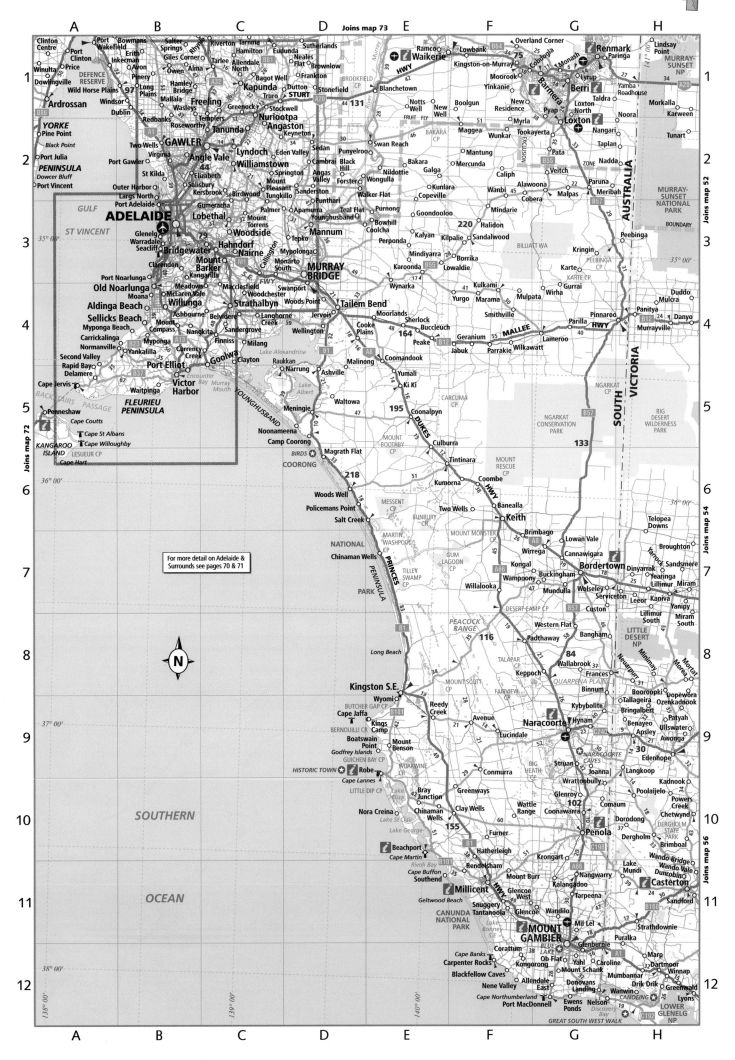

0   20   40   60   80   100 km

Dear Rock and Karnyaka Waterhole, Flinders Ranges

MOUNT GAMBIER *page 82 G12*

i Lady Nelson Discovery Centre
35 Jubilee Hwy East
(08) 8724 9750 or 1800 087 187
www.mountgambier.sa.gov.au

MURRAY BRIDGE *page 70 H11*

i 3 South Tce
(08) 8539 1142 or 1800 442 784
www.murraybridge.sa.gov.au

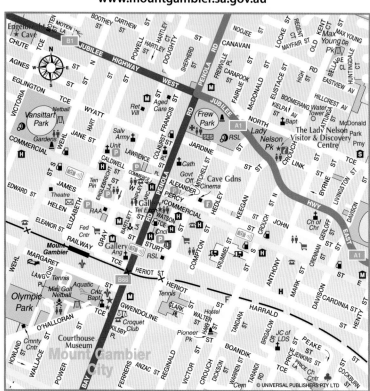

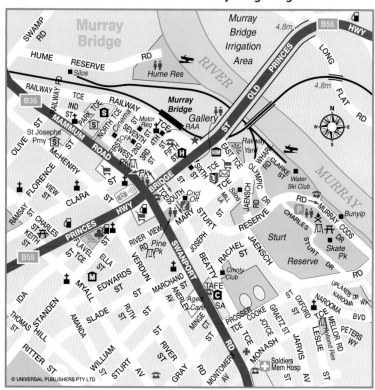

PORT AUGUSTA *page 72 H2*

i Wadlata Outback Centre
41 Flinders Tce
(08) 8641 9194 or 1800 633 060
www.portaugusta.sa.gov.au

PORT LINCOLN *page 72 D8*

i 3 Adelaide Pl
(08) 8683 3544 or 1300 788 378
www.visitportlincoln.net

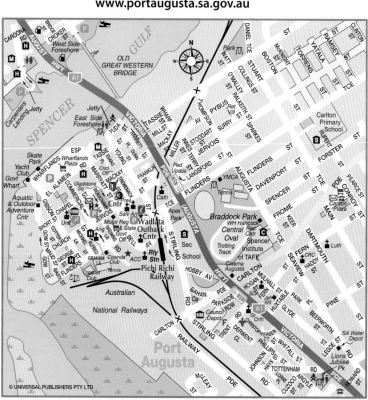

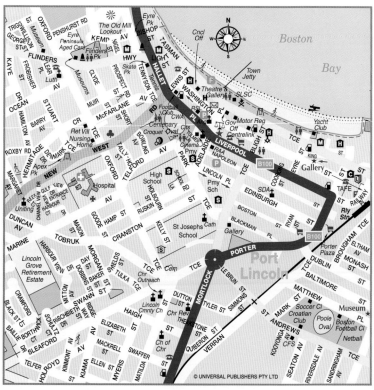

PORT PIRIE *page 73 I4*

3 Mary Elie St
(08) 8633 8700 or 1800 000 424
www.pirie.sa.gov.au

RENMARK *page 73 O7*

84 Murray Av
(08) 8586 6704 or 1300 661 704
www.visitrenmark.com

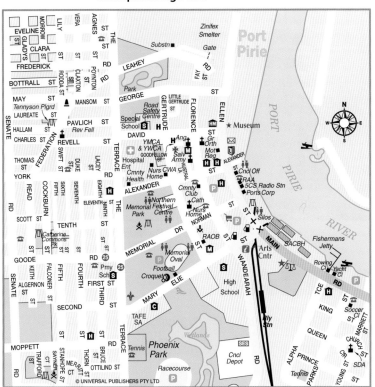

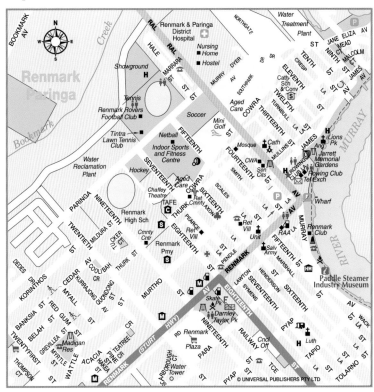

VICTOR HARBOR *page 71 F9*

The Causeway
(08) 8551 0777 or 1800 557 094
www.holidayatvictorharbor.com.au

WHYALLA *page 72 H3*

Lincoln Hwy
(08) 8645 7900 or 1800 088 589
www.whyalla.com

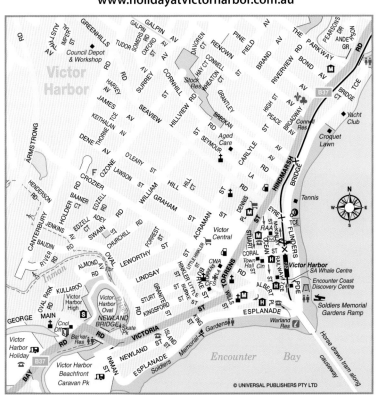

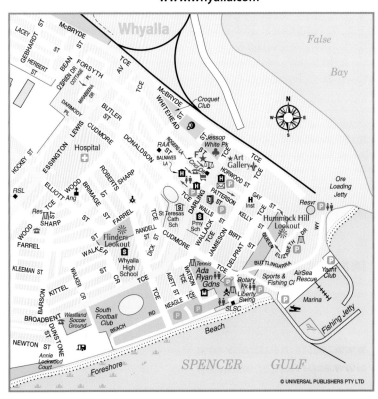

SA

Karri trees, Boranup Forest, Leeuwin–Naturaliste National Park

WESTERN AUSTRALIA

Western Australia is the giant of Australian states and embraces an incredible landscape: rugged northern ranges and dramatic gorges, southern towering forests, arid eastern deserts and a pristine western coastline.

Western Australia's coastline alone offers much to explore: it extends from the remote northern Kimberley region, along the 'iron shoulder' of the Pilbara, past Ningaloo coral reef and Shark Bay to the southern plain of the state's capital, Perth. Heading east, the coastline traces granite shores facing the wild Southern Ocean, and the limestone cliffs of the Great Australian Bight.

Touring this vast state requires planning and time. The south-west area around Perth has good roads and accessible features. The rest of Western Australia has fewer road options. Flying can replace some long drives, but touring by car is a rewarding experience. A four-wheel drive vehicle is essential for touring the Kimberley or the desert tracks of the state's centre.

INFORMATION CENTRE

Western Australian Visitor Centre
55 William St (cnr Hay St), Perth;
(08) 9483 1111 or 1800 812 808
www.westernaustralia.com
www.experienceperth.com

Places of interest

	MAP REF			MAP REF	
The Aquarium of Western Australia (AQWA)	90	B6	Manjimup Timber and Heritage Park	94	F8
Argyle diamond mine	103	O5	Margaret River wineries	94	B7
Broome Bird Observatory	102	H8	Mount Augustus National Park	97	F6
Bungle Bungles (Purnululu National Park)	103	O6	New Norcia	96	C2
			Ningaloo Reef and Marine Park	97	B3
Busselton Jetty	94	B5	Pemberton Tramway	94	F9
Cable Beach, Broome	102	H8	Pinnacles Desert, Nambung National Park	96	A2
Coolgardie Camel Farm	98	H5	Rottnest Island	93	A6
Discovery Bay, Albany	95	M11	St Francis Xavier Cathedral, Geraldton	97	D12
Dolphin Discovery Centre, Bunbury	94	C3	Shark Bay/Monkey Mia	97	B8
Fremantle	91	A8	Stirling Range National Park	95	M8
Geikie Gorge National Park	103	L7	Tunnel Creek National Park	103	K7
Jewel, Lake and Mammoth caves	94	B8	Valley of the Giants	95	I11
Kalbarri National Park	97	D11	Wagin Historical Village	95	J2
Karijini National Park	97	G3	Wave Rock	96	H5
Lake Argyle	103	O5	Wolfe Creek Crater National Park	103	N9
Leeuwin–Naturaliste National Park	94	A5			
Malcolm Douglas Crocodile Park and Animal Refuge, Broome	102	H8			

MAPS

WESTERN AUSTRALIA

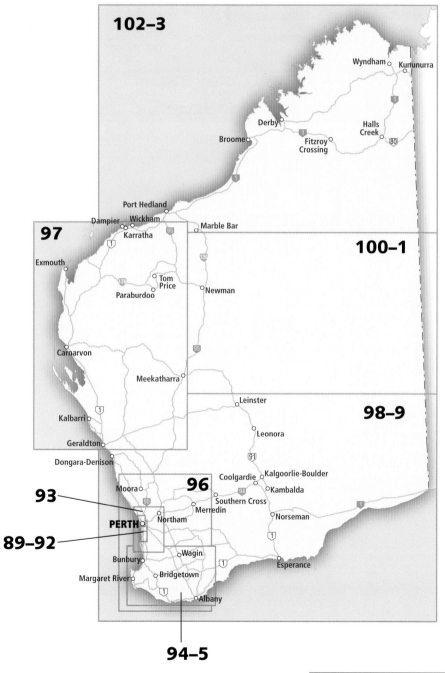

Western Australia

Central Perth	89
Metro Perth, North	90
Metro Perth, Central	91
Metro Perth, South	92
Perth & Surrounds	93
South-west Coast	94–5
South-western Western Australia	96
Central-western Western Australia	97
Southern Western Australia	98–9
Central Western Australia	100–1
Northern Western Australia	102–3

INTER-CITY ROUTES	DISTANCE
Perth–Adelaide via Great Eastern & Eyre hwys 94 1 A1	2700 km
Perth–Darwin via Great Northern Hwy 95 1	4032 km

Cottesloe Beach and the Indiana Tea House

Perth

Perth is a modern city, situated on the banks of the Swan River. It is the most isolated capital city in the world; its nearest neighbour, Adelaide, is 2700 kilometres by road. It is this isolation which has allowed the city to retain its feeling of space and relaxed charm.

Perth was proclaimed on 12 August 1829 and named after the Scottish city of Perth. Convict labour was introduced in the 1850s and many of Perth's early public buildings, roads and bridges were built by convicts. During the 1890s, gold was discovered at Coolgardie and Kalgoorlie, boosting the economy, and people raced to the region to make their fortune.

The Perth Mint offers a visit to the past at its Old Melting House. Gold-bar pouring demonstrations are available every day and visitors can watch mint operations from the public gallery.

Perth's feeling of space is enhanced by the many parks surrounding the city, including well-known Kings Park. This 400 hectare park offers beautiful views overlooking the city and the Swan River. It is noted for its wildflowers in springtime and its bushwalking trails.

The golden surf beaches are another big attraction in Perth, and are within easy reach of the city. With its Mediterranean climate, visitors can enjoy Perth's relaxed, outdoor lifestyle year-round.

Places of interest

	MAP REF			MAP REF	
Art Gallery of Western Australia	89	E5	Parliament House	89	B5
Barrack Square	89	D7	Perth Concert Hall	89	E7
The Bell Tower	89	D7	Perth Mint	89	G7
Fire and Emergency Services Authority			Perth Town Hall	89	E6
Education and Heritage Centre	89	E6	Perth Zoo	89	C12
Hay Street Mall	89	D6	Queens Gardens	89	H7
His Majesty's Theatre	89	C6	Scitech	89	B3
Kings Park and Western Australian			Supreme Court Gardens	89	E7
Botanic Garden	89	A7	Swan River	89	E9
London Court	89	D6	WACA Ground	89	H7
The Old Mill	89	B9	Western Australian Museum	89	E5

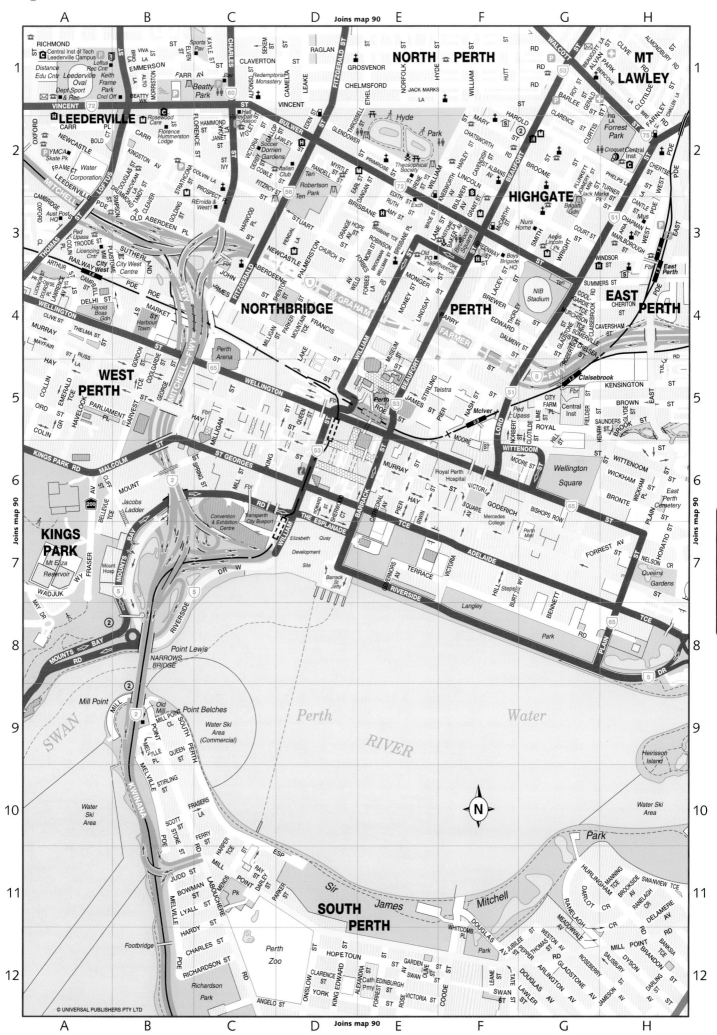

WA

0 2 4 6 8 km

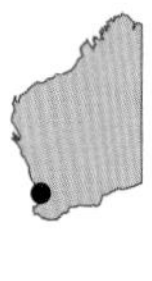

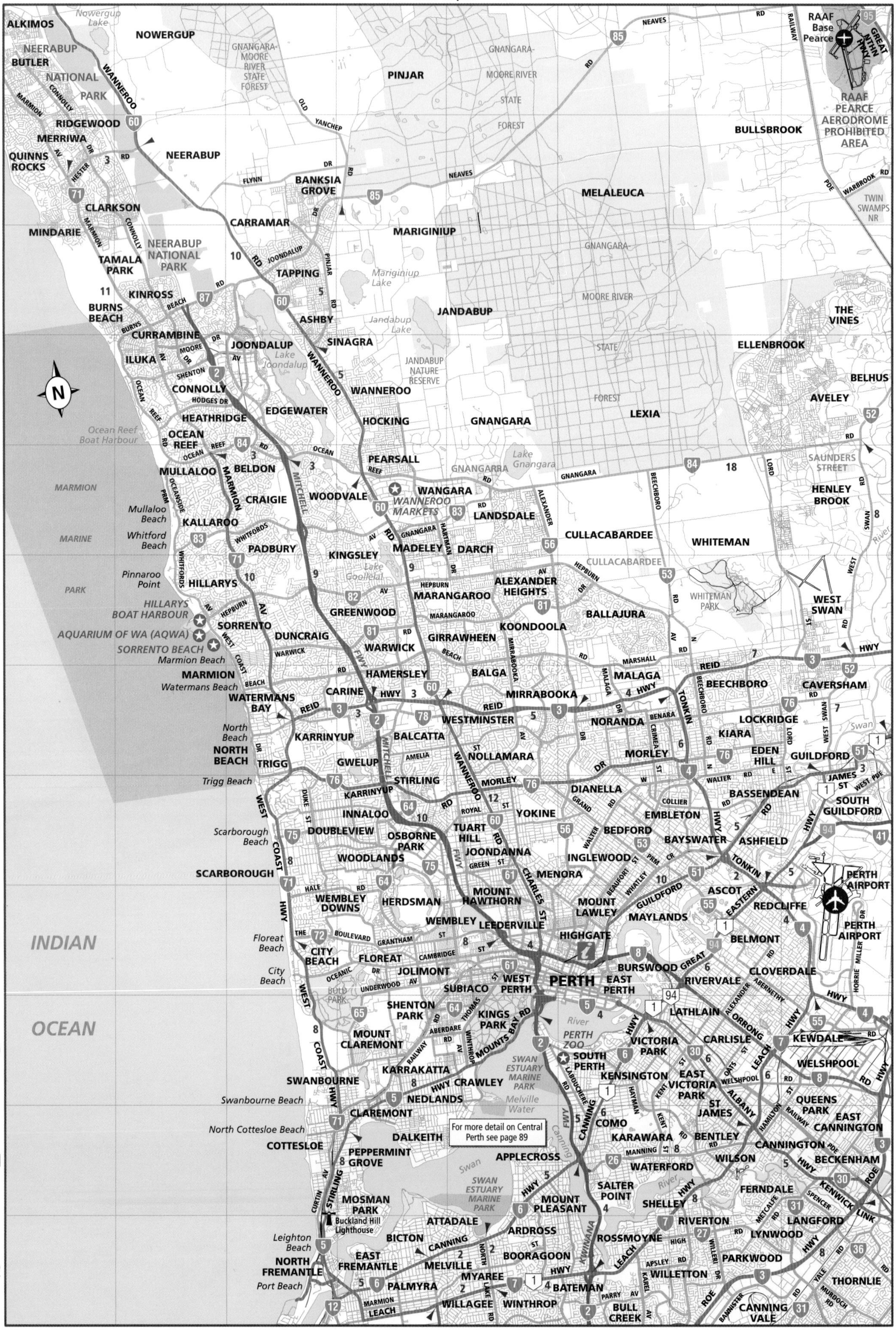

Joins map 93

Joins map 93

Joins map 91

Joins map 91

Joins map 91

A B C D E F G H

1 2 3 4 5 6 7 8 9 10 11 12

ALKIMOS
NOWERGUP
Nowergup Lake
NEERABUP
BUTLER
NATIONAL
PARK
RIDGEWOOD
MERRIWA
QUINNS ROCKS
CLARKSON
MINDARIE
TAMALA PARK
KINROSS
BURNS BEACH
CURRAMBINE
ILUKA
CONNOLLY
HEATHRIDGE
OCEAN REEF
MULLALOO
BELDON
CRAIGIE
KALLAROO
PADBURY
HILLARYS
SORRENTO
DUNCRAIG
WARWICK
GREENWOOD
KINGSLEY
HAMERSLEY
CARINE
WATERMANS BAY
NORTH BEACH
TRIGG
KARRINYUP
GWELUP
STIRLING
INNALOO
DOUBLEVIEW
WOODLANDS
SCARBOROUGH
WEMBLEY DOWNS
HERDSMAN
WEMBLEY
CITY BEACH
FLOREAT
JOLIMONT
SUBIACO
WEST PERTH
SHENTON PARK
MOUNT CLAREMONT
KARRAKATTA
SWANBOURNE
NEDLANDS
CLAREMONT
DALKEITH
PEPPERMINT GROVE
COTTESLOE
MOSMAN PARK
NORTH FREMANTLE
EAST FREMANTLE
PALMYRA
BICTON
ATTADALE
MELVILLE
MYAREE
WILLAGEE
WINTHROP
BATEMAN
BULL CREEK
CANNING VALE
WILLETTON
LEEMING
RIVERTON
ROSSMOYNE
SHELLEY
PARKWOOD
LYNWOOD
LANGFORD
THORNLIE
FERNDALE
BECKENHAM
CANNINGTON
EAST CANNINGTON
QUEENS PARK
WELSHPOOL
KEWDALE
CLOVERDALE
BELMONT
REDCLIFFE
ASCOT
PERTH AIRPORT
SOUTH GUILDFORD
GUILDFORD
BASSENDEAN
EDEN HILL
LOCKRIDGE
KIARA
BEECHBORO
CAVERSHAM
WEST SWAN
WHITEMAN
WHITEMAN PARK
BALLAJURA
MALAGA
NORANDA
MORLEY
EMBLETON
BAYSWATER
ASHFIELD
MAYLANDS
MOUNT LAWLEY
INGLEWOOD
BEDFORD
DIANELLA
YOKINE
MENORA
HIGHGATE
LEEDERVILLE
MOUNT HAWTHORN
JOONDANNA
TUART HILL
OSBORNE PARK
BALCATTA
NOLLAMARA
WESTMINSTER
MIRRABOOKA
BALGA
KOONDOOLA
GIRRAWHEEN
MARANGAROO
ALEXANDER HEIGHTS
CULLACABARDEE
LANDSDALE
DARCH
MADELEY
WANGARA
WANNEROO MARKETS
WOODVALE
PEARSALL
HOCKING
GNANGARA
LEXIA
WHITEMAN
EDGEWATER
WANNEROO
ASHBY
SINAGRA
TAPPING
CARRAMAR
BANKSIA GROVE
MARIGINIUP
JANDABUP
JANDABUP NATURE RESERVE
PINJAR
MELALEUCA
NOWERGUP
NEERABUP NATIONAL PARK
GNANGARA-MOORE RIVER STATE FOREST
MOORE RIVER STATE FOREST
BULLSBROOK
RAAF Base Pearce
RAAF PEARCE AERODROME PROHIBITED AREA
GREAT NTHN HWY
TWIN SWAMPS NR
THE VINES
ELLENBROOK
BELHUS
AVELEY
HENLEY BROOK
CULLACABARDEE
WHITEMAN
ELLENBROOK
PERTH
EAST PERTH
BURSWOOD
RIVERVALE
KINGS PARK
SOUTH PERTH
PERTH ZOO
VICTORIA PARK
KENSINGTON
COMO
KARAWARA
WATERFORD
SALTER POINT
MOUNT PLEASANT
APPLECROSS
ARDROSS
BOORAGOON
LATHLAIN
CARLISLE
EAST VICTORIA PARK
ST JAMES
BENTLEY
WILSON
RIVERTON
CANNING VALE
BENTLEY
INDIAN OCEAN
MARMION MARINE PARK
SWAN ESTUARY MARINE PARK
MELVILLE WATER
SWAN ESTUARY MARINE PARK
Ocean Reef Boat Harbour
Mullaloo Beach
Whitford Beach
Pinnaroo Point
HILLARYS BOAT HARBOUR
AQUARIUM OF WA (AQWA)
SORRENTO BEACH
Marmion Beach
Watermans Beach
North Beach
Trigg Beach
Scarborough Beach
Floreat Beach
City Beach
Swanbourne Beach
North Cottesloe Beach
Leighton Beach
Port Beach
Buckland Hill Lighthouse
Lake Joondalup
Lake Goollelal
Mariginiup Lake
Jandabup Lake
Lake Gnangara
Swan River

For more detail on Central Perth see page 89

N

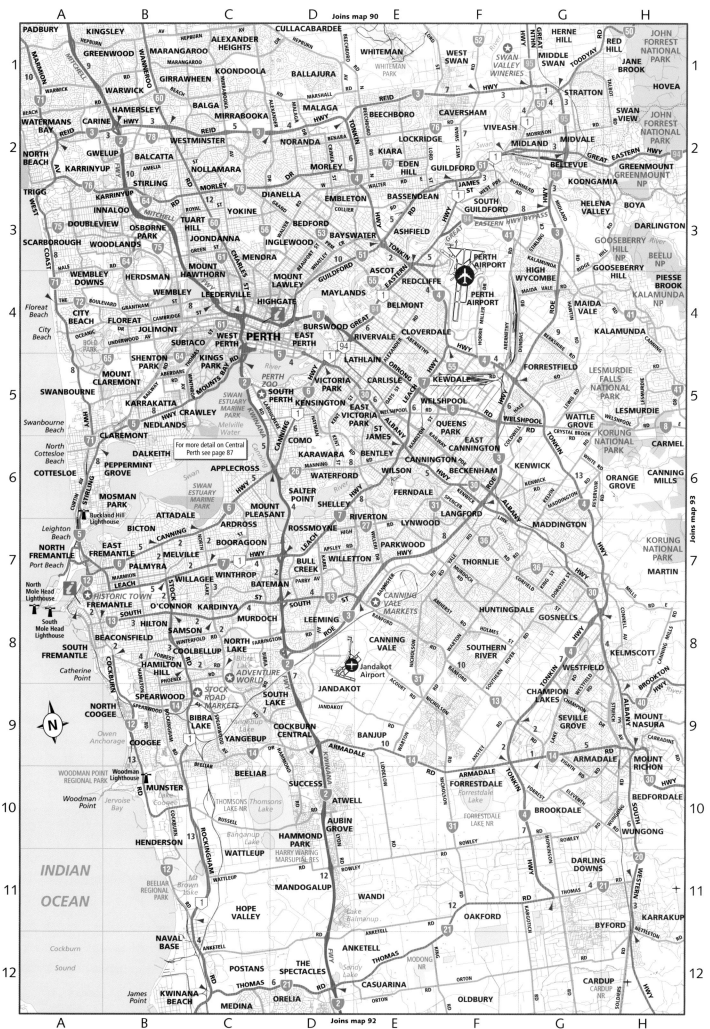

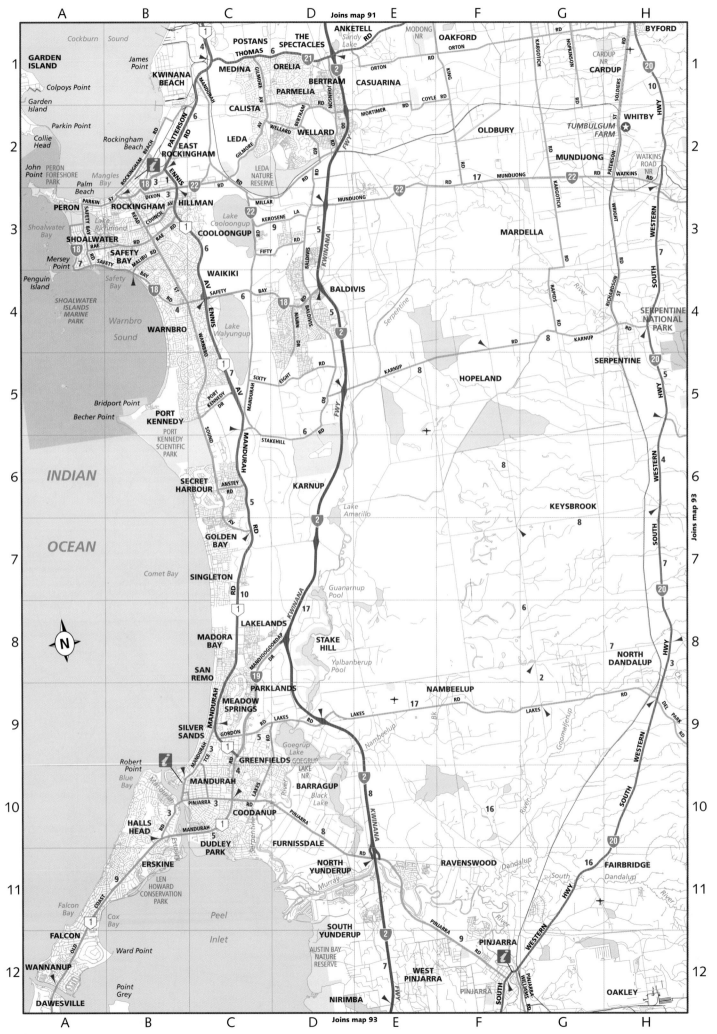

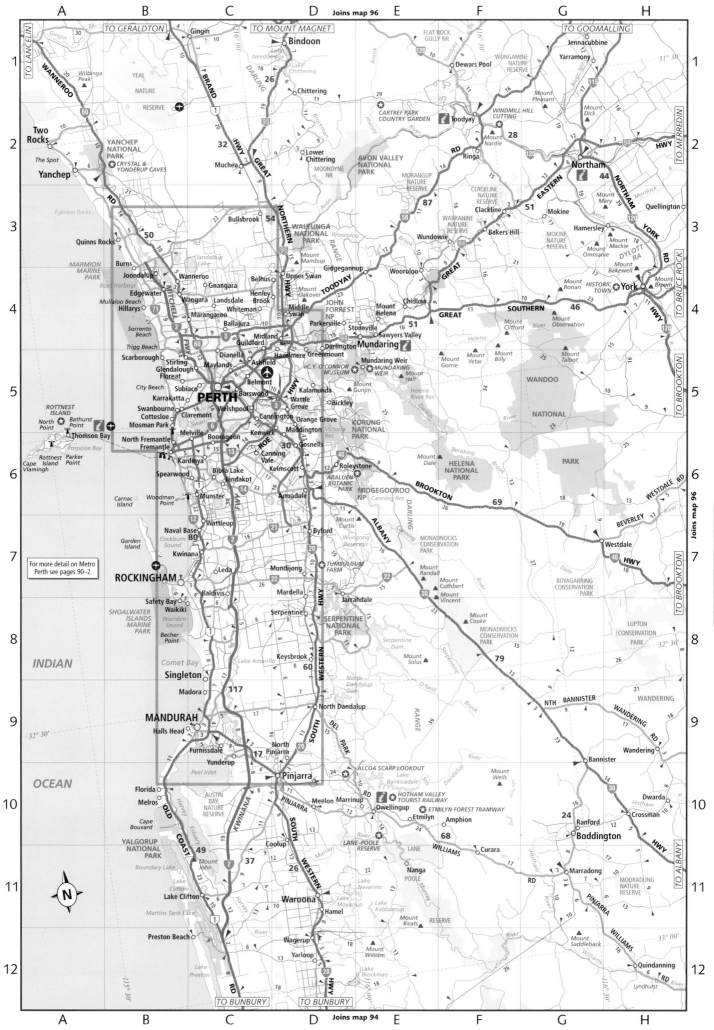

WA

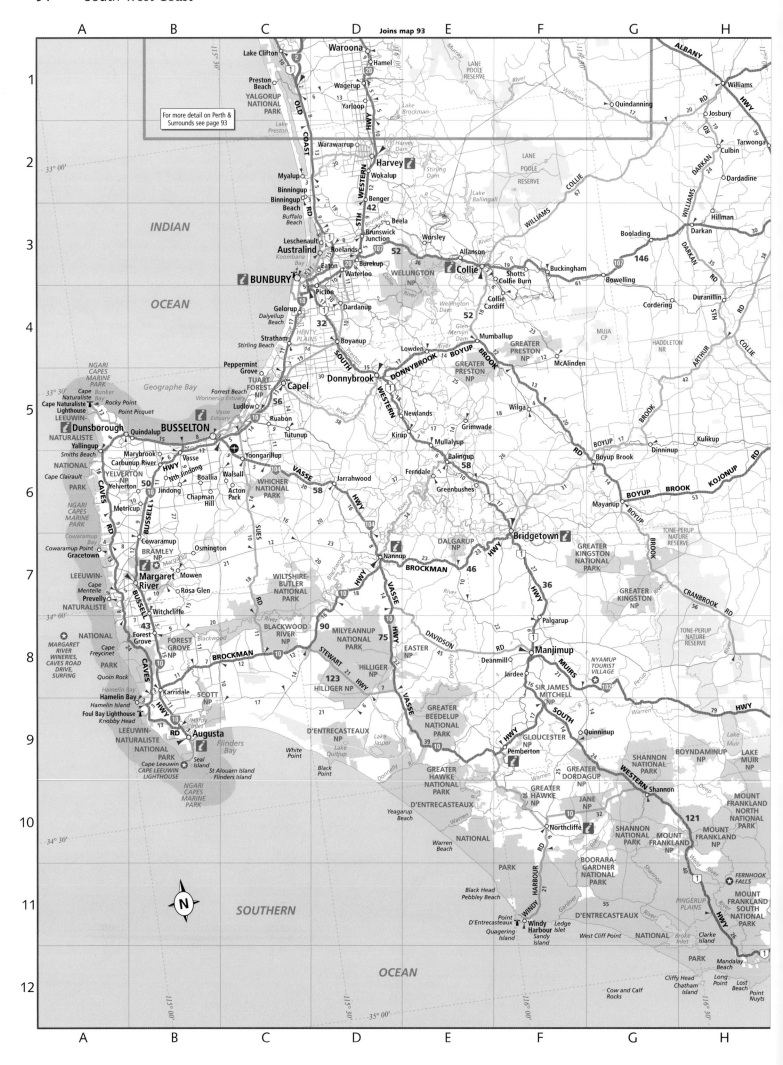

Joins map 93

For more detail on Perth & Surrounds see page 93

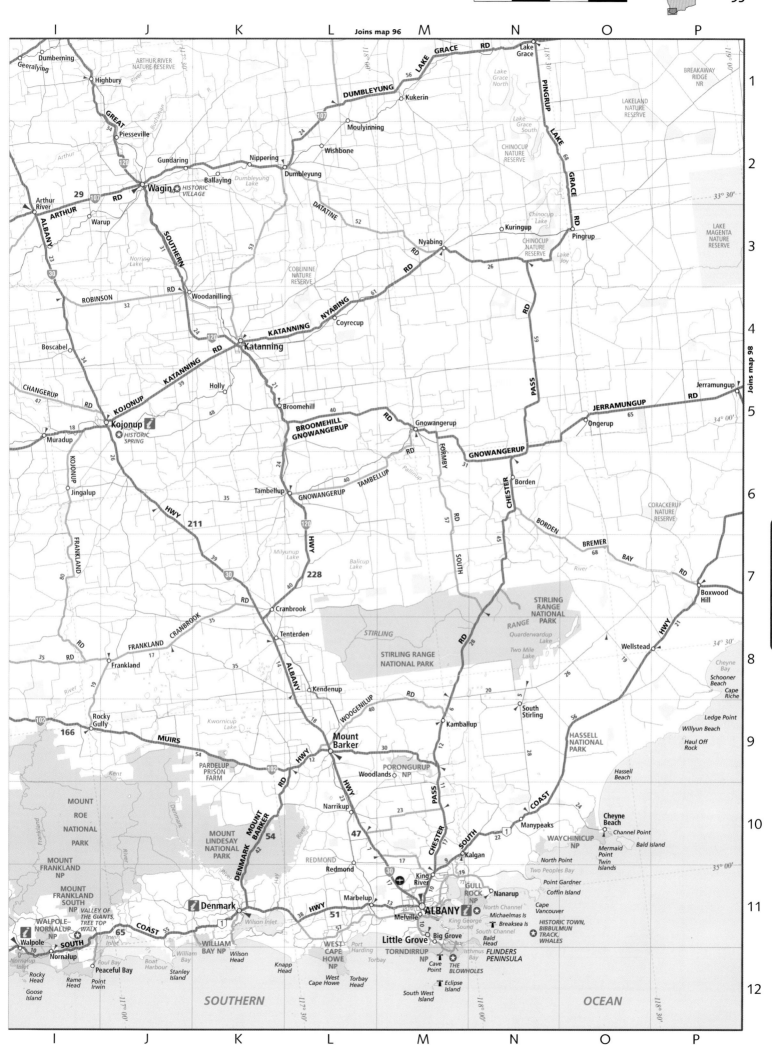

0 10 20 30 40 km

Joins map 96

Joins map 98

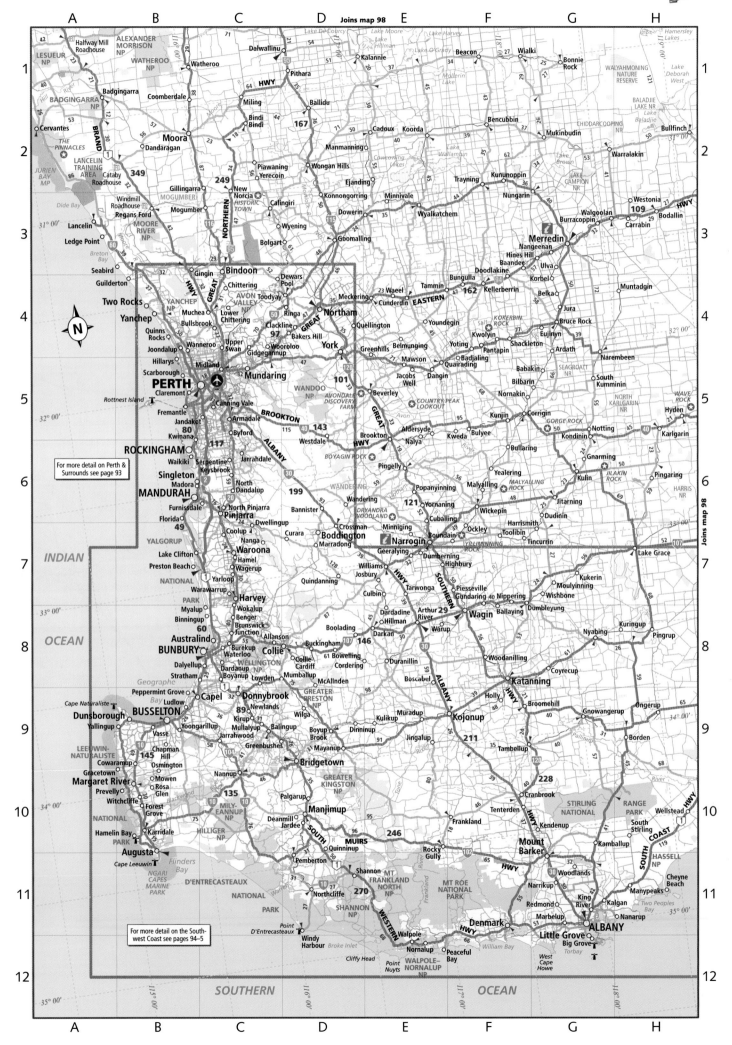

0 20 40 60 80 km

A   B   C   D   Joins map 98   E   F   G   H

Lake De Courcy   Lake Moore   Hamersley Lakes

LESUEUR NP   Halfway Mill Roadhouse   ALEXANDER MORRISON NP   WATHEROO NP   Dalwallinu   Lake O'Grady   Beacon   Wialki   Bonnie Rock   WALYAHMONING NATURE RESERVE   Lake Deborah West   1

Badgingarra   Watheroo   Pithara   Kalannie   Mollerin Lake   Bencubbin   Mukinbudin   CHIDDARCOOPING NR   Bullfinch   BALADJIE LAKE NR   Lake Baladjie

BADGINGARRA NP   Coomberdale   Miling   Ballidu   Cadoux   Koorda   Mukinbudin   Warralakin   2

Cervantes   Moora   Dandaragan   Bindi Bindi   167   Manmanning   Lake Wallambin   Lake Brown   Lake Campion NR

THE PINNACLES   BRAND   349   Gillingarra   Piawaning   Wongan Hills   Ejanding   Trayning   Kununoppin   Nungarin   Westonia   109   HWY   2

LANCELIN TRAINING AREA   Cataby Roadhouse   249   New Norcia HISTORIC TOWN   Calingiri   Konnongorring   Dowerin   Minnivale   Wyalkatchem   Walgoolan   Burracoppin   Bodallin   Carrabin

JURIEN BAY MP   Windmill Roadhouse   Mogumber   MOGUMBER   Yerecoin   Goomalling   Merredin   Nangeenan   3

Lancelin   Regans Ford   MOORE RIVER NP   Wyening   Bolgart   Hines Hill   Baandee   Doodlakine   Ulva   Korbel   Muntadgin

Seabird   Bindoon   Dewars Pool   Meckering   Waeel   Bungulla   Kellerberrin   Belka   Jura   4

Guilderton   Gingin   Chittering   Toodyay   Cunderdin   EASTERN   162   Korbel

Two Rocks   YANCHEP NP   AVON VALLEY NP   Northam   Tammin   Bruce Rock   Narembeen   4

Yanchep   Muchea   Lower Chittering   Clackline   York   Quellington   Youndegin   Kwolyin   KOKERBIN ROCK   Eujinyn   Ardath

Quinns Rocks   Bullsbrook   Bakers Hill   Greenhills   Belmunging   Yoting   Shackleton   South Kumminin   5

Joondalup   Wanneroo   Upper Swan   Gidgegannup   Woooroloo   Mawson   Quairading   Pantapin   Babakin   WAVE ROCK

Hillarys   Midland   Dangin   Bilbarin   Nornakin   NORTH KARLGARIN NR   Hyden

Scarborough   Mundaring   WANDOO NP   Jacobs Well   COUNTRY PEAK LOOKOUT   5

PERTH   Claremont   AVONDALE DISCOVERY FARM   Beverley   Corrigin   GORGE ROCK   Karlgarin

Rottnest Island   Canning Vale   BROOKTON   Aldersyde   Kunjin   Notting   40

Fremantle   Armadale   143   Brookton   Kweda   Bulyee   Kondinin   Pingaring   6

Jandakot   80   Byford   115   40   Westdale   Nalya   Bullaring   Gnarming   HARRIS NR

ROCKINGHAM   117   BOYAGIN ROCK   Pingelly   Yealering   Kulin   JILAKIN ROCK

Waikiki   Jarrahdale   ALBANY   Popanyinning   Malyalling   MALYALLING ROCK   Jitarning   6

Singleton   Serpentine   Keysbrook   North Dandalup   199   Wandering   121   Yornaning   Wickepin   Harrismith   Dudinin

Madora   WANDERING   Bannister   DRYANDRA WOODLAND   Cuballing   Ockley   Toolibin   Tincurrin

MANDURAH   Pinjarra   Dwellingup   Crossman   Minnigin   Boundain   YILLIMINNING ROCK   Lake Grace   107   7

Furnissdale   Coolup   Curara   Boddington   Narrogin   Geeralying   Dumberning   Highbury   Kukerin

Florida   49   Nanga   Marradong   Williams   Tarwonga   Piesseville   Moulyinning   Wishbone

YALGORUP   Waroona   Hamel   Josbury   SOUTHERN   Gundaring   Nippering   Nyabing   Pingrup   8

INDIAN   Lake Clifton   Wagerup   Quindanning   Culbin   Arthur River   29   Wagin   Ballaying   Dumbleyung   Kuringup

Preston Beach   Yarloop   Harvey   Dardadine   Hillman   Warup   Woodanilling   Coyrecup   8

NATIONAL   Warawarrup   Myalup   Benger   Booladung   Darkan   30   Boscabel   Katanning   Ongerup

OCEAN   PARK   Binningup   60   Brunswick Junction   Buckingham   146   Duranillin   Holly   Broomehill   Gnowangerup   65

Australind   Allanson   107   McAlinden   Cordering   Kojonup   211   Tambellup   Borden   9

BUNBURY   Burekup   Waterloo   Collie   Collie Cardiff   61 Bowelling   Mumballup   Kulikup   Muradup   Jingalup   120   228   9

Dalyellup   Dardanup   WELLINGTON NP   Lowden   Wilga   GREATER PRESTON NP   Dinninup   Boyup Brook   Mayanup   Cranbrook   STIRLING NATIONAL   RANGE PARK

Stratham   Boyanup   Donnybrook   Newlands   89   Balingup   Frankland   Tenterden   Kendenup   South Stirling   Wellstead   10

Geographe   Capel   Kirup   Jarrahwood   Greenbushes   Boyup Brook   GREATER KINGSTON NP   Rocky Gully   Mount Barker   Kambalup   HASSELL NP

Peppermint Grove   Ludlow   Yoongarillup   Mullalyup   Bridgetown   246   Woodlands   Cheyne Beach

Dunsborough   Vasse   Chapman Hill   Nannup   Palgarup   SOUTH   Narrikup   King River   Manypeaks

Cape Naturaliste   BUSSELTON   Yallingup   104   58   135   Manjimup   Deanmill Jardee   MUIRS   270   Redmond   Marbelup   Kalgan   Two Peoples Bay

LEEUWIN-NATURALISTE   Cowaramup   Osmington   MILY-EANNUP NP   Pemberton   Quinninup   Denmark   Little Grove   ALBANY   Big Grove   Torbay   35° 00'   11

Margaret River   Gracetown   Mowen   Rosa Glen   145   HILLIGER NP   Northcliffe   SHANNON NP   Walpole   Nornalup   WESTERN   WEST CAPE HOWE   11

Prevelly   Witchcliffe   Forest Grove   Karridale   75   D'ENTRECASTEAUX   MT FRANKLAND NORTH NP   MT ROE NATIONAL PARK   WALPOLE-NORNALUP NP

NATIONAL   Hamelin Bay PARK   Augusta   NATIONAL   Point D'Entrecasteaux   Windy Harbour   Cliffy Head   Point Nuyts   Peaceful Bay   William Bay   12

Cape Leeuwin   NGARI CAPES MARINE PARK   Flinders Bay   PARK   Broke Inlet   SOUTHERN   OCEAN   12

A   B   C   D   E   F   G   H

For more detail on Perth & Surrounds see page 93

For more detail on the South-west Coast see pages 94–5

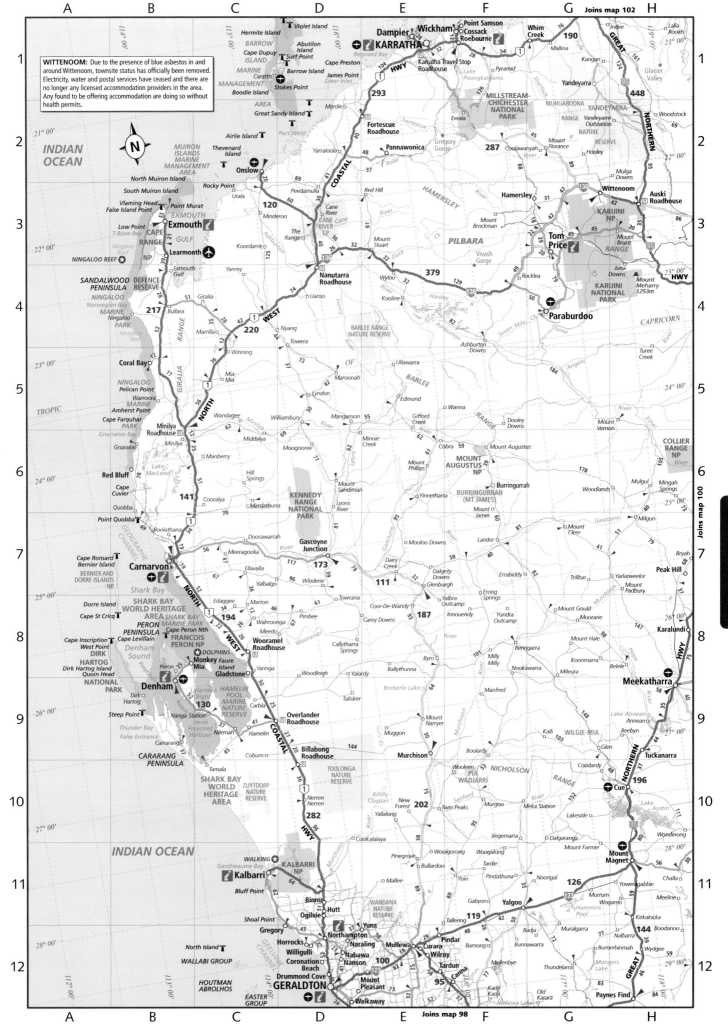

Joins map 102

Joins map 100

W A

0   50   100   150   200 km

INDIAN OCEAN

WITTENOOM: Due to the presence of blue asbestos in and around Wittenoom, townsite status has officially been removed. Electricity, water and postal services have ceased and there are no longer any licensed accommodation providers in the area. Any found to be offering accommodation are doing so without health permits.

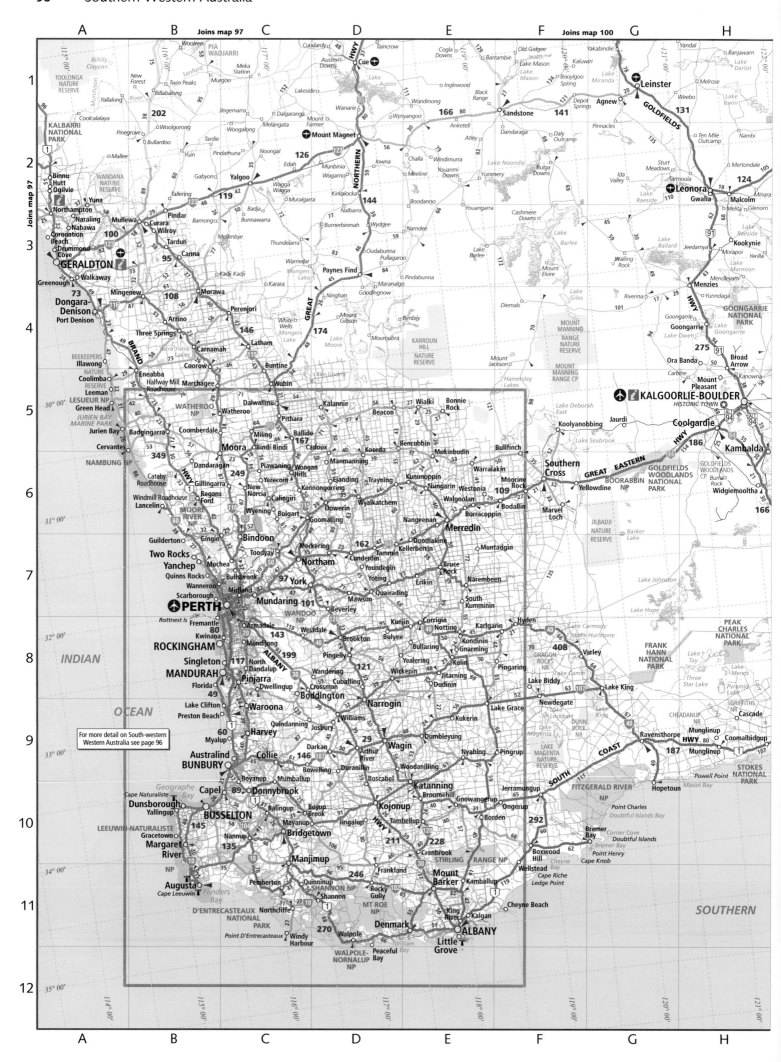

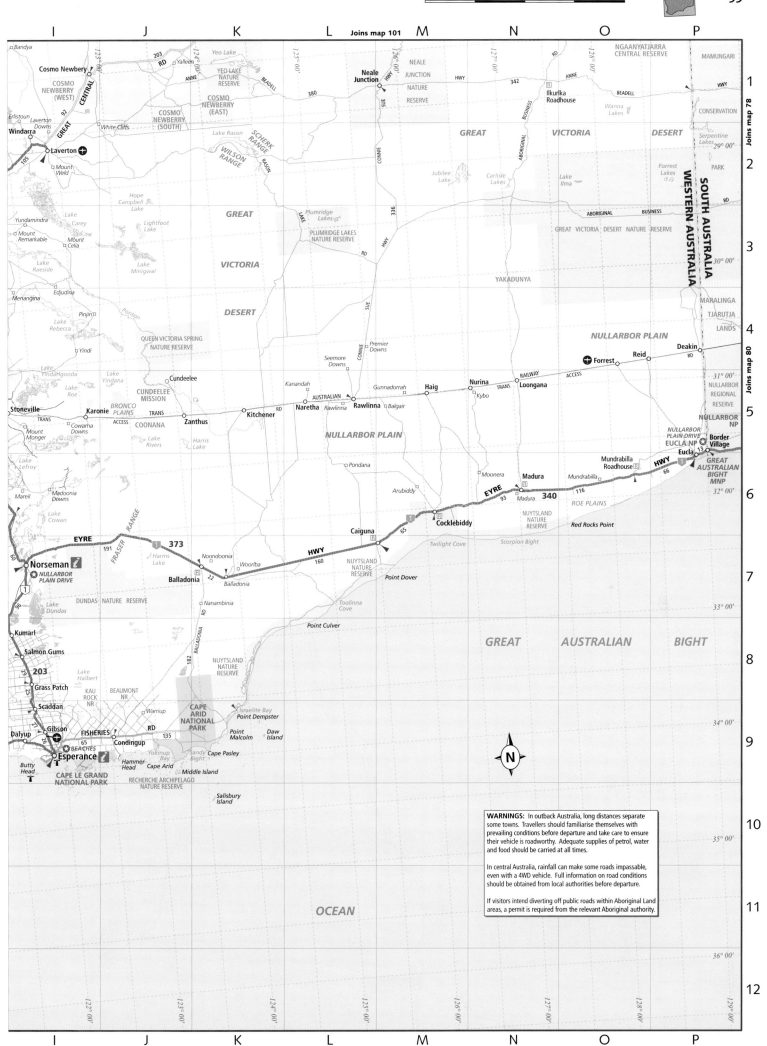

I   J   K   L   Joins map 101   M   N   O   P

Bandya

Cosmo Newbery

203   Yalleen   Yeo Lake

RD

ANNE   BEADELL   380

Neale Junction

NEALE JUNCTION NATURE RESERVE

NGAANYATJARRA CENTRAL RESERVE   MAMUNGARI

ANNE   BEADELL   HWY

COSMO NEWBERY (WEST)

342

Ilkurlka Roadhouse

CONSERVATION

Erliston   Laverton Downs

White Cliffs

COSMO NEWBERY (EAST)

Yeo Lake Nature Reserve

Windarra

92

COSMO NEWBERY (SOUTH)

GREAT   VICTORIA   DESERT

Wanna Lakes

Serpentine Lakes   29° 00'

Laverton

Mount Weld

105

SCHERK RANGE   Lake Rason   WILSON RANGE   RASON LAKE

Jubilee Lake

Carlisle Lakes

Lake Ilma

Forrest Lakes

SOUTH AUSTRALIA

WESTERN AUSTRALIA

RD

PARK

Yundamindra

Lake Carey

Hope Campbell Lake

Lightfoot Lake

GREAT

Plumridge Lakes

ABORIGINAL   BUSINESS

Mount Remarkable

Mount Celia

Lake Minigwal

PLUMRIDGE LAKES NATURE RESERVE

GREAT   VICTORIA   DESERT   NATURE   RESERVE

30° 00'

Lake Raeside

VICTORIA

YAKADUNYA

MARALINGA   TJARUTJA   LANDS

Menangina

Edjudina

Lake Rebecca

Pinjin

Ponton

DESERT

CONNIE   SUE   HWY

Premier Downs

NULLARBOR PLAIN

Deakin

31° 00'

Yindi

QUEEN VICTORIA SPRING NATURE RESERVE

Seemore Downs

Forrest

Reid

RD

NULLARBOR REGIONAL RESERVE

Lake YindaIngooda

Lake Yindana

Cundeelee

Kanandah

Gunnadorrah

Haig

Nurina

Loongana

RAILWAY   ACCESS

TRANS

NULLARBOR NP

Stoneville

Lake Roe

CUNDEELEE MISSION

Ck

AUSTRALIAN   RD

Naretha   Rawlinna   Rawlinna

Kybo

NULLARBOR NP

Karonie

BRONCO PLAINS

TRANS   ACCESS

Zanthus

Kitchener

Balgair

NULLARBOR PLAIN DRIVE   Border Village

Mount Monger

Cowarha Downs

COONANA

Lake Rivers

Harris Lake

Mundrabilla Roadhouse

EUCLA NP   Eucla   13

Lake Lefroy

NULLARBOR PLAIN

Pondana

Moonera

Madura

Mundrabilla

HWY   66

GREAT AUSTRALIAN BIGHT MNP

Mareil

Madoonia Downs

Arubiddy

EYRE   93   Madura   340   116

32° 00'

Lake Cowan

Caiguna

Cocklebiddy

ROE PLAINS

NUYTSLAND NATURE RESERVE

Red Rocks Point

EYRE

FRASER RANGE

191   373

Harms Lake

Noondoonia

Woorlba

HWY   65   160

Twilight Cove

Scorpion Bight

Norseman

NULLARBOR PLAIN DRIVE

1

60

96

Balladonia

22   Balladonia

NUYTSLAND NATURE RESERVE

Point Dover

33° 00'

DUNDAS NATURE RESERVE

Nanambinia

Point Culver

GREAT   AUSTRALIAN   BIGHT

Lake Dundas

BALLADONIA RD

Kumarl

182

NUYTSLAND NATURE RESERVE

Salmon Gums

Lake Halbert

BEAUMONT NR

34° 00'

203

KAU ROCK NR

Warriup

Israelite Bay   Point Dempster

Grass Patch

25

Scaddan

CAPE ARID NATIONAL PARK

Point Malcolm   Daw Island

Dalyup

Gibson

FISHERIES

RD   135

Condingup

65

BEACHES

Esperance

Yokinup Bay   Sandy Bight   Cape Pasley

Butty Head

CAPE LE GRAND NATIONAL PARK

Hammer Head   Cape Arid   Middle Island

RECHERCHE ARCHIPELAGO NATURE RESERVE

Salisbury Island

35° 00'

N

OCEAN

WARNINGS: In outback Australia, long distances separate some towns. Travellers should familiarise themselves with prevailing conditions before departure and take care to ensure their vehicle is roadworthy. Adequate supplies of petrol, water and food should be carried at all times.

In central Australia, rainfall can make some roads impassable, even with a 4WD vehicle. Full information on road conditions should be obtained from local authorities before departure.

If visitors intend diverting off public roads within Aboriginal Land areas, a permit is required from the relevant Aboriginal authority.

36° 00'

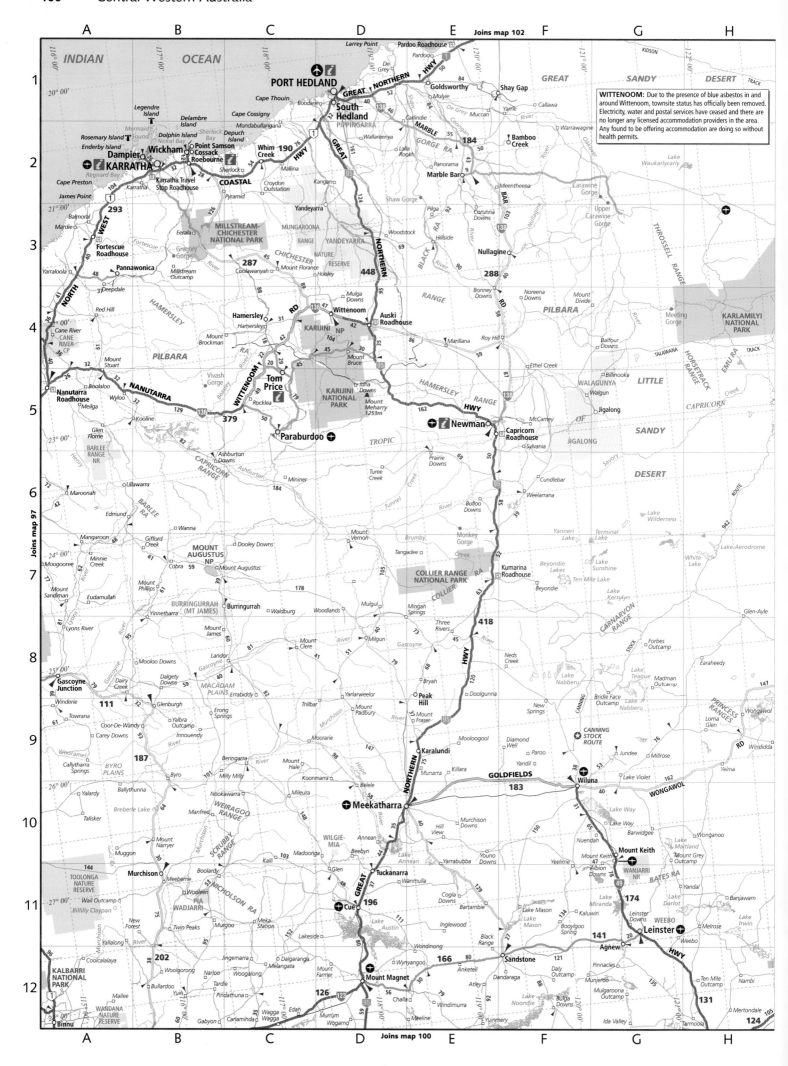

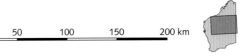

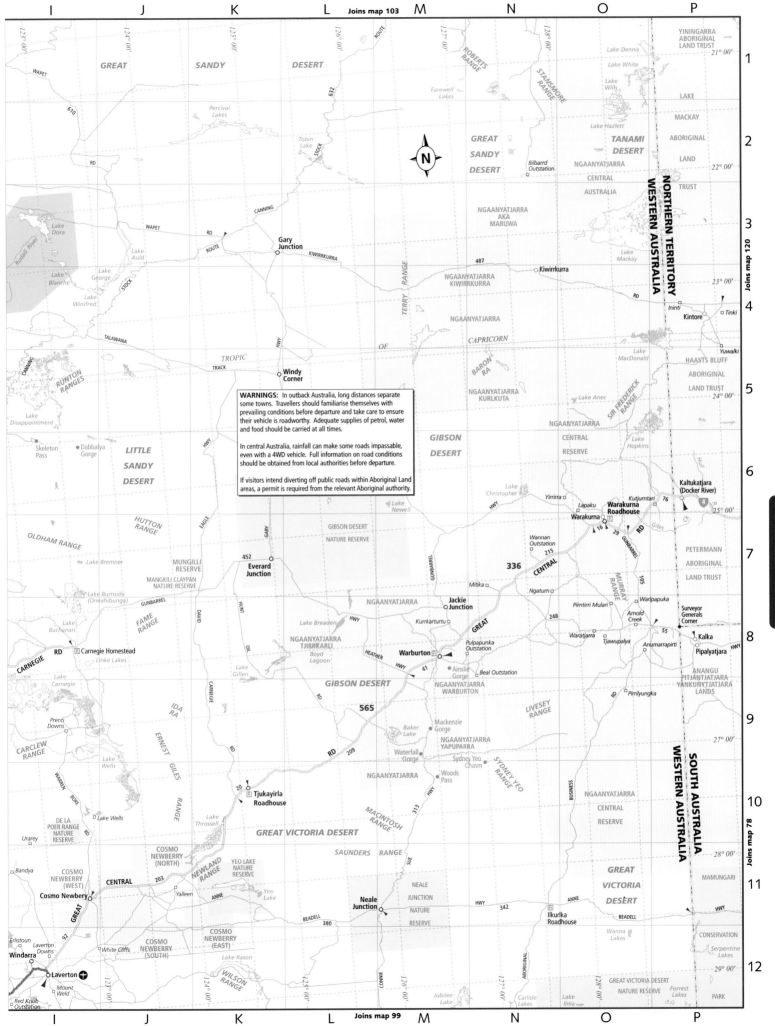

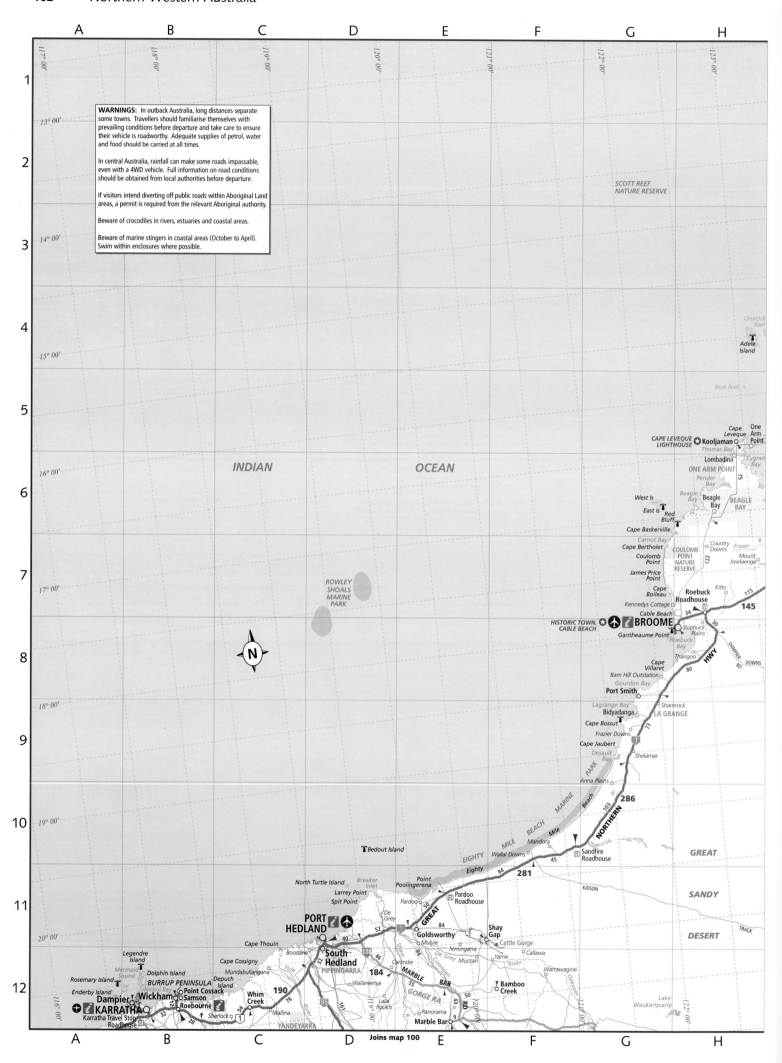

WARNINGS: In outback Australia, long distances separate some towns. Travellers should familiarise themselves with prevailing conditions before departure and take care to ensure their vehicle is roadworthy. Adequate supplies of petrol, water and food should be carried at all times.

In central Australia, rainfall can make some roads impassable, even with a 4WD vehicle. Full information on road conditions should be obtained from local authorities before departure.

If visitors intend diverting off public roads within Aboriginal Land areas, a permit is required from the relevant Aboriginal authority.

Beware of crocodiles in rivers, estuaries and coastal areas.

Beware of marine stingers in coastal areas (October to April). Swim within enclosures where possible.

INDIAN   OCEAN

SCOTT REEF NATURE RESERVE

Churchill Reef

Adele Island

Brue Reef

Cape Leveque   One Arm Point
CAPE LEVEQUE LIGHTHOUSE   Kooljaman
Thomas Bay
Lombadina
ONE ARM POINT
Cygnet Bay
Pender Bay
West Is
Beagle Bay   Beagle Bay   BEAGLE BAY
East Is   Red Bluff
Cape Baskerville
Carnot Bay   Country Downs   Fraser
Cape Bertholet
Coulomb Point   COULOMB POINT NATURE RESERVE   Mount Jowlaenga
James Price Point
Cape Boileau   Roebuck Roadhouse   Kilto
Kennedys Cottage
Cable Beach   145
HISTORIC TOWN, CABLE BEACH   BROOME
Gantheaume Point   Roebuck Plains
Roebuck Bay
Thangoo   HWY
Cape Villaret
Barn Hill Outstation
Gourdon Bay
Port Smith
Lagrange Bay   Shamrock
Bidyadanga   LA GRANGE
Cape Bossut
Frazier Downs
Cape Jaubert
Desault Bay   Shelamar
Anna Plains

ROWLEY SHOALS MARINE PARK

N

GREAT

SANDY

DESERT

286
NORTHERN
Beach
EIGHTY   MILE   BEACH   MARINE   PARK
Mandora
Wallal Downs   Sandfire Roadhouse
Eighty   94   45
281   KIDSON
Bedout Island
North Turtle Island   Breaker Inlet
Larrey Point   Point Poolingerena   Pardoo Roadhouse
Spit Point   Pardoo
De Grey   50
Cape Thouin   52   GREAT   84   Shay Gap
PORT HEDLAND   Goldsworthy   Cattle Gorge
40   Mulyie   Nimingarra   Muccan   TRACK
Cape Cossigny   Boodarie   Shaw   Yarrie   River   Warrawagine
Mundabullangana   32   138   46   Carlindie   Bamboo Creek
Depuch Island   South Hedland   Coongan
Legendre Island   PIPPINGARRA   184   MARBLE   De Grey   Lake Waukarlycarly
Rosemary Island   Whim Creek   Wallareenya   GORGE   BAR   50
Mermaid Sound   Dolphin Island   190   161   RA   43   RD
Nickol Bay   76   Lalla Rookh   Panorama
Enderby Island   BURRUP PENINSULA   Mallina   95   9
Wickham   Point Cossack   54   River   Marble Bar
Samson
Dampier   Roebourne
KARRATHA   28   Sherlock   YANDEYARRA
Karratha Travel Stop   32
Roadhouse

Joins map 100

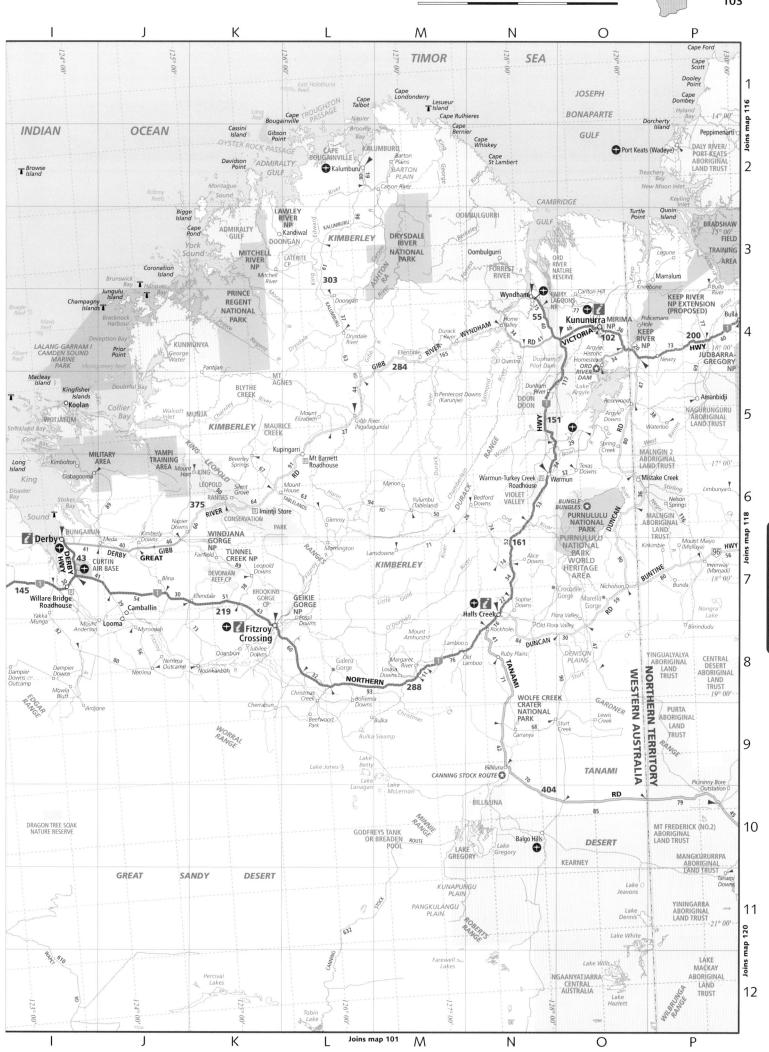

0 50 100 150 200 km

INDIAN OCEAN

TIMOR SEA

WA

Cape Ford
Cape Scott
Dooley Point
Cape Dombey
Hyland Bay
Dorcherty Island
Peppimenarti

JOSEPH BONAPARTE GULF

DALY RIVER/ PORT KEATS ABORIGINAL LAND TRUST

Port Keats (Wadeye)

Cape Londonderry
Cape Talbot
Lesueur Island
Cape Rulhieres
Cape Bernier
Cape Whiskey
Cape St Lambert

Napier Broome Bay
Cape Bougainville
Cassini Island
Gibson Point

OYSTER ROCK PASSAGE
TROUGHTON PASSAGE
East Holothuria Reef

Long Reef

Browse Island

CAMBRIDGE GULF

BRADSHAW FIELD TRAINING AREA

Treachery Bay
New Moon Inlet
Turtle Point
Quoin Island
Keyling Inlet

KALUMBURU
Kalumburu
Barton Plains
BARTON PLAIN
Catson River

CAPE BOUGAINVILLE

Montague Sound
Bigge Island
Cape Pond
Robroy Reefs

ADMIRALTY GULF

LAWLEY RIVER NP
Kandiwal
DOONGAN

KIMBERLEY

OOMBULGURRI

Oombulgurri

DRYSDALE RIVER NATIONAL PARK

ORD RIVER NATURE RESERVE

York Sound
Coronation Island
Brunswick Bay
Hanover Bay
Jungulu Island
Champagny Islands
Brecknock Harbour

ADMIRALTY GULF

MITCHELL RIVER NP
LATERITE CP
Mitchell River

ASHTON RA

KALUMBURU RD

98

303

19

91

37

Carlton Hill
Wyndham
PARRY LAGOONS NR
Home Valley
KEEP RIVER NP EXTENSION (PROPOSED)
Policemans Hole
Newry
Bulla
Kneebone
Marralum
Legune
Forrest River
FORREST RIVER

Beagle Reef
Mavis Reef
Albert Reef
Macleay Island
Kingfisher Islands
Koolan

PRINCE REGENT NATIONAL PARK

KUNMUNYA

George Water
Pantijan

Doongan
Drysdale River
Ellenbrae
El Questro
WYNDHAM
GIBB RIVER RD

55
165
284

VICTORIA HWY

Kununurra
MIRIMA NP
102
Argyle Historic Homestead
ORD RIVER DAM
Dunham Pilot Dam
Lake Argyle
Argyle Downs
Rosewood
Waterloo
Spring Creek
KEEP RIVER NP

200 HWY
JUDBARRA-GREGORY NP

Amanbidji

NAGURUNGURU ABORIGINAL LAND TRUST

Deception Bay
LALANG-GARRAM / CAMDEN SOUND MARINE PARK
Doubtful Bay
Montgomery Reef
Prior Point

Walcott Inlet
Collier Bay
Charnley River
BLYTHE CREEK
MT AGNES

MUNJA
Mount Hart
KIMBERLEY
MAURICE CREEK
Mount Elizabeth
Pentecost Downs (Karunjie)
DURACK RANGE
DOON DOON

151 HWY

Texas Downs
Warmun-Turkey Creek Roadhouse
Warmun
Mistake Creek
Stirling
Limbunya
Nelson Springs

MALNGIN 2 ABORIGINAL LAND TRUST

Stokes Bay
Strickland Bay
Cone Bay
Long Island
King
Disaster Bay
Kimbolton
Gobagooma

MILITARY AREA

YAMPI TRAINING AREA

KING LEOPOLD RANGES

Silent Grove
Mount Hart
KING
LEOPOLD
375 RIVER CONSERVATION PARK
Imintji Store
TABLELANDS
Beverley Springs
Mt Barnett Roadhouse
Kupingarri
Marion
Glenroy
Yulumbu (Tableland)
Bedford Downs
VIOLET VALLEY
BUNGLE BUNGLES
PURNULULU NATIONAL PARK
PURNULULU NATIONAL PARK WORLD HERITAGE AREA

DUNCAN

MALNGIN ABORIGINAL LAND TRUST

Mount Maiyo (Mollaya)
96 HWY
Limbunya

Derby
DERBY HWY
43
CURTIN AIR BASE
Meda
Kimberly Downs
DERBY
GREAT
GIBB
Fairfield
WINDJANA GORGE NP
TUNNEL CREEK NP
Napier Downs
Blina
Leopold Downs
DEVONIAN REEF CP
Mornington
Lansdowne
161
Alice Downs
Kirkimbie
Inverway (Mamadi)
BUNTINE

WILLARE BRIDGE ROADHOUSE
145
30
41
54
Camballin
Looma
Myroodah
Blina
Ellendale
51
BROOKING GORGE
GEIKIE GORGE NP
Fossil Downs
219
Fitzroy Crossing
Quanbun
Jubilee Downs
Noonkanbah
Nerrima
Galeru Gorge
Margaret River
Louisa Downs
Old Lamboo
Lamboo
Halls Creek
Ruby Plains
Sophie Downs
Crocodile Gorge
Flora Valley
Old Flora Valley
Marella Gorge
Nicholson
Bunda
Nongra Lake
Birrindudu

DENISON PLAINS

YINGUALYALYA ABORIGINAL LAND TRUST

CENTRAL DESERT ABORIGINAL LAND TRUST

PURTA ABORIGINAL LAND TRUST

Dampier Downs Outcamp
Mowla Bluff
Ardjorie
EDGAR RANGE

NORTHERN
288
93
Christmas Creek
Bohemia Downs
Beefwood Park
Bulka
Christmas
Mount Amhurst
Rockhole
DUNCAN

WOLFE CREEK CRATER NATIONAL PARK
Carranya
Sturt Creek
Lewis Creek
Sturt

DRAGON TREE SOAK NATURE RESERVE

WORRAL RANGE

Lake Jones
Lake Betty
Lake McLernon
Lake Lanagan

CANNING STOCK ROUTE
Billiluna
404 RD
Pininny Bore Outstation
79
45

MT FREDERICK (NO.2) ABORIGINAL LAND TRUST

GREAT SANDY DESERT

GODFREYS TANK OR BREADEN POOL
MINNIE RANGE
ROBERTS RANGE

LAKE GREGORY
Lake Gregory
Balgo Hills

DESERT
TANAMI

KEARNEY

MANGKURURRPA ABORIGINAL LAND TRUST

Tanami Downs

NORTHERN TERRITORY
WESTERN AUSTRALIA
GARDNER RANGE

Percival Lakes

KUNAPUNGU PLAIN
PANGKULANGU PLAIN
STOCK

Lake Jeavons
Lake Dennis
Lake White

YININGARRA ABORIGINAL LAND TRUST

Tobin Lake
Farewell Lakes
CANNING
632
610

LAKE MACKAY ABORIGINAL LAND TRUST

NGAANYATJARRA CENTRAL AUSTRALIA
Lake Wills
Lake Hazlett
WILBRUNGA RANGE

ALBANY *page 95 M11*

 Old Railway Station
55 Proudlove Pde
(08) 9841 9290
www.amazingalbany.com.au

AUGUSTA *page 94 B9*

75 Blackwood Av
(08) 9758 0166
www.margaretriver.com

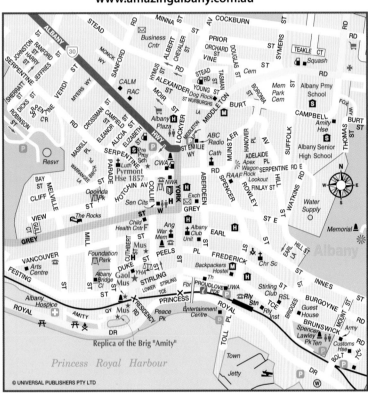

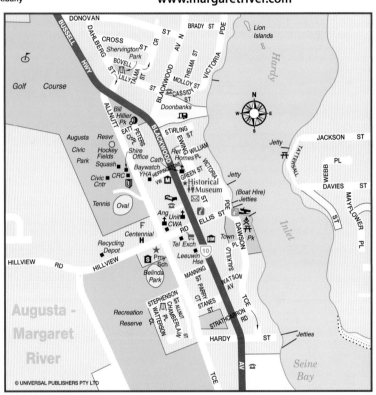

BROOME *page 102 H8*

 1 Hamersley St
(08) 9195 2200
www.visitbroome.com.au

BUNBURY *page 94 C3*

 Old Railway Station
Cnr Carmody Pl and Haley St
(08) 9792 7205 or 1800 286 287
www.visitbunbury.com.au

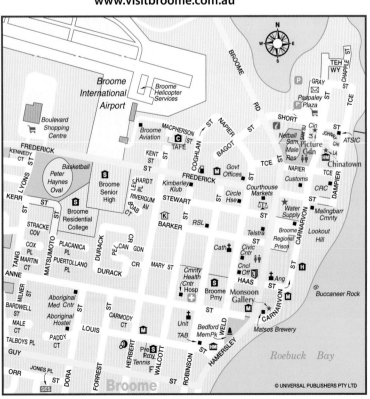

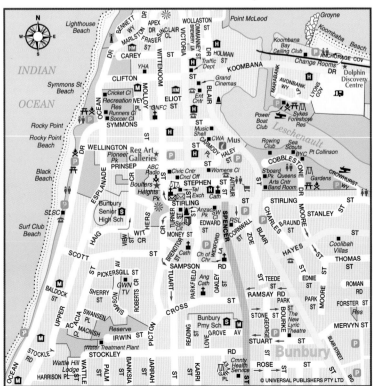

BUSSELTON *page 94 B5*

 Busselton Foreshore
Lot 431 Queen St
(08) 9752 5800
www.margaretriver.com

CARNARVON *page 97 B7*

 21 Robinson St
(08) 9941 1146
www.carnarvon.org.au

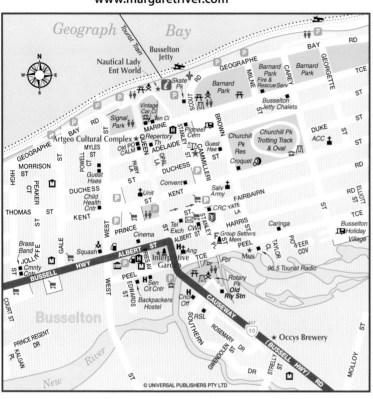

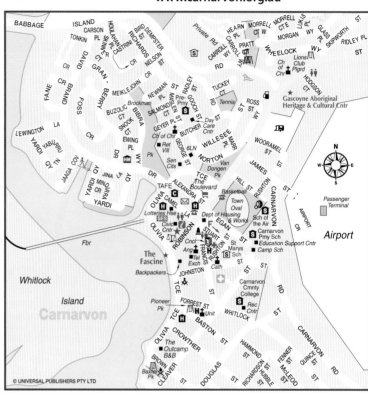

COLLIE *page 94 E3*

 156 Throssell St
(08) 9734 2051
www.collierivervalley.com.au

ESPERANCE *page 99 I9*

 Museum Village
48 Dempster St
(08) 9083 1555 or 1300 664 455
www.visitesperance.com

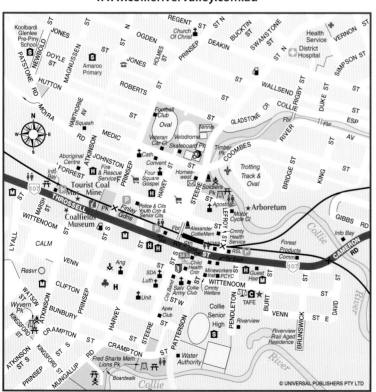

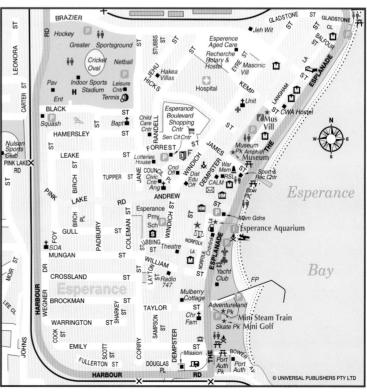

FREMANTLE *page 91 A8*

Kings Square
8 William St
(08) 9431 7878
www.visitfremantle.com.au

GERALDTON *page 98 A3*

246 Marine Tce
(08) 9956 6670 or 1800 847 484
www.visitgeraldton.com.au

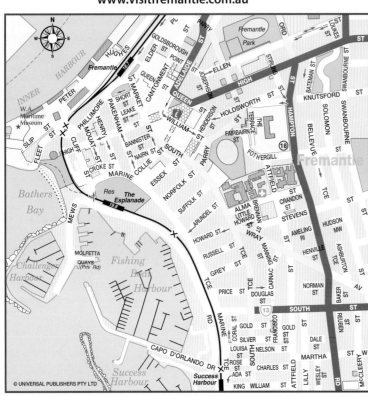

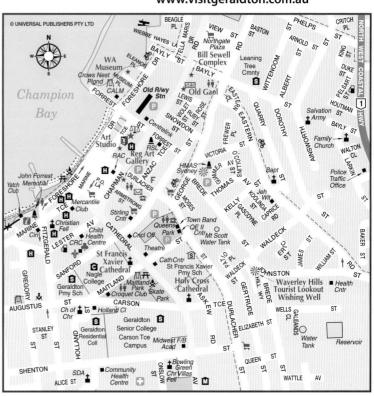

KALGOORLIE *page 98 H5*

316 Hannan St
(08) 9021 1966 or 1800 004 653
www.kalgoorlietourism.com

KUNUNURRA *page 103 O4*

75 Coolibah Dr
(08) 9168 1177 or 1800 586 868
www.visitkununurra.com

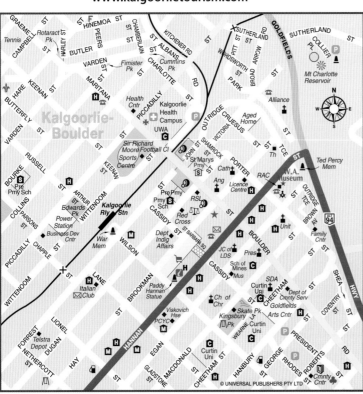

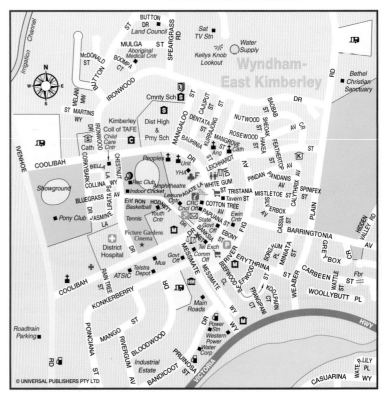

MANDURAH *page 92 B10*

75 Mandurah Tce
(08) 9550 3999
www.visitpeel.com.au

NORSEMAN *page 99 I7*

68 Roberts St
(08) 9039 1071
www.norseman.info

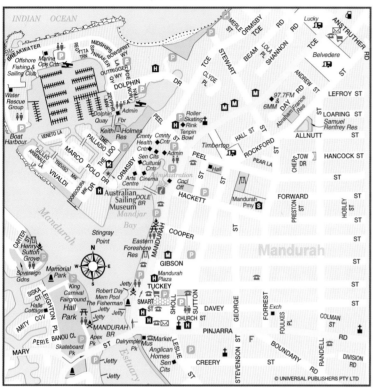

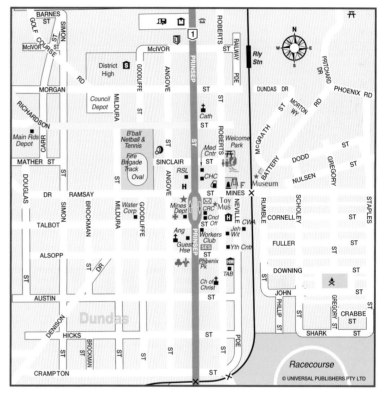

NORTHAM *page 93 G2*

2 Grey St
(08) 9622 2100
www.northam.wa.gov.au

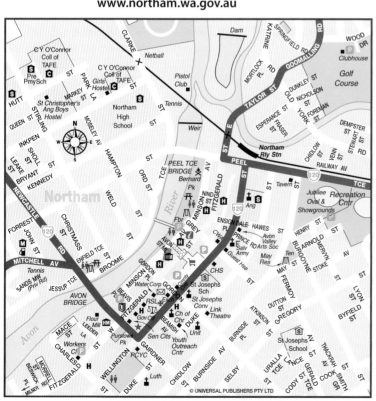

PORT HEDLAND *page 100 D1*

13 Wedge St
(08) 9173 1711
www.visitporthedland.com

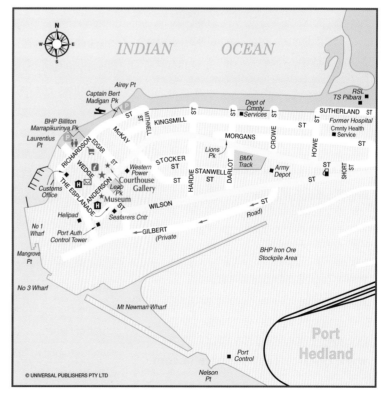

WA

Kata Tjuṯa, Kata Tjuṯa–Uluṟu National Park

NORTHERN TERRITORY

The Northern Territory's rich Aboriginal past dates back some 60,000 years and remains a huge influence today.

Ceremonies, stories and rock art attest to the Aboriginal people's special link with the Territory.

The vibrant sands of the Red Centre characterise the sacred sites of Uluṟu and Kata Tjuṯa. Verdant green rainforests and savannah woodlands cover the Top End. Darwin, the Territory's capital, is a beautiful green city surrounded on three sides by the Timor Sea. And Arnhem Land, in the north-east, is the largest Aboriginal reserve in Australia.

The Northern Territory beckons travellers to explore beyond the beaten track. It is excellent for four-wheel drive touring. The spectacular sights, ancient landscapes and challenging terrain epitomise 'outback Australia'.

INFORMATION CENTRES

www.travelnt.com

Tourism Top End
6 Bennett St, Darwin;
(08) 8980 6000 or 1300 138 886
www.tourismtopend.com.au

Central Australian Visitor Information Centre
Cnr Todd Mall and Parson St, Alice Springs;
(08) 8952 5800 or 1800 645 199
www.discovercentralaustralia.com

Places of interest

	MAP REF	
Alice Springs Telegraph Station		
Historical Reserve	121	I7
Araluen Cultural Precinct	121	I7
Battery Hill Mining Centre	119	J9
Chambers Pillar Historical Reserve	121	I7
Crocodylus Park, Darwin	112	H5
Cutta Cutta Caves Nature Park	116	G9
Howard Springs Nature Park	113	O8
Jim Jim Falls, Kakadu National Park	115	O8
Karlu Karlu (Devils Marbles)		
Conservation Reserve	119	J9
Kata Tjuṯa (The Olgas)	120	E10
Litchfield National Park	114	D9
Mary River National Park	114	H5
Mataranka Hot Springs, Elsey		
National Park	116	H9
National Pioneer Womens		
Hall of Fame	121	I7
Nitmiluk National Park		
(Katherine Gorge)	116	G8

	MAP REF	
Nourlangie Rock, Kakadu National Park	115	O5
Olive Pink Botanic Garden,		
Alice Springs	121	I7
Palm Valley, Finke Gorge National Park	120	G7
Pine Creek	115	I12
Rainbow Valley Conservation Reserve	121	I8
Simpsons Gap, West MacDonnell		
National Park	121	I6
Springvale Homestead Tourist Park,		
Katherine	116	F8
Standley Chasm	121	I7
Territory Wildlife Park	114	D4
Tiwi Islands	116	D3
Tjuwaliyn (Douglas) Hot Springs	114	G12
Ubirr, Kakadu	115	P2
Uluṟu (Ayers Rock)	120	E10
Warradjan Aboriginal Cultural Centre	115	M6
Watarrka National Park (Kings Canyon)	120	F8
Window on the Wetlands	114	F4

MAPS

NORTHERN TERRITORY

111–13

116–17

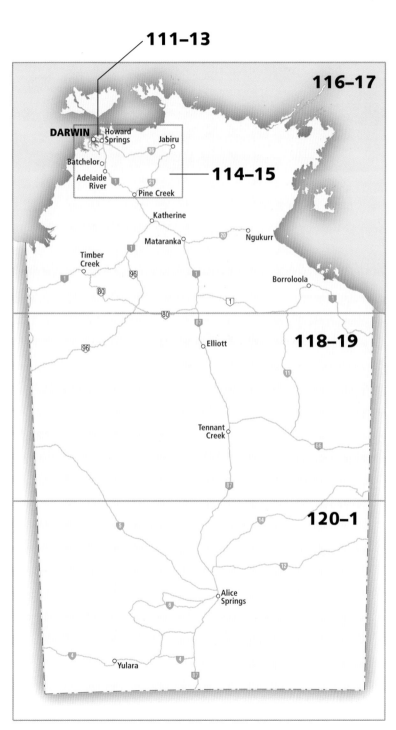

114–15

118–19

120–1

Northern Territory

Central Darwin	111
Metro Darwin	112–13
Darwin & Surrounds	114–15
Top End	116–17
Central Northern Territory	118–19
Southern Northern Territory	120–1

INTER-CITY ROUTES	DISTANCE
Darwin–Adelaide via Stuart Hwy	3026 km
Darwin–Perth via Great Northern Hwy	4032 km
Darwin–Brisbane via Warrego Hwy	3406 km

George Brown Darwin Botanic Gardens

Darwin

Built on the land of the Larrakia Aboriginal people, Darwin is a beautiful green city. Manicured lawns and hedges of bougainvillea and frangipani adorn parks and roadways, while the waters of the Timor Sea lap three sides of the city.

The founding fathers of Darwin laid out the city centre on a small peninsula that juts into one of the finest harbours in northern Australia. In 1864 the first coastal town was established in the Northern Territory and named Palmerston. Located at the mouth of the Adelaide River, it was abandoned after a particularly wet season in 1867. The settlement moved to an area named Port Darwin and although the town was again called Palmerston, locals referred to it as Darwin. The town officially became Darwin in 1911, after the Federal Government took control over the Northern Territory.

Darwin's development was slow due to its isolation from other Australian states. It is now one of Australia's most modern cities since almost every building had to be rebuilt after Japanese wartime air raids in 1942 and after the destruction caused by cyclone Tracy on Christmas Day in 1974.

With so much natural beauty, Darwin is a city where visitors can enjoy the outdoors. The George Brown Darwin Botanic Gardens are over a century old and span 42 hectares. The Mindil Beach Markets operate on the foreshore between late April and October and visitors can watch the spectacular sunset over Fannie Bay whilst browsing through the art and craft stalls.

Places of interest

	MAP REF		MAP REF
Aquascene	111 D10	Government House	111 G12
Chung Wah Temple and		Indo Pacific Marine	111 H12
Chinese Museum	111 G10	Mindil Beach Lookout	111 C7
Crocosaurus Cove	111 F10	Mindil Beach Market	111 D6
Darwin Entertainment Centre	111 E10	Parliament House	111 G11
Darwin Waterfront Precinct	111 H12	SKYCITY Darwin	111 D6
Deckchair Cinema	111 G12	Smith Street Mall	111 G11
Fannie Bay	111 E1	World War II Oil Storage Tunnels	111 G12
Fannie Bay Gaol Museum	111 E1		
George Brown Darwin			
Botanic Gardens	111 E5		

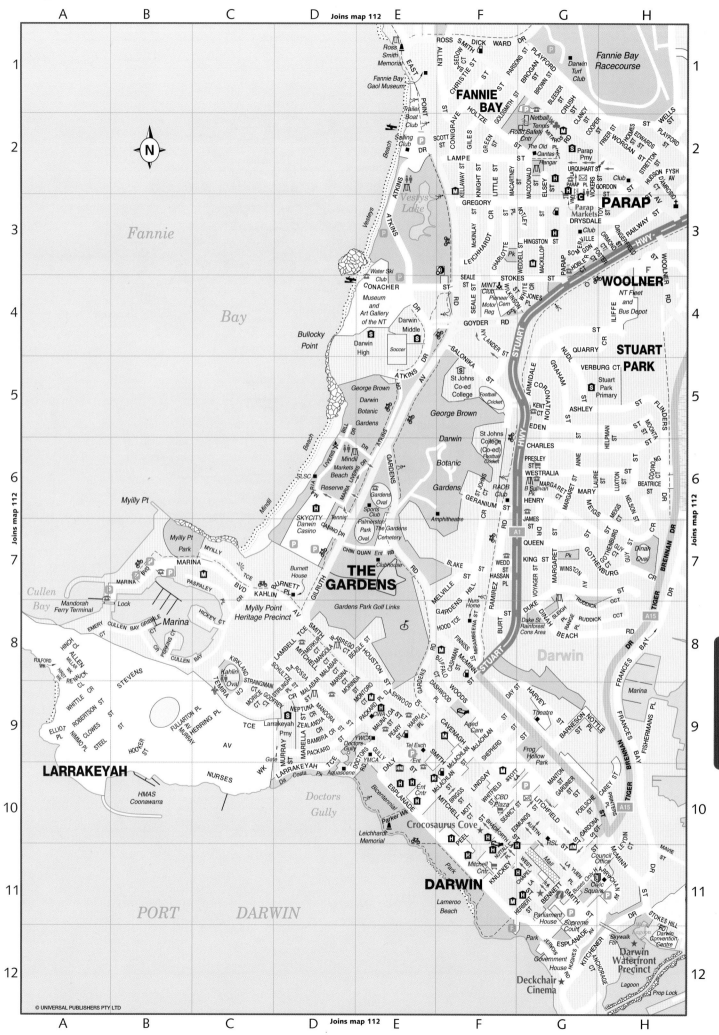

© UNIVERSAL PUBLISHERS PTY LTD

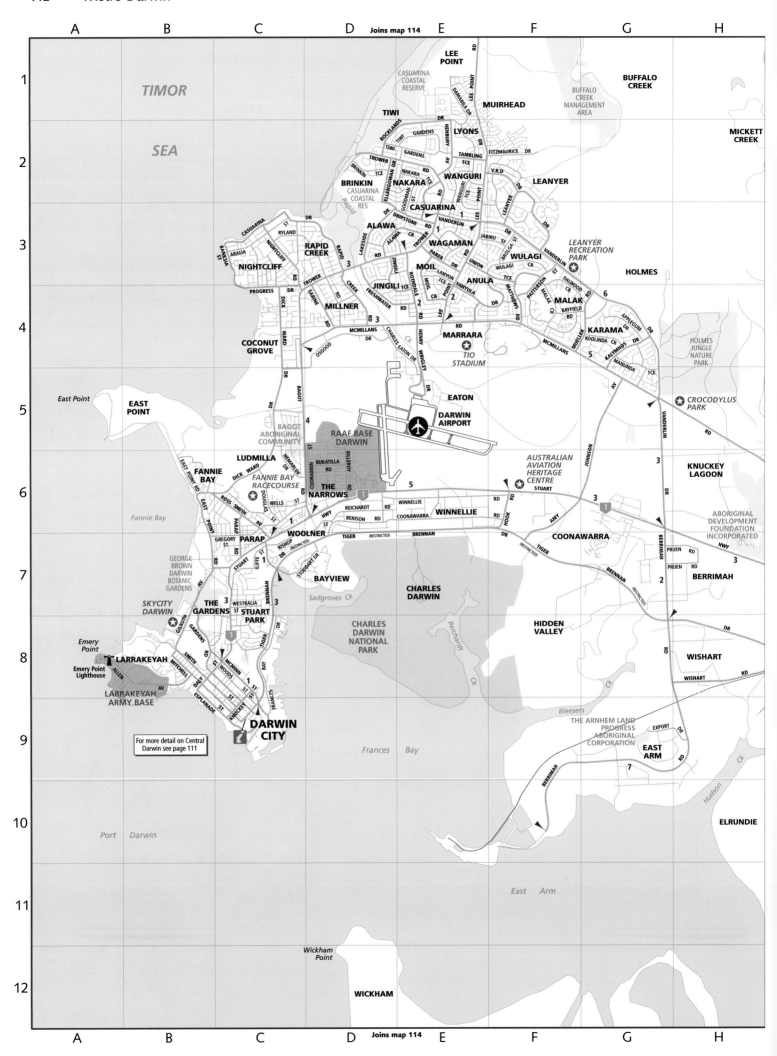

Joins map 114

For more detail on Central Darwin see page 111

Joins map 114

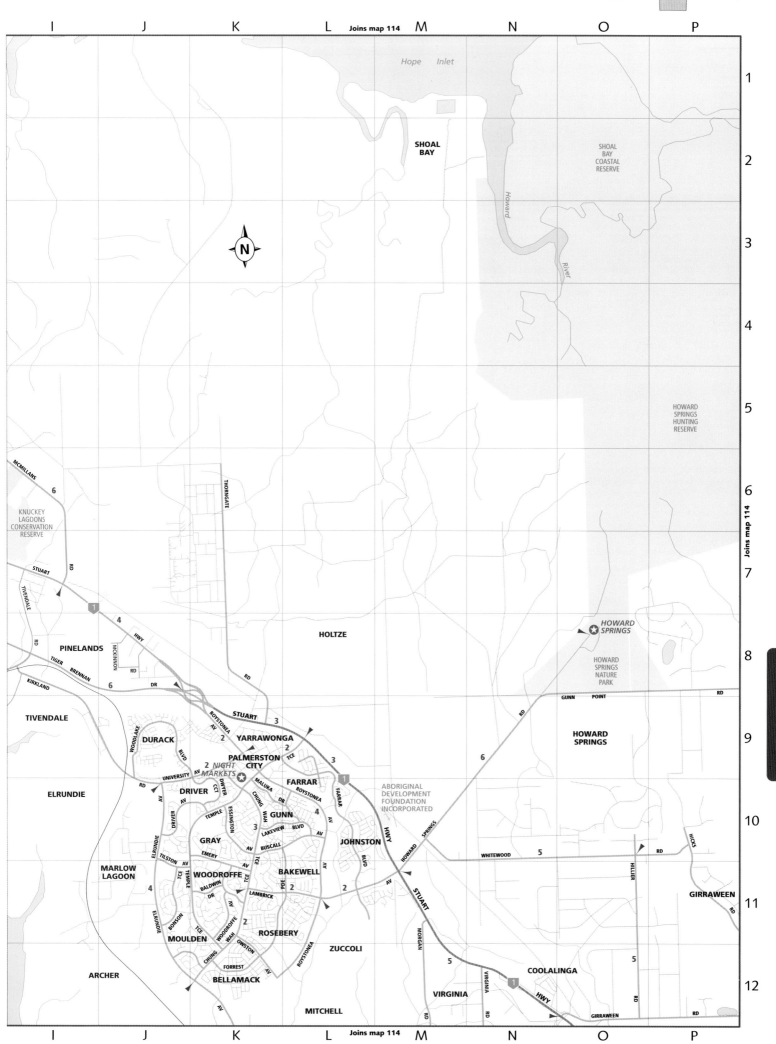

0   1   2   3   4 km

Joins map 114

Hope   Inlet

SHOAL
BAY

SHOAL
BAY
COASTAL
RESERVE

Howard

River

HOWARD
SPRINGS
HUNTING
RESERVE

Joins map 114

MCMILLANS

KNUCKEY
LAGOONS
CONSERVATION
RESERVE

THORNGATE

STUART

RD

TIVENDALE

HWY

1

4

HOLTZE

HOWARD
SPRINGS

HOWARD
SPRINGS
NATURE
PARK

PINELANDS

TIGER

BRENNAN

McKINNON

RD

DR

RD

6

KIRKLAND

RD

STUART

GUNN   POINT

RD

TIVENDALE

ROYSTONEA

STUART

3

RD

HOWARD
SPRINGS

WOODLAKE

DURACK

YARRAWONGA

AV

2

TCE

2

3

6

BLVD

PALMERSTON
CITY

NIGHT
MARKETS

FARRAR

HWY

1

ABORIGINAL
DEVELOPMENT
FOUNDATION
INCORPORATED

ELRUNDIE

UNIVERSITY

RD

DWYER

CCT

2

MALUKA

CHUNG   WAH

DR

ROYSTONEA

FARRAR

FARRAR

AV

DRIVER

AV

DRIVER

TEMPLE

ESSINGTON

GUNN

LAKEVIEW

BLVD

4

AV

HOWARD   SPRINGS

3

AV

JOHNSTON

GRAY

BUSCALL

AV

AV

AV

WHITEWOOD

5

HICKS

ELRUNDIE

TILSTON

EMERY

AV

TCE

BLVD

2

STUART

RD

MARLOW
LAGOON

TCE

WOODROFFE

AV

TCE

BAKEWELL

2

AV

HILLIER

GIRRAWEEN

RD

4

BALDWIN

DR

LAMBRICK

2

ELRUNDIE

BONSON

TCE

WOODROFFE

WAH

2

OWSTON

ROSEBERY

ZUCCOLI

MORGAN

MOULDEN

CHUNG

AV

FORREST

ROYSTONEA

5

COOLALINGA

5

RD

ARCHER

BELLAMACK

VIRGINIA

VIRGINIA

RD

HWY

1

RD

AV

MITCHELL

RD

GIRRAWEEN

RD

Joins map 114

NT

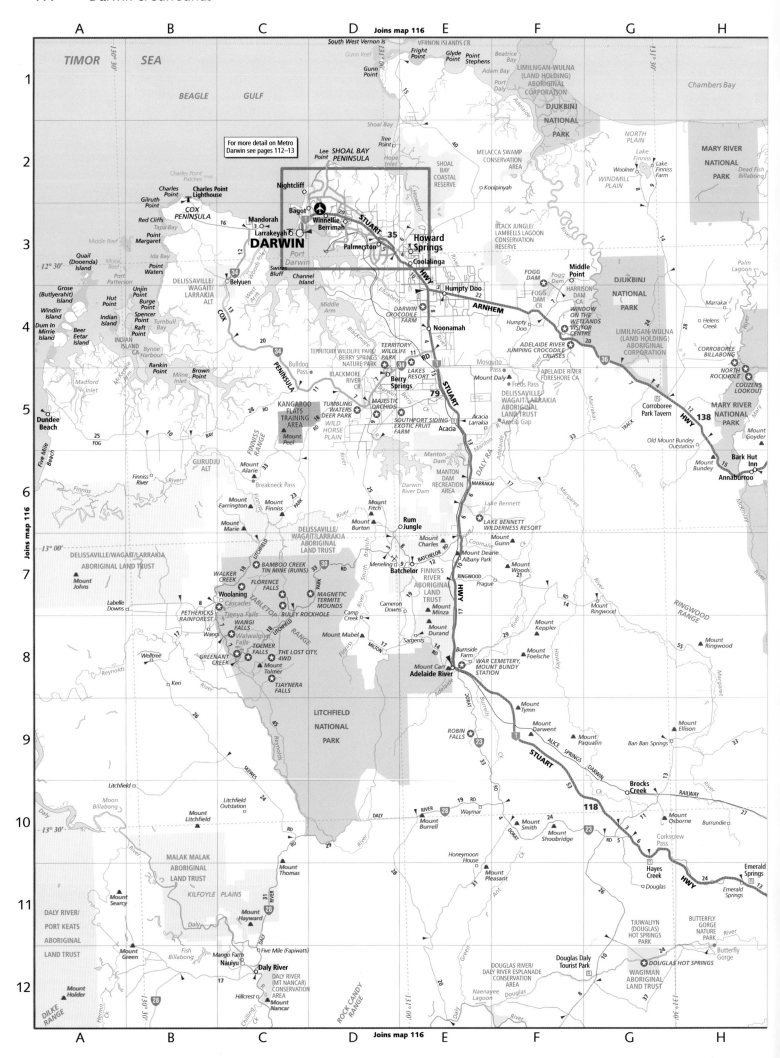

Joins map 116

For more detail on Metro Darwin see pages 112–13

TIMOR SEA

BEAGLE GULF

South West Vernon Is
VERNON ISLANDS CR

Fright Point
Glyde Point
Point Stephens
Beatrice Bay
LIMILNGAN-WULNA (LAND HOLDING) ABORIGINAL CORPORATION
Chambers Bay

Gunn Reef
Gunn Point
Adam Bay
Port Daly
Woolner
Lake Finniss
DJUKBINJ NATIONAL PARK
NORTH PLAIN
Lake Finniss Farm
WINDMILL PLAIN
MARY RIVER NATIONAL PARK
Dead Fish Billabong

Shoal Bay
Tree Point
Lee Point
SHOAL BAY PENINSULA
Hope Inlet
SHOAL BAY COASTAL RESERVE
MELACCA SWAMP CONSERVATION AREA
Koolpinyah

Nightcliff

Charles Point Patches
Charles Point
Charles Point Lighthouse
COX PENINSULA
Bagot
Winnellie
Berrimah
STUART
Howard Springs
BLACK JUNGLE/ LAMBELLS LAGOON CONSERVATION RESERVE

Gilruth Point
Red Cliffs
Tapa Bay
Point Margaret
Mandorah
Larrakeyah
DARWIN
Port Darwin
Palmerston
Coolalinga
FOGG DAM
Fogg Dam
Middle Point

Quail (Dooenda) Island
Moira Reef
Middle Reef
Ida Bay
Point Waters
DELISSAVILLE/ WAGAIT/ LARRAKIA ALT
Belyuen
Swires Bluff
Channel Island
HWY
Humpty Doo
FOGG DAM CR
HARRISON DAM CA
DJUKBINJ NATIONAL PARK
Palm Lagoon

Grose (Butlyerahit) Island
Port Patterson
Hut Point
Unjin Point
Burge Point
COX
West Arm
Woods Inlet
ARNHEM
DARWIN CROCODILE FARM
Humpty Doo
WINDOW ON THE WETLANDS VISITOR CENTRE
LIMILNGAN-WULNA (LAND HOLDING) ABORIGINAL CORPORATION
Marrakai
Helens Creek

Windirr Island
Dum In Mirrie Island
Beer Eetar Island
Indian Island
Spencer Point
Raft Point
Turnbull Bay
Middle Arm
Blackmore
Noonamah
ADELAIDE RIVER JUMPING CROCODILE CRUISES
ADELAIDE RIVER FORESHORE CA
CORROBOREE BILLABONG

INDIAN ISLAND CA
Madford Inlet
Rankin Point
Milne Inlet
Brown Point
PENINSULA
Bulldog Pass
TERRITORY WILDLIFE PARK/ BERRY SPRINGS NATURE PARK
Berry Springs
TERRITORY WILDLIFE PARK
LAKES RESORT
Mosquito Pass
Mount Daly
Freds Pass
DELISSAVILLE WAGAIT/ LARRAKIA ABORIGINAL LAND TRUST
NORTH ROCKHOLE
COUZENS LOOKOUT

Bynoe Harbour
BLACKMORE RIVER CR
MAJESTIC ORCHIDS
SOUTHPORT SIDING EXOTIC FRUIT FARM
Acacia
Acacia Larrakia
Acacia Gap
Corroboree Park Tavern
MARY RIVER NATIONAL PARK
Mount Goyder

Dundee Beach
KANGAROO FLATS TRAINING AREA
TUMBLING WATERS DEER PARK
WILD HORSE PLAIN
Mount Peel
Manton Dam
STUART
Old Mount Bundey Outstation
HWY 138
Bark Hut Inn

Five Mile Beach
FINNISS RANGE
MANTON DAM RECREATION AREA
MARRAKAI
Mount Bundey
Annaburroo

GURUDJU ALT
Mount Alarie
Breakneck Pass
Darwin River Dam
Lake Bennett

Finniss River
Mount Farrington
Mount Finniss
Mount Fitch
Rum Jungle
LAKE BENNETT WILDERNESS RESORT
Mount Gunn
RINGWOOD RANGE

DELISSAVILLE/WAGAIT/LARRAKIA ABORIGINAL LAND TRUST
Mount Marie
Mount Burton
Mount Charles
BATCHELOR RD
Mount Deane
Albany Park
Mount Woods
Mount Keppler
Mount Ringwood

Mount Johns
WALKER CREEK
BAMBOO CREEK TIN MINE (RUINS)
PARK
Meneling
Batchelor
FINNISS RIVER ABORIGINAL LAND TRUST
Prague
RINGWOOD
Mount Foelsche
Mount Ringwood

Labelle Downs
FLORENCE FALLS
MAGNETIC TERMITE MOUNDS
Camp Creek
Cameron Downs
Mount Minza
HWY
Mount Durand
Mount Keppler

Welltree
PETHERICKS RAINFOREST
Woolaning
Cascades
Tjenya Falls
BULEY ROCKHOLE
TABLETOP
Mount Mabel
Sargents
Burnside Farm
Mount Tymn

Keri
Wangi
WANGI FALLS
Walwalgiyn Falls
TOLMER FALLS
LITCHFIELD RANGE
THE LOST CITY, 4WD
MILTON
Mount Carr
Adelaide River
WAR CEMETERY, MOUNT BUNDY STATION
Mount Darwent

Reynolds
GREENANT CREEK
Mount Tolmer
TJAYNERA FALLS
LITCHFIELD NATIONAL PARK
ROBIN FALLS
Mount Paqualin
Ban Ban Springs
Mount Ellison

Litchfield
Moon Billabong
Mount Litchfield
Litchfield Outstation
SKEWES
Reynolds
STUART
Mount Smith
Brocks Creek
RAILWAY
Mount Osborne
Burrundie

DALY
Mount Burrell
Waymar
Mount Shoobridge
HWY 118
Corkscrew Pass
Emerald Springs

MALAK MALAK ABORIGINAL LAND TRUST
Mount Thomas
Honeymoon House
Mount Pleasant
Hayes Creek
Douglas
Emerald Springs

KILFOYLE PLAINS
Mount Searcy
Mount Hayward
TJUWALIYN (DOUGLAS) HOT SPRINGS PARK
BUTTERFLY GORGE NATURE PARK

DALY RIVER/ PORT KEATS ABORIGINAL LAND TRUST
Mount Green
Fish Billabong
Mango Farm
Nauiyu
Five Mile (Fapiwatti)
Daly River
DOUGLAS RIVER/ DALY RIVER ESPLANADE CONSERVATION AREA
Douglas Daly Tourist Park
Douglas Daly
DOUGLAS HOT SPRINGS
Butterfly Gorge

Mount Holder
DILKE RANGE
Hillcrest
DALY RIVER (MT NANCAR) CONSERVATION AREA
Mount Nancar
ROCK CANDY RANGE
Naenayee Lagoon
WAGIMAN ABORIGINAL LAND TRUST

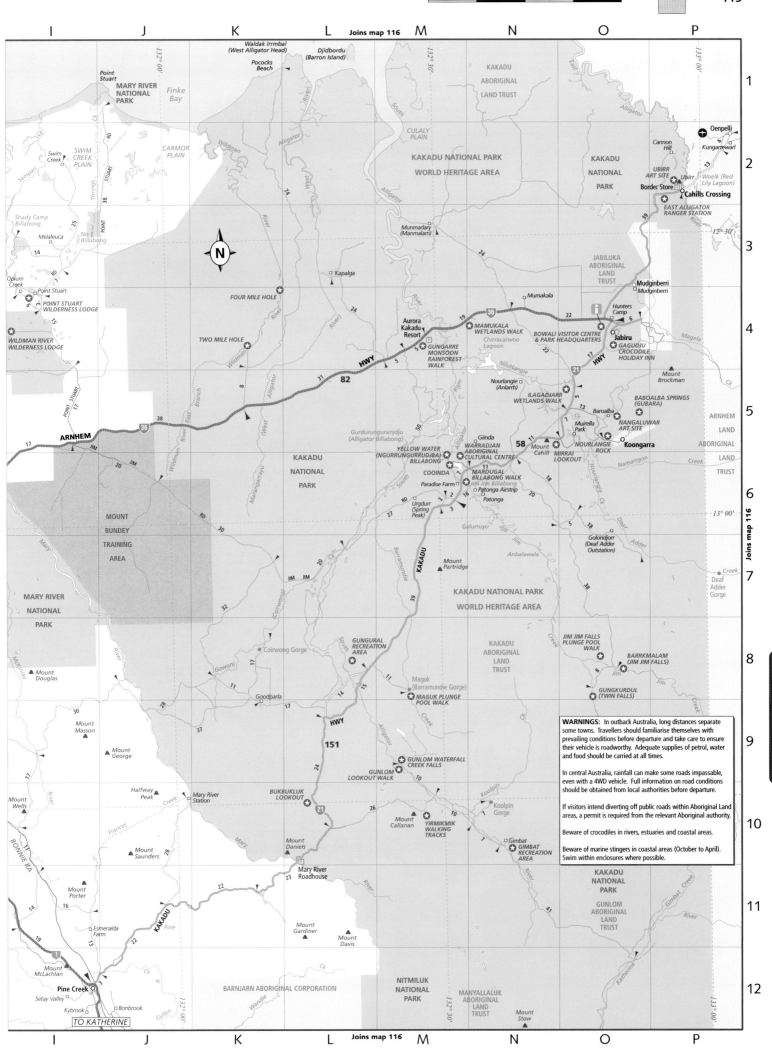

0   10   20   30   40 km

I   J   K   L   M   N   O   P

1

2

3

4

5

6

7

8

9

10

11

12

I   J   K   L   M   N   O   P

NT

Point Stuart
MARY RIVER NATIONAL PARK
Finke Bay

Waldak Irrmbal (West Alligator Head)
Pococks Beach
Djidbordu (Barron Island)

CULALY PLAIN

KAKADU ABORIGINAL LAND TRUST

KAKADU NATIONAL PARK WORLD HERITAGE AREA

KAKADU NATIONAL PARK

Oenpelli
Cannon Hill
Kungarrewarl
UBIRR ART SITE   Ubirr   Woelk (Red Lily Lagoon)
Border Store   Cahills Crossing
EAST ALLIGATOR RANGER STATION

SWIM CREEK PLAIN
CARMOR PLAIN

Swim Creek
Shady Camp Billabong
Melaleuca
No Billabong

Opium Creek
Point Stuart
POINT STUART WILDERNESS LODGE

WILDMAN RIVER WILDERNESS LODGE

ARNHEM

Munmarlary (Manmalarri)

Kapalga

FOUR MILE HOLE

TWO MILE HOLE

Aurora Kakadu Resort
GUNGARRE MONSOON RAINFOREST WALK

HWY
82

MAMUKALA WETLANDS WALK
Chirracarwoo Lagoon
Mumakala

JABILUKA ABORIGINAL LAND TRUST

Mudginberri
Mudginberri

Hunters Camp
BOWALI VISITOR CENTRE & PARK HEADQUARTERS
Jabiru
GAGUDJU CROCODILE HOLIDAY INN
HWY

Mount Brockman

Nourlangie (Anlarrh)
ILAGADJARR WETLANDS WALK

BABOALBA SPRINGS (GUBARA)

ARNHEM LAND

Baroalba
Muirella Park
NANGALUWAR ART SITE
Koongarra

ABORIGINAL LAND TRUST

Gurdurunguranjdju (Alligator Billabong)

Giinda
WARRADJAN ABORIGINAL CULTURAL CENTRE
YELLOW WATER (NGURRUNGURRUDJBA) BILLABONG
COOINDA
Paradise Farm
MARDUGAL BILLABONG WALK
Jim Jim Billabong
Patonga Airstrip
Patonga
Urgdurr (Spring Peak)

Mount Cahill
58
MIRRAI LOOKOUT
NOURLANGIE ROCK

KAKADU NATIONAL PARK

Namarrgon

Golondjorr (Deaf Adder Outstation)

Deaf Adder Gorge

MOUNT BUNDEY TRAINING AREA

MARY RIVER NATIONAL PARK

Mount Douglas

Coirwong Gorge
GUNGURAL RECREATION AREA
Mount Partridge

KAKADU NATIONAL PARK WORLD HERITAGE AREA

KAKADU ABORIGINAL LAND TRUST

JIM JIM FALLS PLUNGE POOL WALK
BARRKMALAM (JIM JIM FALLS)
GUNGKURDUL (TWIN FALLS)

Goodparla
Maguk (Barramundie Gorge)
MAGUK PLUNGE POOL WALK

Mount Masson
Mount George

HWY
151

BUKBUKLUK LOOKOUT

GUNLOM WATERFALL CREEK FALLS
GUNLOM LOOKOUT WALK

Halfway Peak
Mary River Station

Mount Wells

Mount Daniels
Mary River Roadhouse

Mount Callanan
YIRMIKMIK WALKING TRACKS

Koolpin Gorge

Gimbat
GIMBAT RECREATION AREA

KAKADU NATIONAL PARK

GUNLOM ABORIGINAL LAND TRUST

BONNIE RA

Mount Porter
Esmeralda Farm

Mount McLachlan
Pine Creek
Setay Valley
Kybrook
Bonbrook

KAKADU

Mount Gardiner
Mount Davis

BARNJARN ABORIGINAL CORPORATION

NITMILUK NATIONAL PARK

MANYALLALUK ABORIGINAL LAND TRUST

Mount Stow

TO KATHERINE

WARNINGS: In outback Australia, long distances separate some towns. Travellers should familiarise themselves with prevailing conditions before departure and take care to ensure their vehicle is roadworthy. Adequate supplies of petrol, water and food should be carried at all times.

In central Australia, rainfall can make some roads impassable, even with a 4WD vehicle. Full information on road conditions should be obtained from local authorities before departure.

If visitors intend diverting off public roads within Aboriginal Land areas, a permit is required from the relevant Aboriginal authority.

Beware of crocodiles in rivers, estuaries and coastal areas.

Beware of marine stingers in coastal areas (October to April). Swim within enclosures where possible.

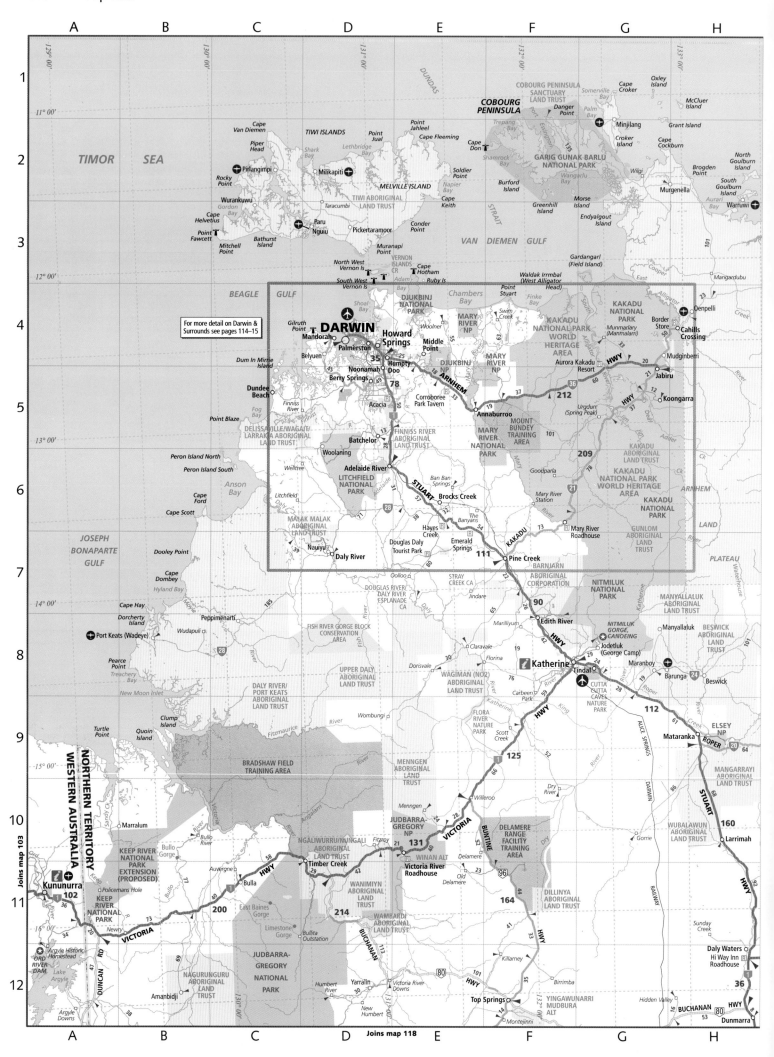

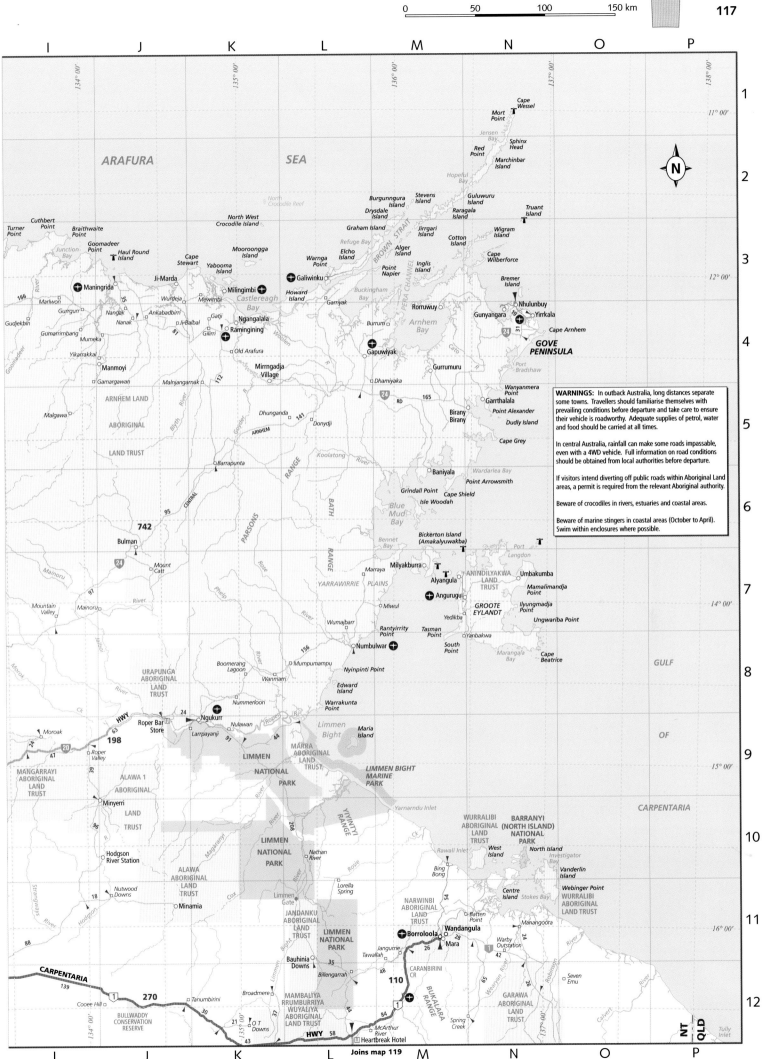

0 50 100 150 km

ARAFURA SEA

Turner Point
Cuthbert Point
Braithwaite Point
Goomadeer Point
Haul Round Island
Junction Bay
Marlwon
Gudjekbin
Gurrgurr
Gumarrirnbang
Mumeka
Yikarrakkal
Gamargawan
Malgawa

Maningrida
Ji-Marda
Wurdeja
Nangak
Nanak
Ankabadbirri
Ji-Balbal
Gatji
Gilirri
Manmoyi

Cape Stewart
Yabooma Island
North West Crocodile Island
North Crocodile Reef
Mooroongga Island

Milingimbi
Mewimbi
Howard Island
Ngangalala
Raminging
Old Arafura
Mirrngadja Village

Castlereagh Bay

Warnga Point
Galiwinku
Garriyak
Elcho Island
Refuge Bay
Point Napier

Burrum

Gapuwiyak
Dhamiyaka

ARNHEM LAND
ABORIGINAL
LAND TRUST

Dhunganda
Donydji
Barrapunta

Bulman
Mount Catt

Burgunngura Island
Drysdale Island
Graham Island
Stevens Island
Guluwuru Island
Raragala Island

Jirrgari Island
Alger Island
Inglis Island
Cotton Island
Wigram Island
Truant Island

Cape Wilberforce
Bremer Island

Rorruwuy
Nhulunbuy
Gunyangara
Yirrkala
Cape Arnhem

GOVE PENINSULA

Gurrumuru

Port Bradshaw

Wanyanmera Point
Garrthalala
Point Alexander
Birany Birany
Dudly Island
Cape Grey

Baniyala
Point Arrowsmith
Wardarlea Bay
Grindall Point
Cape Shield
Isle Woodah

Blue Mud Bay

Arnhem Bay

Pera Channel
Brown Strait
Hopeful Bay
Jensen Bay
Mort Point
Cape Wessel
Red Point
Sphinx Head
Marchinbar Island

Buckingham Bay

WARNINGS: In outback Australia, long distances separate some towns. Travellers should familiarise themselves with prevailing conditions before departure and take care to ensure their vehicle is roadworthy. Adequate supplies of petrol, water and food should be carried at all times.

In central Australia, rainfall can make some roads impassable, even with a 4WD vehicle. Full information on road conditions should be obtained from local authorities before departure.

If visitors intend diverting off public roads within Aboriginal Land areas, a permit is required from the relevant Aboriginal authority.

Beware of crocodiles in rivers, estuaries and coastal areas.

Beware of marine stingers in coastal areas (October to April). Swim within enclosures where possible.

Bennet Bay
Bickerton Island (Amakaluwakba)
Port Langdon
Milyakburra
Marraya
Alyangula
ANINDILYAKWA LAND TRUST
Umbakumba
Mamalimandja Point
Angurugu
Miwul
GROOTE EYLANDT
Yedikba
Ilyungmadja Point
Ungwariba Point
Yanbakwa
South Point
Marangala Bay
Cape Beatrice

Mountain Valley
Mainoru
Mainoru
Marraya
YARRAWIRRIE PLAINS
Wumajbarr
Rantyirrity Point
Tasman Point
Numbulwar
Nyinpinti Point

Boomerang Lagoon
Mumpumampu
Wanmarri
Nummerloori
Edward Island
Warrakunta Point

URAPUNGA ABORIGINAL LAND TRUST

Moroak
Ngukurr
Roper Bar Store
Nulawan
Larrpayanji
Roper Valley
Minyerri

MANGARRAYI ABORIGINAL LAND TRUST

ALAWA 1 ABORIGINAL LAND TRUST

Hodgson River Station
Nutwood Downs
Minamia

ALAWA ABORIGINAL LAND TRUST

Limmen Bight
Maria Island

MARRA ABORIGINAL LAND TRUST

LIMMEN NATIONAL PARK

LIMMEN BIGHT MARINE PARK

Yarnarndu Inlet

YIYINTYI RANGE

Nathan River
Lorella Spring
Limmen Gate

JANDANKU ABORIGINAL LAND TRUST

LIMMEN NATIONAL PARK

Bauhinia Downs
Billengarrah

MAMBALIYA RRUMBURRIYA WUYALIYA ABORIGINAL LAND TRUST

Broadmere
Tanumbirini
Cooee Hill

BULLWADDY CONSERVATION RESERVE

O T Downs

CARPENTARIA

Rawali Inlet

WURRALIBI ABORIGINAL LAND TRUST
West Island
Bing Bong

BARRANYI (NORTH ISLAND) NATIONAL PARK
North Island
Investigator Bay
Vanderlin Island

NARWINBI ABORIGINAL LAND TRUST

Centre Island
Stokes Bay
Webinger Point

WURRALIBI ABORIGINAL LAND TRUST

Batten Point
Borroloola
Wandangula
Mara
Jangurrie
Tawallah
Manangoora
Warby Outstation

CARANBIRINI CR

BUKALARA RANGE

Spring Creek

Seven Emu

GARAWA ABORIGINAL LAND TRUST

McArthur River
Heartbreak Hotel

NT QLD
Tully Inlet

GULF

OF

CARPENTARIA

Joins map 119

NT

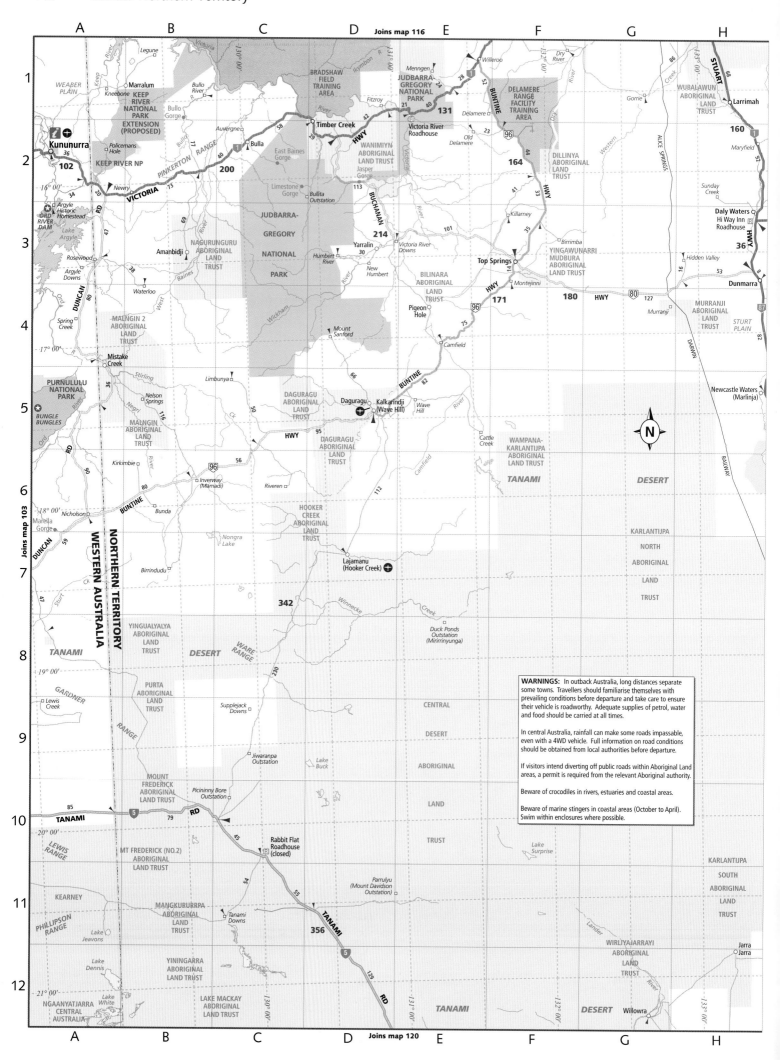

Joins map 116
Joins map 103
Joins map 120

WARNINGS: In outback Australia, long distances separate some towns. Travellers should familiarise themselves with prevailing conditions before departure and take care to ensure their vehicle is roadworthy. Adequate supplies of petrol, water and food should be carried at all times.

In central Australia, rainfall can make some roads impassable, even with a 4WD vehicle. Full information on road conditions should be obtained from local authorities before departure.

If visitors intend diverting off public roads within Aboriginal Land areas, a permit is required from the relevant Aboriginal authority.

Beware of crocodiles in rivers, estuaries and coastal areas.

Beware of marine stingers in coastal areas (October to April). Swim within enclosures where possible.

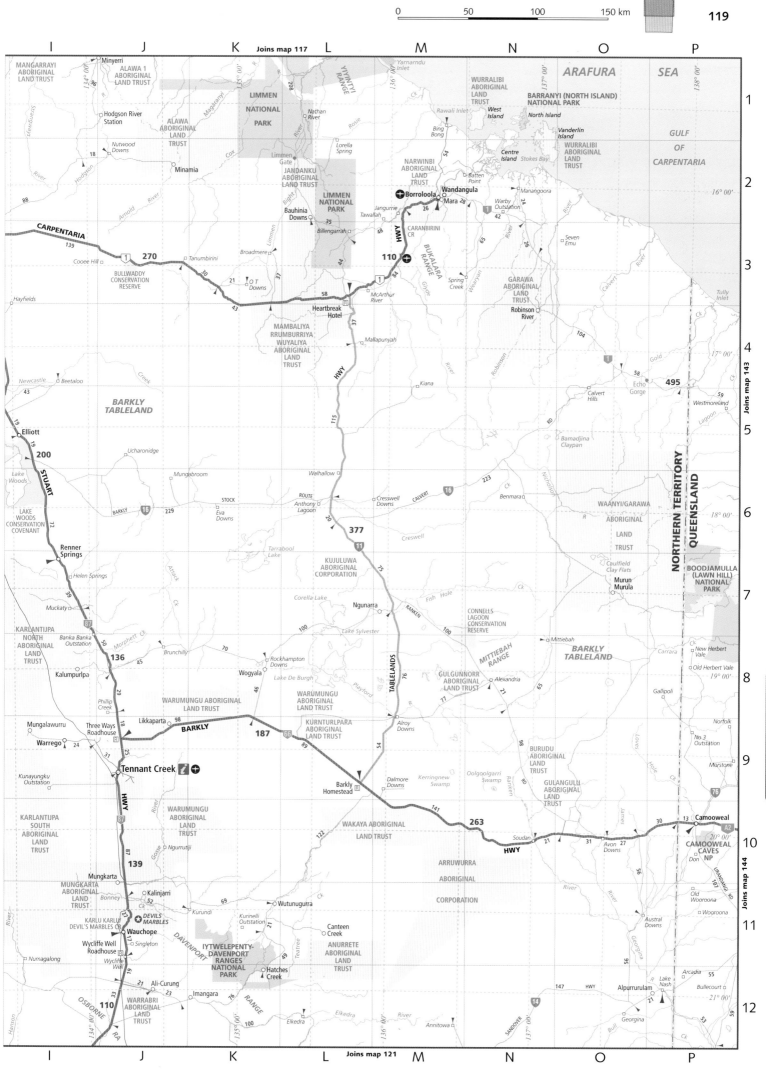

I   J   K   L   M   N   O   P

MANGARRAYI
ABORIGINAL
LAND TRUST

Minyerri
ALAWA 1
ABORIGINAL
LAND TRUST

Hodgson River
Station

ALAWA
ABORIGINAL
LAND
TRUST

Nutwood
Downs

Minamia

LIMMEN
NATIONAL
PARK

YIYINTYI
RANGE

Yarnarndu
Inlet

ARAFURA   SEA

GULF
OF
CARPENTARIA

Nathan
River

Rosie

Lorella
Spring

WURRALIBI
ABORIGINAL
LAND
TRUST

BARRANYI (NORTH ISLAND)
NATIONAL PARK

West
Island

North Island

Centre
Island   Stokes Bay

Vanderlin
Island

Rawali Inlet

Bing
Bong

Batten
Point

WURRALIBI
ABORIGINAL
LAND
TRUST

Manangoora

Hayfields

Cooee Hill

CARPENTARIA

139

270

Bullwaddy
CONSERVATION
RESERVE

Tanumbirini

O T
Downs

Broadmere

JANDANKU
ABORIGINAL
LAND TRUST

LIMMEN
NATIONAL
PARK

Bauhinia
Downs

Billengarrah

Borroloola
Mara

Wandangula

Jangurrie

Tawallah

CARANBIRINI
CR

NARWINBI
ABORIGINAL
LAND
TRUST

Warby
Outstation

Seven
Emu

Newcastle

Beetaloo

Heartbreak
Hotel

McArthur
River

Mallapunyah

MAMBALIYA
RRUMBURRIYA
WUYALIYA
ABORIGINAL
LAND
TRUST

Kiana

BUKALARA
RANGE

Spring
Creek

Robinson
River

GARAWA
ABORIGINAL
LAND
TRUST

Calvert
Hills

Echo
Gorge

495

Westmoreland

Tully
Inlet

BARKLY
TABLELAND

Elliott

200

STUART

Lake
Woods

Ucharonidge

Mungabroom

Walhallow

ROUTE

Anthony
Lagoon

Cresswell
Downs

Benmara

16

WAANYI/GARAWA
ABORIGINAL
LAND
TRUST

Bamadjina
Claypan

LAKE
WOODS
CONSERVATION
COVENANT

Renner
Springs

Helen Springs

STOCK

Eva
Downs

BARKLY   16   229

377

Creswell

11

Tarrabool
Lake

KUJULUWA
ABORIGINAL
CORPORATION

CALVERT   16

223

Caulfield
Clay Flats

Murun
Murula

BOODJAMULLA
(LAWN HILL)
NATIONAL
PARK

Muckaty

KARLANTIJPA
NORTH
ABORIGINAL
LAND
TRUST

87

Banka Banka
Outstation

136

Kalumpurlpa

Brunchilly

Corella Lake

Ngunarra

Lake Sylvester

Rockhampton
Downs

Wogyala

Lake De Burgh

Fish Hole

Ranken

CONNELLS
LAGOON
CONSERVATION
RESERVE

Mittiebah

MITTIEBAH
RANGE

Carrara

New Herbert
Vale

Old Herbert Vale

Gallipoli

BARKLY
TABLELAND

Norfolk

Mungalawurru

Warrego

Three Ways
Roadhouse

Likkaparta

98

BARKLY

187   66

89

WARUMUNGU ABORIGINAL
LAND TRUST

Phillip
Creek

WARUMUNGU
ABORIGINAL
LAND TRUST

Playford

TABLELANDS

KURNTURLPARA
ABORIGINAL
LAND TRUST

GULGUNNORR
ABORIGINAL
LAND TRUST

Alroy
Downs

Alexandria

BURUDU
ABORIGINAL
LAND
TRUST

No 3
Outstation

Morstone

Tennant Creek

Kunayungku
Outstation

HWY

KARLANTIJPA
SOUTH
ABORIGINAL
LAND TRUST

87

139

Mungkarta

WARUMUNGU
ABORIGINAL
LAND
TRUST

Barkly
Homestead

Dalmore
Downs

Kerringnew
Swamp

Oolgoolgarri
Swamp

GULANGULU
ABORIGINAL
LAND
TRUST

Camooweal

76

263

HWY

Soudan

Avon
Downs

CAMOOWEAL
CAVES
NP

Don

URANDANGI RD

MUNGKARTA
ABORIGINAL
LAND
TRUST

Kalinjarri

Bonney

Ngurrutji

WAKAYA ABORIGINAL
LAND TRUST

ARRUWURRA
ABORIGINAL

CORPORATION

Old
Wooroona

Wooroona

KARLU KARLU
DEVIL'S MARBLES CR

DEVILS
MARBLES

Wauchope

Kurundi

Wutunugurra

Kurinelli
Outstation

Canteen
Creek

ANURRETE
ABORIGINAL
LAND
TRUST

Austral
Downs

Wycliffe Well
Roadhouse

DAVENPORT

IYTWELEPENTY-
DAVENPORT
RANGES
NATIONAL PARK

Singleton

Wycliffe
Well

Numagalong

Ali-Curung

Imangara

RANGE

Hatches
Creek

Elkedra

Elkedra

Annitowa

HWY

14

Alpurrurulam

Lake
Nash

Georgina

Arcadia

Bullecourt

Osborne RA

110

WARRABRI
ABORIGINAL
LAND
TRUST

Hanson

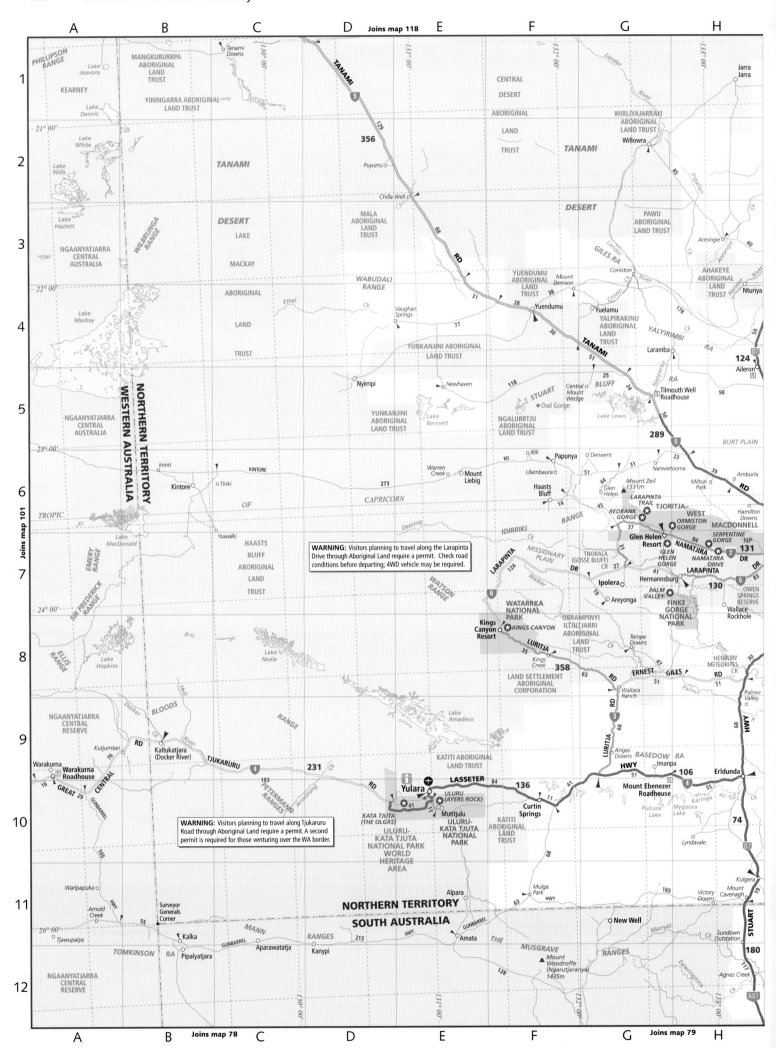

Joins map 118

Joins map 101

WARNING: Visitors planning to travel along the Larapinta Drive through Aboriginal Land require a permit. Check road conditions before departing; 4WD vehicle may be required.

WARNING: Visitors planning to travel along Tjukaruru Road through Aboriginal Land require a permit. A second permit is required for those venturing over the WA border.

NORTHERN TERRITORY
SOUTH AUSTRALIA

Joins map 78

Joins map 79

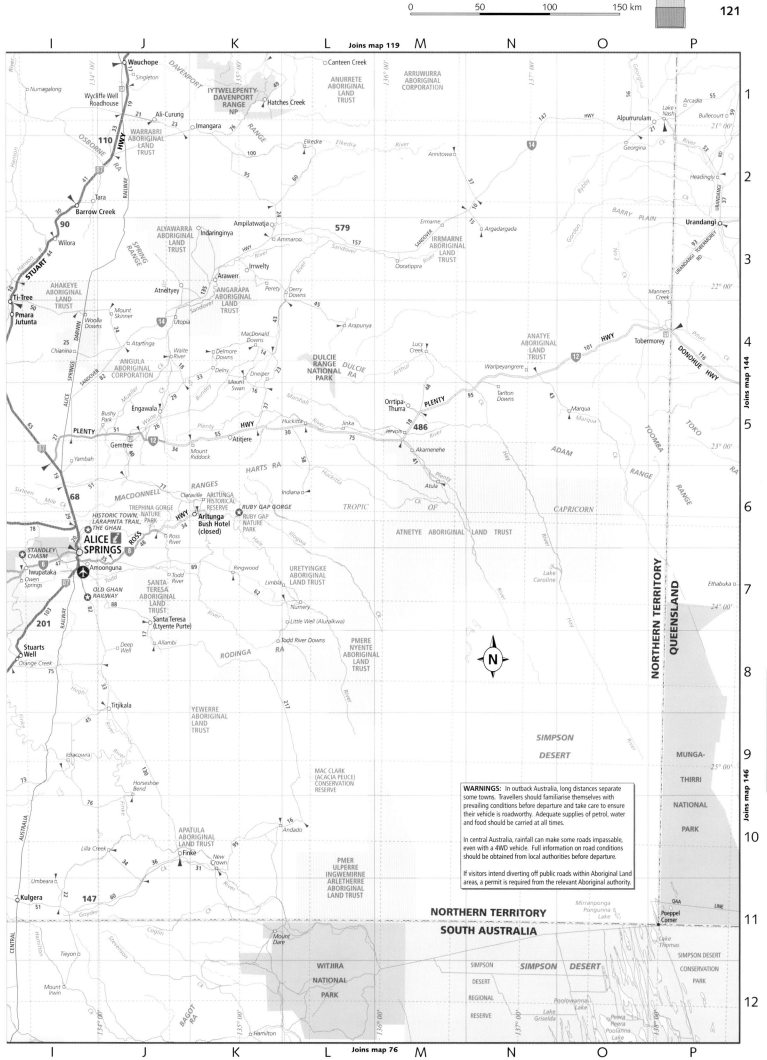

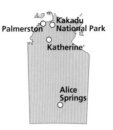

ALICE SPRINGS *page 121 I7*

 41 Todd Mall
(08) 8952 5800 or 1800 645 199
www.discovercentralaustralia.com

KAKADU NATIONAL PARK *page 115 O4*

Bowali Visitor Centre
Kakadu Hwy, Jabiru
(08) 8938 1120
www.travelnt.com

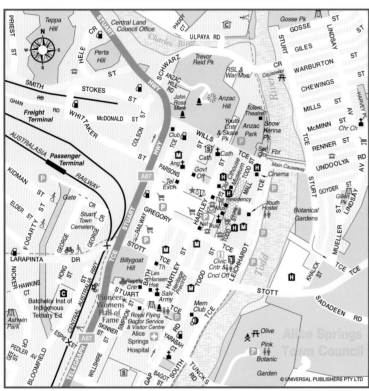

KATHERINE *page 116 F8*

Cnr Lindsay St and Katherine Tce
(08) 8972 2650 or 1800 653 142
www.visitkatherine.com.au

PALMERSTON *page 116 D4*

 6 Bennett St, Darwin
(08) 8980 6000 or 1300 138 886
www.tourismtopend.com.au

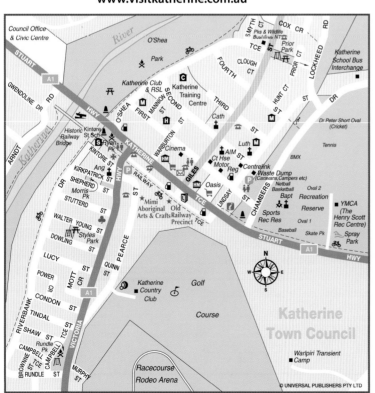

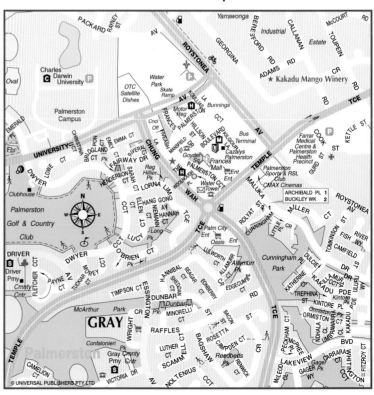

TENNANT CREEK *page 119 J9*

Battery Hill
Peko Rd
(08) 8962 1281
www.barklytourism.com.au

KATA TJUTA (THE OLGAS) *page 120 E10*

Uluru–Kata Tjuta Cultural Centre
Lasseter Hwy
(08) 8956 1128
www.tourismnt.com.au or
www.parksaustralia.gov.au

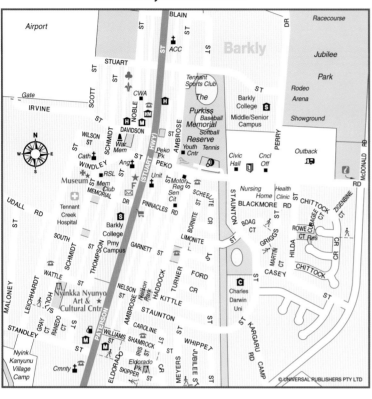

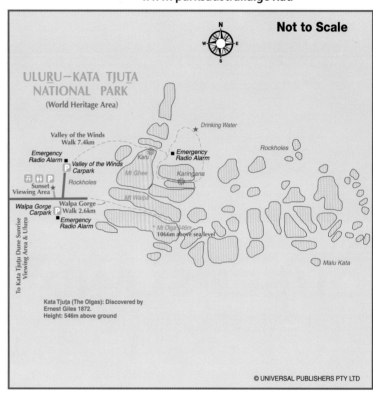

ULURU (AYERS ROCK) *page 120 E10*

Uluru–Kata Tjuta Cultural Centre
Lasseter Hwy
(08) 8956 1128
www.travelnt.com or
www.parksaustralia.gov.au

YULARA (AYERS ROCK RESORT)

Yulara Dr   *page 120 E10*
Yulara
(08) 8957 7324 or 1300 134 044
www.ayersrockresort.com.au

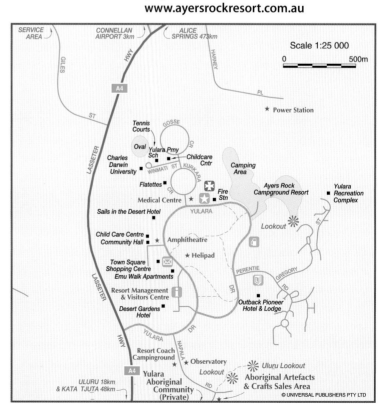

NT

QUEENSLAND

The second largest state in Australia, Queensland is big and incredibly varied, covering 1,730,648 square kilometres. It extends roughly 2100 kilometres north to south, and 1150 kilometres east to west.

Shadowing the coastline for about 2000 kilometres, the stunning Great Barrier Reef is one of the natural wonders of the world and perhaps the state's greatest asset. It offers the ultimate in diving and snorkelling. Its rich fauna, with dugongs, turtles, extensive coral gardens and 1500 species of fish is protected by World Heritage–listing. Even so, the Reef is only one of the fabulous natural attractions found throughout the state. Visitors to Queensland will discover some of the world's most beautiful beaches, luxuriant tropical rainforests, idyllic islands, vast deserts and fascinating towns – enhanced by a relaxed pace, languid lifestyle and a climate that is close to perfect.

Evidence that Aboriginal people have lived in Queensland for many thousands of years can be seen in the traditional rock art found in such places as Carnarvon Gorge in the Central Highlands, and Quinkan Country galleries in the Laura River Valley on Cape York. Visitors can inspect these significant sites with Aboriginal guides and learn about Indigenous lifestyles at cultural centres such as the Dreamtime Cultural Centre near

Rockhampton, or the Tjapukai Aboriginal Culture Park near Cairns.

European settlement of Queensland occurred quite late compared with the rest of Australia. In 1824 a convict station for the most intractable prisoners from the southern gaols was built near Moreton Bay, but after a year of active resistance from Aboriginal tribes it was abandoned and relocated to where Brisbane stands today.

Queensland's capital, Brisbane, is a very cool city, despite its subtropical climate. It is home to a lively young arts scene and is a hotbed of new music and fashion. This has not affected Brisbane's open friendliness or its relaxed way of life, however, making it a perfect holiday destination.

Touring Queensland by car is easy, although a four-wheel drive is required to reach some of the more remote outback regions. The Bruce Highway links Brisbane with Cairns and gives access to all coastal areas in between. Sealed roads continue to Cooktown, but dirt roads take over further north into the pristine wilderness of Cape York. A network of roads covers the

vast outback areas, with convenient links to many points along the Bruce Highway. The enormous distances can also be covered by rail or air. Brisbane, Cairns and Coolangatta have international airports, and there are regional airports at many of the larger towns and cities.

Mt Barney, Gold Coast

Places of interest

	MAP REF		MAP REF
Atherton Tableland	141 L7	Kronosaurus Korner	145 L3
Australia Zoo	134 F5	Kuranda Scenic Railway	141 L6
Australian Stockman's Hall of Fame,		Lamington National Park	135 D11
Longreach	138 B10	Lone Pine Koala Sanctuary	132 G4
The Big Pineapple	134 G4	Mount Coot-tha	132 G2
Birdsville	146 D3	Museum of Tropical Queensland,	
Bundaberg Rum Distillery	137 M3	Townsville	141 N11
Cape York Peninsula	142	Noosa National Park	131 H1
Carnarvon Gorge	136 F3	Outback at Isa	143 D11
Cobb + Co. Museum, Toowoomba	137 L9	Rainbow Beach	137 N61
Currumbin Wildlife Sanctuary	135 G11	reefHQ Aquarium, Townsville	141 N11
Daintree National Park	141 L4	Sea World	135 G9
Dreamtime Cultural Centre	139 M10	Skyrail Rainforest Cableway	141 L6
Dreamworld	135 F8	Surfers Paradise	135 G10
Flinders Discovery Centre	138 B4	Tamborine Mountain	135 E9
Fraser Island	137 O4	Tjapukai Aboriginal Cultural Park	141 L6
Glass House Mountains	134 F6	Undara Lava Tubes	141 J9
Granite Belt Wine Country	137 K12	Underwater World SEALIFE Aquarium,	
Great Barrier Reef	137, 139, 141, 142	Mooloolaba	134 H4
Hervey Bay	137 N4	Warner Bros. Movie World	135 F9
Jupiters Casino, Gold Coast	135 G10	Whitsunday Passage	139 K3

INFORMATION CENTRE

Brisbane Visitor Information Centre
Regent Building, 167 Queen St Mall, Brisbane;
(07) 3006 6290
www.queensland.com
www.visitbrisbane.com.au

Millaa Millaa Falls, Atherton Tablelands, Far North Queensland

MAPS

QUEENSLAND

Queensland

Central Brisbane	129
Metro Brisbane, North	130–1
Metro Brisbane, South	132–3
Brisbane & Surrounds, North	134
Brisbane & Surrounds, South	135
South-eastern Queensland	136–7
North-eastern Queensland	138–9
Far North-eastern Queensland	140–1
Cape York Peninsula	142
Far North-western Queensland	143
North-western Queensland	144–5
South-western Queensland	146–7

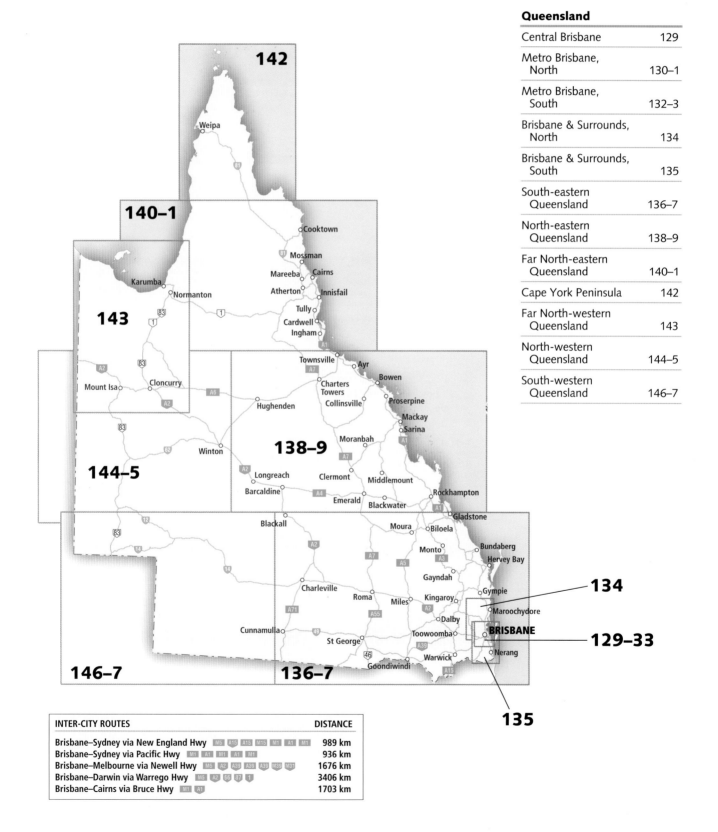

INTER-CITY ROUTES	DISTANCE
Brisbane–Sydney via New England Hwy	989 km
Brisbane–Sydney via Pacific Hwy	936 km
Brisbane–Melbourne via Newell Hwy	1676 km
Brisbane–Darwin via Warrego Hwy	3406 km
Brisbane–Cairns via Bruce Hwy	1703 km

Brisbane city skyline

Brisbane

Brisbane is the northernmost capital on Australia's east coast; a subtropical city on the banks of the Brisbane River. The city lies 14 kilometres inland and the river has always been an integral part of Brisbane life. Paddlesteamers, yachts, floating restaurants, ferries and cruise boats can be seen on the river, and there are restaurants and cafes with beautiful water views lining its shore.

John Oxley, Surveyor-General, sailed up this river in 1823 and named it the Brisbane River after Sir Thomas Brisbane, then Governor of New South Wales. From 1825–42, Brisbane was a penal settlement. The Old Windmill on Wickham Terrace is the city's oldest building, constructed by convicts in 1828. It became known as the 'Tower of Torture' because, when the wind dropped, the convicts had to crush the grain on a treadmill.

Today, Brisbane is a busy, modern city with an extensive transport system, a variety of restaurants, and good entertainment and nightlife. The city has many parks and gardens, with the largest, the City Botanic Gardens, situated on a bend of the Brisbane River. Roma Street Parkland is the world's largest subtropical garden in a city centre. Mount Coot-tha Botanic Gardens, at Toowong, features a scented garden, tropical plant dome and the Sir Thomas Brisbane Planetarium.

Places of interest

	MAP REF		MAP REF
ANZAC Square	129 E6	Queen Street Mall	129 E7
Brisbane Convention & Exhibition Centre	129 C9	Queensland Art Gallery	129 D8
		Queensland Gallery of Modern Art	129 C7
City Botanic Gardens	129 F8	Queensland Maritime Museum	129 E10
Commissariat Store Museum	129 E8	Queensland Museum and Sciencentre	129 D8
Customs House	129 F6	Queensland Performing Arts Centre	129 D8
Fortitude Valley	129 H4	Riverside Centre	129 F6
The Gabba (Brisbane Cricket Ground)	129 H11	Roma Street Parkland	129 D5
Kangaroo Point	129 H10	South Bank Parklands	129 D9
King George Square	129 E7	State Library of Queensland	129 C7
Old Government House	129 F9	Story Bridge	129 G5
Old Windmill	129 E6	Suncorp Stadium	129 B6
Parliament House	129 E8	Treasury Brisbane (Casino)	129 E7

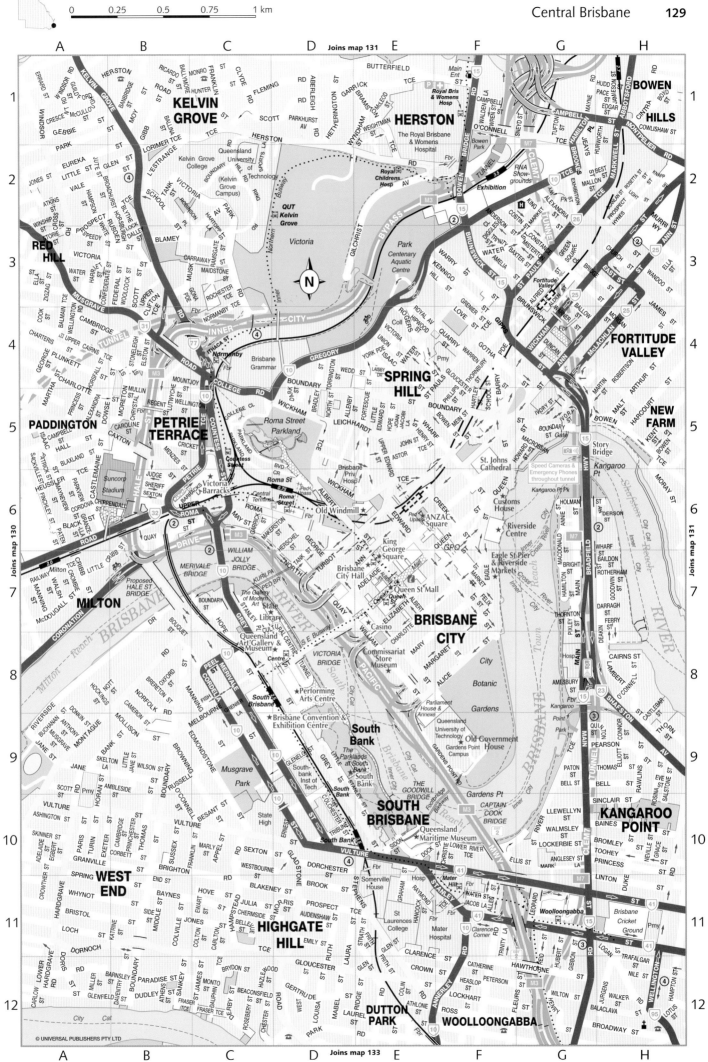

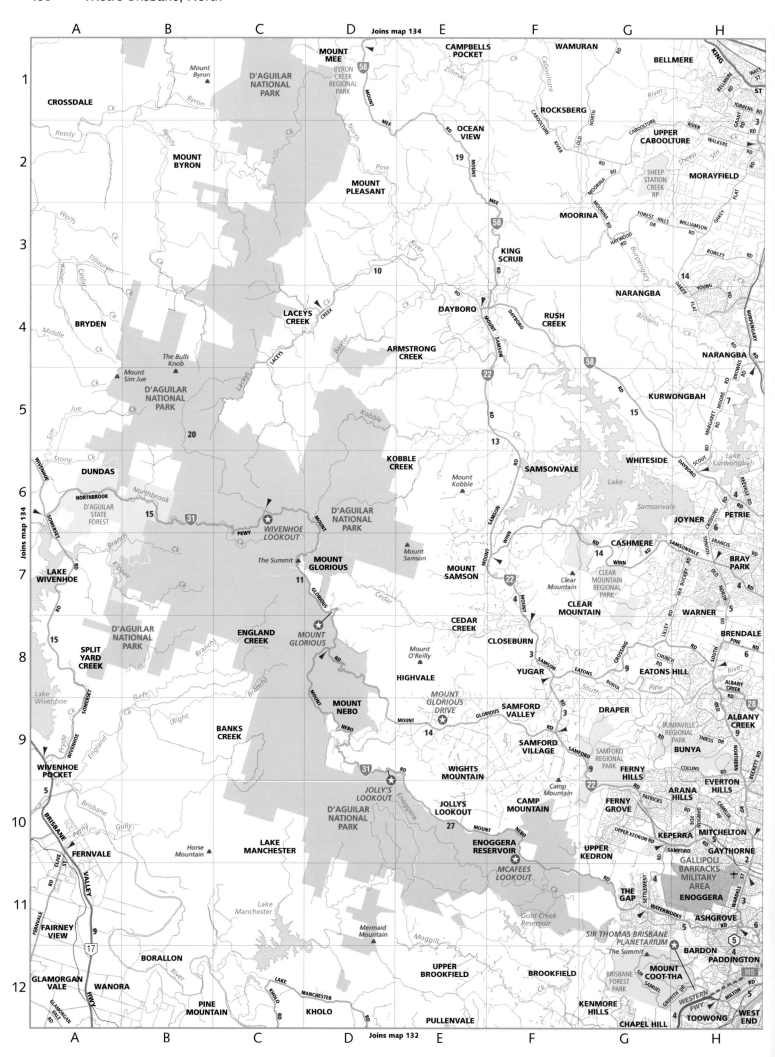

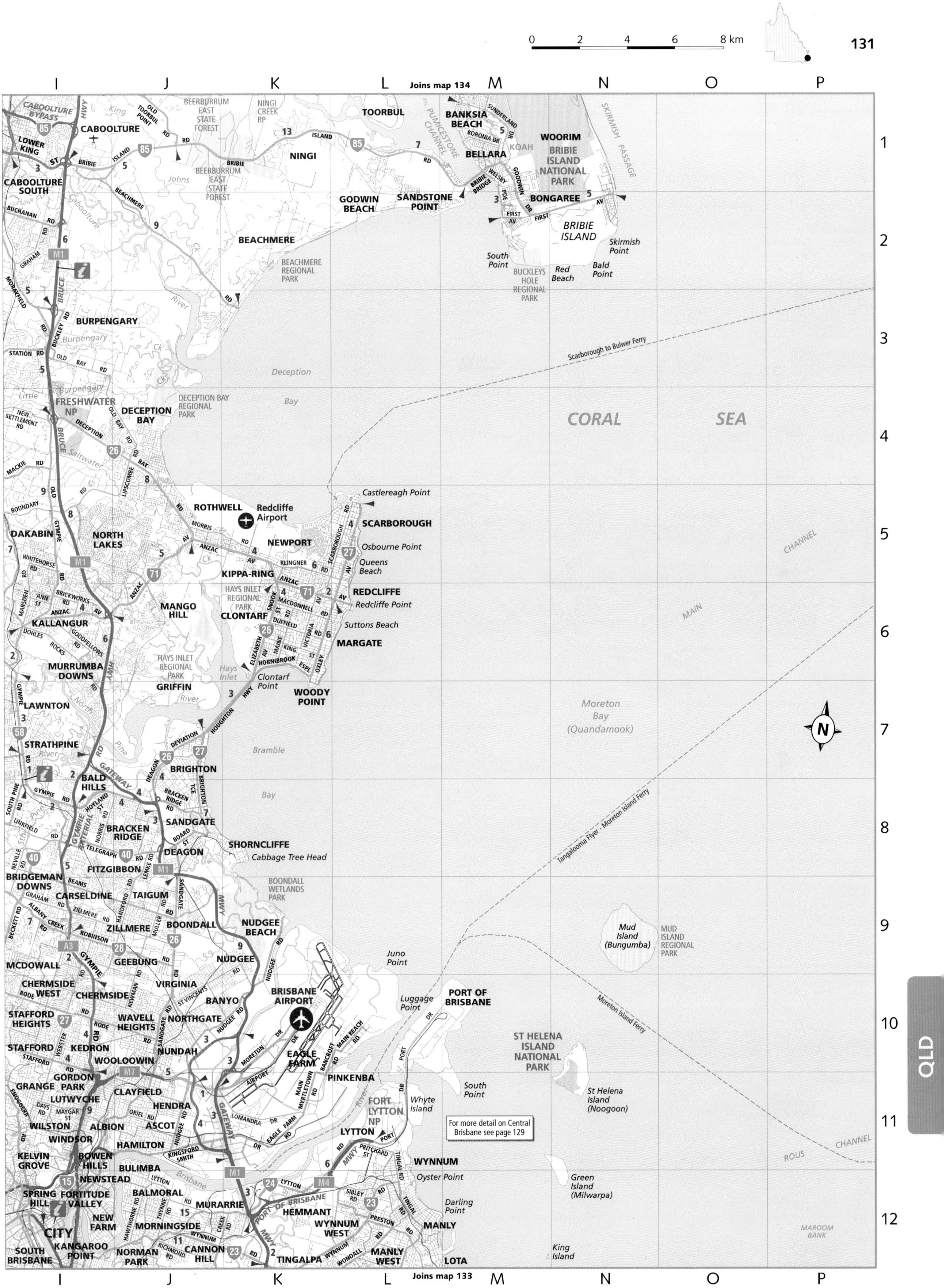

Joins map 134

CABOOLTURE BYPASS
OLD TOORBUL POINT
BEERBURRUM EAST STATE FOREST
NINGI CREEK RP
TOORBUL
BANKSIA BEACH
SUNDERLAND DR
KOAH
WOORIM
BRIBIE ISLAND NATIONAL PARK
LOWER KING
CABOOLTURE
BRIBIE ISLAND
13
ISLAND
85
7
BORONIA DR
GODWIN DR
WELSBY PDE
BELLARA
ST
BRIBIE BRIDGE
BONGAREE
NINGI
85
BEERBURRUM EAST STATE FOREST
CABOOLTURE SOUTH
BUCHANAN RD
BEACHMERE
BRIBIE
Johns
5
BEACHMERE
GODWIN BEACH
SANDSTONE POINT
FIRST AV
FIRST AV
AV

M1
BURPENGARY
BEACHMERE REGIONAL PARK
South Point
BRIBIE ISLAND
BUCKLEYS HOLE REGIONAL PARK
Red Beach
Bald Point
Skirmish Point

Deception
Bay
Scarborough to Bulwer Ferry

CORAL SEA

Little
FRESHWATER NP
DECEPTION BAY
DECEPTION BAY REGIONAL PARK
26
BRUCE
Saltwater

MACKIE RD
BOUNDARY RD
DAKABIN
NORTH LAKES
ROTHWELL
Redcliffe Airport
Castlereagh Point
SCARBOROUGH
Osbourne Point
Queens Beach
CHANNEL

M1
71
NEWPORT
KIPPA-RING
KLINGNER
27
REDCLIFFE
Redcliffe Point
Suttons Beach
MARGATE
MAIN

MANGO HILL
HAYS INLET REGIONAL PARK
CLONTARF
26
SNOOK ST
MACDONNELL
DUFFIELD
VICTORIA ST
ELIZABETH AV
KING
OXLEY
71

KALLANGUR
GOODFELLOWS
DOHLES ROCKS
MURRUMBA DOWNS
HAYS INLET REGIONAL PARK
GRIFFIN
Hays Inlet
Clontarf Point
WOODY POINT
Moreton Bay
(Quandamook)

LAWNTON
58
North
Pine
River
HOUGHTON HWY
DEVIATION
Bramble
Bay

STRATHPINE
Pine River
26
27
BRIGHTON
Tangalooma Flyer - Moreton Island Ferry

BALD HILLS
GYMPIE
BRACKEN RIDGE
SANDGATE
SHORNCLIFFE
Cabbage Tree Head

BRIDGEMAN DOWNS
40
DEAGON
FITZGIBBON
BOONDALL WETLANDS PARK

CARSELDINE
TAIGUM
ZILLMERE
BOONDALL
NUDGEE BEACH
Mud Island (Bungumba)
MUD ISLAND REGIONAL PARK

MCDOWALL
A3
28
GEEBUNG
NUDGEE
Juno Point

CHERMSIDE WEST
CHERMSIDE
VIRGINIA
BANYO
BRISBANE AIRPORT
PORT OF BRISBANE

STAFFORD HEIGHTS
27
WAVELL HEIGHTS
NORTHGATE
Luggage Point
ST HELENA ISLAND NATIONAL PARK

STAFFORD
KEDRON
NUNDAH
M7
EAGLE FARM
South Point
St Helena Island (Noogoon)

GORDON PARK
GRANGE
LUTWYCHE
CLAYFIELD
HENDRA
ASCOT
PINKENBA
FORT LYTTON NP
Whyte Island

WILSTON
WINDSOR
ALBION
HAMILTON
LYTTON
For more detail on Central Brisbane see page 129

KELVIN GROVE
BOWEN HILLS
BULIMBA
WYNNUM
Oyster Point
Green Island (Milwarpa)
CHANNEL
ROUS

SPRING HILL
15
FORTITUDE VALLEY
NEWSTEAD
BALMORAL
24
M4
23
Darling Point
King Island
MAROOM BANK

CITY
KANGAROO POINT
SOUTH BRISBANE
NEW FARM
MORNINGSIDE
23
MURARRIE
HEMMANT
WYNNUM WEST
MANLY
LOTA

NORMAN PARK
CANNON HILL
TINGALPA
MANLY WEST

Joins map 133

QLD

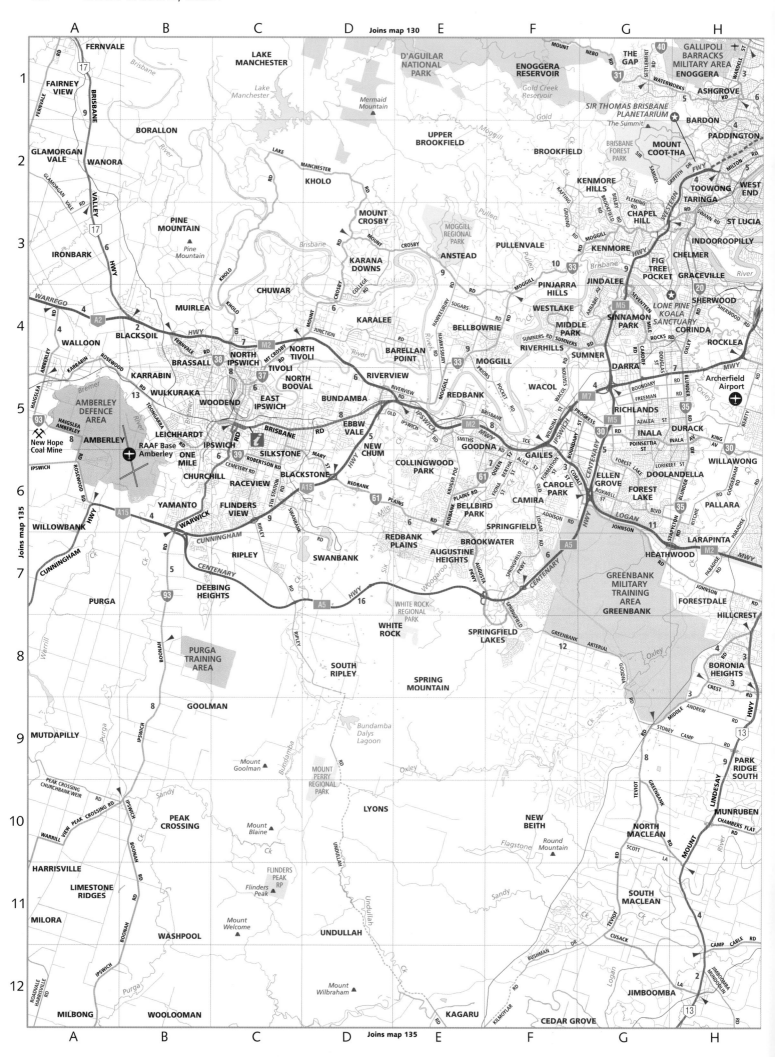

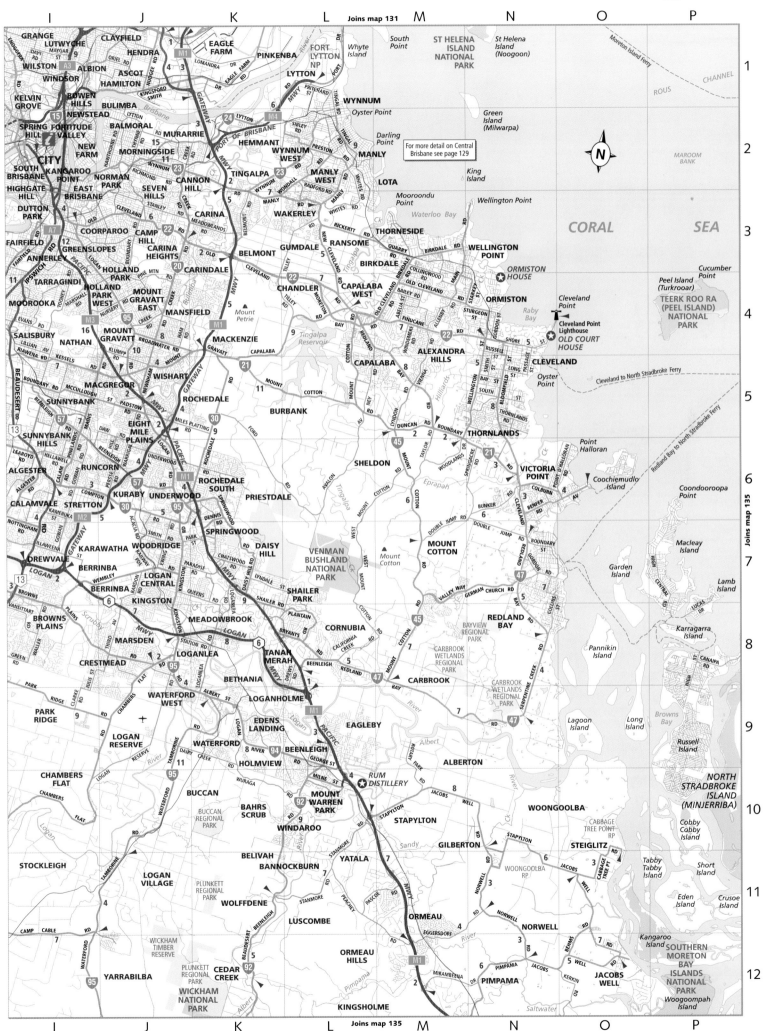

0 2 4 6 8 km

QLD

CORAL **SEA**

I J K L M N O P

1
2
3
4
5
6
7
8
9
10
11
12

ST HELENA ISLAND NATIONAL PARK

St Helena Island (Noogoon)

South Point

Whyte Island

Green Island (Milwarpa)

King Island

MAROOM BANK

Darling Point

Oyster Point

For more detail on Central Brisbane see page 129

GRANGE
LUTWYCHE
CLAYFIELD
HENDRA
EAGLE FARM
PINKENBA
FORT LYTTON NP
LYTTON

WILSTON
ALBION
ASCOT
HAMILTON
MURARRIE
HEMMANT

WINDSOR
BOWEN HILLS
NEWSTEAD
BALMORAL
MORNINGSIDE
WYNNUM
WYNNUM WEST

KELVIN GROVE
SPRING HILL
FORTITUDE VALLEY
NEW FARM
CANNON HILL
TINGALPA
MANLY
MANLY WEST
LOTA

CITY
KANGAROO POINT
NORMAN PARK
SEVEN HILLS
CARINA
WAKERLEY

SOUTH BRISBANE
HIGHGATE HILL
EAST BRISBANE
CAMP HILL
CARINA HEIGHTS
BELMONT
GUMDALE
THORNESIDE

DUTTON PARK
COORPAROO
CARINDALE
RANSOME
BIRKDALE

FAIRFIELD
ANNERLEY
GREENSLOPES
CHANDLER
CAPALABA WEST
WELLINGTON POINT

IPSWICH
TARRAGINDI
HOLLAND PARK
HOLLAND PARK WEST
MANSFIELD
ORMISTON HOUSE

MOOROOKA
MOUNT GRAVATT EAST
CLEVELAND POINT
CUCUMBER POINT

SALISBURY
NATHAN
MOUNT GRAVATT
MACKENZIE
ALEXANDRA HILLS
ORMISTON
CLEVELAND

MACGREGOR
WISHART
ROCHEDALE
CAPALABA

SUNNYBANK
EIGHT MILE PLAINS
ROCHEDALE SOUTH
BURBANK
SHELDON
THORNLANDS

SUNNYBANK HILLS
RUNCORN
PRIESTDALE

ALGESTER
CALAMVALE
STRETTON
KURABY
UNDERWOOD
SPRINGWOOD
VICTORIA POINT

DREWVALE
KARAWATHA
WOODRIDGE
DAISY HILL
MOUNT COTTON

BERRINBA
LOGAN CENTRAL
SHAILER PARK
VENMAN BUSHLAND NATIONAL PARK
REDLAND BAY

BROWNS PLAINS
KINGSTON
MEADOWBROOK
CORNUBIA

MARSDEN
LOGANLEA
TANAH MERAH
CARBROOK

CRESTMEAD
BETHANIA
WATERFORD WEST
LOGANHOLME
EAGLEBY

PARK RIDGE
EDENS LANDING
ALBERTON

LOGAN RESERVE
WATERFORD
BEENLEIGH
HOLMVIEW

CHAMBERS FLAT
BUCCAN
MOUNT WARREN PARK
RUM DISTILLERY
WOONGOOLBA

STOCKLEIGH
LOGAN VILLAGE
BAHRS SCRUB
WINDAROO
STAPYLTON
GILBERTON
STEIGLITZ

BELIVAH
BANNOCKBURN
YATALA

WOLFFDENE
LUSCOMBE
NORWELL

YARRABILBA
CEDAR CREEK
ORMEAU
JACOBS WELL

WICKHAM NATIONAL PARK
ORMEAU HILLS
PIMPAMA

KINGSHOLME

NORTH STRADBROKE ISLAND (MINJERRIBA)

SOUTHERN MORETON BAY ISLANDS NATIONAL PARK

Russell Island
Lamb Island
Macleay Island
Karragarra Island
Coochiemudlo Island
Garden Island
Long Island
Lagoon Island
Pannikin Island
Coondooroopa Point
Cobby Cobby Island
Tabby Tabby Island
Short Island
Eden Island
Crusoe Island
Kangaroo Island
Woogoompah Island

Peel Island (Turkrooar)
TEERK ROO RA (PEEL ISLAND) NATIONAL PARK

Raby Bay
Cleveland Point Lighthouse
OLD COURT HOUSE

Waterloo Bay
Mooroondu Point
Wellington Point

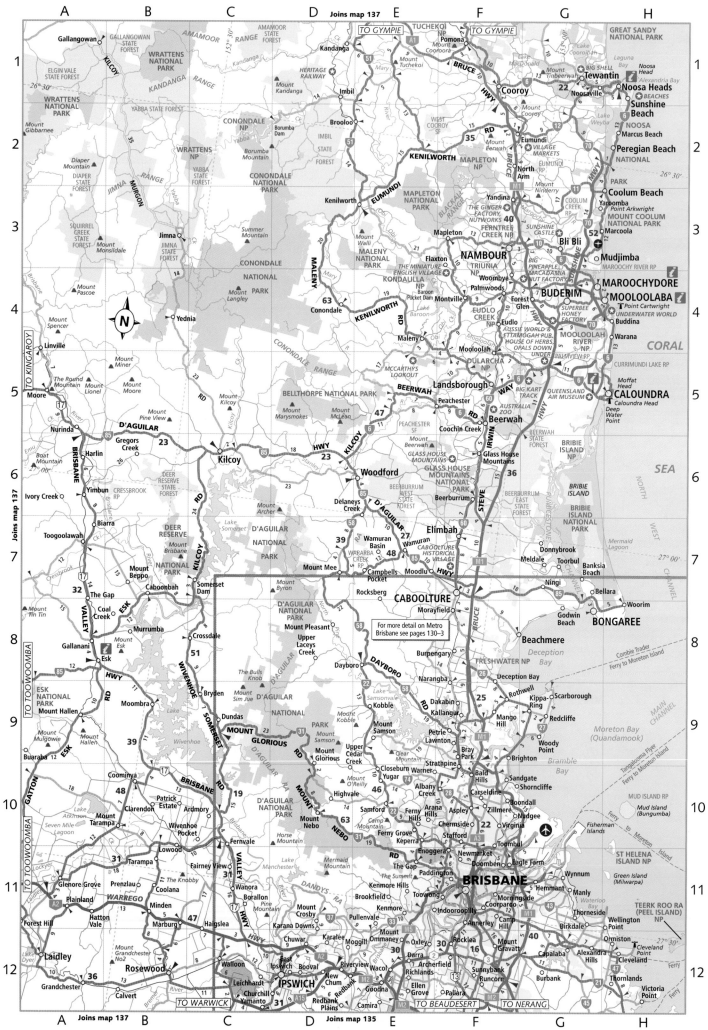

0   10   20   30 km

Joins map 137

GREAT SANDY
NATIONAL PARK

Gallangowan

GALLANGOWAN
STATE
FOREST

WRATTENS
NATIONAL
PARK

ELGIN VALE
STATE FOREST

AMAMOOR
STATE
FOREST

AMAMOOR

RANGE

TUCHEKOI
NP

Kandanga

TO GYMPIE

Pomona
Mount
Cooroora

TO GYMPIE

BIG SHELL

Laguna
Bay

Noosa
Head

Alexandria Bay

Noosa Heads

Tewantin

22

BRUCE

Cooroy

Lake
MacDonald

Mount
Tinbeerwah

Noosaville

BEACHES

Sunshine
Beach

NOOSA

Marcus Beach

Peregian Beach

NATIONAL

Coolum Beach

MOUNT COOLUM
NATIONAL PARK

Marcoola

Mudjimba

MAROOCHYDORE

MOOLOOLABA

CORAL

SEA

WRATTENS
NATIONAL
PARK

KANDANGA RANGE

YABBA STATE FOREST

Mount
Gibbarnee

Mount
Kandanga

Imbil

Brooloo

HERITAGE
RAILWAY

CONONDALE
NP

Borumba
Dam

Borumba
Mountain

IMBIL
STATE
FOREST

Kenilworth

KENILWORTH

35

RD

Mount
Beerwah

North
Arm

Yandina

Eumundi

EUMUNDI

VILLAGE
MARKETS

THE GINGER
FACTORY,
NUTWORKS

40

FERNTREE
CREEK NP

Bli Bli

SUNSHINE
CASTLE

52

Coolum
Beach

CALOUNDRA

BONGAREE

BRISBANE

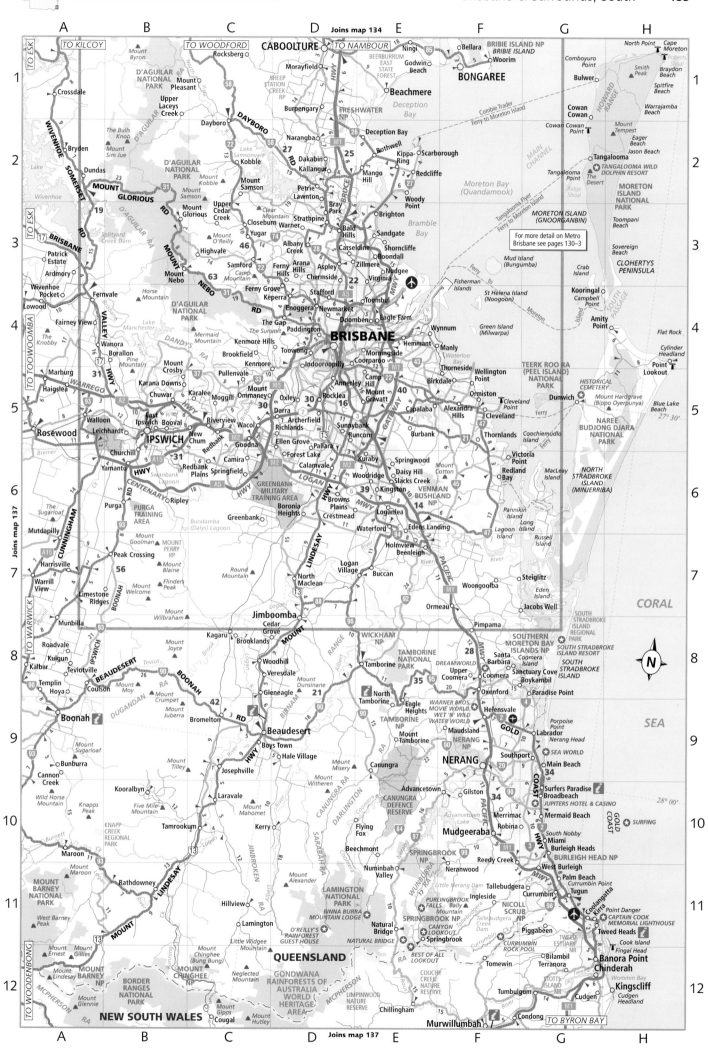

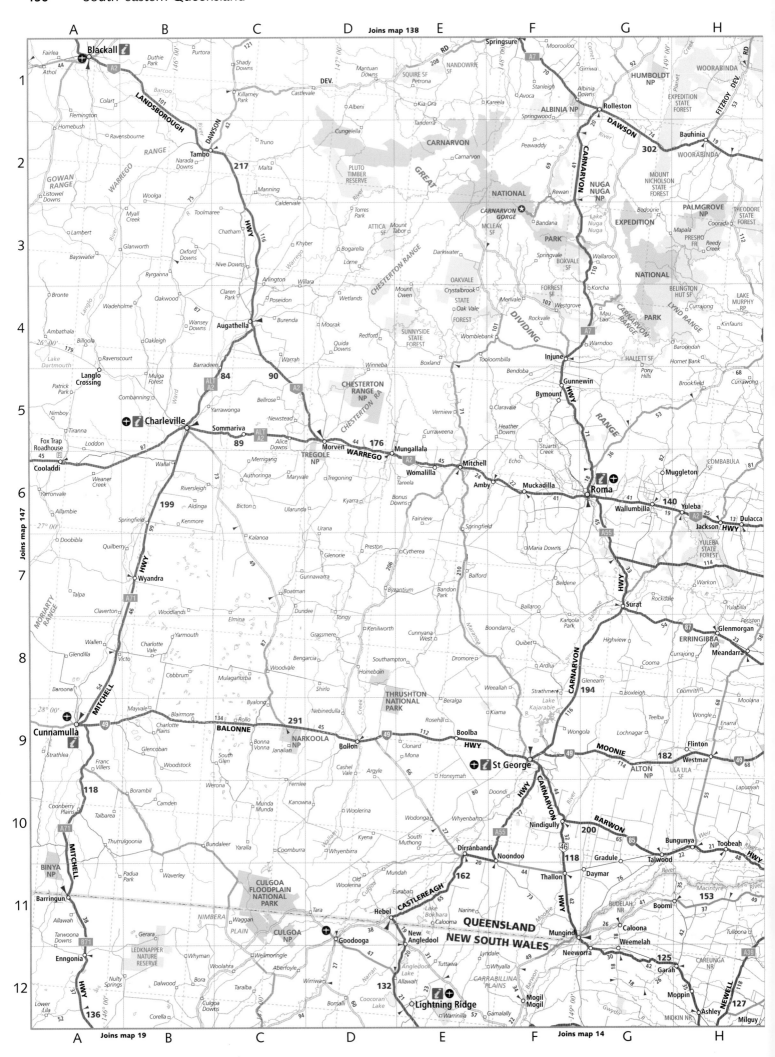

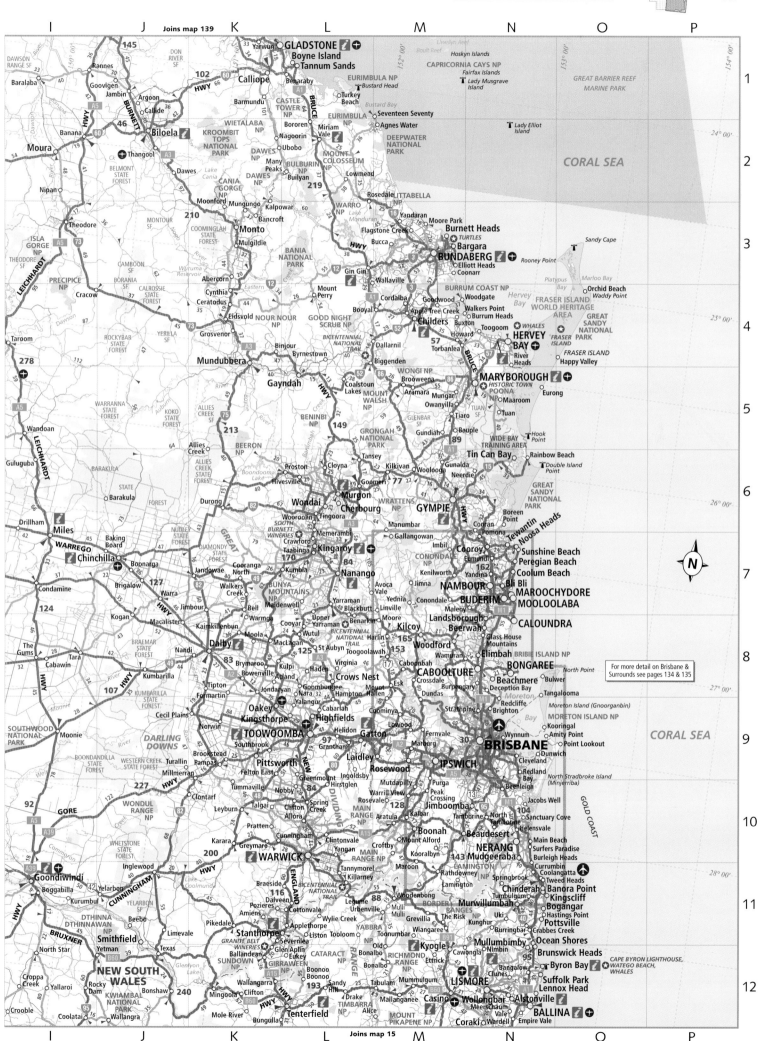

CORAL SEA

GREAT BARRIER REEF
MARINE PARK

CAPRICORNIA CAYS NP

GLADSTONE
Boyne Island
Tannum Sands

Calliope

BUNDABERG

Burnett Heads
Bargara

HERVEY BAY

MARYBOROUGH

Biloela

Moura

Monto

Mundubbera

Gayndah

GYMPIE

Tin Can Bay

Rainbow Beach

Noosa Heads
Sunshine Beach
Peregian Beach
Coolum Beach

Sunshine Beach

Murgon
Cherbourg

Miles

Chinchilla

Kingaroy

Nanango

NAMBOUR
BUDERIM
MAROOCHYDORE
MOOLOOLABA

CALOUNDRA

Dalby

Crows Nest

Kilcoy
Woodford

CABOOLTURE

BONGAREE
Beachmere

BRISBANE

Highfields

TOOWOOMBA

Gatton

IPSWICH

Pittsworth

Laidley
Rosewood

GOLD COAST

Jimboomba

NERANG
Mudgeeraba

Surfers Paradise
Burleigh Heads
Coolangatta

WARWICK

Beaudesert

Goondiwindi

Murwillumbah

Kingscliff

Stanthorpe

Byron Bay

NEW SOUTH WALES

Tenterfield

LISMORE

Casino

BALLINA

CORAL SEA

QLD

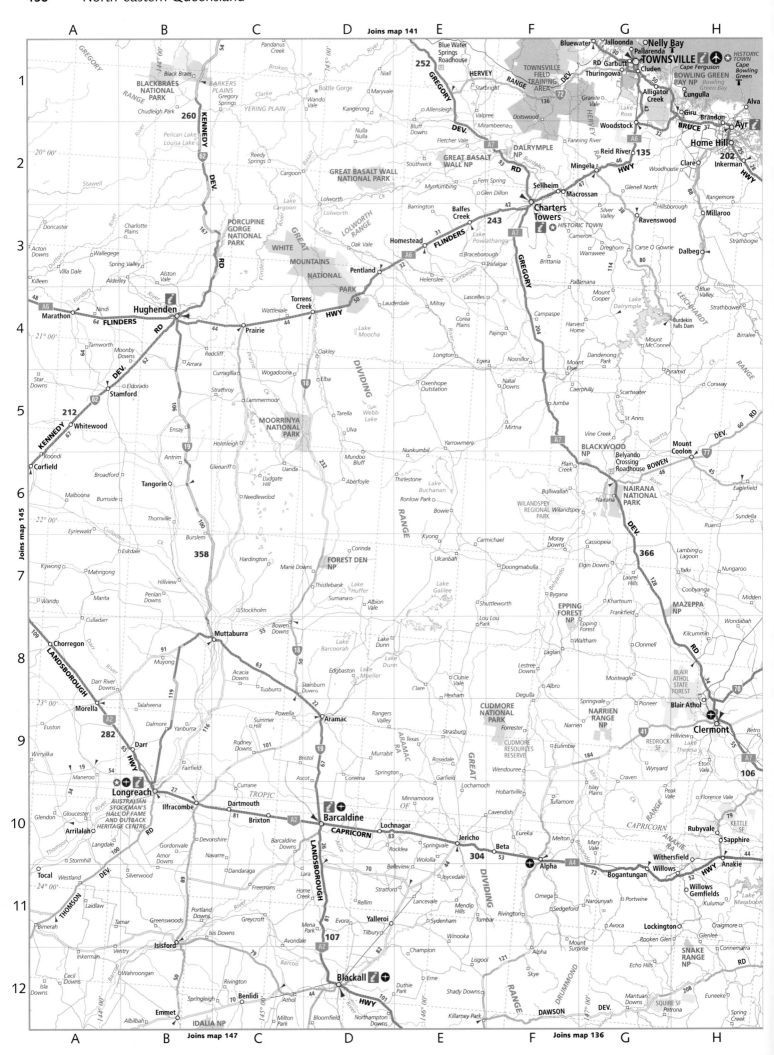

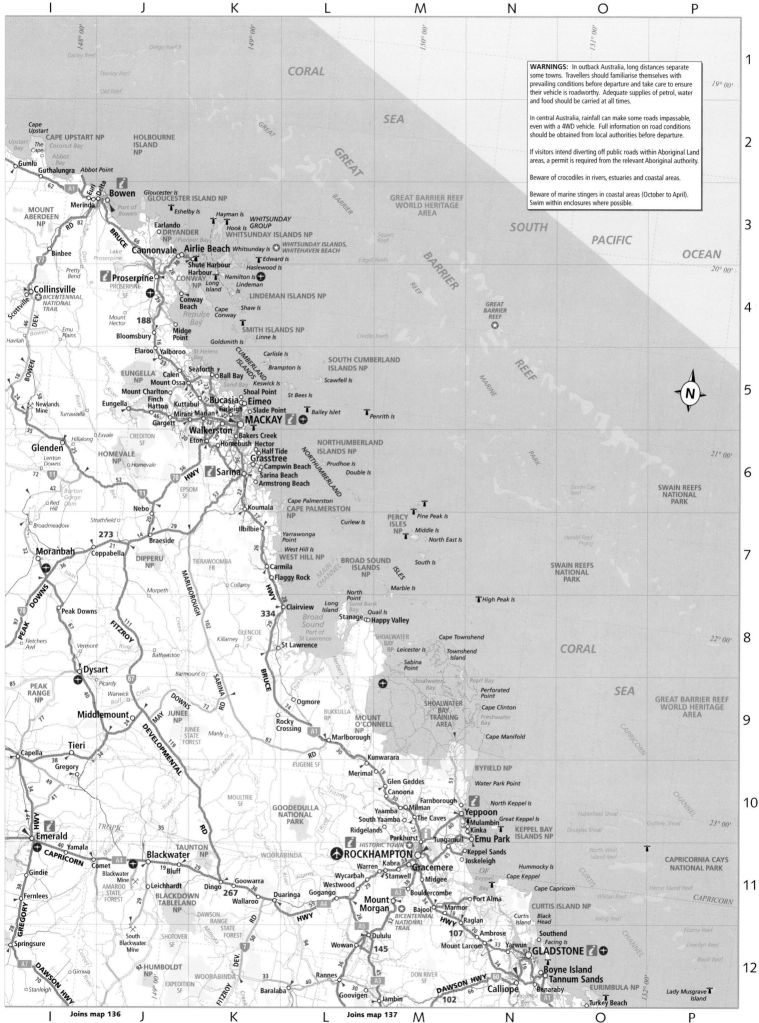

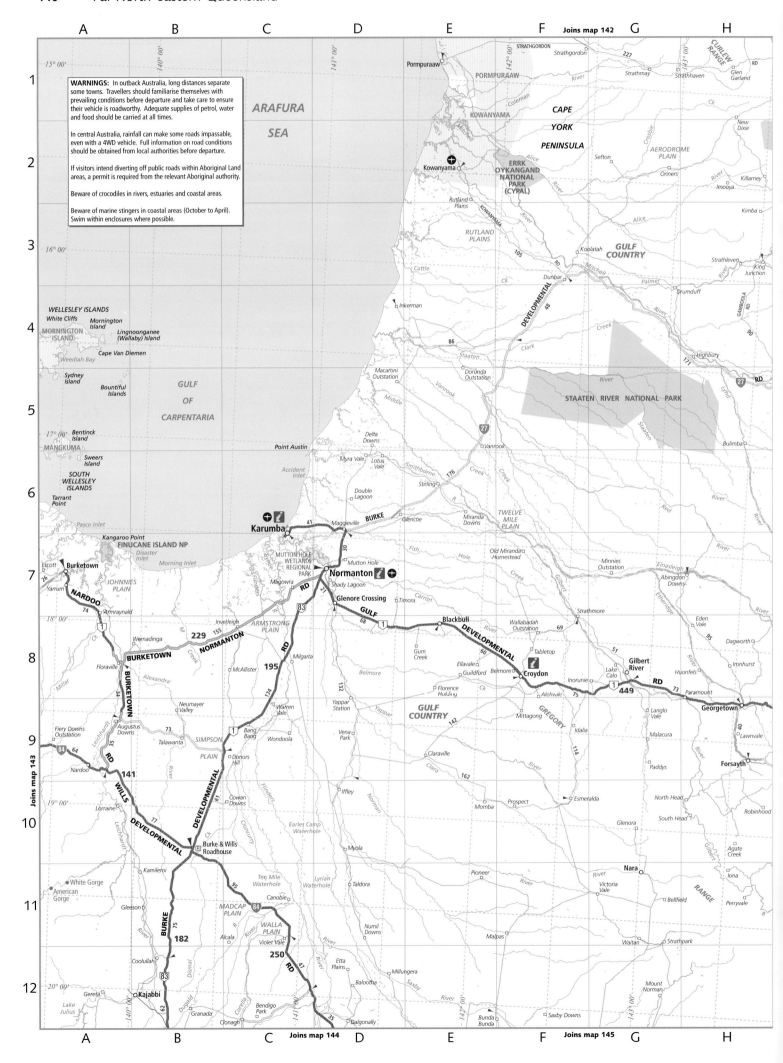

Joins map 142
Joins map 143
Joins map 144
Joins map 145

WARNINGS: In outback Australia, long distances separate some towns. Travellers should familiarise themselves with prevailing conditions before departure and take care to ensure their vehicle is roadworthy. Adequate supplies of petrol, water and food should be carried at all times.

In central Australia, rainfall can make some roads impassable, even with a 4WD vehicle. Full information on road conditions should be obtained from local authorities before departure.

If visitors intend diverting off public roads within Aboriginal Land areas, a permit is required from the relevant Aboriginal authority.

Beware of crocodiles in rivers, estuaries and coastal areas.

Beware of marine stingers in coastal areas (October to April). Swim within enclosures where possible.

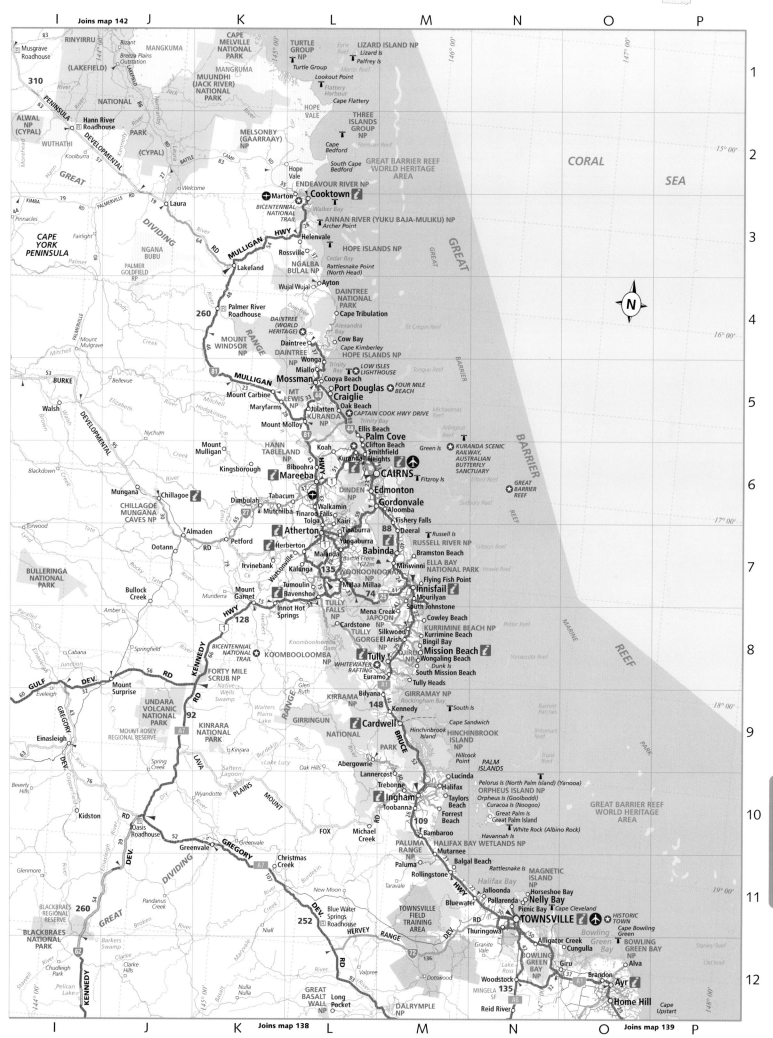

0 25 50 75 100 km

CORAL

SEA

QLD

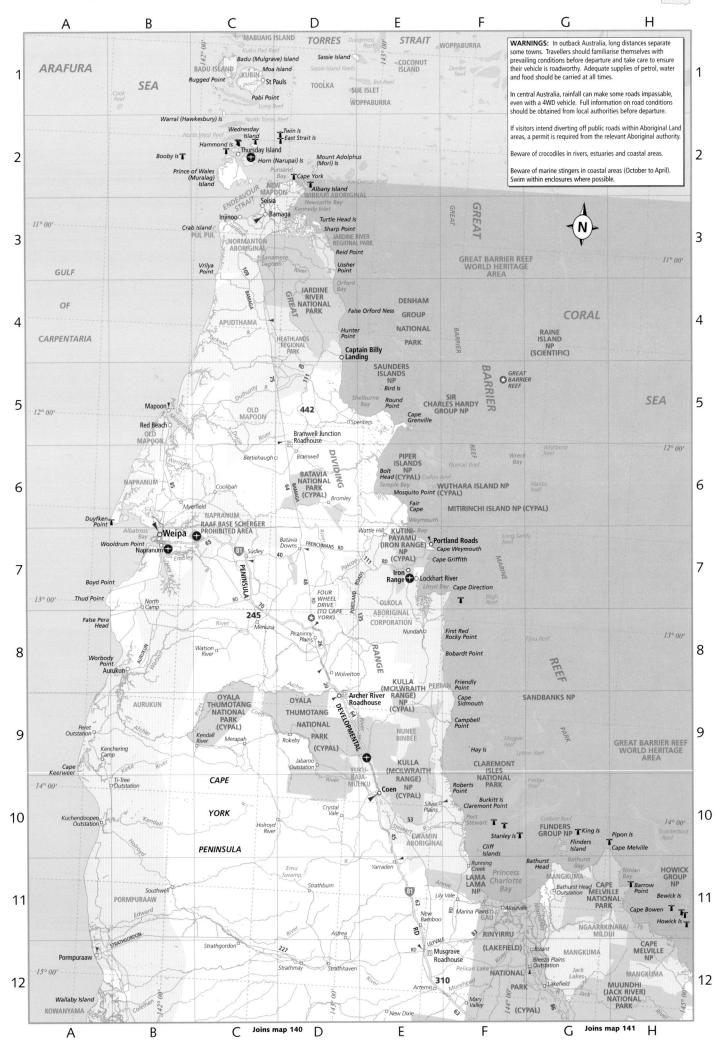

0 25 50 75 100 km

WARNINGS: In outback Australia, long distances separate some towns. Travellers should familiarise themselves with prevailing conditions before departure and take care to ensure their vehicle is roadworthy. Adequate supplies of petrol, water and food should be carried at all times.

In central Australia, rainfall can make some roads impassable, even with a 4WD vehicle. Full information on road conditions should be obtained from local authorities before departure.

If visitors intend diverting off public roads within Aboriginal Land areas, a permit is required from the relevant Aboriginal authority.

Beware of crocodiles in rivers, estuaries and coastal areas.

Beware of marine stingers in coastal areas (October to April). Swim within enclosures where possible.

Joins map 140

Joins map 141

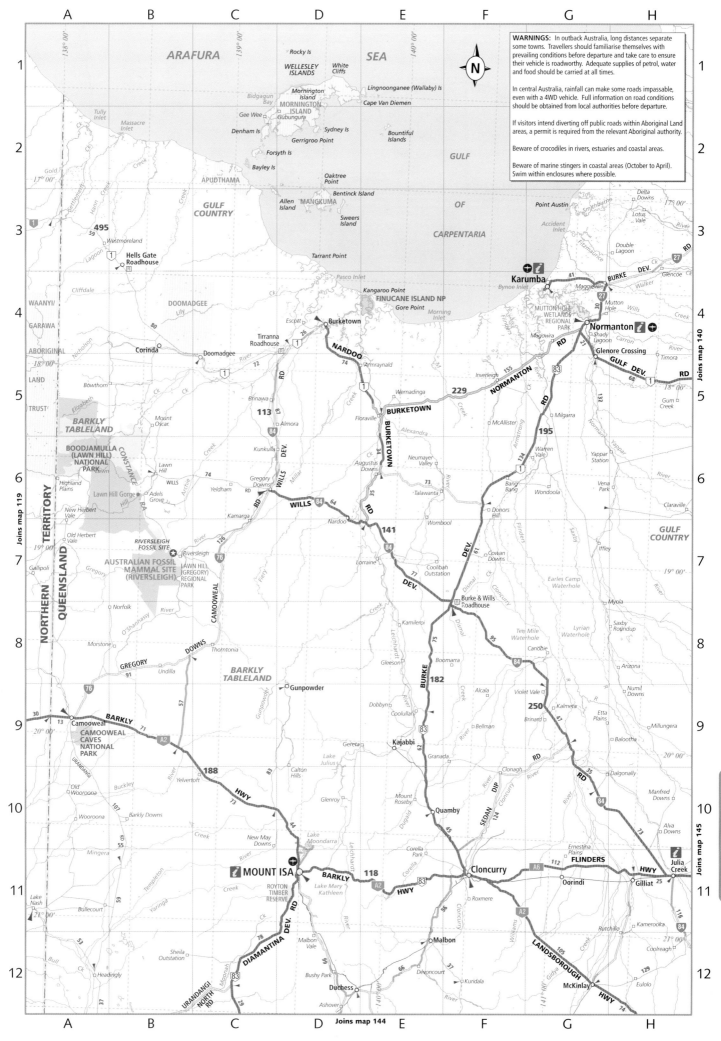

0 25 50 75 100 km

WARNINGS: In outback Australia, long distances separate some towns. Travellers should familiarise themselves with prevailing conditions before departure and take care to ensure their vehicle is roadworthy. Adequate supplies of petrol, water and food should be carried at all times.

In central Australia, rainfall can make some roads impassable, even with a 4WD vehicle. Full information on road conditions should be obtained from local authorities before departure.

If visitors intend diverting off public roads within Aboriginal Land areas, a permit is required from the relevant Aboriginal authority.

Beware of crocodiles in rivers, estuaries and coastal areas.

Beware of marine stingers in coastal areas (October to April). Swim within enclosures where possible.

ARAFURA SEA

WELLESLEY ISLANDS

Rocky Is
White Cliffs

Bidgagun Bay
Mornington Island
Lingnoonganee (Wallaby) Is
Cape Van Diemen

Gee Wee
Gubungura
MORNINGTON ISLAND

Denham Is
Sydney Is
Bountiful Islands

GULF

Tully Inlet
Massacre Inlet

Forsyth Is
Gerrigroo Point

Bayley Is
Oaktree Point

Gold
17° 00'

APUDTHAMA

Bentinck Island

GULF COUNTRY

Allen Island
MANGKUMA
Sweers Island

OF

Delta Downs
17° 00'
Point Austin
Smithburne
Lotus Vale
River

CARPENTARIA

Tarrant Point

Accident Inlet

Double Lagoon

RD 27

WAANYI/ GARAWA

495
59

Westmoreland

DOOMADGEE

Lily

Pasco Inlet

Kangaroo Point
FINUCANE ISLAND NP
Gore Point

Karumba
Bynoe Inlet
Maggieville

Morning Inlet

41
27
MUTTON HOLE WETLANDS REGIONAL PARK
30

BURKE DEV.
Glencoe Ck
Walker
Mutton Hole
Wills
Creek

Hells Gate Roadhouse
R

ABORIGINAL

Cliffdale

Escott
Burketown

Normanton

18° 00'

Hann Creek
Settlement
Ck

LAND

Corinda

Tirranna Roadhouse

NARDOO

Magovira
Shady Lagoon
Carron
Timora
Glenore Crossing

GULF DEV.
68
RD

Nicholson
80
26
1

Doomadgee

74
Armraynald

River
21

Inverleigh
155
83

River

RD

132

Gum Creek

TRUST

Bowthorn

BARKLY TABLELAND

Mount Oscar

Brinawa
113
84
Almora

229
NORMANTON

195

Elizabeth

BOODJAMULLA (LAWN HILL) NATIONAL PARK

Lawn Hill

Kunkulla

Floraville
BURKETOWN

Wernadinga

McAllister

Milgarra

Creek

Gregory Downs
74
Yeldham

Augustus Downs

Neumayer Valley
Alexandra

134
Warren Vale
Yappar Station

Yappar River

Highland Plains

Lawn Hill Gorge

Adels Grove
WILLS
Millar

BURKETOWN

Talawanta
73

1
Bang Bang
Wondoola

Vena Park

GULF COUNTRY

Claraville

New Herbert Vale

Kamarga
126
Nardoo
64
141

Wombool

Donors Hill

19° 00'

Old Herbert Vale

RIVERSLEIGH FOSSIL SITE
Riversleigh
76
84
Lorraine
77

Cowan Downs
Iffley

River

River

Gallipoli

AUSTRALIAN FOSSIL MAMMAL SITE (RIVERSLEIGH)

LAWN HILL (GREGORY) REGIONAL PARK

Coolibah Outstation

Dismal
61

Earles Camp Waterhole

Norfolk
River
CAMOOWEAL

Frey

Burke & Wills Roadhouse

Myola

Saxby Roundup

O'Shanassy River

Kamileroi

DEV.

Ten Mile Waterhole
Lyrian Waterhole

Morstone
DOWNS
Thorntonia

BARKLY TABLELAND

Gleeson
BURKE
75
95

Canobie

Arizona

GREGORY
91
Undilla

Gunpowder

Dobbyn
Coolullah
182

Boomarra
Alcala

84

Numil Downs

30
13
76
57

Camooweal
CAMOOWEAL CAVES NATIONAL PARK

20° 00'

Gunpowder Creek

Violet Vale
250
Kalmeta

Etta Plains

Balootha
Millungera

BARKLY
71
A2

Gereta
83
62
Kajabbi

Bellman

Brinard
47

Clonagh
RD
35

Dalgonally
20° 00'

188

Yelvertoft
73
83

Lake Julius
Calton Hills

Granada

Djip Cloncurry River

Ernestina Plains
84
Manfred Downs

Old Wooroona

Buckley Creek

HWY

Glenroy

Mount Roseby

Clonagh

SEDAN
124

73
Alva Downs

Wooroona
107
Barkly Downs
RD
55

New May Downs

Lake Moondarra
44

Quamby
45

Dugald River

FLINDERS
112

Julia Creek

Mingera
Creek

MOUNT ISA

BARKLY
118

Corella Park

Cloncurry
A6

Oorindi
Gilliat
25

HWY

Lake Nash
21° 00'
59
Templeton Creek

ROYTON TIMBER RESERVE

Lake Mary Kathleen

HWY
83
A2

Roxmere

Kamerooka
84

Bullecourt

Varinga

DIAMANTINA DEV. RD

Malbon Vale

Malbon

Devoncourt
Williams River
A2

Rutchillo
118

37
Headingly
53
78

Sheila Outstation

Bushy Park
66

LANDSBOROUGH
105

Coolreagh
129
Eulolo

Bull
37

URANDANGI NORTH RD
Moorah River
83
29

Duchess
Ashover

Kuridala
Gidya Creek

McKinlay

HWY
74

Joins map 144

QLD

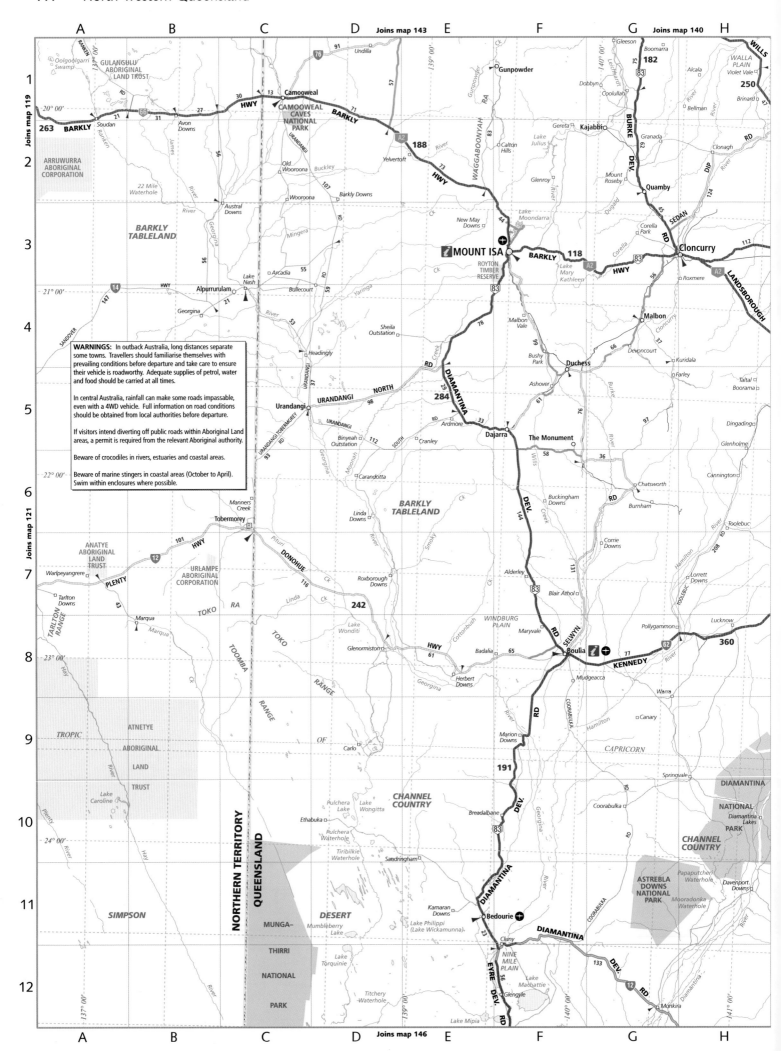

Joins map 143
Joins map 140
Joins map 119
Joins map 121
Joins map 146

WARNINGS: In outback Australia, long distances separate some towns. Travellers should familiarise themselves with prevailing conditions before departure and take care to ensure their vehicle is roadworthy. Adequate supplies of petrol, water and food should be carried at all times.

In central Australia, rainfall can make some roads impassable, even with a 4WD vehicle. Full information on road conditions should be obtained from local authorities before departure.

If visitors intend diverting off public roads within Aboriginal Land areas, a permit is required from the relevant Aboriginal authority.

Beware of crocodiles in rivers, estuaries and coastal areas.

Beware of marine stingers in coastal areas (October to April). Swim within enclosures where possible.

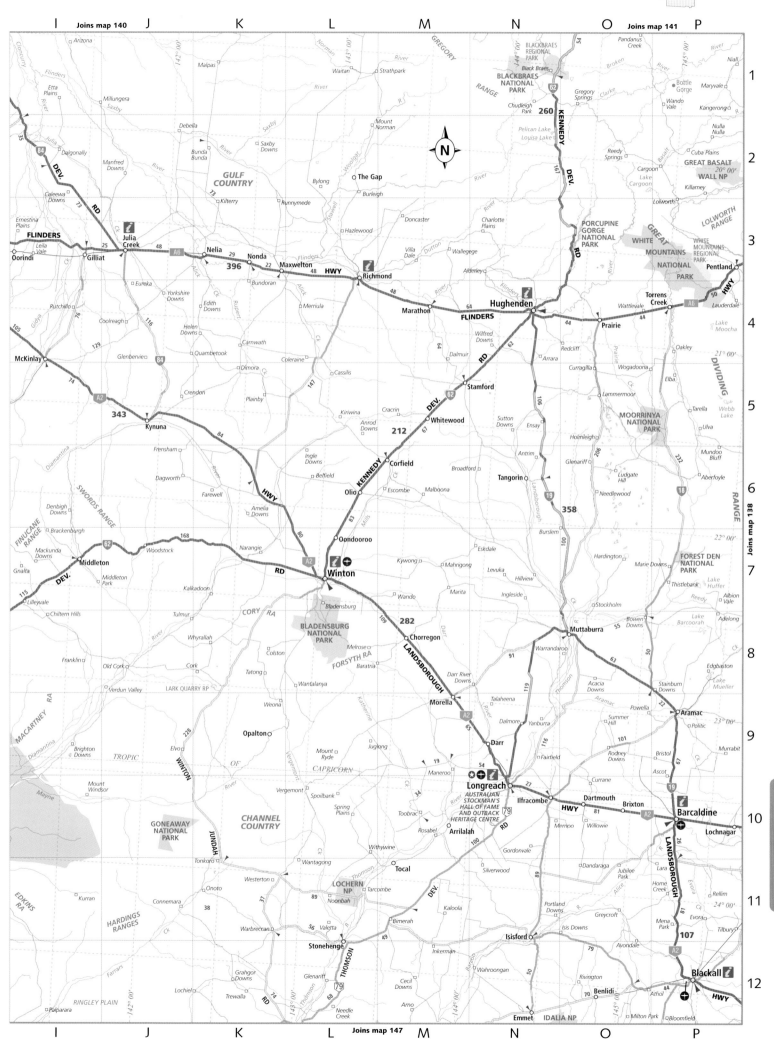

0   25   50   75   100 km

I   J   K   L   M   N   O   P

1
2
3
4
5
6
7
8
9
10
11
12

QLD

Joins map 138

GULF COUNTRY

Arizona
Malpas
Strathpark
Pandanus Creek
Niall
Maryvale

Etta Plains
Millungera
Saxby
Debella
Waitan
BLACKBRAES REGIONAL PARK
Black Braes
Bottle Gorge

Dalgonally
Manfred Downs
Bunda Bunda
Saxby Downs
Mount Norman
BLACKBRAES NATIONAL PARK
Gregory Springs
Wando Vale
Kangerong

Caleewa Downs
73
Bylong
Burleigh
Chudleigh Park
260
Pelican Lake
Louisa Lake
Reedy Springs
Nulla Nulla

Ernestina Plains
Leila Vale
FLINDERS
Julia Creek
Nelia
Nonda
Maxwelton
Richmond
The Gap
Hazlewood
Doncaster
Charlotte Plains
Cargoon
Lake Cargoon
Lolworth
Cuba Plains
Killarney
GREAT BASALT WALL NP

Oorindi
Gilliat
Eureka
Bundoran
Merriula
Villa Dale
Wallegege
Alderley
PORCUPINE GORGE NATIONAL PARK
WHITE MOUNTAINS
Lolworth
LOLWORTH RANGE

Yorkshire Downs
Edith Downs
Coolreagh
Helen Downs
Quambetook
Carnwath
Coleraine
Cassilis
Marathon
Hughenden
Wilfred Downs
Redcliff
Arrara
Curragilla
Wogadoona
Oakley
Elba
Tarella
Webb Lake
WHITE MOUNTAINS NATIONAL PARK
WHITE MOUNTAINS REGIONAL PARK
Pentland
Torrens Creek
Wattlevale
Lauderdale
Prairie

McKinlay
Dimora
Plainby
Stamford
Dalmuir
Ensay
Lammermoor
Holmleigh
Glenariff
Ludgate Hill
Needlewood
MOORRINYA NATIONAL PARK
Mundoo Bluff
Aberfoyle

Kynuna
343
Crendon
Kiriwina
Cracrin
Whitewood
212
Sutton Downs
Antrim
Tangorin
358
GREAT DIVIDING RANGE

Frensham
Anrod Downs
Corfield
Broadford
Malboona
Glenariff

Dagworth
Ingle Downs
Belfield
Escombe
Eskdale
Mahrigong
Levuka
Hillview
Hardington
Marie Downs
Thistlebank
FOREST DEN NATIONAL PARK
Lake Huffer
Albion Vale
Adelong

Denbigh Downs
Brackenburgh
Woodstock
Narangie
Olio
Oondooroo
Kywong
Ingleside
Burslem
Stockholm
Bowen Downs
Lake Barcoorah

Mackunda Downs
Gnalta
Middleton
Middleton Park
Kalkadoon
Winton
Wando
Marita
Muttaburra
Warrandaroo
55
50
Edgbaston
Lake Mueller

Lilleyvale
Chiltern Hills
Tulmur
Whyrallah
BLADENSBURG NATIONAL PARK
Colston
Melrose
Baratria
91
Darr River Downs
119
Acacia Downs
63
Stainburn Downs
Powella
Aramac
Politic

Franklin
Old Cork
Cork
Tatong
Wantalanya
Weona
Chorregon
282
Morella
Talaheena
Dalmore
Yanburra
Summer Hill
Bristol
Murrabit

Verdun Valley
LARK QUARRY RP
Opalton
Jugiong
Juglong
Manerco
Darr
Fairfield
Rodney Downs
101
Ascot

Brighton Downs
Elvo
Mount Ryde
Longreach
AUSTRALIAN STOCKMAN'S HALL OF FAME AND OUTBACK HERITAGE CENTRE
Ilfracombe
Dartmouth
Brixton
Barcaldine
Lochnagar

Mount Windsor
GONEAWAY NATIONAL PARK
Vergemont
Spoilbank
Spring Plains
Toobrac
Rosabel
Arrilalah
Merinoo
Willowie
Currane
Dandaraga
Jubilee Park
Lara
Rellim

CHANNEL COUNTRY
Tonkoro
Wantagong
Withywine
Gordonvale
Portland Downs
Greycroft
Home Creek
Evora
Tilbury

Kurran
Connemara
Onoto
Westerton
Tarcombe
LOCHERN NP
Noonbah
Bimerah
Kaloola
Isis Downs
Mena Park
107
Avondale

EDKINS RA
HARDINGS RANGES
Warbreccan
Valetta
Stonehenge
Inkerman
Isisford
Rivington
Benlidi
Blackall

RINGLEY PLAIN
Palparara
Lochiel
Trewalla
Grahgor Downs
Glenariff
Cecil Downs
Wahroongan
Athol
Bloomfield

Needle Creek
Arno
Emmet
IDALIA NP
Milton Park

FLINDERS HWY
DEV. RD
KENNEDY DEV. RD
LANDSBOROUGH HWY
CAPRICORN HWY
THOMSON DEV. RD
WINTON JUNDAH RD
SWORDS RANGE
FINUCANE RANGE
MACARTNEY RA
CORY RA
FORSYTH RA
Diamantina River
Flinders River
Thomson River
TROPIC OF CAPRICORN

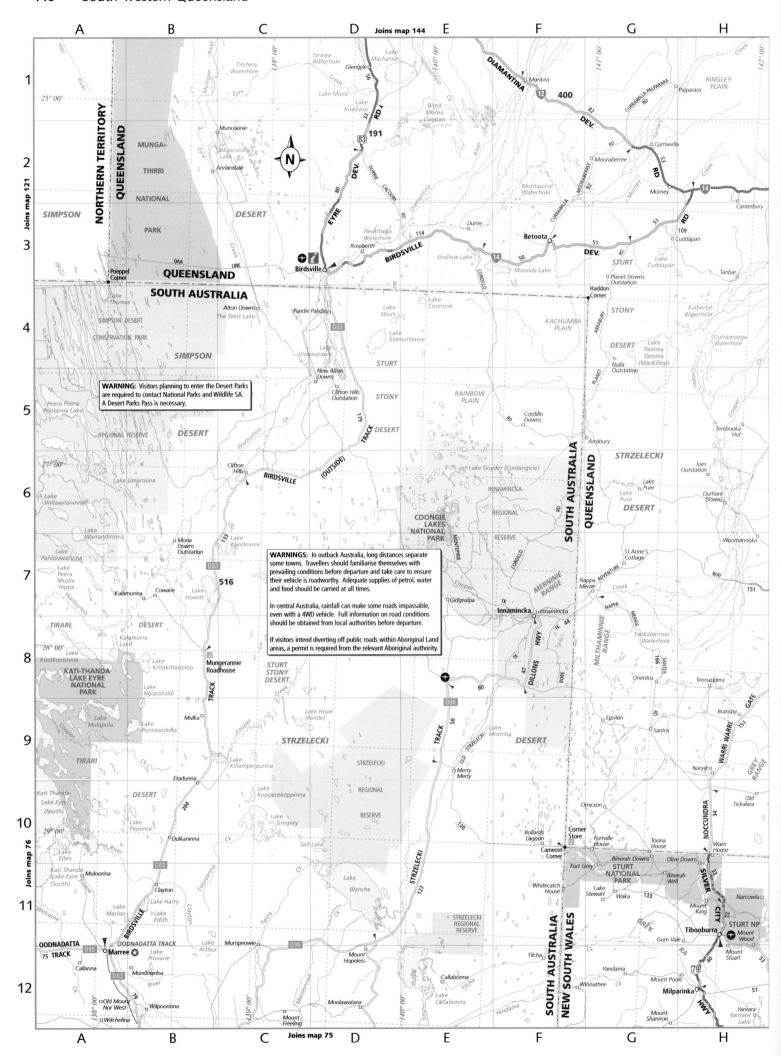

Joins map 144

Joins map 121

Joins map 76

Joins map 75

WARNING: Visitors planning to enter the Desert Parks are required to contact National Parks and Wildlife SA. A Desert Parks Pass is necessary.

WARNINGS: In outback Australia, long distances separate some towns. Travellers should familiarise themselves with prevailing conditions before departure and take care to ensure their vehicle is roadworthy. Adequate supplies of petrol, water and food should be carried at all times.

In central Australia, rainfall can make some roads impassable, even with a 4WD vehicle. Full information on road conditions should be obtained from local authorities before departure.

If visitors intend diverting off public roads within Aboriginal Land areas, a permit is required from the relevant Aboriginal authority.

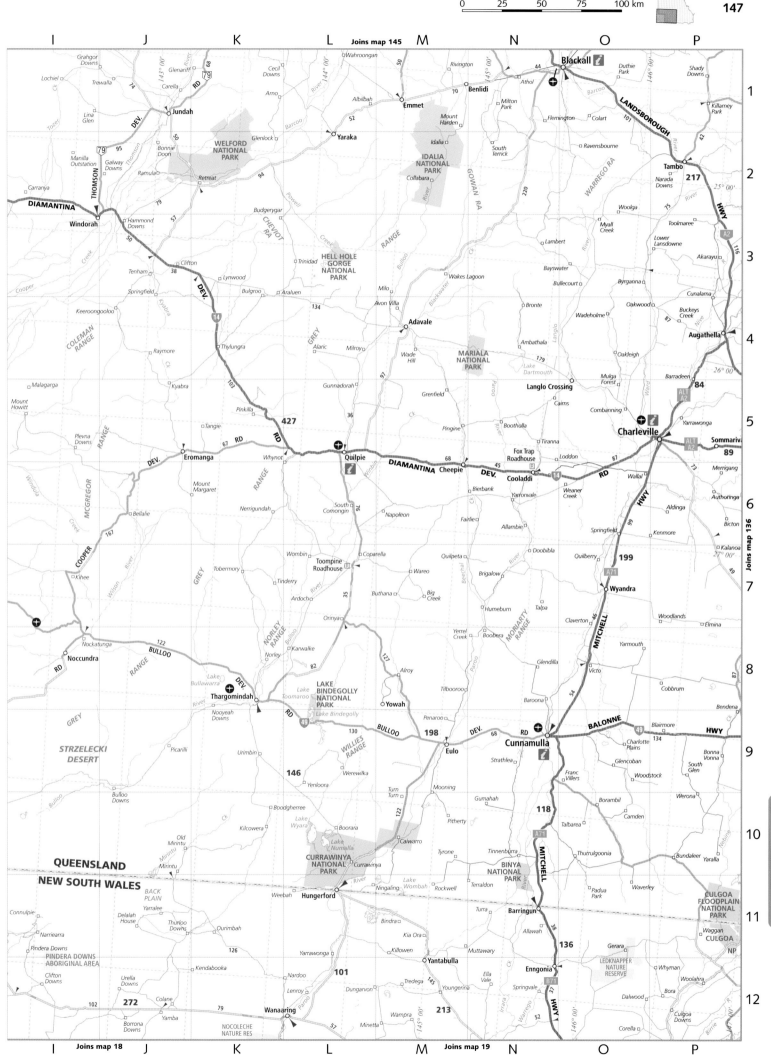

Joins map 145

Blackall

Benlidi

Emmet

Wahroongan

Rivington

Milton Park

Athol

LANDSBOROUGH

Duthie Park

Shady Downs

Killarney Park

Grahgor Downs

Lochiel

Trewalla

Carella

Glenariff

Cecil Downs

Arno

Albilbah

Mount Harden

Idalia

South Terrick

Flemington

Colart

Ravensbourne

Lina Glen

Jundah

Bonnie Doon

Glenlock

Yaraka

IDALIA NATIONAL PARK

Collabara

Woolga

Tambo

Narada Downs

217

Manilla Outstation

Galway Downs

WELFORD NATIONAL PARK

Retreat

Myall Creek

Lambert

Toolmaree

Lower Lansdowne

Akarayu

Carranya

Ramula

Budgerygar

Bayswater

Bullecourt

Byrganna

Cunalama

DIAMANTINA

Windorah

Hammond Downs

Clifton

CHEVIOT RA

Trinidad

HELL HOLE GORGE NATIONAL PARK

Wakes Lagoon

Wadeholme

Oakwood

Buckeys Creek

Tenham

Springfield

Lynwood

Bulgroo

Araluen

Milo

Avon Villa

Bronte

Ambathala

Oakleigh

Augathella

Keeroongooloo

DEV

Thylungra

Kyabra

GREY RANGE

Alaric

Milroy

Wade Hill

MARIALA NATIONAL PARK

Mulga Forest

Barradeen

84

Malagarga

Mount Howitt

Raymore

Pinkilla

Gunnadorah

Grenfield

Lake Dartmouth

Langlo Crossing

Cairns

Combanning

Charleville

Yarrawonga

Sommariva

Plevna Downs

Tangie

427

Pingine

Boothulla

Tiranna

Loddon

89

Bellalie

Eromanga

Whynot

Quilpie

DIAMANTINA Cheepie

68

Fox Trap Roadhouse

45 DEV

Cooladdi

Wallal

Merrigang

Authoringa

Mount Margaret

Nerrigundah

Bierbank

Yarronvale

Weaner Creek

Aldinga

Kenmore

Bicton

Kihee

Tobermory

Tinderry

South Comongin

Napoleon

Fairlie

Allambie

Springfield

199

Kalanoa

Wombin

Coparella

Wareo

Quilpeta

Doobibla

Quilberry

Toompine Roadhouse

Buthana

Big Creek

Brigalow

Humeburn

Talpa

Wyandra

Woodlands

Elmina

COOPER

Nockatunga

Noccundra

BULLOO

Ardoch

Orinya

Yerrel Creek

Boobera

Claverton

Yarmouth

Norley

Karwalke

Alroy

Tilbooroo

Glendilla

Victo

Cobbrum

Bendena

Thargomindah

LAKE BINDEGOLLY NATIONAL PARK

Yowah

Penaroo

Baroona

BALONNE

Blairmore

Nooyeah Downs

Lake Toomaroo

Lake Bindegolly

BULLOO

198

Eulo

Cunnamulla

Charlotte Plains

Bonna Vonna

Picarilli

Urimbin

Werewilka

146

Yenloora

Turn Turn

Mooning

Gumahah

Pitherty

Strathlea

118

Franc Villers

Glencoban

Woodstock

South Glen

Werona

Bulloo Downs

Boodgherree

Kilcowera

Boora

Lake Wyara

Lake Numalla

Caiwarro

Tyrone

Tinnenburra

Borambil

Talbarea

Camden

Thurrulgoonia

Bundaleer

Yaralla

QUEENSLAND

NEW SOUTH WALES

CURRAWINYA NATIONAL PARK

Currawinya

Ningaling

Lake Wombah

Rockwell

Terraldon

BINYA NATIONAL PARK

Padua Park

Waverley

CULGOA FLOODPLAIN NATIONAL PARK

Connulpie

Yarralee

Weebah

Hungerford

Bindra

Kia Ora

Muttawary

Barringun

Waggan CULGOA

NP

Narriearra

Delalah House

Thurloo Downs

Ourimbah

126

Yarrawonga

Dungarvon

Killowen

Yantabulla

Ella Vale

Youngerina

Allawah

Gerara

Whyman

Woolahra

Pindera Downs

272

Kendabooka

101

Nardoo

Tredega

213

Springvale

Ledknapper Nature Reserve

Bora

PINDERA DOWNS ABORIGINAL AREA

Clifton Downs

Urella Downs

Colane

Lenroy

136

Enngonia

Dalwood

Culgoa Downs

Borrona Downs

Yamba

Wanaaring

Minetta

Wampra

NOCOLECHE NATURE RES

Corella

AIRLIE BEACH *page 139 J3*

 Whitsunday Regional Information Centre
192 Main St, Prosperine
(07) 4945 3967
www.tourismwhitsundays.com.au

BUNDABERG *page 137 M3*

 271 Bourbong St
(07) 4153 8888 or 1300 722 099
www.bundabergregion.org

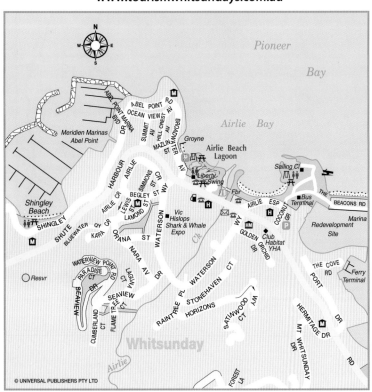

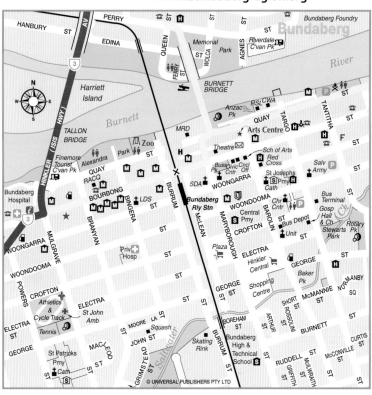

CAIRNS *page 141 L6*

 51 The Esplanade
(07) 4051 3588 or 1800 093 300
www.tropicalnorthqueensland.org.au

GLADSTONE *page 137 K1*

 Marina Ferry Terminal
72 Bryan Jordan Dr
(07) 4972 9000
www.gladstoneregion.info

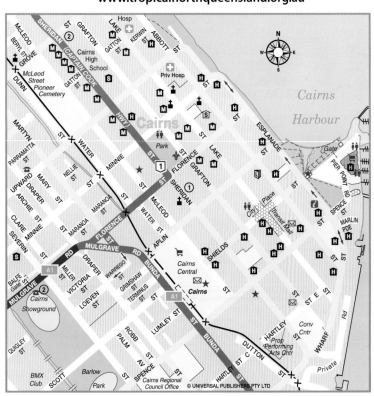

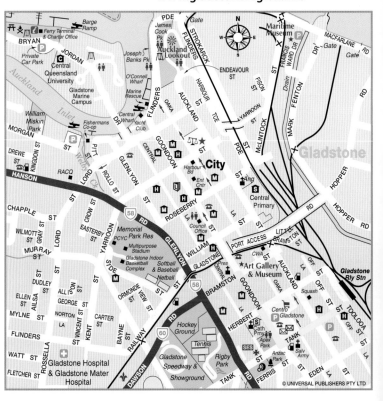

GYMPIE *page 137 M6*

Lake Alford Information Centre
24 Bruce Hwy
1800 444 222
www.cooloola.org.au
www.visitgympieregion.com.au

HERVEY BAY *page 137 N4*

227 Maryborough–Hervey Bay Rd
(07) 4196 9600 or 1800 811 728
www.visitfrasercoast.com

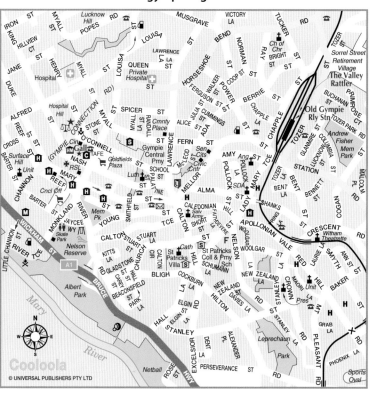

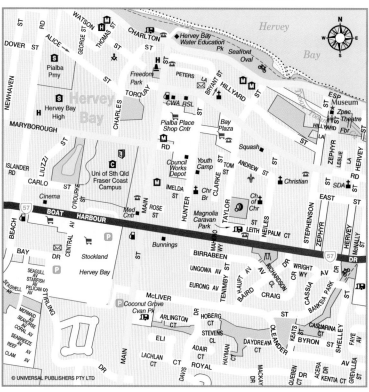

MACKAY *page 139 K5*

320 Nebo Rd
(07) 4944 5888 or 1300 130 001
www.mackayregion.com

MAROOCHYDORE *page 134 G4*

Cnr Melrose Pde and Sixth Ave
(07) 5458 8842 or 1300 847 481
www.visitsunshinecoast.com.au

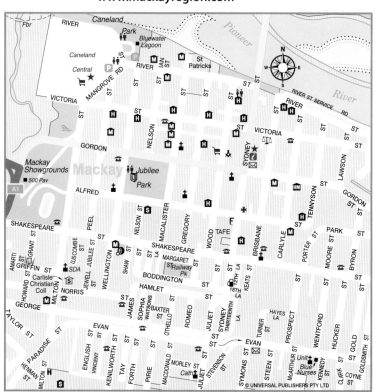

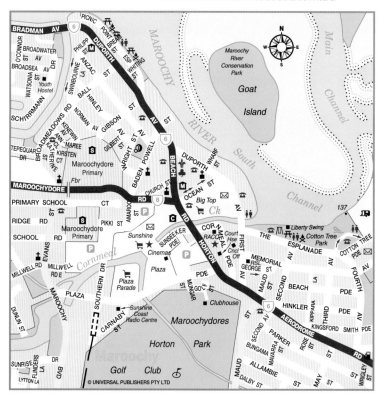

QLD

MARYBOROUGH *page 137 N5*

 City Hall
388–396 Kent St
(07) 4120 5600 or 1800 214 789
www.visitfrasercoast.com

MOUNT ISA *page 144 F3*

Outback at Isa
19 Marian St
(07) 4749 1555 or 1300 659 660
www.mietv.com.au

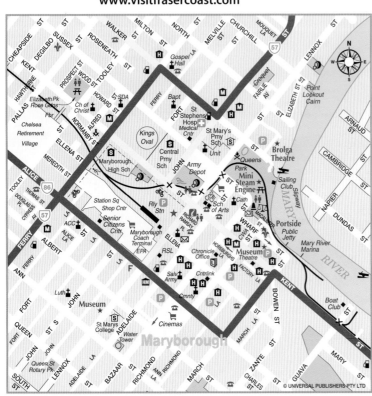

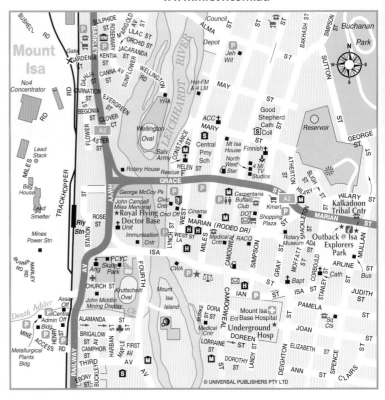

NOOSA HEADS *page 134 H1*

 61 Hastings St
(07) 5430 5020 or 1300 066 672
www.visitnoosa.com.au

ROCKHAMPTON *page 139 M11*

 176 Gladstone Rd
(07) 4921 2311 or 1800 676 701
www.capricornholidays.com.au

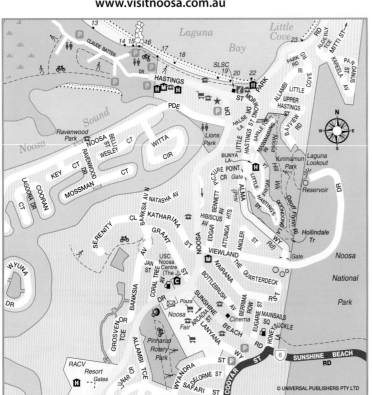

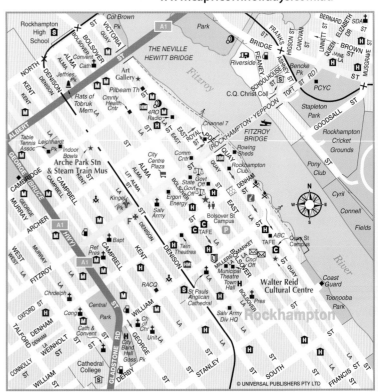

SURFERS PARADISE *page 135 G10*

2 Cavill Ave
(07) 5570 3259 or 1300 309 440
www.visitgoldcoast.com

TOOWOOMBA *page 137 L9*

82–86 James St
(07) 4639 3797 or 1800 331 155
www.southernqueenslandcountry.com.au

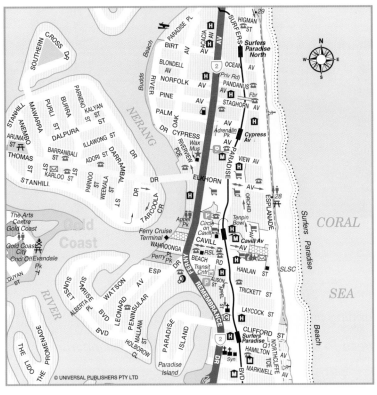

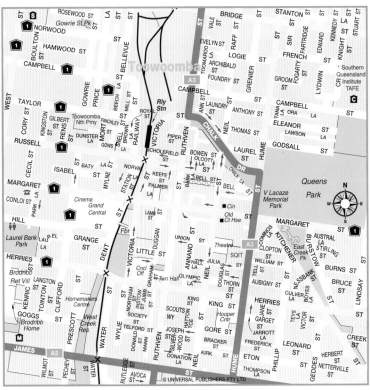

TOWNSVILLE *page 141 N11*

334A Flinders St
(07) 4721 3660 or 1800 801 902
www.townsvillenorthqueensland.com.au

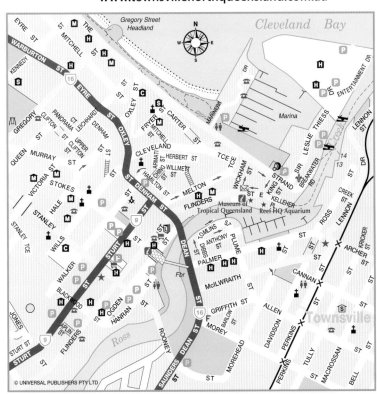

WARWICK *page 137 L10*

49 Albion St
(07) 4661 3122 or 1800 060 877
www.warwickevents.com

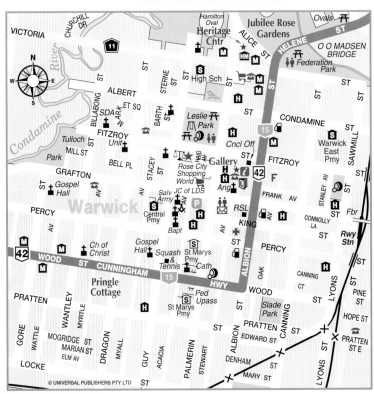

QLD

View from Mt Wellington

TASMANIA

Tasmania is Australia's most mountainous state and boasts stunning and often remote World Heritage areas.

National parks comprise one-third of the state and feature more than 2800 kilometres of world-class walking tracks.

Tasmania, Australia's smallest state, is an island 240 kilometres from the mainland, surrounded by the turbulent Bass Strait, Southern Ocean and Tasman Sea. It's a compact state, making it ideal for touring, as only relatively short distances separate its many attractions.

White settlement in Tasmania began in 1803, when the British set up a penal colony. Historic villages that have hardly changed since the 1800s, convict-built bridges and old gaols are physical reminders of Tasmania's colonial past.

Hobart, Tasmania's capital, lies nestled between the slopes of Mount Wellington and the Derwent estuary. Whaling and sealing initially brought wealth to the town and today, the city's economy still relies heavily on its deep-water harbour.

INFORMATION CENTRE

Tasmanian Travel and Information Centre
20 Davey St, Hobart; (03) 6238 4222
www.discovertasmania.com
www.hobarttravelcentre.com.au

Places of interest

	MAP REF		MAP REF
Australasian Golf Museum, Bothwell	161 J4	Mole Creek Karst National Park	162 G8
Australian Axeman's Hall of Fame, Latrobe	162 H6	Mount Field National Park	158 D2
Bark Mill Museum, Swansea	161 N3	National Automobile Museum of Tasmania	163 K8
Beaconsfield Mine & Heritage Centre	163 J6	The Nut, Stanley	162 D3
Ben Lomond National Park	163 M9	Oatlands	161 K3
Bridestowe Estate Lavender Farm	163 L6	Port Arthur Historic Site	159 M9
Bruny Island	158 H11, 159 I11	Queen Victoria Museum and Art Gallery	163 K8
Burnie Regional Museum	162 F5	Richmond Bridge	159 J3
Cradle Mountain–Lake St Clair National Park	162 F10	Seahorse World/Platypus House	163 J6
Don River Railway, Devonport	162 H6	Tahune AirWalk	158 D7
Franklin–Gordon Wild Rivers National Park	160 F4	Tamar Valley wineries	163 J6
Freycinet National Park	161 O3	Tasmanian Devil Conservation Park	159 M8
Hastings Caves and Thermal Springs	158 E12	Tasmanian Wool Centre, Ross	161 L2
Huon Apple and Heritage Museum	158 G6	The Tin Centre, Derby	163 N6
Maria Island National Park	159 O3	West Coast Wilderness Railway	160 D2

MAPS

TASMANIA

Tasmania

Central Hobart	155
Metro Hobart	156–7
Hobart & Surrounds	158–9
Southern Tasmania	160–1
Northern Tasmania	162–3
Inset: Flinders Island	160
Inset: King Island	161

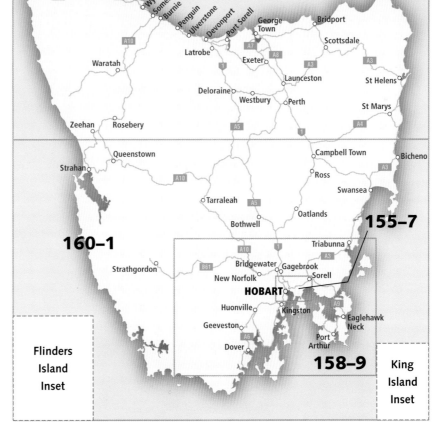

INTER-CITY ROUTES	DISTANCE
Hobart–Launceston via Midland Hwy	197 km
Hobart–Devonport via Midland & Bass hwys	279 km

View of MONA (Museum of Old and New Art)

Hobart

Boasting internationally famed temperate wilderness on its doorstep, Hobart's abundance of natural beauty propelled it to the forefront of environmental politics in 1972, becoming home to the world's first 'green' political party.

Situated on the banks of the Derwent River, Hobart is Australia's smallest state capital and second oldest city. It was founded by Colonel David Collins in 1804, 16 years after the settlement of Sydney. Despite its beginnings as a penal settlement, Hobart quickly became a thriving seaport and its maritime heritage can be seen along its historic waterfront.

Hobart is extremely interesting historically, with over 90 buildings classified by the National Trust, many of them convict-built from sandstone. Some of Australia's oldest buildings are in Hobart, including Anglesea Barracks, the oldest military establishment (1811); and the oldest theatre, the Theatre Royal (1837). Battery Point is Hobart's oldest district. Originally home to sailors, fishermen, prostitutes and shipwrights, today it is a fashionable inner-city neighbourhood.

Cascade Brewery, Australia's oldest brewery, is also in suburban Hobart. They offer daily tours of the brewery and museum. Another visitor favourite, just outside Hobart, is the Cadbury Chocolate factory. Within Hobart, the famous Salamanca Markets, held every Saturday amidst the sandstone warehouses of Salamanca Place, offer an amazing variety of produce, arts and crafts and the opportunity to mingle with Hobart's thriving creative community.

Places of interest

	MAP REF		MAP REF
Australian Army Museum Tasmania		Narryna Heritage Museum	155 E9
(Anglesea Barracks)	155 D9	Parliament House	155 E7
Arthur Circus	155 F8	Queens Domain	155 C1
Battery Point	155 F8	Royal Tasmanian Botanical Gardens	155 E2
Cadbury Visitor Centre	156 B1	Runnymede House	155 D6
Cascade Brewery	156 C8	St David's Park	155 D8
Constitution and Victoria Docks	155 F7	St Mary's Cathedral	155 C6
Elizabeth Mall	155 D7	Salamanca Place	155 E8
Gasworks Cellar Door	155 F6	State Library of Tasmania	155 D7
Government House	155 E3	Sullivans Cove	155 F7
Hobart Convention and		Tasmanian Museum and Art Gallery	155 E7
Entertainment Centre	155 F12	University of Tasmania	155 D12
Maritime Museum of Tasmania	155 F7	Wrest Point Casino	155 F12
MONA (Museum of Old and New Art)	156 B3		

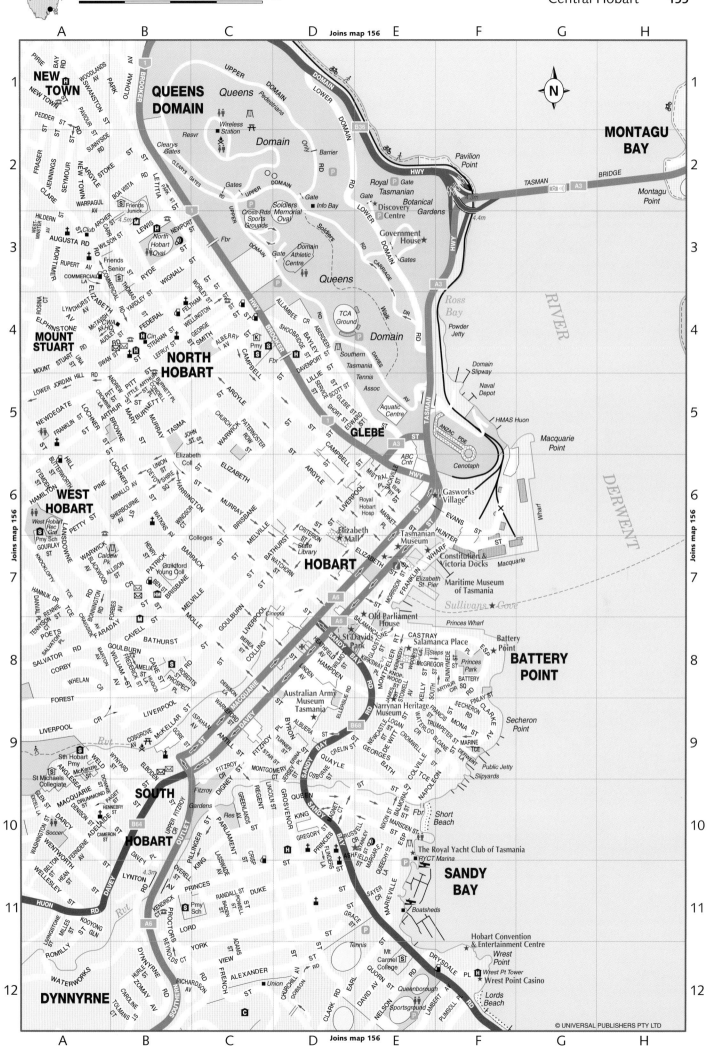

© UNIVERSAL PUBLISHERS PTY LTD

TAS

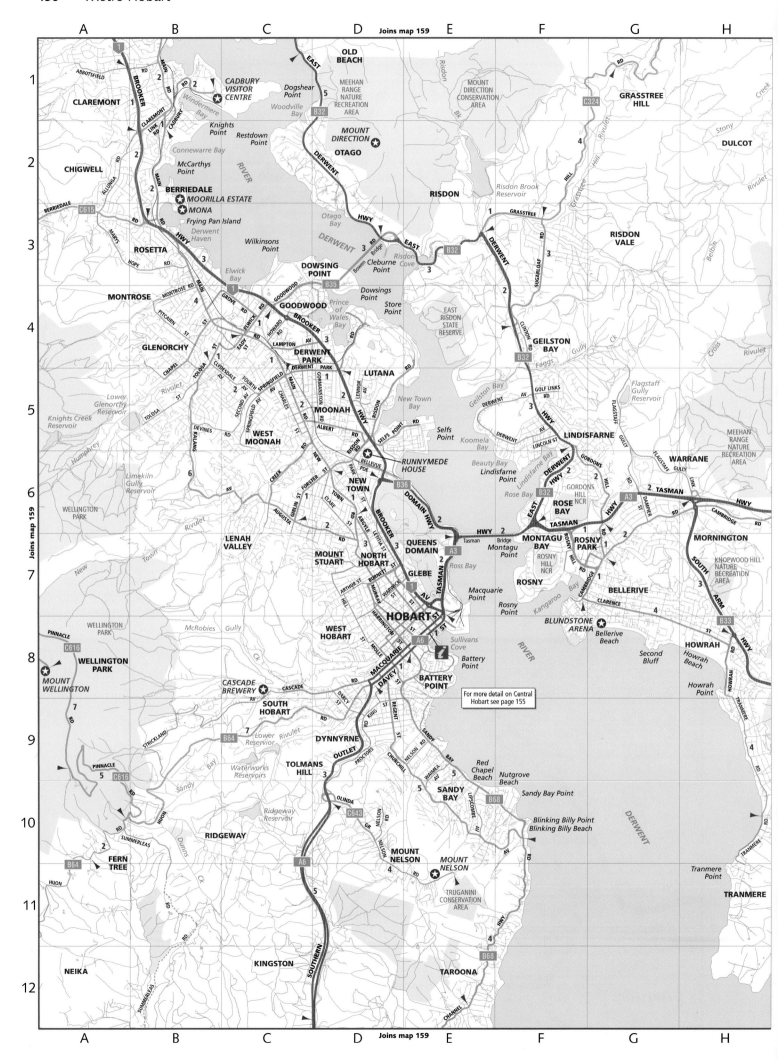

Joins map 159

For more detail on Central
Hobart see page 155

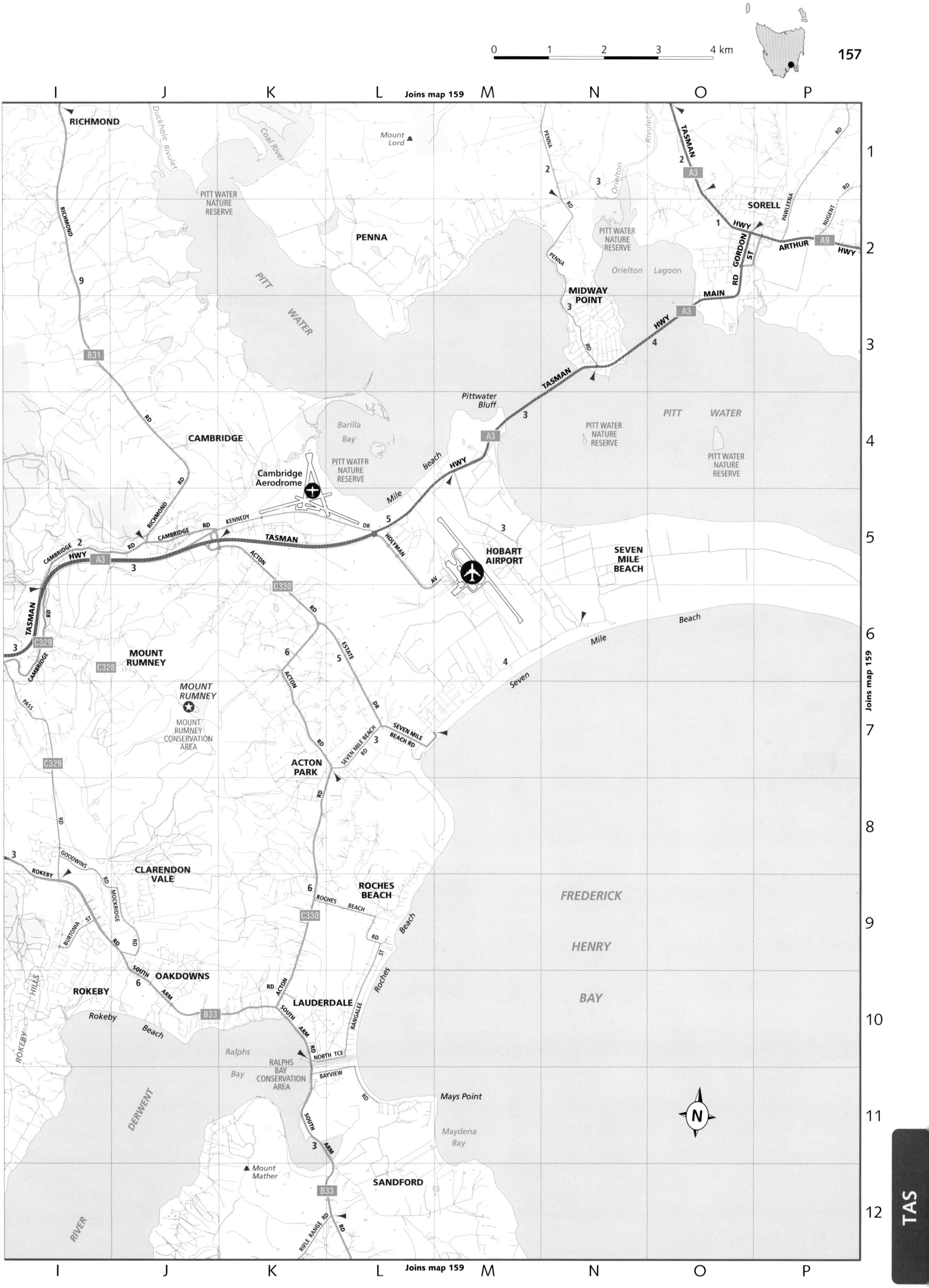

0 1 2 3 4 km

Joins map 159

RICHMOND

Duckhole Rivulet

Coal River

Mount Lord

PITT WATER NATURE RESERVE

PENNA

PENNA

RD

Orielton Rivulet

TASMAN

A3

2

2

1

SORELL

PAWLEENA

NUGENT RD

HWY

ARTHUR

A9

HWY

GORDON ST

PITT WATER NATURE RESERVE

Orielton Lagoon

MIDWAY POINT

RD

MAIN

A3

HWY

TASMAN

4

RD

9

RICHMOND

PITT WATER

B31

RD

CAMBRIDGE

RD

RICHMOND

Barilla Bay

PITT WATER NATURE RESERVE

Pittwater Bluff

A3

TASMAN

3

PITT WATER

PITT WATER NATURE RESERVE

PITT WATER NATURE RESERVE

Cambridge Aerodrome

Mile

beach

HWY

HWY

5

SEVEN MILE BEACH

2

CAMBRIDGE

RD

KENNEDY

RD

CAMBRIDGE

TASMAN

3

HOLYMAN

5

3

HOBART AIRPORT

CAMBRIDGE HWY

A3

3

C330

TASMAN

3

C329

RD

ACTON

AV

Mile

Beach

Seven

Mile

Beach

4

CAMBRIDGE

C328

MOUNT RUMNEY

ESTATE

RD

6

5

ACTON

RD

PASS

MOUNT RUMNEY

MOUNT RUMNEY CONSERVATION AREA

RD

DR

SEVEN MILE BEACH RD

SEVEN MILE BEACH RD

3

C329

ACTON PARK

RD

RD

3

ROKEBY

GOODWINS

RD

CLARENDON VALE

MOCKRIDGE RD

ROCHES BEACH

ROCHES BEACH

6

C330

FREDERICK

HENRY

BAY

BURTONIA ST

ROKEBY

RD

SOUTH ARM

6

OAKDOWNS

RD

ACTON

RD

ST

Roches

Beach

LAUDERDALE

ROKEBY HILLS

Rokeby Beach

B33

SOUTH ARM RD

BANGALEE

NORTH TCE

BAYVIEW

RD

Ralphs Bay

RALPHS BAY CONSERVATION AREA

Mays Point

N

DERWENT

SOUTH ARM

Maydena Bay

RIVER

3

Mount Mather

B33

RIFLE RANGE RD

SANDFORD

Joins map 159

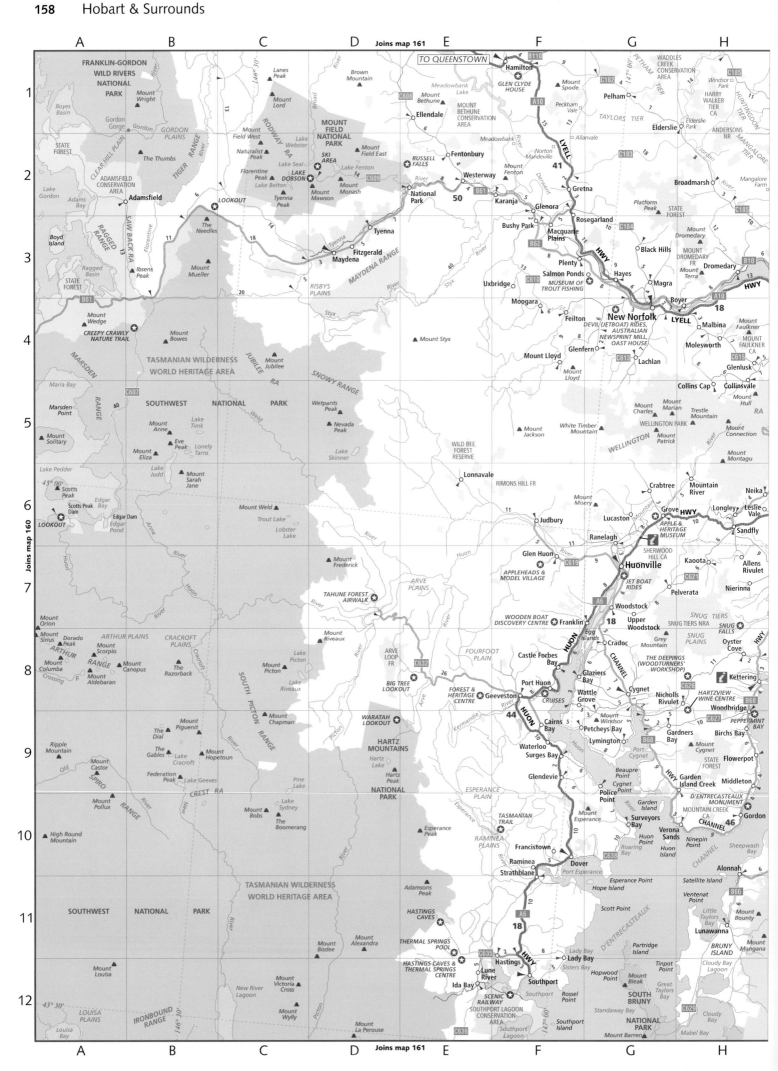

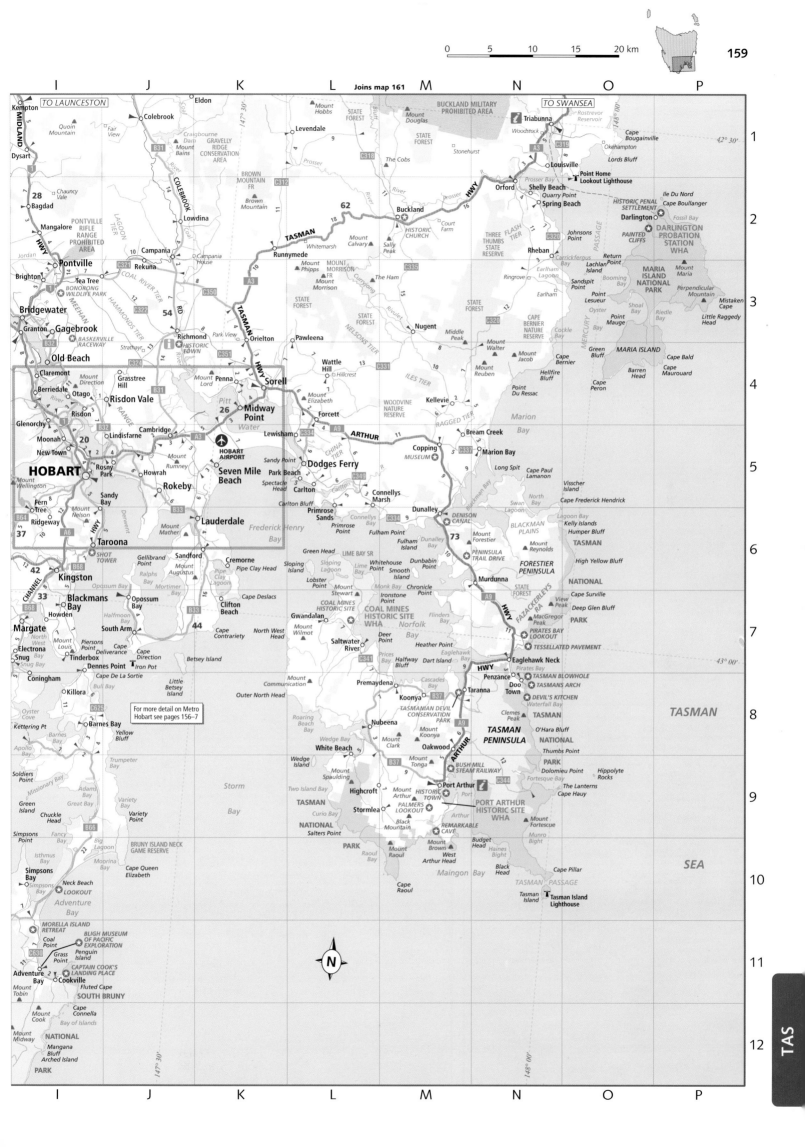

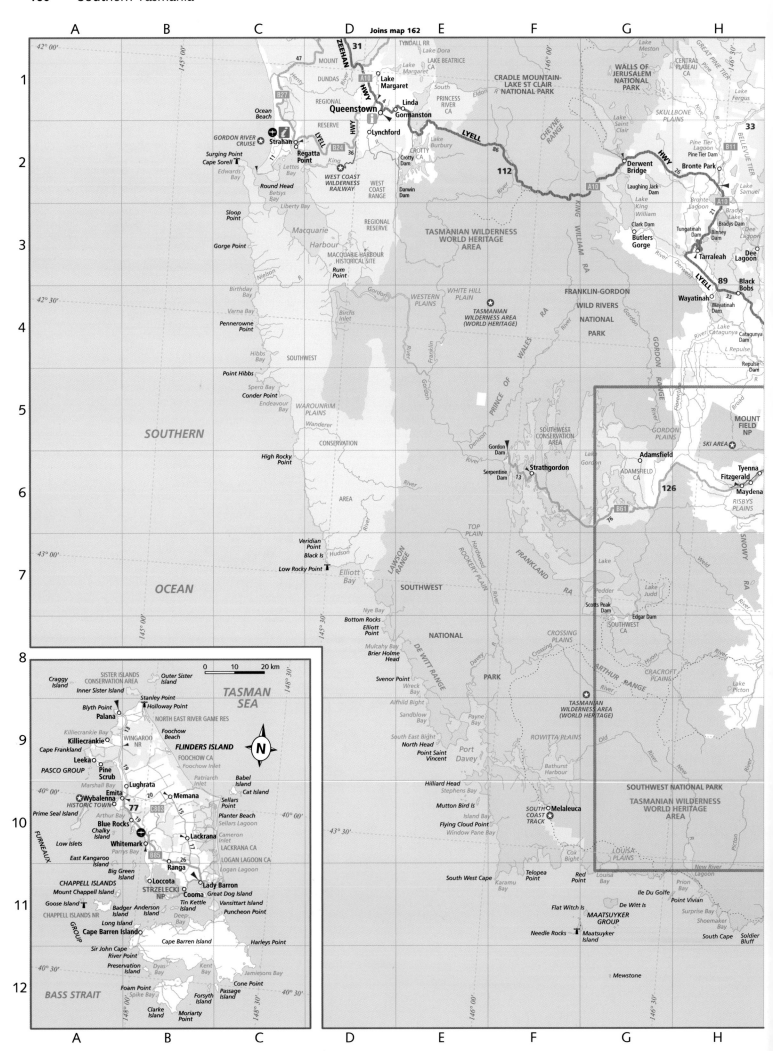

Joins map 162

A B C D E F G H

1

ZEEHAN **31**
TYNDALL RR
Lake Dora
MOUNT *Lake Beatrice*
DUNDAS *Lake Margaret* CA
47
Henty River
Lake Margaret
Lake Meston
WALLS OF JERUSALEM NATIONAL PARK
CENTRAL PLATEAU CA
Lake Fergus
B27
REGIONAL
A10
South *Eldon River*
CRADLE MOUNTAIN-LAKE ST CLAIR NATIONAL PARK

2
Ocean Beach
Queenstown
Linda
Gormanston
PRINCESS RIVER CA
CHEYNE RANGE
SKULLBONE PLAINS
146° 00'
33
GORDON RIVER CRUISE
Strahan
Lynchford
LYELL
LYELL
86
Derwent Bridge
Bronte Park
B11
Surging Point
Cape Sorell
Regatta Point
B24 36
King River
112
Laughing Jack Dam
Pine Tier Lagoon
Pine Tier Dam
A10

3
Round Head
Betsys Bay
Liberty Bay
WEST COAST WILDERNESS RAILWAY
WEST COAST RANGE
Darwin Dam
Clark Dam
Butlers Gorge
Tungatinah Dam
Brady's Lake
Brady Dam
Binney Dam
Dee Lagoon
Sloop Point
Macquarie Harbour
WHITE HILL PLAIN
TASMANIAN WILDERNESS WORLD HERITAGE AREA
Tarraleah
Dee Lagoon
Gorge Point
MACQUARIE HARBOUR HISTORICAL SITE
REGIONAL RESERVE
KING WILLIAM RA
89
Black Bobs

4
42° 30'
Nielson R
Birthday Bay
Rum Point
WESTERN PLAINS
TASMANIAN WILDERNESS AREA (WORLD HERITAGE)
FRANKLIN-GORDON WILD RIVERS NATIONAL PARK
Wayatinah
33
Wayatinah Dam
Lake Catagunya
Catagunya Dam
L Repulse
Varna Bay
Pennerowne Point
Franklin River
Gordon River
OF WALES RA
PRINCE
Repulse Dam

5
SOUTHERN
Hibbs Bay
SOUTHWEST
Point Hibbs
Spero Bay
Conder Point
Endeavour Bay
WAROUNRIM PLAINS
Wanderer River
MOUNT FIELD NP
SKI AREA
GORDON PLAINS
GORDON RANGE

6
High Rocky Point
CONSERVATION
AREA
Denison River
Gordon Dam
Strathgordon
Serpentine Dam
13
ADAMSFIELD CA
Adamsfield
126
Tyenna
Fitzgerald
Maydena
B61
RISBYS PLAINS
Lake Gordon
76

7
43° 00'
Veridian Point
Black Is
Low Rocky Point
Hudson R
Elliott Bay
LAWSON RANGE
SOUTHWEST
NATIONAL
TOP PLAIN
Hardwood River
ROOKERY PLAIN
FRANKLAND RA
Davey River
Crossing River
CROSSING PLAINS
Scotts Peak Dam
Edgar Dam
Huon River
SOUTHWEST CA
Lake Judd
Lake Pedder
Weld River
SNOWY RA
Lake Picton

8
OCEAN
Nye Bay
Bottom Rocks
Elliott Point
PARK
Old River
ARTHUR RANGE
CRACROFT PLAINS
Lake Picton
0 10 20 km
TASMAN SEA
Mulcahy Bay
Brier Holme Head
DE WITT RANGE

Inset map (A–C, 8–12):

SISTER ISLANDS CONSERVATION AREA
Craggy Island
Outer Sister Island
Inner Sister Island
Stanley Point
Holloway Point
Blyth Point
Palana
73
WINGAROO NR
NORTH EAST RIVER GAME RES

9
Killiecrankie Bay
Killiecrankie
Cape Frankland
Leeka
Pine Scrub
PASCO GROUP
Foochow Beach
FLINDERS ISLAND
FOOCHOW CA
Foochow Inlet
Svenor Point
Wreck Bay
Alfhild Bight
Sandblow Bay
TASMANIAN WILDERNESS AREA (WORLD HERITAGE)

10
40° 00'
Marshall Bay
Lughrata
Emita
Wybalenna
HISTORIC TOWN
77
20
C803
Memana
15
Patriarch Inlet
Babel Island
Cat Island
Sellars Point
Planter Beach
Sellars Lagoon
Arthur Bay
Prime Seal Island
Blue Rocks
Chalky Island
19
Whitemark
Parrys Bay
Lackrana
LACKRANA CA
Cameron Inlet
LOGAN LAGOON CA
South East Bight
North Head
Point Saint Vincent
Port Davey
Hilliard Head
Stephens Bay
Mutton Bird Is
Island Bay
Flying Cloud Point
Window Pane Bay
South Coast Track
Melaleuca
SOUTH COAST TRACK
SOUTHWEST NATIONAL PARK
TASMANIAN WILDERNESS WORLD HERITAGE AREA

11
FURNEAUX
Low Islets
East Kangaroo Island
B85
Ranga
26
17
Big Green Island
Loccota
STRZELECKI NP
Cooma
Tin Kettle Island
Great Dog Island
Vansittart Island
Puncheon Point
CHAPPELL ISLANDS
Mount Chappell Island
Goose Island
CHAPPELL ISLANDS NR
Badger Island
Anderson Island
Long Island
Cape Barren Island
Deep Bay
Lady Barron
South West Cape
Karamu Bay
Telopea Point
Red Point
Louisa Bay
LOUISA PLAINS
Ile Du Golfe
Flat Witch Is
De Witt Is
MAATSUYKER GROUP
Point Vivian
Surprise Bay
Shoemaker Bay

12
40° 30'
BASS STRAIT
Sir John Cape River Point
Preservation Island
Foam Point
Spike Bay
Clarke Island
GROUP
Dyas Bay
Kent Bay
Jamiesons Bay
Forsyth Island
Cone Point
40° 30'
Passage Island
Moriarty Point
Cape Barren Island
Harleys Point
Mewstone
Needle Rocks
Maatsuyker Island
South Cape
Soldier Bluff

A B C D E F G H

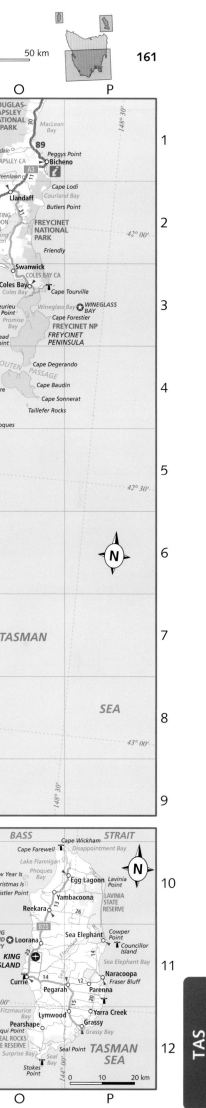

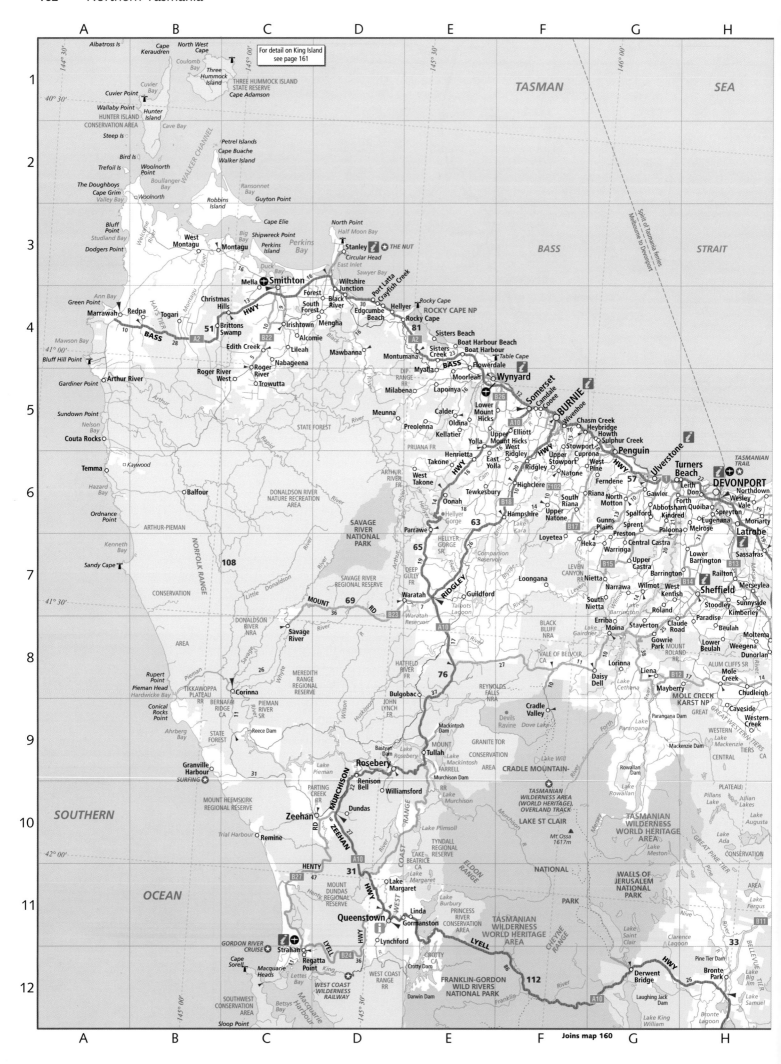

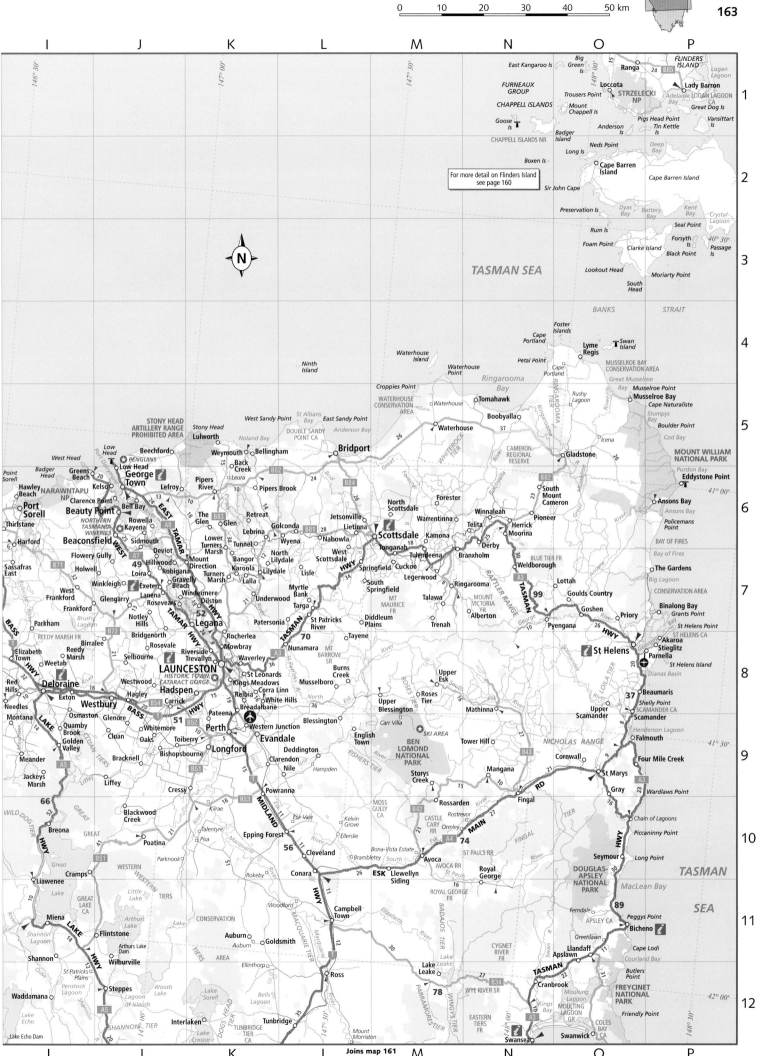

0   10   20   30   40   50 km

TASMAN SEA

BANKS   STRAIT

FLINDERS ISLAND

East Kangaroo Is
Big Green Is
Ranga
Loccota
STRZELECKI NP
Lady Barron
LOGAN LAGOON CA
Logan Lagoon
Great Dog Is
Adelaide Bay
Vansittart Is

FURNEAUX GROUP
Trousers Point
Mount Chappell Is
Pigs Head Point
Tin Kettle Is

CHAPPELL ISLANDS
Goose Is
Badger Island
Anderson Is

CHAPPELL ISLANDS NR
Boxen Is
Long Is
Neds Point
Deep Bay

For more detail on Flinders Island see page 160

Sir John Cape
Cape Barren Island
Cape Barren Island

Preservation Is
Dyas Bay
Battery Bay
Kent Bay
Crystal Lagoon

Rum Is
Seal Point
40° 30'
Foam Point
Forsyth Is
Passage Is
Lookout Head
Clarke Island
Black Point
Moriarty Point
South Head

Waterhouse Island
Foster Islands
Cape Portland
Lyme Regis
Swan Island

Ninth Island
Waterhouse Point
Petal Point
Cape Portland
MUSSELROE BAY CONSERVATION AREA

Croppies Point
Ringarooma Bay
Great Musselroe
Musselroe Bay
Musselroe Point
Cape Naturaliste

West Sandy Point
St Albans Bay
East Sandy Point
Tomahawk
Rushy Lagoon
Stumpys Bay
Boulder Point

WATERHOUSE CONSERVATION AREA
Anderson Bay
Boobyalla
37
Icena
Cod Bay

Stony Head
DOUBLE SANDY POINT CA
Waterhouse
WHITEROCK TIER
CAMERON REGIONAL RESERVE
Gladstone
MOUNT WILLIAM NATIONAL PARK

STONY HEAD ARTILLERY RANGE PROHIBITED AREA
Lulworth
Noland Bay
26
Purdon Bay
Eddystone Point
41° 00'

West Head
Low Head
Beechford
Weymouth
Bellingham
Bridport
South Mount Cameron
Ansons Bay

Low Head
PENGUINS
George Town
Lefroy
Pipers River
Leura
Pipers Brook
North Scottsdale
Forester
Winnaleah
Pioneer
Herrick
Ansons Bay
Policemans Point

Greens Beach
Kelso
Bell Bay
The Glen
Glen
Retreat
Jetsonville
Lietinna
Scottsdale
Warrentinna
Telita
Moorina
BAY OF FIRES

Clarence Point
Sidmouth
Lebrina
Golconda
Wyena
West Scottsdale
Tonganah
Kamona
Derby
Branxholm
Weldborough
The Gardens

Beauty Point
Rowella
Kayena
Lower Turners Marsh
North Lilydale
Nabowla
Lisle
Springfield
Cuckoo
Tulendeena
Ringarooma
Legerwood
BLUE TIER FR
Lottah
Big Lagoon
BAY OF FIRES CONSERVATION AREA

Beaconsfield
Deviot
Hillwood
Bangor
Karoola
Lilydale
South Springfield
Talawa
Goulds Country

Flowery Gully
Holwell
49
Robigana
Gravelly Beach
Lalla
Myrtle Bank
MT MAURICE FR
Trenah
99
Goshen
Priory
Binalong Bay
Grants Point

West Frankford
Winkleigh
Exeter
Lanena
Windermere
Targa
Underwood
MT VICTORIA FR
Alberton
Pyengana
St Helens Point
St Helens CA

Frankford
Glengarry
Rosevears
Dilston
52
Patersonia
St Patricks River
Diddleum Plains
MOUNT VICTORIA FR
George
St Helens
Akaroa
Stieglitz

Parkham
Notley Hills
Legana
Rocherlea
Nunamara
MT BARROW SR
Tayene
RATTLER RANGE
Parnella
St Helens Island

BASS
Birralee
Bridgenorth
Riverside
Mowbray
Waverley
Burns Creek
TASMAN
LOILA TIER
Dianas Basin

Elizabeth Town
Reedy Marsh
Rosevale
Selbourne
Trevallyn
LAUNCESTON
St Leonards
Musselboro
Upper Esk
70
37
Beaumaris

Deloraine
Weetah
Exton
Westwood
Hagley
Hadspen
Kings Meadows
Relbia
Corra Linn
White Hills
Breadalbane
North Esk
Upper Blessington
Roses Tier
Mathinna
Scamander
SCAMANDER CA
Shelly Point

Red Hills
Needles
Osmaston
Carrick
Pateena
Western Junction
51
Blessington
Mangana
Cornwall
Upper Scamander
41° 30'

Montana
Quamby Brook
Glenore
Whitemore
Perth
Evandale
Deddington
ENGLISH TOWN
BEN LOMOND NATIONAL PARK
SKI AREA
Tower Hill
St Marys
Four Mile Creek

Meander
Golden Valley
Cluan
Oaks
Toiberry
Longford
Clarendon
Nile
Hampden
FISHERS TIER
Carr Villa
Storys Creek
Rossarden
Fingal
Gray
Falmouth

Jackeys Marsh
Bracknell
Bishopsbourne
Cressy
Powranna
Kilrae
Esk Vale
Kelvin Grove
Ellerslie
MOSS GULLY CA
CASTLE CARY RR
Ormley
NICHOLAS RANGE
Wardlaws Point
Chain of Lagoons

66
Breona
Blackwood Creek
Poatina
Talentyre
Pisa
Epping Forest
Cleveland
Bona-Vista Estate
Brambletey
Avoca
AVOCA RR
Royal George
FINGAL TIER
Seymour
Piccaninny Point

Liawenee
Cramps
WESTERN TIERS
Parknook
Rokeby
56
Conara
ESK
Llewellyn Siding
ROYAL GEORGE FR
DOUGLAS-APSLEY NATIONAL PARK
Long Point
TASMAN SEA

Miena
Flintstone
Arthurs Lake Dam
GREAT LAKE CA
Auburn
Goldsmith
Woodford
Campbell Town
Elizabeth
APSLEY CA
89
Ferndale
Peggys Point
Bicheno

Shannon
Wilburville
Arthurs Lake
CONSERVATION AREA
Auburn
Ellinthorp
Ross
Lake Leake
CYGNET RIVER FR
Greenlawn
Llandaff
Apslawn
Cape Lodi

Waddamana
St Patricks Plains
Steppes
Woods Lake
Lake Sorell
Bells Lagoon
Lake Leake
WYE RIVER SR
WINGYS TIER
Cranbrook
Butlers Point
FREYCINET NATIONAL PARK
42° 00'

Lake Echo
Penstock Lagoon
Interlaken
DOGS HEAD
TUNBRIDGE TIER CA
Tunbridge
Mount Morriston
78
PARRAMORE TIER
EASTERN TIERS FR
MOULTING LAGOON GR
COLES BAY CA
Friendly Point

Lake Echo Dam
SHANNON TIER
Swansea
Swanwick

TAS

BICHENO *page 161 O1*

41B Foster St
(03) 6375 1500
www.eastcoasttasmania.com

BURNIE *page 162 F5*

Makers Workshop
2 Bass Hwy
(03) 6430 5831
www.discoverburnie.net

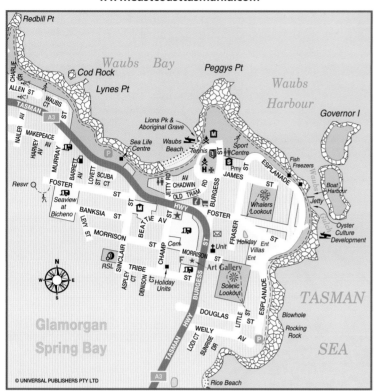

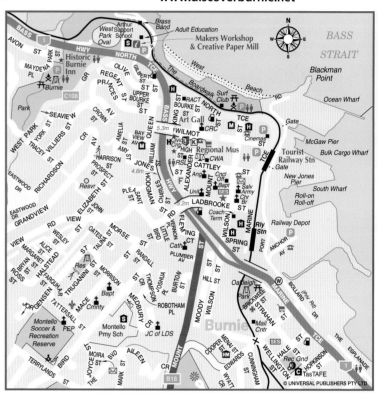

DEVONPORT *page 162 H6*

92 Formby Rd
(03) 6424 4466 or 1800 649 514
www.devonporttasmania.travel

GEORGE TOWN *page 163 J6*

92–96 Main Rd
(03) 6382 1700
www.provincialtamar.com.au

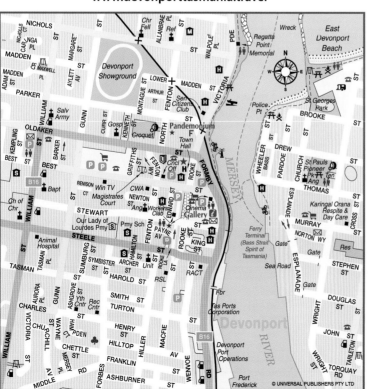

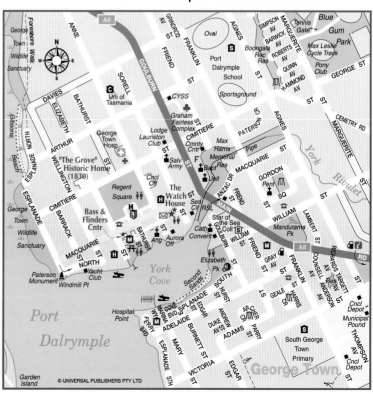

HUONVILLE *page 158 G7*

i Huon Valley Visitor Centre
2273 Huon Hwy
(03) 6264 0326
www.huonvalleyvisitorcentre.com.au

LAUNCESTON *page 163 K8*

i 68–72 Camerson St
(03) 6323 3000 or 1800 651 827
www.destinationlaunceston.com.au

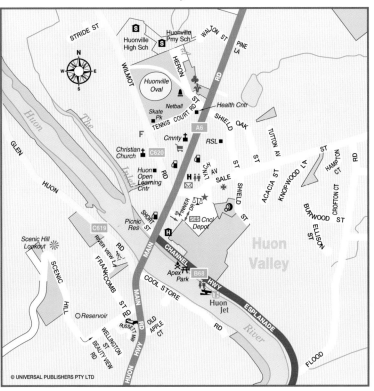

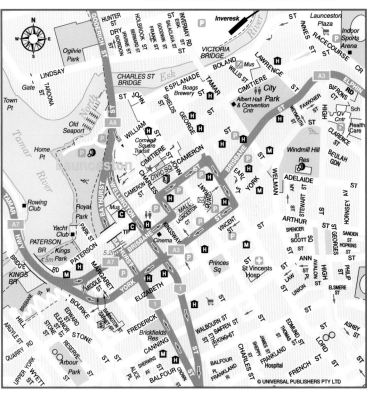

PORT ARTHUR *page 159 M9*

i Port Arthur and Tasman Region
Visitor Information Centre
6973 Arthur Hwy
(03) 6251 2371
www.portarthur.org.au

QUEENSTOWN *page 160 D1*

i Eric Thomas Galley Museum
1–7 Driffield St
(03) 6471 1483
www.westernwilderness.com.au

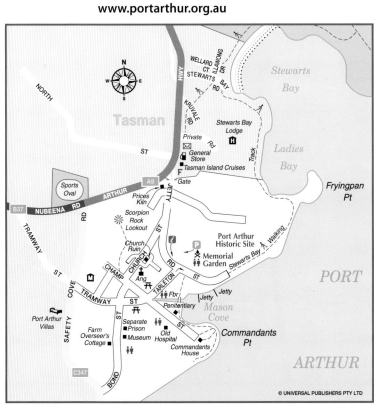

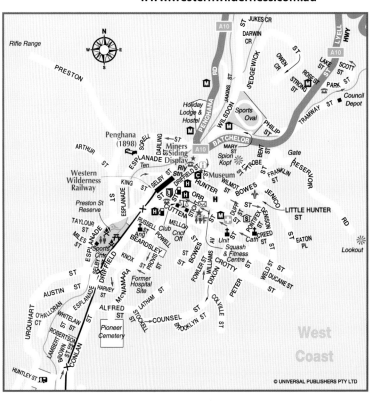

TAS

RICHMOND *page 159 J3*

Old Hobart Town Model Village
21 Bridge St
(03) 6260 2502
www.richmondvillage.com.au

STRAHAN *page 160 C2*

Wharf Complex
12 Esplanade
(03) 6472 6800 or 1800 352 200
www.westernwilderness.com.au

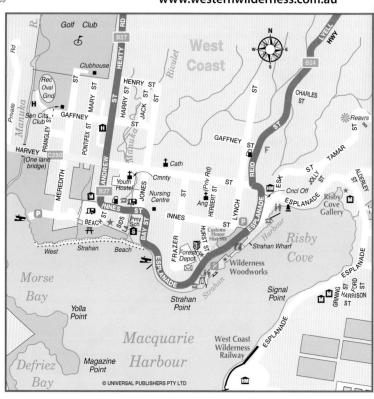

SWANSEA *page 161 N3*

Cnr Noyes St and Tasman Hwy
(03) 6256 5072
www.eastcoasttasmania.com

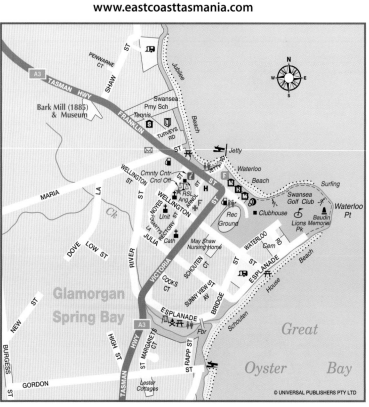

ULVERSTONE *page 162 G6*

13–15 Alexandra Rd
(03) 6425 2839
www.coasttocanyon.com.au

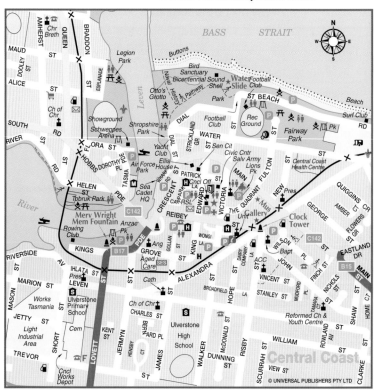

Planning your trip

BEFORE YOU LEAVE

- organise pet care
- pay essential bills early or organise for them to be paid electronically
- cancel deliveries
- mow the lawn
- turn off at the power point all unnecessary electric appliances (TVs, microwaves, clocks, etc.) to reduce power consumption of devices on 'standby' mode
- secure your home: lock windows, sheds, gates, etc.
- leave a blind partly open and a light on a timer
- leave contact details and spare keys with your neighbour; ask them to collect the mail, keep an eye on the place and occasionally park in your driveway

IF YOU ARE CAMPING, DON'T FORGET

- tent, tent pegs, tarps
- rope, shovel, axe and hammer/mallet
- mattress and bedding
- folding table, chairs, lamp and torches
- camp oven, gas stove, gas bottle and attachments
- matches (preferably waterproof)
- oven mitt
- saucepans, frying pan and billy
- drink bottles and water containers
- mixing bowl, crockery, cutlery
- can opener, knives, cutting board
- airtight food storage containers
- washing up equipment
- esky and/or car fridge

PASSES AND PERMITS

Passes and permits are necessary for travelling through many Indigenous areas and the Woomera Prohibited Area in South Australia. Organise permits well before you begin the journey as approval can take some time.

The main Land Councils are:
- Central Land Council, 27 Stuart Hwy, Alice Springs; (08) 8951 6211; www.clc.org.au
- Northern Land Council, 45 Mitchell St, Darwin; (08) 8920 5100; www.nlc.org.au
- For Woomera Prohibited Area: Woomera Test Range Operations Office, Woomera; (08) 8674 3370 or 1300 727 420; www.defence.gov.au/woomera/permit-tourist.htm

You may need a Desert Parks Pass if travelling into the desert parks of northern South Australia. The passes are issued by the Department for Environment, Water and Natural Resources and are an alternative to the daily camping permits issued for entering the parks. They include detailed maps, information on first aid and survival skills. Level 1, 100 Pirie St, Adelaide; (08) 8648 5328; www.environment.sa.gov.au.

PACKING

Since much of your holiday will be spent driving in the car, take lots of comfortable clothes. Even if travelling in summer, take warm clothing as nights can still be cool, or even cold in desert regions. Also, take extra changes of clothes if the area you will be exploring is cold and wet. Thermal clothing is particularly useful in very cold weather.

In a sedan, put as much as possible in the boot; it is dangerous to have loose luggage in the cabin – in an accident even light objects such as books can cause serious injury. Soft baggage is ideal for car journeys as it can be squashed into tight spaces in the vehicle.

Pack items you are likely to need first (such as warm jumpers or a tent) near the top, so they are easily accessible. Pack heavy items in the boot or a trailer, not on a roof rack. The weight of heavy items on the roof could easily throw the car off balance. When packing a roof rack, make the load lower at the front and higher at the back so there is less wind resistance.

Cover a trailer with a cargo net and place a high-quality tarp over items you would like to protect from the elements.

Keep tissues, extra water and snacks, maps and a compass within easy reach.

The glove box can be used to keep important papers such as vehicle registration, the number of your insurance policy and medical prescriptions.

FIRST AID

Your first-aid kit is almost useless if you don't know how to use it. On an extended trip someone in your group should have completed a basic first-aid course, particularly if you are travelling to remote areas.

Keep your first-aid kit well stocked. Ensure it's easily accessible and that everyone knows where it is. Commercially prepared kits are available from chemists and camping equipment shops. Alternatively, make up your own kit in a clean, waterproof container. The following are recommended inclusions:
- saline solution
- sterile dressings
- non-adherent dressings for use when you don't want a bandage to stick to the wound, such as burns
- bandages – triangular and conforming
- alcoholic swabs, gauze swabs
- safety pins
- antihistamine (for insect stings)
- aspirin or paracetamol
- car-sickness tablets
- soothing lotion for bites
- clinical thermometer
- scissors, tweezers
- first-aid book
- latex gloves
- thermo blanket

CAR PREPARATION

Before you leave home, book your car in for a thorough service by a qualified mechanic. If you are towing a caravan or trailer, get it serviced as well – particularly the tyres, lights and indicators.

Before you leave and during the trip, check:
- battery and mountings
- tyre condition and pressure (remember the spare!)
- windscreen wipers – blades and reservoir
- heater and demister
- air-conditioning
- lights
- oil and coolant

Extras to take

Carry a spare set of keys, a set of spanners and screwdrivers, jumper leads, WD lubricant, spare engine drive belt(s), radiator hoses, light globes and fuses, a jack and tools for changing tyres. A fire extinguisher is also recommended.

Motoring hints

BEATING FATIGUE

Research has shown that the best way to beat fatigue on long journeys is to be well rested and have occasional naps; napping is more effective than a quick bout of exercise (such as a brisk walk), but napping should not replace main sleep. The best times to nap are in the body's natural 'sleepy' periods, such as 2–4pm or 12–6am.

Naps should last 10–30 minutes (after that you might enter a deep sleep phase, which may make you more drowsy when you wake). After waking, allow 15 minutes or so before driving. This is the best time to go for a walk.

Other tips for beating fatigue:

- *every two hours take a break from driving*
- *change drivers regularly*
- *pull over and stop when drowsiness or discomfort occurs*
- *wear comfortable clothes and sit upright with good back support*
- *keep the windscreen clean and clear*
- *wear sunglasses to avoid glare*
- *avoid eating a heavy meal before driving*
- *get a good night's sleep before a long drive*

TRAVELLING WITH CHILDREN

To prevent boredom, keep some toys and activities in the car. You can also:

- *use back-seat DVD players*
- *play music and sing together*
- *stop for frequent breaks at places where they can run around, such as playgrounds*
- *have healthy snacks available – carrot and celery sticks, cut-up fruit*

Carsickness is common in children. To lessen the symptoms you should:

- *drive smoothly with windows open*
- *restrict intake of greasy foods and milkshakes*
- *don't let susceptible children read or write while the car is moving*
- *put those at risk in the front seat or in the middle of the back seat where they can see ahead*
- *have a bag or container for them in case they are sick*

OFF THE BEATEN TRACK

Four-wheel drivers heading off-road should also consider taking:

- service and repair manual
- extra water and water filter
- oil and metal jerry cans of fuel (stored on the back of the four-wheel drive or in a trailer)
- towing hooks, heavy rope or tow cable
- flares for signals
- EPIRB or satellite phone
- breakdown warning reflector
- cooling system leak sealer
- glue, insulating tape
- radiator insect screen
- plastic sheet, water bucket
- fuel filter
- shovel and axe
- spark plugs
- heater hoses and clamps
- brake fluid
- tyres or tube repair kit
- tyre pump – 12V
- inflatable bull bag (an inflatable jack)

FUEL ECONOMY

Fuel consumption is affected by the condition of the car and where it is driven. The following tips can increase your fuel efficiency by up to a third:

- avoid delays (peak-hour traffic or scheduled bridge closures)
- distribute weight evenly throughout the vehicle

- if you are based somewhere for longer than a couple of days, remove all excess weight from the vehicle
- if held up in traffic, turn off the engine (if safe to do so)
- drive smoothly, accelerate slowly
- ensure tyres are inflated to the ideal pressure and wheel alignment and balance are correct
- avoid driving at very high speeds
- use the air-conditioner only when necessary
- once you reach a destination, consider whether you really need to use the car; walk or use bikes or public transport

Fuel consumption

When covering long distances on remote roads, it is helpful to know your car's fuel consumption. Here is a basic formula:

Total litres ÷ (total km ÷ 100) = litres per 100 km

or

100 × total litres ÷ total km = litres per 100 km

Example: 60 litres ÷ (300km ÷ 100) = 20 litres per 100 km

Driving on the Indian Ocean Drive, Western Australia

Motoring survival

DRIVING IN FOG

▶ *It may be safer to pull off the road and wait for the fog to lift if you are in zero or near-zero visibility. It is better to get to your destination late than not at all.*

▶ *Drive slowly and put low beam, hazard lights and fog lights on if you have them. High beams usually make it harder to see.*

▶ *Keep seatbelts fastened.*

▶ *Avoid crossing roads or busy highways if visibility is dramatically reduced.*

SURVIVAL HINTS

▶ *Stay with your vehicle – it provides shelter and greatly increases chances of survival. Spotting a car is easier than finding a person. Only leave a vehicle if you know there is help nearby and you know exactly how to get there.*

▶ *Conserve food and water. Carry enough food and water to keep you supplied for a few days (minimum 4 litres of water per person, per day).*

▶ *Avoid drinking alcohol – it can dehydrate you and make you think less clearly.*

▶ *Stay in the shade – keep clothes on to help protect against exposure.*

▶ *Prepare adequate signals – you can use a mirror to attract an aircraft, use flares or light a fire.*

▶ *Stay calm and think through the options.*

SURVIVING A BUSHFIRE

If you get caught in a bushfire and can't retreat, don't panic. The car may be the safest place; unlike in the movies, there is little risk of the petrol tank exploding in a bushfire.

▶ *In dense smoke pull to the side of the road, away from the leading edge of the fire and stop. If possible, park behind a solid structure to protect the car and yourself from as much heat as possible.*

▶ *Switch on your headlights and hazard lights and close all windows and air vents. Leave the engine running, and the air-conditioning on recirculate.*

▶ *Stay in the car. Put on covered shoes (for after) and if possible have water nearby to drink. Crouch in the car, under a woollen blanket. Stay there until the fire passes (usually just 5–10 minutes), then get out of the car.*

DRIVING IN NORTHERN AUSTRALIA

The climate can dictate when to travel around northern Australia. There are two distinct seasons in northern Australia: the wet season (November–April) and the dry season (May–October). Generally, the dry season is the best time of year to explore the Northern Territory, Far North Queensland and northern Western Australia, because it has comfortable daytime temperatures and cool nights. The wet season is not a pleasant time for a driving holiday as it is characterised by monsoonal rainfall and it is quite common for roads to become impassable after heavy rainfall.

DRIVING IN ALPINE REGIONS

• Have tyres and brakes checked.
• Add anti-freeze to radiator.
• Renew windscreen wiper blades.
• Check heater and demister are working properly.
• Carry warm blankets and/or sleeping-bags.
• Buy or hire chains if travelling in snowy areas, and make sure you have gloves to use when putting the chains on or taking them off in freezing conditions. In some areas, in winter, signs will indicate chains are compulsory and you may be turned back if you do not have them.
• Use brakes as little as possible to avoid skidding; use lower gears to control speed.
• Use higher gears when driving uphill, as over-revving can cause wheel slip.
• Don't use the handbrake to park, as it could freeze in the engaged position. Park on the flat and use wheel chocks if necessary. Also lift windscreen wipers off the windscreen after parking.

OUTBACK MOTORING

• On dirt roads, drive carefully at a safe speed.
• When overtaking, beware of soft or loose edges and the dust from road trains. If stuck behind a road train, pull over to the side of the road and wait a few minutes until the dust has settled.
• When making a creek crossing, drive slowly in the centre of the crossing, keep the wheels straight and do not change gear midstream. If it is safe to do so (bearing in mind crocodiles), check out the crossing on foot first, assessing depth and creek flow. Do not cross if the flow is deep and fast.
• On sand, keep the four-wheel drive in as straight a line as possible. Lower tyre pressure as necessary, but be careful not to lower them too much in desert areas with spinifex and hard wooden roots.
• Generally you don't need to brake on sand – let the sand retard the vehicle.
• If stuck in sand, use floor mats or old blankets to give support and traction. Use a shovel to dig out tyres as much as possible.
• Hub caps can be used as jack supports in an emergency.

Bunyeroo Valley Lookout Drive, South Australia

Index

A1 Mine Settlement Vic. 47 P4, 48 H3
Abbeyard Vic. 51 J10
Abbotsbury NSW 6 E10, 8 E2
Abbotsford NSW 7 K11, 9 K3
Abbotsford Vic. 42 H8, 43 I8
Abbotsham Tas. 162 G6
Abercorn Qld 137 K3
Abercrombie River NP NSW 12 H7, 20 E1
Aberdeen NSW 13 K1, 14 H12
Aberfeldie Vic. 42 F6
Aberfeldy Vic. 48 H4
Aberfoyle Park SA 69 D6
Abergowrie Qld 141 L9
Abermain NSW 13 L4
Acacia NT 114 E5, 116 D5
Acacia Gardens NSW 6 F7
Acacia Ridge Qld 132 H5, 133 I5
Acheron Vic. 47 N1, 48 F1, 50 F12
Acland Qld 137 K8
Acton ACT 33 B4, 34 D5
Acton Park Tas. 157 K5
Acton Park WA 94 C6
Adaminaby NSW 12 E12, 20 B6, 58 D2
Adamsfield Tas. 158 A2, 160 G6
Adavale Qld 147 M4
Addington Vic. 46 C2, 57 L3
Adelaide SA 67 E8, 68 D11, 69 D1, 70 B9, 71 F2, 73 J9, 82 B3
Adelaide Airport SA 68 B12, 69 B3
Adelaide Lead Vic. 55 L12
Adelaide River NT 114 E8, 116 D6
Adelong NSW 12 D10, 20 A4, 51 P2
Adjungbilly NSW 12 E10, 20 B4
Advancetown Qld 135 F10
Adventure Bay Tas. 159 I11, 161 K10
Agery SA 72 H7
Agnes Vic. 48 H10
Agnes Banks NSW 6 B3, 10 H4
Agnes Water Qld 137 M2
Agnew WA 98 G1, 100 G11
Aileron Roadhouse NT 120 H5
Ailsa Vic. 54 G7
Ainslie ACT 33 H1, 34 F4
Airds NSW 8 C9
Aireys Inlet Vic. 46 D10, 57 N9
Airlie Beach Qld 139 J3
Airly Vic. 49 K6
Airport West Vic. 42 F5
Akaroa Tas. 163 P8
Alawa NT 112 D3
Alawoona SA 16 A7, 52 A8, 73 N9, 82 G2
Albacutya Vic. 16 D11, 54 F4
Albanvale Vic. 42 D6
Albany WA 95 M11, 96 G11, 98 E11
Albany Creek Qld 130 H8, 134 F10, 135 D3
Albert NSW 12 C1, 14 A12, 19 P12
Albert Park SA 68 B10, 70 B8, 71 E1
Albert Park Vic. 41 D12, 42 G9
Alberton Qld 133 M9
Alberton SA 68 B9
Alberton Tas. 163 N7
Alberton Vic. 49 I9
Alberton West Vic. 49 I9
Albina Rock Tas. 160 C3
Albinia NP Qld 136 F1, 139 I12
Albion Qld 131 I11, 133 I1

Albion Vic. 42 E7
Albury NSW 12 A12, 17 O12, 51 K6
Alcomie Tas. 162 C4
Alderley Qld 130 H11, 131 I10, 132 H1, 133 I1
Aldersyde WA 96 E5
Aldgate SA 69 G4, 70 C10, 71 G3
Aldinga SA 69 A12, 70 A12, 71 E5
Aldinga Beach SA 69 A12, 70 A12, 71 E6, 73 J10, 82 B4
Alectown NSW 12 E3
Alexander Heights WA 90 E6, 91 C1
Alexander Morrison NP WA 96 A1, 98 B5
Alexandra Vic. 47 N1, 48 F1, 50 F12
Alexandra Hills Qld 133 M5, 134 G12, 135 F5
Alexandria NSW 9 L5
Alford SA 73 I6
Alfords Point NSW 8 H6
Alfred Cove WA 90 E12, 91 C6
Alfred NP Vic. 20 C11, 58 F10
Alfred Town NSW 12 C10, 17 P10, 51 N1
Algester Qld 132 H6, 133 I6
Ali–Curung NT 119 J12, 121 J1
Alice NSW 15 M4, 137 M12
Alice Springs NT 121 I7
Alkimos WA 90 A1
Allambee Vic. 47 O9, 48 G7
Allambee South Vic. 47 O10, 48 G8
Allambie Heights NSW 7 N8, 9 N1
Allans Flat Vic. 51 K7
Allansford Vic. 56 H8
Allanson WA 94 E3, 96 C8
Allawah NSW 9 J6
Alleena NSW 12 B6, 17 P6
Allenby Gardens SA 68 C11, 69 C1
Allendale Vic. 46 D2, 57 M3
Allendale East SA 56 A6, 82 G12
Allendale North SA 70 E2, 73 K7, 82 C1
Allens Rivulet Tas. 158 H7
Allenvale Vic. 46 D11, 57 M9
Allies Creek Qld 137 K6
Alligator Creek Qld 138 G1, 141 N12
Allora Qld 137 L10
Alma SA 70 C2, 73 J7, 82 B1
Alma Vic. 55 L11, 57 L1
Alma Park NSW 12 A11, 17 N11, 51 K3
Almaden Qld 141 J7
Almonds Vic. 50 H6
Alonnah Tas. 158 H10, 161 J10
Aloomba Qld 141 M6
Alpara NT 78 G2, 120 E11
Alpha Qld 138 F10
Alpha Rock Qld 142 D2
Alphadale NSW 15 O3
Alphington Vic. 43 I7
Alpine NP Vic. 20 A9, 49 J2, 50 H12, 51 J12, 58 A6
Alpurrurulam NT 119 P12, 121 P1, 144 C4
Alstonville NSW 15 O3, 137 N12
Alton NP Qld 136 G9
Altona Vic. 42 D9, 47 I6, 48 B5
Altona Meadows Vic. 42 C9
Altona North Vic. 42 E8
Alva Qld 138 H1, 141 O12

Alvie Vic. 46 A8, 57 K7
Alwal NP (CYPAL) Qld 141 I2, 142 E12
Alyangula NT 117 M7
Amamoor NP Qld 137 M6
Amanbidji NT 103 P5, 116 B12, 118 B3
Amaroo ACT 34 E1
Amata SA 78 G2, 120 E11
Ambarvale NSW 8 B9
Amberley Qld 132 A5
Amboyne Crossing Vic. 20 B10, 58 C7
Ambrose Qld 139 N12
Amby Qld 136 F6
American Beach SA 73 I11
American River SA 72 H11
Amherst Vic. 55 L12, 57 L1
Amiens Qld 15 K2, 137 K11
Amity Point Qld 135 H4, 137 N9
Amoonguna NT 121 I7
Amosfield NSW 15 L2
Amphion WA 93 F10
Amphitheatre Vic. 55 K12, 57 K2
Ampilatwatja NT 121 K3
Anakie Qld 138 H10
Anakie Vic. 46 F6, 57 N6
Anakie East Vic. 46 F6, 57 O6
Anakie Junction Vic. 46 F6, 57 N6
Ancona Vic. 50 G10
Andamooka SA 74 F3
Anderson Vic. 47 L11, 48 E8
Ando NSW 20 C9, 58 F6
Andover Tas. 161 L4
Andrews Vic. 73 J5
Andrews Farm SA 68 F4
Anembo NSW 12 G12, 20 D6, 31 G11, 58 G1
Angas Valley SA 70 H7, 73 L8, 82 D2
Angaston SA 70 F4, 73 K8, 82 C2
Angip Vic. 16 D12, 54 G6
Angle Park SA 68 C9
Angle Vale SA 68 E2, 70 C6, 73 J8, 82 B2
Anglers Reach NSW 12 E12, 20 B6, 58 D2
Anglers Rest Vic. 49 M1, 51 M11
Anglesea Vic. 46 E10, 57 N9
Angleside Vic. 51 I8
Angourie NSW 15 O5
Angurugu NT 117 M7
Angustown Vic. 50 D9
Anketell WA 91 D11, 92 D1
Anna Bay NSW 13 M4
Annaburroo NT 114 H6, 116 E5
Annan River (Yuku Baja–Muliku) NP Qld 141 L3
Annandale NSW 7 L12, 9 L4
Annangrove NSW 6 G5, 11 J6
Annerley Qld 133 I3, 134 F11, 135 D5
Annuello Vic. 16 F8, 53 J9
Ansons Bay Tas. 163 P6
Anstead Qld 132 E3
Anthony Qld 132 A12
Antill Ponds Tas. 161 L3
Antwerp Vic. 16 D12, 54 F7
Anula NT 112 E3
Apamurra SA 70 G8, 73 K9, 82 D3
Aparawatatja SA 78 D2, 120 C11
Apollo Bay Vic. 46 B12, 57 L10
Appila SA 73 J3, 74 H11
Appin NSW 8 B11, 13 J8, 20 H2

Appin Vic. 16 H11, 55 M5
Appin South Vic. 55 N5
Apple Tree Creek Qld 137 M4
Apple Tree Flat NSW 10 C7, 13 I9, 15 M5, 20 F3
Applecross WA 90 E11, 91 C6
Applethorpe Qld 15 L2, 137 L11
Apslawn Tas. 161 O2, 163 O11
Apsley Tas. 161 J4
Apsley Vic. 54 B10, 82 H9
Arakoon NP NSW 15 M9
Arakwal NP NSW 15 O3, 137 N12
Araluen NSW 12 H12, 20 E6
Aramac Qld 138 D9, 145 P9
Aramara Qld 137 M5
Arana Hills Qld 130 G10, 134 E10, 135 D3
Aranda ACT 34 D4
Arapiles Vic. 54 E9
Ararat Vic. 55 I12, 57 I2
Aratula Qld 137 M10
Arawata Vic. 47 N10, 48 F8
Arawerr NT 121 K3
Arcadia NSW 7 J3, 11 K5
Arcadia Vic. 50 E8
Arch Rock Vic. 48 F10
Archdale Vic. 55 L10
Archer NT 112 H12, 113 I11
Archer River Roadhouse Qld 142 D9
Archerfield Qld 132 H4, 133 I5, 134 F12, 135 D5
Archies Creek Vic. 47 L11, 48 E9
Ardath WA 96 G4
Ardeer Vic. 42 D7, 47 I5, 57 P5
Ardglen NSW 14 H11
Ardlethan NSW 12 B7, 17 O7
Ardmona Vic. 50 E7
Ardmory Qld 134 C10, 135 A3
Ardross WA 90 F12, 91 C6
Ardrossan SA 73 I7, 82 A1
Areegra Vic. 55 I7
Areyonga NT 120 G7
Argalong NSW 12 E10, 20 B4
Argoon Qld 137 J1
Argyle Vic. 50 B10, 55 P11, 57 P1
Ariah Park NSW 12 B7, 17 P7
Arkaroola SA 75 K3
Arkona Vic. 16 D12, 54 F7
Arltunga Bush Hotel NT 121 K6
Armadale Vic. 43 I9
Armadale WA 91 G10, 93 D6, 96 C5, 98 C8
Armatree NSW 14 C10
Armidale NSW 15 J8
Armstrong Vic. 55 I12, 57 I2
Armstrong Beach Qld 139 K6
Armstrong Creek Qld 130 E3
Armytage Vic. 46 C8, 57 M8
Arncliffe NSW 9 K5, 11 L10
Arno Bay SA 72 F6
Arnold Vic. 55 M9
Arnold West Vic. 55 M9
Arrawarra NSW 15 N7
Arrilalah Qld 138 A10, 145 M10
Arrino WA 98 B4
Artarmon NSW 7 L10, 9 L2
Arthur River Tas. 162 A5
Arthur River WA 95 I3, 96 E8, 98 D9
Arthurs Creek Vic. 43 L1, 47 K4, 48 D3
Arthurton SA 72 H7

Arthurville NSW 12 F2
Ascot Qld 131 J11, 133 J1
Ascot Vic. 46 C2, 57 M3
Ascot WA 90 G8, 91 E3
Ascot Park SA 69 C3
Ascot Vale Vic. 42 F7
Ashbourne SA 69 H12, 71 G6, 73 J10, 82 C4
Ashburton Vic. 43 J10
Ashbury NSW 7 J12, 9 K5
Ashby WA 90 C3
Ashcroft NSW 6 F12, 8 F4
Ashens Vic. 54 H9
Ashfield NSW 7 K12, 9 K5
Ashfield WA 90 G8, 91 E3, 93 C5
Ashford NSW 15 I4
Ashford SA 68 D12, 69 D2
Ashgrove Qld 130 H11, 131 I11, 132 H1, 133 I1
Ashley NSW 14 F4, 136 H12
Ashton SA 68 G12, 69 G2
Ashville SA 73 L11, 82 D5
Ashwood Vic. 43 K10
Aspendale Vic. 44 D4, 47 J8, 48 C5
Aspendale Gardens Vic. 44 E4
Aspley Qld 131 I9, 134 F10, 135 D3
Asquith NSW 7 L6, 11 L6
Astrebla Downs NP Qld 144 G11
Athelstone SA 68 G10
Atherton Qld 141 L7
Athlone Vic. 47 N9, 48 F7
Athol Park SA 68 C9
Atitjere NT 121 K5
Atneltyey NT 121 J3
Attadale WA 90 D11, 91 B6
Attunga NSW 14 H9
Attwood Vic. 42 F4
Atwell WA 91 D9
Aubin Grove WA 91 D11
Aubrey Vic. 54 G7
Auburn NSW 6 H10, 7 I11, 8 H2, 9 I2, 11 K8
Auburn SA 73 J6
Auburn Tas. 161 K1, 163 K11
Auburn River NP Qld 137 K5
Auchenflower Qld 130 H12, 132 H2
Augathella Qld 136 C4, 147 P4
Augusta WA 94 B9, 96 B10, 98 B11
Augustine Heights Qld 132 E7
Auldana SA 68 F11, 69 F1
Aurora Kakadu Resort NT 115 M4, 116 G4
Aurukun Qld 142 B8
Auski Roadhouse WA 97 H3, 100 D4
Austins Ferry Tas. 156 B1
Austral NSW 6 C12, 8 C4, 10 H9, 13 J7, 20 H1
Australia Plains SA 73 K7
Australian National University ACT 33 C3
Australind WA 94 D3, 96 C8, 98 C9
Avalon NSW 7 P4, 11 N6
Aveley WA 90 H4
Avenel Vic. 50 D10
Avenue SA 82 F9
Avoca Tas. 163 M10
Avoca Vic. 55 L12, 57 L1
Avoca Beach NSW 11 O3
Avoca Vale Qld 137 L7
Avon SA 73 J7, 82 B1
Avon Plains Vic. 55 J8

Avon Valley NP WA 93 E2, 96 C4, 98 C7
Avondale NSW 13 J8, 20 H3
Avondale Heights Vic. 42 F6
Avonsleigh Vic. 45 L1
Awonga Vic. 54 C10, 82 H9
Axe Creek Vic. 50 A9, 55 O10
Axedale Vic. 50 B9, 55 P10
Ayr Qld 138 H2, 141 O12
Ayrford Vic. 57 I8
Ayton Qld 141 L4

Baan Baa NSW 14 F7
Baandee WA 96 F3
Baarmutha Vic. 51 J8
Babakin WA 96 G5
Babinda Qld 141 M7
Bacchus Marsh Vic. 46 G4, 48 A3, 57 O5
Back Creek Tas. 163 K5
Baddaginnie Vic. 50 G8
Baden Tas. 161 L4
Badger Island Tas. 160 A11, 163 N1
Badgerys Creek NSW 6 B10, 8 B2, 10 H8, 13 J7, 20 H1
Badgingarra WA 96 A1, 98 B5
Badgingarra NP WA 96 A1, 98 B5
Badjaling WA 96 F5
Badu (Mulgrave) Island Qld 142 C1
Baerami NSW 13 J2
Bagdad Tas. 159 I2, 161 K5
Bagnoo NSW 15 L11
Bago Bluff NP NSW 15 L11
Bagot NT 114 D3
Bagot Well SA 70 F2, 73 K7, 82 C1
Bagshot Vic. 50 A8, 55 O9
Bahrs Scrub Qld 133 K9
Bailieston Vic. 50 D9
Baird Bay SA 72 A4, 81 N11
Bairnsdale Vic. 49 M5
Bajool Qld 139 M11
Bakara SA 73 M8, 82 E2
Baker Vic. 54 E6
Bakers Creek Qld 139 K6
Bakers Hill WA 93 F3, 96 D4
Bakers Swamp NSW 12 F3
Bakewell NT 113 K10
Baking Board Qld 137 J7
Balaclava Vic. 42 H10
Balaklava SA 73 J7
Balcatta WA 90 D7, 91 C2
Bald Hills Qld 131 I7, 134 F10, 135 D3
Bald Rock Vic. 17 I12, 50 A5, 55 O6
Bald Rock NP NSW 15 L3, 137 L12
Baldivis WA 92 D2, 93 C7
Baldry NSW 12 E3
Balfes Creek Qld 138 E3
Balfour Tas. 162 B6
Balga WA 90 D6, 91 C2
Balgal Beach Qld 141 M11
Balgo Hills WA 103 N10
Balgowan SA 72 H7
Balgowlah NSW 7 N9, 9 N1, 11 M8
Balgowlah Heights NSW 7 N10, 9 N2
Balhannah SA 70 D9, 71 H3
Balingup WA 94 E6, 96 C9, 98 C10
Balintore Vic. 46 B8, 57 L8
Ball Bay Qld 139 K5
Balladonia WA 99 K7
Balladonia Roadhouse WA 99 K7

Balladoran NSW 14 C11
Ballajura WA 90 E6, 91 C1, 93 C4
Ballalaba NSW 12 G11, 20 E5
Ballan Vic. 46 F3, 57 N4
Ballan North Vic. 46 F3, 57 N4
Ballandean Qld 15 K3, 137 K12
Ballangeich Vic. 56 H7
Ballarat Vic. 46 D3, 57 M4
Ballark Vic. 46 E4, 57 N5
Ballaying WA 95 K2, 96 F8
Ballbank NSW 16 H10, 55 N3
Balldale NSW 17 N11, 51 J4
Ballendella Vic. 50 B6, 55 P8
Balliang Vic. 46 F5, 48 A4, 57 O5
Balliang East Vic. 46 F5, 48 A4, 57 O5
Ballidu WA 96 D1, 98 C5
Ballimore NSW 12 F1, 14 D12
Ballina NSW 15 O3, 137 N12
Ballyrogan Vic. 57 J3
Balmain NSW 7 L11, 9 L3
Balmain East NSW 5 B3, 7 L11, 9 L3
Balmattum Vic. 50 F9
Balmoral Qld 131 J12, 133 J2
Balmoral Vic. 54 E12, 56 E2
Balnarring Vic. 47 J10, 48 C7
Balook Vic. 49 I8
Balranald NSW 16 H7, 53 M9
Balrootan North Vic. 16 C12, 54 E7
Balumbah SA 72 E4, 74 D11
Balwyn Vic. 43 J8
Balwyn North Vic. 43 J7
Bamaga Qld 142 C3
Bamawm Vic. 17 I12, 50 B6, 55 P7
Bamawm Extension Vic. 50 B6, 55 P7
Bambaroo Qld 141 M10
Bambill Vic. 16 C6, 52 E7, 73 P8
Bamboo Creek WA 100 F2, 102 F12
Bambra Vic. 46 D9, 57 M8
Bamganie Vic. 46 D6, 57 M6
Ban Ban NP Qld 137 L5
Banana Qld 137 I2
Bancroft Qld 137 K3
Bandiana Vic. 12 A12, 51 K6
Bandon Grove NSW 13 M2
Banealla SA 73 N12, 82 F6
Bangadilly NP NSW 13 I8, 20 F2
Bangalow NSW 15 O3, 137 N12
Bangerang Vic. 54 H6
Bangham SA 54 B8, 82 G8
Bangholme Vic. 44 E4
Bangor NSW 8 H7, 9 I7
Bangor Tas. 163 K7
Bania NP Qld 137 L3
Baniyala NT 117 M6
Banjup WA 91 D11
Banks ACT 34 C12
Banks Creek Qld 130 C9
Banksia NSW 9 K6, 11 L10
Banksia Beach Qld 131 L1, 134 G7
Banksia Grove WA 90 C3
Banksia Park SA 68 G8
Banksmeadow NSW 9 L6
Bankstown NSW 6 H12, 7 I12, 8 H4, 9 I5, 11 K9
Bankstown Aerodrome NSW 6 G12, 8 G4
Bannaby NSW 12 H8, 20 F2
Bannerton Vic. 16 F7, 53 J9
Bannister NSW 12 G8, 20 E2

Bannister WA 93 G9, 96 D6
Bannockburn Qld 133 K10
Bannockburn Vic. 46 E7, 57 N7
Banora Point NSW 15 O2, 135 G12, 137 N11
Banyan Vic. 55 I3
Banyena Vic. 55 I9
Banyo Qld 131 J9
Bar Point NSW 7 M1
Barabba SA 70 B2
Baradine NSW 14 D8
Barakee NP NSW 15 J11
Barakula Qld 137 J6
Baralaba Qld 137 I1, 139 L12
Baranduda Vic. 51 K6
Barangaroo NSW 5 C4
Barayamal NP NSW 15 I5
Barcaldine Qld 138 D10, 145 P10
Barden Ridge NSW 8 G8
Bardon Qld 130 H11, 132 H1
Bardwell Park NSW 9 J5
Bardwell Valley NSW 9 K5
Barellan NSW 12 A7, 17 N7
Barellan Point Qld 132 E5
Barfold Vic. 50 A11, 55 P12, 57 P1
Bargara Qld 137 M3
Bargo NSW 13 J8, 20 G2
Barham NSW 17 I10, 50 A2, 55 O4
Baring Vic. 16 D9, 52 G12, 54 G2
Baringhup Vic. 55 N11, 57 N1
Barjarg Vic. 50 G10
Bark Hut Inn NT 114 H6
Barkers Creek Vic. 50 A10, 55 O11, 57 O1
Barkly Vic. 55 K11
Barkly Homestead NT 119 L9
Barkstead Vic. 46 E2, 57 N3
Barmah Vic. 17 J12, 50 D5
Barmah NP Vic. 17 K11, 50 D4
Barmedman NSW 12 C6, 17 P6
Barmera SA 16 A6, 73 N7, 82 G1
Barmundu Qld 137 K1
Barnadown Vic. 50 B8, 55 P9
Barnard Island Group NP Qld 141 M8
Barnawartha Vic. 12 A12, 17 N12, 51 J6
Barnawartha North Vic. 51 K6
Barnes NSW 17 J12, 50 C5
Barnes Bay Tas. 159 I8, 161 K8
Barnes Caravans NSW 6 G12
Barongarook Vic. 46 B10, 57 L9
Barongarook West Vic. 46 B9, 57 K8
Barooga NSW 17 L11, 50 G4
Barool NP NSW 15 L5
Baroota SA 73 I3, 74 G11
Barpinba Vic. 46 B7, 57 L7
Barraba NSW 14 H7
Barragup WA 92 D9
Barrakee Vic. 55 L7
Barramunga Vic. 46 B11, 57 L9
Barranyi (North Island) NP NT 117 N10, 119 N1
Barraport Vic. 16 H11, 55 M6
Barringo Vic. 48 B2, 50 B12
Barrington NSW 13 M1, 15 J12
Barrington Tas. 162 H7
Barrington Tops NP NSW 13 L1, 15 I12
Barringun NSW 19 M2, 136 A11, 147 N11
Barron Gorge NP Qld 141 L6
Barrow Creek NT 121 I2

Barrow Island WA 97 C1
Barrow Island Marine Management Area WA 97 C1
Barrow Island Marine Park WA 97 C1
Barry NSW 12 G5, 15 I11
Barrys Reef Vic. 46 F2, 48 A2, 57 O3
Barton ACT 33 F10, 34 E7
Barton Vic. 57 I2
Barunga NT 116 G8
Barunga Gap SA 73 I6
Barwidgee Creek Vic. 51 K8
Barwo Vic. 50 D5
Barwon Bluff Marine Sanctuary Vic. 46 G9, 48 A7, 57 O8
Barwon Downs Vic. 46 C10, 57 L9
Barwon Heads Vic. 46 G9, 48 A7, 57 O8
Baryulgil NSW 15 M4
Basin Pocket Qld 132 C5
Baskerville WA 90 H4
Basket Range SA 68 H12, 69 H3
Basket Swamp NP NSW 15 L3, 137 L12
Bass Vic. 47 L11, 48 E8
Bass Hill NSW 6 G12, 8 H4
Bassendean WA 90 G7, 91 E2
Batavia NP (CYPAL) Qld 142 D6
Batchelor NT 114 E7, 116 D5
Batchica Vic. 16 E12, 54 H6
Bateau Bay NSW 11 P2
Batehaven NSW 12 H12
Bateman WA 90 F12, 91 C7
Batemans Bay NSW 12 H12, 20 F6
Bates SA 81 J3
Batesford Vic. 46 F7, 57 N7
Bathumi Vic. 50 H5
Bathurst NSW 12 H5
Bathurst Island NT 116 C3
Batlow NSW 12 D11, 20 A5, 51 P3
Battery Point Tas. 155 F8, 156 E8
Bauhinia Qld 136 H2
Bauhinia Downs NT 117 L11, 119 L2
Baulkham Hills NSW 6 H6, 7 I8, 11 J7
Bauple Qld 137 M5
Baw Baw NP Vic. 47 P6, 48 H5, 49 I5
Bawley Point NSW 13 I11, 20 F5
Baxter Vic. 44 E9, 47 J9, 48 D6
Bay Rock Qld 141 N11
Bayles Vic. 45 M9, 47 M9, 48 E6
Baynton Vic. 50 B11, 55 P12, 57 P2
Bayswater Vic. 43 M10
Bayswater WA 90 G7, 91 E2
Bayswater North Vic. 43 N9
Bayview NSW 7 O5, 11 N6
Bayview NT 112 C7
Beachmere Qld 131 J1, 134 F8, 135 E1, 137 N8
Beachport SA 82 E10
Beacon WA 96 F1, 98 D5
Beacon Hill NSW 7 N8, 9 N1
Beaconsfield NSW 9 L5
Beaconsfield Tas. 163 J6
Beaconsfield Vic. 45 J5, 47 K7, 48 E6
Beaconsfield WA 91 A8
Beaconsfield Upper Vic. 45 L4
Beagle Bay WA 102 H6
Bealiba Vic. 55 L10
Beardmore Vic. 49 I5

Beargamil NSW 12 E3
Bearii Vic. 17 K11, 50 E4
Bears Lagoon Vic. 16 H12, 55 N7
Beauchamp Vic. 55 L3
Beaudesert Qld 15 N1, 135 C9, 137 M10
Beaufort SA 73 I6
Beaufort Vic. 46 A2, 57 K3
Beaumaris Tas. 163 O8
Beaumaris Vic. 44 C3
Beaumont SA 68 F12, 69 F3
Beaumont Hills NSW 6 G5
Beauty Point NSW 20 E8
Beauty Point Tas. 163 J6
Beazleys Bridge Vic. 55 J9
Beckenham WA 90 H12, 91 F5
Beckom NSW 12 B7, 17 O7
Bedarra Island Qld 141 M8
Bedford WA 90 F8, 91 D3
Bedford Park SA 69 C4
Bedfordale WA 91 H10
Bedgerebong NSW 12 D4
Bedourie Qld 144 E11
Beeac Vic. 46 B8, 57 L7
Beebo Qld 15 I2, 137 J11
Beech Forest Vic. 46 B11, 57 K10
Beechboro WA 90 G6, 91 D2
Beechford Tas. 163 J5
Beechmont Qld 135 E10
Beechwood NSW 15 L11
Beechworth Vic. 51 J7
Beecroft NSW 7 J7
Beela WA 94 D3
Beelbangera NSW 17 M7
Beeliar WA 91 B9
Beelu NP WA 91 H3, 93 D5, 96 C5, 98 C7
Beenak Vic. 45 O1
Beenleigh Qld 133 K9, 135 E7, 137 N10
Beerburrum Qld 134 F6
Beeron NP Qld 137 K5
Beerwah Qld 134 F5, 137 N8
Bega NSW 20 E9, 58 H6
Beggan Beggan NSW 12 D8, 20 B2
Beilpajah NSW 16 H2
Belair SA 69 D4, 70 C9, 71 F3, 73 J9
Belair NP SA 69 E4, 70 B9, 71 F3, 73 J9, 82 B3
Belalie North SA 73 J4, 75 I11
Belbora NSW 13 N1, 15 K12
Belconnen ACT 12 F10, 20 C4, 31 D4, 34 C3
Beldon WA 90 C4
Belfield NSW 7 J12, 9 J5
Belford NSW 13 L3
Belford NP NSW 13 L3
Belgrave Vic. 43 O11, 45 J1, 47 K6, 48 E5
Belgrave Heights Vic. 43 O12, 45 J1
Belgrave South Vic. 43 O12, 45 I2, 47 K7
Belhus WA 90 H4, 93 D4
Belivah Qld 133 K10
Belka WA 96 G4
Bell NSW 10 D2, 13 I5
Bell Qld 137 K7
Bell Bay Tas. 163 J6
Bella Vista NSW 6 G7
Bellamack NT 113 K11
Bellara Qld 131 M1, 134 G7, 135 F1

Bellarine Vic. 46 G8, 48 B6, 57 P7
Bellarwi NSW 12 B6, 17 P6
Bellata NSW 14 F5
Bellbird NSW 13 L4
Bellbird Creek Vic. 20 B12, 58 C11
Bellbird Park Qld 132 E6
Bellbowrie Qld 132 E4
Bellbrae Vic. 46 E9, 57 N8
Bellbridge Vic. 51 L6
Bellbrook NSW 15 L9
Bellellen Vic. 55 I12, 57 I1
Bellerive Tas. 156 G6
Bellevue WA 91 G2
Bellevue Heights SA 69 C5
Bellevue Hill NSW 7 M12, 9 M4
Bellfield Vic. 43 I6
Bellingen NSW 15 M8
Bellinger River NP NSW 15 M8
Bellingham Tas. 163 K5
Bellmere Qld 130 F1
Bellmount Forest NSW 12 F9,
   20 D3
Bellthorpe NP Qld 134 D5, 137 M8
Belltrees NSW 11 N2, 13 K1, 15 I12
Belmont NSW 18 B10
Belmont Qld 133 K3
Belmont Vic. 46 F8, 48 A6, 57 O7
Belmont WA 90 G9, 91 E4, 93 C5
Belmore NSW 9 J5, 11 K9
Belmunging WA 96 E4
Beloka NSW 20 B8, 58 D5
Belowra NSW 20 E7, 58 H3
Belrose NSW 7 M7, 11 M7
Beltana SA 74 H4
Beltana Roadhouse SA 74 H4
Belton SA 73 K1, 75 I9
Belvidere SA 82 C4
Belyando Crossing Roadhouse
   Qld 138 G6
Belyuen NT 114 C3, 116 D4
Bemboka NSW 20 D9, 58 G5
Bemm River Vic. 20 B12, 58 D11
Ben Boyd NP NSW 20 E10, 58 H9
Ben Bullen NSW 13 I4
Ben Halls Gap NP NSW 15 I11
Ben Lomond NSW 15 J6
Ben Lomond NP Tas. 163 M9
Ben Nevis Vic. 55 J12, 57 J2
Bena NSW 12 B5, 17 P5
Bena Vic. 47 M10, 48 F8
Benalla Vic. 50 G8
Benambra Vic. 49 N1, 51 N11
Benambra NSW 12 B11,
   17 O11, 51 L4
Benaraby Qld 137 L1, 139 N12
Benarkin Qld 137 L8
Benarkin NP Qld 137 L7
Benayeo Vic. 54 B10, 82 H9
Bencubbin WA 96 F2, 98 D5
Bend of Islands Vic. 43 N5
Bendalong NSW 13 I11, 20 G5
Bendemeer NSW 15 I9
Bendick Murrell NSW 12 E7, 20 B1
Bendidee NP Qld 14 H1, 137 I10
Bendigo Vic. 50 A9, 55 O10
Bendoc Vic. 20 B10, 58 D8
Bendolba NSW 13 M2
Beneree NSW 12 G5
Benetook Vic. 16 D6, 52 G7
Benger WA 94 D2, 96 C8
Bengworden Vic. 49 M6
Beni NSW 12 F1, 14 C12
Beninbi NP Qld 137 L5
Benjeroop Vic. 16 H10, 55 M3

Benlidi Qld 138 C12, 145 O12,
   147 M1
Bennett Rock Qld 139 K4
Bennies Vic. 51 I11
Bentinck Island Qld 140 A5,
   143 D2
Bentleigh Vic. 43 I11, 44 C1
Bentleigh East Vic. 43 J11, 44 D1
Bentley NSW 15 N3
Bentley WA 90 F10, 91 D5
Benwerrin Vic. 46 D10, 57 M9
Berala NSW 7 I11, 9 I3
Berambing NSW 10 E3
Berat Qld 15 L1
Beremboke Vic. 46 E5, 57 N5
Berendebba NSW 12 D6
Beresfield NSW 13 L4
Bergalia NSW 20 F7
Berkeley Vale NSW 11 P2
Berkshire Park NSW 6 C4
Bermagui NSW 20 E8
Bermagui South NSW 20 E8
Bernier Island WA 97 B7
Berowra NSW 7 L5, 11 L5
Berowra Creek NSW 7 K1
Berowra Heights NSW 7 L3, 11 L5
Berowra Valley NP NSW 7 K4
Berowra Waters NSW 7 K3, 11 L5
Berri SA 16 A6, 52 A6, 73 N7, 82 G1
Berridale NSW 20 B8, 58 D4
Berriedale Tas. 156 B2, 159 I4,
   161 K6
Berrigan NSW 17 L11, 50 G3
Berrilee NSW 7 K3
Berrima NSW 13 I8, 20 G2
Berrimah NT 112 F5, 113 I7,
   114 D3
Berrimal Vic. 55 L8
Berrinba Qld 133 I7
Berringa Vic. 46 C5, 57 L5
Berringama Vic. 51 N7
Berriwillock Vic. 16 F10, 55 J3
Berry NSW 13 J9, 20 G3
Berry Springs NT 114 D5, 116 D5
Berrybank Vic. 46 A6, 57 K6
Bertram WA 91 D12, 92 D1
Berwick Vic. 45 J4, 47 K7, 48 D6
Bessiebelle Vic. 56 E7
Beswick NT 116 H8
Bet Bet Vic. 55 M11
Beta Qld 138 F10
Bete Bolong Vic. 20 A12, 49 P5,
   58 B11
Bethanga Vic. 51 L6
Bethania Qld 133 K9
Bethungra NSW 12 D8, 20 A3
Betley Vic. 55 M11
Betoota Qld 77 N1, 146 F3
Beulah Tas. 162 H8
Beulah Vic. 16 E11, 54 H5
Beulah East Vic. 16 E11, 54 H5
Beulah Park SA 68 E11, 69 E1
Beulah West Vic. 16 E11, 54 G5
Bevendale NSW 12 F8, 20 D2
Beverford Vic. 16 G9, 53 L12, 55 L1
Beveridge Vic. 47 J3, 48 C2
Beverley SA 68 C10, 69 C1
Beverley WA 96 E5, 98 D7
Beverley Park NSW 9 J7
Beverly Hills NSW 9 I5, 11 K10
Beware Reef Marine Sanctuary
   Vic. 20 B12, 58 C12
Beware Rocks Qld 139 L7
Bexhill NSW 15 O3

Bexley NSW 9 J6
Bexley North NSW 9 J5
Bezout Rock WA 97 F1, 100 B2,
   102 B12
Biala NSW 12 G8, 20 D2
Biamanga NP NSW 20 E8, 58 H5
Biarra Qld 134 A7
Bibaringa SA 68 H2
Bibbenluke NSW 20 C9, 58 F6
Biboohra Qld 141 L6
Bibra Lake WA 91 B8, 93 C6
Bicheno Tas. 161 O1, 163 O11
Bickerton Island
   (Amakalyuwakba) NT 117 M6
Bickley WA 93 D5
Bicton WA 90 D11, 91 B6
Biddon NSW 14 D10
Bidwill NSW 6 D6
Bidyadanga WA 102 G9
Big Caroline Rock Tas. 160 E9
Big Grove WA 95 M11, 96 G12
Big Pats Creek Vic. 47 N5
Big Rocky NSW 13 M4
Bigga NSW 12 G7, 20 D1
Biggara Vic. 20 A7, 51 P7, 58 A3
Bigge Island WA 103 K2
Biggenden Qld 137 L4
Biggs Flat SA 69 H6
Bilambil NSW 135 G12
Bilbarin WA 96 G5
Bilbul NSW 17 M7
Bilgola NSW 7 P5
Billabong Vic. 16 E6, 52 G6
Billabong Roadhouse WA 97 D10
Billimari NSW 12 E5
Billinudgel NSW 15 O2
Billys Creek NSW 15 M7
Biloela Qld 137 J2
Bilpin NSW 10 F3, 13 J5
Bilyana Qld 141 M9
Bimbaya NSW 58 G6
Bimberamala NP NSW 12 H11,
   20 F5
Bimbi NSW 12 D6
Bimbimbie NSW 12 H12, 20 F6
Binalong NSW 12 E8, 20 C2
Binalong Bay Tas. 163 P7
Binbee Qld 139 I3
Binda NSW 12 G8, 20 D2
Bindarri NP NSW 15 M7
Bindi Vic. 49 N1, 51 N12
Bindi Bindi WA 96 C2, 98 C5
Bindoon NSW 93 D1, 96 C3, 98 C7
Bingara NSW 14 H6
Bingera NP Qld 137 M3
Bingil Bay Qld 141 M8
Binginwarri Vic. 48 H9
Binjour Qld 137 K4
Binnaway NSW 14 E10
Binningup WA 94 C2, 96 C8
Binningup Beach WA 94 C2
Binnu WA 97 D11, 98 A2, 100 A12
Binnum SA 54 B9, 82 G8
Binya NSW 17 N7
Binya NP Qld 19 L1, 136 A10,
   147 N11
Birany Birany NT 117 N5
Birchgrove NSW 7 L11, 9 L3
Birchip Vic. 16 F11, 55 J5
Birchs Bay Tas. 158 H9, 161 J9
Bird Island SA 72 H6
Bird Island WA 93 B7
Birdsville Qld 77 K2, 146 D3

Birdwood NSW 15 L10
Birdwood SA 70 E8, 73 K9, 82 C2
Birdwoodton Vic. 52 G6
Biriwal Bulga NP NSW 15 K11
Birkdale Qld 133 L3, 134 G11,
   135 F5
Birkenhead SA 68 B9
Birralee Tas. 163 J8
Birrego NSW 12 A9, 17 N9
Birregurra Vic. 46 C9, 57 L8
Birriwa NSW 12 H1, 14 E12
Birrong NSW 6 H12, 7 I12, 8 H4,
   9 I4, 11 K9
Bishop Rock WA 99 I10
Bishopsbourne Tas. 163 J9
Bittern Vic. 47 J10, 48 D7
Black Bobs Tas. 160 H4
Black Forest SA 69 D3
Black Hill SA 73 L8, 82 D2
Black Hills Tas. 158 G3, 161 J6
Black Mountain NSW 15 J7
Black Mountain (Kalkajaka) NP
   Qld 141 L3
Black River Tas. 162 D4
Black Rock NSW 15 N7
Black Rock SA 72 H6, 73 J3, 75 I10
Black Rock Vic. 44 C3
Black Rock WA 96 H11, 98 B11,
   99 I9
Black Springs NSW 12 H6, 14 H12,
   15 I5
Black Springs SA 73 K6
Blackall Qld 136 A1, 138 D12,
   145 P12, 147 O1
Blackbraes NP Qld 138 B1,
   141 I11, 145 N1
Blackbull Qld 140 E8
Blackburn Vic. 43 K8
Blackburn North Vic. 43 K8
Blackburn South Vic. 43 K10
Blackbutt Qld 137 L8
Blackdown Tableland NP
   Qld 139 J11
Blackett NSW 6 D6
Blackfellow Caves SA 82 F12
Blackfellows Creek SA 69 F12
Blackheath NSW 10 C4, 13 I6
Blackheath Vic. 54 G8
Blackmans Bay Tas. 159 I7, 161 K8
Blacksoil Qld 132 B4
Blackstone Qld 132 D5
Blacktown NSW 6 F7, 8 F1, 11 J7,
   13 J6
Blackville NSW 14 G11
Blackwall NSW 7 P1
Blackwarry Vic. 49 I8
Blackwater Qld 139 J11
Blackwood SA 69 D4, 70 B10,
   71 F3
Blackwood Vic. 46 F2, 48 A2,
   57 O3
Blackwood Creek Tas. 163 J10
Blackwood NP Qld 138 G6
Blackwood River NP WA 94 D7,
   96 B10, 98 B10
Bladensburg NP Qld 145 L8
Blair Athol NSW 8 C8
Blair Athol Qld 138 H9
Blair Athol SA 68 D9
Blairgowrie Vic. 46 H10, 48 B7,
   57 P9
Blairmount NSW 8 C7
Blakehurst NSW 9 J7
Blakeview SA 68 G3

Blakeville Vic. 46 E3, 57 N4
Blampied Vic. 46 E2
Blanchetown SA 73 L7, 82 E1
Bland NSW 12 C6
Blandford NSW 14 H11
Blanket Flat NSW 12 G7, 20 D1
Blaxland NSW 6 A6, 10 G6, 13 J6
Blaxlands Ridge NSW 10 H3
Blayney NSW 12 G5
Bleak House Vic. 16 C12, 54 D7
Blessington Tas. 163 L9
Bletchley SA 70 E12
Blewitt Springs SA 69 C9, 70 B11,
   71 F4
Bli Bli Qld 134 G3, 137 N7
Bligh Park NSW 6 D3
Blighty NSW 17 K10, 50 E3
Blind Bight Vic. 45 I9
Blinman SA 75 I5
Bloomsbury Qld 139 J4
Blow Clear NSW 12 B5, 17 P5
Blue Mountains NP NSW 10 E7,
   12 H7, 13 I5, 20 F1
Blue Rocks Tas. 160 B10
Blue Water Springs Roadhouse
   Qld 138 E1, 141 L11
Bluewater Qld 138 G1, 141 N11
Blueys Beach NSW 13 O3
Bluff Qld 139 J11
Bluff Beach SA 72 H8
Bluff Hill NP Qld 139 J5
Bluff Rock NSW 15 L4
Bluff Rock (Iron Pot Rock)
   Qld 139 N10
Blyth SA 73 J6
Blythewood WA 92 F12
Boallia WA 94 B6
Boambee NSW 15 N8
Boat Harbour Tas. 162 E4
Boat Harbour Beach Tas. 162 E4
Boatswain Point SA 82 E9
Bobadah NSW 12 B1, 17 O1,
   19 N12
Bobbin Head NSW 11 L6
Bobin NSW 13 N1, 15 K12
Bobinawarrah Vic. 51 I8
Bodalla NSW 20 E7
Bodallin WA 96 H3, 98 F6
Boddington WA 93 G10, 96 D7,
   98 C8
Bogan Gate NSW 12 D3
Bogangar NSW 15 O2, 137 N11
Bogantungan Qld 138 G11
Boggabilla NSW 14 H2, 137 I11
Boggabri NSW 14 G8
Bogong Vic. 51 L10
Boho Vic. 50 G9
Boho South Vic. 50 G9
Boigbeat Vic. 16 F10, 55 J3
Boiler Rock WA 97 E1, 100 B2,
   102 B12
Boinka Vic. 16 C9, 52 E11, 54 C12,
   73 P10
Boisdale Vic. 49 K5
Bolgart WA 96 D3, 98 C6
Bolinda Vic. 46 H2, 48 B2
Bolivar SA 68 D6, 70 B6
Bolivia NSW 15 K4
Bollon Qld 136 D9
Bolton Vic. 16 F8, 53 J10
Bolwarra Vic. 56 D7
Bolwarrah Vic. 46 E3, 57 N4
Bomaderry NSW 13 I9, 20 G4
Bombala NSW 20 C9, 58 F7

Bonalbo NSW 15 M3, 137 M12
Bonang Vic. 20 B10, 58 C8
Bonbeach Vic. 44 E5, 47 J7
Bondi NSW 9 N5
Bondi Beach NSW 7 N12, 9 N5
Bondi Junction NSW 7 M12, 9 M5, 11 M9
Bondo NSW 12 E10, 20 B4
Bonegilla Vic. 12 A12, 51 L6
Boneo Vic. 47 I10, 48 C8
Bongaree Qld 131 M1, 134 G8, 135 F1, 137 N8
Bongil Bongil NP NSW 15 N8
Bonner ACT 34 F1
Bonnet Bay NSW 9 I7
Bonnie Doon Vic. 50 G11
Bonnie Rock WA 96 G1, 98 E5
Bonny Hills NSW 15 M11
Bonnyrigg NSW 6 E11, 8 E3
Bonnyrigg Heights NSW 6 E11, 8 E3
Bonshaw NSW 15 J3, 137 J12
Bonville NSW 15 M8
Bonython ACT 34 C10
Booborowie SA 73 K5, 75 I12
Boobyalla Tas. 163 N5
Boodalan Island WA 93 C10
Booderee NP NSW 20 G5
Boodjamulla (Lawn Hill) NP Qld 119 P7, 143 A6
Bookabie SA 81 K7
Bookar Vic. 57 J7
Bookham NSW 12 E9, 20 B3
Boolading WA 94 G3, 96 D8
Boolarra Vic. 47 P10, 48 H8
Boolba Qld 136 E9
Booleroo SA 73 J3, 74 H10
Booleroo Centre SA 73 J3, 74 H10
Boolgun SA 73 M8, 82 F1
Booligal NSW 17 K5
Boomahnoomoonah Vic. 50 H6
Boomi NSW 14 F2, 136 H11
Boonah Qld 15 M1, 135 A9, 137 M10
Boonah Vic. 46 D10, 57 M9
Boonarga Qld 137 J7
Boondall Qld 131 J8, 134 F10, 135 E3
Boonoo Boonoo NSW 15 L3, 137 L12
Boonoo Boonoo NP NSW 15 L3, 137 L12
Boonoonar Vic. 16 E7, 52 G8
Boorabbin NP WA 98 G6
Booragoon WA 90 F12, 91 C7, 93 C6
Booral NSW 13 M3
Boorara–Gardner NP WA 94 F10, 96 D11, 98 C11
Boorcan Vic. 57 I7
Boorhaman Vic. 51 I6
Boorindal NSW 19 M6
Boorongie Vic. 52 H11
Boorongie North Vic. 16 E8, 52 H11
Booroopki Vic. 54 C9, 82 H8
Booroorban NSW 17 J8
Boorowa NSW 12 E8, 20 C2
Boort Vic. 16 H12, 55 M6
Boosey Vic. 50 G5
Booti Booti NP NSW 13 N2
Booval Qld 132 C5, 134 D12, 135 B5
Booyal Qld 137 M4

Boppy Mountain NSW 19 M9
Borallon Qld 130 A11, 132 A1, 134 C11, 135 B4
Boralma Vic. 51 I6
Borambil NSW 13 I1, 14 F12
Borden WA 95 N6, 96 H9, 98 E10
Border Ranges NP NSW 15 N2, 135 B12, 137 M11
Border Store NT 115 P2, 116 H4
Border Village SA 80 C7, 99 P5
Bordertown SA 16 A12, 54 A7, 82 G7
Boree NSW 12 F4, 13 K4
Boree Creek NSW 12 A9, 17 N9
Boreen Point Qld 137 N6
Borenore NSW 12 F4
Boro NSW 12 G10, 20 E4
Boronia Vic. 43 N10, 47 K6, 48 D5
Boronia Heights Qld 132 H8, 135 D6
Bororen Qld 137 L2
Borrika SA 73 M9, 82 F3
Borroloola NT 117 M11, 119 M2
Borung Vic. 16 H12, 55 M7
Boscabel WA 95 I4, 96 E8, 98 D10
Bossley Park NSW 6 E10, 8 E2
Bostobrick NSW 15 M7
Bostock Creek Vic. 57 J8
Botany NSW 9 L6, 11 L10, 13 K7
Botany Bay NSW 9 K6
Botany Bay NP NSW 13 K7
Bothwell Tas. 161 J4
Bottom Rocks Tas. 160 D8
Bouddi NP NSW 11 O4, 13 K6
Boulder Rock Qld 142 G10
Bouldercombe Qld 139 M11
Boulia Qld 144 F8
Boulka Vic. 52 H11
Boundain WA 96 F7
Boundary Bend Vic. 16 G7, 53 K9
Boundary Island WA 93 C9
Bourke NSW 19 M5
Bournda NP NSW 20 E9, 58 H7
Bow NSW 13 J1, 14 G12
Bow Bowing NSW 8 D7
Bowan Park NSW 12 F4
Bowden SA 67 A1, 68 D11, 69 D1, 70 B8, 71 F2
Bowelling WA 94 G3, 96 D8, 98 C9
Bowen Qld 139 J3
Bowen Hills Qld 129 H1, 131 I11, 133 I1
Bowen Mountain NSW 6 A1, 10 G4
Bowenfels NSW 10 B2
Bowenvale Vic. 55 L11, 57 L1
Bowenville Qld 137 K8
Bower SA 73 L7
Boweya Vic. 50 H7
Bowhill SA 73 L9, 82 E3
Bowling Alley Point NSW 15 I10
Bowling Green Bay NP Qld 138 G1, 141 N12
Bowman Vic. 51 J8
Bowmans SA 73 I7, 82 A1
Bowna NSW 12 B12, 17 O12, 51 L5
Bowning NSW 12 F9, 20 C3
Bowral NSW 13 I8, 20 G2
Bowraville NSW 15 M9
Bowser Vic. 51 I7
Box Head NSW 7 P2
Box Hill NSW 6 G5
Box Hill Vic. 43 K8, 47 J6, 48 D4
Box Hill North Vic. 43 K8

Box Hill South Vic. 43 K9
Box Tank NSW 18 D11
Boxwood Vic. 50 G7
Boxwood Hill WA 95 P7, 98 F10
Boya WA 91 H2
Boyanup WA 94 D4, 96 C8, 98 C10
Boydtown NSW 20 E10, 58 H8
Boyer Tas. 158 H4, 161 J6
Boykambil Qld 135 F8
Boyndaminup NP WA 94 G9, 96 E11, 98 D11
Boyne Island Qld 137 L1, 139 N12
Boys Town Qld 135 C9
Boyup Brook WA 94 G6, 96 D9, 98 C10
Bracken Ridge Qld 131 J7
Brackendale NSW 15 J10
Bracknell Tas. 163 J9
Bradbury NSW 8 C9
Bradbury SA 69 F6
Braddon ACT 33 F1, 34 E5
Bradvale Vic. 46 A5, 57 K5
Braefield NSW 14 H11
Braeside Qld 15 L2, 137 L11, 139 J7
Braeside Vic. 44 E3
Brahma Lodge SA 68 E7
Braidwood NSW 12 H11, 20 E5
Bramfield SA 72 C5, 74 A12, 81 P12
Bramley NP WA 94 B7, 96 B10, 98 B10
Brampton Island Qld 139 K5
Brampton Islands NP Qld 139 K5
Bramston Beach Qld 141 M7
Bramwell Junction Roadhouse Qld 142 D6
Brandon Qld 138 H2, 141 O12
Brandy Creek Vic. 47 N8, 48 G6
Branxholm Tas. 163 M7
Branxholme Vic. 56 E5
Branxton NSW 13 L3
Brassall Qld 132 B5
Brawlin NSW 12 D8, 20 A2
Bray Junction SA 82 E10
Bray Park Qld 130 H7, 131 I7, 134 F9, 135 D3
Braybrook Vic. 42 E7
Breadalbane NSW 12 G9, 20 E3
Breadalbane Tas. 163 K8
Break O Day Vic. 47 L2, 48 E2, 50 E12
Breakfast Creek NSW 12 F7, 13 I3, 20 C1
Breakfast Point NSW 7 J11, 9 J2
Bream Creek Tas. 159 M5, 161 M7
Breamlea Vic. 46 F9, 48 A7, 57 O8
Bredbo NSW 12 F12, 20 C6, 58 F2
Breelong NP NSW 14 C11
Breeza NSW 14 G10
Bremer Bay WA 98 G10
Brendale Qld 130 H7, 131 I7
Brentwood SA 72 H9
Brentwood Vic. 16 D11, 54 G5
Brentwood WA 90 F12, 91 C7
Breona Tas. 163 I10
Bretti NSW 13 M1, 15 K12
Brewarrina NSW 19 O5
Brewongle NSW 12 H5
Brewster Vic. 46 B2, 57 L3
Briagolong Vic. 49 K5
Briar Hill Vic. 43 K5
Bribbaree NSW 12 D7, 20 A1

Bribie Island Qld 134 G7, 135 F1, 137 N8
Bribie Island NP Qld 131 M1, 134 G7, 135 F1, 137 N8
Bridge Creek Vic. 50 H10
Bridge Inn Vic. 55 I11, 57 I1
Bridgeman Downs Qld 130 H8, 131 I8
Bridgenorth Tas. 163 J7
Bridgetown WA 94 F6, 96 D9, 98 C10
Bridgewater SA 69 H4, 70 D10, 71 G3, 73 J9, 82 C3
Bridgewater Tas. 159 I3, 161 K6
Bridgewater On Loddon Vic. 55 N9
Bridport Tas. 163 L5
Brigalow Qld 137 J7
Bright Vic. 51 K9
Brighton Qld 131 J7, 134 F9, 135 E3, 137 N9
Brighton SA 69 B4, 70 B10, 71 E3, 73 J9
Brighton Tas. 159 I3, 161 K6
Brighton Vic. 42 H10, 44 C1, 47 J6, 48 C5
Brighton East Vic. 42 H11, 43 I11, 44 C1
Brighton-Le-Sands NSW 9 K6
Brim Vic. 16 E11, 54 H6
Brimbago SA 16 A11, 82 F7
Brimboal Vic. 56 C2, 82 H10
Brimin Vic. 51 I5
Brimpaen Vic. 54 G11
Brindabella NP NSW 12 E10, 20 C4, 31 A3
Bringagee NSW 17 L7
Bringalbert Vic. 54 C10, 82 H9
Bringelly NSW 6 B12, 8 A3, 10 H9
Brinkin NT 112 C2
Brinkley SA 70 G12, 73 K10
Brinkworth SA 73 J5
Brisbane Qld 134 F11, 135 D4, 137 N9
Brisbane City Qld 129 F7, 131 I12, 133 I2
Brisbane Ranges NP Vic. 46 F5, 48 A4, 57 N5
Brisbane Water NP NSW 7 M1, 11 N4, 13 K5
Brit Brit Vic. 56 E3
Brittons Swamp Tas. 162 B4
Brixton Qld 138 C10, 145 O10
Broad Arrow WA 98 H4
Broad Sound Islands NP Qld 139 L7
Broadbeach Qld 15 O1, 135 G10
Broadford Vic. 47 J1, 48 D1, 50 D11
Broadmarsh Tas. 158 H2, 161 J6
Broadmeadows Vic. 42 G4, 47 I4, 48 C3
Broadview SA 68 E10
Broadwater NSW 15 O4
Broadwater Vic. 56 F6
Broadwater NP NSW 15 O4
Broadway NSW 5 B11
Brocklehurst NSW 12 F1, 14 C12
Brocklesby NSW 12 A11, 17 N11, 51 J4
Brockman NP WA 94 E9, 96 D11, 98 C11
Brocks Creek NT 114 G10, 116 E6
Brodies Plains NSW 15 J5

Brodribb River Vic. 20 A12, 58 B11
Brogo NSW 20 E8, 58 H5
Broke NSW 13 K3
Broken Hill NSW 18 B10, 73 P1, 75 O8
Bromelton Qld 135 C9
Bromley Vic. 55 M10
Brompton SA 68 C11, 69 C1
Bronte NSW 9 N5
Bronte Park Tas. 160 H2, 162 H12
Bronzewing Vic. 16 E9, 52 H11, 54 H1
Brook Islands NP Qld 141 M9
Brookdale WA 91 G10
Brooker SA 72 D6
Brookfield NSW 13 M3
Brookfield Qld 130 F11, 132 F1, 134 E11, 135 C4
Brooklands Qld 135 C8
Brooklyn NSW 7 N4, 11 M4
Brooklyn Vic. 42 E8
Brooklyn Park SA 68 C12, 69 C2
Brookside Vic. 51 K10
Brookstead Qld 137 K9
Brookton WA 96 E5, 98 D8
Brookvale NSW 7 N8, 9 N1, 11 M7
Brookville Vic. 49 N3
Brookwater Qld 132 E6
Brooloo Qld 134 E2
Broome WA 102 H8
Broomehill WA 95 K5, 96 F9, 98 E10
Broomfield Vic. 46 D2, 57 M3
Brooms Head NSW 15 N6
Brooweena Qld 137 M5
Broughton Vic. 16 C12, 54 D6, 82 H7
Broughton Island NSW 13 N3
Broula NSW 12 E6
Broulee NSW 12 H12, 20 F6
Brown Hill Vic. 46 D3
Brown Hill Creek SA 69 E3
Brownlow SA 70 H1, 72 H11, 73 L7, 82 D1
Browns Plains Qld 133 I7, 135 D6
Browns Plains Vic. 51 J6
Bruarong Vic. 51 K8
Bruce ACT 34 D3
Bruce SA 73 I2, 74 H9
Bruce Rock WA 96 G4, 98 E7
Brucefield SA 72 H6
Brucknell Vic. 57 I9
Brukunga SA 70 E9
Brungle NSW 12 D10, 20 A4
Brunswick Vic. 42 H6, 47 I5, 48 C4
Brunswick East Vic. 42 H7
Brunswick Heads NSW 15 O3, 137 N12
Brunswick Junction WA 94 D3, 96 C8
Brunswick West Vic. 42 G6
Bruny Island Tas. 158 H11, 159 I10, 161 K10
Brushgrove NSW 15 I8
Bruthen Vic. 49 N5
Bryden Qld 130 A2, 134 C9, 135 A2
Brymaroo Qld 137 K8
Buangor Vic. 57 J3
Buaraba Qld 134 A9
Bucasia Qld 139 K5
Bucca Qld 137 M3
Buccan Qld 133 J9, 135 E7
Buccleuch SA 73 M10, 82 E4

Buchan Vic. 20 A11, 49 P4, 58 A10
Buchan South Vic. 49 O4
Bucheen Creek Vic. 51 N8
Buchfelde SA 68 G1
Buckenderra NSW 20 B7, 58 D3
Bucketty NSW 13 K4
Buckingham SA 16 A12, 82 G7
Buckingham WA 94 F3, 96 D8
Buckland Tas. 159 M2, 161 M5
Buckland Vic. 51 K10
Buckland Park SA 68 B6
Buckleboo SA 72 E3, 74 D10
Buckley Vic. 46 E8, 57 N8
Buckrabanyule Vic. 16 G12, 55 L7
Budawang NP NSW 12 H11, 20 F5
Buddabaddah NSW 19 O11
Budderoo NP NSW 13 J9, 20 G3
Buddigower NSW 12 B6, 17 O6
Buddina Qld 134 H4
Buderim Qld 134 G4, 137 N7
Budgeree Vic. 47 P11, 48 H8
Budgeree East Vic. 48 H8
Budgerum Vic. 55 L4
Buffalo Vic. 47 O12, 48 G9
Buffalo Creek NT 112 G1
Buffalo Creek Vic. 51 J9
Buffalo River Vic. 51 J9
Bugaldie NSW 14 D9
Bugilbone NSW 14 D5
Bugong NP NSW 13 I9, 20 G3
Builyan Qld 137 L2
Bukalong NSW 20 C9, 58 E6
Bukkulla NSW 15 I5
Bulahdelah NSW 13 N3
Bulart Vic. 56 F3
Bulburin NP Qld 137 L2
Buldah Vic. 20 C10, 58 E9
Bulga NSW 13 K3
Bulgandramine NSW 12 E2
Bulgobac Tas. 162 E8
Bulimba Qld 131 J11, 133 J1
Bull Creek SA 69 H11
Bull Creek WA 90 F12, 91 D7
Bulla NT 103 P4, 116 C11, 118 C2
Bulla Vic. 42 D1, 47 I4, 48 B3
Bullaburra NSW 10 E6
Bullala NP NSW 14 H4, 137 I12
Bullarah NSW 14 E4
Bullaring WA 96 F6, 98 E8
Bullarook Vic. 46 D3, 57 M4
Bullarto Vic. 46 F2, 57 N3
Bullarto South Vic. 46 F2
Bulleen Vic. 43 J7
Bullengarook Vic. 46 G3, 48 A2, 57 O4
Bullengarook East Vic. 46 G3, 48 A2
Bulleringa NP Qld 141 I7
Bullfinch WA 96 H2, 98 F6
Bullhead Creek Vic. 51 M8
Bullioh Vic. 51 M7
Bullock Creek Qld 141 J7
Bullocks Flat NSW 58 B4
Bullsbrook WA 90 G2, 93 C3, 96 C4, 98 C7
Bullumwaal Vic. 49 M4
Bulman NT 117 J6
Buln Buln Vic. 47 N8, 48 G6
Buln Buln East Vic. 47 O8, 48 G6
Bulwer Qld 135 G1, 137 N8
Bulyee WA 96 F5, 98 D8
Bumbaldry NSW 12 E6
Bumberry NSW 12 E4
Bumbunga SA 73 I6

Bunbartha Vic. 17 K12, 50 E6
Bunburra Qld 135 A9
Bunbury WA 94 C3, 96 C8, 98 C9
Bundaberg Qld 137 M3
Bundaburrah NSW 12 D5
Bundalaguah Vic. 49 K6
Bundalong Vic. 17 M12, 50 H5
Bundalong South Vic. 50 H6
Bundamba Qld 132 C5
Bundanoon NSW 13 I9, 20 G3
Bundarra NSW 15 I7
Bundeena NSW 9 J10, 11 L12, 13 K7
Bundella NSW 14 F10
Bunding Vic. 46 E3, 57 N4
Bundjalung NP NSW 15 N5
Bundook NSW 13 N1, 15 K12
Bundoora Vic. 43 J4
Bundure NSW 17 M9
Bung Bong Vic. 55 L12, 57 L1
Bunga NSW 20 E8
Bungador Vic. 57 K8
Bungal Vic. 46 E4, 57 N5
Bungarby NSW 20 C9, 58 E5
Bungaree Vic. 46 D3, 57 M4
Bungawalbin NP NSW 15 N4, 137 N12
Bungeet Vic. 50 H7
Bungendore NSW 12 G10, 20 D4, 31 H5
Bungil Vic. 12 B12, 51 M6
Bungonia NSW 12 H9, 20 F3
Bungonia NP NSW 12 H9, 20 F3
Bungowannah NSW 12 A12, 51 K5
Bungulla NSW 15 L4, 137 L12
Bungulla WA 96 F4
Bunguluke Vic. 16 G12, 55 L6
Bungunya Qld 14 F1, 136 H10
Bungwahl NSW 13 N3
Buninyong Vic. 46 D4, 57 M4
Bunnaloo NSW 17 J11, 50 B3, 55 P5
Bunnan NSW 13 J1, 14 G12
Bunurong Marine NP Vic. 47 M12, 48 E9
Bunurong Marine Park Vic. 47 L12, 48 E9
Bunya Qld 130 G8
Bunya Mountains NP Qld 137 K7
Bunyah NSW 13 N2
Bunyan NSW 20 C7, 58 F3
Bunyip Vic. 45 P6, 47 M8, 48 F6
Bunyip North Vic. 45 P6
Buraja NSW 17 M11, 51 I4
Burbank Qld 133 K5, 134 G12, 135 E5
Burbong NSW 31 G5
Burcher NSW 12 C5, 17 P5
Burekup WA 94 D3, 96 C8
Burgooney NSW 12 A4, 17 N4
Burke and Wills Roadhouse Qld 140 B10, 143 F8
Burkes Flat Vic. 55 L9
Burketown Qld 140 A7, 143 D4
Burleigh Head NP Qld 15 O1, 135 G10, 137 N11
Burleigh Heads Qld 15 O1, 135 G10, 137 N11
Burnbank Vic. 55 L12, 57 L2
Burnett Heads Qld 137 M3
Burnie Tas. 162 F5
Burnley Vic. 43 I9
Burns WA 93 B4

Burns Beach WA 90 A3
Burns Creek Tas. 163 L8
Burnside SA 68 F12, 69 F2
Burnside Vic. 42 C6
Burnside Heights Vic. 42 D5
Burnt Yards NSW 12 F5
Buronga NSW 52 G6
Burpengary Qld 130 H3, 131 I2, 134 F8, 135 D1, 137 N8
Burra SA 73 K5
Burraboi NSW 17 I10, 50 A1, 55 O2
Burracoppin WA 96 G3, 98 E6
Burraga NSW 12 G6
Burragate NSW 58 G8
Burral Yurrul NP NSW 15 I3, 137 J12
Burramine South Vic. 50 G5
Burrandana NSW 12 B10, 17 P10, 51 M2
Burrawang NSW 13 I9, 20 G3
Burrell Creek NSW 13 N1, 15 K12
Burren Junction NSW 14 D6
Burrereo Vic. 55 I8
Burrill Lake NSW 13 I11, 20 G5
Burringbar NSW 15 O2, 137 N11
Burringurrah WA 97 F6, 100 C7
Burrinjuck NSW 12 E9, 20 B3
Burroin Vic. 16 E10, 54 H3
Burrowa–Pine Mountain NP Vic. 12 C12, 17 P12, 51 N6
Burroway NSW 14 B11
Burrowye Vic. 12 C12, 17 P12, 51 N6
Burrum Vic. 55 I9
Burrum Coast NP Qld 137 M4
Burrum Heads Qld 137 N4
Burrumbeet Vic. 46 C2, 57 L3
Burrumbuttock NSW 12 A11, 17 N11, 51 K4
Burswood WA 90 F9, 91 D4, 93 C5
Burton SA 68 D6
Burton Rocks WA 99 I9
Burwood NSW 7 J11, 9 J3
Burwood Vic. 43 K10, 47 J6
Burwood East Vic. 43 K10
Burwood Heights NSW 7 J12, 9 J4
Busby NSW 6 E12, 8 E4
Bushfield Vic. 56 G8
Bushy Park Tas. 158 F3, 161 I6
Bushy Park Vic. 49 K5
Busselton WA 94 B5, 96 B9, 98 B10
Butchers Ridge Vic. 20 A10, 49 P2, 58 A8
Bute SA 73 I6
Butler WA 90 A1
Butler Tanks SA 72 E6
Butlers Gorge Tas. 160 G3
Butmaroo NSW 12 G10, 20 D4
Butterleaf NP NSW 15 K5
Buxton NSW 13 I8, 20 G2
Buxton Qld 137 M4
Buxton Vic. 47 N3, 48 F2
Byabarra NSW 15 L11
Byaduk Vic. 56 E5
Byaduk North Vic. 56 E5
Byawatha Vic. 51 J7
Byfield NP Qld 139 N10
Byford WA 91 H12, 92 G1, 93 D7, 96 C5
Bylands Vic. 47 J2, 48 C2, 50 C12
Bylong NSW 13 I2
Bymount Qld 136 F5
Byrne Vic. 51 I8
Byrneside Vic. 50 D7

Byrnestown Qld 137 L4
Byrneville Vic. 54 G8
Byrock NSW 19 N7
Byron Bay NSW 15 O3, 137 N12

Cabarita NSW 7 K11, 9 K3
Cabarita Vic. 16 D6, 52 G6
Cabarlah Qld 137 L9
Cabawin Qld 137 I8
Cabbage Tree Creek Vic. 20 B12, 58 C11
Caboolture Qld 130 H1, 131 I1, 134 F7, 135 D1, 137 N8
Caboolture South Qld 130 H1, 131 I1
Caboonbah Qld 134 B7, 137 M8
Cabramatta NSW 6 F11, 8 F4, 11 J9, 13 J7, 20 H1
Cabramatta West NSW 6 F11, 8 F3
Cabramurra NSW 12 D12, 20 B6, 58 B1
Cadell SA 73 M6
Cadney Homestead SA 79 N7
Cadoux WA 96 E2, 98 D6
Cahills Crossing NT 115 P2, 116 H4
Caiguna WA 99 M7
Caiguna Roadhouse WA 99 L7
Cairnlea Vic. 42 D6
Cairns Qld 141 L6
Cairns Bay Tas. 158 F9, 161 I9
Calala NSW 15 I9
Calamvale Qld 133 I6, 135 D6
Calca SA 72 A3, 81 N11
Calder Tas. 162 E5
Calder Park Vic. 42 D4
Caldermeade Vic. 45 M10
Caldwell NSW 17 I10, 50 B2, 55 P4
Calen Qld 139 J5
Calga NSW 11 M3
Calingiri WA 96 C3, 98 C6
Caliph SA 73 N8, 82 F2
Calista WA 92 C1
Calivil Vic. 55 N7
Callala Bay NSW 13 J10, 20 G4
Callawadda Vic. 55 I10
Calleen NSW 12 B5, 17 O5
Callide Qld 137 J1
Callignee Vic. 49 I8
Callignee North Vic. 49 I8
Callington SA 70 F11, 73 K10, 82 C3
Calliope Qld 137 K1, 139 N12
Caloona NSW 14 E2, 136 G11
Caloote SA 70 H9, 73 K9
Caloundra Qld 134 H5, 137 N8
Caltowie SA 73 J4, 74 H11
Calulu Vic. 49 M5
Calvert Qld 134 B12
Calvert Vic. 57 I3
Calwell ACT 34 D11
Camballin WA 103 J7
Cambarville Vic. 47 O4, 48 G3
Camberwell NSW 13 K2
Camberwell Vic. 43 I9, 47 J6
Cambewarra NSW 13 I9, 20 G3
Cambrai SA 70 H6, 73 L8, 82 D2
Cambrian Hill Vic. 46 C4
Cambridge Tas. 156 G5, 157 I1, 159 J5, 161 K7
Cambridge Gardens NSW 6 B6
Cambridge Park NSW 6 B6
Camdale Tas. 162 F5

Camden NSW 8 A7, 10 G11, 13 J7, 20 H1
Camden Park NSW 8 A9
Camden Park SA 69 C3
Camden South NSW 8 A8
Camellia NSW 7 I10, 9 I1
Cameron Corner NSW 18 B1, 77 N11, 146 F10
Camira Qld 132 F6, 134 E12, 135 C6
Camira Creek NSW 15 N4
Cammeray NSW 7 M10, 9 M2
Camooweal Qld 119 P10, 143 A9, 144 C1
Camooweal Caves NP Qld 119 P10, 143 A9, 144 C1
Camp Coorong SA 73 L12, 82 D5
Camp Hill Qld 133 J3, 134 F11, 135 E5
Camp Mountain Qld 130 E10
Campania Tas. 159 J2, 161 K6
Campbell ACT 33 H5, 34 F5
Campbell Town Tas. 161 L1, 163 L11
Campbellfield Vic. 42 G3
Campbells Bridge Vic. 55 I10
Campbells Creek Vic. 55 N12, 57 N1
Campbells Forest Vic. 55 N9
Campbells Pocket Qld 130 E1, 134 E7
Campbelltown NSW 8 C8, 10 H11, 13 J7, 20 H1
Campbelltown SA 68 E10, 69 F1
Campbelltown Vic. 55 M12, 57 M2
Camperdown NSW 7 L12, 9 L4
Camperdown Vic. 57 J7
Campsie NSW 7 J12, 9 J5
Campwin Beach Qld 139 K6
Camurra NSW 14 G4
Canada Bay NSW 7 K11, 9 K3
Canadian Vic. 46 D3
Canbelego NSW 19 M9
Canberra ACT 12 F10, 20 D4, 31 E5
Canberra City ACT 34 E5
Candelo NSW 20 D9, 58 H6
Cangai NSW 15 L5
Cania Gorge NP Qld 137 K2
Caniambo Vic. 50 F8
Canley Heights NSW 6 F11, 8 F3
Canley Vale NSW 6 G11, 8 G3
Cann River Vic. 20 C11, 58 E10
Canna WA 97 F12, 98 B3
Cannawigara SA 16 A12, 54 A6, 82 G7
Cannie Vic. 16 G11, 55 L4
Canning Mills WA 91 H6
Canning Vale WA 90 G12, 91 E7, 93 C6, 96 C5
Cannington WA 90 G11, 91 E5, 93 C5
Cannon Creek Qld 15 K2, 135 A9
Cannon Hill Qld 131 J12, 133 J2
Cannons Creek Vic. 44 H9, 45 I9
Cannonvale Qld 139 J3
Cannum Vic. 54 G7
Canoelands NSW 7 K1
Canomodine NSW 12 F5
Canonba NSW 19 P9
Canoona Qld 139 M10
Canowie SA 73 K4, 75 I12
Canowindra NSW 12 F5
Canteen Creek NT 119 L11, 121 L1
Canterbury NSW 9 J5, 11 L9

Canterbury Vic. 43 J8
Canunda NP SA 82 F11
Canungra Qld 135 E9
Capalaba Qld 133 L5, 134 G12, 135 E5
Capalaba West Qld 133 L3
Cape Woolamai Vic. 47 K11, 48 D8
Cape Arid NP WA 99 K9
Cape Barren Island Tas. 160 B12, 163 O2
Cape Borda SA 72 F11
Cape Bridgewater Vic. 56 C8
Cape Clear Vic. 46 B5, 57 L5
Cape Hillsborough NP Qld 139 K5
Cape Howe Marine NP Vic. 20 E11, 58 H11
Cape Jaffa SA 82 E9
Cape Jervis SA 71 A9, 73 I11, 82 A5
Cape Le Grand NP WA 99 I9
Cape Melville NP Qld 141 K1, 142 H11
Cape Palmerston NP Qld 139 K6
Cape Paterson Vic. 47 L12, 48 E9
Cape Range NP WA 97 B3
Cape Rock Qld 142 G10
Cape Tribulation Qld 141 L4
Cape Upstart NP Qld 139 I2, 141 P12
Capel WA 94 C5, 96 B9, 98 C10
Capella Qld 139 I9
Capels Crossing Vic. 55 N4
Capertee NSW 13 I4
Capertee NP NSW 13 I4
Capietha SA 72 B2, 74 A10, 81 O10
Capital Hill ACT 33 D10, 34 E6
Capoompeta NP NSW 15 K5
Capricorn Coast NP Qld 139 N10
Capricorn Roadhouse WA 100 E5
Capricornia Cays NP Qld 137 N1, 139 P11
Captain Billy Landing Qld 142 D4
Captains Flat NSW 12 G11, 20 D5, 31 G9
Carabooda WA 90 A1
Carabost NSW 12 C11, 17 P11, 51 O4
Caragabal NSW 12 D6
Caralue SA 72 E4, 74 D12
Caralulup Vic. 55 L12, 57 L2
Caramut Vic. 56 H6
Carapooee Vic. 55 K9
Carapook Vic. 56 D3
Carawa SA 72 A1, 81 N9
Carboor Vic. 51 J9
Carboor Upper Vic. 51 J9
Carbrook Qld 133 M8
Carbunup River WA 94 B6
Carcoar NSW 12 G5
Cardigan Village Vic. 46 C3, 57 L3
Cardinia Vic. 45 J7, 47 L8, 48 E6
Cardross Vic. 52 G6
Cardstone Qld 141 L8
Cardup WA 91 H12, 92 G1
Cardwell Qld 141 M9
Carey Gully SA 69 H3
Cargerie Vic. 46 D5, 57 M5
Cargo NSW 12 F5
Carina Qld 131 J12, 133 J2
Carina Heights Qld 133 J3
Carinda NSW 14 A6
Carindale Qld 133 J3
Carine WA 90 C7, 91 A1
Caringbah NSW 9 J8, 11 K11

Carisbrook Vic. 55 M11, 57 M1
Carlingford NSW 7 I8, 9 I1, 11 K7
Carlisle WA 90 G10, 91 E5
Carlisle Island Qld 139 K5
Carlisle River Vic. 46 A11, 57 K9
Carlsruhe Vic. 46 G1, 48 A1, 50 A12, 57 O3
Carlton NSW 9 J6
Carlton Tas. 159 L5, 161 L7
Carlton Vic. 41 E1, 42 H8
Carlton North Vic. 42 H7
Carlwood NSW 12 H5
Carmel WA 91 H6
Carmila Qld 139 K7
Carnac Island WA 93 B6
Carnamah WA 98 B4
Carnarvon WA 97 B7
Carnarvon NP Qld 136 E2
Carnegie Vic. 43 I11, 44 D1
Carnegie Homestead WA 101 I8
Carngham Vic. 46 B3, 57 L4
Carole Park Qld 132 F5
Caroline SA 56 A5, 82 G12
Caroline Springs Vic. 42 C5
Caroona NSW 14 G10
Carpa SA 72 F5
Carpendeit Vic. 57 J8
Carpenter Rocks SA 82 F12
Carrabin WA 96 H3
Carrai NP NSW 15 L9
Carrajung Vic. 49 I8
Carrajung South Vic. 49 J8
Carramar NSW 6 G11, 8 G3
Carramar WA 90 C3
Carranballac Vic. 57 J4
Carraragarmungee Vic. 51 I7
Carrathool NSW 17 L7
Carrick Tas. 163 J8
Carrickalinga SA 71 C7, 73 I10, 82 B4
Carrieton SA 73 J2, 75 I9
Carroll NSW 14 G9
Carron Vic. 16 F12, 55 I7
Carrum Vic. 44 E5, 47 J8, 48 D6
Carrum Downs Vic. 44 F5, 47 J8, 48 D6
Carseldine Qld 131 I8, 134 F10, 135 D3
Carss Park NSW 9 J7
Cartwright NSW 6 E12, 8 E4
Carwarp Vic. 16 E7, 52 G7
Carwoola NSW 34 H9
Cascade WA 98 H9
Cascade NP NSW 15 M7
Cashmere Qld 130 F6
Cashmore Vic. 56 D7
Casino NSW 15 N3, 137 M12
Cassilis NSW 13 I1, 14 F12
Cassilis Vic. 49 M2, 51 M12
Castambul SA 68 H10
Castella Vic. 47 L3, 48 E3
Casterton Vic. 56 C3, 82 H11
Castle Cove NSW 7 M9, 9 M1
Castle Forbes Bay Tas. 158 F8, 161 I8
Castle Hill NSW 6 H6, 7 I6, 11 K7
Castle Rock NSW 13 K2
Castle Tower NP Qld 137 L1
Castleburn Vic. 49 L4
Castlecrag NSW 7 M10, 9 M1
Castlemaine Vic. 55 N12, 57 N1
Castlemaine Diggings National Heritage Park Vic. 50 A10, 55 O12, 57 N1

Castlereagh NSW 6 A4, 10 G5
Casuarina NT 112 E2
Casuarina WA 91 D12, 92 D1
Casula NSW 8 E5, 11 I9
Cataby Roadhouse WA 96 B2, 98 B6
Catamaran Tas. 161 I11
Catani Vic. 45 N9, 47 M9
Cataract NP NSW 15 L3, 137 L12
Cathcart NSW 20 D9, 58 F7
Cathcart Vic. 57 I2
Cathedral Rock NP NSW 15 L8
Catherine Field NSW 8 B5
Catherine Hill Bay NSW 13 L5
Cathkin Vic. 47 M1, 48 F1, 50 F11
Cathundral NSW 14 A11
Cattai NSW 6 G1, 11 J4
Cattai NP NSW 6 G1, 11 J4, 13 J6
Catumnal Vic. 16 G12, 55 L6
Caulfield Vic. 43 I10, 47 J6, 48 C5
Caulfield East Vic. 43 I10
Caulfield North Vic. 42 H10, 43 I10
Caulfield South Vic. 43 I11
Cavan SA 68 D8
Caveat Vic. 50 E11
Cavendish Vic. 56 F3
Caversham WA 90 G6, 91 E2
Caveside Tas. 162 H9
Cawdor NSW 8 A8, 10 G11
Cawongla NSW 15 N3, 137 N12
Cecil Hills NSW 6 D11, 8 D3
Cecil Park NSW 6 D10, 8 D2, 11 I8
Cecil Plains Qld 137 K9
Cedar Creek Qld 130 D7, 133 K12
Cedar Grove Qld 132 F12, 135 D8
Ceduna SA 81 M8
Centennial Park NSW 7 M12, 9 M5
Central SA 5 D10
Central Castra Tas. 162 G7
Central Colo NSW 11 I2, 13 J5
Central Mangrove NSW 11 N1, 13 K5
Central Tilba NSW 20 E8
Centre Island NT 117 N10, 119 N2
Centre Rock WA 103 L2
Ceratodus Qld 137 K4
Ceres NSW 12 E1, 14 B12
Ceres Vic. 46 F8, 57 N7
Cervantes WA 96 A2, 98 A5
Cessnock NSW 13 L4
Chadstone Vic. 43 K10
Chaelundi NP NSW 15 L6
Chakola NSW 20 C7, 58 F2
Chambers Flat Qld 132 H10, 133 I9
Champion Lakes WA 91 G8
Chandada SA 72 B2, 81 O10
Chandler Qld 133 K3
Chandler SA 79 L4
Chandlers Creek Vic. 20 C11, 58 E9
Chandlers Hill SA 69 D6
Channel Island WA 93 C9
Chapel Hill Qld 130 G3, 132 G2
Chapel Hill SA 69 H6
Chapman ACT 34 B7
Chapman Hill WA 94 B6, 96 B9
Chapple Vale Vic. 57 K10
Charam Vic. 54 D10
Charles Darwin NT 112 D6
Charles Darwin NP NT 112 D7, 114 D3, 116 D4
Charleston SA 70 E9, 71 H2, 73 K9
Charleville Qld 136 B5, 147 P5

Charlotte Pass NSW 20 A8, 58 B4
Charlton NSW 12 H6, 19 O6
Charlton Vic. 16 G12, 55 K7
Charnwood ACT 34 B2
Charters Towers Qld 138 F2
Chasm Creek Tas. 162 F5
Chatsbury NSW 12 H8, 20 E2
Chatswood NSW 7 L9, 9 L1, 11 L8
Chatswood West NSW 7 L9, 9 L1
Chatsworth NSW 15 N5
Chatsworth Vic. 56 H5
Cheepie Qld 147 M6
Cheero Point NSW 7 M1
Cheesemans Creek NSW 12 F4
Chelmer Qld 132 H3
Chelsea Vic. 44 E5, 47 J7, 48 D6
Chelsea Heights Vic. 44 E4
Cheltenham NSW 7 J8
Cheltenham SA 68 B10, 70 B8, 71 E1
Cheltenham Vic. 43 I12, 44 D3, 47 J7, 48 C5
Chepstowe Vic. 46 B3, 57 L4
Cherbourg Qld 137 L6
Cherbourg NP Qld 137 L6
Chermside Qld 131 I9, 134 F10, 135 D3
Chermside West Qld 131 I9
Cherokee Vic. 46 H2, 48 B2
Cherry Gardens SA 69 E6
Cherrybrook NSW 7 I6
Cherryville SA 68 H11, 69 H1
Cheshunt Vic. 51 I10
Chesney Vale Vic. 50 H7
Chester Hill NSW 6 H11, 8 H3
Chesterton Range NP Qld 136 D5
Chetwynd Vic. 54 D12, 56 D2, 82 H10
Chewton Vic. 50 A10, 55 O12, 57 O1
Cheyne Beach WA 95 O10, 96 H11, 98 F11
Chidlow WA 93 E4
Chifley ACT 34 C8
Chifley NSW 9 M7
Chigwell Tas. 156 A2
Childers NSW 12 E1, 14 B12
Childers Qld 137 M4
Childers Vic. 47 O10, 48 G7
Chillagoe Qld 141 J6
Chillagoe Mungana Caves NP Qld 141 J6
Chillingham NSW 135 E12
Chillingollah Vic. 16 F9, 53 J12, 55 J1
Chilpanunda SA 72 A2, 81 O10
Chiltern Vic. 17 N12, 51 J6
Chiltern–Mount Pilot NP Vic. 12 A12, 17 N12, 51 J7
Chiltern Valley Vic. 51 J6
Chinaman Wells SA 72 H7, 82 E10
Chinbingina SA 72 A1, 81 N8
Chinchilla Qld 137 J7
Chinderah NSW 15 O2, 135 G12, 137 N11
Chinkapook Vic. 16 F9, 53 J11, 55 J1
Chinnock WA 93 D1, 96 C4
Chippendale NSW 5 A11, 7 L12, 9 L4
Chipping Norton NSW 6 G12, 8 F4
Chirnside Park Vic. 43 N6
Chisholm ACT 34 D10
Chiswick NSW 7 K11, 9 K3
Chittering WA 93 D1, 96 C4
Chorregon Qld 138 A8, 145 M8

Christie Downs SA 69 A8, 70 A11, 71 E4
Christies Beach SA 69 A8, 70 A11, 71 E4
Christmas Creek Qld 141 K11
Christmas Hills Tas. 162 C4
Christmas Hills Vic. 43 O3, 47 K4
Chudleigh Tas. 162 H8
Chullora NSW 7 I12, 9 I4
Church Point NSW 7 O5, 11 N6
Churchill Qld 132 B5, 134 D12, 135 B6
Churchill Vic. 48 H8
Churchill Island Vic. 47 K11, 48 D8
Churchill Island Marine NP Vic. 47 K11, 48 D8
Churchill NP Vic. 43 M12, 44 H2, 47 K7, 48 D5
Churchlands WA 90 D8, 91 B3
Chute Vic. 46 A1, 57 K2
Chuwar Qld 132 C3, 134 D12, 135 B5
Circular Quay NSW 5 E4
City ACT 33 E3
City Beach WA 90 C8, 91 A3
Clackline WA 93 F3, 96 D4
Clairview Qld 139 L8
Clandulla NSW 13 I3
Clapham SA 69 D4
Clare Qld 138 H2
Clare SA 73 J6
Claremont Tas. 156 A1, 159 I4, 161 K6
Claremont Vic. 51 I9
Claremont WA 90 D10, 91 A5, 93 B5, 96 B5
Claremont Isles NP Qld 142 F10
Claremont Meadows NSW 6 C7
Clarence NSW 10 C2, 13 I5
Clarence Gardens SA 69 D3
Clarence Park SA 69 D3
Clarence Point Tas. 163 J6
Clarence Town NSW 13 M3
Clarendon NSW 6 D2, 11 I5
Clarendon Qld 134 B10
Clarendon SA 69 D7, 70 B11, 71 F4, 73 J9, 82 B3
Clarendon Tas. 163 K9
Clarendon Vic. 46 D4, 57 M5
Clarendon Vale Tas. 157 I8
Clarinda Vic. 43 J12, 44 E1
Clarke Island Tas. 160 B12, 163 O3
Clarkefield Vic. 46 H3, 48 B2, 57 P4
Clarkes Hill Vic. 46 D3, 57 M3
Clarkson WA 90 A3
Claude Road Tas. 162 G8
Clay Wells SA 82 F10
Clayfield Qld 131 J10, 133 I1
Claymore NSW 8 C8
Clayton SA 71 H8, 73 K11, 82 C4
Clayton Vic. 43 J11, 44 E1, 47 J6
Clayton South Vic. 43 J12, 44 E1
Clear Lake Vic. 54 E10
Clear Mountain Qld 130 F7
Clear Ridge NSW 12 C5, 17 P5
Clearview SA 68 E9
Cleland SA 69 F3
Clematis Vic. 43 P12, 45 K2, 47 L7
Clemton Park NSW 9 J5
Clermont Qld 138 H9
Cleve SA 72 F5
Cleveland Qld 133 N5, 134 H12, 135 F5, 137 N9
Cleveland Tas. 163 L10

Cliff Island NP Qld 142 F10
Clifton NSW 15 K3, 137 K12
Clifton Qld 137 L10
Clifton Beach Qld 141 L6
Clifton Beach Tas. 159 K7, 161 L8
Clifton Creek Vic. 49 M5
Clifton Hill Vic. 42 H7, 43 I7
Clifton Springs Vic. 46 G8, 48 A6, 57 O7
Clinton Centre SA 73 I7, 82 A1
Clintonvale Qld 15 L1, 137 L10
Clonbinane Vic. 47 J2, 48 D2, 50 D12
Cloncurry Qld 143 F11, 144 H3
Clontarf NSW 7 N10, 9 N2
Clontarf Qld 131 J6, 137 K10
Closeburn Qld 130 E7, 134 E10, 135 C3
Clouds Creek NSW 15 M7
Clovelly NSW 9 N5
Clovelly Park SA 69 C4, 70 B9, 71 F3
Cloven Hills Vic. 57 J6
Cloverdale WA 90 G9, 91 E4
Cloyna Qld 137 L6
Cluan Tas. 163 J9
Club Terrace Vic. 20 B11, 58 D10
Cluden Qld 138 G1
Clump Mountain NP Qld 141 M8
Clunes NSW 15 O3, 137 N12
Clunes Vic. 46 C1, 57 M2
Clybucca NSW 15 M9
Clyde NSW 6 H10, 7 I10, 8 H2, 9 I2
Clyde Vic. 45 I7, 47 K8, 48 D6
Clyde North Vic. 45 I6
Clyde River NP NSW 12 H12, 20 F6
Clydebank Vic. 49 L6
Clydesdale Vic. 55 N12
Coal Creek Qld 134 B8
Coaldale NSW 15 M5
Coalfalls Qld 132 B5
Coalstoun Lakes Qld 137 L5
Coalstoun Lakes NP Qld 137 L5
Coalville Vic. 47 P9, 48 H7
Coasters Retreat NSW 7 O4
Cobains Vic. 49 K7
Cobar NSW 19 L9
Cobargo NSW 20 E8
Cobaw Vic. 46 H1, 48 B1, 50 B12
Cobbadah NSW 14 H7
Cobbannah Vic. 49 L4
Cobbitty NSW 8 A4, 10 G10, 13 J7, 20 H1
Cobboboonee NP Vic. 56 C6, 82 H12
Cobbora NSW 12 G1, 14 D12
Cobden Vic. 57 J8
Cobdogla SA 16 A6, 73 N7, 82 F1
Cobera SA 16 A7, 73 N9, 82 F2
Cobram Vic. 17 L12, 50 F4
Cobrico Vic. 57 I8
Cobungra Vic. 49 M1, 51 M12
Coburg Vic. 42 H6, 47 I5
Coburg North Vic. 42 H5
Cocamba Vic. 16 F9, 53 J11
Cochranes Creek Vic. 55 L9
Cockaleechie SA 72 D7
Cockatoo Vic. 45 M2, 47 L7, 48 E5
Cockburn SA 18 A10, 73 O1, 75 N8
Cockburn Central WA 91 D9
Cockle Creek Tas. 161 I11
Cocklebiddy WA 99 M6
Cocklebiddy Roadhouse WA 99 M6

Coconut Grove NT 112 C4
Cocoparra NP NSW 17 M6
Cocoroc Vic. 42 A11
Codrington Vic. 56 E7
Coen Qld 142 E10
Coffin Bay SA 72 D8
Coffin Bay NP SA 72 C7
Coffs Harbour NSW 15 N8
Coghills Creek Vic. 46 C2, 57 M3
Cogra Bay NSW 7 N1
Cohuna Vic. 17 I11, 50 A3, 55 O5
Coimadai Vic. 46 G4, 48 A3, 57 O4
Colac Vic. 46 B9, 57 L8
Colac Colac Vic. 51 O7
Colbinabbin Vic. 50 C8
Colbinabbin West Vic. 50 C8
Coldstream Vic. 43 O5, 47 L5, 48 E4
Coleambally NSW 17 M8
Colebee NSW 6 E6
Colebrook Tas. 159 J1, 161 K5
Coleraine Vic. 56 E3
Coles Bay Tas. 161 O3
Colignan Vic. 16 E7, 52 H8
Colinroobie NSW 12 A7, 17 N7
Colinton NSW 12 F12, 20 C6, 31 D12, 58 F1
Collarenebri NSW 14 D4
Collaroy NSW 7 O7, 13 I1, 14 F12
Collaroy Plateau NSW 11 N7
Collector NSW 12 G9, 20 D3
College Park SA 68 E11, 69 E1
Collerina NSW 19 O4
Colley SA 72 B3, 81 O11
Collie NSW 14 B10
Collie WA 94 E3, 96 D8, 98 C9
Collie Burn WA 94 F3
Collie Cardiff WA 94 F4, 96 D8
Collier Range NP WA 97 H6, 100 E7
Collier Rocks WA 100 B2, 102 B12
Collingullie NSW 12 B9, 17 O9
Collingwood Vic. 42 H8
Collingwood Park Qld 132 E5
Collins Cap Tas. 158 H5
Collinsfield SA 73 I5
Collinsvale Tas. 156 A3, 158 H4, 161 J7
Collinsville Qld 139 I4
Collinswood SA 68 D10, 69 D1
Collombatti Rail NSW 15 M10
Colly Blue NSW 14 G10
Colo NSW 11 I2, 13 J5
Colo Heights NSW 11 I1, 13 J5
Colo Vale NSW 13 I8, 20 G2
Colonel Light Gardens SA 69 D3
Colquhoun NSW 49 O5
Colton SA 72 B5, 74 A12, 81 P12
Columbey NP NSW 13 M3
Colyton NSW 6 C8
Comara NSW 15 L9
Comaum SA 54 B12, 56 B1, 82 G10
Combara NSW 14 C9
Combienbar Vic. 20 C11, 58 D9
Comboyne NSW 15 L11
Come-by-Chance NSW 14 C6
Comet Qld 139 I11
Como NSW 9 I7, 11 K10
Como WA 90 F10, 91 C5
Compton Downs NSW 19 N6
Conara Tas. 161 L1, 163 L10
Conargo NSW 17 K10, 50 E1
Concord NSW 7 J11, 9 J2, 11 K8
Concord West NSW 7 J10, 9 J2

Concordia SA 68 H1
Condah Vic. 56 E5
Condamine Qld 137 I7
Condell Park NSW 8 H4
Conder ACT 34 C11
Condingup WA 99 J9
Condobolin NSW 12 B3, 17 P3
Condong NSW 15 O2, 135 F12
Condowie SA 73 J5
Cone Rock WA 103 I5
Congo NSW 20 F7
Congupna Vic. 50 E7
Conical Rocks Qld 139 N10
Conimbla NP NSW 12 E5
Coningham Tas. 159 I8, 161 K8
Conjola NSW 13 I11, 20 G5
Conjola NP NSW 13 I10, 20 G5
Conmurra SA 82 F9
Connangorach Vic. 54 F10
Connells Point NSW 9 J7
Connellys Marsh Tas. 159 L5, 161 L7
Connemarra NSW 14 F10
Connewarre Vic. 46 F9, 48 A7, 57 O8
Connolly WA 90 B4
Conondale Qld 134 D4, 137 M7
Conondale NP Qld 134 C4, 137 M7
Constitution Hill NSW 6 H8, 8 H1
Conway Beach Qld 139 J4
Conway NP Qld 139 J4
Coober Pedy SA 76 A10, 79 O10
Coobowie SA 72 H9
Coochin Creek Qld 134 F5
Coodanup WA 92 C10
Cooee Tas. 162 F5
Coogee NSW 9 M5
Coogee WA 91 B9
Coojar Vic. 56 E2
Cook ACT 34 C4
Cook SA 80 F4
Cookamidgera NSW 12 E4
Cookardinia NSW 12 B11, 17 O11, 51 M3
Cooke Plains SA 73 L10, 82 D4
Cooks Gap NSW 12 H2
Cooktown Qld 141 L3
Cookville Tas. 159 I11, 161 K10
Coolabah NSW 19 N8
Coolac NSW 12 D9, 20 A3
Cooladdi Qld 136 A6, 147 N6
Coolah NSW 14 F11
Coolah Tops NP NSW 14 F11
Coolalie NSW 12 F9, 20 C3
Coolalinga NT 113 N11, 114 E3
Coolamon NSW 12 B8, 17 O8
Coolana Qld 134 B11
Coolangatta Qld 15 O1, 135 G11, 137 N11
Coolaroo Vic. 42 G3
Coolatai NSW 15 I4, 137 I12
Coolbellup WA 91 B8
Coolbinia WA 90 E8, 91 C3
Coolcha SA 73 L9, 82 D3
Coolgardie WA 98 H5
Coolimba WA 98 A5
Coolongolook NSW 13 N2
Cooloongup WA 92 C2
Cooltong SA 16 A5, 52 A5, 73 O7
Coolum Beach Qld 134 G3, 137 N7
Coolup WA 93 D10, 96 C7
Cooma NSW 20 C7, 58 E3
Cooma Tas. 160 B11
Cooma Vic. 50 D7

Cooma West NSW 20 C7, 58 E3
Coomalbidgup WA 98 H9
Coomandook SA 73 L11, 82 E4
Coomba NSW 13 N2
Coombah Roadhouse NSW 16 C2, 75 O11
Coombe SA 73 M12, 82 F6
Coombell NSW 15 N4
Coomberdale WA 96 B1, 98 C5
Coomera Qld 135 F8
Coominya Qld 134 B10, 137 M9
Coomoora Vic. 46 E1, 57 N3
Coonabarabran NSW 14 E9
Coonalpyn SA 73 M11, 82 E5
Coonamble NSW 14 C8
Coonarr Qld 137 M3
Coonawarra NT 112 F6
Coonawarra SA 54 A12, 56 A2, 82 G10
Coonerang NSW 20 C8, 58 F4
Coongie Lakes NP SA 77 M6, 146 E6
Coongulla Vic. 49 J5
Coongulmerang Vic. 49 L5
Coonong NSW 17 M9
Coonooer Bridge Vic. 55 K8
Coopernook NSW 13 O1, 15 L12
Coopers Creek Vic. 49 I6
Coopers Plains Qld 133 I5
Cooplacurripa NSW 15 K11
Coopracambra NP Vic. 20 C11, 58 F9
Coorabakh NP NSW 13 O1, 15 L12
Coorabie SA 81 J8
Cooran Qld 137 N6
Cooranbong NSW 13 L4
Cooranga North Qld 137 K7
Coorong NP SA 71 G8, 73 K11, 82 D6
Coorow WA 98 B4
Cooroy Qld 134 F1, 137 N7
Coorparoo Qld 131 I12, 133 I2, 134 F11, 135 D4
Cootamundra NSW 12 D8, 20 A2
Cooya Beach Qld 141 L5
Cooyal NSW 12 H2
Cooyar Qld 137 L8
Copacabana NSW 11 O4
Cope Cope Vic. 55 J8
Copeland NSW 13 M1, 15 J12
Copeville SA 73 M9, 82 E2
Copley SA 75 I4
Copmanhurst NSW 15 M5
Coppabella Qld 139 I7
Copping Tas. 159 M5, 161 M7
Coppins Crossing ACT 31 D5
Cora Lynn Vic. 45 N8, 47 M8, 48 E6
Corack Vic. 16 F12, 55 J7
Corack East Vic. 16 F12, 55 J6
Coragulac Vic. 46 A8, 57 K8
Coraki NSW 15 O4, 137 N12
Coral Bank Vic. 51 L9
Coral Bay WA 97 B5
Coram Vic. 46 B9, 57 L8
Coramba NSW 15 M7
Corang NSW 12 H10, 20 F4
Corattum SA 82 F12
Cordalba Qld 137 M4
Cordalba NP Qld 137 M4
Cordering WA 94 G4, 96 E8
Coreen NSW 17 M11, 51 I4
Corfield Qld 138 A6, 145 M6
Corinda Qld 132 H4, 143 B4
Corindhap Vic. 46 C5, 57 L6

Corindi NSW 15 N7
Corindi Beach NSW 15 N7
Corinella Vic. 47 L10, 48 E8
Corinna Tas. 162 C8
Corio Vic. 46 F7, 48 A6, 57 O7
Corner Inlet Marine and Coastal Park Vic. 48 H10
Corner Inlet Marine NP Vic. 48 H10
Corner Store Qld 18 B1, 77 N11, 146 F10
Cornubia Qld 133 L7
Cornwall Tas. 163 O9
Cornwallis NSW 6 D1
Corny Point SA 72 G9
Corobimilla NSW 17 N8
Coromandel East SA 69 E5
Coromandel Valley SA 69 D5
Coromby Vic. 54 H8
Coronation Beach WA 97 D12, 98 A3
Coronet Bay Vic. 47 L11, 48 E8
Corop Vic. 50 C7
Cororooke Vic. 46 A9, 57 K8
Corowa NSW 17 M12, 51 I5
Corra Linn Tas. 163 K8
Corrigin WA 96 F5, 98 E8
Corringle NSW 12 C5, 17 P5
Corroboree Park Tavern NT 114 C3, 116 E5
Corryong Vic. 51 O7
Cosgrove Vic. 50 F7
Cosmo Newbery WA 99 I1, 101 I11
Cossack WA 97 F1, 100 B2, 102 B12
Costerfield Vic. 50 C9
Cottage Point NSW 7 M4
Cottan–Bimbang NP NSW 15 K10
Cottesloe WA 90 C11, 91 A5, 93 B5
Cottles Bridge Vic. 43 M2, 47 K4
Cottonvale Qld 15 L2, 137 L11
Couangalt Vic. 46 H3, 48 B3, 57 P4
Cougal NSW 15 N2, 135 C12
Coulson Qld 135 A8
Coulta SA 72 D7
Countegany NSW 20 D7, 58 G3
Couradda NP NSW 14 G6
Couta Rocks Tas. 162 A5
Coutts Crossing NSW 15 M6
Cow and Calf Rocks WA 98 C12
Cow Bay Qld 141 L4
Cowabbie West NSW 12 A8, 17 O8
Cowan NSW 7 L1, 11 M5, 13 K6
Cowan Cowan Qld 135 G1
Cowandilla SA 68 C12, 69 C2
Cowangie Vic. 16 C9, 52 D11, 54 D1, 73 P10
Cowaramup WA 94 B7, 96 B9
Cowell SA 72 G5
Cowes Vic. 47 K11, 48 D8
Cowley Beach Qld 141 M8
Cowleys Creek Vic. 57 J9
Cowper NSW 15 N5
Cowra NSW 12 F6
Cowwarr Vic. 49 J6
Coyrecup WA 95 L4, 96 G8
Crabbes Creek NSW 15 O2, 137 N11
Crabtree Tas. 158 G6, 161 J7
Cracow Qld 137 I4
Cradle Mountain–Lake St Clair NP Tas. 160 F2, 162 F9
Cradle Valley Tas. 162 F9
Cradoc Tas. 158 G8, 161 J8
Cradock SA 73 J1, 75 I8

Crafers SA 69 G3
Crafers West SA 69 F3
Craigburn Farm SA 69 D5
Craigie NSW 20 C10, 58 E8
Craigie Vic. 55 M12, 57 M1
Craigie WA 90 B5
Craigieburn Vic. 42 G1, 47 I4,
48 C3
Craiglie Qld 141 L5
Craigmore SA 68 G5
Cramenton Vic. 16 E8, 52 H9
Cramps Tas. 161 I1, 163 I10
Cranbourne Vic. 44 H6, 47 K8,
48 D6
Cranbourne East Vic. 44 H6, 45 I6
Cranbourne North Vic. 44 H6,
45 I6
Cranbourne South Vic. 44 G7,
47 K8, 48 D6
Cranbourne West Vic. 44 G6
Cranbrook Tas. 161 N2, 163 N12
Cranbrook WA 95 K7, 96 F10,
98 E10
Cranebrook NSW 6 B6
Crater Lakes NP Qld 141 L7
Craven NSW 13 M2
Cravensville Vic. 51 N8
Crawford Qld 137 L7
Crawley WA 90 E10, 91 B5
Crawney Pass NP NSW 15 I11
Crayfish Creek Tas. 162 D4
Creek Junction Vic. 50 G9
Creery Island WA 93 C9
Creighton Vic. 50 E9
Cremorne NSW 7 M10, 9 M2
Cremorne Tas. 159 K6, 161 L8
Cremorne Vic. 42 H9
Cremorne Point NSW 7 M11, 9 M3
Crescent Head NSW 15 M10
Cressy Tas. 163 K9
Cressy Vic. 46 B7, 57 L6
Crestmead Qld 133 I9, 135 D6
Crestwood NSW 34 G8
Creswick Vic. 46 D2, 57 M3
Crib Point Vic. 47 J10, 48 D7
Croajingolong NP Vic. 20 C12,
58 E11
Croftby Qld 15 M1, 137 M10
Croker Island NT 116 G1
Cromer NSW 7 N7
Cronulla NSW 9 K9, 11 L11, 13 K7
Crooble NSW 14 H4, 137 I12
Crooked River Vic. 49 K3
Crookwell NSW 12 G8, 20 E2
Croppa Creek NSW 14 H3, 137 I12
Crossdale Qld 130 A1, 134 C8,
135 A1, 137 M8
Crossley Vic. 56 G8
Crossman WA 93 H10, 96 D7,
98 C8
Crossover Vic. 47 O8, 48 G6
Crowdy Bay NP NSW 13 O1,
15 L12
Crowlands Vic. 55 J12, 57 J1
Crown Rock NT 117 O11, 119 O2
Crows Nest NSW 7 M10, 9 M2
Crows Nest Qld 137 L8
Crows Nest NP Qld 137 L8
Crowther NSW 12 E7, 20 B1
Croxton East Vic. 56 F5
Croydon NSW 7 K11, 9 J3, 11 L9
Croydon Qld 140 F8
Croydon SA 68 C11, 69 C1, 70 B8,
71 F2

Croydon Vic. 43 N7, 47 K5
Croydon Hills Vic. 43 N7
Croydon North Vic. 43 N7
Croydon Park NSW 7 J12, 9 J4
Croydon Park SA 68 C10
Croydon South Vic. 43 N9
Crymelon Vic. 16 E12, 54 G6
Cryon NSW 14 D5
Crystal Brook SA 73 I4, 74 H12
Cuballing WA 96 E6, 98 D8
Cubbaroo NSW 14 E6
Cuckoo Tas. 163 M7
Cudal NSW 12 F4
Cuddell NSW 17 N8
Cudgee Vic. 56 H8
Cudgen NSW 135 G12
Cudgewa Vic. 51 O7
Cudgewa North Vic. 51 O6
Cudmore NP Qld 138 F9
Cue WA 97 H10, 98 D1, 100 D11
Culbin WA 94 H2, 96 E7
Culburra NSW 13 J10, 20 H4
Culburra SA 73 M12, 82 E5
Culcairn NSW 12 B11, 17 O11,
51 L4
Culgoa Vic. 16 F10, 55 K4
Culgoa Floodplain NP Qld 14 A2,
19 O2, 136 C11, 147 P11
Culgoa NP NSW 14 A2, 19 O2,
136 C11, 147 P11
Cullacabardee WA 90 E5, 91 D1
Cullen Bullen NSW 13 I5
Cullendulla NSW 12 H12
Culloden Vic. 49 K5
Cullulleraine Vic. 16 C6, 52 E6,
73 P7
Cumberland Park SA 69 D3
Cumberland Rock WA 96 B11,
98 B11
Cumborah NSW 14 B4
Cummins SA 72 D7
Cumnock NSW 12 F3
Cundeelee WA 99 J5
Cunderdin WA 96 E4, 98 D7
Cundletown NSW 13 N2
Cungena SA 72 B2, 81 O9
Cungulla Qld 138 H1, 141 O12
Cunliffe SA 72 H6
Cunnamulla Qld 136 A9, 147 N9
Cunnawarra NP NSW 15 L8
Cunningar NSW 12 E8, 20 B2
Cunningham Qld 15 K1, 137 K10
Cunningham SA 72 H7
Cunninyeuk NSW 16 H9, 53 N12,
55 N1
Cuprona Tas. 162 F6
Curara WA 93 F11, 96 D7, 97 E12,
98 B3
Curban NSW 14 C10
Curdie Vale Vic. 57 I9
Curl Curl NSW 7 O9, 9 O1
Curlewis NSW 14 G9
Curlwaa NSW 16 D5, 52 G5
Currabubula NSW 14 H10
Curramble NSW 90 B3
Curramulka SA 72 H8
Currans Hill NSW 8 B7
Currarong NSW 13 J10, 20 H4
Currawang NSW 12 G10, 20 E4
Currawarna NSW 12 B9, 17 O9
Currawinya NP Qld 19 I1, 147 L10
Currency Creek SA 71 G7, 73 J10,
82 C4
Currie Tas. 161 O11

Currowan Creek NSW 12 H12,
20 F6
Currumbin Qld 15 O1, 135 G11,
137 N11
Curtain Fig NP Qld 141 L7
Curtin ACT 34 C7
Curtin Springs NT 120 F10
Curtis Island Qld 137 L1, 139 N11
Curtis Island NP Qld 139 N11
Curyo Vic. 16 F11, 55 I5
Custon SA 16 B12, 54 B7, 82 G7
Cuttabri NSW 14 E6
Cygnet Tas. 158 G8, 161 J9
Cygnet River SA 72 H11
Cynthia Qld 137 K4

Daceyville NSW 9 M5
Dadswells Bridge Vic. 54 H10
Daglish WA 90 D9, 91 B4
D'Aguilar NP Qld 130 F10, 132 E1,
134 D7, 135 B2, 137 M8
Daguragu NT 118 D5
Dahlen Vic. 54 G9
Dahwilly NSW 17 J10, 50 D1
Daintree Qld 141 L4
Daintree NP Qld 141 L4
Daisy Dell Tas. 162 G8
Daisy Hill Qld 133 K6, 135 E6
Daisy Hill Vic. 55 M12, 57 M1
Dajarra Qld 144 F5
Dakabin Qld 130 H5, 131 I5,
134 F9, 135 D2
Dalbeg Qld 138 H3
Dalby Qld 137 K8
Dalgarup NP WA 94 E7, 96 C9,
98 C10
Dalgety NSW 20 B8, 58 D4
Dalkeith WA 90 D11, 91 B6
Dallarnil Qld 137 M4
Dallas Vic. 42 G4
Dalmalee Vic. 16 D11, 54 G5
Dalmeny NSW 20 F7
Dalmore Vic. 45 J9
Dalmorton NSW 15 L6
Dalrymple NP Qld 138 F2,
141 M12
Dalton NSW 12 F9, 20 D3
Dalveen Qld 15 L2, 137 L11
Dalwallinu WA 96 D1, 98 C5
Daly River NT 114 C12, 116 D7
Daly Waters NT 116 H12, 118 H3
Dalyellup WA 96 C8
Dalyston Vic. 47 L12, 48 E9
Dalyup WA 99 I9
Dampier WA 97 E1, 100 B2,
102 B12
Dampiers Monument WA
103 I5
Dan Dan NP Qld 137 K1, 139 N12
Danbulla NP Qld 141 L6
Dandaloo NSW 12 D1, 14 A12,
19 P12
Dandaragan WA 96 B2, 98 B6
Dandenong Vic. 44 G3, 47 K7,
48 D5
Dandenong North Vic. 43 L12,
44 G2
Dandenong Ranges NP
Vic. 43 O11, 45 J1, 47 L6, 48 E5
Dandenong South Vic. 44 F4
Dandongadale Vic. 51 J10
Dangarfield NSW 13 K1, 14 H12
Dangarsleigh NSW 15 J8
Dangin WA 96 E5

Danyo Vic. 16 C9, 52 D11, 54 D1,
73 P10, 82 H4
Darby Falls NSW 12 F6
Darbyshire Vic. 51 M6
Darch WA 90 D5, 91 B1
Dardadine WA 94 H2, 96 E8
Dardanup WA 94 D4, 96 C8
Dareton NSW 16 D5, 52 G5
Dargo Vic. 49 L3
Dargo High Plains Vic. 49 L1
Dark Corner NSW 12 H5
Darkan WA 94 H3, 96 E8, 98 D9
Darke Peak SA 72 E5, 74 D12
Darkes Forest NSW 8 D12
Darkwood NSW 15 M8
Darley Vic. 46 G4, 48 A3, 57 O4
Darling Downs WA 91 G10
Darling Harbour NSW 5 B8
Darling Point NSW 7 M12, 9 M4
Darlinghurst NSW 5 F9, 7 M12,
9 M4
Darlington NSW 5 A12, 7 L12, 9 L4
Darlington SA 69 C5
Darlington Tas. 159 P2, 161 N5
Darlington Vic. 57 J6
Darlington WA 91 H3, 93 D4
Darlington Point NSW 17 M7
Darnick NSW 16 H2
Darnum Vic. 47 O9, 48 G7
Daroobalgie NSW 12 D4
Darr Qld 138 B9, 145 N9
Darra Qld 132 G5, 134 E12, 135 D5
Darraweit Guim Vic. 47 I2, 48 C2,
50 C12
Darriman Vic. 49 J9
Dart Dart Vic. 16 D12, 54 G7
Dartmoor Vic. 56 C5, 82 H12
Dartmouth Qld 138 C10, 145 O10
Dartmouth Vic. 51 M9
Darwin NT 111 F11, 112 C9,
114 C3, 116 D4
Dattuck Vic. 16 E10, 54 G3
Davidson NSW 7 M7, 11 M7
Davies Creek NP Qld 141 L6
Davis Creek NSW 13 L2
Davistown NSW 11 O4
Davoren Park SA 68 F5
Daw Park SA 69 D3
Dawes Qld 137 J2
Dawes NP Qld 137 K2
Dawes Point NSW 5 D2, 7 M11,
9 M4
Dawesville WA 92 A12
Dawson SA 73 K3, 75 J10
Dawson Vic. 49 J6
Dawsons Hill NSW 13 L2
Dayboro Qld 130 E3, 134 E8,
135 C2
Daylesford Vic. 46 E1, 57 N3
Daymar Qld 14 E1, 136 G11
Daysdale NSW 17 M11, 51 I3
Daytrap Vic. 16 F9, 53 J12, 55 J1
Daytrap Corner Vic. 16 F9, 53 I12,
55 I2
De Witt Island Tas. 160 G11
Deagon Qld 131 J8
Deakin ACT 33 B11, 34 D7
Deakin WA 80 C4, 99 P4
Dean Vic. 46 D2, 57 M3
Dean Park NSW 6 E6
Deanmill WA 94 F8, 96 D10
Deans Marsh Vic. 46 C10, 57 M8
Deception Bay Qld 131 I3, 134 F8,
135 E2, 137 N8

Deddick Vic. 20 A10, 58 B7
Deddington Tas. 163 L9
Dederang Vic. 51 L8
Dee Lagoon Tas. 160 H3
Dee Why NSW 7 O8, 9 O1
Deebing Heights Qld 132 B7
Deep Lead Vic. 55 I11
Deepwater NSW 15 K5
Deepwater NP Qld 137 L2
Deer Park Vic. 42 D6, 46 H5, 48 B4,
57 P5
Deer Reserve NP Qld 134 B7,
135 A1, 137 M8
Deeral Qld 141 M7
Delahey Vic. 42 D5
Delamere SA 71 B9, 73 I11, 82 A5
Delaneys Creek Qld 134 E6
Delatite Vic. 47 P1, 48 H1, 50 H11
Delburn Vic. 47 P10, 48 H8
Delegate NSW 20 C10, 58 D7
Delegate River Vic. 20 B10, 58 D8
Dellicknora Vic. 20 B10, 58 C8
Deloraine Tas. 163 I8
Delta Qld 139 J3
Delungra NSW 15 I5
Denham WA 97 B9
Denham Court NSW 8 D5
Denham Group NP Qld 142 E4
Denicull Creek Vic. 57 I2
Deniliquin NSW 17 J10, 50 D2
Denison Vic. 49 J6
Denistone NSW 7 J9, 9 J1
Denistone East NSW 7 J9, 9 J1
Denistone West NSW 7 J9, 9 J1
Denman NSW 13 J2
Denman SA 80 E4
Denmark WA 95 K11, 96 F11,
98 E11
Dennes Point Tas. 159 I7, 161 K8
Dennington Vic. 56 G8
D'Entrecasteaux NP WA 94 D9,
96 C11, 98 C11
Denver Vic. 46 F1, 48 A1, 50 A12,
57 O2
Deptford Vic. 49 N4
Derby Tas. 163 N6
Derby Vic. 55 N9
Derby WA 103 I7
Dereel Vic. 46 C5, 57 L5
Dergholm Vic. 56 C2, 82 H10
Dering Vic. 16 D9, 52 G12, 54 G2
Deringulla NSW 14 E10
Dernancourt SA 68 F10
Derrimut Vic. 42 D7
Derrinal Vic. 50 B9, 55 P11
Derrinallum Vic. 57 J6
Derriwong NSW 12 C3, 17 P3
Derwent Bridge Tas. 160 G2,
162 G12
Derwent Park Tas. 156 D5
Detpa Vic. 16 D12, 54 F6
Deua NP NSW 12 G12, 20 E7,
58 H1
Devenish Vic. 50 G7
Deviot Tas. 163 J7
Devon Vic. 49 I9
Devon Meadows Vic. 44 H9, 45 I8
Devon Park SA 68 D11
Devondale Vic. 57 J10
Devonport Tas. 162 H6
Dewars Pool WA 93 F1, 96 C4
Dewhurst Vic. 45 L4
Dharawal NP NSW 8 C11, 9 J7,
10 H12

Dharruk NSW 6 D7
Dharug NP NSW 11 L2, 13 K5
Dhulura NSW 12 B9, 17 P9
Dhuragoon NSW 17 I9, 53 O12, 55 O1
Diamantina NP Qld 144 H10, 145 I10
Diamond Beach NSW 13 O2
Diamond Creek Vic. 43 L3, 47 K4
Dianella WA 90 E7, 91 C2, 93 C5
Diapur Vic. 16 C12, 54 D7
Dickson ACT 34 E4
Diddleum Plains Tas. 163 L7
Digby Vic. 56 D5
Diggers Rest Vic. 42 A1, 46 H4, 48 B3, 57 P4
Diggora Vic. 50 B7, 55 P8
Dilston Tas. 163 K7
Dimboola Vic. 54 F8
Dimbulah Qld 141 K6
Dinden NP Qld 141 L6
Dingabledinga SA 69 D12
Dingee Vic. 50 A7, 55 O8
Dingley Village Vic. 44 E3
Dingo Qld 139 K11
Dingwall Vic. 16 H11, 55 M5
Dinmont Vic. 46 B11, 57 K10
Dinmore Qld 132 D5
Dinner Plain Vic. 49 L1, 51 L11
Dinninup WA 94 G5, 96 D9
Dinoga NSW 14 H6
Dinyarrak Vic. 16 B12, 54 B7, 82 H7
Dipperu NP (Scientific) Qld 139 J7
Direk SA 68 E6, 70 B6
Dirk Hartog Island WA 97 A8
Dirk Hartog NP WA 97 A8
Dirranbandi Qld 14 C1, 136 E10
Discovery Bay Marine NP Vic. 56 C8
Dixie Vic. 57 I8
Dixons Creek Vic. 47 L4, 48 E3
Djidbordu (Barron Island) NT 115 L1, 116 G4
Djiru NP Qld 141 M8
Djukbinj NP NT 114 F1, 116 E4
Dobie Vic. 57 J2
Docker Vic. 51 I8
Docklands Vic. 41 A6, 42 G8
Doctors Flat Vic. 49 N2
Dodges Ferry Tas. 159 L5, 161 L7
Dolans Bay NSW 9 J9
Dolls Point NSW 9 K7
Don Tas. 162 H6
Don Valley Vic. 47 M5
Donald Vic. 16 F12, 55 J7
Doncaster Vic. 43 K7, 47 J5, 48 D4
Doncaster East Vic. 43 K7
Dongara–Denison WA 98 A4
Donington Reef SA 72 E8
Donnybrook Qld 134 G7
Donnybrook Vic. 42 H1, 43 I1, 47 J3, 48 C3
Donnybrook WA 94 D5, 96 C9, 98 C10
Donovans Landing SA 56 B6, 82 G12
Donvale Vic. 43 L7
Doo Town Tas. 159 N8, 161 M8
Dooboobetic Vic. 55 K8
Doodlakine WA 96 F4, 98 E7
Dooen Vic. 54 G9
Dookie Vic. 50 F7

Doolandella Qld 132 G6
Doomadgee Qld 143 C5
Doomben Qld 134 F11, 135 E4
Doonside NSW 6 E7, 11 I7
Dooragan NP NSW 13 O1, 15 L11
Dopewora Vic. 54 C9, 82 H8
Doreen Vic. 43 K1
Dorodong Vic. 54 B12, 56 B2, 82 H10
Dorre Island WA 97 B7
Dorrien SA 70 F4
Dorrigo NSW 15 M8
Dorrigo NP NSW 15 M8
Dorset Vale SA 69 F6
Double Bay NSW 7 M12, 9 M4
Doubleview WA 90 C8, 91 A3
Douglas Vic. 54 E11
Douglas–Apsley NP Tas. 161 O1, 163 O10
Douglas Daly Tourist Park NT 114 G12, 116 E7
Douglas Park NSW 8 A11
Dover Tas. 158 F10, 161 J10
Dover Gardens SA 69 B5
Dover Heights NSW 7 N12, 9 N4
Doveton Vic. 44 G3
Dowe NP NSW 14 H8
Dowerin WA 96 E3, 98 D6
Dowlingville SA 73 I7, 82 A1
Downer ACT 34 E4
Dowsing Point Tas. 156 C3
Doyalson NSW 13 L5
Drake NSW 15 L3, 137 L12
Draper Qld 130 F8
Dreeite Vic. 46 A8, 57 K7
Drewvale Qld 133 I7
Drik Drik Vic. 56 C6, 82 H12
Drillham Qld 137 I6
Drillwarrina NP NSW 14 C11
Dripstone NSW 12 G2
Driver NT 113 J9
Dromana Vic. 44 B12, 47 I10, 48 C7
Dromedary Tas. 158 H3, 161 J6
Dropmore Vic. 50 E11
Drouin Vic. 47 N8, 48 F6
Drouin South Vic. 47 N9, 48 F7
Drouin West Vic. 47 N8, 48 F6
Drovers Cave NP WA 96 A1, 98 A5
Drumborg Vic. 56 D6
Drummartin Vic. 50 A7, 55 O8
Drummond Vic. 46 F1, 48 A1, 50 A11, 57 O2
Drummond Cove WA 97 D12, 98 A3
Drummoyne NSW 7 L11, 9 K3, 11 L8
Drung Drung Vic. 54 G9
Drung Drung South Vic. 54 G10
Dry Creek SA 68 C7, 70 B8, 71 F1
Dry Creek Vic. 50 G10
Dryander NP Qld 139 J3
Drysdale Vic. 46 G8, 48 A6, 57 O7
Drysdale River NP WA 103 M3
Dthinna Dthinnawan NP NSW 15 I3, 137 J11
Duaringa Qld 139 K11
Dubbo NSW 12 F1, 14 C12
Dublin SA 73 J8, 82 B1
Duchess Qld 143 D12, 144 F5
Duddo Vic. 16 C9, 52 D11, 73 P10, 82 H4
Dudinin WA 96 G6, 98 E8
Dudley Vic. 47 L12, 48 E9
Dudley Park SA 68 D10

Dudley Park WA 92 B10
Duffholme Vic. 54 E9
Duffy ACT 34 B7
Duffys Forest NSW 7 M5, 11 M6
Dulacca Qld 136 H6
Dularcha NP Qld 134 F5, 137 N7
Dulcie Range NP NT 121 L4
Dulcot Tas. 156 H1, 157 I1
Dululu Qld 139 L12
Dulwich SA 68 E12, 69 E2
Dulwich Hill NSW 7 K12, 9 K5
Dum In Mirrie Island NT 114 A4, 116 C5
Dumbalk Vic. 47 O12, 48 G9
Dumberning WA 95 I1, 96 E7
Dumbleyung WA 95 K2, 96 F7, 98 E9
Dumosa Vic. 16 G11, 55 K5
Dunach Vic. 55 M12, 57 M2
Dunalley Tas. 159 M6, 161 M7
Duncraig WA 90 C6, 91 A1
Dundas NSW 7 I9, 9 I1
Dundas Qld 130 B3, 134 C9, 135 A2, 137 M9
Dundas Tas. 162 D10
Dundas Valley NSW 7 I9, 9 I1
Dundee NSW 15 K5
Dundee Beach NT 114 A5, 116 C5
Dundonnell Vic. 57 I5
Dundurrabin NSW 15 L7
Dunedoo NSW 12 H1, 14 E12
Dunggir NP NSW 15 L8
Dungog NSW 13 M2
Dungowan NSW 15 I10
Dunk Island Qld 141 M8
Dunkeld NSW 12 G5
Dunkeld Vic. 56 G4
Dunlop ACT 34 C1
Dunluce Vic. 55 L11
Dunmarra NT 116 H12, 118 H3
Dunneworthy Vic. 55 J12, 57 J2
Dunnstown Vic. 46 D3, 57 M4
Dunolly Vic. 55 M10
Dunoon NSW 15 O3
Dunorlan Tas. 162 H8
Dunrobin Vic. 56 C3, 82 H11
Dunsborough WA 94 A5, 96 B9, 98 B10
Dunwich Qld 135 G5, 137 N9
Durack NT 113 J8
Durack Qld 132 G5
Dural NSW 6 H6, 7 I5, 11 K6
Duranillin WA 94 H4, 96 E8, 98 D9
Durdidwarrah Vic. 46 E5, 57 N5
Durham Lead Vic. 46 D4, 57 M5
Durham Ox Vic. 16 H12, 55 N6
Duri NSW 14 H10
Durong Qld 137 K6
Durran Durra NSW 12 H11, 20 E5
Durras NSW 13 I12, 20 F6
Dutson Vic. 49 K7
Dutton SA 70 G3, 73 K7, 82 D1
Dutton Park Qld 129 E12, 133 I3
Duverney Vic. 46 B6, 57 L6
Dwarda WA 93 H10
Dwellingup WA 93 E10, 96 C7, 98 C8
Dwyers NSW 19 M6
Dyer Island WA 93 A6
Dynnyrne Tas. 155 A12, 156 D8
Dysart Qld 139 I8
Dysart Tas. 159 I1, 161 K5

Eagle Farm Qld 131 K9, 133 J1, 134 F11, 135 E4
Eagle Heights Qld 135 E9
Eagle Point Vic. 49 M6
Eagle Rock Marine Sanctuary Vic. 46 D10, 57 N9
Eagle Vale NSW 8 C7
Eagleby Qld 133 L9
Eaglehawk Vic. 50 A8, 55 O10
Eaglehawk Neck Tas. 159 N7, 161 M8
Eaglemont Vic. 43 J7
Earlando Qld 139 J3
Earlston Vic. 50 F8
Earlwood NSW 9 J5
East Arm NT 112 G8
East Bairnsdale Vic. 49 M5
East Boyd NSW 20 E10, 58 H8
East Brisbane Qld 131 I12, 133 I2
East Cannington WA 90 H10, 91 F5
East Fremantle WA 90 D12, 91 A7
East Gresford NSW 13 L2
East Hills NSW 8 G6, 11 J10
East Ipswich Qld 132 C5, 134 D12, 135 B5
East Island SA 72 B5, 74 A12, 81 O12
East Jindabyne NSW 20 B8, 58 C4
East Killara NSW 7 L8
East Kurrajong NSW 11 I3
East Lindfield NSW 7 L8, 9 L1
East Lynne NSW 20 F6
East Melbourne Vic. 41 H4, 42 H8
East Perth WA 89 H4, 90 F9, 91 D4
East Point NT 112 A4
East Pyramids Tas. 160 E10
East Rockingham WA 92 B2
East Ryde NSW 7 K10, 9 K1
East Victoria Park WA 90 F10, 91 D5
East Yolla Tas. 162 E6
Easter NP WA 94 E8, 96 C10, 98 C10
Eastern Creek NSW 6 D8, 8 D1, 11 I7
Eastern Heights Qld 132 C5
Eastern View Vic. 46 D10, 57 M9
Eastgardens NSW 9 M6
Eastlakes NSW 9 L5
Eastville Vic. 55 N10
Eastwood NSW 7 J9, 9 J1, 11 K7
Eastwood SA 68 E12, 69 E2
Eaton NT 112 C4
Eaton WA 94 D3
Eatons Hill Qld 130 G8
Eatonsville NSW 15 M6
Eba SA 73 L6
Ebbw Vale Qld 132 D5
Ebden Vic. 51 L6
Ebenezer NSW 6 F1, 11 J4
Ebor NSW 15 L8
Eccleston NSW 13 L2
Echuca Vic. 17 J12, 50 C5
Echuca Village Vic. 17 J12, 50 C5
Echunga SA 69 H8, 70 D11, 71 G4, 73 J9
Ecklin South Vic. 57 I8
Eddington Vic. 55 M11
Eddystone Point Tas. 163 P6
Eden NSW 20 E10, 58 H8
Eden Hill WA 90 G7, 91 E2
Eden Hills SA 69 D4, 70 B10, 71 F3
Eden Park Vic. 47 J3, 48 D3

Eden Valley SA 70 G6, 73 K8, 82 C2
Edenhope Vic. 54 C11, 82 H9
Edens Landing Qld 133 K9, 135 E6
Edgcumbe Beach Tas. 162 D4
Edgecliff NSW 7 M12, 9 M4, 11 M9
Edgeroi NSW 14 F6
Edgewater WA 90 C4, 93 B4
Edi Vic. 51 I9
Edi Upper Vic. 51 I9
Edillilie SA 72 D7
Edinburgh SA 68 F5
Edith NSW 12 H6
Edith Creek Tas. 162 C4
Edith River NT 116 F8
Edithburgh SA 72 H9
Edithvale Vic. 44 E4, 47 J7, 48 D6
Edmondson Park NSW 8 D5
Edmonton Qld 141 L6
Edwardstown SA 69 C3, 70 B9, 71 F3
Eganstown Vic. 46 E2, 57 N3
Egg Lagoon Tas. 161 P10
Eidsvold Qld 137 K4
Eight Mile Plains Qld 133 J5
Eildon Vic. 47 O1, 48 G1, 50 G12
Eimeo Qld 139 K5
Einasleigh Qld 141 I9
Ejanding WA 96 E2, 98 D6
El Arish Qld 141 M8
Elaine Vic. 46 D5, 57 M5
Elands NSW 15 K11
Elanora Heights NSW 7 N7, 11 N6
Elaroo Qld 139 J5
Elbow Hill SA 72 F5
Elcombe NSW 14 H5
Elderslie NSW 8 A8
Elderslie Tas. 158 H1, 161 J5
Eldon Tas. 159 J1, 161 L5
Eldorado Vic. 51 J7
Electrona Tas. 159 I7
Elimbah Qld 134 F7, 137 N8
Elingamite Vic. 57 I8
Elizabeth SA 68 F5, 70 C6, 73 J8, 82 B2
Elizabeth Bay NSW 7 M12, 9 M4
Elizabeth Beach NSW 13 N2
Elizabeth Downs SA 68 F5
Elizabeth East SA 68 F5
Elizabeth Grove SA 68 F6
Elizabeth North SA 68 F5
Elizabeth Park SA 68 F5
Elizabeth South SA 68 F5
Elizabeth Town Tas. 163 I8
Elizabeth Vale SA 68 F6
Elizabeth West SA 68 F5
Ella Bay NP Qld 141 M7
Ella Rock SA 72 G9
Ellalong NSW 13 L4
Ellam Vic. 16 D11, 54 F5
Ellen Grove Qld 132 G6, 134 E12, 135 D5
Ellenborough NSW 15 L11
Ellenbrook WA 90 G3
Ellendale Tas. 158 E1, 161 I5
Ellerslie Vic. 56 H7
Ellerston NSW 13 L1, 15 I12
Elliminyt Vic. 46 B9, 57 L8
Ellinbank Vic. 47 N9, 48 G7
Elliott NT 119 I5
Elliott Tas. 162 F5
Elliott Heads Qld 137 M3
Ellis Beach Qld 141 L5
Ellis Lane NSW 8 A7

Elliston SA 72 B5
Elmhurst Vic. 55 K12, 57 K1
Elmore Vic. 50 B7, 55 P9
Elong Elong NSW 12 G1, 14 D12
Elphick Nob WA 100 A2, 102 A12
Elphinstone Vic. 50 A11, 55 O12, 57 O1
Elrundie NT 112 H9, 113 I9
Elsey NP NT 116 H9
Elsmore NSW 15 J6
Elsternwick Vic. 42 H10, 43 I11, 47 J6, 48 C5
Eltham Vic. 43 K5, 47 J5, 48 D4
Eltham North Vic. 43 K5
Elvina Bay NSW 7 O5
Elwood Vic. 42 H10
Embleton WA 90 F8, 91 E2
Emerald Qld 139 I10
Emerald Vic. 43 P12, 45 K1, 47 L7, 48 E5
Emerald Beach NSW 15 N7
Emerald Hill NSW 14 G8
Emerald Springs NT 114 H11, 116 E7
Emerton NSW 6 D6
Emita Tas. 160 B10
Emmaville NSW 15 K5
Emmdale Roadhouse NSW 19 I9
Emmes Reef SA 72 F10
Emmet Qld 138 B12, 145 N12, 147 M1
Empire Bay NSW 11 O4
Empire Vale NSW 15 O4, 137 N12
Emu Vic. 55 L10
Emu Bay SA 72 H11
Emu Creek Vic. 50 A9, 55 O10
Emu Downs SA 73 K6
Emu Heights NSW 6 A6
Emu Park Qld 139 N10
Emu Plains NSW 6 A6, 10 G6, 17 N9, 51 J1
Endeavour Hills Vic. 43 M12, 44 G2
Endeavour River NP Qld 141 L2
Eneabba WA 98 B5
Enfield NSW 7 J12, 9 J4
Enfield SA 68 D9
Enfield Vic. 46 C4, 57 M5
Engadine NSW 8 G8, 11 J11
Engawala NT 121 J5
England Creek Qld 130 C8
Englefield Vic. 54 E12, 56 E2
English Town Tas. 163 L9
Englorie Park NSW 8 C9
Enmore NSW 7 L12, 9 L5
Enngonia NSW 19 M3, 136 A12, 147 N12
Enoggera Qld 130 H11, 131 I10, 132 G1, 133 I1, 134 F11, 135 D4
Enoggera Reservoir Qld 130 D10, 132 F1
Ensay Vic. 49 N3
Ensay North Vic. 49 N3
Ensay South Vic. 49 N3
Environa NSW 34 F9
Eppalock Vic. 50 A9, 55 O10
Epping NSW 7 J8, 9 J1, 11 K7
Epping Vic. 42 H2, 43 I3, 47 J4, 48 C3
Epping Forest Tas. 163 L10
Epping Forest NP (Scientific) Qld 138 F8
Epsom Vic. 50 A8, 55 O10
Ercildoun Vic. 46 B2, 57 L3

Erica Vic. 48 H6
Erigolia NSW 17 N5
Erikin WA 98 E7
Erina NSW 11 O3
Erindale SA 68 F12, 69 F2
Erith SA 70 A1, 73 J7, 82 B1
Erldunda NT 120 H9
Ermington NSW 7 I9, 9 I1
Eromanga Qld 147 J5
Erriba Tas. 162 G8
Erringibba NP Qld 136 H8
Errinundra Vic. 20 B11, 58 D9
Errinundra NP Vic. 20 B11, 58 D9
Errk Oykangand NP (CYPAL) Qld 140 F2
Erskine WA 92 B10
Erskine Park NSW 6 D8, 8 C1, 10 H7
Erskineville NSW 9 L5
Eschol Park NSW 8 C7
Esk Qld 134 A8, 137 M8
Esk NP Qld 134 A9, 137 M8
Eskdale Vic. 51 L8
Esmond Vic. 17 M12, 50 H6
Esperance WA 99 I9
Essendon Vic. 42 F6, 47 I5, 48 C4
Essendon North Vic. 42 F6
Essendon West Vic. 42 F6
Ethelton SA 68 A9
Etmilyn WA 93 E10
Eton Qld 139 K6
Ettalong Beach NSW 7 P1, 11 N4
Ettamogah NSW 12 A12, 17 O12, 51 L6
Ettrick NSW 15 N3, 137 M12
Euabalong NSW 12 A3, 17 N3
Euabalong West NSW 12 A3, 17 N3
Eubenangee Swamp NP Qld 141 M7
Euchareena NSW 12 G3
Eucla WA 80 C7, 99 P6
Eucla NP WA 80 C7, 99 P5
Eucumbene NSW 20 B7, 58 C2
Eudlo Qld 134 F4
Eudlo Creek NP Qld 134 F4, 137 N7
Eudunda SA 70 G1, 73 K7, 82 C1
Eugenana Tas. 162 H6
Eugowra NSW 12 E5
Eujinyn WA 96 G4
Eukey Qld 15 L3, 137 L12
Eulo Qld 147 M9
Eumemmerring Vic. 44 H3
Eumundi Qld 134 F2, 137 N7
Eumungerie NSW 14 C11
Eungai Creek NSW 15 M9
Eungella Qld 139 J5
Eungella NP Qld 139 J5
Eurack Vic. 46 B8, 57 L7
Euramo Qld 141 M8
Euratha NSW 12 A6, 17 N6
Eurelia SA 73 J2, 75 I9
Euri Qld 139 I3
Eurimbula NP Qld 137 L1, 139 O12
Euroa Vic. 50 F9
Eurobin Vic. 51 K9
Eurobodalla NSW 20 E7
Eurobodalla NP NSW 20 F7
Euroka NSW 10 C6
Eurong Qld 137 N5
Eurongilly NSW 12 C9
Euston NSW 16 F7, 53 I8

Evandale SA 68 E11, 69 E1
Evandale Tas. 163 K9
Evans Head NSW 15 O4
Evans Plains NSW 12 G5
Evansford Vic. 46 B1, 57 L2
Evanston SA 68 H2
Evanston Gardens SA 68 G2
Evanston Park SA 68 H2
Evanston South SA 68 G3
Evatt ACT 34 D2
Eveleigh NSW 7 L12, 9 L5
Everard Junction WA 101 K7
Everard Park SA 69 D3
Eversley Vic. 55 J12, 57 J2
Everton Vic. 51 J8
Everton Hills Qld 130 H10
Everton Park Qld 130 H10, 131 I10
Ewens Ponds SA 56 A6, 82 G12
Exeter NSW 13 I9, 20 G3
Exeter SA 68 B9
Exeter Tas. 163 J7
Exford Vic. 46 G5, 48 A4, 57 P5
Exmouth WA 97 B3
Expedition NP Qld 136 G3
Exton Tas. 163 I8

Fadden ACT 34 D10
Fairbridge WA 92 G10
Fairfield NSW 6 G11, 8 G2
Fairfield Qld 133 I3
Fairfield Vic. 43 I7
Fairfield East NSW 6 G11, 8 G3
Fairfield Heights NSW 6 G11, 8 G3
Fairfield West NSW 6 F11, 8 F2
Fairhaven Vic. 47 K10, 48 D7
Fairholme NSW 12 C4, 17 P4
Fairley Vic. 16 H10, 55 N4
Fairlies Knob NP Qld 137 M5
Fairlight NSW 7 N9, 9 N1
Fairney View Qld 130 A11, 132 A1, 134 C11, 135 A4
Fairview Vic. 16 G12, 55 K6
Fairview Park SA 68 G8
Fairy Dell Vic. 50 C7
Fairy Hill NSW 15 N3
Falcon WA 92 A11
Falls Creek NSW 13 I10, 20 G4
Falls Creek Vic. 51 L10
Falmouth Tas. 163 O9
Family Islands NP Qld 141 M8
Fannie Bay NT 111 F1, 112 B6
Faraday Vic. 50 A10, 55 O12, 57 O1
Farleigh Qld 139 K5
Farnborough Qld 139 M10
Farnham NSW 12 G3
Farrar NT 113 K9
Farrell Flat SA 73 K6
Farrer ACT 34 D8
Faulconbridge NSW 10 F5
Fawcett Vic. 48 F1, 50 F11
Fawkner Vic. 42 H5, 47 I5, 48 C4
Feilton Tas. 158 F4, 161 I6
Felixstow SA 68 E10, 69 E1
Felton East Qld 137 K9
Fentonbury Tas. 158 E2, 161 I5
Fentons Creek Vic. 55 L9
Ferguson Vic. 46 A11, 57 K10
Fern Hill Vic. 46 G2, 48 A2, 50 A12
Fern Tree Tas. 156 A10, 159 I6, 161 K7
Fernbank Vic. 49 L5
Ferndale NSW 12 A11, 17 N11, 51 J3
Ferndale WA 90 G12, 91 E6, 94 E6

Ferndene Tas. 162 G6
Fernihurst Vic. 55 M7
Fernlees Qld 139 I11
Ferntree Creek NP Qld 134 F3, 137 N7
Ferntree Gully Vic. 43 M10, 44 H1, 45 I1, 47 K6, 48 D5
Fernvale Qld 130 B10, 132 A1, 134 C10, 135 A4, 137 M9
Ferny Creek Vic. 43 O10, 45 J1
Ferny Grove Qld 130 G10, 134 E10, 135 D4
Ferny Hills Qld 130 F10, 134 E10, 135 D3
Ferryden Park SA 68 C10
Fiddletown NSW 7 J1
Fiery Flat Vic. 55 M8
Fifield NSW 12 C2
Fig Tree NSW 12 F4
Fig Tree Pocket Qld 132 H4
Finch Hatton Qld 139 J5
Findon SA 68 B11, 69 B1
Fingal Tas. 163 N9
Finke NT 121 J10
Finke Gorge NP NT 120 H8
Finley NSW 17 L11, 50 F3
Finniss SA 71 H7, 73 K10, 82 C4
Finucane Island NP Qld 140 A7, 143 E4
Firle SA 68 E11, 69 E1
Fish Creek Vic. 48 G10
Fish Point Vic. 16 H10, 55 M2
Fisher ACT 34 C8
Fisher SA 80 G4
Fishery Falls Qld 141 M6
Fiskville Vic. 46 F4, 57 N5
Fitzgerald Tas. 158 D3, 160 H6
Fitzgerald River NP WA 98 F10
Fitzgibbon Qld 131 I8
Fitzroy SA 67 B1, 68 D11, 69 D1
Fitzroy Vic. 41 H2, 42 H8
Fitzroy Crossing WA 103 K8
Fitzroy Island Qld 141 M6
Fitzroy Island NP Qld 141 M6
Fitzroy North Vic. 42 H7
Five Dock NSW 7 K11, 9 K3
Five Rocks Qld 139 N9
Five Trees Cays Qld 139 M8
Five Ways NSW 12 A10, 17 O10, 19 O11, 51 L2
Flaggy Rock Qld 139 K7
Flagstaff Hill SA 69 C5
Flagstone Creek Qld 137 M3
Flat Rock Qld 135 H4, 137 O9, 139 N11
Flaxton Qld 134 F3
Fletcher Qld 15 K3
Flinders Vic. 47 I11, 48 C8
Flinders Chase NP SA 72 F12
Flinders Group NP Qld 142 G10
Flinders Island Qld 142 G10
Flinders Island SA 72 A5
Flinders Island Tas. 160 B9, 163 O1
Flinders Park SA 68 C11, 69 C1
Flinders Ranges NP SA 75 I6
Flinders View Qld 132 B6
Flinton Qld 136 H9
Flintstone Tas. 161 J1, 163 J11
Floreat WA 90 D9, 91 A4, 93 B5
Florey ACT 34 C3
Florida NSW 19 M9
Florida WA 93 B10, 96 B6, 98 B8

Florieton SA 73 L6
Flowerdale Tas. 162 E4
Flowerdale Vic. 47 K2, 48 D2, 50 D12
Flowerpot Tas. 158 H9, 161 K9
Flowery Gully Tas. 163 J7
Flying Fish Point Qld 141 M7
Flying Fox Qld 135 E10
Flynn ACT 34 C2
Flynn Vic. 49 J7
Flynns Creek Vic. 49 I7
Foam Rocks WA 99 J9
Footscray Vic. 42 F7, 47 I5, 48 C4
Forbes NSW 12 D4
Forcett Tas. 159 L4, 161 L7
Forde ACT 34 F1
Fords SA 70 E3
Fords Bridge NSW 19 L4
Fordwich NSW 13 K3
Forest Tas. 162 D4
Forest Hill NSW 12 C10, 17 P10, 51 N1
Forest Den NP Qld 138 D7, 145 P7
Forest Glen NSW 7 I1, 11 K4
Forest Glen Qld 134 G4
Forest Grove WA 94 B8, 96 B10
Forest Grove NP WA 94 B8, 96 B10, 98 B10
Forest Hill Qld 134 A11
Forest Hill Vic. 43 L10
Forest Lake Qld 132 G5, 135 D6
Forest Lodge NSW 7 L12, 9 L4
Forest Reefs NSW 12 G5
Forestdale Qld 132 G7
Forester Tas. 163 M6
Forestville NSW 7 M8, 9 M1
Forestville SA 68 D12, 69 D3
Forge Creek Vic. 49 M6
Formartin Qld 137 K8
Forrest ACT 33 D12, 34 E7
Forrest Vic. 46 B10, 57 L9
Forrest WA 80 A5, 99 O4
Forrest Beach Qld 141 M10
Forrestdale WA 91 G10
Forrestfield WA 90 H9, 91 F4
Forreston SA 70 E7, 71 H1
Forsayth Qld 140 H9
Forster SA 73 L8, 82 D2
Forster–Tuncurry NSW 13 O2
Fort Denison NSW 11 M9, 13 K7
Fort Lytton NP Qld 131 L11, 133 L1, 134 G11, 135 E4, 137 N9
Fortescue Roadhouse WA 97 E2, 100 A3
Forth Tas. 162 G6
Fortis Creek NP NSW 15 M5
Fortitude Valley Qld 129 H4, 131 I12, 133 I2
Forty Mile Scrub NP Qld 141 K8
Foster Vic. 48 G9
Fosterville Vic. 50 B8, 55 P10
Fountaindale NSW 11 O2
Four Hummocks SA 72 C8
Four Mile Creek Tas. 163 O9
Fowlers Bay SA 81 J8
Fox Ground NSW 13 J9, 20 H3
Fox Trap Roadhouse Qld 136 A6, 147 N6
Foxhow Vic. 46 A7, 57 K6
Framlingham Vic. 56 H7
Framlingham East Vic. 56 H7
Frampton NSW 12 D8, 20 A2

Frances SA 54 B9, 82 G8
Francistown Tas. 158 F10, 161 I9
Francois Peron NP WA 97 B8
Frank Hann NP WA 98 G8
Frankford Tas. 163 I7
Frankland WA 95 J8, 96 F10, 98 D11
Frankland Group NP Qld 141 M7
Franklin ACT 34 F2
Franklin Tas. 158 G7, 161 J8
Franklin–Gordon Wild Rivers NP Tas. 158 A1, 160 E5, 162 E12
Franklinford Vic. 46 E1, 57 N2
Frankston Vic. 44 E7, 47 J8, 48 D6
Frankston North Vic. 44 E7
Frankston South Vic. 44 D8
Frankton SA 70 H2, 73 K7, 82 D1
Fraser ACT 34 C1
Fraser Island Qld 137 O4
Frederickton NSW 15 M10
Freds Pass NT 113 O12
Freeburgh Vic. 51 K10
Freeling SA 70 D4, 73 K8, 82 C1
Freemans Reach NSW 6 D1, 11 I4, 13 J6
Freestone Qld 15 L1
Fregon SA 79 I4
Fremantle WA 90 C12, 91 A8, 93 B6, 96 B5, 98 B8
French Island Vic. 44 H12, 45 I12, 47 K10, 48 D7
French Island Marine NP Vic. 44 H12, 45 I12, 47 K9, 48 D7
French Island NP Vic. 44 H12, 45 I12, 47 L10, 48 E7
Frenchs Forest NSW 7 M8, 9 M1, 11 M7, 13 K6
Freshwater Creek Vic. 46 E9, 57 N8
Freshwater NP Qld 131 I4, 134 F8, 135 D1, 137 N8
Frewville SA 68 E12, 69 E2
Freycinet NP Tas. 161 O2, 163 O12
Frogmore NSW 12 F7, 20 C1
Fryerstown Vic. 50 A11, 55 O12, 57 O2
Fulham SA 68 B12, 69 B1
Fulham Vic. 49 K7
Fulham Gardens SA 68 B11, 69 B1
Fullarton SA 68 E12, 69 E3
Fullerton NSW 12 G7, 20 E1
Fumina Vic. 47 P7, 48 G5
Fur Rock WA 99 I9
Furner SA 82 F10
Furnissdale WA 92 C10, 93 C9, 96 C6
Fyansford Vic. 46 F8, 57 N7
Fyshwick ACT 31 E5, 34 F7

Gaagal Wanggaan (South Beach) NP NSW 15 M9
Gabo Island Vic. 20 E11, 58 H11
Gadayim Pyramid WA 103 I5
Gaffneys Creek Vic. 47 P3, 48 H3
Gagebrook Tas. 159 I3, 161 K6
Gailes Qld 132 F5
Galah Vic. 16 D8, 52 G11
Galaquil Vic. 16 E11, 54 H5
Galaquil East Vic. 54 H5
Galga SA 73 M8, 82 E2
Galiwinku NT 117 L3
Gallanani Qld 134 A8
Gallangowan Qld 134 A1, 137 M7
Galong NSW 12 E8, 20 B2

Galston NSW 7 J5, 11 K5, 13 K6
Gama Vic. 16 E10, 54 H3
Ganmain NSW 12 B8, 17 O8
Gapsted Vic. 51 J8
Gapuwiyak NT 117 L4
Garah NSW 14 F3, 136 H12
Garbutt Qld 138 G1
Garden Island NSW 5 H3
Garden Island WA 91 A12, 92 A1, 93 B7, 96 B5, 98 B8
Garden Island Creek Tas. 158 H9, 161 J9
Gardens of Stone NP NSW 13 I4
Gardenvale Vic. 42 H11, 43 I11
Gardners Bay Tas. 158 G9, 161 J9
Garema NSW 12 D5
Garfield Vic. 45 P6, 47 M8, 48 F6
Garfield North Vic. 45 P5, 47 M8, 48 F6
Gargett Qld 139 J5
Garibaldi Vic. 46 D4, 57 M5
Garig Gunak Barlu NP NT 116 F2
Garigal NP NSW 7 N7, 9 M1, 11 M6, 13 K6
Garra NSW 12 F4
Garran ACT 34 D7
Garrawilla NP NSW 14 F9
Garrthalala NT 117 N5
Garvoc Vic. 57 I8
Gary Junction WA 101 K3
Gascoyne Junction WA 97 D7, 100 A8
Gatton Qld 137 L9
Gatton NP Qld 137 L9
Gatum Vic. 56 E2
Gawler SA 68 H1, 70 D5, 73 J8, 82 C2
Gawler Tas. 162 G6
Gawler Belt SA 68 G1
Gawler East SA 68 H1
Gawler Ranges NP SA 72 C1, 74 B9, 81 P9
Gawler River SA 68 E1
Gawler South SA 68 H1
Gawler West SA 68 H2
Gayndah Qld 137 L5
Gaythorne Qld 130 H10, 132 H1
Geebung Qld 131 I9
Geehi NSW 20 A8, 51 P8, 58 A4
Geelong Vic. 46 F8, 48 A6, 57 O7
Geeralying WA 95 I1, 96 E7
Geeveston Tas. 158 F8, 161 I9
Geham NP Qld 137 L9
Geikie Gorge NP WA 103 L7
Geilston Bay Tas. 156 E5
Gelantipy Vic. 20 A10, 49 P2, 58 A4
Gellibrand Vic. 46 A10, 57 K9
Gelliondale Vic. 49 I9
Gelorup WA 94 C4
Gembrook Vic. 45 M4, 47 M7, 48 E5
Gemtree NT 121 J5
Genoa Vic. 20 D11, 58 G10
George Rocks Tas. 163 P5
George Town Tas. 163 J6
Georges Creek Vic. 51 M6
Georges Hall NSW 6 G12, 8 G4
Georges Plains NSW 12 H5
Georges River NP NSW 8 G6, 9 I6, 11 J10, 13 K7, 20 H1
Georgetown Qld 140 H9
Georgetown SA 73 J4, 74 H12
Georgica NSW 15 N3

Gepps Cross SA 68 D9
Geraldton WA 97 D12, 98 A3
Gerang Gerung Vic. 16 D12, 54 F7
Gerangamete Vic. 46 C10, 57 L9
Geranium SA 73 M10, 82 F4
Geranium Plain SA 73 K6
Germantown Vic. 51 K10
Gerogery NSW 12 A12, 17 O12, 51 L5
Gerogery West NSW 12 A12, 17 O12, 51 L5
Gerringong NSW 13 J9, 20 H3
Geurie NSW 12 F2
Gheringhap Vic. 46 E7, 57 N7
Ghin Ghin Vic. 47 L1, 48 E1, 50 E11
Ghin-doo-ee NP NSW 13 M2
Giant Rocks WA 99 I10
Gibraltar Range NP NSW 15 L5
Gibson WA 99 I9
Gibsonvale NSW 12 A5, 17 O5
Gidgegannup WA 93 E4, 96 C4
Gidginbung NSW 12 C7, 17 P7
Giffard Vic. 49 K8
Gig Rocks WA 99 I9
Gilbert River Qld 140 G8
Gilberton Qld 133 M10
Gilberton SA 67 G1, 68 D11, 69 D1
Gilberts SA 71 G7
Gilead NSW 8 B11
Giles Corner SA 70 C1, 73 J7, 82 C1
Gilgai NSW 15 I6
Gilgandra NSW 14 C10
Gilgooma NSW 14 C8
Gilgunnia NSW 17 M1, 19 M12
Gillenbah NSW 12 A8, 17 N8
Gilles Plains SA 68 F9
Gilliat Qld 143 H11, 145 I3
Gillieston Vic. 50 E7
Gillingarra WA 96 C2, 98 C6
Gillman SA 68 B8
Gilmore ACT 34 E10
Gilmore NSW 12 D10, 20 A4
Gilston Qld 135 F10
Gin Gin NSW 14 B11
Gin Gin Qld 137 L3
Gindie Qld 139 I11
Gingin WA 93 C1, 96 B3, 98 C7
Ginninderra ACT 31 E3
Gipsy Point Vic. 20 D11, 58 G10
Gir-um-bit NP NSW 13 M3
Giralang ACT 34 D2
Girgarre Vic. 50 D7
Girilambone NSW 19 O9
Girral NSW 12 B5, 17 O5
Girramay NP Qld 141 M9
Girraween NSW 6 G9, 8 G1
Girraween NT 113 P10
Girraween NP Qld 15 L3, 137 K12
Girrawheen WA 90 D6, 91 B1
Girringun NP Qld 141 L9
Giru Qld 138 H1, 141 O12
Gisborne Vic. 46 H3, 48 B2, 57 P4
Gisborne South Vic. 42 B1
Gladesville NSW 7 K10, 9 K2
Gladfield Vic. 16 H12, 55 N6
Gladstone NSW 15 M10
Gladstone Qld 137 K1, 139 N12
Gladstone SA 73 J4, 74 H12
Gladstone Tas. 163 O5
Gladstone WA 97 C8
Gladstone Park Vic. 42 F4
Gladysdale Vic. 45 P1, 47 M6, 48 F5

Glamorgan Vale Qld 130 A12, 132 A2
Glandore SA 69 C3
Glanmire NSW 12 H5
Glanville SA 68 A9
Glass House Mountains Qld 134 F6, 137 N8
Glass House Mountains NP Qld 134 F6, 137 N8
Glastonbury NP Qld 137 M6
Glaziers Bay Tas. 158 F8, 161 J8
Glebe NSW 5 A9, 7 L12, 9 L4
Glebe Tas. 155 E5, 156 D7
Glen Tas. 163 K6
Glen Alice NSW 13 I4
Glen Alpine NSW 8 B9
Glen Aplin Qld 15 K3, 137 K12
Glen Creek Vic. 51 K8
Glen Davis NSW 13 I4
Glen Forbes Vic. 47 L11, 48 E8
Glen Forrest WA 91 H2
Glen Geddes Qld 139 M10
Glen Helen Resort NT 120 G7
Glen Huntly Vic. 43 I11
Glen Huon Tas. 158 F7, 161 I8
Glen Innes NSW 15 K5
Glen Iris Vic. 43 I9
Glen Oak NSW 13 M3
Glen Osmond SA 69 E3
Glen Valley Vic. 51 M10
Glen Waverley Vic. 43 L10, 44 F1, 47 J6, 48 D5
Glen Wills Vic. 51 M10
Glenaire Vic. 46 A12, 57 K10
Glenaladale Vic. 49 L5
Glenalbyn Vic. 55 M8
Glenalta SA 69 E4, 70 B10, 71 F3
Glenariff NSW 19 N7
Glenaroua Vic. 50 C11
Glenbar NP Qld 137 M5
Glenbrae Vic. 46 B1, 57 L3
Glenbrook NSW 6 A6, 10 G6, 13 J6
Glenburn Vic. 47 L3, 48 E2
Glenburnie SA 56 A5, 82 G12
Glencoe NSW 15 K6
Glencoe SA 82 G11
Glencoe West SA 82 F11
Glendalough WA 90 D8, 91 B3, 93 C5
Glendambo SA 74 C5
Glenden Qld 139 I6
Glendenning NSW 6 E7
Glendevie Tas. 158 F9, 161 I9
Glendon Brook NSW 13 L3
Gleneagle Qld 135 C8
Glenelg SA 69 B3, 70 B9, 71 E2, 73 J9, 82 B3
Glenelg East SA 69 B3
Glenelg North SA 69 B3
Glenelg South SA 69 B3
Glenfern Tas. 158 G4, 161 J6
Glenfield NSW 8 E5
Glenfyne Vic. 57 I8
Glengarry Tas. 163 J7
Glengarry Vic. 49 I7
Glengower Vic. 55 M12, 57 M2
Glengowrie SA 69 B3
Glenhaven NSW 6 H6, 7 I6, 11 K6
Glenisla Vic. 54 G12, 56 G1
Glenlee Vic. 16 D12, 54 E7
Glenlofty Vic. 55 K12, 57 K1
Glenloth Vic. 16 G12, 55 K6
Glenluce Vic. 55 N12, 57 N2
Glenlusk Tas. 158 H4

Glenlyon Vic. 46 F1, 57 N2
Glenmaggie Vic. 49 J5
Glenmore NSW 10 F11
Glenmore Vic. 46 F4, 48 A3, 49 O2, 57 O5, 58 A8
Glenmore Park NSW 6 A7
Glenmorgan Qld 136 H8
Glenora Tas. 158 F2, 161 I6
Glenorchy Tas. 156 A6, 159 I4, 161 K7
Glenorchy Vic. 54 H10
Glenore Tas. 163 J9
Glenore Crossing Qld 140 D7, 143 G5
Glenore Grove Qld 134 A11
Glenorie NSW 6 H1, 7 I1, 11 K4
Glenormiston Vic. 57 I7
Glenormiston North Vic. 57 I7
Glenpatrick Vic. 55 K12, 57 K1
Glenreagh NSW 15 M7
Glenrowan Vic. 50 H8
Glenrowan West Vic. 50 H8
Glenroy NSW 10 B3, 12 C11, 13 I5, 20 A6, 51 O4
Glenroy SA 54 A12, 56 A1, 82 G10
Glenroy Vic. 42 G5
Glenshee Vic. 55 K12, 57 K1
Glenside SA 68 E12, 69 E2
Glenthompson Vic. 56 H4
Glenunga SA 68 E12, 69 E3
Glenvale Vic. 47 J3, 48 D2
Glenwood NSW 6 G6
Gliddon Reef SA 81 M9
Globe Derby Park SA 68 D7
Glossodia NSW 6 D1, 11 I3
Glossop SA 16 A6, 52 A6, 73 N7
Gloucester NSW 13 M1, 15 K12
Gloucester Island Qld 139 J3
Gloucester Island NP Qld 139 J3
Gloucester NP WA 94 F9, 96 D11, 98 C11
Glynde SA 68 E11, 69 E1
Gnangara WA 90 D4, 93 C4
Gnarming WA 96 G6, 98 E8
Gnarwarre Vic. 46 E8, 57 N7
Gnotuk Vic. 57 J7
Gnowangerup WA 95 M5, 96 G9, 98 E10
Gobondery NSW 12 C2
Gobur Vic. 50 F11
Gocup NSW 12 D10, 20 A4
Godfreys Creek NSW 12 F7, 20 C1
Godwin Beach Qld 131 L1, 134 G8, 135 E1
Gogango Qld 139 L11
Gol Gol NSW 16 E6, 52 G6
Golconda Tas. 163 L6
Golden Bay WA 92 C6
Golden Beach Vic. 49 L7
Golden Grove SA 68 H6
Golden Point Vic. 50 A10, 55 M12
Golden Valley Tas. 163 I9
Goldfields Woodlands NP WA 98 G6
Goldsborough Vic. 55 L10
Goldsmith Tas. 161 K1, 163 K11
Goldsmith Island Qld 139 K4
Goldsworthy WA 100 E1, 102 E11
Gollan NSW 12 G1, 14 D12
Golspie NSW 12 H8, 20 E2
Goneaway NP Qld 145 J10
Gongolgon NSW 19 O6
Gonn Crossing Vic. 55 N3
Goobang NP NSW 12 E2

Goobarragandra NSW 12 E11, 20 B5
Good Night Scrub NP Qld 137 L4
Goodedulla NP Qld 139 L10
Goodna Qld 132 E5, 134 E12, 135 C5
Goodnight NSW 16 G8, 53 L10
Goodooga NSW 14 A2, 136 D11
Goodwood Qld 137 M4
Goodwood SA 69 D3, 70 B9, 71 F2
Goodwood Tas. 156 C3
Googong NSW 34 G9
Goolawah NP NSW 15 M10
Goold Island NP Qld 141 M9
Goolgowi NSW 17 L6
Goolma NSW 12 G2
Goolman Qld 132 B8
Goolmangar NSW 15 N3
Gooloogong NSW 12 E5
Goolwa SA 71 G8, 73 J11, 82 C4
Goomalibee Vic. 50 G8
Goomalling WA 96 D3, 98 C6
Goomboorian NP Qld 137 N6
Goombungee Qld 137 L8
Goomburra Qld 15 L1
Goomeri Qld 137 L6
Goon Nure Vic. 49 M6
Goondah NSW 12 E9, 20 C3
Goondiwindi Qld 14 H1, 137 I11
Goondooloo SA 73 M9, 82 E3
Goonengerry NP NSW 15 O3, 137 N12
Goongarrie WA 98 H4
Goongarrie NP WA 98 H4
Goongerah Vic. 20 B11, 58 C9
Goonoo NP NSW 12 F1, 14 C11
Goonumbla NSW 12 E3
Gooram Vic. 50 F10
Goorambat Vic. 50 G7
Goornong Vic. 50 B8, 55 P9
Gooroc Vic. 55 K8
Gooseberry Hill WA 91 G3
Gooseberry Hill NP WA 91 H3, 93 D5, 96 C5, 98 C7
Goovigen Qld 137 J1, 139 L12
Goowarra Qld 139 K11
Gorae Vic. 56 D7
Gorae West Vic. 56 D7
Gordon ACT 34 C11
Gordon NSW 7 K8, 9 L1
Gordon SA 73 J1, 74 H8
Gordon Tas. 158 H10, 161 J9
Gordon Vic. 46 E3, 57 N4
Gordon Park Qld 131 I10, 133 I1
Gordonvale Qld 141 L6
Gormandale Vic. 49 J8
Gormanston Tas. 160 E1, 162 E11
Gorokan NSW 11 P1
Goroke Vic. 54 D9
Gosford NSW 11 O3, 13 L5
Goshen Tas. 163 O7
Gosnells WA 91 F7, 93 D6
Goughs Bay Vic. 47 P1, 48 H1, 50 H12
Goulburn NSW 12 H9, 20 E3
Goulburn River NP NSW 13 I2, 14 F12
Goulburn Weir Vic. 50 D9
Gould Creek SA 68 G5
Gould Island Qld 139 J4
Goulds Country Tas. 163 O7
Gourock NP NSW 12 G12, 20 D6, 31 G12, 58 G1
Gowanbrae Vic. 42 F5

Gowanford Vic. 16 G10, 55 K2
Gowangardie Vic. 50 F8
Gowar Vic. 55 N11, 57 N1
Gowar East Vic. 55 K9
Gowrie ACT 34 D10
Gowrie Park Tas. 162 G8
Goyura Vic. 16 E11, 54 H4
Grabben Gullen NSW 12 G8, 20 D2
Grabine NSW 12 F6
Gracemere Qld 139 M11
Gracetown WA 94 A7, 96 B9, 98 B10
Graceville Qld 132 H4
Gradgery NSW 14 B9
Gradule Qld 14 E1, 136 G10
Grafton NSW 15 M6
Graman NSW 15 I4
Grampians NP Vic. 54 G12, 56 G2
Grandchester Qld 134 A12
Grange Qld 131 I10, 133 I1
Grange SA 68 A11, 69 A1, 70 A8, 71 E2
Granite Flat Vic. 51 M9
Granite Island SA 71 F9, 73 J11, 82 B5
Grantham Qld 137 L9
Granton Tas. 159 I3, 161 K6
Grantville Vic. 47 L10, 48 E8
Granville NSW 6 H10, 7 I10, 8 H2, 9 I2, 11 K8
Granville Harbour Tas. 162 B9
Granya Vic. 12 B12, 17 O12, 51 M6
Grasmere NSW 8 A8, 10 G11
Grass Flat Vic. 54 E9
Grass Patch WA 99 I8
Grassdale Vic. 56 D5
Grassmere Junction Vic. 56 H8
Grasstree Qld 139 K6
Grasstree Hill Tas. 156 F1, 159 J4
Grassy Tas. 161 P12
Gravelly Beach Tas. 163 J7
Gravesend NSW 14 H5
Grawin NSW 14 B4
Grawlin NSW 12 D5
Grawlin Plains NSW 12 D5
Gray NT 113 J10
Gray Tas. 163 O9
Grays Point NSW 9 I9
Graytown Vic. 50 C9
Gre Gre Vic. 55 J9
Great Australian Bight Marine NP SA 80 D7, 81 I7, 99 P6
Great Barrier Reef Marine Park Qld 137 O2, 138 H1, 139 N4, 141 N7, 142 F5
Great Basalt Wall NP Qld 138 D2, 141 L12, 145 P2
Great Keppel Island Qld 139 N10
Great Mackeral Beach NSW 7 O4
Great Northern Vic. 51 J6
Great Otway NP Vic. 46 C11, 57 K9
Great Palm Island Qld 141 N10
Great Sandy NP Qld 134 G1, 137 N6
Great Western Vic. 55 I12, 57 I1
Greater Beedelup NP WA 94 E8, 96 C10, 98 C11
Greater Bendigo NP Vic. 50 A8, 55 O9
Greater Dordagup NP WA 94 F9, 96 D11, 98 C11
Greater Hawke NP WA 94 F10, 96 D11, 98 C11

Greater Kingston NP WA 94 G7, 96 D10, 98 D10
Greater Preston NP WA 94 F4, 96 D8, 98 C10
Gredgwin Vic. 16 G11, 55 L5
Green Fields SA 68 D7, 70 B7
Green Head WA 98 A5
Green Hill NSW 15 M10
Green Hill Creek Vic. 55 K12, 57 K2
Green Island (Cairns region) Qld 141 M6
Green Island (Mackay region) Qld 139 K5
Green Island (Milwarpa) (Brisbane region) Qld 131 M11, 133 M1, 134 H11, 135 F4, 137 N9
Green Island NP Qld 141 M6
Green Point NSW 11 O3, 13 O2
Green Valley NSW 6 E11, 8 E3
Greenacre NSW 7 I12, 9 I4
Greenacres SA 68 E10
Greenbank Qld 132 G8, 135 C6
Greenbushes WA 94 E6, 96 C9
Greendale NSW 6 A11, 8 A3
Greendale Vic. 46 F3, 48 A3, 57 O4
Greenethorpe NSW 12 E6
Greenfield Park NSW 6 E11, 8 E3
Greenfields SA 92 C9
Greenhill SA 68 F12, 69 F3
Greenhills WA 96 E4
Greenleigh NSW 34 H8
Greenmantle NSW 12 F6
Greenmount Qld 137 L9
Greenmount Vic. 49 I9
Greenmount WA 91 G2, 93 D4
Greenmount NP WA 91 H2, 93 D4, 96 C5, 98 C7
Greenock SA 70 E4, 73 K8, 82 C1
Greenough WA 98 A3
Greens Beach Tas. 163 I6
Greens Creek Vic. 55 J11
Greensborough Vic. 43 J5, 47 J5, 48 D4
Greenslopes Qld 133 I3
Greenvale Qld 141 K10
Greenvale Vic. 42 F2
Greenwald Vic. 56 C5, 82 H12
Greenway ACT 34 C9
Greenways SA 82 F10
Greenwell Point NSW 13 J10, 20 G4
Greenwich NSW 7 L10, 9 L2
Greenwith SA 68 G6
Greenwood WA 90 C6, 91 A1
Greg Greg NSW 12 D12, 20 A6, 51 P6, 58 A2
Gregors Creek Qld 134 B6
Gregory Qld 139 I10
Gregory WA 97 D12
Gregory NP NT 103 P4
Greigs Flat NSW 20 E10, 58 H7
Grenfell NSW 12 D6
Grenville Vic. 46 D5, 57 M5
Gresford NSW 13 L2
Greta Vic. 51 I8
Greta South Vic. 50 H9
Greta West Vic. 50 H8
Gretna Tas. 158 F2, 161 J6
Grevillia NSW 15 N2, 137 M11
Grey Peaks NP Qld 141 M6
Greymare Qld 15 K1, 137 K10
Greystanes NSW 6 G9, 8 G1
Griffin Qld 131 J6

Griffith ACT 33 F12, 34 E7
Griffith NSW 17 M7
Grimwade WA 94 E5
Gringegalgona Vic. 56 E2
Gritjurk Vic. 56 E3
Grogan NSW 12 D7, 20 A1
Grong Grong NSW 12 A8, 17 O8
Grongah NP Qld 137 L5
Groote Eylandt NT 117 N7
Grose Vale NSW 6 A1, 10 G4
Grose Wold NSW 6 A1
Grosvenor Qld 137 K4
Grove Tas. 158 G6, 161 J7
Grovedale Vic. 46 F8, 57 O8
Gruyere Vic. 47 L5
Gubbata NSW 12 A5, 17 N5
Guilderton WA 96 B4, 98 B7
Guildford NSW 6 G10, 8 H2, 11 J8
Guildford Tas. 162 E7
Guildford Vic. 55 N12, 57 N2
Guildford WA 90 H7, 91 E2, 93 C4
Guildford West NSW 6 G10, 8 G2
Gulaga NP NSW 20 E8
Gular NSW 14 C9
Gulargambone NSW 14 C9
Gulf Creek NSW 14 H7
Gulfview Heights SA 68 F7
Gulgong NSW 12 H2
Gull Rock WA 96 G11, 98 E11
Gull Rock NP WA 95 M11, 96 G11, 98 E11
Gulnare SA 73 J5, 74 H12
Guluguba Qld 137 I6
Gum Lake NSW 16 G1, 18 F12
Gumbaynggirr NP NSW 15 L8
Gumble NSW 12 F4
Gumbowie SA 73 K3, 75 I11
Gumdale Qld 133 K3
Gumeracha SA 70 E8, 71 H1, 73 K9, 82 C2
Gumlu Qld 139 I2
Gumly Gumly NSW 12 C9, 17 P9, 51 N1
Gunalda Qld 137 M6
Gunbar NSW 17 L6
Gunbower Vic. 17 I11, 50 A4, 55 O6
Gunbower NP Vic. 17 I11, 50 A4, 55 O5
Gundabooka NP NSW 19 L6
Gundagai NSW 12 D9, 20 A3, 51 P1
Gundaring WA 95 J2, 96 F7
Gundaroo NSW 12 G10, 20 D4, 31 F2
Gundary NSW 12 H9, 20 E3
Gunderman NSW 11 L3
Gundiah Qld 137 M5
Gundillion NSW 12 G12, 20 E6, 58 H1
Gundowring Vic. 51 L8
Gundowring North Vic. 51 L7
Gundowring Upper Vic. 51 L8
Gundy NSW 13 K1, 14 H12
Gunebang NSW 12 A3, 17 O3
Gungahlin ACT 12 F10, 31 E3, 34 F1
Gungal NSW 13 J2
Gunn NT 113 K10
Gunnary NSW 12 F7, 20 C2
Gunnedah NSW 14 G9
Gunnewin Qld 136 F5
Gunning NSW 12 G9, 20 D3
Gunningbland NSW 12 D4

Gunns Plains Tas. 162 G6
Gunpowder Qld 143 D9, 144 F1
Gunyangara NT 117 N4
Gunyerwarildi NP NSW 14 H4, 137 I12
Gurley NSW 14 F5
Gurrai SA 16 A8, 52 A10, 73 N10, 82 G4
Gurrumuru NT 117 M4
Gurrundah NSW 12 G9, 20 D3
Guthalungra Qld 139 I2
Guthega NSW 20 A8, 58 B4
Guy Fawkes River NP NSW 15 L7
Guyong NSW 12 G5
Guyra NSW 15 J7
Guys Forest Vic. 12 C12, 51 N6
Guys Hill Vic. 45 J5
Gwabegar NSW 14 D7
Gwalia WA 98 H2
Gwandalan Tas. 159 L7, 161 L8
Gwelup WA 90 D7, 91 A3
Gwydir River NP NSW 14 H6, 15 I6
Gymbowen Vic. 54 D9
Gymea NSW 9 I8
Gymea Bay NSW 9 I8
Gympie Qld 137 M6
Gympie NP Qld 137 M6
Gypsum Vic. 16 E9, 52 H12, 54 H1

Haasts Bluff NT 120 F6
Haberfield NSW 7 K12, 9 K3
Hackett ACT 34 F4
Hackham SA 69 B8
Hackham West SA 69 B8
Hackney SA 67 H4, 68 E11, 69 E1
Haddon Vic. 46 C3, 57 L4
Haddon Corner Qld 77 O2, 146 G4
Haden Qld 137 L8
Hadfield Vic. 42 G5
Hadspen Tas. 163 K8
Hagley Tas. 163 J8
Hahndorf SA 70 D10, 71 H3, 73 K9, 82 C3
Haig WA 99 M5
Haigslea Qld 130 A12, 132 A2, 134 C11, 135 A5
Halbury SA 73 J6
Hale Village Qld 135 D9
Half Tide Qld 139 K6
Halfway Creek NSW 15 N6
Halfway Mill Roadhouse WA 96 A1, 98 B5
Halidon SA 73 M9, 82 F3
Halifax Qld 141 M10
Halifax Bay Wetlands NP Qld 141 M10
Hall ACT 31 D3, 34 C1
Hallam Vic. 44 H3, 45 I4, 47 K7
Hallett SA 73 K5, 75 I12
Hallett Cove SA 69 A6
Hallidays Point NSW 13 O2
Halls Creek WA 103 N7
Halls Gap Vic. 54 H12, 56 H1
Halls Head WA 92 B10, 93 B9
Hallston Vic. 47 O10, 48 G8
Halton NSW 13 L2
Hamel WA 93 D11, 94 D1, 96 C7
Hamelin Bay WA 94 B9, 96 B10
Hamelin Pool Marine Nature Reserve WA 97 C9
Hamersley WA 90 D6, 91 B1, 93 H3, 97 G3, 100 C4
Hamilton Qld 131 I11, 133 I1
Hamilton SA 70 E1, 73 K7, 82 C1

Hamilton Tas. 158 F1, 161 I5
Hamilton Vic. 56 F4
Hamilton Hill WA 91 B8
Hamilton Island Qld 139 K4
Hamley Bridge SA 70 C3, 73 J7, 82 B1
Hammond SA 73 J2, 74 H9
Hammond Park WA 91 D11
Hammondville NSW 8 G5
Hampden SA 73 K7
Hampshire Tas. 162 F6
Hampstead Gardens SA 68 E10
Hampton NSW 10 A4, 13 I6
Hampton Qld 137 L9
Hampton Vic. 42 H12, 43 I12, 44 C1, 47 J6
Hampton East Vic. 43 I12, 44 C1
Hampton NP Qld 137 L9
Hampton Park Vic. 44 H4, 47 K7
Hanging Rock Vic. 49 P1, 51 P12, 58 B7
Hann River Roadhouse Qld 141 I2
Hann Tableland NP Qld 141 K6
Hannahs Bridge NSW 14 E11
Hannan NSW 12 A5, 17 N5
Hansborough SA 70 F1, 73 K7
Hanson SA 73 K6
Hansonville Vic. 51 I8
Hanwood NSW 17 M7
Happy Valley Qld 137 O4, 139 L8
Happy Valley SA 69 C6
Happy Valley Vic. 16 F7, 46 B4, 51 K9, 53 I9, 57 L5
Harbord NSW 7 N9, 9 N1
Harcourt Vic. 50 A10, 55 O11, 57 O1
Harcourt North Vic. 50 A10, 55 O11, 57 O1
Harden NSW 12 E8, 20 B2
Hardwicke Bay SA 72 H9
Harefield NSW 12 C9, 17 P9
Harford Tas. 163 I6
Hargraves NSW 12 H3
Harkaway Vic. 45 I3, 47 K7
Harlin Qld 134 A6, 137 M8
Harrietville Vic. 51 L10
Harrington NSW 13 O1, 15 L12
Harrington Park NSW 8 A7
Harris Park NSW 6 H10, 7 I10, 8 H1, 9 I2
Harrismith WA 96 G7
Harrison ACT 34 F2
Harrisville Qld 132 A11, 135 A7
Harrogate SA 70 F9
Harrow Vic. 49 L6, 54 D11, 56 D1
Harrys Creek Vic. 50 F9
Harston Vic. 50 D7
Hart SA 73 J6
Hartley NSW 10 B3, 13 I5
Hartley SA 70 F12
Hartley Vale NSW 10 C3
Hartz Mountains NP Tas. 158 D9, 160 H9, 161 I9
Harvey WA 94 D2, 96 C7, 98 C9
Harwood NSW 15 N5
Haslam SA 72 A2, 81 N9
Hassall Grove NSW 6 E6
Hassell NP WA 95 N10, 96 H10, 98 F11
Hasties Swamp NP Qld 141 L7
Hastings Tas. 158 F11, 161 I10
Hastings Vic. 44 F12, 47 J9, 48 D7
Hastings Point NSW 15 O2, 137 N11

Hat Head NSW 15 M10
Hat Head NP NSW 15 M10
Hatches Creek NT 119 K12, 121 K1
Hatfield NSW 16 H5, 53 N4
Hatherleigh SA 82 F10
Hattah Vic. 16 E7, 52 H9
Hattah–Kulkyne NP Vic. 16 E7, 52 H8
Hatton Vale Qld 134 A11
Haul Off Rock WA 98 F11
Havelock Vic. 55 M11
Haven Vic. 54 G9
Havilah Vic. 51 K9
Hawker ACT 34 B4
Hawker SA 74 H8
Hawkesbury Heights NSW 6 A4, 10 G5
Hawkesdale Vic. 56 G6
Hawks Nest NSW 13 N3
Hawley Beach Tas. 163 I6
Hawthorn SA 69 D3
Hawthorn Vic. 43 I8
Hawthorn East Vic. 43 I8
Hawthorndene SA 69 E4
Hawthorne Qld 131 J12, 133 J2
Hay NSW 17 J7
Haydens Bog Vic. 20 B10, 58 D8
Hayes Tas. 158 G3, 161 J6
Hayes Creek NT 114 G10, 116 E6
Haymarket NSW 5 D9, 7 L12, 9 L4
Haysdale Vic. 16 G8, 53 K10
Hazel Park Vic. 47 P12, 48 H9
Hazelbrook NSW 10 E6
Hazeldene Vic. 47 K2, 48 D2, 50 D12
Hazelmere WA 90 H7, 91 F2, 93 D4
Hazelwood Vic. 48 H7
Hazelwood Park SA 68 F12, 69 F2
Healesville Vic. 47 L4, 48 E4
Heartbreak Hotel NT 117 L12, 119 L3
Heath Hill Vic. 45 P10, 47 M9, 48 F7
Heathcote NSW 8 G10, 11 J11, 13 K7, 20 H1
Heathcote Vic. 50 B10, 55 P11
Heathcote Junction Vic. 47 J2, 48 C2, 50 C12
Heathcote NP NSW 8 G10, 11 J12, 13 J7, 20 H1
Heathcote–Graytown NP Vic. 50 C9, 55 P11, 57 P1
Heatherton Vic. 43 J12, 44 E3
Heathfield SA 69 G4, 70 C10, 71 G3
Heathmere Vic. 56 D7
Heathmont Vic. 43 M9
Heathpool SA 68 E12, 69 E2
Heathridge WA 90 B4
Heathwood Qld 132 G6
Hebden NSW 13 K2
Hebel Qld 14 B2, 136 D11
Hebersham NSW 6 E6
Heckenberg NSW 6 E12, 8 E4
Hector Qld 139 K6
Hectorville SA 68 F11, 69 F1
Hedley Vic. 49 I9
Heidelberg Vic. 43 J6, 47 J5
Heidelberg Heights Vic. 43 I6
Heidelberg West Vic. 43 I6
Heka Tas. 162 F7
Helena NP WA 93 E5, 96 C5, 98 C7
Helena Valley WA 91 G2

Helensburgh NSW 8 G11, 13 K8, 20 H2
Helensvale Qld 15 O1, 135 F9, 137 N10
Helenvale Qld 141 L3
Helidon Qld 137 L9
Hell Hole Gorge NP Qld 147 L3
Hells Gate Roadhouse Qld 143 B3
Hellyer Tas. 162 D4
Hemmant Qld 131 K11, 133 K1, 134 G11, 135 E4
Henderson WA 91 B11
Hendon SA 68 B10, 70 B8, 71 E1
Hendra Qld 131 J11, 133 J1
Henley NSW 7 K11, 9 K3
Henley Beach SA 68 A11, 69 A1
Henley Beach South SA 68 B12, 69 B2
Henley Brook WA 90 H4, 91 E1, 93 D4
Henrietta Tas. 162 E6
Hensley Park Vic. 56 F4
Henty NSW 12 B11, 17 O11, 51 L3
Henty Vic. 56 D4
Hepburn Springs Vic. 46 E1, 57 N2
Herberton Qld 141 L7
Herberton Range NP Qld 141 L7
Herdsman WA 90 D8, 91 B3
Heritage Park Qld 133 I9
Hermannsburg NT 120 H7
Hermidale NSW 19 N10
Hernani NSW 15 L7
Herne Hill WA 90 H5, 91 G1
Heron Island Qld 139 O11
Herons Creek NSW 15 L11
Herrick Tas. 163 N6
Herston Qld 129 E1, 131 I11, 133 I1
Hervey Bay Qld 137 N4
Hervey Rocks NT 117 N10, 119 N1
Hesket Vic. 46 H2, 48 B2, 50 B12, 57 P3
Hesso SA 72 H1, 74 F8
Hewett SA 68 H1
Hexham NSW 13 L4
Hexham Vic. 56 H6
Heybridge Tas. 162 F5
Heyfield Vic. 49 J6
Heywood Vic. 56 D6
Hi Way Inn Roadhouse NT 116 H12, 118 H3
Hiamdale Vic. 49 J7
Hiawatha Vic. 49 I9
Hibbs Pyramid Tas. 160 C5
Hidden Valley NT 112 E6
Higgins ACT 34 B3
High Black Rock NT 116 F2
High Camp Vic. 48 C1, 50 C11
High Range NSW 13 I8, 20 G2
High Wycombe WA 90 H8, 91 F3
Highbury SA 68 G9
Highbury WA 95 I1, 96 E7
Highclere Tas. 162 F6
Highcroft Tas. 159 L9, 161 M9
Highett Vic. 43 I12, 44 C2, 47 J7
Highfields Qld 137 L9
Highgate SA 69 E3
Highgate WA 89 G2, 90 F9, 91 C4
Highgate Hill Qld 129 D11, 131 I12, 133 I2
Highlands Vic. 50 E11
Highvale Qld 130 E10, 134 D10, 135 C3
Hilgay Vic. 56 D4

Hill End NSW 12 G4
Hill End Vic. 47 P7, 48 H6
Hillarys WA 90 B6, 91 A1, 93 B4, 96 B5
Hillbank SA 68 G5
Hillcrest Qld 132 H7, 133 I7
Hillcrest SA 68 E10
Hillcrest Vic. 46 B3
Hillgrove NSW 15 K8
Hillier SA 68 F2
Hilliger NP WA 94 D8, 96 C10, 98 C11
Hillman WA 92 B2, 94 H3, 96 E8
Hillsdale NSW 9 M6
Hillside Vic. 42 C4, 49 M5
Hillston NSW 17 L4
Hilltop NSW 13 I8, 20 G2
Hilltown SA 73 J5
Hillview Qld 15 N1, 135 C11
Hillwood Tas. 163 J7
Hilton SA 68 C12, 69 C2
Hilton WA 91 B8
Hinchinbrook NSW 6 E12, 8 E4
Hinchinbrook Island Qld 141 M9
Hindmarsh SA 68 C11, 69 C1
Hindmarsh Island SA 71 H8
Hindmarsh Valley SA 71 F8
Hines Hill WA 96 G3
Hinnomunjie Vic. 49 N1, 51 N11
Hippolyte Rocks Tas. 159 O9, 161 N9
Hirstglen Qld 137 L10
Hivesville Qld 137 L6
Hobart Tas. 155 D7, 156 D7, 159 I5, 161 K7
Hobartville NSW 6 C2
Hobbys Yards NSW 12 G6
Hocking WA 90 D4
Hoddle Vic. 48 G10
Hoddles Creek Vic. 45 O1, 47 M6, 48 E5
Hodgson River Station NT 117 J10, 119 J1
Holbourne Island NP Qld 139 J2
Holbrook NSW 12 B11, 17 O11, 51 M4
Holden Hill SA 68 F9
Holder ACT 34 B7
Holgate NSW 11 O2
Holland Park Qld 133 J3
Holland Park West Qld 133 I3
Hollow Tree Tas. 161 J5
Holly WA 95 K5, 96 F9
Hollydeen NSW 13 J2
Holmes NT 112 F2
Holmview Qld 133 K9, 135 E7
Holmwood NSW 12 F6
Holroyd NSW 6 H10, 8 H2
Holsworthy NSW 8 G10
Holt ACT 34 B3
Holtze NT 113 J6
Holwell Tas. 163 J7
Home Hill Qld 138 H2, 141 O12
Homebush NSW 7 J11, 9 J3
Homebush Qld 139 K6
Homebush Vic. 55 L11, 57 L1
Homebush Bay NSW 7 I10, 9 I2
Homebush West NSW 7 I11, 9 I3
Homecroft Vic. 16 E12, 54 H7
Homerton Vic. 56 E6
Homestead Qld 138 E3
Homevale NP Qld 139 J6
Homewood Vic. 47 L1, 48 E1, 50 E11

Hook Island Qld 139 K3
Hope Forest SA 69 D12
Hope Islands NP Qld 141 L3
Hope Vale Qld 141 K2
Hope Valley SA 68 F9
Hope Valley WA 91 C11, 92 C1
Hopeland WA 92 E4
Hopetoun Vic. 16 E10, 54 H4
Hopetoun WA 98 G10
Hopetoun West Vic. 16 D10, 54 G3
Hopevale Vic. 16 E11, 54 G4
Hoppers Crossing Vic. 42 B9, 46 H6, 48 B5, 57 P6
Hordern Vale Vic. 46 A12, 57 K10
Horn (Narupai) Island Qld 142 C2
Horningsea Park NSW 8 D5
Hornsby NSW 7 J6, 11 L6, 13 K6
Hornsby Heights NSW 7 J5, 11 L6
Hornsdale SA 73 J4, 75 I11
Horrocks WA 97 D12
Horse Lake NSW 18 D11, 75 P9
Horseshoe Bay Qld 141 N11
Horsfield Bay NSW 7 P1
Horsham Vic. 54 G9
Horsley Park NSW 6 D9, 8 E1, 11 I8
Horsnell Gully SA 68 F12, 69 G3
Horton Falls NP NSW 14 G7
Hoskinstown NSW 12 G11, 20 D5, 31 H7
Hotham Heights Vic. 49 L1, 51 L11
Hotspur Vic. 56 D5
Houghton SA 68 H9, 70 D8, 71 G1
Houtman Abrolhos Islands WA 97 C12
Hove SA 69 B4, 70 B10, 71 E3
Hovea WA 91 H2
Howard Qld 137 M4
Howard Springs NT 113 O9, 114 E3, 116 D4
Howden Tas. 159 I7, 161 K8
Howes Valley NSW 13 K3
Howick Group NP Qld 142 H11
Howick Island Qld 142 H11
Howlong NSW 12 A12, 17 N12, 51 J5
Howqua Vic. 47 P1, 48 H1, 50 H12
Howrah Tas. 156 G7, 157 I8, 159 J5
Howth Tas. 162 G5
Hoxton Park NSW 6 D12, 8 D4
Hoya Qld 135 A8
Hoyleton SA 73 J6
Huddleston SA 73 J4, 74 H12
Hughenden Qld 138 B4, 145 N4
Hughes ACT 34 D7
Hughes SA 80 D4
Hughesdale Vic. 43 J11, 44 D1
Hull River NP Qld 141 M8
Humboldt NP Qld 136 G1, 139 J12
Hume NSW 34 F8
Humevale Vic. 43 L1, 47 K3, 48 D3
Humpty Doo NT 114 E4, 116 D4
Humula NSW 12 C11, 51 O3
Hunter Vic. 50 B7, 55 P8
Hunter Island Tas. 162 B2
Hunter Wetlands NP NSW 13 L4
Hunters Hill NSW 7 K10, 9 K2
Hunterston Vic. 49 J9
Huntfield Heights SA 69 B9
Huntingdale Vic. 43 J11, 44 E1
Huntingdale WA 90 H12, 91 F7
Huntingwood NSW 6 E8, 8 E1
Huntleys Cove NSW 7 K11, 9 K2
Huntleys Point NSW 7 K11, 9 K3

Huntly Vic. 50 A8, 55 O9
Huon Vic. 51 L7
Huonville Tas. 158 G7, 161 J8
Hurlstone Park NSW 9 K5
Hurstbridge Vic. 43 L3, 47 K4, 48 D3
Hurstville NSW 9 J6, 11 K10
Hurstville Grove NSW 9 J6
Huskisson NSW 13 J10, 20 G4
Hutt WA 97 D11, 98 A2
Hyde Park SA 69 D3
Hyden WA 96 H5, 98 F8
Hyland Park NSW 15 M9
Hynam SA 54 A10, 82 G9

Icy Creek Vic. 47 O6, 48 G5
Ida Bay Tas. 158 E12, 161 I10
Idalia NP Qld 138 B12, 145 N12, 147 M2
Ilbilbie Qld 139 K7
Ile des Phoques Tas. 161 N4
Ile du Golfe Tas. 160 G11
Ile du Nord Tas. 159 P2, 161 N5
Ilford NSW 12 H4
Ilfracombe Qld 138 B10, 145 N10
Ilkurlka Roadhouse WA 99 N1, 101 N11
Illabarook Vic. 46 B5, 57 L5
Illabo NSW 12 C9
Illalong Creek NSW 12 E9, 20 C3
Illawarra Vic. 55 I11, 57 I1
Illawong NSW 8 H6, 9 I6, 11 J10
Illawong WA 98 A4
Illowa Vic. 56 G8
Iluka NSW 15 O5
Iluka WA 90 B3
Imangara NT 119 K12, 121 K1
Imanpa NT 120 G9
Imbil Qld 134 D1, 137 M7
Imintji Store WA 103 K6
Impimi NSW 16 H8, 53 M9
Inala Qld 132 G5
Indaringinya NT 121 K3
Indented Head Vic. 46 H8, 48 B6, 57 P7
Indigo Vic. 51 J6
Indigo Upper Vic. 51 K7
Indooroopilly Qld 130 G12, 132 G2, 134 E11, 135 D4
Indwarra NP NSW 15 J6
Ingham Qld 141 M10
Ingle Farm SA 68 E8
Ingleburn NSW 8 D6
Ingleby Vic. 46 C9, 57 M8
Ingleside NSW 7 N6, 11 N6
Ingleside Qld 135 F11
Inglewood Qld 15 J1, 137 J11
Inglewood SA 68 H9
Inglewood Tas. 161 L4
Inglewood Vic. 55 M9
Inglewood WA 90 F8, 91 C3
Ingliston Vic. 46 F4, 57 O4
Ingoldsby Qld 137 L9
Injinoo Qld 142 C3
Injune Qld 136 F4
Inkerman NT 138 H2
Inkerman SA 73 I7, 82 A1
Innaloo WA 90 D8, 91 A3
Innamincka SA 77 N7, 146 F8
Inner Rock NSW 13 N3
Innes NP SA 72 F10
Inneston SA 72 F10
Innisfail Qld 141 M7
Innot Hot Springs Qld 141 K7

Interlaken Tas. 161 K2, 163 K12
Inverell NSW 15 I5
Invergordon Vic. 50 F6
Inverleigh Vic. 46 D7, 57 M7
Inverloch Vic. 47 M12, 48 F9
Invermay Vic. 46 D3
Iona Vic. 45 P8, 47 M8
Ipolera NT 120 G7
Ipswich Qld 132 B5, 134 D12, 135 B5, 137 M9
Irishtown Tas. 162 C4
Irishtown Vic. 55 N12, 57 N2
Iron Baron SA 72 G3, 74 F11
Iron Knob SA 72 G2, 74 F10
Iron Pot Tas. 159 J7, 161 K8
Iron Range Qld 142 E7
Ironbank SA 69 F5
Ironbark Qld 132 A3
Irrewarra Vic. 46 B9, 57 L8
Irrewillipe Vic. 46 A9, 57 K8
Irrwelty NT 121 K3
Irvinebank Qld 141 K7
Irymple Vic. 16 E6, 52 G6
Isaacs ACT 34 D8
Isabella NSW 12 H7, 20 E1
Isabella Plains ACT 34 C10
Isisford Qld 138 B11, 145 N11
Isla Gorge NP Qld 137 I3
Island Bend NSW 58 C3
Island Head Qld 139 M8
Ivanhoe NSW 17 I2
Ivanhoe Vic. 43 I7
Ivanhoe East Vic. 43 J7
Ivory Creek Qld 134 A6
Iwantja (Indulkana) SA 79 L4
Iwupataka NT 121 I7
Iytwelepenty–Davenport Ranges NP NT 119 K11, 121 K1

Jabiru NT 115 O4, 116 G5
Jabuk SA 73 M10, 82 F4
Jacana Vic. 42 G4
Jack River Vic. 49 I9
Jackadgery NSW 15 M5
Jackeys Marsh Tas. 163 I9
Jackie Junction WA 101 M8
Jackson Qld 136 H6
Jacobs Well Qld 133 O11, 135 F7, 137 N10
Jacobs Well WA 96 E5
Jalloonda Qld 138 G1, 141 N11
Jallumba Vic. 54 F10
Jamberoo NSW 13 J9, 20 H3
Jambin Qld 137 J1, 139 M12
Jamboree Heights Qld 132 G4
Jamestown SA 73 J4, 75 I11
Jamieson Vic. 47 P2, 48 H2, 50 H12
Jamisontown NSW 6 A7
Jancourt Vic. 57 J8
Jancourt East Vic. 57 J8
Jandabup WA 90 D3
Jandakot WA 91 D8, 93 C6, 96 C5
Jandowae Qld 137 K7
Jane Brook WA 91 G1
Jane NP WA 94 G10, 96 D11, 98 C11
Jannali NSW 9 I7
Japoon NP Qld 141 M8
Jardee WA 94 F8, 96 D10
Jardine River NP Qld 142 D4
Jarklin Vic. 16 H12, 55 N7
Jarra Jarra NT 118 H12, 120 H1
Jarrahdale WA 92 H2, 93 D7, 96 C6
Jarrahmond Vic. 49 P5, 58 B11

Jarrahwood WA 94 D6, 96 C9
Jarvis Creek Vic. 51 L6
Jaurdi WA 98 G5
Jawbone Marine Sanctuary Vic. 47 I6, 48 C4
Jeebropilly Qld 132 A5
Jeffcott Vic. 16 F12, 55 J7
Jeffcott North Vic. 55 J7
Jellat Jellat NSW 58 H6
Jemalong NSW 12 D4
Jennacubbine WA 93 G1
Jenolan Caves NSW 13 I6
Jeogla NSW 15 K8
Jeparit Vic. 16 D12, 54 F6
Jerangle NSW 12 F12, 20 D6, 31 F12, 58 G1
Jericho Qld 138 E10
Jericho Tas. 161 K4
Jericho Vic. 48 H4
Jerilderie NSW 17 L10, 50 G1
Jerrabomberra NSW 31 E6, 34 G8
Jerramungup WA 95 P5, 98 F10
Jerrawa NSW 12 F9, 20 D3
Jerrawangala NP NSW 13 I10, 20 G4
Jerrys Plains NSW 13 K2
Jerseyville NSW 15 M9
Jervis Bay JBT 13 J10, 20 G4
Jervis Bay NP NSW 13 J10, 20 H4
Jervois SA 73 L10, 82 D4
Jetsonville Tas. 163 L6
Ji-Marda NT 117 J3
Jigalong WA 100 G5
Jil Jil Vic. 55 J4
Jimaringle NSW 17 I9, 50 A1, 53 O12, 55 O2
Jimboomba Qld 132 F11, 133 I11, 135 D8, 137 N10
Jimbour Qld 137 K7
Jimna Qld 134 B3, 137 M7
Jindabyne NSW 20 B8, 58 C4
Jindalee Qld 132 G3
Jindalee WA 90 A1
Jindera NSW 12 A12, 17 O12, 51 K5
Jindivick Vic. 47 N8, 48 G6
Jindong WA 94 B6
Jingalup WA 95 I6, 96 E9, 98 D10
Jingellic NSW 12 C12, 17 P12, 51 N5
Jingili NT 112 D3
Jitarning WA 96 G6, 98 E8
Joanna SA 54 A11, 82 G9
Jodetluk (George Camp) NT 116 G8
Joel Joel Vic. 55 J11, 57 J1
Joel South Vic. 55 J11, 57 J1
Johanna Vic. 46 A12, 57 K10
John Forrest NP WA 91 H1, 93 D4, 96 C5, 98 C7
Johnburgh SA 73 J2, 75 I9
Johns River NSW 13 O1, 15 L12
Johnsonville Vic. 49 N5
Johnston NT 113 L10
Jolimont WA 90 D9, 91 B4
Jollys Lookout Qld 130 E10
Jondaryan Qld 137 K8
Joondalup WA 90 B3, 93 B4, 96 B4
Joondanna WA 90 E8, 91 C3
Josbury WA 94 H1, 96 E7, 98 D9
Josephville Qld 15 N1, 135 C9
Joskeleigh Qld 139 M11
Joslin SA 68 E11, 69 E1

Joyces Creek Vic. 55 N12, 57 N1
Joyner Qld 130 G6
Judbarra–Gregory NP NT 116 C12, 118 C3
Judbury Tas. 158 F6, 161 I8
Jugiong NSW 12 E9, 20 B3
Julatten Qld 141 L5
Julia SA 73 K7
Julia Creek Qld 143 H11, 145 J3
Jumbuk Vic. 49 I8
Jumbunna Vic. 47 M11, 48 F8
Junction Hill NSW 15 M6
Junction Village Vic. 44 H7
Jundah Qld 147 J1
Junee NSW 12 C9, 17 P9
Junee NP Qld 139 J9
Junee Reefs NSW 12 C8, 17 P8
Jung Vic. 54 G9
Junortoun Vic. 50 A9, 55 O10
Junuy Juluum NP NSW 15 M7
Jupiter Creek SA 69 G7
Jura WA 96 G4
Jurien Bay WA 98 A5
Jurien Bay Marine Park WA 96 A1, 98 A5
Jurunjung Vic. 46 H4, 48 B3, 57 P5
Juunju Daarrba NP Qld 141 K1

Kaarimba Vic. 17 K12, 50 E6
Kabra Qld 139 M11
Kadina SA 72 H6
Kadnook Vic. 54 C11, 56 C1, 82 H10
Kadungle NSW 12 D2
Kagaru Qld 132 E12, 135 C8
Kai-Kudulug Qld 142 C2
Kaimkillenbun Qld 137 K8
Kain NSW 12 G12, 20 D6, 31 H11, 58 H1
Kainton SA 73 I7
Kairi Qld 141 L6
Kajabbi Qld 140 B12, 143 E9, 144 G2
Kakadu NP NT 115 N3, 116 G4
Kalamunda WA 91 G4, 93 D5
Kalamunda NP WA 91 H4, 93 D5, 96 C5, 98 C7
Kalangadoo SA 56 A3, 82 G11
Kalannie WA 96 D1, 98 D5
Kalaru NSW 20 E9
Kalbar Qld 135 A8, 137 M10
Kalbarri WA 97 C11
Kalbarri NP WA 97 D11, 98 A2, 100 A12
Kaleen ACT 34 D3
Kaleentha Loop NSW 16 G1, 18 F12
Kalgan WA 95 M10, 96 G11, 98 E11
Kalgoorlie–Boulder WA 98 H5
Kalimna Vic. 49 O6
Kalimna West Vic. 49 N6
Kalinjarri NT 119 J11
Kalka SA 78 C2, 101 P8, 120 B11
Kalkallo Vic. 47 I3, 48 C3
Kalkarindji (Wave Hill) NT 118 D5
Kalkee Vic. 54 G8
Kalkite NSW 58 C3
Kallangur Qld 131 I5, 134 F9, 135 D2
Kallaroo WA 90 B5
Kallista Vic. 43 P11, 45 J1
Kalorama Vic. 43 P9
Kalpienung Vic. 16 G11, 55 K4
Kalpowar Qld 137 K2

Kaltukatjara (Docker River) NT 101 P6, 120 B9
Kalumburu WA 103 L2
Kalumpurlpa NT 119 I8
Kalunga Qld 141 L7
Kalyan SA 73 M9, 82 E3
Kamarah NSW 12 A7, 17 O7
Kamarooka Vic. 50 A7, 55 O8
Kamay Botany Bay NP NSW 9 M7, 11 M11
Kambah ACT 34 B8
Kambalda WA 98 H5
Kamballup WA 95 M9, 96 G10, 98 E11
Kameruka NSW 20 D9, 58 H6
Kamona Tas. 163 M6
Kananggra–Boyd NP NSW 10 A7, 12 H6, 13 I7, 20 F1
Kancoona South Vic. 51 K9
Kandanga Qld 134 D1
Kandiwal WA 103 K3
Kandos NSW 13 I3
Kangarilla SA 69 E8, 70 C11, 71 F4, 73 J10, 82 B3
Kangaroo Valley NSW 13 I9, 20 G3
Kangaroo Flat NSW 12 F6
Kangaroo Flat SA 70 C5
Kangaroo Flat Vic. 50 A9, 55 O10
Kangaroo Ground Vic. 43 M4
Kangaroo Island SA 71 A10, 72 G12, 82 A5
Kangaroo Point NSW 9 J7
Kangaroo Point Qld 129 H10, 131 I12, 133 I2
Kangawall Vic. 54 D10
Kangiara NSW 12 F8, 20 C2
Kaniva Vic. 16 B12, 54 C7, 82 H7
Kanmantoo SA 70 F10
Kanumbra Vic. 50 F11
Kanya Vic. 55 J10
Kanyapella Vic. 17 J12, 50 C5
Kanypi SA 78 E2, 120 D11
Kaoota Tas. 158 H7, 161 J8
Kapinnie SA 72 D7
Kapooka NSW 12 B10, 17 P10, 51 M1
Kapril (Black) Rock Qld 142 C1
Kapunda SA 70 E2, 73 K7, 82 C1
Kara Kara NP Vic. 55 K10
Karabar NSW 34 G8
Karabeal Vic. 56 F3
Karadoc Vic. 16 E6, 52 H6
Karalee Qld 132 D5, 134 D12, 135 C5
Karalundi WA 97 H8, 100 E9
Karama NT 112 F4
Karana Downs Qld 132 D3, 134 D11, 135 B5
Karanja Tas. 158 F2, 161 I6
Karara Qld 15 K1, 137 K10
Karatta SA 72 G12
Karawara WA 90 F11, 91 D6
Karawinna Vic. 16 D6, 52 E7
Karawatha Qld 133 J6
Kardinya WA 90 E12, 91 C7, 93 C6
Kareela NSW 9 I8
Kariah Vic. 57 J7
Karijini NP WA 97 G3, 100 D5
Kariong NSW 11 N3
Karkoo SA 72 D6
Karlamilyi NP WA 100 H4, 101 I3
Karlgarin WA 96 H5, 98 F8
Karn Vic. 50 H9
Karnak Vic. 54 D10

Karnup WA 92 C5
Karonie WA 99 I5
Karoola Tas. 163 K7
Karoonda SA 73 M10, 82 E3
Karoonda Roadhouse Vic. 20 A10, 49 P2, 58 A8
Karrabin Qld 132 A5
Karrakatta WA 90 D10, 91 B5, 93 B5
Karrakup WA 91 H11, 92 H1
Karratha WA 97 E1, 100 B2, 102 B12
Karratha Travel Stop Roadhouse WA 97 E1, 100 B2, 102 B12
Karridale WA 94 B8, 96 B10
Karrinyup WA 90 C7, 91 A3
Kars Springs NSW 13 J1, 14 G12
Karte SA 16 A8, 52 A10, 73 N9, 82 G3
Karuah NSW 13 M3
Karuah NP NSW 13 M3
Karumba Qld 140 C7, 143 G4
Karween Vic. 16 C6, 52 C6, 73 P8, 82 H1
Katamatite Vic. 17 L12, 50 F5
Katandra Vic. 50 F6
Katandra West Vic. 50 F6
Katanning WA 95 K4, 96 F8, 98 E9
Katherine NT 116 F8
Katoomba NSW 10 D5, 13 I6
Katunga Vic. 17 K12, 50 F5
Katyil Vic. 54 G7
Kawarren Vic. 46 B10, 57 L9
Kay Reef Cay A Qld 142 E6
Kay Reef Cay B Qld 142 E6
Kayena Tas. 163 J6
Kealba Vic. 42 E5
Kearns NSW 8 C7
Kedron Qld 131 I10, 133 I1
Keep River NP NT 103 O4, 116 A11, 118 A2
Keep River NP Extension NT 103 P4, 116 A10, 118 B1
Keilor Vic. 42 E4, 47 I5, 48 B4
Keilor Downs Vic. 42 D5
Keilor East Vic. 42 E5
Keilor Lodge Vic. 42 E4
Keilor North Vic. 42 D4
Keilor Park Vic. 42 E5
Keith SA 82 F6
Kellalac Vic. 16 E12, 54 H7
Kellatier Tas. 162 E5
Kellerberrin WA 96 F4, 98 D7
Kellevie Tas. 159 M4, 161 M7
Kellyville NSW 6 G5
Kellyville Ridge NSW 6 G5
Kelmscott WA 91 G8, 93 D6
Kelso Tas. 163 J6
Kelvin NSW 14 G8
Kelvin Grove Qld 129 B1, 131 I11, 133 I1
Kelvin NP Qld 139 K6
Kelvin View Vic. 50 F9
Kemendok NP NSW 16 E7, 52 H7
Kemps Creek NSW 6 C9, 8 C2
Kempsey NSW 15 M10
Kempton Tas. 159 I1, 161 K5
Kendall NSW 15 L11
Kendenup WA 95 L8, 96 G10
Kenebri NSW 14 D8
Kenilworth Qld 134 E3, 137 M7
Kenmare Vic. 16 D11, 54 G5
Kenmore NSW 12 H9, 20 E3

Kenmore Qld 132 G3, 134 E11, 135 D5
Kenmore Hills Qld 130 F12, 132 F2, 134 E11, 135 D4
Kennedy Qld 141 M9
Kennedy Range NP WA 97 D6, 100 A8
Kennedys Creek Vic. 57 J9
Kennett River Vic. 46 C12, 57 M10
Kennys Creek NSW 12 F8, 20 C2
Kensington NSW 9 M5
Kensington SA 68 E12, 69 E1
Kensington Vic. 42 G7
Kensington WA 90 F10, 91 D5
Kensington Gardens SA 68 F11, 69 F1
Kensington Park SA 68 E11, 69 E1
Kent Town SA 67 H6, 68 E12, 69 E1
Kentbruck Vic. 56 C6
Kenthurst NSW 6 H5, 7 I5, 11 K5
Kentlyn NSW 8 D8, 11 I11
Kentucky NSW 15 J8
Kenwick WA 90 H12, 91 F5, 93 D5
Keperra Qld 130 G10, 132 G1, 134 E10, 135 D4
Keppel Bay Islands NP Qld 139 N10
Keppel Rocks Qld 139 N11
Keppel Sands Qld 139 N11
Keppoch SA 82 G8
Kerang Vic. 16 H11, 55 N4
Kerang East Vic. 16 H11, 55 N4
Kerang South Vic. 16 H11, 55 N5
Kergunyah Vic. 51 L7
Kergunyah South Vic. 51 L8
Kernot Vic. 47 L10, 48 E8
Kerrabee NSW 13 J2
Kerrie Vic. 48 B2, 50 B12
Kerrisdale Vic. 48 D1, 50 D11
Kerrs Creek NSW 12 G4
Kerry Qld 15 N1, 135 D10
Kersbrook SA 70 D7, 73 K9, 82 C2
Keswick SA 67 A12, 68 D12, 69 D2, 70 B9, 71 F2
Keswick Terminal SA 67 A11, 68 D12, 69 D2
Kettering Tas. 158 H8, 161 K8
Keverstone NP NSW 12 G7, 20 D1
Kevington Vic. 47 P2, 48 H2
Kew NSW 15 L11
Kew Vic. 42 H8, 43 I7
Kew East Vic. 43 I7
Kewdale WA 90 G9, 91 E4
Kewell Vic. 54 H8
Keyneton SA 70 G5, 73 K8, 82 C2
Keysborough Vic. 44 F4
Keysbrook WA 92 G5, 93 D8, 96 C6
Khancoban NSW 20 A7, 51 P7, 58 A3
Kholo Qld 130 B12, 132 B2
Ki Ki SA 73 M11, 82 E5
Kiah NSW 20 E10, 58 H8
Kialla NSW 12 G8, 20 E2
Kialla Vic. 50 E7
Kialla West Vic. 50 E7
Kiama NSW 13 J9, 20 H3
Kiamil Vic. 16 E8, 52 H10
Kiana SA 72 C6
Kiandra NSW 12 E12, 20 B6, 58 C1
Kiara WA 90 G7, 91 E2
Kiata Vic. 16 C12, 54 E7
Kidman Park SA 68 B11, 69 B1
Kidston Qld 141 I10
Kielpa SA 72 E5, 74 D12

Kiewa Vic. 51 L7
Kikoira NSW 12 A5, 17 O5
Kilburn SA 68 D9, 70 B8, 71 F1
Kilcoy Qld 134 C6, 137 M8
Kilcunda Vic. 47 L11, 48 E9
Kilkenny SA 68 C10
Kilkivan Qld 137 M6
Killabakh NSW 13 N1, 15 L12
Killara NSW 7 L8, 9 K1, 11 L7
Killarney Qld 15 L1, 137 L11
Killarney Vic. 56 G8
Killarney Heights NSW 7 M9, 9 M1
Killawarra Vic. 51 I6
Killiecrankie Tas. 160 A9
Killora Tas. 159 I8, 161 K8
Kilmany Vic. 49 J7
Kilmany South Vic. 49 J7
Kilmore Vic. 47 J1, 48 C1, 50 C12
Kilpalie SA 73 M9, 82 F3
Kilsyth Vic. 43 O10
Kilsyth South Vic. 43 N10
Kimba SA 72 F4, 74 D11
Kimberley Tas. 162 H7
Kinalung NSW 18 D10, 75 P8
Kincaid Vic. 46 A11, 57 K10
Kinchega NP NSW 16 E1, 18 D12, 75 P10
Kinchela NSW 15 M10
Kincumber NSW 11 O3, 13 L6
Kindred Tas. 162 G6
King Island Tas. 161 O11
King River WA 95 M11, 96 G11, 98 E11
King Scrub Qld 130 E2
King Valley Vic. 51 I9
Kingaroy Qld 137 L7
Kinglake Vic. 43 O1, 47 L3, 48 E3
Kinglake Central Vic. 43 O1, 47 K3, 48 E3
Kinglake East Vic. 47 L3
Kinglake NP Vic. 43 O1, 47 K2, 48 D2, 50 D12
Kinglake West Vic. 43 M1, 47 K3, 48 D2
Kingoonya SA 74 B5, 81 P5
Kingower Vic. 55 M9
Kings Camp SA 82 E9
Kings Canyon Resort NT 120 F8
Kings Cross NSW 11 M9
Kings Langley NSW 6 G7
Kings Meadows Tas. 163 K8
Kings Park NSW 6 F7
Kings Park SA 69 D3
Kings Park Vic. 42 D5
Kings Park WA 89 A7, 90 E10, 91 C4
Kings Plains NP NSW 15 J5
Kings Point NSW 13 I11, 20 G5
Kingsborough Qld 141 K6
Kingsbury Vic. 43 I5
Kingscliff NSW 15 O2, 135 H12, 137 N11
Kingscote SA 72 H11
Kingsdale NSW 12 H9, 20 E3
Kingsford NSW 9 M5, 11 M10
Kingsford SA 68 H1
Kingsgrove NSW 9 J5
Kingsholme Qld 133 L12
Kingsley WA 90 C5, 91 B1
Kingsthorpe Qld 137 L9
Kingston ACT 33 H11, 34 E7
Kingston Qld 133 J7, 135 E6

Kingston Tas. 156 A11, 159 I6, 161 K8
Kingston Vic. 46 D2, 57 M3
Kingston Park SA 69 B5
Kingston S.E. SA 82 E8
Kingston-on-Murray SA 16 A6, 73 N7, 82 F1
Kingstown NSW 15 I8
Kingsvale NSW 12 E8, 20 B2
Kingsville Vic. 42 F8
Kingswood NSW 6 B7, 10 H6
Kingswood SA 69 D3, 73 I2, 74 H9
Kinimakatka Vic. 54 D7
Kinka Qld 139 N10
Kinnabulla Vic. 16 F11, 55 I5
Kinrara NP Qld 141 L8
Kinross WA 90 A3
Kintore NT 101 P4, 120 B6
Kioloa NSW 13 I12, 20 F6
Kippa-Ring Qld 131 K6, 134 G9, 135 E2
Kirkham NSW 8 A7
Kirkstall Vic. 56 G7
Kirra Qld 135 G11
Kirrama NP Qld 141 L8
Kirrawee NSW 9 I8, 11 K11
Kirribilli NSW 5 F1, 7 M11, 9 M3
Kirup WA 94 E5, 96 C9
Kitchener WA 99 K5
Kithbrook Vic. 50 F10
Kiwirrkurra WA 101 N4
Klemzig SA 68 E10
Knockrow NSW 15 O3
Knockwood Vic. 47 P3, 48 H3
Knowsley Vic. 50 B9, 55 P10
Knoxfield Vic. 43 M10, 44 H1
Knuckey Lagoon NT 112 H4, 113 I6
Koah Qld 141 L6
Kobble Qld 134 E9, 135 C2
Kobble Creek Qld 130 D5
Koetong Vic. 51 N6
Kogan Qld 137 J8
Kogarah NSW 9 K6, 11 L10
Kogarah Bay NSW 9 J7
Koimbo Vic. 16 F8, 53 J10
Kojonup WA 95 J5, 96 F9, 98 D10
Koloona NSW 14 H5
Kolora Vic. 57 I7
Komungla NSW 12 G9, 20 E3
Konagaderra Vic. 47 I3
Kondalilla NP Qld 134 E4, 137 N7
Kondinin WA 96 G5, 98 E8
Kongal SA 16 A12, 82 G7
Kongorong SA 82 F12
Kongwak Vic. 47 M11, 48 F8
Konnongorring WA 96 D3, 98 C6
Konong Wootong Vic. 56 E3
Konong Wootong North Vic. 56 E2
Koo Wee Rup Vic. 45 K8, 47 L9, 48 E7
Koo Wee Rup North Vic. 45 M8
Koojarra Shoal WA 103 L1
Kookynie WA 98 H3
Koolan WA 103 I5
Koolewong NSW 11 N3
Kooljaman WA 102 H5
Kooloonong Vic. 16 G8, 53 K10
Koolunga SA 73 J5, 74 H12
Koolyanobbing WA 98 F5
Koolywurtie SA 72 H8
Koombooloomba NP Qld 141 L8
Koonda Vic. 50 F8

Koondoola WA 90 E6, 91 C1
Koondrook Vic. 17 I10, 50 A2, 55 O4
Koongamia WA 91 G2
Koongarra NT 115 O5, 116 G5
Koongawa SA 72 D4, 74 C11
Kooniba SA 81 L7
Kooninderie SA 70 F1
Koonoomoo Vic. 17 L11, 50 F4
Koonwarra Vic. 47 N12, 48 G9
Koonya Tas. 159 M8, 161 M8
Kooraban NP NSW 20 E8, 58 H3
Kooralbyn Qld 15 N1, 135 B10, 137 M10
Koorawatha NSW 12 E6
Koorda WA 96 E2, 98 D6
Kooreh Vic. 55 K9
Kooringal Qld 135 G4, 137 N9
Koorkab Vic. 16 G8, 53 K9
Koorlong Vic. 52 G6
Kootingal NSW 15 I9
Kooyong Vic. 43 I9
Koppio SA 72 D7
Korbel WA 96 G4
Koreelah NP NSW 15 M2, 137 L11
Koriella Vic. 47 M1, 48 F1, 50 F11
Korobeit Vic. 46 F3, 48 A3, 57 O4
Koroit Vic. 56 G7
Korong Vale Vic. 55 M8
Koroop Vic. 55 N4
Korora NSW 15 N7
Korumburra Vic. 47 N11, 48 F8
Korung NP WA 91 H5, 93 E5, 96 C5, 98 C7
Korunye SA 68 B1
Korweinguboora Vic. 46 E2, 57 N3
Kosciuszko NP NSW 12 E11, 20 A7, 31 A9, 51 P8, 58 B2
Kotta Vic. 17 I12, 50 B6, 55 P7
Kotupna Vic. 17 K12, 50 D6
Koumala Qld 139 K6
Kowanyama Qld 140 E2
Koyuga Vic. 50 C6
Krambach NSW 13 N2
Kringin SA 16 A8, 52 B10, 73 O9, 82 G3
Krongart SA 56 A3, 82 G10
Kroombit Tops NP Qld 137 K2
Krowera Vic. 47 M11, 48 F8
Ku-ring-gai Chase NSW 7 N4
Ku-ring-gai Chase NP NSW 7 N4, 11 M5, 13 K6
Kudla SA 68 G2
Kuitpo SA 69 F9
Kukerin WA 95 M1, 96 G7, 98 E9
Kulgera NT 79 L1, 121 I11
Kulgun Qld 135 A8
Kulikup WA 94 H5, 96 E9
Kulin WA 96 G6, 98 E8
Kulkami SA 73 N10, 82 F4
Kulkyne Vic. 16 E7, 52 H8
Kulla (Mcilwraith Range) NP (CYPAL) Qld 142 E10
Kulnine Vic. 16 C6, 52 E6, 73 P7
Kulnine East Vic. 16 C6, 52 E6, 73 P7
Kulnura NSW 13 K5
Kulpara SA 73 I6
Kulpi Qld 137 K8
Kulwin Vic. 16 E8, 53 I10
Kumarina Roadhouse WA 100 E7
Kumarl WA 99 I8
Kumbarilla Qld 137 J8
Kumbatine NP NSW 15 L10

Kumbia Qld 137 L7
Kumorna SA 73 M12, 82 F6
Kunama NSW 12 D11, 20 A5, 51 P3
Kunat Vic. 55 L3
Kundabung NSW 15 M10
Kungala NSW 15 N7
Kunghur NSW 15 O2, 137 N11
Kunjin WA 96 F5, 98 E8
Kunlara SA 73 M8, 82 E2
Kununoppin WA 96 F2, 98 E6
Kununurra WA 103 O4, 116 A11, 118 A2
Kunwarara Qld 139 L10
Kupingarri WA 103 L6
Kuraby Qld 133 J6, 135 E6
Kuranda Qld 141 L6
Kuranda NP Qld 141 L5
Kuringup WA 95 N3, 96 H8
Kurmond NSW 6 B1, 10 H4
Kurnell NSW 9 J7, 11 L11, 13 K7
Kurraba Point NSW 5 G1
Kurraca Vic. 55 L9
Kurraca West Vic. 55 L8
Kurrajong NSW 6 A1, 10 G4
Kurrajong Heights NSW 10 G3, 13 J5
Kurrajong Hills NSW 6 A1
Kurralta Park SA 68 C12, 69 C3
Kurri Kurri NSW 13 L4
Kurrimine Beach Qld 141 M8
Kurrimine Beach NP Qld 141 M8
Kurting Vic. 55 M9
Kurumbul Qld 14 H2, 137 I11
Kurunjang Vic. 42 A3
Kurwongbah Qld 130 F4, 131 I5
Kutini–Payamu (Iron Range) NP (CYPAL) Qld 142 E7
Kuttabul Qld 139 K5
Kweda WA 96 F5
Kwiambal NP NSW 15 I3, 137 J12
Kwinana WA 93 C7, 96 B5, 98 C8
Kwinana Beach WA 91 B12, 92 B1
Kwinana Town Centre WA 92 C1
Kwolyin WA 96 F4
Kyabram Vic. 50 D6
Kyalite NSW 16 G8, 53 L10
Kyancutta SA 72 D4, 74 B11
Kybeyan NSW 20 D8, 58 G4
Kybunga SA 73 J6
Kybybolite SA 54 B10, 82 G9
Kydra NSW 20 D8, 58 F4
Kyeamba NSW 12 C10, 17 P10, 51 N3
Kyeema SA 69 E12
Kyeemagh NSW 9 K6
Kyle Bay NSW 9 J7
Kyndalyn Vic. 16 F7, 53 J9
Kyneton Vic. 46 G1, 48 A1, 50 A11, 57 O2
Kynuna Qld 145 J5
Kyogle NSW 15 N3, 137 M12
Kyup Vic. 56 F3
Kyvalley Vic. 50 D6
Kywong NSW 12 A9, 17 N9

La Perouse NSW 9 M7
Laanecoorie Vic. 55 M10
Laang Vic. 57 I8
Labertouche Vic. 47 N8, 48 F6
Labrador Qld 15 O1, 135 G9
Laceys Creek Qld 130 C3
Lachlan Tas. 158 G4, 161 J7
Lachlan Valley NP NSW 17 J7, 53 P7

Lackrana Tas. 160 B10
Lady Barron Tas. 160 B11, 163 P1
Lady Bay Tas. 158 F11, 161 I10
Lady Elliot Island Qld 137 N2
Lady Julia Percy Island Vic. 56 E8
Lady Musgrave Island Qld 137 M1, 139 P12
Ladysmith NSW 12 C10, 17 P10, 51 N1
Laen Vic. 55 I8
Laen North Vic. 55 I7
Laggan NSW 12 G8, 20 E2
Lah Vic. 16 E12, 54 H6
Laharum Vic. 54 G10
Laheys Creek NSW 12 G1, 14 D12
Laidley Qld 134 A12, 137 M9
Lajamanu (Hooker Creek) NT 118 D7
Lake Bathurst NSW 12 G10, 20 E4
Lake Biddy WA 98 F8
Lake Bindegolly NP Qld 147 L8
Lake Boga Vic. 16 H10, 55 M3
Lake Bolac Vic. 57 I4
Lake Buloke Vic. 16 F12, 55 J7
Lake Cargelligo NSW 12 A4, 17 N4
Lake Cathie NSW 15 M11
Lake Charm Vic. 16 H10, 55 M4
Lake Clifton WA 93 C11, 94 C1, 96 B7, 98 C9
Lake Condah Vic. 56 E6
Lake Conjola NSW 13 I11, 20 G5
Lake Cowal NSW 12 C5, 17 P5
Lake Eildon NP Vic. 47 O1, 48 G1, 50 G11
Lake Eppalock Vic. 50 B9, 55 P11
Lake Eyre NP SA 74 F1, 76 H8, 146 A8
Lake Gairdner NP SA 72 E1, 74 C7, 81 P6
Lake Goldsmith Vic. 46 A3, 57 K4
Lake Grace WA 95 N1, 96 H7, 98 E9
Lake Hindmarsh Vic. 16 D11, 54 E6
Lake King WA 98 G8
Lake Leake Tas. 161 M2, 163 M12
Lake Manchester Qld 130 C10, 132 C1
Lake Margaret Tas. 160 D1, 162 D11
Lake Marmal Vic. 16 G12, 55 L6
Lake Muir NP WA 94 H9, 95 I9, 96 E11, 98 D11
Lake Mundi Vic. 56 B3, 82 H11
Lake Munmorah NSW 13 L5
Lake Rowan Vic. 50 G7
Lake Torrens NP SA 74 G4
Lake Tyers Vic. 49 O6
Lake View SA 73 I5
Lake Wivenhoe Qld 130 A7
Lakeland Qld 141 K3
Lakelands WA 92 C7
Lakemba NSW 9 I5
Lakes Entrance Vic. 49 O6
Lakesland NSW 10 E12
Lal Lal Vic. 46 D4, 57 M4
Lalbert Vic. 16 G10, 55 L4
Lalbert Road Vic. 16 G10, 55 L3
Lalla Tas. 163 K7
Lallat Vic. 55 I8
Lalor Vic. 42 H4, 43 I4, 47 J4
Lalor Park NSW 6 G7
Lama Lama NP (CYPAL) Qld 142 F11

Lameroo SA 16 A9, 73 N10, 82 G4
Lamington Qld 15 N1, 135 C11, 137 M11
Lamington NP Qld 15 N2, 135 D12, 137 N11
Lamplough Vic. 55 L12, 57 L1
Lancaster Vic. 50 D6
Lancefield Vic. 46 H1, 48 B1, 50 B12, 57 P2
Lancelin WA 96 A3, 98 B6
Landsborough Qld 134 F5, 137 N8
Landsborough Vic. 55 J11, 57 J1
Landsdale WA 90 D5, 91 C1, 93 C4
Lane Cove NSW 7 K10, 9 K2, 11 L8
Lane Cove NP NSW 7 J7, 9 K1, 11 L7, 13 K6
Lane Cove North NSW 7 K9, 9 K1
Lane Cove West NSW 7 K10, 9 K1
Lanena Tas. 163 J7
Lang Lang Vic. 45 M11, 47 L9, 48 E7
Lang Lang East Vic. 45 O12
Langford WA 90 H12, 91 E6
Langhorne Creek SA 73 K10, 82 C4
Langi Logan Vic. 57 I2
Langkoop Vic. 54 B11, 56 B1, 82 H9
Langley Vic. 50 A11, 55 P12, 57 P2
Langlo Crossing Qld 136 A5, 147 O5
Langloh Tas. 161 I5
Langsborough Vic. 49 I10
Langville Vic. 16 H11, 55 M5
Langwarrin Vic. 44 F7, 47 J8
Langwarrin South Vic. 44 F9
Lankeys Creek NSW 12 C12, 17 P12, 51 N5
Lannercost Qld 141 M10
Lansdowne NSW 6 G12, 8 G4, 13 O1, 15 L12
Lansvale NSW 6 G12, 8 G4
Lapoinya Tas. 162 E5
Lapstone NSW 10 G7
Lara Vic. 46 F7, 48 A5, 57 O7
Laramba NT 120 H4
Larapinta Qld 132 H6
Laravale Qld 15 N1, 135 C10
Largs Bay SA 68 A8
Largs North SA 68 A8, 70 A7, 71 E1, 73 J9, 82 B2
Larpent Vic. 46 A9, 57 K8
Larrakeyah NT 111 A10, 112 A8, 114 C3
Larras Lee NSW 12 F3
Larrimah NT 116 H10, 118 H1
Lascelles Vic. 16 E10, 54 H3
Latham ACT 34 B2
Latham WA 98 C4
Lathlain WA 90 G9, 91 D4
Latrobe Tas. 162 H6
Lauderdale Tas. 157 K10, 159 K6, 161 L7
Laughtondale NSW 11 K2
Launceston Tas. 163 K8
Launching Place Vic. 47 M5, 48 E4
Laura Qld 141 J3
Laura SA 73 J4, 74 H11
Laurel Hill NSW 12 D11, 20 A5, 51 P4
Laurieton NSW 13 O1, 15 L12
Lauriston Vic. 46 F1, 48 A1, 50 A11, 57 O2

Lavender Bay NSW 7 M11, 9 M3
Lavers Hill Vic. 46 A12, 57 K10
Laverton Vic. 42 C9, 46 H6, 48 B4, 57 P6
Laverton WA 99 I2, 101 I12
Laverton North Vic. 42 D8
Lawler Vic. 16 E12, 55 I7
Lawley River NP WA 103 L3
Lawloit Vic. 16 C12, 54 D7
Lawnton Qld 130 H6, 131 I7, 134 F9, 135 D2
Lawrence NSW 15 N5
Lawrence Vic. 46 D1, 57 M2
Lawrence Road NSW 15 N5
Lawrence Rocks Vic. 56 D8
Lawrenny Tas. 161 I5
Lawson ACT 34 D3
Lawson NSW 10 E6, 13 I6
Layard Vic. 46 E9, 57 N8
Le Roy Vic. 49 I8
Leabrook SA 68 F12, 69 F2
Leadville NSW 12 H1, 14 E12
Leaghur Vic. 16 H11, 55 M5
Leanyer NT 112 E2
Learmonth Vic. 46 C2, 57 L3
Learmonth WA 97 B3
Leasingham SA 73 J6
Leawood Gardens SA 69 F3
Lebrina Tas. 163 K6
Leda WA 92 C2, 93 C7
Ledge Point WA 96 A3
Lee Point NT 112 D1
Leederville WA 89 A2, 90 E9, 91 C4
Leeka Tas. 160 A9
Leeman WA 98 A5
Leeming WA 90 G12, 91 D7
Leeor Vic. 16 B12, 54 B7, 82 H7
Leeton NSW 17 N8
Leets Vale NSW 11 J2
Leeuwin–Naturaliste NP WA 94 A7, 96 A9, 98 B10
Leeville NSW 15 N4
Lefroy Tas. 163 J6
Legana Tas. 163 K7
Legerwood Tas. 163 M7
Legume NSW 15 L2, 137 L11
Leichardt Vic. 55 N10
Leichhardt NSW 7 K12, 9 K4
Leichhardt Qld 132 B5, 134 C12, 135 B5, 139 J11
Leigh Creek SA 74 H4
Leigh Creek Vic. 46 D3, 57 M4
Leighton SA 73 K5
Leinster WA 98 G1, 100 G11
Leitchville Vic. 17 I11, 50 A4, 55 O5
Leith Tas. 162 H6
Lemnos Vic. 50 E7
Lemon Rock Tas. 161 O3
Lemon Tree Passage NSW 13 M4
Lemont Tas. 161 L4
Lenah Valley Tas. 156 A6
Leneva Vic. 51 K6
Lennox Head NSW 15 O3, 137 N12
Leonay NSW 6 A7
Leongatha Vic. 47 N11, 48 G8
Leongatha South Vic. 47 N11, 48 F9
Leonora WA 98 H2
Leopold Vic. 46 G8, 48 A6, 57 O7
Leppington NSW 8 B5, 10 H9
Leprena Tas. 161 I11
Leschenault WA 94 D3

Leslie Manor Vic. 46 A7, 57 K7
Leslie Vale Tas. 156 A12, 158 H6, 161 K7
Lesmurdie WA 91 G5
Lesmurdie Falls NP WA 91 H5, 93 D5, 96 C5, 98 C7
Lesueur NP WA 96 A1, 98 A5
Lethbridge Vic. 46 E6, 57 N6
Lethbridge Park NSW 6 D6
Leumeah NSW 8 D8, 10 H11
Leura NSW 10 D5, 13 I6
Levendale Tas. 159 L1, 161 L5
Lewis Ponds NSW 12 G4
Lewisham NSW 7 K12, 9 K4
Lewisham Tas. 159 L5, 161 L7
Lewiston SA 68 D1, 70 B5
Lexia WA 90 E4
Lexton Vic. 46 B1, 57 L2
Leyburn Qld 137 K10
Liawenee Tas. 161 I1, 163 I11
Liberty Grove NSW 7 J10, 9 J2
Licola Vic. 49 J4
Lidcombe NSW 7 I10, 9 I2, 11 K8
Liena Tas. 162 G8
Lietinna Tas. 163 L6
Liffey Tas. 163 J9
Lightning Ridge NSW 14 B3, 136 E12
Likkaparta NT 119 J9
Lileah Tas. 162 C4
Lilford Rock WA 96 E12, 98 D11
Lilli Pilli NSW 9 J9
Lillicur Vic. 55 L12, 57 L1
Lillimur Vic. 16 B12, 54 C7, 82 H7
Lillimur South Vic. 16 B12, 54 C7, 82 H7
Lilydale Tas. 163 K7
Lilydale Vic. 43 O6, 47 L5, 48 E4
Lilyfield NSW 7 L11, 9 K3
Lilyvale NSW 8 G12, 9 I12
Lima Vic. 50 G9
Lima East Vic. 50 G9
Lima South Vic. 50 G10
Limeburners Creek NSW 13 M3
Limeburners Creek NP NSW 15 M11
Limekilns NSW 12 H4
Limestone Vic. 47 M1, 48 E1, 50 E12
Limestone Ridges Qld 132 A11, 135 B7
Limevale Qld 15 J2, 137 J11
Limmen NP NT 117 K9, 119 K1
Limpet Rock WA 99 I9
Lincoln NP SA 72 D9
Lincolnfields SA 73 I6
Lind NP Vic. 20 B11, 58 D10
Linda Tas. 160 E1, 162 E11
Lindeman Island Qld 139 K4
Lindeman Islands NP Qld 139 K4
Linden NSW 10 F6
Linden Park SA 68 E12, 69 E2
Lindenow Vic. 49 M5
Lindenow South Vic. 49 M5
Lindfield NSW 7 K9, 9 K1
Lindisfarne Tas. 156 E5, 159 J5, 161 K7
Lindsay Point Vic. 16 B5, 52 C5, 73 O7, 82 H1
Linga Vic. 16 C9, 52 E11, 54 E1
Linley Point NSW 7 K10, 9 K2
Linton Vic. 46 B4, 57 L4
Linville Qld 134 A4, 137 M7

Linwood SA 70 D3, 73 J7
Lipson SA 72 E7
Lisarow NSW 11 O2
Lisle Tas. 163 L7
Lismore NSW 15 O3, 137 N12
Lismore Vic. 46 A6, 57 K6
Liston NSW 15 L2, 137 L11
Litchfield Vic. 16 F12, 55 I7
Litchfield NP NT 114 D9, 116 D6
Littabella NP Qld 137 M2
Little Bay NSW 9 M7
Little Billabong NSW 12 C11, 17 P11, 51 N3
Little Desert NP Vic. 16 C12, 54 B8, 82 H8
Little Grove WA 95 M11, 96 G12, 98 E11
Little Hampton Vic. 46 F2, 48 A2, 50 A12, 57 O3
Little Hard Hills Vic. 46 C4
Little Hartley NSW 10 C3
Little Island WA 93 B4
Little River Vic. 46 G6, 48 A5, 57 O6
Little Snowy Creek Vic. 51 L8
Little Swanport Tas. 161 N4
Little Topar Roadhouse NSW 18 D9
Little Wobby NSW 7 O1
Littlehampton SA 70 D10, 71 H3
Liverpool NSW 6 F12, 8 F4, 11 J9, 13 J7, 20 H1
Livingstone NP NSW 12 B10, 17 P10, 51 M2
Lizard Island Qld 141 L1
Lizard Island NP Qld 141 L1
Llandaff Tas. 161 O2, 163 O11
Llandeilo Vic. 46 E3, 57 N4
Llandilo NSW 6 B6
Llanelly Vic. 55 M10
Llangothlin NSW 15 K7
Llewellyn Siding Tas. 161 M1, 163 M10
Lobethal SA 70 E8, 71 H2, 73 K9, 82 C3
Loccota Tas. 160 B11, 163 O1
Loch Vic. 47 M10, 48 F8
Loch Sport Vic. 49 M6
Lochern NP Qld 145 L11
Lochiel NSW 58 H7
Lochiel SA 73 I6
Lochinvar NSW 13 L3
Lochnagar Qld 138 D10, 145 P10
Lock SA 72 D5, 74 C12
Lockhart NSW 12 A10, 17 N10, 51 K1
Lockhart River Qld 142 E7
Lockington Qld 138 H11
Lockington Vic. 17 I12, 50 B6, 55 P7
Lockleys SA 68 B11, 69 B1
Lockridge WA 90 G7, 91 E2
Locksley NSW 12 H5
Locksley Vic. 50 E9
Lockwood Vic. 55 N10
Lockwood South Vic. 55 N10
Lockyer NP Qld 137 L9
Locust Rock Qld 140 A6, 143 D3
Loddon Vale Vic. 16 H11, 55 N6
Loftus NSW 8 H8, 9 I8, 11 K11
Logan Vic. 55 L9
Logan Central Qld 133 J7
Logan Reserve Qld 133 J9

Logan Village Qld 133 I10, 135 E7
Loganholme Qld 133 K9
Loganlea Qld 133 K9, 135 E6
Logie Brae NSW 17 L10, 50 F2
Loira Tas. 163 J7
Lombadina WA 102 H6
Londonderry NSW 6 B3, 10 H5
Londrigan Vic. 51 I7
Long Beach NSW 20 F6
Long Flat NSW 12 G11, 13 I8, 15 L11, 20 E5
Long Jetty NSW 11 P2, 13 L5
Long Plains SA 70 A2, 73 J7, 82 B1
Long Plains Vic. 55 J2
Long Pocket Qld 141 L12
Long Point NSW 8 E7
Long Rock Qld 139 K4
Longerenong Vic. 54 G9
Longford Tas. 163 K9
Longford Vic. 49 K7
Longlea Vic. 50 A9, 55 O10
Longley Tas. 158 H6, 161 J7
Longreach Qld 138 B10, 145 N10
Longueville NSW 7 L10, 9 L2
Longwarry Vic. 47 N8, 48 F6
Longwood SA 69 G5
Longwood Vic. 50 E9
Longwood East Vic. 50 E9
Lonnavale Tas. 158 E6, 161 I7
Lonsdale SA 69 A7, 70 A11, 71 E4, 73 J9
Looma WA 103 J7
Loongana Tas. 162 F7
Loongana WA 99 N5
Loorana Tas. 161 O11
Lorinna Tas. 162 G8
Lorne NSW 15 L11
Lorne Vic. 46 D11, 57 M9
Lorquon Vic. 16 C12, 54 E6
Lorquon West Vic. 54 E6
Lostock NSW 13 L2
Lota Qld 131 M12, 133 M2
Lottah Tas. 163 O7
Louisville Tas. 159 N1, 161 M5
Louth NSW 19 K6
Louth Bay SA 72 D8
Loveday SA 73 N7
Low Head Tas. 163 J6
Low Rock NT 117 L8
Low Rock WA 99 I9, 103 J3
Lowaldie SA 73 M9, 82 E3
Lowan Vale SA 16 A12, 54 A6, 82 G7
Lowanna NSW 15 M7
Lowbank SA 73 M7, 82 F1
Lowden WA 94 E4, 96 C8
Lowdina Tas. 159 J2, 161 K5
Lower Acacia Creek NSW 15 L2
Lower Barrington Tas. 162 H7
Lower Beulah Tas. 162 H8
Lower Boro NSW 12 H10, 20 E4
Lower Bucca NSW 15 N7
Lower Chittering WA 93 D2, 96 C4
Lower Creek NSW 15 L9
Lower Gellibrand Vic. 57 J10
Lower Glenelg NP Vic. 56 B6, 82 H12
Lower Goulburn NP Vic. 17 K12, 50 D5
Lower Hermitage SA 68 H8
Lower Heytesbury Vic. 57 I9
Lower Light SA 68 A1
Lower Mangrove NSW 11 M2
Lower Marshes Tas. 161 K4

Lower Mitcham SA 69 D3
Lower Mookerawa NSW 12 G3
Lower Mount Hicks Tas. 162 F5
Lower Norton Vic. 54 F10
Lower Plenty Vic. 43 K6
Lower Quipolly NSW 14 H10
Lower Turners Marsh Tas. 163 K6
Lowesdale NSW 17 M11, 51 I4
Lowlands NSW 10 H4, 17 L3
Lowmead Qld 137 L2
Lowood Qld 134 B10, 135 A4, 137 M9
Lowther NSW 10 B4, 13 I6
Loxton SA 16 A6, 52 A7, 73 N8, 82 G2
Loxton North SA 16 A6, 52 A7, 73 N8, 82 G1
Loyetea Tas. 162 F7
Lubeck Vic. 54 H9
Lucas Heights NSW 8 G8, 11 J11
Lucaston Tas. 158 G6, 161 J7
Lucinda Qld 141 M10
Lucindale SA 82 F9
Lucknow NSW 12 G5
Lucknow Vic. 49 M5
Lucky Bay SA 72 G5
Lucyvale Vic. 51 N7
Luddenham NSW 6 A9, 8 A2, 10 G8
Ludlow WA 94 C5, 96 B9
Ludmilla NT 112 B5
Lue NSW 12 H3
Lugarno NSW 8 H7, 9 I6
Lughrata Tas. 160 B10
Lulworth Tas. 163 K5
Lunawanna Tas. 158 H11, 161 J10
Lune River Tas. 158 E12, 161 I10
Lurg Vic. 50 H8
Lurg Upper Vic. 50 H8
Lurnea NSW 8 F4
Luscombe Qld 133 K11
Lutana Tas. 156 D5
Lutwyche Qld 131 I11, 133 I1
Lyme Regis Tas. 163 O4
Lymington Tas. 158 G9, 161 J9
Lymwood Tas. 161 P12
Lynbrook Vic. 44 H5
Lynchford Tas. 160 D2, 162 D11
Lynchs Creek NSW 15 N2
Lyndhurst NSW 12 F5
Lyndhurst SA 74 H3
Lyndhurst Vic. 44 G5, 47 K7, 48 D6
Lyndoch SA 70 E5, 73 K8, 82 C2
Lyneham ACT 34 E3
Lynton SA 69 D4
Lynwood WA 90 G12, 91 E6
Lyons ACT 34 C7
Lyons NT 112 E2
Lyons Qld 132 C9
Lyons Vic. 56 D6, 82 H12
Lyonville Vic. 46 F2, 57 O3
Lyrup SA 16 A6, 52 A6, 73 N7, 82 G1
Lysterfield Vic. 43 N11, 44 H2, 45 I1, 47 K6, 48 D5
Lysterfield South Vic. 43 M12, 44 H2, 45 I2
Lytton Qld 131 L11, 133 K1

Ma'alpiku Island NP (CYPAL) Qld 142 E7
Maaroom Qld 137 N5
McAlinden WA 94 F4, 96 D8

Macalister Qld 137 J8
Macalister Range NP Qld 141 L5
Macarthur ACT 34 E10
Macarthur Vic. 56 F6
Macclesfield SA 70 D11, 71 H5, 73 K10, 82 C4
Macclesfield Vic. 45 L1, 47 L6, 48 E5
McCullys Gap NSW 13 K2
MacDonald Park SA 68 E3
McDowall Qld 130 H10, 131 I9
Macedon Vic. 46 G2, 48 B2, 50 B12, 57 P3
McGraths Hill NSW 6 E2, 11 I5
Macgregor ACT 34 B2
Macgregor Qld 133 I5
McHarg Creek SA 69 G12
McIntyre Vic. 55 M9
Mackay Qld 139 K5
McKellar ACT 34 D3
Mackenzie Qld 133 K5
McKenzie Creek Vic. 54 G9
McKinlay Qld 143 G12, 145 I4
Mckinnon Vic. 43 I11, 44 C1
Macks Creek Vic. 49 I9
Macksville NSW 15 M9
Maclagan Qld 137 K8
McLaren Flat SA 69 C10, 70 B12, 71 F5
McLaren Vale SA 69 B9, 70 B12, 71 E5, 73 J10, 82 B4
Maclean NSW 15 N5
Macleod Vic. 43 J5
McLoughlins Beach Vic. 49 J9
McMahons Creek Vic. 47 N5, 48 F4
McMahons Point NSW 5 C1, 7 M11, 9 M3
McMahons Reef NSW 12 E8, 20 B2
McMillans Vic. 50 A4, 55 O5
McMinns Lagoon NT 113 O12
Macorna Vic. 16 H11, 55 N5
Macquarie ACT 34 C4
Macquarie Fields NSW 8 E6, 11 I10
Macquarie Links NSW 8 E6
Macquarie Park NSW 7 K8, 9 K1
Macquarie Pass NP NSW 13 J9, 20 G3
Macquarie Plains Tas. 158 F3, 161 I6
Macrossan Qld 138 F2
Macs Cove Vic. 47 P1, 48 H1, 50 H12
Madalya Vic. 49 I9
Maddington WA 91 F6, 93 D6
Madeley WA 90 D5, 91 B1
Madora WA 93 C9, 96 B6
Madora Bay WA 92 C8
Madura WA 99 N6
Madura Roadhouse WA 99 N6
Mafeking Vic. 56 H2
Maffra Vic. 49 K6
Maggea SA 73 M8, 82 F2
Magill SA 68 F11, 69 F1
Magistrate Rocks WA 99 I9
Magnetic Island Qld 138 G1, 141 N11
Magnetic Island NP Qld 138 G1, 141 N11
Magpie Vic. 46 C3
Magra Tas. 158 G3, 161 J6
Magrath Flat SA 73 L12, 82 D6
Maianbar NSW 9 J10, 11 K12

Maida Vale WA 91 G3
Maiden Gully Vic. 55 O10
Maidenwell Qld 137 L7
Maidstone Vic. 42 F7
Mailors Flat Vic. 56 G7
Maimuru NSW 12 D7, 20 B1
Main Beach Qld 15 O1, 135 G9, 137 N10
Main Lead Vic. 46 A1, 57 K3
Main Range NP Qld 15 M1, 137 L10
Maindample Vic. 50 G11
Maitland NSW 13 L3
Maitland SA 72 H7
Major Plains Vic. 50 G7
Majorca Vic. 55 M12, 57 M1
Majors Creek NSW 12 G11, 20 E5
Malaan NP Qld 141 L7
Malabar NSW 9 M6
Malaga WA 90 F6, 91 C2
Malak NT 112 F3
Malanda Qld 141 L7
Malbina Tas. 158 H4, 161 J6
Malbon Qld 143 E12, 144 G4
Malcolm WA 98 H2
Maldon NSW 10 F12
Maldon Vic. 55 N11, 57 N1
Maleny Qld 134 E4, 137 N7
Maleny NP Qld 134 E3, 137 M7
Malinong SA 73 L11, 82 D5
Mallacoota Vic. 20 D11, 58 G11
Mallala SA 70 B3, 73 J7, 82 B1
Mallan NSW 16 H9, 53 M11, 55 M1
Mallanganee NSW 15 M3, 137 M12
Mallanganee NP NSW 15 M3, 137 M12
Mallee Cliffs NP NSW 16 F6, 52 H6, 53 I6
Mallum Vic. 50 H9
Malmsbury Vic. 48 A1, 50 A11, 55 O12, 57 O2
Malpas SA 16 A7, 52 A8, 73 N9, 82 G2
Malua Bay NSW 12 H12, 20 F6
Malvern SA 69 D3
Malvern Vic. 43 I9
Malvern East Vic. 43 J11
Malyalling WA 96 F6
Mambray Creek SA 73 I3, 74 G10
Manangatang Vic. 16 F8, 53 J11
Manara NSW 17 I1, 18 H12
Mandagery NSW 12 E4
Mandogalup WA 91 C11
Mandorah NT 114 C3, 116 D4
Mandurah WA 92 C10, 93 C9, 96 B6, 98 C8
Mandurama NSW 12 F5
Mandurang Vic. 50 A9, 55 O10
Mangalo SA 72 F5, 74 E12
Mangalore Tas. 159 I2, 161 K6
Mangalore Vic. 50 D10
Mangana Tas. 163 N9
Mango Hill Qld 131 J6, 134 F9, 135 E2
Mangoola NSW 13 J2
Mangoplah NSW 12 B10, 17 O10, 51 M2
Mangrove Creek NSW 11 M1, 13 K5
Mangrove Mountain NSW 11 M1, 13 K5
Manguri SA 79 N10
Manildra NSW 12 F4

Manilla NSW 14 H8
Maningrida NT 117 J3
Manjimup WA 94 F8, 96 D10, 98 C10
Manly NSW 7 N9, 9 N1, 11 M8, 13 K6
Manly Qld 131 L12, 133 L2, 134 G11, 135 E4
Manly Vale NSW 7 N9, 9 N1
Manly West Qld 131 L12, 133 L2
Manmanning WA 96 E2, 98 D6
Manmoyi NT 117 J4
Mannahill SA 73 M2, 75 L9
Mannanarie SA 73 J3, 75 I11
Mannerim Vic. 46 G8, 48 A6
Mannering Park NSW 13 L5
Mannibadar Vic. 46 A4, 57 K5
Manning WA 90 F11, 91 D6
Manning Point NSW 13 O1, 15 L12
Manningham SA 68 E10
Manns Beach Vic. 49 J10
Mannum SA 70 H9, 73 L9, 82 D3
Manobalai NSW 13 J1, 14 H12
Manoora SA 73 K6
Mansfield Qld 133 J4
Mansfield Vic. 50 H11
Mansfield Park SA 68 C9
Mantung SA 73 M8, 82 F2
Manumbar Qld 137 M6
Many Peaks Qld 137 L2
Manyallaluk NT 116 G8
Manypeaks WA 95 N10, 96 H11
Mapleton Qld 134 F3
Mapleton Falls NP Qld 134 E3, 137 N7
Mapoon Qld 142 B5
Mara NT 117 M11, 119 M2
Maralinga SA 80 H3
Marama SA 73 M10, 82 F4
Maranboy NT 116 G8
Marangaroo WA 90 D6, 91 B1, 93 C4
Marathon Qld 138 A4, 145 M4
Maraylya NSW 6 G1, 11 J4
Marayong NSW 6 F7
Marbelup WA 95 L11, 96 G11
Marble Bar WA 100 E2, 102 E12
Marble Hill SA 68 H12, 69 H1
Marburg Qld 134 B11, 135 A5, 137 M9
Marchagee WA 98 B5
Marcoola Qld 134 G3
Marcus Beach Qld 134 H2
Marcus Hill Vic. 46 G9, 48 A7
Mardella WA 92 E2, 93 D7
Marden SA 68 E11, 69 E1
Mareeba Qld 141 L6
Marengo NSW 15 L7
Marengo Vic. 46 B12, 57 L11
Marengo Reefs Marine Sanctuary Vic. 46 B12, 57 L11
Margaret River WA 94 B7, 96 B10, 98 B10
Margate Qld 131 L6
Margate Tas. 159 I7, 161 K8
Maria Creek NP Qld 141 M8
Maria Island NP Tas. 159 O3, 161 N6
Maria NP NSW 15 M10
Mariala NP NSW 147 N4
Marian Qld 139 K5
Maribyrnong Vic. 42 F6
Mariginiup WA 90 C3

Marino SA 69 B5
Marion SA 69 C4, 70 B9, 71 E3
Marion Bay SA 72 G10
Marion Bay Tas. 159 N5, 161 M7
Markwell NSW 13 N2
Markwood Vic. 51 I8
Marla SA 79 M5
Marlborough Qld 139 L9
Marlee NSW 13 N1, 15 K12
Marleston SA 68 C12, 69 C2
Marlo Vic. 20 A12, 58 B11
Marlow Lagoon NT 112 H12, 113 J9
Marma Vic. 54 H9
Marmion WA 90 C6, 91 A1
Marmion Marine Park WA 93 B4, 96 B4, 98 B7
Marmor Qld 139 M11
Marnoo Vic. 55 I9
Marong Vic. 55 N10
Maroochydore Qld 134 G4, 137 N7
Maroon Qld 15 N1, 135 A10, 137 M10
Maroona Vic. 57 I3
Maroota NSW 11 K3, 13 K5
Maroubra NSW 9 M6
Marp Vic. 56 C5, 82 H12
Marrabel SA 73 K7
Marradong WA 93 G11, 96 D7
Marralum NT 103 P3, 116 B10, 118 B1
Marramarra NP NSW 7 K2, 11 K3, 13 K5
Marrangaroo NSW 10 B1, 13 I5
Marrangaroo NP NSW 10 B1, 13 I5
Marrar NSW 12 B9, 17 P9
Marrara NT 112 D4
Marrawah Tas. 162 A4
Marraweeny Vic. 50 F9
Marree SA 74 H1, 76 H12, 146 A12
Marrickville NSW 7 K12, 9 K5, 11 L9
Marrinup WA 93 E10
Marryatville SA 68 E12, 69 E2
Marsden NSW 12 C5, 17 P5
Marsden Qld 133 J7
Marsden Park NSW 6 D6
Marsfield NSW 7 J8, 9 J1
Marshall Vic. 46 F8, 48 A6, 57 O7
Marshdale NSW 13 M3
Martin WA 91 G6
Martindale NSW 13 J2
Martins Creek NSW 13 L3
Marton Qld 141 L3
Marulan NSW 12 H9, 20 F3
Marulan South NSW 12 H9, 20 F3
Marungi Vic. 17 L12, 50 F6
Marvel Loch WA 98 F6
Mary River NP NT 114 H2, 115 J1, 116 E4
Mary River Roadhouse NT 115 L10, 116 F6
Maryborough Qld 137 N5
Maryborough Vic. 55 M11, 57 M1
Marybrook WA 94 B6
Maryfarms Qld 141 K5
Maryknoll Vic. 45 N5, 47 M7, 48 E6
Maryland NP NSW 15 L2, 137 L11
Marysville Vic. 47 N3, 48 F3
Maryvale NSW 12 F2
Mascot NSW 9 K5, 11 L9
Maslin Beach SA 69 A11, 70 A12, 71 E5

Massey Vic. 16 F12, 55 I7
Matakana NSW 17 M3
Mataranka NT 116 H9
Matcham NSW 11 O3
Matheson NSW 15 J5
Mathinna Tas. 163 N8
Mathoura NSW 17 J11, 50 D4
Matlock Vic. 47 P4, 48 H4
Matong NSW 12 B8, 17 O8, 20 B9, 58 D6
Matraville NSW 9 M6
Maude NSW 17 I7, 53 P8
Maude Vic. 46 E6, 57 N6
Maudsland Qld 135 F9
Mawbanna Tas. 162 D4
Mawson ACT 34 D8
Mawson WA 96 E5, 98 D7
Mawson Lakes SA 68 D8
Maxwelton Qld 145 K3
Mayanup WA 94 G6, 96 D9, 98 D10
Mayberry Tas. 162 H8
Maydena Tas. 158 D3, 160 H6
Maylands SA 68 E11, 69 E1
Maylands WA 90 F8, 91 D3, 93 C5
Mayrung NSW 17 K10, 50 E2
Mays Hill NSW 6 H10, 8 H1
Mazeppa NP Qld 138 G7
Meadow Creek Vic. 51 I8
Meadow Heights Vic. 42 G3
Meadow Springs WA 92 C8
Meadowbank NSW 7 J10, 9 J2, 11 K8
Meadowbrook Qld 133 K7
Meadows SA 69 H8, 70 D11, 71 G5, 73 J10, 82 C4
Meandarra Qld 136 H8
Meander Tas. 163 I9
Meatian Vic. 16 G10, 55 K3
Mebbin NP NSW 15 N2, 137 N11
Meckering WA 96 E4, 98 D7
Medina WA 91 C12, 92 C1
Medindie SA 67 F1, 68 D11, 69 D1
Medindie Gardens SA 68 D11, 69 D1
Medlow Bath NSW 10 C5, 13 I6
Meekatharra WA 97 H9, 100 E10
Meelon WA 93 D10
Meeniyan Vic. 47 O12, 48 G9
Meerlieu Vic. 49 L6
Meerschaum Vale NSW 15 O4, 137 N12
Megalong NSW 10 C5
Megan NSW 15 M7
Meggi–Kudulug Qld 142 C2
Melaleuca Tas. 160 F10
Melaleuca WA 90 F2
Melba ACT 34 C2
Melbourne Vic. 41 E5, 42 G8, 47 I5, 48 C4
Melbourne Airport Vic. 42 E3
Meldale Qld 134 G7
Mella Tas. 162 C4
Mellis Vic. 54 H7
Melros WA 93 B10
Melrose SA 73 I3, 74 H10
Melrose Tas. 162 H6
Melrose Park NSW 7 J9, 9 J1
Melrose Park SA 69 D3
Melsonby (Gaarraay) NP Qld 141 K2
Melton SA 73 I6
Melton Vic. 42 A3, 46 G4, 48 B3, 57 P5
Melton Mowbray Tas. 161 K4

Melton South Vic. 42 A4, 46 G4, 48 B4, 57 P5
Melville WA 90 D12, 91 B7, 93 C6, 95 M11
Melville Forest Vic. 56 E3
Melville Island NT 116 C2
Memana Tas. 160 B10
Memerambi Qld 137 L6
Mena Creek Qld 141 M8
Mena Park Vic. 46 A3, 57 K4
Menai NSW 8 G7, 11 J11
Menangle NSW 8 A11, 10 G12, 13 J7, 20 H1
Menangle Park NSW 8 A9, 10 H11
Mendooran NSW 14 D11
Mengha Tas. 162 D4
Menindee NSW 18 E11
Meningie SA 73 L11, 82 D5
Menora WA 90 F8, 91 C3
Mentone Vic. 44 D3, 47 J7, 48 C5
Menzies WA 98 H3
Menzies Creek Vic. 43 P11, 45 K1, 47 L6
Mepunga East Vic. 56 H8
Mepunga West Vic. 56 H8
Merah North NSW 14 E6
Merbein Vic. 16 D6, 52 G6
Merbein South Vic. 16 D6, 52 G6
Merbein West Vic. 52 G5
Mercunda SA 73 M8, 82 F2
Merebene NSW 14 D7
Meredith Vic. 46 E5, 57 N5
Meribah SA 16 B7, 52 B8, 73 O8, 82 G2
Merildin SA 73 K6
Merimal Qld 139 M10
Merimbula NSW 20 E9, 58 H7
Merinda Qld 139 I3
Meringo NSW 20 F7
Meringur Vic. 16 C6, 52 D7, 73 P8
Meringur North Vic. 16 C6, 52 D6, 73 P7
Merino Vic. 56 D4
Mermaid Beach Qld 135 G10
Mernda Vic. 43 J1, 47 J4, 48 D3
Meroo NP NSW 13 I11, 20 F5
Merredin WA 96 G3, 98 E6
Merri Marine Sanctuary Vic. 56 G8
Merriang Vic. 51 J8
Merriang South Vic. 51 J9
Merricks North Vic. 44 D12, 47 J10, 48 C7
Merrigum Vic. 50 D7
Merrijig Vic. 48 H1, 50 H11
Merrimac Qld 135 F10
Merrinee Vic. 16 D6, 52 F7
Merrinee North Vic. 16 D6, 52 F6
Merriton SA 73 I5, 74 H12
Merriwa NSW 13 J1, 14 G12
Merriwa WA 90 A1
Merriwagga NSW 17 L5
Merrygoen NSW 14 D11
Merrylands NSW 6 G10, 8 H1, 11 J8
Merrylands West NSW 6 G10, 8 G2
Merseylea Tas. 162 H7
Merton Vic. 50 F10
Metcalfe Vic. 50 A11, 55 O12, 57 O1
Metricup WA 94 B6
Metung Vic. 49 N6
Meunna Tas. 162 D5

Mewstone Tas. 160 G12
Mia Mia Vic. 50 B10, 55 P11, 57 P1
Miallo Qld 141 L5
Miami Qld 135 G10
Miandetta NSW 19 O10
Michael Creek Qld 141 L10
Michaelmas and Upolu Cays NP Qld 141 M5
Michelago NSW 12 F12, 20 C6, 31 E10
Mickett Creek NT 112 H1, 113 I1
Mickleham Vic. 42 F1, 47 I3, 48 C3
Middle Beach SA 68 A1
Middle Brother NP NSW 13 O1, 15 L12
Middle Cove NSW 7 M9, 9 M1
Middle Creek Vic. 57 K3
Middle Dural NSW 7 I5, 11 K5
Middle Harbour NSW 7 M8, 9 M1
Middle Indigo Vic. 51 J6
Middle Park Qld 132 F4
Middle Park Vic. 42 G9
Middle Point NT 114 F3, 116 E4
Middle Rock WA 99 I10
Middle Swan WA 90 H6, 91 F2, 93 D4
Middlemount Qld 139 J9
Middleton Qld 145 I7
Middleton SA 71 G8
Middleton Tas. 158 H9, 161 J9
Middleton Grange NSW 6 D12, 8 D4
Middlingbank NSW 20 B7, 58 D3
Midge Point Qld 139 J4
Midgee Qld 139 M11
Midgee SA 72 G4, 74 F12
Midgegooroo NP WA 93 D6, 96 C5, 98 C8
Midland WA 90 H7, 91 F2, 93 D4, 96 C5, 98 C7
Midvale WA 91 G2
Midway Point Tas. 157 N2, 159 K4, 161 L7
Miena Tas. 161 I1, 163 I11
Miepoll Vic. 50 E8
Miga Lake Vic. 54 D10
Mil Lel SA 56 A4, 82 G11
Mila NSW 20 C10, 58 E8
Milabena Tas. 162 E5
Milang SA 73 K10, 82 C4
Milawa Vic. 51 I8
Milbong Qld 132 A12
Milbrulong NSW 12 A10, 17 O10, 51 K1
Mildura Vic. 16 E6, 52 G6
Mile End SA 67 A8, 68 C12, 69 C1
Mile End South SA 68 C12, 69 C2
Miles Qld 137 I7
Milguy NSW 14 G4, 136 H12
Milikapiti NT 116 D2
Miling WA 96 C1, 98 C5
Milingimbi NT 117 K3
Mill Park Vic. 43 I4
Millaa Millaa Qld 141 L7
Millaroo Qld 138 H3
Millbrook Vic. 46 E3
Millendon WA 90 H5
Miller NSW 6 E12, 8 E4
Millers Point NSW 5 C4, 7 L11, 9 L3
Millfield NSW 13 L4
Millgrove Vic. 47 M5, 48 F4
Millicent SA 82 F11

Millie NSW 14 F5
Millmerran Qld 137 K9
Millner NT 112 D3
Milloo Vic. 50 A6, 55 O8
Millstream–Chichester NP WA 97 F2, 100 C3
Millstream Falls NP Qld 141 L7
Millswood SA 69 D3
Millthorpe NSW 12 G5
Milltown Vic. 56 D6
Millwood NSW 12 B9, 17 O9
Milman Qld 139 M10
Milora Qld 132 A11
Milparinka NSW 18 D3, 75 P2, 146 H12
Milperra NSW 8 G5
Milsons Passage NSW 7 M1
Milsons Point NSW 5 D1, 7 M11, 9 M3
Miltalie SA 72 F5, 74 E12
Milton NSW 13 I11, 20 G5
Milton Qld 129 A7, 130 H12, 131 I12, 132 H2, 133 I2
Milvale NSW 12 D7, 20 A1
Milyakburra NT 117 M7
Milyeannup NP WA 94 D8, 96 C10, 98 C10
Mimili SA 79 K5
Mimmindie Vic. 16 H12, 55 M6
Mimosa NSW 12 B8, 17 P8
Mimosa Rocks NP NSW 20 E9, 58 H6
Minamia NT 117 J11, 119 J2
Mincha Vic. 16 H11, 55 N6
Minchinbury NSW 6 D8
Mindarie SA 73 M9, 82 F3
Mindarie WA 90 A3
Minden Qld 134 B11
Mindiyarra SA 73 M9, 82 E3
Miners Rest Vic. 46 C2, 57 M3
Minerva Hills NP Qld 138 H12, 139 I12
Mingary SA 18 A10, 73 O1, 75 M8
Mingay Vic. 46 A5, 57 K5
Mingela Qld 138 G2
Mingenew WA 98 B4
Mingoola NSW 15 K3, 137 K12
Minhamite Vic. 56 G6
Minilya Roadhouse WA 97 B6
Minimay Vic. 54 C9, 82 H8
Mininera Vic. 57 I4
Minjary NP NSW 12 D10, 20 A4, 51 P2
Minjilang NT 116 G1
Minlaton SA 72 H8
Minnie Water NSW 15 N6
Minniging WA 96 E7
Minnipa SA 72 C3, 74 A10, 81 P10
Minnivale WA 96 E3
Minore NSW 12 E1, 14 C12
Mintabie SA 79 L5
Mintaro SA 73 J6
Minto NSW 8 D7, 11 I10
Minto Heights NSW 8 E7
Minyerri NT 117 J10, 119 J1
Minyip Vic. 54 H8
Miowera NSW 19 P10
Miralie Vic. 53 L11, 55 L1
Miram Vic. 16 C12, 54 C7, 82 H7
Miram South Vic. 54 D7, 82 H7
Miranda NSW 9 J8, 11 K11
Mirani Qld 139 K5
Mirannie NSW 13 L2
Mirboo Vic. 47 P11, 48 H8

Mirboo North Vic. 47 P11, 48 G8
Miriam Vale Qld 137 L2
Mirima NP WA 103 O4, 116 A11, 118 A2
Mirimbah Vic. 49 I1, 51 I11
Miriwinni Qld 141 M7
Mirrabooka WA 90 E6, 91 C2
Mirranatwa Vic. 56 G3
Mirrngadja Village NT 117 K4
Mirrool NSW 12 B7, 17 O7
Missabotti NSW 15 M8
Mission Beach Qld 141 M8
Mistake Creek NT 103 O6, 118 A4
Mitcham SA 69 E3, 70 B9, 71 F2
Mitcham Vic. 43 L8
Mitchell ACT 31 E4, 34 E3
Mitchell NT 113 K12
Mitchell Qld 136 E6
Mitchell Park SA 69 C4
Mitchell River NP Vic. 49 L4
Mitchell River NP WA 103 K3
Mitchellville SA 72 G5, 74 F12
Mitchelton Qld 130 H10, 132 H1
Mitiamo Vic. 17 I12, 50 A6, 55 O7
Mitirinchi Island NP (CYPAL) Qld 142 F6
Mitre Vic. 54 E9
Mitta Mitta Vic. 51 M9
Mittagong NSW 13 I8, 20 G2
Mittyack Vic. 16 F9, 53 I11, 55 I1
Moa Island Qld 142 C1
Moama NSW 17 J12, 50 C5
Moana SA 69 A10, 73 J10, 82 B4
Mockinya Vic. 54 F10
Moculta SA 70 G4
Modanville NSW 15 O3
Modbury SA 68 F9
Modbury Heights SA 68 F8
Modbury North SA 68 F8
Modella Vic. 45 P9, 47 M9, 48 F7
Modewarre Vic. 46 E9, 57 N8
Moe Vic. 47 P9, 48 H7
Moema NP NSW 14 F6
Moffat Vic. 56 H5
Mogendoura NSW 20 F6
Moggill Qld 132 E5, 134 D12, 135 C5
Mogil Mogil NSW 14 D3, 136 F12
Moglonemby Vic. 50 F8
Mogo NSW 20 F6
Mogriguy NSW 12 F1, 14 C12
Mogriguy NP NSW 12 F1, 14 C12
Mogumber WA 96 C3
Moil NT 112 E3
Moina Tas. 162 G8
Moira NSW 17 J11, 50 C4
Mokepilly Vic. 54 H11, 56 H1
Mokine WA 93 G3
Mole Creek Tas. 162 H8
Mole Creek Karst NP Tas. 162 G8
Mole River NSW 15 K4, 137 K12
Molesworth Tas. 158 H4
Molesworth Vic. 47 M1, 48 F1, 50 F11
Moliagul Vic. 55 L10
Molle Islands NP Qld 139 K3
Mollongghip Vic. 46 E2
Mologa Vic. 50 A5, 55 O7
Molong NSW 12 F4
Moltema Tas. 162 H8
Molyullah Vic. 50 H9
Mona Rock Qld 142 D2
Mona Vale NSW 7 O6, 11 N6, 13 K6
Monak NSW 52 H6

Monarto SA 70 G10, 73 K9
Monarto South SA 70 G11, 73 K10, 82 C3
Monash ACT 34 C10
Monash SA 16 A6, 52 A6, 73 N7, 82 G1
Monbulk Vic. 43 P10, 45 K1, 47 L6, 48 E5
Monea Vic. 50 E10
Monegeetta Vic. 46 H2, 48 B2, 50 B12, 57 P3
Monga NSW 12 H11, 20 E5
Monga NP NSW 12 H12, 20 E6
Mongarlowe NSW 12 H11, 20 E5
Monkey Mia WA 97 B8
Monomeith Vic. 45 L10, 47 L9, 48 E7
Mont Albert Vic. 43 J8
Mont Albert North Vic. 43 K8
Montacute SA 68 G10, 69 G1
Montagu Tas. 162 B3
Montagu Bay Tas. 155 H2, 156 F6
Montague Island NSW 20 F8
Montana Tas. 163 I9
Montarra SA 69 D12
Monteagle NSW 12 E7, 20 B1
Montebello Islands Marine Park WA 97 C1
Monterey NSW 9 K6
Montgomery Vic. 49 K6
Montgomery Rocks Tas. 160 C6
Montmorency Vic. 43 K5
Monto Qld 137 K3
Montrose Tas. 156 A3
Montrose Vic. 43 O10
Montumana Tas. 162 E4
Montville Qld 134 F4
Mooball NP NSW 15 O2, 137 N11
Moockra SA 73 J2, 74 H9
Moodlu Qld 130 H1, 134 E7
Moogara Tas. 158 F4, 161 I6
Moogerah Qld 15 M1
Moogerah Peaks NP Qld 15 M1, 135 A8, 137 M10
Moola Qld 137 K8
Moolap Vic. 46 F8
Mooloolaba Qld 134 H4, 137 N7
Mooloolah Qld 134 F5
Mooloolah River NP Qld 134 G4, 137 N7
Moolort Vic. 55 M12, 57 M1
Moolpa NSW 16 H8, 53 M11
Moombooldool NSW 12 A7, 17 N7
Moombra Qld 134 B9
Moona Plains NSW 15 K9
Moonah Tas. 156 D5, 159 I5
Moonambel Vic. 55 K11
Moonan Flat NSW 13 L1, 15 I12
Moonbah NSW 20 B8, 58 C4
Moonbi NSW 15 I9
Moondarra Vic. 48 H6
Moonee Beach NSW 15 N7
Moonee Ponds Vic. 42 G6
Mooney Mooney NSW 7 M1, 11 M4
Mooney Mooney Creek NSW 7 M1
Moonford Qld 137 K3
Moonie Qld 137 I9
Moonlight Flat SA 72 C3, 74 A11, 81 P11
Moonta SA 72 H6
Moonta Bay SA 72 H6

Moora WA 96 B2, 98 B6
Moorabbin Vic. 43 I12, 44 D1, 47 J6, 48 C5
Moorabbin Airport Vic. 44 E3
Mooralla Vic. 56 F2
Moore Qld 134 A5, 137 M8
Moore Park NSW 5 G12, 7 M12, 9 M5
Moore Park Qld 137 M3
Moore River NP WA 96 B3, 98 B6
Moorebank NSW 8 F4
Moores Flat Vic. 55 L11, 57 L1
Moores Pocket Qld 132 C5
Moorilda NSW 12 G5
Moorilim Vic. 50 E8
Moorina Qld 130 F2
Moorina Tas. 163 N6
Moorine Rock WA 98 F6
Moorland NSW 13 O1, 15 L12
Moorlands SA 73 L10, 82 E4
Moorleah Tas. 162 E5
Moorngag Vic. 50 H9
Moorooduc Vic. 44 E9, 47 J9, 48 C7
Moorook SA 73 N7, 82 F1
Moorooka Qld 132 H4, 133 I3
Moorookyle Vic. 46 D1, 57 M2
Mooroolbark Vic. 43 O7, 47 K5
Mooroopna Vic. 50 E7
Moorrinya NP Qld 138 C5, 145 O5
Moppin NSW 14 F3, 136 H12
Moranbah Qld 139 I7
Morangarell NSW 12 C7
Morans Crossing NSW 20 D9, 58 G6
Morawa WA 98 B4
Morayfield Qld 130 H1, 131 I1, 134 F8, 135 D1
Morchard SA 73 J2, 75 I10
Mordialloc Vic. 44 D3, 47 J7, 48 C5
Morea Vic. 54 C9, 82 H8
Moree NSW 14 G4
Moree Vic. 54 D12, 56 D1
Morella Qld 138 A9, 145 M9
Moresby Range NP Qld 141 M7
Moreton Bay Qld 131 M12, 133 N5
Moreton Island (Gnoorganbin) Qld 135 G3, 137 N9
Moreton Island NP Qld 135 H2, 137 N9
Morgan SA 73 L6
Moriac Vic. 46 E8, 57 N8
Moriarty Tas. 162 H6
Morisset NSW 13 L4
Morkalla Vic. 16 B6, 52 C6, 73 P8, 82 H1
Morley WA 90 F7, 91 D2
Morning Bay NSW 7 O4
Morningside Qld 131 J11, 133 J1, 134 F11, 135 E4
Mornington Tas. 156 G6, 157 I6
Mornington Vic. 44 D9, 47 J9, 48 C7
Mornington Island Qld 140 A4, 143 C1
Mornington Peninsula NP Vic. 46 H10, 47 I10, 48 B8, 57 P8
Morongla NSW 12 F6
Morpeth NSW 13 L3
Morphett Vale SA 69 B7, 70 B11, 71 E4
Morphettville SA 69 C3
Morrisons Vic. 46 E5, 57 N5
Morrl Morrl Vic. 55 J10

Mortat Vic. 54 D9, 82 H8
Mortchup Vic. 46 B3, 57 L4
Mortdale NSW 9 I6
Mortlake NSW 7 J10, 9 J2
Mortlake Vic. 57 I6
Morton NP NSW 12 H10, 13 I10, 20 F4
Morton Plains Vic. 16 F12, 55 J6
Morundah NSW 17 M9
Moruya NSW 20 F7
Moruya Heads NSW 20 F7
Morven NSW 12 B11, 17 O11, 51 L4
Morven Qld 136 D5
Morwell Vic. 48 H7
Morwell NP Vic. 48 H8
Mosman NSW 7 M10, 9 M2, 11 M8
Mosman Park WA 90 C11, 91 B6, 93 B5
Moss Glen Tas. 161 I11
Moss Vale NSW 13 I9, 20 G3
Mossgiel NSW 17 J3
Mossiface Vic. 49 N5
Mossman Qld 141 L5
Moulamein NSW 17 I9, 53 N11, 55 N1
Moulden NT 113 J10
Moulyinning WA 95 L1, 96 G7
Mount Aberdeen NP Qld 139 I3
Mount Adrah NSW 12 D10, 20 A4, 51 P1
Mount Alford Qld 15 M1, 137 M10
Mount Alfred Vic. 12 C12, 51 N6
Mount Annan NSW 8 B9
Mount Archer NP Qld 139 M11
Mount Augustus NP WA 97 F6, 100 B7
Mount Barker SA 70 D10, 71 H3, 73 K9, 82 C3
Mount Barker WA 95 L9, 96 G11, 98 E11
Mount Barnett Roadhouse WA 103 L6
Mount Barney NP Qld 15 M1, 135 A12, 137 M11
Mount Bauple NP (Scientific) Qld 137 M5
Mount Baw Baw Vic. 47 P6, 48 H5
Mount Beauty Vic. 51 L10
Mount Beckworth Vic. 46 C1, 57 L2
Mount Benson SA 82 E9
Mount Beppo Qld 134 B7
Mount Best Vic. 47 P12, 48 H9
Mount Binga NP Qld 137 L8
Mount Blue Cow NSW 58 B4
Mount Bryan SA 73 K5, 75 I12
Mount Bryan East SA 73 K5, 75 J12
Mount Buffalo NP Vic. 51 J9
Mount Buller Vic. 49 I1, 51 I12
Mount Burnett Vic. 45 M4
Mount Burr SA 82 F11
Mount Bute Vic. 46 A5, 57 K5
Mount Byron Qld 130 A1
Mount Carbine Qld 141 K5
Mount Charlton Qld 139 J5
Mount Chinghee NP Qld 15 N2, 135 C12, 137 M11
Mount Claremont WA 90 C10, 91 A4
Mount Clunie NP NSW 15 M2, 137 M11
Mount Colah NSW 7 K5, 11 L6

Mount Colosseum NP Qld 137 L2
Mount Compass SA 71 F6, 73 J10, 82 B4
Mount Cook NP Qld 141 L3
Mount Coolon Qld 138 H6
Mount Coolum NP Qld 134 G3, 137 N7
Mount Coot-tha Qld 130 G11, 132 G1
Mount Cotton Qld 133 L6
Mount Cottrell Vic. 42 A6, 46 H5, 48 B4, 57 P5
Mount Crosby Qld 130 D12, 132 D2, 134 D11, 135 B5
Mount Damper SA 72 C4, 74 A11, 81 P11
Mount Dandenong Vic. 43 O10
Mount David NSW 12 H6
Mount Direction Tas. 163 K7
Mount Doran Vic. 46 D4, 57 M5
Mount Druitt NSW 6 D7, 11 I7
Mount Ebenezer NT 120 G10
Mount Eccles Vic. 47 O10, 48 G8
Mount Eccles NP Vic. 56 E6
Mount Egerton Vic. 46 E4, 57 N4
Mount Eliza Vic. 44 D8, 47 J8, 48 C6
Mount Emu Vic. 46 A3, 57 K4
Mount Etna Caves NP Qld 139 M10
Mount Evelyn Vic. 43 P7, 47 L5
Mount Fairy NSW 12 G10, 20 E4
Mount Field NP Tas. 158 D2, 160 H5, 161 I5
Mount Frankland NP WA 94 G10, 95 I10, 96 E11, 98 D11
Mount Frankland North NP WA 94 H9, 95 I10, 96 E11, 98 D11
Mount Frankland South NP WA 94 H10, 95 I11, 96 E11, 98 D11
Mount Franklin Vic. 46 E1, 57 N2
Mount Gambier SA 56 A5, 82 G12
Mount Garnet Qld 141 K7
Mount George NSW 13 N1, 15 K12
Mount George SA 69 H3
Mount Glorious Qld 130 D6, 134 D9, 135 B3
Mount Gravatt Qld 133 I4, 134 F12, 135 E5
Mount Gravatt East Qld 133 J4
Mount Hallen Qld 134 A9, 137 M9
Mount Hawthorn WA 90 E9, 91 C3
Mount Helen Vic. 46 D4, 57 M4
Mount Helena WA 93 E4
Mount Hope NSW 17 M2
Mount Hope SA 72 C6
Mount Horeb NSW 12 D10, 20 A4, 51 P1
Mount Hunter NSW 10 F11
Mount Hypipamee NP Qld 141 L7
Mount Imlay NP NSW 20 D10, 58 G8
Mount Irvine NSW 10 E2
Mount Isa Qld 143 D11, 144 F3
Mount Jerusalem NP NSW 15 O2, 137 N11
Mount Jim Crow NP Qld 139 M10
Mount Kaputar NP NSW 14 G6
Mount Keith WA 100 G10
Mount Kuring-Gai NSW 7 K5, 11 L6
Mount Lambie NSW 10 A1, 13 I5
Mount Larcom Qld 139 N12

Mount Lawley WA 89 H1, 90 F8, 91 C3
Mount Lewis NSW 9 I5
Mount Lewis NP Qld 141 L5
Mount Liebig NT 120 E6
Mount Lindesay NP WA 95 J10, 96 F11, 98 D11
Mount Lloyd Tas. 158 F4, 161 I7
Mount Lofty SA 70 C10, 71 G3
Mount Lonarch Vic. 55 K12, 57 K2
Mount Macedon Vic. 46 H2, 48 B2, 50 B12, 57 P3
Mount Mackay NP Qld 141 M8
Mount Magnet WA 97 H11, 98 D2, 100 D12
Mount Martha Vic. 44 B11, 47 I9, 48 C7
Mount Martin NP Qld 139 K5
Mount Mary SA 73 L7
Mount Mee Qld 130 D1, 134 D7
Mount Mercer Vic. 46 D5, 57 M5
Mount Molloy Qld 141 L5
Mount Morgan Qld 139 M11
Mount Moriac Vic. 46 E8, 57 N8
Mount Mulligan Qld 141 K6
Mount Nasura WA 91 H9
Mount Nebo Qld 130 D8, 134 D10, 135 B3
Mount Nelson Tas. 156 D9
Mount Nothofagus NP NSW 15 M2, 135 A12, 137 M11
Mount O'Connell NP Qld 139 L9
Mount Ommaney Qld 132 F4, 134 E12, 135 C5
Mount Osmond SA 69 E3
Mount Ossa Vic. 139 J5
Mount Ossa NP Qld 139 J5
Mount Perry Qld 137 L4
Mount Pikapene NP NSW 15 M4, 137 M12
Mount Pinbarren NP Qld 137 N6
Mount Pleasant Qld 130 D1, 134 D8, 135 C1
Mount Pleasant SA 70 F7, 73 K9, 82 C2
Mount Pleasant WA 90 F12, 91 C6, 97 D12, 98 H5
Mount Pritchard NSW 6 E12, 8 F3
Mount Remarkable NP SA 73 I3, 74 H10
Mount Richmond Vic. 56 C7
Mount Richmond NP Vic. 56 C7
Mount Richon WA 91 H10
Mount Riverview NSW 6 A6
Mount Roe NP WA 95 J10, 96 F11, 98 D11
Mount Rowan Vic. 46 D3, 57 M3
Mount Royal NP NSW 13 L2
Mount Rumney Tas. 157 I5
Mount Samson Qld 130 E6, 134 E9, 135 C2
Mount Schank SA 56 A5, 82 G12
Mount Seaview NSW 15 K11
Mount Seymour Tas. 161 L4
Mount Spurgeon NP Qld 141 K5
Mount Stuart Tas. 155 A4, 156 D6
Mount Surprise Qld 141 J8
Mount Tamborine Qld 135 E9
Mount Tarampa Qld 134 B10
Mount Taylor Vic. 49 M5
Mount Templeton SA 73 J6
Mount Thorley NSW 13 K3
Mount Tomah NSW 10 E3

Mount Torrens SA 70 E8, 73 K9, 82 C3
Mount Vernon NSW 6 C10, 8 C2
Mount Victoria NSW 10 C4, 13 I6
Mount Wallace Vic. 46 E5, 57 N5
Mount Walsh NP Qld 137 L5
Mount Warren Park Qld 133 L10
Mount Waverley Vic. 43 K10, 44 E1
Mount Webb NP Qld 141 L2
Mount Wedge SA 72 C5, 74 A12, 81 P12
Mount White NSW 11 M3, 13 K5
Mount William NP Tas. 163 P5
Mount Wilson NSW 10 D3, 13 I5
Mount Windsor NP Qld 141 K4
Mountain River Tas. 158 H6, 161 J7
Moura Qld 137 I2
Mourilyan Qld 141 M7
Moutajup Vic. 56 G4
Mowbray Tas. 163 K8
Mowbray NP Qld 141 L5
Mowbray Park NSW 10 E12
Mowen WA 94 B7, 96 B10
Moyhu Vic. 51 I8
Moyreisk Vic. 55 K10
Moyston Vic. 57 I2
Muchea WA 93 C2, 96 C4, 98 C7
Muckadilla Qld 136 F6
Mudamuckla SA 81 N8
Mudgee NSW 12 H2
Mudgeeraba Qld 15 O1, 135 F10, 137 N10
Mudgegonga Vic. 51 K8
Mudginberri NT 115 O3, 116 G4
Mudjimba Qld 134 G3
Mudlo NP Qld 137 M6
Muggleton Qld 136 G6
Muirhead NT 112 E2
Muirlea Qld 132 B3
Muiron Islands Marine Management Area WA 97 B2
Mukinbudin WA 96 G2, 98 E6
Muknab Rock Qld 142 C1
Mulambin Qld 139 N10
Mulcra Vic. 16 B9, 52 C11, 73 O10, 82 H4
Mulgildie Qld 137 K3
Mulgoa NSW 6 A9, 8 A2, 10 G8, 13 J6
Mulgrave NSW 6 E3
Mulgrave Vic. 43 K11, 44 G2
Mullaley NSW 14 F9
Mullaloo WA 90 B5
Mullalyup WA 94 E5, 96 C9
Mullaway NSW 15 N7
Mullenderee NSW 12 H12
Mullengandra NSW 12 B12, 17 O12, 51 L5
Mullengudgery NSW 14 A10, 19 P10
Mullewa WA 97 E12, 98 B3
Mulli Mulli NSW 15 M2, 137 M11
Mullindolingong Vic. 51 L9
Mullion NSW 34 A1
Mullion Creek NSW 12 G4
Mullumbimby NSW 15 O3, 137 N12
Mulpata SA 16 A8, 73 N10, 82 F4
Mulwala NSW 17 M12, 50 H5
Mumballup WA 94 E4, 96 D8, 98 C9
Mumbannar Vic. 56 C5, 82 H12

Mumbil NSW 12 G3
Mumblin Vic. 57 I8
Mummel Gulf NP NSW 15 J10
Mummulgum NSW 15 M3, 137 M12
Munbilla Qld 135 A8
Mundaring WA 93 E4, 96 C5, 98 C7
Mundaring Weir WA 93 E5
Mundijong WA 92 G1, 93 D7, 98 C8
Mundoona Vic. 50 E6
Mundoora SA 73 I5, 74 H12
Mundrabilla Roadhouse WA 80 A8, 99 O6
Mundubbera Qld 137 K4
Mundulla SA 16 A12, 54 A7, 82 G7
Munga–Thirri NP Qld 77 I1, 121 P9, 144 C12
Mungalawurru NT 119 I9
Mungallala Qld 136 D6
Mungana Qld 141 J6
Mungar Qld 137 M5
Mungerannie Roadhouse SA 77 I8, 146 B8
Mungeribar NSW 12 E1, 14 B12
Mungery NSW 12 D2
Mungindi NSW 14 E2, 136 F11
Mungkarta NT 119 J11
Munglinup WA 98 H9
Mungo NP NSW 16 F3, 53 K1
Mungungo Qld 137 K3
Munno Para SA 68 G3
Munno Para Downs SA 68 F3
Munno Para West SA 68 F3
Munro Vic. 49 L6
Munruben Qld 132 H9, 133 I10
Munster WA 91 B9, 93 C6
Muntadgin WA 96 H4, 98 E7
Muradup WA 95 I5, 96 E9
Murarrie Qld 131 K11, 133 J2
Murchison Vic. 50 D8
Murchison WA 97 E9, 100 B11
Murchison East Vic. 50 E8
Murdinga SA 72 D5
Murdoch WA 90 F12, 91 C7
Murdunna Tas. 159 N6, 161 M8
Murga NSW 12 E4
Murgenella NT 116 G2
Murgheboluc Vic. 46 E7, 57 N7
Murgon Qld 137 L6
Murmungee Vic. 51 J8
Murphys Creek Qld 55 M10
Murra Warra Vic. 54 G8
Murrabit Vic. 16 H10, 55 N3
Murramarang NP NSW 12 H12, 13 I12, 20 F6
Murrami NSW 17 N7
Murrawal NSW 14 E10
Murray Bridge SA 70 H11, 73 K10, 82 D3
Murray River NP SA 16 A6, 52 B5, 73 N8, 82 G1
Murray Town SA 73 I3, 74 H11
Murray Valley NP NSW 17 K11, 50 D3
Murray–Sunset NP Vic. 16 C7, 52 D9, 73 P9, 82 H2
Murrays Run NSW 13 K4
Murrayville Vic. 16 B9, 52 C11, 54 C1, 73 O10, 82 H4
Murrindal Vic. 20 A11, 49 P3, 58 A9

Murrindindi Vic. 47 M2, 48 E2, 50 E12
Murringo NSW 12 E7, 20 B1
Murroon Vic. 46 C10, 57 L9
Murrumba Qld 134 B8
Murrumba Downs Qld 131 I7
Murrumbateman NSW 12 F9, 20 C3, 31 D1
Murrumbeena Vic. 43 I11, 44 D1
Murrumburrah NSW 12 E8, 20 B2
Murrungowar Vic. 20 B11, 58 C10
Murrurundi NSW 14 H11
Murrurundi Pass NP NSW 14 H11
Murtoa Vic. 54 H9
Murun Murula NT 119 O7
Murwillumbah NSW 15 O2, 135 F12, 137 N11
Musgrave Roadhouse Qld 142 E12
Mushroom Reef Marine Sanctuary Vic. 47 I11, 48 C8
Musk Vic. 46 E2, 57 N3
Muskerry East Vic. 50 B8, 55 P10
Musselboro Tas. 163 L8
Musselroe Bay Tas. 163 O5
Muswellbrook NSW 13 K2
Mutarnee Qld 141 M10
Mutawintji NP NSW 18 E7
Mutchilba Qld 141 K6
Mutdapilly Qld 132 A9, 135 A7, 137 M10
Mutitjulu NT 120 E10
Muttaburra Qld 138 C8, 145 O8
Muttama NSW 12 D9, 20 A3
Mutton Bird Island Vic. 57 J10
Muttonbird Island NSW 15 N8
Muundhi (Jack River) NP Qld 141 K1, 142 H12
Myall Vic. 16 H10, 55 N3
Myall Lakes NP NSW 13 N3
Myall Mundi NSW 14 B11
Myall Plains NSW 17 M10, 50 H2
Myalla Tas. 162 E5
Myalup WA 94 C2, 96 C8, 98 C9
Myamyn Vic. 56 E6
Myaree WA 90 E12, 91 C7
Mylestom NSW 15 M8
Mylor SA 69 G5, 70 D10, 71 G3
Myola Vic. 50 B8, 55 P9
Mypolonga SA 70 H10, 73 L9, 82 D3
Myponga SA 71 E7, 73 J10, 82 B4
Myponga Beach SA 71 D7, 73 J10, 82 B4
Myrla SA 73 N8, 82 F2
Myrniong Vic. 46 F4, 48 A3, 57 O4
Myrrhee Vic. 47 P6, 48 H4, 51 I9
Myrtle Bank SA 69 E3
Myrtle Bank Tas. 163 L7
Myrtle Creek Vic. 50 A10, 55 O11, 57 O1
Myrtleford Vic. 51 J8
Myrtleville NSW 12 H8, 20 E2
Mysia Vic. 16 H12, 55 M7
Mystic Park Vic. 16 H10, 55 M3
Mywee Vic. 50 F4

Nabageena Tas. 162 C4
Nabawa WA 97 D12, 98 A3
Nabiac NSW 13 N2
Nabowla Tas. 163 L6
Nackara SA 73 L3, 75 J10
Nadda SA 16 B7, 52 B8, 73 O8, 82 H2

Nagambie Vic. 50 D9
Nagoorin Qld 137 K2
Nailsworth SA 68 D10, 69 D1
Nairana NP Qld 138 G6
Nairne SA 70 E10, 71 H3, 73 K9, 82 C3
Nakara NT 112 D2
Nala Tas. 161 L4
Nalangil Vic. 46 A9, 57 K8
Nalinga Vic. 50 G7
Nalya WA 96 E5
Namadgi NP ACT 12 F12, 20 C5, 31 C8, 58 E1
Namadgi NP NSW 34 A11
Nambeelup WA 92 E7
Nambour Qld 134 F3, 137 N7
Nambrok Vic. 49 J6
Nambucca Heads NSW 15 M9
Nambung NP WA 96 A2, 98 B5
Nana Glen NSW 15 M7
Nanango Qld 137 L7
Nanarup WA 95 N11, 96 H11
Nandaly Vic. 16 F9, 53 I12, 55 I1
Nandi Qld 137 K8
Nanga WA 93 E11, 96 C7
Nangana Vic. 45 M1, 47 L6, 48 E5
Nangar NP NSW 12 E5
Nangari SA 16 B6, 52 B7, 73 O8, 82 H2
Nangeenan WA 96 G3, 98 E6
Nangiloc Vic. 16 E7, 52 H7
Nangkita SA 71 F6, 73 J10, 82 B4
Nangur NP Qld 137 L6
Nangus NSW 12 D9, 20 A3, 51 P1
Nangwarry SA 56 A3, 82 G11
Nanneella Vic. 50 C6
Nannup WA 94 D7, 96 C10, 98 C10
Nanson WA 97 D12
Nantabibbie SA 73 K3, 75 J10
Nantawarra SA 73 I6
Nanutarra Roadhouse WA 97 D4, 100 A5
Napoleons Vic. 46 C4, 57 M4
Napperby SA 73 I4, 74 H11
Napranum Qld 142 B7
Nar Nar Goon Vic. 45 M6, 47 M8, 48 E6
Nar Nar Goon North Vic. 45 M4
Nara Qld 13 / L8, 140 G11
Naracoopa Tas. 161 P11
Naracoorte SA 54 A10, 82 G9
Naracoorte Caves NP SA 54 A11, 82 G9
Naradhan NSW 17 N5
Naraling WA 97 D12, 98 A3
Narangba Qld 130 F3, 131 I4, 134 F9, 135 D2
Narara NSW 11 O2
Narawntapu NP Tas. 163 I6
Narbethong Vic. 47 M4, 48 F3
Naree Budjong Djara NP Qld 135 H5, 137 N9
Nareen Vic. 56 D2
Narellan NSW 8 A7, 10 G10, 13 J7, 20 H1
Narellan Vale NSW 8 B7
Narembeen WA 96 G4, 98 E7
Naremburn NSW 7 L10, 9 L2
Naretha WA 99 L5
Nariel Vic. 51 O8
Naringal Vic. 56 H8
Narkoola NP Qld 136 C9
Naroghid Vic. 57 J7
Narooma NSW 20 F8

Narrabeen NSW 7 N7
Narrabri NSW 14 F7
Narrabri West NSW 14 F7
Narrabundah ACT 34 E7
Narracan Vic. 47 P10, 48 H7
Narrandera NSW 12 A8, 17 N8
Narraport Vic. 16 F11, 55 J5
Narrawa Tas. 162 G7
Narraweena NSW 7 N8, 11 M7
Narrawong Vic. 56 D7
Narre Warren Vic. 44 H4, 45 I5, 47 K7, 48 D6
Narre Warren East Vic. 45 I2
Narre Warren North Vic. 44 H3, 45 I3, 47 K7
Narre Warren South Vic. 44 H4, 45 I5
Narrewillock Vic. 55 L6
Narridy SA 73 J5, 74 H12
Narrien Range NP Qld 138 G9
Narrikup WA 95 L10, 96 G11
Narrogin WA 96 E7, 98 D9
Narromine NSW 12 E1, 14 B12
Narrung SA 73 K11, 82 C5
Narrung Vic. 16 G8, 53 K9
Narwee NSW 9 I5
Nashdale NSW 12 F4
Nathalia Vic. 17 K12, 50 E5
Nathan Qld 133 I5
Natimuk Vic. 54 F9
National Park Tas. 158 E2, 161 I6
Natone Tas. 162 F6
Nattai NSW 10 D11, 13 I7, 20 G1
Nattai NP NSW 10 D12, 13 I8, 20 G2
Natte Yallock Vic. 55 L11
Natural Bridge Qld 15 O1, 135 E11
Natya Vic. 16 G8, 53 K10
Nauiyu NT 114 C12, 116 D7
Naval Base WA 91 B11, 92 B1, 93 C7
Navarre Vic. 55 J10
Navigators Vic. 46 D3, 57 M4
Nayook Vic. 47 O7, 48 G5
Neale Junction WA 99 M1, 101 M11
Neales Flat SA 70 G1, 73 K7, 82 D1
Nebo Qld 139 J7
Nectar Brook SA 73 I2, 74 G10
Nedlands WA 90 D10, 91 B5
Neds Corner Vic. 16 C6, 52 E6, 73 P7
Needle Rock WA 103 J4
Needle Rocks Tas. 160 F11
Needles Tas. 163 I8
Neerabup WA 90 B3
Neerabup NP WA 90 A1, 93 B3, 96 B4, 98 B7
Neerdie Qld 137 N6
Neerim Vic. 47 O7, 48 G5
Neerim East Vic. 47 O7, 48 G6
Neerim Junction Vic. 47 O7, 48 G5
Neerim South Vic. 47 O7, 48 G6
Neeworra NSW 14 E3, 136 G12
Neika Tas. 156 A11, 158 H6, 161 K7
Neilborough Vic. 50 A8, 55 O9
Neilborough East Vic. 50 A7, 55 O9
Neilrex NSW 14 E11
Nelia Qld 145 K3
Nelligen NSW 12 H12, 20 F6
Nelly Bay Qld 138 G1, 141 N11
Nelshaby SA 73 I4, 74 H11
Nelson NSW 6 G5, 11 J5

Nelson Vic. 56 B6, 82 G12
Nelson Bay NSW 13 N4
Nelson Rocks WA 100 B2, 102 B12
Nelungaloo NSW 12 D4
Nemingha NSW 15 I9
Nene Valley SA 82 F12
Nepabunna SA 75 J4
Nerang Qld 15 O1, 135 F9, 137 N10
Nerang NP Qld 15 O1, 135 F9, 137 N10
Neranwood Qld 135 F11
Nerriga NSW 12 H10, 20 F4
Nerrigundah NSW 20 E7
Nerrin Nerrin Vic. 57 J5
Nerrina Vic. 46 D3, 57 M4
Nerring Vic. 46 A2, 57 K3
Netherby SA 69 E3
Netherby Vic. 16 C11, 54 E6
Nethercote NSW 20 E10, 58 H8
Netley SA 68 C12, 69 C3
Neuarpurr Vic. 54 B9, 82 H8
Neurea NSW 12 F3
Neuroodla SA 74 H7
Neutral Bay NSW 7 M11, 9 M2
Nevertire NSW 14 A11, 19 P11
Neville NSW 12 G6
New Angledool NSW 14 B2, 136 E11
New Beith Qld 132 F9
New Chum Qld 132 D5, 134 D12, 135 C5
New England NP NSW 15 L8
New Farm Qld 129 H5, 131 I12, 133 I2
New Gisborne Vic. 46 H3, 48 B2, 57 P3
New Italy NSW 15 N4
New Mollyann NSW 14 E10
New Norcia WA 96 C2, 98 C6
New Norfolk Tas. 158 G4, 161 J6
New Residence SA 16 A6, 73 N7, 82 F1
New Town Tas. 155 A1, 156 D5, 159 I5
New Well SA 73 M7, 79 I2, 82 E1, 120 G11
Newborough Vic. 47 P9, 48 H7
Newbridge NSW 12 G5
Newbridge Vic. 55 M10
Newbury Vic. 46 F2, 48 A2, 50 A12, 57 O3
Newcastle NSW 13 M4
Newcastle Waters (Marlinja) NT 118 H5
Newdegate WA 98 F8
Newfield Vic. 57 I9
Newham Vic. 46 H1, 48 B1, 50 B12, 57 P3
Newhaven Vic. 47 K11, 48 D8
Newington NSW 7 I10, 9 I2
Newlands WA 94 D5, 96 C9
Newlyn Vic. 46 D2, 57 M3
Newman WA 100 E5
Newmarket Qld 130 H11, 131 I11, 132 H1, 133 I1, 134 F11, 135 D4
Newmerella Vic. 20 A12, 49 P5, 58 B11
Newnes NSW 13 I4
Newnes Junction NSW 10 C2
Newport NSW 7 O5, 11 N6, 13 K6
Newport Qld 131 K5
Newport Vic. 42 F9, 47 I6
Newry Vic. 49 J6

Newry Islands NP Qld 139 K5
Newrybar NSW 15 O3
Newstead Qld 131 I11, 133 I1
Newstead Vic. 55 N12, 57 N1
Newton SA 68 F10
Newton Boyd NSW 15 L6
Newtown NSW 7 L12, 9 L5, 11 L9
Newtown Qld 132 C5
Newtown Vic. 46 B4, 57 L4
Ngalba Bulal NP Qld 141 L3
Ngangalala NT 117 K4
Nguiu NT 116 D3
Ngukurr NT 117 K9
Ngunarra NT 119 M7
Ngunnawal ACT 34 E1
Nhill Vic. 16 C12, 54 E7
Nhulunbuy NT 117 N4
Niagara Park NSW 11 O2
Niangala NSW 15 J10
Nicholls ACT 34 D1
Nicholls Point Vic. 52 G6
Nicholls Rivulet Tas. 158 H8, 161 J9
Nicholson Vic. 49 N5
Nicoll Scrub NP Qld 15 O1, 135 F11, 137 N11
Niddrie Vic. 42 F6
Niemur Vic. 17 I9, 53 O12, 55 O1
Nierinna Tas. 158 H7
Nietta Tas. 162 G7
Nightcap NP NSW 15 O2, 137 N11
Nightcliff NT 112 C3, 114 C2
Nildottie SA 73 L8, 82 E2
Nile Tas. 163 L9
Nileye Vic. 47 O9, 48 G7
Nilma Vic. 47 O9, 48 G7
Nimbin NSW 15 O3, 137 N12
Nimmitabel NSW 20 D8, 58 F5
Ninda Vic. 16 F10, 55 I2
Nindigully Qld 136 F10
Nine Mile Vic. 55 L8
Ninety Mile Beach Marine NP Vic. 49 K8
Ningaloo Marine Park WA 97 B4
Ningi Qld 131 J1, 134 G7, 135 E1
Ninnes SA 73 I6
Ninyeunook Vic. 16 G11, 55 L5
Nipan Qld 137 I2
Nippering WA 95 K2, 96 F7
Nirimba WA 92 D12
Nirranda Vic. 56 H9
Nirranda South Vic. 57 I9
Nitmiluk NP NT 115 M12, 116 G7
Noarlunga Centre SA 69 A8, 70 A11, 71 E4
Noarlunga Downs SA 69 A8
Nobby Qld 137 L10
Noble Park Vic. 43 L12, 44 G2, 47 J7
Noble Park North Vic. 43 L12, 44 G2
Noccundra Qld 147 I8
Nollamara WA 90 E7, 91 C2
Nonda Qld 145 K3
Noojee Vic. 47 O7, 48 G5
Noonamah NT 114 E4, 116 D5
Noonameena SA 73 K11, 82 D5
Noonbinna NSW 12 E6
Noondoo Qld 14 D1, 136 F10
Noora SA 16 B6, 52 B7, 73 O8, 82 H2
Nooramunga Vic. 50 G7
Nooramunga Marine and Coastal Park Vic. 48 H10, 49 I10

Noorat Vic. 57 I7
Noorinbee Vic. 20 C11, 58 E10
Noorinbee North Vic. 20 C11, 58 E10
Noorong NSW 16 H9, 53 N12, 55 N2
Noorongong Vic. 51 L7
Noosa Heads Qld 134 H1, 137 N7
Noosa NP Qld 134 G2, 137 N7
Noosaville Qld 134 G1
Nora Creina SA 82 E10
Noradjuha Vic. 54 F10
Norah Head NSW 13 L5
Noranda WA 90 F7, 91 D2
Norman Park Qld 131 I12, 133 I2
Normanhurst NSW 7 J7, 11 L6
Normanton Qld 140 D7, 143 G4
Normanville SA 71 C7, 73 I10, 82 B4
Normanville Vic. 55 M5
Nornakin WA 96 F5
Nornalup WA 95 I12, 96 E12
Norseman WA 99 I7
North Adelaide SA 67 B4, 68 D11, 69 D1, 70 B8, 71 F2
North Arm Qld 134 F2
North Balgowlah NSW 7 N9, 9 N1
North Beach SA 72 H6
North Beach WA 90 C7, 91 A2
North Bondi NSW 7 N12, 9 N4, 11 M9
North Booval Qld 132 C5
North Bourke NSW 19 M5
North Brig Rock Tas. 161 P12
North Brighton SA 69 B4
North Coogee WA 91 A8
North Curl Curl NSW 7 O9, 9 O1
North Dandalup WA 92 G7, 93 D9, 96 C6, 98 C8
North Epping NSW 7 J8
North Fremantle WA 90 C12, 91 A7, 93 B6
North Harbour NSW 7 N10, 9 N2
North Haven NSW 15 M12
North Haven SA 68 A7, 70 A7
North Hobart Tas. 155 B4, 156 D6
North Ipswich Qld 132 C5
North Island NT 117 N10, 119 N1
North Jindong WA 94 B6
North Keppel Island Qld 139 N10
North Lake WA 91 C8
North Lakes Qld 131 J6
North Lilydale Tas. 163 K7
North Maclean Qld 132 G10, 135 D7
North Manly NSW 7 N9, 9 N1
North Melbourne Vic. 41 B2, 42 G7
North Motton Tas. 162 G6
North Narrabeen NSW 7 O7
North Neptunes SA 72 E10
North Page SA 71 C11, 73 I11, 82 A4
North Parramatta NSW 6 H9, 7 I8, 8 H1, 9 I1
North Perth WA 89 E1, 90 E8, 91 C3
North Pinjarra WA 93 D9, 96 C6
North Plympton SA 69 C3
North Richmond NSW 6 B1, 10 H4
North Rock NSW 13 N3, 15 N7
North Rock Qld 139 J3
North Rock WA 103 L2

North Rocks NSW 6 H8, 7 I8, 8 H1, 9 I1
North Rothbury NSW 13 L3
North Ryde NSW 7 K9, 9 K1
North St Marys NSW 6 C7
North Scottsdale Tas. 163 M6
North Shields SA 72 D8
North Solitary Island NSW 15 N7
North Star NSW 14 H3, 137 I12
North Stradbroke Island (Minjerriba) Qld 133 P9, 135 G6, 137 N9
North Strathfield NSW 7 J11, 9 J3
North Sydney NSW 7 M11, 9 M2, 11 M8
North Tamborine Qld 135 E9, 137 N10
North Tivoli Qld 132 C4
North Turramurra NSW 7 L5
North Wahroonga NSW 7 K6
North Warrandyte Vic. 43 L6
North West Rock NSW 15 N7
North West Rock WA 96 G12, 98 E12
North Willoughby NSW 7 M9, 9 M1
North Yunderup WA 92 D11
Northam WA 93 G2, 96 D4, 98 C7
Northampton WA 97 D12, 98 A3
Northbridge NSW 7 M10, 9 M2
Northbridge WA 89 D4, 90 E9, 91 C4
Northcliffe WA 94 F10, 96 D11, 98 C11
Northcote Vic. 42 H7, 43 I7
Northdown Tas. 162 H6
Northfield SA 68 E9, 70 B8, 71 F1
Northgate Qld 131 J10
Northgate SA 68 E9
Northmead NSW 6 H8, 7 I8, 8 H1, 11 J7
Northumberland Islands NP Qld 139 L6
Northwood NSW 7 L10, 9 L2
Norton Summit SA 68 G11, 69 G1
Norval Vic. 55 I12, 57 I2
Norwell Qld 133 M11
Norwin Qld 137 K9
Norwood SA 68 E11, 69 E1
Notley Hills Tas. 163 J7
Notting WA 96 G5, 98 E8
Notting Hill Vic. 43 K11, 44 F1
Notts Well SA 73 M8, 82 E1
Nour Nour NP Qld 137 L4
Novar Gardens SA 69 B3
Nowa Nowa Vic. 49 O5
Nowendoc NSW 15 J11
Nowendoc NP NSW 15 J11
Nowergup WA 90 A1
Nowie North Vic. 53 L12, 55 L1
Nowingi Vic. 16 E7, 52 G8
Nowley NSW 14 E5
Nowra NSW 13 I10, 20 G4
Nowra Hill NSW 13 I10, 20 G4
Nturiya NT 120 H4
Nubba NSW 12 D8, 20 B2
Nubeena Tas. 159 L8, 161 L8
Nudgee Qld 131 J9, 134 F10, 135 E3
Nudgee Beach Qld 131 K8
Nug Nug Vic. 51 J9
Nuga Nuga NP Qld 136 G2
Nugent Tas. 159 M3, 161 M6
Nuggetty Vic. 55 N11

Nullagine WA 100 F3
Nullamanna NP NSW 15 J5
Nullan Vic. 54 H8
Nullarbor SA 80 G6
Nullarbor NP WA 80 D6, 99 P5
Nullarbor Roadhouse SA 80 G7
Nullawarre Vic. 56 H9
Nullawil Vic. 16 G11, 55 K5
Numbla Vale NSW 20 B8, 58 D5
Numbugga NSW 20 D9, 58 H6
Numbulwar NT 117 L8
Numeralla NSW 20 D7, 58 F3
Numinbah Valley Qld 15 O1, 135 E11
Numurkah Vic. 17 K12, 50 F5
Nunamara Tas. 163 L8
Nunawading Vic. 43 L8
Nundah Qld 131 J10, 133 J1
Nundle NSW 15 I10
Nundroo Roadhouse SA 81 J7
Nunga Vic. 16 E9, 52 H11
Nungarin WA 96 G2, 98 E6
Nungurner Vic. 49 N6
Nunjikompita SA 72 A1, 81 N9
Nurcoung Vic. 54 E9
Nurina WA 99 N5
Nurinda Qld 134 A5
Nuriootpa SA 70 F4, 73 K8, 82 C1
Nurom SA 73 I4, 74 H12
Nurrabiel Vic. 54 F10
Nutfield Vic. 43 L2, 47 K4, 48 D3
Nyabing WA 95 M3, 96 G8, 98 E9
Nyah Vic. 16 G9, 53 L11, 55 L1
Nyah West Vic. 16 G9, 53 L11, 55 L1
Nyarrin Vic. 16 F9, 53 I12, 55 I2
Nyirripi NT 120 D5
Nymagee NSW 19 M11
Nymboi–Binderay NP NSW 15 M7
Nymboida NSW 15 M6
Nymboida NP NSW 15 L5
Nyngan NSW 19 O10
Nyora Vic. 45 O12, 47 M10, 48 F7
Nypo Vic. 16 D10, 54 F4

Oak Beach Qld 141 L5
Oak Park Vic. 42 G5
Oakbank SA 70 D9, 71 H3
Oakdale NSW 10 E11, 13 J7, 20 G1
Oakden SA 68 E9
Oakdowns Tas. 157 J9
Oakey Qld 137 K9
Oakey Creek NSW 14 F11
Oakford WA 91 G10, 92 E1
Oakhurst NSW 6 E6
Oaklands NSW 17 M10, 51 I3
Oaklands SA 72 H9
Oaklands Junction Vic. 42 E1
Oaklands Park SA 69 C4
Oakleigh Vic. 43 J11, 44 E1, 47 J6, 48 C5
Oakleigh East Vic. 43 J11, 44 E1
Oakleigh South Vic. 43 J11, 44 D1
Oakley WA 92 H11
Oaks Tas. 163 J9
Oaks Estate NSW 34 H8
Oakvale Vic. 16 G11, 55 L5
Oakview NP Qld 137 M6
Oakville NSW 6 F2
Oakwood Tas. 159 M8, 161 M9
Oasis Roadhouse Qld 141 J10
Oatlands NSW 7 I9, 9 I1
Oatlands Tas. 161 K3
Oatley NSW 9 I6, 11 K10

Ob Flat SA 56 A5, 82 G12
Oberne NSW 12 C10, 51 O3
Oberon NSW 12 H6
Obley NSW 12 F2
Obx Creek NSW 15 M6
Ocean Grove Vic. 46 G9, 48 A7, 57 O8
Ocean Reef WA 90 B4
Ocean Shores NSW 15 O2, 137 N11
Ocean View Qld 130 D1
Ockley WA 96 F7
O'Connor ACT 34 D4
O'Connor WA 90 D12, 91 B7
Oenpelli NT 115 P2, 116 H4
Officer Vic. 45 J5, 47 L8, 48 E6
Officer South Vic. 45 J6
Ogilvie WA 97 D11, 98 A2
Ogmore Qld 139 L9
Ohalloran Hill SA 69 C5
Olary SA 73 N1, 75 M9
Old Adaminaby NSW 20 B7, 58 D2
Old Bar NSW 13 O1, 15 L12
Old Beach Tas. 156 C1, 159 I4, 161 K6
Old Bonalbo NSW 15 M3, 137 M12
Old Bowenfels NSW 10 B2
Old Guildford NSW 6 H11, 8 H3
Old Junee NSW 12 C9, 17 P9
Old Man Rock NT 114 D3, 116 D4
Old Noarlunga SA 69 B10, 70 A11, 71 E5, 73 J10, 82 B4
Old Reynella SA 69 B7
Old Tallangatta Vic. 51 M7
Old Toongabbie NSW 6 H8, 8 G1
Old Warrah NSW 14 H11
Oldbury WA 91 E12, 92 E1
Oldina Tas. 162 E5
Olinda NSW 13 I3
Olinda Vic. 43 O10, 47 L6, 48 E5
Olio Qld 145 L6
Olympic Dam Village SA 74 E3
O'Malley ACT 34 D8
O'Malley SA 80 G4
Ombersley Vic. 46 C8, 57 M7
Omeo Vic. 49 M1, 51 M12
Ondit Vic. 46 B8, 57 L8
One Arm Point WA 102 H5
One Mile Qld 132 B5
One Tree NSW 17 J6
One Tree Hill SA 68 G5
Ongerup WA 95 O5, 96 H9, 98 F10
Onkaparinga Hills SA 69 C7
Onkaparinga River NP SA 69 D8, 70 A11, 71 E4, 73 J10, 82 B3
Onslow WA 97 C2
Oodla Wirra SA 73 K3, 75 J10
Oodnadatta SA 76 B6
Oolambeyan NP NSW 17 K8
Ooldea SA 81 I3
Oombulgurri WA 103 N3
Oonah Tas. 162 E6
Oondooroo Qld 145 L7
Oorindi Qld 143 G11, 145 I3
Ootann Qld 141 J7
Ootha NSW 12 C3, 17 P3
Opalton Qld 145 K9
Ophir NSW 12 G4
Opossum Bay Tas. 159 J7, 161 K8
Ora Banda WA 98 H4
Oran Park NSW 8 B5
Orange NSW 12 G4
Orange Grove WA 91 G5, 93 D5

Orangeville NSW 10 F10, 13 J7, 20 G1
Oranmeir NSW 12 G12, 20 E6
Orbost Vic. 20 A12, 58 B11
Orchard Hills NSW 6 B7, 8 A1
Orchard Rocks Qld 141 N11
Orchid Beach Qld 137 O4
Orelia WA 91 C12, 92 C1
Orford Tas. 159 N2, 161 M5
Orford Vic. 56 F7
Organ Pipes NP Vic. 42 D4, 46 H4, 48 B3, 57 P5
Orielton Tas. 159 K3, 161 L6
Ormeau Qld 133 L11, 135 F7
Ormeau Hills Qld 133 L12
Ormiston Qld 133 N3, 134 H12, 135 F5
Ormond Vic. 43 I11, 44 C1
Orpheus Island (Goolboddi) Qld 141 N10
Orpheus Island NP Qld 141 N10
Orroroo SA 73 J3, 75 I10
Orrtipa-Thurra NT 121 M5
Orton Park NSW 12 H5
Osborne SA 68 B7, 70 A7
Osborne Park WA 90 D8, 91 B3
Osbornes Flat SA 51 K7
Osmaston Tas. 163 I8
Osmington WA 94 B7, 96 B10
Osprey Rock Qld 139 M7
Osterley Tas. 161 I3
Osullivan Beach SA 69 A8
Otago Tas. 156 C1, 159 I4, 161 K7
Ottoway SA 68 B9
Oura NSW 12 C9, 17 P9, 51 N1
Ourimbah NSW 11 O2, 13 L5
Ournie NSW 12 C12, 51 O5
Ouse Tas. 161 I4
Outer Harbor SA 68 A7, 70 A7, 73 J8, 82 B2
Outer Rocks Qld 139 N10
Outtrim Vic. 47 M11, 48 F8
Ouyen Vic. 16 E8, 52 H11
Ovens Vic. 51 J9
Overhanging Rock WA 97 D1
Overland Corner SA 16 A5, 73 N7, 82 F1
Overlander Roadhouse WA 97 D9
Ovingham SA 67 B1, 68 D11, 69 D1, 70 B8, 71 F2
Owanyilla Qld 137 M5
Owen SA 70 B2, 73 J7, 82 B1
Owens Gap NSW 13 K1, 14 H12
Oxenford Qld 135 F8
Oxford Falls NSW 7 N7
Oxley ACT 34 C10
Oxley NSW 17 I6, 53 O6
Oxley Qld 132 H4, 134 E12, 135 D5
Oxley Vic. 51 I8
Oxley Park NSW 6 D7
Oxley Wild Rivers NP NSW 15 K9
Oyala Thumotang NP (CYPAL) Qld 142 C9
Oyster Bay NSW 9 I7
Oyster Cove Tas. 158 H8, 161 J8
Oyster Rocks Tas. 160 B11, 163 O1
Ozenkadnook Vic. 54 C10, 82 H9

Paaratte Vic. 57 I9
Pacific Palms NSW 13 N3
Packsaddle Roadhouse NSW 18 D6, 75 P4
Padbury WA 90 C5, 91 A1

Paddington NSW 5 H10, 7 M12, 9 M4, 19 K11
Paddington Qld 129 A5, 130 H11, 131 I12, 132 H1, 133 I2, 134 F11, 135 D4
Padstow NSW 8 H5, 9 I5
Padstow Heights NSW 8 H6, 9 I6
Padthaway SA 82 F8
Page ACT 34 C3
Pagewood NSW 9 M5
Paignie Vic. 16 D8, 52 G11
Painswick Vic. 55 M10
Pakenham Vic. 45 L4, 47 L8, 48 E6
Pakenham South Vic. 45 L7
Pakenham Upper Vic. 45 L4
Palana Tas. 160 A9
Palgarup WA 94 F8, 96 D10
Pallamallawa NSW 14 G4
Pallara Qld 132 G6, 134 F12, 135 D5
Pallarenda Qld 138 G1, 141 N11
Palm Beach NSW 7 P4, 11 N5, 13 K6
Palm Beach Qld 15 O1, 135 G11
Palm Cove Qld 141 L5
Palm Dale NSW 11 O1
Palm Grove NSW 11 N1
Palmer SA 70 G8, 73 K9, 82 D3
Palmer River Roadhouse Qld 141 K4
Palmers Island NSW 15 N5
Palmers Oakey NSW 12 H4
Palmerston ACT 34 E2
Palmerston NT 114 D3, 116 D4
Palmerston City NT 113 K9
Palmerston Rocks NP Qld 141 M7
Palmgrove NP (Scientific) Qld 136 H3
Palmwoods Qld 134 F4
Palmyra WA 90 D12, 91 B7
Paloona Tas. 162 H6
Paluma Qld 141 M11
Paluma Range NP Qld 138 F1, 141 M10
Pambula NSW 20 E10, 58 H7
Pambula Beach NSW 20 E10, 58 H7
Pampas Qld 137 K9
Panania NSW 8 G5
Pandora Reef Qld 141 M10
Panitya Vic. 16 B9, 52 B11, 54 B1, 73 O10, 82 H4
Panmure Vic. 56 H8
Pannawonica WA 97 E2, 100 A3
Panorama SA 69 D4
Pantapin WA 96 F4
Panton Hill Vic. 43 M3, 47 K4
Papunya NT 120 F6
Para Hills SA 68 E8, 70 C7
Para Hills West SA 68 E8
Para Vista SA 68 F8
Paraburdoo WA 97 G4, 100 C5
Parachilna SA 74 H5
Paracombe SA 68 H9
Paradise SA 68 F10
Paradise Tas. 162 H8
Paradise Vic. 46 B12, 55 J10, 57 L10
Paradise Beach Vic. 49 L7
Paradise Point Qld 15 O1, 135 G8
Parafield SA 68 E7, 70 C7
Parafield Gardens SA 68 D7, 70 B7
Paralowie SA 68 D6

Parap NT 111 H3, 112 C6
Paraparap Vic. 46 E9, 57 N8
Parattah Tas. 161 L4
Pardoo Roadhouse WA 100 E1, 102 E11
Parenna Tas. 161 P11
Parilla SA 16 A9, 52 A11, 54 A1, 73 N10, 82 G4
Paringa SA 16 B5, 52 B5, 73 O7, 82 G1
Paris Creek SA 69 H10
Park Beach Tas. 159 L5
Park Holme SA 69 C3
Park Orchards Vic. 43 L7
Park Ridge Qld 132 H8, 133 I9
Park Ridge South Qld 132 H9, 133 I9
Parkdale Vic. 44 D3
Parkers Corner Vic. 48 H6
Parkerville WA 93 D4
Parkes ACT 33 E8, 34 E5
Parkes NSW 12 E4
Parkham Tas. 163 I7
Parkhurst Qld 139 M10
Parkinson Qld 132 H6, 133 I6
Parklands WA 92 C8
Parklea NSW 6 F6
Parkside SA 67 G12, 68 D12, 69 E3
Parkville NSW 13 K1, 14 H12
Parkville Vic. 41 C1, 42 G7
Parkwood WA 90 G12, 91 E7
Parmelia WA 91 D12, 92 D1
Parndana SA 72 G11
Parnella Tas. 163 P8
Paroo–Darling NP NSW 18 G7, 19 I8
Parrakie SA 73 N10, 82 F4
Parramatta NSW 6 H9, 7 I9, 8 H1, 9 I1, 11 J8, 13 K6
Parrawe Tas. 162 E6
Paru NT 116 D3
Paruna SA 16 A7, 52 A8, 73 O8, 82 G2
Parwan Vic. 46 G4, 48 A4, 57 O5
Pasadena SA 69 D4
Paschendale Vic. 56 D4
Pascoe Vale Vic. 42 G5
Pascoe Vale South Vic. 42 G6
Paskeville SA 73 I6
Pata SA 16 A7, 52 A7, 73 N8, 82 G2
Patchewollock Vic. 16 D9, 52 G12, 54 G2
Pateena Tas. 163 K9
Paterson NSW 13 L3
Patersonia Tas. 163 L7
Patho Vic. 50 B5, 55 P6
Patonga NSW 7 O1, 11 N4
Patrick Estate Qld 134 B10, 135 A3
Patterson Lakes Vic. 44 E5
Patyah Vic. 54 C10, 82 H9
Paupong NSW 20 B8, 58 C5
Pawleena Tas. 157 P1, 159 L3, 161 L6
Pawtella Tas. 161 L3
Payneham SA 68 E11, 69 E1
Payneham South SA 68 E11, 69 E1
Paynes Crossing NSW 13 K4
Paynes Find WA 97 H12, 98 D3
Paynesville Vic. 49 N6
Peaceful Bay WA 95 I12, 96 E12, 98 D11
Peachester Qld 134 F5
Peak Charles NP WA 98 H8

Peak Crossing Qld 132 A8, 135 B7, 137 M10
Peak Downs Qld 139 I8
Peak Hill NSW 12 E2
Peak Hill WA 97 H7, 100 E8
Peak Range NP Qld 139 I9
Peak View NSW 20 D7, 58 G2
Peake SA 73 M10, 82 E4
Peakhurst NSW 9 I6
Peakhurst Heights NSW 9 I6
Pearce ACT 34 C8
Pearcedale Vic. 44 F9, 47 K9, 48 D7
Pearl Beach NSW 7 P2, 11 N4
Pearsall WA 90 D5
Pearshape Tas. 161 O12
Peats Ridge NSW 11 N1, 13 K5
Pebbly Beach NSW 13 I12, 20 F6
Peebinga SA 16 B8, 52 B9, 73 O9, 82 H3
Peechelba Vic. 17 M12, 51 I6
Peechelba East Vic. 51 I6
Peel NSW 12 H5
Peelwood NSW 12 G7, 20 E1
Pegarah Tas. 161 P11
Pekina SA 73 J3, 75 I10
Pelham Tas. 158 G1, 161 J5
Pelican Rock Qld 139 M8
Pelican Rocks WA 97 F1, 100 B2, 102 B12
Pella Vic. 16 D11, 54 F4
Pelverata Tas. 158 G7, 161 J8
Pemberton WA 94 F9, 96 D11, 98 C11
Pembroke NSW 15 L11
Pemulwuy NSW 6 F9, 8 F1
Penarie NSW 16 H7, 53 M7
Penderlea NSW 20 B8, 58 C4
Pendle Hill NSW 6 G9, 8 G1, 11 J7
Penfield SA 68 F5
Penfield Gardens SA 68 D2
Penguin Tas. 162 G6
Penguin Island WA 93 B8, 96 B6, 98 B8
Penna Tas. 157 K1, 159 K4
Pennant Hills NSW 7 J7, 11 K7
Penneshaw SA 73 I11, 82 A5
Pennington SA 68 C9
Pennyroyal Vic. 46 C10, 57 M9
Penola SA 56 A2, 82 G10
Penong SA 81 K8
Penrice SA 70 F4
Penrith NSW 6 A6, 10 H6, 13 J6
Penrose NSW 13 I9, 20 F3
Penshurst NSW 9 I6, 11 K10
Penshurst Vic. 56 G5
Pentland Qld 138 D3, 145 P3
Penwortham SA 73 J6
Penzance Tas. 159 N8, 161 M8
Peppermint Grove WA 90 C11, 91 A6, 94 C5, 96 B9
Peppers Plains Vic. 16 D12, 54 G6
Peppimenarti NT 103 P2, 116 C8
Percy Isles NP Qld 139 M7
Percydale Vic. 55 K11, 57 K1
Peregian Beach Qld 134 H2, 137 N7
Perekerten NSW 16 H8, 53 N10
Perenjori WA 98 C4
Perenna Vic. 16 C11, 54 E5
Pericoe NSW 20 D10, 58 G8
Perisher NSW 20 A8, 58 B4
Perkins Island Tas. 162 C3
Perkins Reef Vic. 55 N11, 57 N1

Peron WA 92 A2
Peron Island North NT 116 C6
Peron Island South NT 116 C6
Peronne Vic. 54 C9
Perponda SA 73 M9, 82 E3
Perroomba SA 73 J3, 74 H10
Perry Bridge Vic. 49 L6
Perth Tas. 163 K9
Perth WA 89 F4, 90 F9, 91 C4, 93 C5, 96 C5, 98 C7
Perth Airport WA 90 H8, 91 E3
Perthville NSW 12 H5
Petcheys Bay Tas. 158 F9, 161 J9
Peterborough SA 73 K3, 75 I11
Peterborough Vic. 57 I9
Peterhead SA 68 B9, 70 A8, 71 E1
Petersham NSW 7 K12, 9 K4
Petersville SA 73 I7
Petford Qld 141 K7
Petina SA 72 A2, 81 N9
Petrie Qld 130 H6, 131 I7, 134 F9, 135 D2
Petrie Terrace Qld 129 B5
Pheasant Creek Vic. 47 K3, 48 D3
Phegans Bay NSW 7 P1
Phillip ACT 34 D7
Phillip Bay NSW 9 M7
Phillip Island Vic. 47 J10, 48 C8
Piallaway NSW 14 H9
Pialligo ACT 34 F7
Piambie Vic. 16 G8, 53 K9
Piangil Vic. 16 G8, 53 L11
Piangil North Vic. 53 L11
Piawaning WA 96 C2, 98 C6
Piccadilly SA 69 G3
Pickertaramoor NT 116 D3
Picnic Bay Qld 141 N11
Picnic Point NSW 8 H6, 17 J11, 50 D4
Picola Vic. 17 K12, 50 D5
Picola North Vic. 50 D5
Picton NSW 10 F12, 13 J7, 20 G1
Picton WA 94 D4
Pidna NP Qld 137 L7
Pier Millan Vic. 16 F9, 53 I12, 55 I1
Piesse Brook WA 91 H3
Piesseville WA 95 J2, 96 F7
Pigeon Hole NT 118 E4
Pigeon Ponds Vic. 54 E12, 56 E2
Piggabeen NSW 135 G11
Piggoreet Vic. 46 B4, 57 L5
Pikedale Qld 15 K2, 137 K11
Pilchers Bridge Vic. 50 A10, 55 O11
Pile Siding Vic. 46 A11
Pillar Valley NSW 15 N6
Pilliga NSW 14 D6
Pilliga NP NSW 14 D7
Pilliga West NP NSW 14 D7
Pilot Hill NSW 12 D11, 20 A5, 51 P4
Pimba SA 74 E6
Pimpama Qld 133 M12, 135 F8
Pimpinio Vic. 54 F8
Pindar WA 97 E12, 98 B3
Pine Creek NT 115 I12, 116 F7
Pine Islets Qld 139 M7
Pine Lodge Vic. 50 F7
Pine Mountain Qld 130 A12, 132 A2
Pine Point SA 73 I8, 82 A2
Pine Ridge NSW 12 G6, 14 G10
Pine Scrub Tas. 160 A9
Pinelands NT 113 I7

Pinery SA 70 A2, 73 J7, 82 B1
Pingaring WA 96 H6, 98 F8
Pingelly WA 96 E6, 98 D8
Pingrup WA 95 O3, 96 H8, 98 F9
Pinjar WA 90 C1
Pinjarra WA 92 F11, 93 D10, 96 C6, 98 C8
Pinjarra Hills Qld 132 F3
Pinkenba Qld 131 L9, 133 K1
Pinnaroo SA 16 B9, 52 B11, 54 B1, 73 O10, 82 H4
Pioneer Tas. 163 N6
Pioneer Peaks NP Qld 139 K5
Pipalyatjara SA 78 C2, 101 P8, 120 B12
Pipeclay NP Qld 137 N6
Piper Islands NP Qld 142 E6
Pipers Brook Tas. 163 K6
Pipers River Tas. 163 K6
Pira Vic. 16 G9, 53 L12, 55 L1
Piries Vic. 47 P1, 48 H1, 50 H11
Pirlangimpi NT 116 C2
Pirlta Vic. 16 D6, 52 F7
Pirron Yallock Vic. 46 A9, 57 K8
Pithara WA 96 D1, 98 C5
Pitt Town NSW 6 F1, 11 I4
Pitt Town Bottoms NSW 6 E2
Pittong Vic. 46 B4, 57 K4
Pittsworth Qld 137 K9
Pittwater NSW 7 O4
Plainland Qld 134 A11
Pleasant Hills NSW 12 A10, 17 N10, 51 K2
Pleasure Point NSW 8 G6
Plenty Tas. 158 F3, 161 J6
Plenty Vic. 43 J4, 47 J4
Plumpton NSW 6 E7
Plumpton Vic. 42 B3
Plympton SA 69 C3
Plympton Park SA 69 C3
Pmara Jutunta NT 121 I4
Poatina Tas. 163 J10
Poeppel Corner NT 76 H2, 121 P11, 146 A3
Point Addis Marine NP Vic. 46 E10, 57 N8
Point Clare NSW 11 N3
Point Cook Vic. 42 C9, 46 H6, 48 B5, 57 P6
Point Cooke Marine Sanctuary Vic. 46 H6, 48 B5, 57 P6
Point Danger Marine Sanctuary Vic. 46 F9, 57 N8
Point Grey WA 92 A12
Point Hicks Marine NP Vic. 20 C12, 58 E12
Point Leo Vic. 47 J10, 48 C8
Point Lonsdale Vic. 46 G9, 48 B7, 57 P8
Point Lookout Qld 135 H4, 137 O9
Point Nepean NP Vic. 46 H9, 48 B7, 57 P8
Point Pass SA 73 K6
Point Piper NSW 7 N12, 9 N4
Point Samson WA 97 F1, 100 B2, 102 B12
Point Turton SA 72 G9
Pokataroo NSW 14 D4
Police Point Tas. 158 G9, 161 J9
Policemans Point SA 73 L12, 82 D6
Pomborneit Vic. 57 K8
Pomborneit East Vic. 46 A9
Pomona Qld 134 F1, 137 N7

Pomonal Vic. 54 H12, 56 H1
Pompapiel Vic. 55 N8
Pompoota SA 73 L9
Ponde SA 70 H9, 73 L9
Pontville Tas. 159 I3, 161 K6
Pontypool Tas. 161 N4
Poochera SA 72 B2, 74 A10, 81 O10
Poolaijelo Vic. 54 B12, 56 B1, 82 H10
Poona NP Qld 137 N5
Pooncarie NSW 16 F3, 53 I1
Poonindie SA 72 D8
Pooraka SA 68 E8, 70 B8, 71 F1
Pootilla Vic. 46 D3
Pootnoura SA 79 N9
Poowong Vic. 47 M10, 48 F7
Poowong East Vic. 47 N10, 48 F7
Popanyinning WA 96 E6
Popran NP NSW 7 M1, 11 M2, 13 K5
Porcupine Gorge NP Qld 138 C3, 145 O3
Porcupine Ridge Vic. 46 F1, 57 N2
Porepunkah Vic. 51 K9
Pormpuraaw Qld 140 E1, 142 A12
Porongurup NP WA 95 M9, 96 G11, 98 E11
Port Adelaide SA 68 B8, 70 A8, 71 E1, 73 J9, 82 B3
Port Albert Vic. 49 I10
Port Alma Qld 139 N11
Port Arthur Tas. 159 M9, 161 M9
Port Augusta SA 72 H2, 74 G9
Port Bonython SA 72 H3, 74 G11
Port Botany NSW 9 L7
Port Broughton SA 73 I5, 74 G12
Port Campbell Vic. 57 I9
Port Campbell NP Vic. 57 J10
Port Clinton SA 73 I7, 82 A1
Port Davis SA 73 I4, 74 G11
Port Denison WA 98 A4
Port Douglas Qld 141 L5
Port Elliot SA 71 F8, 73 J11, 82 B5
Port Fairy Vic. 56 F8
Port Franklin Vic. 48 H10
Port Gawler SA 68 A2, 70 A6, 73 J8, 82 B2
Port Germein SA 73 I3, 74 G11
Port Gibbon SA 72 F6
Port Hedland WA 100 D1, 102 D11
Port Hughes SA 72 H6
Port Huon Tas. 158 F8, 161 I9
Port Julia SA 73 I8, 82 A2
Port Keats (Wadeye) NT 103 P2, 116 B8
Port Kembla NSW 13 J8, 20 H2
Port Kennedy WA 92 C4
Port Kenny SA 72 B4, 81 O11
Port Latta Tas. 162 D4
Port Lincoln SA 72 D8
Port MacDonnell SA 56 A6, 82 G12
Port Macquarie NSW 15 M11
Port Melbourne Vic. 41 A11, 42 F8
Port Minlacowie SA 72 H9
Port Neill SA 72 E6
Port Noarlunga SA 69 A8, 70 A11, 71 E4, 73 J10, 82 B3
Port Noarlunga South SA 69 A9
Port of Brisbane Qld 131 M9, 133 L1
Port Phillip Heads Marine NP Vic. 46 G9, 48 B7, 57 P8

Port Pirie SA 73 I4, 74 H11
Port Rickaby SA 72 H8
Port Smith WA 102 G8
Port Sorell Tas. 163 I6
Port Victoria SA 72 H8
Port Vincent SA 73 I8, 82 A2
Port Wakefield SA 73 I7, 82 A1
Port Welshpool Vic. 48 H10
Port Willunga SA 69 A12, 70 A12, 71 E5
Portarlington Vic. 46 H8, 48 B6, 57 P7
Porters Retreat NSW 12 H7, 20 E1
Portland NSW 13 I5
Portland Vic. 56 D8
Portland Roads Qld 142 E7
Portsea Vic. 46 H9, 48 B7, 57 P8
Poruma Qld 142 E1
Possession Island NP Qld 142 C2
Postans WA 91 C12, 92 C1
Potato Point NSW 20 F7
Potts Hill NSW 7 I12, 9 I4
Potts Point NSW 5 H6, 7 M11, 9 M3
Pottsville NSW 15 O2, 137 N11
Pound Creek Vic. 47 N12, 48 F9
Powelltown Vic. 47 N6, 48 F5
Powers Creek Vic. 54 C12, 56 C1, 82 H10
Powlett River Vic. 47 L12, 48 E9
Powranna Tas. 163 K9
Pozieres Qld 15 K2, 137 K11
Prahran Vic. 42 H9, 43 I9
Prairie Qld 138 C4, 145 O4
Prairie Vic. 17 I12, 50 A6, 55 O7
Prairiewood NSW 6 F10, 8 F2
Pratten Qld 15 K1, 137 K10
Precipice NP Qld 137 I3
Premaydena Tas. 159 M8, 161 M8
Premer NSW 14 F10
Prenzlau Qld 134 B11
Preolenna Tas. 162 E5
Preston Tas. 162 G7
Preston Vic. 42 H6, 43 I6, 47 J5, 48 C4
Preston Beach WA 93 C12, 94 C1, 96 B7, 98 C9
Prestons NSW 8 E4
Prevelly WA 94 A7, 96 B10
Price SA 73 I7, 82 A1
Priestdale Qld 133 K6
Primrose Sands Tas. 159 L5, 161 L7
Prince of Wales (Muralag) Island Qld 142 C2
Prince Regent NP WA 103 K4
Princes Hill Vic. 42 H7
Princetown Vic. 57 J10
Priory Tas. 163 O7
Prooinga Vic. 16 F8, 53 J10
Propodollah Vic. 54 D6
Proserpine Qld 139 J4
Prospect NSW 6 F8, 8 E1
Prospect SA 68 D10, 69 D1
Prospect Hill SA 69 G10
Proston Qld 137 L6
Prudhoe Island Qld 139 L6
Puckapunyal Vic. 50 D10
Pullabooka NSW 12 D5
Pullenvale Qld 130 E12, 132 E2, 134 E11, 135 C5
Pullut Vic. 16 D11, 54 F5

Punchbowl NSW 9 I5
Punthari SA 70 H8, 73 L9, 82 D3
Punyelroo SA 73 L8, 82 E2
Pura Pura Vic. 57 J5
Puralka Vic. 56 B5, 82 H12
Purfleet NSW 13 N1, 15 L12
Purga Qld 132 A6, 135 B6, 137 M9
Purlewaugh NSW 14 E10
Purnim Vic. 56 H7
Purnong SA 73 L9, 82 E3
Purnululu NP WA 103 O6, 118 A5
Putney NSW 7 J10, 9 J2
Putty NSW 13 J4
Pyalong Vic. 50 C11
Pyap SA 16 A6, 52 A7, 73 N8, 82 G1
Pyengana Tas. 163 N7
Pygery SA 72 C3, 74 B11
Pymble NSW 7 K7, 11 L7
Pyramid Hill Vic. 17 I12, 55 N6
Pyrmont NSW 5 A6, 7 L12, 9 L3

Quaama NSW 20 E8, 58 H5
Quairading WA 96 E5, 98 D7
Quakers Hill NSW 6 F6, 11 I6
Qualco SA 73 M7
Quambatook Vic. 16 G11, 55 L5
Quambone NSW 14 B8
Quamby Qld 143 E10, 144 G2
Quamby Brook Tas. 163 I9
Quandary NSW 12 B7, 17 P7
Quandialla NSW 12 D6
Quandong Roadhouse NSW 18 C11, 75 P9
Quantong Vic. 54 F9
Queanbeyan NSW 12 F11, 20 D5, 31 F6, 34 H8
Queanbeyan East NSW 34 H7
Queanbeyan West NSW 34 G8
Queens Domain Tas. 155 B1, 156 D6
Queens Park NSW 9 M5
Queens Park WA 90 G10, 91 E5
Queenscliff NSW 7 N9, 9 N1
Queenscliff Vic. 46 H9, 48 B7, 57 P8
Queenstown SA 68 B9
Queenstown Tas. 160 D1, 162 D11
Quellington WA 93 H3, 96 D4
Quilpie Qld 147 L5
Quindalup WA 94 B5
Quindanning WA 93 H12, 94 G1, 96 D7, 98 C9
Quinninup WA 94 F9, 96 D10, 98 C11
Quinns Rocks WA 90 A1, 93 B3, 96 B4, 98 B7
Quirindi NSW 14 H10
Quoiba Tas. 162 H6
Quoin Rock WA 96 B10, 98 B11
Quorn SA 73 I1, 74 H9

Rabbit Flat Roadhouse NT 118 C10
Rabbit Rock Vic. 48 H11
Raby NSW 8 C7
Raceview Qld 132 C6
Raglan Qld 139 M11
Raglan Vic. 46 A1, 57 K3
Railton Tas. 162 H7
Rainbow Vic. 16 D11, 54 F5
Rainbow Beach Qld 137 N6
Rainbow Flat NSW 13 N2
Raine Island NP Qld 142 G4
Raleigh NSW 15 M8

Ramco SA 73 M7, 82 E1
Raminea Tas. 158 F10, 161 I10
Ramingining NT 117 K4
Ramornie NP NSW 15 M6
Ramsbotham Rocks Vic. 48 G12
Ramsgate NSW 9 K7
Ramsgate Beach NSW 9 K7
Ranceby Vic. 47 N10, 48 F8
Rand NSW 12 A11, 17 N11, 51 J3
Randwick NSW 9 M5, 11 M9, 13 K7
Ranelagh Tas. 158 G6, 161 J8
Ranford WA 93 G10
Ranga Tas. 160 B10, 163 O1
Rankins Springs NSW 17 N5
Rannes Qld 137 I1, 139 L12
Ransome Qld 133 L3
Rapid Bay SA 71 B8, 73 I11, 82 A5
Rapid Creek NT 112 B2
Rappville NSW 15 N4
Rathdowney Qld 15 N1, 135 B11, 137 M11
Rathmines NSW 13 L4
Rathscar Vic. 55 L11
Raukkan SA 82 C5
Ravenhall Vic. 42 C6
Ravensbourne NP Qld 137 L9
Ravenshoe Qld 141 L7
Ravensthorpe WA 98 G9
Ravenswood Qld 138 G3
Ravenswood Vic. 55 N11
Ravenswood WA 92 E10
Ravenswood South Vic. 50 A10, 55 O11
Ravensworth NSW 13 K2
Rawdon Vale NSW 13 M1, 15 J12
Rawlinna WA 99 L5
Raymond Terrace NSW 13 M4
Raywood Vic. 50 A7, 55 O9
Red Banks SA 73 K5
Red Beach Qld 142 B5
Red Bluff WA 97 B6
Red Cliffs Vic. 16 E6, 52 G6
Red Hill ACT 34 D7
Red Hill Qld 129 A3, 130 H11, 131 I11, 132 H1, 133 I1
Red Hill Vic. 47 I10, 48 C7
Red Hill WA 91 H1
Red Hill South Vic. 47 I10
Red Hills Tas. 163 I8
Red Jacket Vic. 48 H4
Red Range NSW 15 K6
Red Rock NSW 15 J4
Redan Vic. 46 C3
Redbank Qld 132 E5, 134 D12, 135 C5
Redbank Vic. 55 K11
Redbank Plains Qld 132 D6, 134 D12, 135 C6
Redbanks SA 70 B4, 72 F6, 73 J8, 82 B1
Redcastle Vic. 50 C9
Redcliffe Qld 131 L6, 134 G9, 135 E2, 137 N9
Redcliffe WA 90 G8, 91 E3
Redesdale Vic. 50 B10, 55 P11, 57 P1
Redfern NSW 5 C12, 7 L12, 9 M5, 11 L9
Redhill SA 73 I5, 74 H12
Redland Bay Qld 133 N6, 135 F6, 137 N9
Redmond WA 95 L10, 96 G11
Redpa Tas. 162 B4
Redwood Park SA 68 G8

Reedy Creek Qld 135 F10
Reedy Creek SA 82 E9
Reedy Creek Vic. 47 K1, 48 D1, 50 D12
Reedy Dam Vic. 16 E11, 55 I5
Reedy Flat Vic. 49 O3
Reedy Marsh Tas. 163 I8
Reefton NSW 12 C7, 17 P7
Reekara Tas. 161 O10
Reeves Plains SA 68 D1
Regans Ford WA 96 B3, 98 B6
Regatta Point Tas. 160 C2, 162 C12
Regency Park SA 68 C9
Regents Park NSW 6 H11, 7 I11, 8 H3, 9 I3, 11 K9
Regents Park Qld 132 H7, 133 I7
Regentville NSW 6 A7
Reid ACT 33 H3, 34 E5
Reid SA 68 H1
Reid WA 80 A5, 99 O4
Reid River Qld 138 G2, 141 N12
Reids Creek Vic. 51 J7
Reids Flat NSW 12 F7, 20 D1
Reidsdale NSW 12 H11, 20 E5
Rekuna Tas. 159 J3, 161 K6
Relbia Tas. 163 K8
Reliance Creek NP Qld 139 K5
Remine Tas. 162 C10
Rendelsham SA 82 F11
Renison Bell Tas. 162 D9
Renmark SA 16 A5, 52 B5, 73 O7, 82 G1
Renner Springs NT 119 I7
Rennie NSW 17 M11, 50 H4
Renown Park SA 68 C11, 69 D1
Repulse Islands NP Qld 139 K4
Research Vic. 43 L5
Reservoir Vic. 42 H5, 43 I5, 47 J5
Restoration Rock Qld 142 E7
Retreat Tas. 163 K6
Revesby NSW 8 H5, 11 J10
Revesby Heights NSW 8 H6
Reynella SA 69 B7, 70 B10, 71 E4
Reynella East SA 69 C7
Rheban Tas. 159 N2, 161 M6
Rheola Vic. 55 M9
Rhodes NSW 7 J10, 9 J2, 11 K8
Rhyll Vic. 47 K11, 48 D8
Rhymney Reef Vic. 55 I12, 57 I2
Rhyndaston Tas. 161 K5
Rhynie SA 73 J7, 82 B1
Riachella Vic. 55 I10
Riana Tas. 162 F6
Rich Avon Vic. 55 I8
Richardson ACT 34 D10
Richlands NSW 12 H8, 20 E2
Richlands Qld 132 G5, 134 E12, 135 D5
Richmond NSW 6 C1, 10 H4, 13 J6
Richmond Qld 145 L3
Richmond SA 68 C12, 69 C2
Richmond Tas. 156 F1, 157 I1, 159 J3, 161 K6
Richmond Vic. 42 H8, 43 I8, 47 J5, 48 C4
Richmond Lowlands NSW 6 C1
Richmond Range NP NSW 15 M2, 137 M12
Ricketts Point Marine Sanctuary Vic. 47 J7, 48 C5
Riddells Creek Vic. 46 H3, 48 B2, 57 P3
Ridgehaven SA 68 G8

Ridgelands Qld 139 M10
Ridgeway Tas. 156 B9, 159 I6
Ridgewood WA 90 A1
Ridgley Tas. 162 F6
Ridleyton SA 68 C11, 69 C1
Riggs Creek Vic. 50 F8
Ringa WA 93 F2, 96 D4
Ringarooma Tas. 163 M7
Ringwood Vic. 43 M8, 47 K6, 48 D4
Ringwood East Vic. 43 M8
Ringwood North Vic. 43 M8
Rinyirru (Lakefield) NP (CYPAL) Qld 141 I1, 142 F12
Ripley Qld 132 C6, 135 B6
Ripplebrook Vic. 47 N9, 48 F7
Ripponlea Vic. 42 H10
Risdon Tas. 156 D1, 159 I4
Risdon Vale Tas. 156 F2, 159 J4, 161 K7
River Heads Qld 137 N4
Riverhills Qld 132 F4
Riverside Tas. 163 K8
Riverstone NSW 6 G5, 11 I6
Riverton SA 73 J7, 82 C1
Riverton WA 90 F12, 91 D6
Rivervale WA 90 F9, 91 D4
Riverview NSW 7 L10, 9 L2
Riverview Qld 132 D5, 134 D12, 135 C5
Riverwood NSW 9 I5, 11 K10
Rivett ACT 34 B7
Roadvale Qld 135 A8
Rob Roy Vic. 47 K4
Robbins Island Tas. 162 B2
Robe SA 82 E9
Robertson NSW 13 J9, 20 G3
Robertson Qld 133 I5
Robertstown SA 73 K6
Robigana Tas. 163 J7
Robina Qld 135 G10
Robinson River NT 119 N4
Robinvale Vic. 16 F7, 53 J8
Rochedale Qld 133 J5
Rochedale South Qld 133 J6
Rocherlea Tas. 163 K8
Roches Beach Tas. 157 L8
Rochester SA 73 J5
Rochester Vic. 50 C7
Rochford Vic. 46 H1, 48 B1, 50 B12, 57 P3
Rock Dunder WA 96 H11, 98 E11
Rock Flat NSW 20 C8, 58 F4
Rockbank Vic. 42 A4, 46 H5, 48 B4, 57 P5
Rockdale NSW 9 K6
Rockhampton Qld 139 M11
Rockingham WA 92 B3, 93 B7, 96 B6, 98 B8
Rocklea Qld 132 H4, 133 I4, 134 F12, 135 D5
Rockleigh SA 70 F9
Rockley NSW 12 H6
Rocklyn Vic. 46 E2, 57 N3
Rocksberg Qld 130 E1, 134 E7, 135 C1
Rocky Cape Tas. 162 D4
Rocky Cape NP Tas. 162 E4
Rocky Creek NSW 14 G6
Rocky Crossing Qld 139 K9
Rocky Dam NSW 15 I3, 137 I12
Rocky Glen NSW 14 E9
Rocky Gully WA 95 I9, 96 E10, 98 D11
Rocky Hall NSW 20 D10, 58 G7

Rocky River NSW 15 J8
Rocky River SA 72 F12
Rodd Point NSW 7 K11, 9 K3
Roe Rocks WA 98 F10
Roebourne WA 97 F1, 100 B2, 102 B12
Roebuck Roadhouse WA 102 H7
Roelands WA 94 D3
Roger River Tas. 162 C4
Roger River West Tas. 162 C5
Rokeby Tas. 156 H11, 157 I7, 159 J5, 161 K7
Rokeby Vic. 47 N8, 48 G6
Rokewood Vic. 46 C6, 57 L6
Rokewood Junction Vic. 46 B5, 57 L5
Roland Tas. 162 G7
Roleystone WA 91 H8, 93 D6
Rollands Plains NSW 15 L10
Rolleston Qld 136 G1
Rollingstone Qld 141 M11
Roly Rock WA 97 E1, 100 A2, 102 A12
Roma Qld 136 G6
Romsey Vic. 46 H2, 48 B2, 50 B12, 57 P3
Rookhurst NSW 13 M1, 15 J12
Rookwood NSW 7 I11, 9 I3
Rooty Hill NSW 6 E7, 11 I7
Roper Bar Store NT 117 J9
Ropes Crossing NSW 6 C6
Rorruwuy NT 117 M4
Rosa Glen WA 94 B7, 96 B10
Rosanna Vic. 43 J6
Rose Bay NSW 7 N12, 9 N4
Rose Bay Tas. 156 F6
Rose Park SA 68 E12, 69 E2
Rosebery NSW 9 L5
Rosebery NT 113 K11
Rosebery Tas. 162 D9
Rosebery Vic. 16 E11
Rosebrook Vic. 56 G8
Rosebud Vic. 47 I10, 48 C7
Rosedale NSW 20 F6
Rosedale Qld 137 L2
Rosedale SA 70 D5
Rosedale Vic. 49 J7
Rosegarland Tas. 158 F2, 161 J6
Rosehill NSW 6 H10, 7 I10, 8 H2, 9 I2
Roselands NSW 9 I5
Rosemeadow NSW 8 B9
Rosenthal NSW 13 N2
Roses Tier Tas. 163 M8
Rosetta Tas. 156 A3
Rosevale Qld 137 M10
Rosevale Tas. 163 J8
Rosevears Tas. 163 J7
Roseville NSW 7 L9, 9 L1
Roseville Chase NSW 7 M9, 9 M1
Rosewater SA 68 B9
Rosewhite Vic. 51 K9
Rosewood NSW 12 C11, 51 O4
Rosewood Qld 134 B12, 135 A5, 137 M9
Roseworthy SA 70 D4, 73 J8, 82 C2
Roslyn NSW 12 G8, 20 E2
Roslynmead Vic. 17 I12, 50 B5, 55 P6
Rosny Tas. 156 F7
Rosny Park Tas. 156 F6, 159 J5, 161 K7
Ross Tas. 161 L2, 163 L12

Ross Creek Vic. 46 C4, 57 L4
Rossarden Tas. 163 M10
Rossbridge Vic. 57 I3
Rossi NSW 12 G11, 20 D5, 31 H7
Rosslyn Park SA 68 F12, 69 F1
Rossmore NSW 6 B12, 8 B4, 10 H9
Rossmoyne WA 90 F12, 91 D6
Rossville Qld 141 L3
Rostrevor SA 68 F11, 69 F1, 70 C8, 71 G1
Rostron Vic. 55 J10
Rothbury NSW 13 L3
Rothwell Qld 131 J4, 134 F9, 135 E2
Roto NSW 17 L3
Rottnest Island WA 93 A6, 96 B5, 98 B7
Round Corner NSW 11 K6
Round Rock Qld 139 M8
Round Top Island NP Qld 139 K6
Rouse Hill NSW 6 G5
Rowella Tas. 163 J6
Rowena NSW 14 D5
Rowland Flat SA 70 E5
Rowley Shoals Marine Park 102 D7
Rowsley Vic. 46 F4, 48 A4, 57 O5
Rowville Vic. 43 M11, 44 G2, 45 I1, 47 K6
Roxburgh NSW 13 K2
Roxburgh Park Vic. 42 G2
Roxby Downs SA 74 E4
Royal George Tas. 161 N1, 163 N11
Royal NP NSW 8 H11, 9 I8, 11 J12, 13 K7, 20 H1
Royal Park SA 68 B10
Royalla NSW 12 F11, 20 D5, 31 E7, 34 E11
Royston Park SA 68 E11, 69 E1
Rozelle NSW 7 L11, 9 L3
Ruabon WA 94 C5
Rubicon Vic. 47 N2, 48 G2, 50 G12
Ruby Vic. 47 N11, 48 F8
Rubyvale Qld 138 H10
Rudall SA 72 E5
Ruffy Vic. 50 E10
Rufus River NSW 16 C5, 52 D5, 73 P7
Rug Rock WA 99 I9
Rugby NSW 12 F8, 20 C2
Rukenvale NSW 15 N2
Rules Point NSW 12 E12, 20 B6
Rum Jungle NT 114 E6
Runcorn Qld 133 I5, 134 F12, 135 D5
Rundle Range NP Qld 139 N11
Running Creek Vic. 51 L8
Running Stream NSW 12 H4
Runnymede Tas. 159 K2, 161 L6
Rupanyup Vic. 54 H9
Rupanyup North Vic. 54 H8
Rupanyup South Vic. 54 H9
Ruse NSW 8 D8
Rush Creek Qld 130 F3
Rushcutters Bay NSW 7 M12, 9 M4
Rushworth Vic. 50 D8
Russell ACT 33 H7, 34 F6
Russell Island Qld 133 O9, 135 G6, 137 N9, 141 M7
Russell Lea NSW 7 K11, 9 K3
Russell River NP Qld 141 M7
Russell Rock WA 99 I9

Rutherglen Vic. 17 N12, 51 J6
Ryanby Vic. 53 K12, 55 K1
Ryans Creek Vic. 50 H9
Rydal NSW 10 A2
Rydalmere NSW 7 I9, 9 I1
Ryde NSW 7 J9, 9 J1, 11 L8
Rye Vic. 46 H10, 48 B7, 57 P9
Rye Park NSW 12 F8, 20 C2
Rylstone NSW 13 I3
Rythdale Vic. 45 K8
Ryton Vic. 48 H9

Sackville North NSW 11 J3
Saddleworth SA 73 K6
Sadleir NSW 6 E12, 8 E4
Sadliers Crossing Qld 132 B5
Safety Bay WA 92 A3, 93 B8
Safety Beach NSW 15 N7
Safety Beach Vic. 44 B12, 47 I9, 48 C7
Sail Rock WA 99 J9
St Agnes SA 68 G9
St Albans NSW 13 K5
St Albans Vic. 42 D5, 47 I5, 48 B4, 57 P5
St Andrews NSW 8 D7
St Andrews Vic. 43 N1, 47 K4, 48 D3
St Arnaud Vic. 55 K9
St Aubyn Qld 137 L8
St Clair NSW 6 C8, 8 C1, 13 L2
St Fillans Vic. 47 M4, 48 F3
St George Qld 136 F9
St Georges SA 69 E3
St Georges Basin NSW 13 I10, 20 G4
St Helena Vic. 43 K5
St Helena Island (Noogoon) Qld 131 M10, 133 M1, 134 H10, 135 F4, 137 N9
St Helena Island NP Qld 131 M10, 133 M1, 134 H10, 135 F4, 137 N9
St Helens Tas. 163 O8
St Helens Vic. 56 F7
St Helens Park NSW 8 C9
St Ives NSW 7 L6, 11 L7
St Ives Chase NSW 7 L6
St James Vic. 50 G7
St James WA 90 G10, 91 E5
St Johns Park NSW 6 F11, 8 F3
St Kilda SA 68 B6, 70 B7, 73 J8, 82 B2
St Kilda Vic. 42 H9, 47 I6, 48 C5
St Kilda East Vic. 42 H10, 43 I10
St Kilda West Vic. 42 H9
St Kitts SA 70 F3
St Lawrence Qld 139 K8
St Leonards NSW 7 L10, 9 L2, 11 L8
St Leonards Tas. 163 K8
St Leonards Vic. 46 H8, 48 B6, 57 P7
St Lucia Qld 130 H12, 132 H2, 133 I3
St Marys NSW 6 C6, 10 H7
St Marys SA 69 D4
St Marys Tas. 163 O9
St Morris SA 68 E11, 69 E1
St Patricks River Tas. 163 L7
St Pauls Qld 142 C1
St Peter Island SA 81 M9
St Peters NSW 9 L5
St Peters SA 67 H2, 68 E11, 69 E1
Sale Vic. 49 K7

Salisbury NSW 13 L2
Salisbury Qld 133 I5
Salisbury SA 68 E6, 70 C7, 73 J8, 82 B2
Salisbury Vic. 16 C12, 54 E7
Salisbury Downs SA 68 E7
Salisbury East SA 68 F7
Salisbury Heights SA 68 F6
Salisbury North SA 68 E6
Salisbury Park SA 68 F6
Salisbury Plain SA 68 F7
Salisbury South SA 68 E7
Salisbury West Vic. 55 N8
Sallys Flat NSW 12 H4
Salmon Gums WA 99 I8
Salmon Ponds Tas. 158 G3
Salt Creek SA 82 E6
Salter Point WA 90 F12, 91 D6
Salter Springs SA 70 C1, 73 J7, 82 B1
Saltwater NP NSW 13 O2
Saltwater River Tas. 159 L7, 161 L8
Samaria Vic. 50 H9
Samford Qld 134 E10, 135 C3
Samford Valley Qld 130 E8
Samford Village Qld 130 F9
Samson WA 91 B8
Samsonvale Qld 130 F4
San Remo Vic. 47 K11, 48 D8
San Remo WA 92 C8
Sanctuary Cove Qld 135 F8, 137 N10
Sand Bank No.7 Qld 142 F9
Sand Bank No.8 Qld 142 F9
Sandalwood SA 73 M9, 82 F3
Sandbanks NP Qld 142 F9
Sandergrove SA 71 H6, 82 C4
Sanderston SA 70 H7, 73 K8, 82 D2
Sandfire Roadhouse WA 102 F10
Sandfly Tas. 158 H6, 161 J8
Sandford Tas. 157 J11, 159 K6, 161 L7
Sandford Vic. 56 D3, 82 H11
Sandgate Qld 131 J8, 134 F10, 135 E3
Sandhill Lake Vic. 16 H11, 55 M4
Sandhurst Vic. 44 F6
Sandigo NSW 12 A9, 17 N9
Sandilands SA 72 H8
Sandon Vic. 55 N12, 57 N2
Sandringham NSW 9 K7
Sandringham Vic. 42 H12, 43 I12, 44 C2, 47 J6, 48 C5
Sandsmere Vic. 16 B12, 54 C7, 82 H7
Sandstone WA 98 F1, 100 F12
Sandstone Point Qld 131 L1
Sandy Bay Tas. 155 F11, 156 D8, 159 I6, 161 K7
Sandy Beach NSW 15 N7
Sandy Creek SA 70 D5
Sandy Creek Vic. 51 L7
Sandy Creek Upper Vic. 51 L7
Sandy Flat NSW 15 L4
Sandy Hill NSW 15 L3, 137 L12
Sandy Hollow NSW 13 J2
Sandy Point NSW 8 G6, 11 J10, 12 H10, 20 E4
Sandy Point Vic. 20 A11, 48 G10, 49 P4, 58 A10
Sangar NSW 17 M11, 50 H3
Sans Souci NSW 9 J7

Santa Barbara Qld 135 F8
Santa Teresa (Ltyente Purte) NT 121 J7
Sapphire NSW 15 J5
Sapphire Qld 138 H10
Sapphiretown SA 72 H11
Sarabah NP Qld 15 N1, 135 D10, 137 N10
Saratoga NSW 11 O3
Sarina Qld 139 K6
Sarina Beach Qld 139 K6
Sarsfield Vic. 49 N5
Sassafras NSW 13 I10, 20 F4
Sassafras Tas. 162 H7
Sassafras Vic. 43 O10
Sassafras East Tas. 163 I7
Saunders Islands NP Qld 142 E5
Savage River Tas. 162 C8
Savage River NP Tas. 162 D7
Savenake NSW 17 M11, 50 H4
Sawmill Settlement Vic. 49 I1, 51 I11
Sawpit Creek NSW 58 C3
Sawtell NSW 15 N8
Sawyers Valley WA 93 E4
Sayers Lake NSW 16 G1, 18 F12
Scaddan WA 99 I9
Scamander Tas. 163 O8
Scarborough NSW 13 J8, 20 H2
Scarborough Qld 131 K5, 134 G9, 135 E2
Scarborough WA 90 C8, 91 A3, 93 B5, 96 B5, 98 B7
Scarsdale Vic. 46 B4, 57 L4
Scawfell Island Qld 139 L5
Sceale Bay SA 72 A3, 81 N11
Scheyville NSW 6 F2, 11 J5
Scheyville NP NSW 6 F2, 11 J4, 13 J6
Schofields NSW 6 E6, 11 I6
Schouten Island Tas. 161 O4
Scone NSW 13 K1, 14 H12
Scone Mountain NP NSW 13 K1, 14 H12
Scoresby Vic. 43 L11, 44 G1
Scotsburn Vic. 46 D4, 57 M4
Scott Creek SA 69 G5
Scott NP WA 94 B8, 96 B10, 98 B11
Scotts Creek Vic. 57 J9
Scotts Head NSW 15 M9
Scottsdale Tas. 163 M6
Scottville Qld 139 I4
Scullin ACT 34 C3
Sea Elephant Tas. 161 P11
Sea Lake Vic. 16 F10, 55 J3
Seabird WA 96 B3
Seabrook Vic. 42 C10
Seacliff SA 69 B5, 70 B10, 71 E3, 82 B3
Seacliff Park SA 69 B5
Seacombe Vic. 49 L7
Seacombe Gardens SA 69 C5
Seacombe Heights SA 69 C5
Seaford SA 69 A10, 70 A11, 71 E5
Seaford Vic. 44 E6, 47 J8, 48 D6
Seaford Heights SA 69 A10
Seaford Meadows SA 69 A9
Seaford Rise SA 69 A10
Seaforth NSW 7 M9, 9 M1
Seaforth Qld 139 K5
Seaham NSW 13 M3
Seaholme Vic. 42 E9
Seal Island WA 93 B7
Seal Rock Tas. 161 O12

Seal Rock WA 99 I9
Seal Rocks NSW 13 N3
Seal Rocks Vic. 47 J11, 48 C8
Seaspray Vic. 49 K8
Seaton SA 68 B10, 69 B1
Seaton Vic. 49 J6
Seaview WA 47 N10, 48 G7
Seaview Downs SA 69 B5
Sebastian Vic. 55 O9
Sebastopol NSW 12 C8, 17 P8
Sebastopol Vic. 46 C3
Second Valley SA 71 B8, 73 I11, 82 A4
Secret Harbour WA 92 B6
Sedan SA 70 H5, 73 L8, 82 D2
Seddon Vic. 42 F8
Sedgwick Vic. 50 A9, 55 O11
Seelands NSW 15 M5
Sefton NSW 6 H11, 8 H3
Sefton Park SA 68 D10
Seisia Qld 142 C3
Selbourne Tas. 163 J8
Selby Vic. 43 P11, 45 J1
Seldom Seen Roadhouse Vic. 20 A10, 49 P2, 51 P12, 58 A8
Sellheim Qld 138 F2
Sellicks Beach SA 71 D6, 73 J10, 82 B4
Semaphore SA 68 A9, 70 A8, 71 E1
Semaphore Park SA 68 A9
Semaphore South SA 68 A9
Separation Creek Vic. 46 C11, 57 M10
Seppeltsfield SA 70 E4, 73 K8
Serpentine Vic. 55 N8
Serpentine WA 92 F4, 93 D8, 96 C6
Serpentine NP WA 92 H3, 93 D8, 96 C6, 98 C8
Serviceton Vic. 16 B12, 54 B7, 82 H7
Seven Hills NSW 6 F8, 8 G1
Seven Hills Qld 131 J12, 133 J2
Seven Mile Beach Tas. 157 M5, 159 K5, 161 L7
Seven Mile Beach NP NSW 13 J9, 20 G3
Sevenhill SA 73 J6
Seventeen Mile Rocks Qld 132 G4
Seventeen Seventy Qld 137 M1
Severnlea Qld 15 K2, 137 K11
Seville Vic. 47 L5, 48 E4
Seville Grove WA 91 G9
Seymour Tas. 163 O10
Seymour Vic. 50 D10
Shackleton WA 96 F4
Shadforth NSW 12 G5
Shady Creek Vic. 47 O8, 48 G6
Shailer Park Qld 133 K7
Shallow Inlet Marine and Coastal Park Vic. 48 G11
Shalvey NSW 6 D6
Shanes Park NSW 6 C6
Shannon Tas. 161 I2, 163 I11
Shannon WA 94 G10, 96 D11, 98 D11
Shannon NP WA 94 G9, 96 D11, 98 D11
Shannons Flat NSW 12 F12, 20 C6, 31 B12, 58 E1
Shark Bay Marine Park WA 97 B8
Shay Gap WA 100 E1, 102 E11
Shays Flat Vic. 55 J11, 57 J1
Sheans Creek Vic. 50 F9
Sheep Hills Vic. 16 E12, 54 H7

Sheffield Tas. 162 H7
Sheidow Park SA 69 B6
Shelbourne Vic. 55 N10
Sheldon Qld 133 L5
Shelford Vic. 46 D7, 57 M6
Shelley Vic. 51 N7
Shelley WA 90 F12, 91 D6
Shellharbour NSW 13 J9, 20 H3
Shelly Beach Tas. 159 N2, 161 M5
Shenton Park WA 90 D9, 91 B4
Sheoaks Vic. 46 E6, 57 N6
Shepherds Flat Vic. 46 E1, 57 N2
Shepparton Vic. 50 E7
Sherbrooke Vic. 43 O11, 45 J1
Sheringa SA 72 C6
Sherlock SA 73 M10, 82 E4
Sherwood Qld 132 H4
Shipley NSW 10 C5
Shirley Vic. 57 J3
Shoal Bay NSW 13 N4
Shoal Bay NT 113 L5
Shoal Point Qld 139 K5
Shoalhaven Heads NSW 13 J10, 20 H4
Shoalwater WA 92 A3
Shoalwater Islands Marine Park WA 93 B8, 96 B6, 98 B8
Shooters Hill NSW 12 H6
Shoreham Vic. 47 J10, 48 C8
Shorncliffe Qld 131 J8, 134 F10, 135 E3
Shotts WA 94 F3
Shute Harbour Qld 139 K3
Sidmouth Tas. 163 J6
Sidonia Vic. 50 B11, 55 P12, 57 P2
Silkstone Qld 132 C5
Silkwood Qld 141 M8
Silloth Rocks Qld 139 L5
Silvan Vic. 43 P10, 47 L6
Silver Creek Vic. 51 J7
Silver Sands SA 71 D6
Silver Sands WA 92 C9
Silverdale NSW 10 F8, 13 J7, 20 H1
Silverton NSW 18 B10, 75 N8
Silverwater NSW 7 I10, 9 I2
Simmie Vic. 50 C6
Simpson Vic. 57 J9
Simpson Desert NP Qld 76 H1, 146 B1
Simpsons Bay Tas. 159 I10, 161 K9
Sinagra WA 90 D4
Single NP NSW 15 J6
Singleton NSW 13 K3
Singleton WA 92 C7, 93 C8, 96 B6, 98 C8
Sinnamon Park Qld 132 G3
Sir Charles Hardy Group NP Qld 142 F5
Sir James Mitchell NP WA 94 F8, 96 D10, 98 C11
Sisters Beach Tas. 162 E4
Sisters Creek Tas. 162 E4
Skenes Creek Vic. 46 B12, 57 L10
Skenes Creek North Vic. 46 B12, 57 L10
Skipton Vic. 46 A4, 57 K4
Skye SA 68 F12, 69 G1
Skye Vic. 44 F6
Slacks Creek Qld 133 J6, 135 E6
Slade Point Qld 139 K5
Slaty Creek Vic. 55 K8
Sloop Rocks Tas. 160 C3, 162 C12
Smeaton Vic. 46 D1, 57 M3
Smeaton Grange NSW 8 B7

Smiggin Holes NSW 20 B8, 58 B4
Smith Islands NP Qld 139 K4
Smith Rock WA 99 I9
Smithfield NSW 6 F10, 8 F2
Smithfield Qld 15 I2, 137 J11
Smithfield SA 68 G5, 70 C6
Smithfield Heights Qld 141 L6
Smithfield Plains SA 68 F4
Smiths Gully Vic. 43 N3, 47 K4, 48 D3
Smiths Lake NSW 13 N3
Smithton Tas. 162 C4
Smithtown NSW 15 M10
Smithville SA 16 A9, 73 N10, 82 F4
Smoko Vic. 51 L10
Smoky Bay SA 81 M9
Smooth Rocks WA 98 F10
Smythesdale Vic. 46 C4, 57 L4
Snake Island Vic. 48 H10, 49 I10
Snake Range NP Qld 138 H12
Snake Valley Vic. 46 B3, 57 L4
Snobs Creek Vic. 47 O2, 48 G2, 50 G12
Snowtown SA 73 I6
Snowy River NP Vic. 20 A10, 49 P3, 51 P12, 58 B8
Snug Tas. 159 I7, 161 K8
Snuggery SA 82 F11
Sodwalls NSW 10 A2
Sofala NSW 12 H4
Somers Vic. 47 J10, 48 D8
Somersby NSW 11 N2
Somerset Tas. 162 F5
Somerset Dam Qld 134 C7
Somerton NSW 14 H9
Somerton Vic. 42 G3
Somerton NP NSW 14 H9
Somerton Park SA 69 B4
Somerville Vic. 44 F9, 47 J9, 48 D7
Sommariva Qld 136 C5, 147 P5
Sorell Tas. 157 P2, 159 K4, 161 L6
Sorrento Vic. 46 H9, 48 B7, 57 P8
Sorrento WA 90 B6, 91 A1
South Arm Tas. 159 J7, 161 K8
South Bank Qld 129 D9
South Brig Rock Tas. 161 P12
South Brighton SA 69 B5
South Brisbane Qld 129 E10, 131 I12, 133 I2
South Bruny NP Tas. 158 G12, 159 I12, 161 J11
South Coogee NSW 9 N6
South Cumberland Islands NP Qld 139 L5
South East Forests NP NSW 20 D10, 58 F8
South Forest Tas. 162 D4
South Fremantle WA 91 A8
South Granville NSW 6 H10, 8 H2
South Guildford WA 90 H7, 91 F2
South Gundagai NSW 12 D9, 20 A4, 51 P1
South Hedland WA 100 D1, 102 D12
South Hobart Tas. 155 B10, 156 C9
South Hurstville NSW 9 J6
South Johnstone Qld 141 M7
South Kilkerran SA 72 H7
South Kingsville Vic. 42 F8
South Kumminin WA 96 G5, 98 E7
South Lake WA 91 D8
South Maclean Qld 132 G10
South Maroota NSW 6 H1, 7 I1

South Melbourne Vic. 41 C9, 42 G9
South Mission Beach Qld 141 M8
South Molle Island Qld 139 K3
South Morang Vic. 43 J3
South Mount Cameron Tas. 163 N6
South Neptunes SA 72 E10
South Page SA 71 C11, 73 I11, 82 A5
South Penrith NSW 6 A7
South Perth WA 89 D11, 90 E10, 91 C5
South Plympton SA 69 C3
South Riana Tas. 162 F6
South Ripley Qld 132 C7
South Springfield Tas. 163 L7
South Stirling WA 95 N9, 96 H10
South Stradbroke Qld 133 P12
South Stradbroke Island Qld 15 O1, 135 G8, 137 N10
South Turramurra NSW 7 J8
South Wentworthville NSW 6 G9, 8 G1
South West Rocks NSW 15 M9
South Wharf Vic. 41 B8
South Windsor NSW 6 D3
South Yaamba Qld 139 M10
South Yarra Vic. 41 H11, 42 H9, 43 I9
South Yunderup WA 92 B11
Southbank Vic. 41 E7, 42 G8
Southbrook Qld 137 K9
Southend Qld 139 N12
Southend SA 82 E11
Southern Cross Vic. 56 G7
Southern Cross WA 98 F6
Southern Moreton Bay Islands NP Qld 133 P12, 135 G8, 137 N10
Southern River WA 91 F8
Southport Qld 135 G9
Southport Tas. 158 F12, 161 I10
Southwest NP Tas. 158 B5, 160 E8, 161 I10
Southwood NP Qld 136 H9, 137 I9
Spalding SA 73 J5, 75 I12
Spalford Tas. 162 G6
Spargo Creek Vic. 46 E2, 57 N3
Spearwood WA 91 B8, 93 C6
Speed Vic. 16 E9, 52 H12, 54 H2
Speewa Vic. 53 L12, 55 L1
Spence ACT 34 C2
Spencer NSW 11 L3
Spicers Creek NSW 12 G2
Split Yard Creek Qld 130 A7
Spotswood Vic. 42 F8, 47 I6
Sprent Tas. 162 G6
Spreyton Tas. 162 H6
Spring Beach Tas. 159 N2, 161 M5
Spring Creek Qld 137 L10
Spring Farm NSW 8 A8
Spring Hill NSW 12 G5
Spring Hill Qld 129 E4, 131 I12, 133 I1
Spring Hill Vic. 46 F1, 48 A1, 50 A12, 57 O2
Spring Mountain Qld 132 E8
Spring Ridge NSW 12 G1, 14 G10
Springbrook Qld 15 O1, 135 E11, 137 N11
Springbrook NP Qld 15 O1, 135 E11, 137 N11
Springdale NSW 12 C8

Springfield Qld 132 F6, 135 C6
Springfield SA 69 E3
Springfield Tas. 163 L7
Springfield Lakes Qld 132 E7
Springhurst Vic. 51 I6
Springmount Vic. 46 D2
Springsure Qld 136 F1, 139 I12
Springton SA 70 F6, 73 K8, 82 C2
Springvale Vic. 43 K12, 44 G2, 47 J7, 48 D5, 56 H9
Springvale South Vic. 44 F2
Springwood NSW 10 F5, 13 J6
Springwood Qld 133 K6, 135 E6
Square Rock WA 99 I9
Staaten River NP Qld 140 G5
Stafford Qld 131 I10, 133 I1, 134 F10, 135 D4
Stafford Heights Qld 131 I10
Staghorn Flat Vic. 51 K7
Stake Hill WA 92 D7
Stamford Qld 138 A5, 145 M5
Stanage Qld 139 L8
Stanborough NSW 15 I6
Stanhope Vic. 50 D7
Stanhope Gardens NSW 6 G6
Stanley Tas. 162 D3
Stanley Vic. 51 K8
Stanmore NSW 7 K12, 9 K4
Stannifer NSW 15 J6
Stannum NSW 15 K4
Stansbury SA 72 H9
Stanthorpe Qld 15 L2, 137 L11
Stanwell Qld 139 M11
Stanwell Park NSW 13 J8, 20 H2
Stapylton Qld 133 L9
Starcke NP Qld 142 H12
Statis Rock NSW 13 N3
Staughton Vale Vic. 46 F5, 57 N6
Stavely Vic. 56 H4
Staverton Tas. 162 G8
Stawell Vic. 55 I11, 57 I1
Steels Creek Vic. 43 P3, 47 L4
Steep Rocks WA 99 I9
Steepcut Rock NT 117 N11, 119 N2
Steiglitz Qld 133 O10, 135 F7
Steiglitz Vic. 46 E6, 57 N6
Stenhouse Bay SA 72 G10
Stephens Creek NSW 18 C9, 75 O8
Stepney SA 68 E11, 69 E1
Steppes Tas. 161 J2, 163 J12
Stieglitz Tas. 163 P8
Stirling ACT 34 C7
Stirling SA 69 G4, 70 C9, 71 G3
Stirling Vic. 49 N3
Stirling WA 90 D7, 91 B3, 93 B5
Stirling North SA 73 I2, 74 G9
Stirling Range NP WA 95 L7, 96 G10, 98 E10
Stockdale Vic. 49 L5
Stockinbingal NSW 12 D8, 20 A2
Stockleigh Qld 132 H10, 133 I10
Stockmans Reward Vic. 47 O4, 48 G3
Stockport SA 70 D2
Stockwell SA 70 F3, 73 K8, 82 C1
Stockyard Hill Vic. 46 A3, 57 K4
Stokers Siding NSW 15 O2
Stokes Bay SA 72 G11
Stokes NP WA 98 H9
Stone Hut SA 73 J4, 74 H11
Stonefield SA 70 H3, 73 L7, 82 D1
Stonehenge NSW 15 K6
Stonehenge Qld 145 L12

Stonehenge Tas. 161 L4
Stoneville WA 93 E4, 99 I5
Stoneyford Vic. 57 K8
Stonor Tas. 161 K4
Stony Creek Vic. 47 O12, 48 G9
Stony Crossing NSW 16 D3, 52 F1, 53 M11, 75 P12
Stony Point Vic. 47 J10, 48 D7
Stonyfell SA 68 F12, 69 F2
Stoodley Tas. 162 H7
Store Creek NSW 12 G3
Stormlea Tas. 159 M9, 161 M9
Storys Creek Tas. 163 M9
Stowport Tas. 162 F5
Stradbroke Vic. 49 K8
Stradbroke West Vic. 49 K8
Strahan Tas. 160 C2, 162 C12
Stratford NSW 13 M2
Stratford Vic. 49 K6
Strath Creek Vic. 47 K1, 48 D1, 50 D12
Strathalbyn SA 70 E12, 71 H5, 73 K10, 82 C4
Strathallan Vic. 50 C6
Stratham WA 94 C4, 96 C8
Strathblane Tas. 158 F11, 161 I10
Strathbogie Vic. 50 F10
Strathdownie Vic. 56 B4, 82 H11
Strathewen Vic. 43 N1, 47 K3, 48 D3
Strathfield NSW 7 I11, 9 I3
Strathfield South NSW 7 I12, 9 I4
Strathfieldsaye Vic. 50 A9, 55 O10
Strathgordon Tas. 160 F6
Strathkellar Vic. 56 F4
Strathlea Vic. 55 M12, 57 M1
Strathmerton Vic. 17 K11, 50 F4
Strathmore Vic. 42 F5
Strathmore Heights Vic. 42 F5
Strathpine Qld 130 H7, 131 I7, 134 F10, 135 D3, 137 N9
Stratton WA 91 G2
Streaky Bay SA 72 A3, 81 N10
Streatham Vic. 57 J4
Stretton Qld 133 I6
Strickland Tas. 161 I4
Stroud NSW 13 M3
Stroud Road NSW 13 M2
Struan SA 54 A11, 82 G9
Strzelecki Vic. 47 N10, 48 F7
Strzelecki NP Tas. 160 B11, 163 O1
Stuart Mill Vic. 55 K10
Stuart Park NT 111 H4, 112 C7
Stuart Town NSW 12 G3
Stuarts Point NSW 15 M9
Stuarts Well NT 121 I8
Sturt SA 69 C5
Sturt NP NSW 18 B1, 75 P1, 77 O11, 146 G11
Subiaco WA 90 D9, 91 B4, 93 C5
Success WA 91 D9
Sue City NSW 12 D12, 20 B6
Suffolk Park NSW 15 O3, 137 N12
Sugarloaf Rock Tas. 160 E10
Sugarloaf Rock WA 96 A9, 98 B10
Suggan Buggan Vic. 20 A9, 49 P1, 51 P11, 58 B7
Sulphur Creek Tas. 162 G5
Summer Hill NSW 7 K12, 9 K4, 11 L9
Summerfield Vic. 50 A7, 55 O9
Summertown SA 68 G12, 69 G3, 70 C9, 71 G2

Summervale NSW 19 O9
Sumner Qld 132 G5
Sunbury Vic. 42 B1, 46 H3, 48 B3, 57 P4
Sunday Creek Vic. 47 J1, 50 D12
Sunday Island Vic. 49 I10
Sundown NP Qld 15 K3, 137 K12
Sunny Cliffs Vic. 16 E6, 52 G6
Sunnybank Qld 133 I5, 134 F12, 135 D5
Sunnybank Hills Qld 133 I5
Sunnyside Tas. 162 H7
Sunnyside Vic. 51 M10
Sunshine Vic. 42 E7, 47 I5
Sunshine Beach Qld 134 H1, 137 N7
Sunshine North Vic. 42 E6
Sunshine West Vic. 42 D7
Surat Qld 136 G7
Surfers Paradise Qld 15 O1, 135 G10, 137 N10
Surges Bay Tas. 158 F9, 161 I9
Surrey Downs SA 68 G7
Surrey Hills Vic. 43 J8
Surry Hills NSW 5 E10, 7 L12, 9 L4
Surveyor Generals Corner WA 78 B2, 101 P8, 120 B11
Surveyors Bay Tas. 158 G10, 161 J9
Sussex Inlet NSW 13 I10, 20 G4
Sutherland NSW 8 H8, 9 I8, 11 K11
Sutherlands SA 73 K7, 82 D1
Sutton NSW 12 F10, 20 D4, 31 F3, 34 G1
Sutton Vic. 16 F11, 55 J4
Sutton Forest NSW 13 I9, 20 G3
Sutton Grange Vic. 50 A10, 55 O11, 57 O1
Swain Reefs NP Qld 139 O7
Swan Estuary Marine Park WA 93 C5, 96 B5, 98 C7
Swan Hill Vic. 16 G9, 53 L12, 55 L2
Swan Marsh Vic. 46 A9, 57 K8
Swan Reach SA 73 L8, 82 E2
Swan Reach Vic. 49 N5
Swan View WA 91 G2
Swanbank Qld 132 C6
Swanbourne WA 90 C10, 91 A5, 93 B5
Swanhaven NSW 13 I10, 20 G4
Swanpool Vic. 50 G9
Swanport SA 70 H11, 73 L10, 82 D4
Swansea NSW 13 L4
Swansea Tas. 161 N3, 163 N12
Swanwater West Vic. 55 J8
Swanwick Tas. 161 O3, 163 O12
Sweers Island Qld 140 A5, 143 D3
Swell Rocks WA 99 I9
Swifts Creek Vic. 49 N2
Sydenham NSW 9 L5
Sydenham Vic. 42 D4, 46 H4, 48 B4, 57 P5
Sydney NSW 5 D7, 7 M11, 9 M4, 11 L9, 13 K7
Sydney Harbour NP NSW 7 O10, 9 O2, 11 M8, 13 K7
Sylvania NSW 9 J7
Sylvania Waters NSW 9 J8
Sylvaterre Vic. 17 I12, 50 A5, 55 O6
Symonston ACT 34 F7

Taabinga Qld 137 L7
Tabacum Qld 141 L6

Tabbara Vic. 20 A12, 58 B11
Tabberabbera Vic. 49 L4
Tabbimoble NSW 15 N4
Tabbita NSW 17 M6
Tabilk Vic. 50 D9
Table Top NSW 12 A12, 17 O12, 51 L5
Tabor Vic. 56 F5
Tabourie Lake NSW 13 I11, 20 F5
Tabulam NSW 15 M3, 137 M12
Tacoma NSW 11 P1
Taggerty Vic. 47 N2, 48 F2, 50 F12
Tahara Vic. 56 E4
Tahara Bridge Vic. 56 D4
Taigum Qld 131 J8
Tailem Bend SA 73 L10, 82 D4
Taillefer Rocks Tas. 161 O4
Takone Tas. 162 E6
Talawa Tas. 163 M7
Talbingo NSW 12 D11, 20 A5
Talbot Vic. 55 L12, 57 L2
Taldra SA 16 B6, 52 B6, 73 O7, 82 G1
Talgai Qld 137 K10
Talgarno Vic. 12 B12, 17 O12, 51 L6
Talia SA 72 B4, 74 A12, 81 O12
Tallaganda NP NSW 12 G11, 20 D5, 31 H10, 58 G1
Tallageira Vic. 54 B10, 82 H9
Tallandoon Vic. 51 L8
Tallangatta Vic. 51 L7
Tallangatta East Vic. 51 M7
Tallangatta Valley Vic. 51 M7
Tallarook Vic. 50 D11
Tallebudgera Qld 135 G11
Tallebung NSW 12 A2, 17 O2
Tallimba NSW 12 B6, 17 O6
Tallong NSW 12 H9, 20 F3
Tallygaroopna Vic. 50 E6
Talmalmo NSW 12 B12, 17 P12, 51 N5
Talwood Qld 14 F1, 136 G10
Tamala Park WA 90 A3
Tamarama NSW 9 N5
Tamarang NSW 14 G10
Tambar Springs NSW 14 F10
Tambaroora NSW 12 G4
Tambellup WA 95 L6, 96 F9, 98 E10
Tambo Qld 136 B2, 147 P2
Tambo Crossing Vic. 49 N4
Tambo Upper Vic. 49 N5
Tamboon Vic. 20 C12, 58 E11
Tamborine Qld 133 I12, 135 E8, 137 N10
Tamborine NP Qld 15 O1, 135 E8, 137 N10
Tamboy NSW 13 N3
Taminick Vic. 50 H7
Tamleugh Vic. 50 F8
Tamleugh North Vic. 50 F8
Tamleugh West Vic. 50 F8
Tammin WA 96 F4, 98 D7
Tamrookum Qld 15 N1, 135 C10
Tamworth NSW 14 H9
Tanah Merah Qld 133 K9
Tandarook Vic. 57 J8
Tandarra Vic. 50 A7, 55 O8
Tangalooma Qld 135 G2, 137 N8
Tangambalanga Vic. 51 L7
Tangmangaroo NSW 12 F8, 20 C2
Tangorin Qld 138 B6, 145 N6
Tanja NSW 20 E9

Tanjil Bren Vic. 47 P6, 48 H5
Tanjil South Vic. 47 P8, 48 H6
Tankerton Vic. 47 K10, 48 D8
Tannum Sands Qld 137 L1, 139 N12
Tannymorel Qld 15 L1, 137 L11
Tansey Qld 137 L6
Tantanoola SA 82 F11
Tanunda SA 70 E4, 73 K8, 82 C2
Tanwood Vic. 55 K11, 57 K1
Tanybryn Vic. 46 B11, 57 L10
Taperoo SA 68 B8, 70 A7, 71 E1
Tapin Tops NP NSW 13 N1, 15 K11
Taplan SA 16 B7, 52 B7, 73 O8, 82 H2
Tapping WA 90 C3
Tara NT 121 I2
Tara Qld 137 I8
Taradale Vic. 50 A11, 55 O12, 57 O2
Tarago NSW 12 G10, 20 E4
Tarago Vic. 47 N8, 48 G6
Taralga NSW 12 H8, 20 E2
Tarampa Qld 134 B11
Tarana NSW 12 H5
Taranna Tas. 159 M8, 161 M8
Tarcoola SA 81 O4
Tarcoon NSW 19 O6
Tarcowie SA 73 J3, 75 I11
Tarcutta NSW 12 C10, 51 O2
Tardun WA 97 E12, 98 B3
Taree NSW 13 N1, 15 L12
Taren Point NSW 9 J8
Targa Tas. 163 L7
Taringa Qld 130 H12, 132 H2
Tarlee SA 70 D2, 73 J7, 82 C1
Tarlo NSW 12 H8, 20 E3
Tarlo River NP NSW 12 H8, 20 F2
Tarnagulla Vic. 55 M10
Tarndanya SA 67 E9
Tarneit Vic. 42 B7, 46 H6, 48 B4, 57 P6
Tarnma SA 82 C1
Tarnook Vic. 50 G8
Tarong NP Qld 137 L7
Taroom Qld 137 I4
Taroona Tas. 156 D11, 159 I6, 161 K7
Tarpeena SA 56 A3, 82 G11
Tarra–Bulga NP Vic. 49 I8
Tarragal Vic. 56 C7
Tarragindi Qld 133 I3
Tarraleah Tas. 160 H3
Tarranginnie Vic. 54 D7
Tarrango Vic. 16 D6, 52 E7
Tarranyurk Vic. 16 D12, 54 F6
Tarraville Vic. 49 I9
Tarrawingee Vic. 51 I7
Tarrayoukyan Vic. 54 D12, 56 D2
Tarrington Vic. 56 F4
Tarrion NSW 19 O5
Tarwin Vic. 47 N12, 48 G9
Tarwin Lower Vic. 48 F10
Tarwin Meadows Vic. 48 F10
Tarwonga WA 94 H2, 96 E7
Tascott NSW 11 N3
Tasman NP Tas. 159 L9, 161 M8
Tatachilla SA 69 A11
Tatham NSW 15 N4
Tathra NSW 20 E9
Tathra NP WA 98 B4
Tatong Vic. 50 H9
Tatura Vic. 50 E7
Tatyoon Vic. 57 I3

Taunton NP (Scientific) Qld 139 K11
Tawonga Vic. 51 L9
Tawonga South Vic. 51 L9
Tayene Tas. 163 L8
Taylor Rock WA 99 I9
Taylors Arm NSW 15 M9
Taylors Beach Qld 141 M10
Taylors Flat NSW 12 F7, 20 D1
Taylors Hill Vic. 42 C5
Taylors Lakes Vic. 42 D4, 47 I4, 57 P5
Taylorville SA 73 M7
Tea Gardens NSW 13 N3
Tea Tree Tas. 159 I3, 161 K6
Tea Tree Gully SA 68 G8, 70 C7, 71 G1
Teal Flat SA 73 L9, 82 D3
Tecoma Vic. 43 O11, 45 J1, 47 K6
Teddywaddy Vic. 16 G12, 55 K7
Teerk Roo Ra NP Qld 133 P4, 134 H12, 135 G5, 137 N9
Teesdale Vic. 46 D7, 57 M6
Telegraph Point NSW 15 M11
Telford Vic. 17 L12, 50 G6
Telita Tas. 163 N6
Telopea NSW 7 I9, 9 I1
Telopea Downs Vic. 16 B11, 54 C6, 82 H7
Temma Tas. 162 A6
Temora NSW 12 C7, 17 P7
Tempe NSW 9 K5, 11 L9
Templers SA 70 D4, 73 J8, 82 C1
Templestowe Vic. 43 K6, 47 J5, 48 D4
Templestowe Lower Vic. 43 J7
Templin Qld 135 A8
Tempy Vic. 16 E9, 52 H12, 54 H2
Ten Mile Vic. 47 P3, 48 H2
Tennant Creek NT 119 J9
Tennyson NSW 6 C1, 10 H3
Tennyson Qld 132 H4
Tennyson SA 68 A10, 69 A1
Tennyson Vic. 50 B6, 55 P7
Tennyson Point NSW 7 K10, 9 K2
Tenterden WA 95 K8, 96 F10
Tenterfield NSW 15 L4, 137 L12
Tepko SA 70 G9, 73 K9, 82 D3
Terang Vic. 57 I7
Teridgerie NSW 14 D8
Teringie SA 68 F11, 69 F1
Terip Terip Vic. 50 F10
Terka SA 73 I2, 74 H10
Termeil NSW 13 I11, 20 F5
Terowie NSW 12 D2
Terowie SA 73 K4, 75 I11
Terranora NSW 15 O2, 135 G12
Terrey Hills NSW 7 M6, 11 M6
Terrick Terrick Vic. 17 I12, 50 A5, 55 O6
Terrick Terrick NP Vic. 17 I12, 50 A5, 55 O6
Terrigal NSW 11 P3, 13 L5
Terry Hie Hie NSW 14 G5
Tesbury Vic. 57 J8
Teviotville Qld 135 A8
Tewantin Qld 134 G1, 137 N7
Tewkesbury Tas. 162 E6
Texas Qld 15 J3, 137 J12
Thallon Qld 14 E1, 136 F11
Thanes Creek Qld 15 K1
Thangool Qld 137 J2
Tharbogang NSW 17 M7
Thargomindah Qld 147 K8

Tharwa ACT 12 F11, 20 C5, 31 D7
The Arches Marine Sanctuary
    Vic. 57 I10
The Basin Vic. 43 N10, 47 K6,
    49 M4
The Brothers SA 72 C8
The Carbuncle Tas. 163 I6
The Cascade Vic. 51 M7
The Caves Qld 139 M10
The Channon NSW 15 O3
The Child Qld 139 N10
The Cove Vic. 56 H9
The Devils Wilderness NSW 6 A2
The Doughboys Tas. 162 A2
The Entrance NSW 11 P2, 13 L5
The Entrance North NSW 11 P2
The Friars Tas. 161 K11
The Gap NSW 12 B9, 17 P9
The Gap Qld 130 G10, 132 G1,
    134 E11, 135 D4, 145 L2
The Gap Vic. 46 H3, 48 B3, 57 P4
The Gardens NT 111 E7, 112 B7
The Gardens Tas. 163 P7
The Glen Tas. 163 K6
The Gulf NSW 15 J4
The Gums Qld 137 I8
The Gurdies Vic. 47 L10, 48 E8
The Heart Vic. 49 K7
The Highlands Vic. 46 F4, 48 A3,
    57 O4
The Hungry Mile NSW 5 C5
The Images Tas. 161 I11
The Lakes NP Vic. 49 M6
The Lanterns Tas. 159 N9, 161 M9
The Monument Qld 144 F5
The Narrows NSW 112 D6
The Nobbies Vic. 47 J11, 48 C8
The Nuggets Tas. 161 O3
The Oaks NSW 10 F11, 13 J7,
    20 G1
The Pages SA 71 C11, 73 I11,
    82 A5
The Palms NP Qld 137 L8
The Patch Vic. 43 P11, 45 K1, 47 L6
The Pines SA 72 G9
The Range SA 69 D11
The Ridgeway NSW 34 H7
The Risk NSW 15 N2, 137 M11
The Rock NSW 12 B10, 14 G4,
    17 O10, 51 L1
The Rocks NSW 5 E3, 7 M11, 9 M3
The Sisters Vic. 57 I7
The Skerries Vic. 20 D12, 58 F12
The Spectacles WA 91 D12, 92 D1
The Summit Qld 15 L2
The Vines WA 90 H3
The Watchers SA 72 B5, 81 O12
Thebarton SA 68 C11, 69 C1
Theodore ACT 34 D11
Theodore Qld 137 I3
Theresa Park NSW 10 G10
Thevenard SA 81 M8
Thirlmere NSW 10 F12, 13 J7,
    20 G2
Thirlmere Lakes NP NSW 13 I8,
    20 G2
Thirlstane Tas. 163 I6
Thistle Island SA 72 E9
Thologolong Vic. 12 B12, 17 P12,
    51 M5
Thomas Plains SA 73 I6
Thomastown Vic. 42 H4, 43 I4,
    47 J4, 48 C4
Thomson Vic. 46 F8, 49 I6

Thomson Bay WA 93 A6
Thoona Vic. 50 H7
Thora NSW 15 M8
Thornbury Vic. 42 H6, 43 I6
Thorneside Qld 133 L3, 134 G11,
    135 F5
Thorngate SA 67 D1, 68 D11,
    69 D1
Thornlands Qld 133 M5, 134 H12,
    135 F5
Thornleigh NSW 7 J6
Thornlie WA 90 H12, 91 F6
Thornton Vic. 47 N1, 48 F1, 50 F12
Thorpdale Vic. 47 P10, 48 H7
Thowgla Vic. 51 O7
Thowgla Upper Vic. 51 O8
Thredbo NSW 20 A8, 58 B4
Three Bridges Vic. 45 P1, 47 M6,
    48 F5
Three Hummock Island
    Tas. 162 B1
Three Hummocks NT 117 N5
Three Islands Group NP
    Qld 141 L2
Three Rocks Qld 139 L5
Three Springs WA 98 B4
Three Ways Roadhouse NT 119 J9
Thrushton NP Qld 136 D8
Thuddungra NSW 12 D7, 20 A1
Thulimbah Qld 15 L2
Thulloo NSW 12 A5, 17 O5
Thuringowa Qld 138 G1, 141 N11
Thurla Vic. 52 G6
Thursday (Waiben) Island
    Qld 142 C2
Ti-Tree NT 121 I4
Tia NSW 15 J10
Tiaro Qld 137 M5
Tiberias Tas. 161 K4
Tibooburra NSW 18 D2, 146 H11
Tichborne NSW 12 D4
Tickera SA 72 H6
Tidal River Vic. 48 H12
Tiega Vic. 16 E8, 52 G11
Tieri Qld 139 I9
Tilba Tilba NSW 20 E8
Tilligerry NP NSW 13 M4
Tilmouth Well Roadhouse
    NT 120 G5
Tilpa NSW 19 I7
Timallallie NP NSW 14 E8
Timbarra Vic. 49 O3
Timbarra NP NSW 15 L4, 137 L12
Timber Creek NT 116 D10, 118 D2
Timberoo Vic. 16 D9, 52 G11
Timberoo South Vic. 16 D9,
    52 G11, 54 G1
Timbillica NSW 20 D11, 58 G10
Timboon Vic. 57 I9
Timmering Vic. 50 C7
Timor Vic. 55 M11, 57 M1
Timor West Vic. 55 L11
Tin Can Bay Qld 137 N6
Tinaburra Qld 141 L7
Tinamba Vic. 49 J6
Tinaroo Falls Qld 141 L6
Tincurrin WA 96 F7
Tindal NT 116 G8
Tinderbox Tas. 159 I7, 161 K8
Tingalpa Qld 131 K12, 133 K2
Tingha NSW 15 I6
Tingoora Qld 137 L6
Tinkrameanah NP NSW 14 F10
Tinonee NSW 13 N1, 15 L12

Tintaldra Vic. 12 C12, 51 O6
Tintinara SA 73 M12, 82 E6
Tiona NSW 13 N2
Tiparra West SA 72 H7
Tipton Qld 137 K8
Tirranna Roadhouse Qld 143 D4
Titjikala NT 121 J8
Tittybong Vic. 55 K4
Tivendale NT 112 H8, 113 I8
Tivoli Qld 132 C5
Tiwi NT 112 D2
Tjoritja–West MacDonnell NP
    NT 120 H6, 121 I7
Tjukayirla Roadhouse
    WA 101 K10
Tobermorey NT 121 P4, 144 C6
Tocal Qld 138 A11, 145 M11
Tocumwal NSW 17 L11, 50 F4
Togari Tas. 162 B4
Toiberry Tas. 163 J9
Tolga Qld 141 L7
Tolmans Hill Tas. 156 C9
Tolmie Vic. 50 H10
Tom Groggin NSW 20 A8, 51 P9,
    58 A4
Tom Price WA 97 G3, 100 C5
Tomahawk Tas. 163 N5
Tomahawk Creek Vic. 46 A9, 57 K8
Tomaree NP NSW 13 N4
Tombong NSW 20 C9, 58 D7
Tomewin Qld 135 F12
Tomingley NSW 12 E2
Tongala Vic. 17 J12, 50 D6
Tonganah Tas. 163 M7
Tonghi Creek Vic. 20 C11, 58 D10
Tongio Vic. 49 N2, 51 N12
Tongio West Vic. 49 N2
Tonimbuk Vic. 45 P4, 47 M7, 48 F6
Tooan Vic. 54 E9
Toobanna Qld 141 M10
Toobeah Qld 14 G1, 136 H10
Tooborac Vic. 50 C10
Toodyay WA 93 F2, 96 D4, 98 C7
Toogong NSW 12 F4
Toogoolawah Qld 134 A7, 137 M8
Toogoom Qld 137 N4
Tookayerta SA 16 A6, 52 A7,
    73 N8, 82 G2
Toolamba Vic. 50 E8
Toolangi Vic. 47 L4, 48 E3
Toolern Vale Vic. 42 A1, 46 G4,
    48 B3, 57 P4
Tooleybuc Vic. 16 G8, 53 L11
Toolibin WA 96 F7
Tooligie SA 72 D6
Toolleen Vic. 50 B9, 55 P10
Toolondo Vic. 54 F11
Toolong Vic. 56 F8
Tooloom NSW 15 M2, 137 L11
Tooloom NP NSW 15 M2, 137 L11
Tooma NSW 12 D12, 20 A6, 51 P6,
    58 A1
Toombul Qld 134 F10, 135 E4
Toombullup Vic. 50 H10
Toompine Roadhouse Qld 147 L7
Toongabbie NSW 6 G8, 8 G1
Toongabbie Vic. 49 I6
Toongi NSW 12 F2
Toonumbar NSW 15 M2, 137 M11
Toonumbar NP NSW 15 M2,
    137 M11
Tooperang SA 71 G7
Toora Vic. 48 H9
Tooradin Vic. 45 I9, 47 K9, 48 E7

Toorak Vic. 42 H9, 43 I9
Toorak Gardens SA 68 E12, 69 E2
Toorale NP NSW 19 L6
Tooraweenah NSW 14 D10
Toorbul Qld 131 K1, 134 G7
Toorongo Vic. 47 P6, 48 H5
Tootool NSW 12 B10, 17 O10,
    51 L1
Toowong Qld 130 H12, 132 H2,
    134 F11, 135 D4
Toowoomba Qld 137 L9
Toowoon Bay NSW 11 P2
Top Rocks Tas. 160 D7
Top Springs NT 116 F12, 118 F3
Topaz Road NP Qld 141 L7
Torbanlea Qld 137 M4
Torndirrup NP WA 95 M11,
    96 G12, 98 E11
Toronto NSW 13 L4
Torquay Vic. 46 F9, 57 N8
Torrens ACT 34 C8
Torrens Creek Qld 138 D4, 145 P4
Torrens Island SA 70 B7, 71 E1,
    73 J8, 82 B2
Torrens Park SA 69 D3, 70 B9,
    71 F2
Torrensville SA 68 C11, 69 C1
Torrington NSW 15 K4
Torrita Vic. 16 D9, 52 F11
Torrumbarry Vic. 17 I12, 50 B5,
    55 P6
Tostaree Vic. 20 A12, 49 O5,
    58 A11
Tottenham NSW 12 C1, 17 P1,
    19 P12
Tottenham Vic. 42 E8
Tottington Vic. 55 J10
Toukley NSW 13 L5
Tourello Vic. 46 C1, 57 M3
Towallum NSW 15 M7
Towamba NSW 20 D10, 58 G8
Towaninny Vic. 16 G11, 55 L5
Towarri NP NSW 13 K1, 14 H12
Tower Hill Tas. 163 N9
Tower Hill Vic. 56 G8
Towitta SA 70 H5
Towlers Bay NSW 7 O5
Towong Vic. 20 A7, 51 O7, 58 A2
Towong Upper Vic. 20 A7, 51 P7,
    58 A2
Towrang NSW 12 H9, 20 E3
Tracy SA 73 K5, 75 J12
Trafalgar Vic. 47 P9, 48 G7
Tragowel Vic. 55 N5
Tralee NSW 34 E10
Trangie NSW 14 B11
Tranmere SA 68 F11, 69 F1
Tranmere Tas. 156 H10, 157 I10
Traralgon Vic. 49 I7
Traralgon South Vic. 49 I7
Travancore Vic. 42 G7
Trawalla Vic. 46 B2, 57 K3
Trawool Vic. 50 D11
Trayning WA 96 F2, 98 D6
Traynors Lagoon Vic. 55 J9
Trebonne Qld 141 M10
Tregear NSW 6 D6
Tregole NP Qld 136 D6
Tremont Vic. 43 N10, 45 I1
Trenah Tas. 163 M7
Trentham Vic. 46 F2, 48 A2,
    50 A12, 57 O3
Trentham Cliffs NSW 52 H6

Trentham East Vic. 46 F2
Tresco Vic. 16 H10, 55 M3
Tresco West Vic. 55 M3
Trevallyn NSW 13 L3
Trevallyn Tas. 163 K8
Trewalla Vic. 56 D8
Trewilga NSW 12 E3
Triabunna Tas. 159 N1, 161 M5
Trida NSW 17 K3
Trida Vic. 47 N10, 48 G7
Trigg WA 90 C7, 91 A3
Trinita Vic. 16 E8, 52 H10
Trinity Gardens SA 68 E11, 69 E1
Triunia NP Qld 134 F3, 137 N7
Trott Park SA 69 B6
Trowutta Tas. 162 C5
Truganina Vic. 42 B6, 46 H5, 48 B4,
    57 P6
Trundle NSW 12 D3
Trunkey NSW 12 G6
Truro SA 70 G3, 73 K7, 82 C1
Tuan Qld 137 N5
Tuart Forest NP WA 94 C5, 96 B9,
    98 B10
Tuart Hill WA 90 E8, 91 B3
Tubbut Vic. 20 B10, 58 C7
Tucabia NSW 15 N6
Tuchekoi NP Qld 134 F1, 137 N7
Tuckanarra WA 97 H9, 100 D11
Tucklan NSW 12 H1, 14 E12
Tuena NSW 12 G7, 20 D1
Tuerong Vic. 44 C11
Tuft Rock Qld 142 C1
Tuggerah NSW 11 P1, 13 L5
Tuggeranong ACT 12 F11, 20 C5,
    31 D6
Tuggerawong NSW 11 P1
Tugun Qld 135 G11
Tulendeena Tas. 163 M7
Tulkara Vic. 55 J11
Tullah Tas. 162 E9
Tullamarine Vic. 42 F4
Tullamore NSW 12 C2
Tullibigeal NSW 12 A4, 17 O4
Tulloh Vic. 46 B9, 57 L8
Tully Qld 141 M8
Tully Falls NP Qld 141 L8
Tully Gorge NP Qld 141 L8
Tully Heads Qld 141 M8
Tumbarumba NSW 12 D12, 20 A6,
    51 P5
Tumbi Umbi NSW 11 P2
Tumblong NSW 12 D10, 20 A4,
    51 P1
Tumbulgum NSW 15 O2, 135 G12,
    137 N11
Tumby Bay SA 72 E7
Tummaville Qld 137 K10
Tumorrama NSW 12 E10, 20 B4
Tumoulin Qld 141 L7
Tumut NSW 12 D10, 20 A4
Tunart Vic. 16 B6, 52 C7, 73 P8,
    82 H2
Tunbridge Tas. 161 L2, 163 L12
Tungamah Vic. 17 L12, 50 G6
Tungamull Qld 139 M11
Tungkillo SA 70 F8, 73 K9, 82 C3
Tunnack Tas. 161 L4
Tunnel Tas. 163 K6
Tunnel Creek NP WA 103 K7
Tura Beach NSW 20 E9
Turallin Qld 137 J9
Turill NSW 13 I1, 14 F12
Turkey Beach Qld 137 L1, 139 O12

Turlinjah NSW 20 F7
Turner ACT 33 D1, 34 E5
Turners Beach Tas. 162 G6
Turners Marsh Tas. 163 K7
Turon NP NSW 12 H4, 13 I4
Turondale NSW 12 H4
Tuross Head NSW 20 F7
Turramurra NSW 7 K7
Turrawan NSW 14 F7
Turrella NSW 9 K5
Turriff Vic. 16 E10, 54 H2
Turriff East Vic. 55 I2
Turriff West Vic. 54 H2
Turtle Group NP Qld 141 L1
Turtons Creek Vic. 47 P12, 48 H9
Tusmore SA 68 E12, 69 E2
Tutunup WA 94 C5
Tutye Vic. 16 C9, 52 D11, 54 D1, 73 P10
Tweed Heads NSW 15 O1, 135 G11, 137 N11
Twelve Apostles Marine NP Vic. 57 J10
Twelve Mile NSW 12 G2, 13 I10, 20 G4
Twin Rocks WA 99 I10
Two Mile Flat NSW 12 G2
Two Rocks WA 93 A2, 96 B4, 98 B7
Two Round Rocks No. 1 Qld 139 M8
Two Round Rocks No. 2 Qld 139 M8
Two Sisters WA 96 G11, 98 E11
Two Wells SA 68 B1, 70 B5, 73 M12, 82 B2
Tyaak Vic. 47 K1, 48 D1, 50 D12
Tyabb Vic. 44 E11, 47 J9, 48 D7
Tyagarah NSW 15 O3
Tyagong NSW 12 E6
Tyalgum NSW 15 O2
Tyenna Tas. 158 D3, 160 H6
Tyers Vic. 49 I7
Tyers Junction Vic. 48 H6
Tylden Vic. 46 G1, 48 A1, 50 A12, 57 O3
Tyndale NSW 15 N5
Tynong Vic. 45 O6, 47 M8, 48 E6
Tynong North Vic. 45 N4
Tyntynder Central Vic. 53 L12, 55 L1
Tyntynder South Vic. 53 L12, 55 L2
Tyrendarra Vic. 56 E7
Tyrendarra East Vic. 56 E7
Tyringham NSW 15 L7
Tyrrell Downs Vic. 16 F9, 53 J12, 55 J2

Uarbry NSW 12 H1, 14 F12
Ubobo Qld 137 K2
Ucolta SA 73 K3, 75 J11
Uki NSW 15 O2, 137 N11
Ulamambri NSW 14 E10
Ulan NSW 12 H2
Uleybury SA 68 G5
Ulidarra NP NSW 15 N7
Ulinda NSW 14 E10
Ulladulla NSW 13 I11, 20 G5
Ullina Vic. 46 D1, 57 M2
Ullswater Vic. 54 C10, 82 H9
Ulmarra NSW 15 N6
Ulong NSW 15 M7
Ulooloo SA 73 K4, 75 I12
Ultima Vic. 16 G10, 55 K3

Ultimo NSW 5 B9, 7 L12, 9 L4
Ulupna Vic. 17 K11, 50 E4
Uluru–Kata Tjuṯa NP NT 120 E10
Ulva WA 96 G3
Ulverstone Tas. 162 G6
Umbakumba NT 117 N7
Umina NSW 11 N4, 13 K6
Umina Beach NSW 7 P1
Undalya SA 73 J6
Undara Volcanic NP Qld 141 J9
Undera Vic. 50 E6
Undera North Vic. 50 E6
Underbool Vic. 16 D9, 52 F11, 54 F1
Underdale SA 68 C11, 69 C1
Underwood Qld 133 J6
Underwood Tas. 163 K7
Undullah Qld 132 D10
Ungarie NSW 12 B5, 17 O5
Ungarra SA 72 E7
Unley SA 67 E12, 68 D12, 69 D3
Unley Park SA 69 D3, 70 B9, 71 F2
Upper Natone Tas. 162 F6
Upper Beaconsfield Vic. 47 L7, 48 E5
Upper Bingara NSW 14 H6
Upper Blessington Tas. 163 M8
Upper Bowman NSW 13 M1, 15 J12
Upper Brookfield Qld 130 D11, 132 D1
Upper Bylong NSW 13 I2
Upper Caboolture Qld 130 G1
Upper Castra Tas. 162 G7
Upper Cedar Creek Qld 134 D10, 135 C3
Upper Colo NSW 10 H2, 13 J5
Upper Coomera Qld 135 F8
Upper Esk Tas. 163 M8
Upper Ferntree Gully Vic. 43 N11, 45 I1
Upper Gellibrand Vic. 46 B11, 57 L9
Upper Hermitage SA 68 H7
Upper Horton NSW 14 H6
Upper Kedron Qld 130 F10, 132 F1
Upper Laceys Creek Qld 134 D8, 135 B1
Upper Macdonald NSW 13 K5
Upper Mangrove NSW 11 M1
Upper Manilla NSW 14 H8
Upper Mount Gravatt Qld 133 J5
Upper Mount Hicks Tas. 162 E5
Upper Myall NSW 13 N2
Upper Plenty Vic. 47 J2, 48 D2
Upper Scamander Tas. 163 O8
Upper Stowport Tas. 162 F6
Upper Sturt SA 69 F4, 70 C10, 71 G3
Upper Swan WA 90 H3, 93 D4, 96 C4
Upper Woodstock Tas. 158 G7
Upper Yarraman Qld 137 L7
Upwey Vic. 43 N11, 45 I1, 47 K6
Uraidla SA 68 H12, 69 H3, 70 C9, 71 G2
Uralla NSW 15 J8
Urana NSW 17 M10, 51 I1
Urandangi Qld 121 P3, 144 C5
Urangeline East NSW 12 A10, 17 N10, 51 K2
Urania SA 72 H8
Uranno SA 72 D7

Uranquinty NSW 12 B10, 17 O10, 51 M1
Urbenville NSW 15 M2, 137 M11
Uriarra NSW 34 A2
Urrbrae SA 69 E3
Urunga NSW 15 M8
Uxbridge Tas. 158 F3, 161 I6

Vacy NSW 13 L3
Vale Park SA 68 E10, 69 E1
Valencia Creek Vic. 49 K5
Valla Beach NSW 15 M8
Valley Heights NSW 10 F6
Valley View SA 68 E9
Vancouver Rock WA 96 G12, 98 E11
Vanderlin Island NT 117 N10, 119 N2
Varley WA 98 F8
Varroville NSW 8 C6
Vasey Vic. 56 E2
Vasse WA 94 B6, 96 B9
Vaucluse NSW 7 N11, 9 N3
Vaughan Vic. 55 N12, 57 N2
Vectis Vic. 54 F9
Veitch SA 16 A7, 52 A8, 73 N8, 82 G2
Venman Bushland NP Qld 133 L7, 135 E6, 137 N9
Ventnor Vic. 47 J11, 48 D8
Venus Bay SA 72 B4, 81 O11
Venus Bay Vic. 48 F9
Veresdale Qld 135 C8
Vermont Vic. 43 L10
Vermont South Vic. 43 L10
Vernor Qld 130 A11, 132 A1
Verona Sands Tas. 158 H10, 161 J9
Verran SA 72 E6
Vervale Vic. 45 O8
Victor Harbor SA 71 F9, 73 J11, 82 B5
Victoria Park WA 89 H10, 90 F10, 91 D5
Victoria Point Qld 133 N5, 134 H12, 135 F6
Victoria River Roadhouse NT 116 E10, 118 E1
Victoria Valley Tas. 161 I3
Viewbank Vic. 43 J6
Villawood NSW 6 G11, 8 G3, 11 J9
Vincentia NSW 13 J10, 20 G4
Vineyard NSW 6 E3, 11 I5
Vinifera Vic. 53 L12, 55 L1
Violet Town Vic. 48 H4, 50 F8
Virginia NT 113 M11
Virginia Qld 131 J9, 134 F10, 135 E3, 137 L8
Virginia SA 68 C3, 70 B6, 82 B2
Vista SA 68 G9
Vite Vite Vic. 57 J5
Vite Vite North Vic. 57 J5
Viveash WA 90 H6, 91 F2
Vivonne Bay SA 72 G12
Voyager Point NSW 8 G5
Vulkathunha–Gammon Ranges NP SA 75 J3

W Tree Vic. 20 A10, 49 P3, 58 A9
Waaia Vic. 17 K12, 50 E5
Waarre Vic. 57 I9
Wacol Qld 132 F5, 134 E12, 135 C5
Wadbilliga NP NSW 20 D8, 58 G4
Waddamana Tas. 161 I2, 163 I12
Waddi NSW 17 M8

Waddikee SA 72 E4, 74 D12
Waeel WA 96 E4
Wagaman NT 112 E3
Wagant Vic. 16 E8, 52 H11
Wagerup WA 93 D12, 94 D1, 96 C7
Wagga Wagga NSW 12 B9, 17 P9, 51 M1
Wagin WA 95 J2, 96 F8, 98 D9
Wahgunyah Vic. 17 M12, 51 I5
Wahring Vic. 50 D9
Wahroonga NSW 7 K6
Waikerie SA 73 M7, 82 F1
Waikiki WA 92 B3, 93 B8, 96 B6
Wail Vic. 54 F8
Wairewa Vic. 20 A11, 49 O5, 58 A11
Waitara NSW 7 K6
Waitchie Vic. 16 F9, 53 K12, 55 K2
Waitpinga SA 71 E9, 73 J11, 82 B5
Wakeley NSW 6 F11, 8 F3
Wakerley Qld 133 K3
Wakool NSW 17 I10, 50 B2, 55 P3
Wal Wal Vic. 54 H10
Walbundrie NSW 12 A11, 17 N11, 51 K4
Walcha NSW 15 J9
Walcha Road NSW 15 J9
Walgett NSW 14 B5
Walgoolan WA 96 G3, 98 E6
Walhalla Vic. 49 I5
Walkamin Qld 141 L6
Walkaway WA 97 D12, 98 A3
Walker Flat SA 73 L9, 82 D2
Walkers Creek Qld 137 K7
Walkers Point Qld 137 M4
Walkers Rock SA 72 B5, 74 A12, 81 O12
Walkerston Qld 139 K5
Walkerville SA 68 E10, 69 E1
Walkerville Vic. 48 G10
Walkerville South Vic. 48 G10
Walkley Heights SA 68 E9
Walla Walla NSW 12 A11, 17 O11, 51 K4
Wallabadah NSW 14 H11
Wallabi Point NSW 13 O1
Wallabrook SA 54 A9, 82 G8
Wallace Vic. 46 E3, 57 N4
Wallace Island WA 93 A6
Wallace Rockhole NT 120 H7
Wallacedale Vic. 56 E5
Wallacia NSW 6 A10, 8 A2, 10 G8, 13 J7
Wallaloo Vic. 55 I9
Wallaloo East Vic. 55 J10
Wallan Vic. 47 J2, 48 C2
Wallangarra Qld 15 K3, 137 K12
Wallangra NSW 15 I4, 137 J12
Wallarah NP NSW 13 L5
Wallarobba NSW 13 M3
Wallaroo NSW 34 A1
Wallaroo Qld 139 K11
Wallaroo SA 72 H6
Wallaroo NP NSW 13 M3
Wallaville Qld 137 L3
Wallendbeen NSW 12 D8, 20 A2
Wallerawang NSW 10 A1, 13 I5
Walli NSW 12 F5
Wallinduc Vic. 46 B5, 57 K5
Wallingat NP NSW 13 N2
Wallington Vic. 46 G8, 48 A6, 57 O8
Walliston WA 91 H5

Walloon Qld 132 A5, 134 C12, 135 A5
Walloway SA 73 J2, 75 I10
Walls of Jerusalem NP Tas. 160 G1, 162 G11
Wallumbilla Qld 136 G6
Wallup Vic. 16 D12, 54 G7
Walmer NSW 12 F2
Walmer Vic. 55 N11, 57 N1
Walpa Vic. 49 M5
Walpeup Vic. 16 D9, 52 F11
Walpole WA 95 I12, 96 E12, 98 D11
Walpole–Nornalup Inlets Marine Park WA 96 E12, 98 D11
Walpole–Nornalup NP WA 94 H12, 95 I12, 96 E12, 98 D12
Walsall WA 94 C6
Walsh Qld 141 I5
Waltowa SA 73 L11, 82 D5
Walwa Vic. 12 C12, 17 P12, 51 O6
Walyunga NP WA 93 D3, 96 C4, 98 C7
Wamberal NSW 11 P3
Wambidgee NSW 12 D9, 20 A3
Wamboyne NSW 12 C5, 17 P5
Wamoon NSW 17 N7
Wampoony SA 16 A12, 82 G7
Wamuran Qld 130 F1, 134 E7, 137 N8
Wamuran Basin Qld 134 E7
Wanaaring NSW 19 I3, 147 L12
Wanalta Vic. 50 C8
Wanbi SA 73 N9, 82 F2
Wandangula NT 117 M11, 119 M2
Wandearah SA 73 I4, 74 H12
Wandearah West SA 73 I4, 74 G12
Wandella NSW 20 E8, 58 H4
Wandering WA 93 H9, 96 D6, 98 D8
Wandi WA 91 D11
Wandiligong Vic. 51 K10
Wandilo SA 56 A4, 82 G11
Wandin North Vic. 47 L5, 48 E4
Wando Bridge Vic. 56 D3, 82 H11
Wando Vale Vic. 56 D3, 82 H11
Wandoan Qld 137 I5
Wandong Vic. 47 J2, 48 C2, 50 C12
Wandoo NP WA 93 G5, 96 D5, 98 C7
Wandsworth NSW 15 J6
Wang Wauk NSW 13 N2
Wanganella NSW 17 J9
Wangara WA 90 D5, 93 B4
Wangarabell NSW 20 D11, 58 F10
Wangaratta Vic. 51 I7
Wangary SA 72 D8
Wangerrip Vic. 57 K10
Wangoom Vic. 56 H8
Wanguri NT 112 E2
Wanilla SA 72 D8
Wannanup WA 92 A12
Wanneroo WA 90 C3, 93 B4, 96 B4, 98 B7
Wanniassa ACT 34 C9
Wannon Vic. 56 H3
Wanora Qld 130 A11, 132 A1, 134 C11, 135 A4
Wantabadgery NSW 12 C9, 51 O1
Wantirna Vic. 43 L10
Wantirna South Vic. 43 L10
Wanwin Vic. 56 B6, 82 H12
Wapengo NSW 20 E9
Wappinguy NSW 13 J1, 14 G12

Warakurna WA 101 O7, 120 A9
Warakurna Roadhouse WA 101 O7, 120 A9
Waramanga ACT 34 C7
Warana Qld 134 H4
Waratah Tas. 162 E7
Waratah Bay Vic. 48 G10
Waratah North Vic. 48 G10
Warawarrup WA 94 D2, 96 C7
Warburton Vic. 47 M5, 48 F4
Warburton WA 101 M8
Warburton East Vic. 47 N5
Warburton Roadhouse WA 101 M8
Warby–Ovens NP Vic. 17 M12, 50 H7, 51 I6
Ward Belt SA 68 E1
Wardell NSW 15 O4, 137 N12
Wards River NSW 13 M2
Wareek Vic. 55 L11, 57 L1
Wareemba NSW 7 K11, 9 K3
Warialda NSW 14 H5
Warialda NP NSW 14 H5
Warialda Rail NSW 14 H5
Warkton NSW 14 E10
Warkworth NSW 13 K3
Warmga Qld 137 K8
Warmun WA 103 N6
Warmun–Turkey Creek Roadhouse WA 103 N6
Warnbro WA 92 B4
Warncoort Vic. 46 C9, 57 L8
Warne Vic. 16 F11, 55 K4
Warneet Vic. 44 H10, 45 I10, 47 K9, 48 D7
Warner Qld 130 H7, 134 E10, 135 D3
Warnertown SA 73 I4, 74 H11
Warooka SA 72 H9
Waroona WA 93 D11, 94 D1, 96 C7, 98 C9
Warra Qld 137 J7
Warra NP NSW 15 K6
Warra Yadin Vic. 55 J12, 57 J2
Warrabah NP NSW 15 I8
Warraber Qld 142 D1
Warracknabeal Vic. 16 E12, 54 H7
Warradale SA 69 B4, 70 B10, 71 E3, 82 B3
Warraderry NSW 12 E6
Warragamba NSW 10 F8, 13 J7, 20 H1
Warragul Vic. 47 N9, 48 G7
Warrah Creek NSW 14 H11
Warrak Vic. 55 J12, 57 J2
Warralakin WA 96 G2, 98 E6
Warrambine Vic. 46 C6, 57 M6
Warramboo SA 72 D4, 74 B11
Warrandyte Vic. 43 L6, 47 K5, 48 D4
Warrandyte South Vic. 43 M7
Warrane Tas. 156 G5
Warranwood Vic. 43 M7
Warrawee NSW 7 K7, 11 L7
Warrayure Vic. 56 G4
Warrego NT 119 I9
Warrell Creek NSW 15 M9
Warren NSW 14 A10
Warren Qld 139 M11
Warren NP WA 94 E9, 96 C11, 98 C11
Warrenbayne Vic. 50 G9
Warrenmang Vic. 55 K11, 57 K1
Warrentinna Tas. 163 M6

Warriewood NSW 7 O6
Warrill View Qld 135 A7, 137 M10
Warrimoo NSW 6 A6, 10 G6
Warringa Tas. 162 G7
Warrion Vic. 46 B8, 57 L7
Warrnambool Vic. 56 G8
Warro NP Qld 137 L2
Warrong Vic. 56 G7
Warrow SA 72 C7
Warrumbungle NP NSW 14 D9
Warruwi NT 116 H2
Wartook Vic. 54 G11
Warup WA 95 I3, 96 E8
Warwick Qld 15 L1, 137 L10
Warwick WA 90 D6, 91 A1
Warwick Farm NSW 6 F12, 8 F4, 11 J9
Washpool Qld 132 B11
Washpool SA 73 J4, 75 I12
Washpool NP NSW 15 L4
Wasleys SA 70 C4, 82 B1
Watagans NP NSW 13 L4
Watarrka NP NT 120 F8
Watchem Vic. 16 F12, 55 I6
Watchman SA 73 J6
Watchupga Vic. 16 F11, 55 I4
Waterfall NSW 8 G10, 11 J12, 13 K7
Waterfall Gully SA 69 F3, 70 C9, 71 F2, 72 H3, 74 G10
Waterford Qld 133 J9, 135 E6
Waterford Vic. 49 L3
Waterford WA 90 F11, 91 D6
Waterford Park Vic. 47 J2, 48 D1, 50 D12
Waterford West Qld 133 J9
Waterhouse Tas. 163 M5
Waterloo NSW 9 L5
Waterloo SA 73 K6
Waterloo Tas. 158 F9, 161 I9
Waterloo Vic. 46 A1, 57 K3
Waterloo WA 94 D3, 96 C8
Waterloo Corner SA 68 C6
Watermans Bay WA 90 C7, 91 A2
Watervale SA 73 J6
Waterview Heights NSW 15 M6
Waterways Vic. 44 E4
Watheroo WA 96 B1, 98 B5
Watheroo NP WA 96 B1, 98 B5
Watson ACT 34 F3
Watson SA 80 H3
Watsonia Vic. 43 J5
Watsonia North Vic. 43 J5
Watsons Bay NSW 7 N11, 9 N3
Watsons Creek NSW 15 I8
Watsons Creek Vic. 43 N4, 47 K4
Watsonville Qld 141 L7
Wattamondara NSW 12 E6
Wattle Flat NSW 12 H4, 17 P5, 20 F4
Wattle Glen Vic. 43 L4, 47 K4
Wattle Grove NSW 8 F5
Wattle Grove Tas. 158 F8, 161 J9
Wattle Grove WA 90 H10, 91 F5, 93 D5
Wattle Hill Tas. 159 L4, 161 L6
Wattle Hill Vic. 57 J10
Wattle Park SA 68 F12, 69 F2
Wattle Range SA 82 F10
Wattleup WA 91 C11, 93 C7
Waubra Vic. 46 B1, 57 L3
Wauchope NSW 15 L11
Wauchope NT 119 J11, 121 J1
Wauraltee SA 72 H8

Waurn Ponds Vic. 46 F8, 57 N8
Wave Hill NSW 19 N6
Wavell Heights Qld 131 I10
Waverley NSW 9 M5, 11 M9
Waverley Tas. 163 K8
Waverton NSW 7 L11, 9 L3
Wayatinah Tas. 160 H4
Waychinicup NP WA 95 N10, 96 H11, 98 E11
Waygara Vic. 49 P5, 58 A11
Wayville SA 67 C12, 68 D12, 69 D2
Webbs NSW 12 E1, 14 B12
Webbs Creek NSW 11 J1
Wedderburn NSW 8 C11, 10 H12
Wedderburn Vic. 55 L8
Wedderburn Junction Vic. 55 M8
Weddin Mountains NP NSW 12 D6
Wedge Island SA 72 F9
Wedge Rock NT 117 M6
Wedge Rocks Qld 142 G10
Wee Jasper NSW 12 E10, 20 B4, 31 A2
Wee Waa NSW 14 E6
Weeaproinah Vic. 46 A11
Weegena Tas. 162 H8
Weemelah NSW 14 E3, 136 G12
Weeragua Vic. 20 C11, 58 E9
Weerite Vic. 57 J7
Weetah Tas. 163 I8
Weetaliba NSW 14 E11
Weetangera ACT 34 C4
Weethalle NSW 12 A6, 17 N6
Weetulta SA 72 H7
Wehla Vic. 55 L9
Weipa Qld 142 B7
Weismantels NSW 13 M2
Weja NSW 12 B5, 17 O5
Welaregang NSW 12 C12, 51 O6, 58 A1
Weldborough Tas. 163 N7
Welford NP Qld 145 L12, 147 K2
Welland SA 68 C11, 69 C1
Wellard WA 92 E1
Wellingrove NSW 15 J5
Wellington NSW 12 F2
Wellington SA 73 L10, 82 D4
Wellington NP WA 94 E3, 96 C8, 98 C9
Wellington Park Tas. 156 A6
Wellington Point Qld 131 M12, 133 M2, 134 H11, 135 F5
Wellstead WA 95 P8, 96 H10, 98 F10
Welshmans Reef Vic. 55 N12, 57 N1
Welshpool Vic. 48 H10
Welshpool WA 90 G10, 91 E5, 93 C5
Wembley WA 90 D9, 91 B4
Wembley Downs WA 90 C8, 91 A3
Wemen Vic. 16 F8, 53 I9
Wendouree Vic. 46 C3
Wentworth NSW 16 D5, 52 F5
Wentworth Falls NSW 10 D5, 13 I6
Wentworthville NSW 6 G9, 8 G1, 11 J8
Wepowie SA 73 J3, 75 I10
Werakata NP NSW 13 L3
Wereboldera NSW 12 D10, 20 A5
Werneth Vic. 46 B6, 57 L6
Werombi NSW 10 F9, 13 J7, 20 G1
Werona Vic. 46 E1
Werrap Vic. 16 D11, 54 F5

Werribee Vic. 42 A9, 46 H6, 48 B5, 57 P6
Werribee South Vic. 42 B12, 46 H7, 48 B5, 57 P6
Werrikimbe NP NSW 15 K10
Werrimull Vic. 16 C6, 52 E7, 73 P8
Werrington NSW 6 B7
Werrington County NSW 6 C6
Werrington Downs NSW 6 B6
Werris Creek NSW 14 H10
Wesburn Vic. 47 M5
Wesley Vale Tas. 162 H6
West Beach SA 68 B12, 69 B3
West Burleigh Qld 135 G11
West Cape Howe NP WA 95 L12, 96 G12, 98 E11
West Croydon SA 68 C10, 69 C1
West End Qld 129 B11, 130 H12, 131 I12, 132 H2, 133 I2
West Footscray Vic. 42 F7
West Frankford Tas. 163 I7
West Hill NP Qld 139 K7
West Hindmarsh SA 68 C11, 69 C1
West Hobart Tas. 155 A6, 156 C7
West Hoxton NSW 6 D12, 8 D4
West Ipswich Qld 132 B5
West Island NT 116 N10, 117 N10, 119 N1
West Kentish Tas. 162 G7
West Lakes SA 68 B9, 69 A1
West Lakes Shore SA 68 A10
West Leederville WA 90 E9, 91 C4
West Melbourne Vic. 41 B3, 42 G8
West Molle (Daydream) Island Qld 139 K3
West Montagu Tas. 162 B3
West Moonah Tas. 156 B6
West Pennant Hills NSW 7 I7
West Perth WA 89 A5, 90 E9, 91 C4
West Pine Tas. 162 F6
West Pinjarra WA 92 E12
West Pymble NSW 7 K8, 9 K1
West Pyramid Tas. 160 E9
West Richmond SA 68 C12, 69 C2
West Ridgley Tas. 162 F6
West Rock WA 103 L2
West Ryde NSW 7 J9, 9 J1
West Scottsdale Tas. 163 L6
West Swan WA 90 H5, 91 E1
West Takone Tas. 162 E6
West Wyalong NSW 12 B6, 17 P6
Westbourne Park SA 69 D3
Westbury Tas. 163 J8
Westbury Vic. 47 P9, 48 H6
Westby Vic. 16 H10, 55 N4
Westdale NSW 14 H9
Westdale WA 93 G7, 96 D5, 98 C8
Western Creek Tas. 162 H9
Western Flat SA 54 A8, 82 G8
Western Junction Tas. 163 K9
Western Rocks SA 160 F11
Westerway Tas. 158 E2, 161 I6
Westfield WA 91 G8
Westlake Qld 132 F4
Westleigh NSW 7 J6
Westmar Qld 136 H9
Westmead NSW 6 H9, 8 H1
Westmeadows Vic. 42 F4
Westmere Vic. 57 I4
Westminster WA 90 D7, 91 C2
Weston ACT 34 C7
Weston NSW 13 L4
Westonia WA 96 H3, 98 E6

Westwood Qld 139 L11
Westwood Tas. 163 J8
Wetherill Park NSW 6 E10, 8 F1
Weymouth Tas. 163 K5
Whalan NSW 6 D7
Whale Rock WA 99 I9
Wharminda SA 72 E6
Wharparilla Vic. 17 J12, 50 B5, 55 P7
Wharparilla North Vic. 50 B5, 55 P6
Wheatsheaf Vic. 46 F1
Wheelers Hill Vic. 43 K11, 44 F1
Wheeo NSW 12 G8, 20 D2
Whicher NP WA 94 C6, 96 B9, 98 B10
Whim Creek WA 97 G1, 100 C2, 102 C12
Whiporie NSW 15 N5
Whirily Vic. 55 J5
Whitby WA 91 H12, 92 H1
White Beach Tas. 159 L8, 161 L9
White Cliffs NSW 18 F7
White Flat SA 72 D8
White Gum Valley WA 91 B8
White Hills Tas. 163 K8
White Mountains NP Qld 138 C3, 145 P3
White Patch Qld 131 L1
White Rock Qld 132 D7, 139 K3
White Rock (Albino Rock) Qld 141 N10
Whitefoord Tas. 161 L4
Whiteheads Creek Vic. 50 D10
Whiteman WA 90 F5, 91 D1, 93 C4
Whitemark Tas. 160 B10
Whitemore Tas. 163 J9
Whites Valley SA 69 A12
Whiteside Qld 130 G5
Whitewood Qld 138 A5, 145 M5
Whitfield Vic. 51 I9
Whitlands Vic. 51 I9
Whitsunday Group Qld 139 K3
Whitsunday Islands NP Qld 139 K3
Whittlesea Vic. 47 J3, 48 D3
Whitton NSW 17 M7
Whitwarta SA 73 J7
Whoorel Vic. 46 C9, 57 M8
Whorouly Vic. 51 J8
Whorouly East Vic. 51 J8
Whorouly South Vic. 51 J8
Whroo Vic. 50 D8
Whyalla SA 72 H3, 74 G11
Whyte Yarcowie SA 73 K4, 75 I11
Wialki WA 96 F1, 98 E5
Wiangaree NSW 15 N2, 137 M11
Wickepin WA 96 F6, 98 D8
Wickham NT 112 D12
Wickham WA 97 F1, 100 B2, 102 B12
Wickham NP Qld 133 K12, 135 E8, 137 N10
Wickliffe Vic. 56 H4
Widgiemooltha WA 98 H6
Widgiewa NSW 17 M9
Wietalaba NP Qld 137 K2
Wights Mountain Qld 130 E10
Wilberforce NSW 6 E1, 11 I4, 13 J6
Wilburville Tas. 161 J2, 163 J11
Wilby Vic. 17 M12, 50 H6
Wilcannia NSW 18 G9
Wild Cattle Island NP Qld 137 L1, 139 N12

Index **199**

Wild Horse Plains SA 73 I7, 82 B1
Wildwood Vic. 42 D1
Wiley Park NSW 9 I5, 11 K9
Wilga WA 94 F5, 96 D9
Wilgul Vic. 46 B6, 57 L6
Wilkawatt SA 73 N10, 82 F4
Wilkur Vic. 16 E11, 55 I6
Willa Vic. 16 E10, 54 G2
Willagee WA 90 D12, 91 B7
Willalooka SA 82 F7
Willandra NP NSW 17 K3
Willare Bridge Roadhouse WA 103 I7
Willaston SA 68 H1
Willatook Vic. 56 G7
Willaura Vic. 57 I3
Willawarrin NSW 15 L9
Willawong Qld 132 H5, 133 I6
Willbriggie NSW 17 M7
Willenabrina Vic. 16 D11, 54 G6
Willetton WA 90 F12, 91 D7
Willi Willi NP NSW 15 L10
William Bay NP WA 95 K11, 96 F12, 98 D11
William Creek SA 76 D10
Williams WA 94 H1, 96 E7, 98 D9
Williamsdale ACT 12 F11, 20 C5, 31 E8
Williamsford Tas. 162 D10
Williamstown SA 70 E6, 73 K8, 82 C2
Williamstown Vic. 42 E9, 47 I6, 48 C4
Williamstown North Vic. 42 E9
Willigulli WA 97 D12
Willina NSW 13 N2
Willmot NSW 6 D6
Willoughby NSW 7 L10, 9 M1
Willoughby East NSW 7 M9, 9 M1
Willow Grove Vic. 47 P8, 48 H6
Willow Tree NSW 14 H11
Willow Vale Qld 133 M12
Willowbank Qld 132 A6
Willowie SA 73 J2, 74 H10
Willowmavin Vic. 47 I1, 48 C1, 50 C12
Willowra NT 118 G12, 120 G2
Willows Qld 138 H11
Willows Gemfields Qld 138 H11
Willowvale Qld 15 L1
Willowvale Vic. 46 A5, 57 K5
Willung Vic. 49 J7
Willung South Vic. 49 J8
Willunga SA 69 B12, 70 B12, 71 E6, 73 J10, 82 B4
Wilmington SA 73 I2, 74 H10
Wilmot Tas. 162 G7
Wilora NT 121 I3
Wilpena SA 75 I6
Wilroy WA 97 E12, 98 B3
Wilson WA 90 G11, 91 E6
Wilsons Promontory Marine NP Vic. 48 H12
Wilsons Promontory Marine Park Vic. 48 G11, 49 I11
Wilsons Promontory Marine Reserve Vic. 48 H12
Wilsons Promontory NP Vic. 48 H11, 49 I11
Wilsons Valley NSW 58 C3
Wilston Qld 131 I11, 133 I1
Wilton NSW 13 J8, 20 H2
Wiltshire–Butler NP WA 94 C7, 96 B10, 98 B10

Wiltshire Junction Tas. 162 D4
Wiluna WA 100 F10
Wimba Vic. 46 B11, 57 K9
Winchelsea Vic. 46 D8, 57 M8
Windang NSW 13 J9, 20 H3
Windaroo Qld 133 K10
Windarra WA 99 I2, 101 I12
Windermere Tas. 163 J7
Windermere Vic. 46 C2
Windeyer NSW 12 H3
Windjana Gorge NP WA 103 K7
Windmill Roadhouse WA 96 B3, 98 B6
Windorah Qld 147 I3
Windowie NSW 12 D10, 20 A4, 51 P2
Windsor NSW 6 D2, 11 I5, 13 J6
Windsor Qld 131 I11, 133 I1
Windsor SA 73 J7, 82 B1
Windsor Vic. 42 H9
Windsor Downs NSW 6 D4
Windsor Gardens SA 68 E10
Windy Corner WA 101 K5
Windy Harbour WA 94 F11, 96 D11, 98 C11
Wingeel Vic. 46 C7, 57 M7
Wingello NSW 13 I9, 20 F3
Wingen NSW 13 K1, 14 H12
Wingfield SA 68 C9
Wingham NSW 13 N1, 15 K12
Winiam Vic. 16 C12, 54 E7
Winiam East Vic. 54 E7
Winjallok Vic. 55 K10
Winkie SA 52 A6, 73 N7
Winkleigh Tas. 163 J7
Winmalee NSW 6 A4, 10 G5
Winnaleah Tas. 163 N6
Winnambool Vic. 16 F8, 53 I10
Winnap Vic. 56 C5, 82 H12
Winnellie NT 112 D6, 114 D3
Winnindoo Vic. 49 J6
Winninowie SA 73 I2, 74 G10
Winnunga NSW 12 B5, 17 O5
Winslow Vic. 56 G7
Winston Hills NSW 6 G8, 8 H1
Winthrop WA 90 F12, 91 C7
Winton Qld 145 L7
Winton Vic. 50 H8
Winton North Vic. 50 H8
Winulta SA 73 I7, 82 A1
Wirha SA 16 A8, 73 N10, 82 G4
Wirlinga NSW 12 A12, 51 L6
Wirrabara SA 73 J3, 74 H11
Wirrega SA 16 A12, 54 A6, 82 G7
Wirrida SA 79 O12, 81 O1
Wirrimah NSW 12 E7, 20 B1
Wirrinya NSW 12 D5
Wirrulla SA 72 B1, 81 O9
Wiseleigh Vic. 49 N5
Wisemans Creek NSW 12 H6
Wisemans Ferry NSW 11 K2, 13 K5
Wishart NT 112 G7, 113 I8
Wishart Qld 133 J5
Wishbone WA 95 L2, 96 G7
Wistow SA 70 E11, 71 H4
Witchcliffe WA 94 B7, 96 B10
Withersfield Qld 138 H10
Witjira NP SA 76 C2, 79 P2, 121 L12
Wittenoom WA 97 G3, 100 D4
Wivenhoe Tas. 162 F5
Wivenhoe Pocket Qld 130 A9, 134 C10, 135 A4

Wodonga Vic. 12 A12, 17 N12, 51 K6
Wogyala NT 119 K8
Wokalup WA 94 D2, 96 C8
Woko NP NSW 13 M1, 15 J11
Wokurna SA 73 I5
Wolfe Creek Crater NP WA 103 N9
Wolffdene Qld 133 K11
Wollar NSW 13 I2
Wollemi NP NSW 10 G1, 11 I2, 13 J3
Wollert Vic. 42 H1, 43 I1, 47 J4, 48 C3
Wolli Creek NSW 9 K5
Wollombi NSW 13 K4
Wollomombi NSW 15 K8
Wollongbar NSW 15 O3, 137 N12
Wollongong NSW 13 J8, 20 H2
Wollstonecraft NSW 7 L10, 9 L2
Wollumbin NP NSW 15 O2, 137 N11
Wollun NSW 15 J9
Wolseley SA 16 B12, 54 B7, 82 G7
Wolumla NSW 20 E9, 58 H7
Womalilla Qld 136 E6
Wombat NSW 12 D8, 20 B2
Wombelano Vic. 54 D11
Wombeyan Caves NSW 12 H8, 20 F2
Womboota NSW 17 J11, 50 B4, 55 P5
Won Wron Vic. 49 I9
Wonboyn NSW 20 E11
Wonboyn Lake NSW 58 H9
Wondabyne NSW 7 N1
Wondai Qld 137 L6
Wondalga NSW 12 D10, 20 A5, 51 P3
Wondul Range NP Qld 137 J10
Wonga Qld 141 L5
Wonga Park Vic. 43 M6
Wongaling Beach Qld 141 M8
Wongan Hills WA 96 D2, 98 C6
Wongarbon NSW 12 F1, 14 C12
Wongi NP Qld 137 M5
Wongulla SA 73 L8, 82 D2
Wonthaggi Vic. 47 L12, 48 E9
Wonwondah East Vic. 54 G10
Wonwondah North Vic. 54 F10
Wonyip Vic. 48 H9
Woocoo NP Qld 137 M5
Wood Wood Vic. 16 G9, 53 L11, 55 L1
Woodanilling WA 95 J4, 96 F8, 98 D9
Woodbine NSW 8 C8
Woodbridge Tas. 158 H9, 161 J9
Woodbridge WA 90 H7, 91 F2
Woodburn NSW 15 O4
Woodbury Tas. 161 L3
Woodchester SA 70 E12, 73 K10, 82 C4
Woodcroft NSW 6 F7
Woodcroft SA 69 C7
Woodenbong NSW 15 M2, 137 M11
Woodend Qld 132 B5
Woodend Vic. 46 G2, 48 B2, 50 B12, 57 P3
Woodfield Vic. 50 G11
Woodford NSW 10 E6
Woodford Qld 134 E6, 137 M8
Woodford Vic. 56 G8
Woodforde SA 68 F11, 69 F1

Woodgate Qld 137 M4
Woodglen Vic. 49 L5
Woodhill Qld 135 C8
Woodhouse Rocks NT 117 N6
Woodhouselee NSW 12 G8, 20 E2
Woodlands WA 90 D8, 91 B3, 95 M9, 96 G11
Woodleigh Vic. 47 M10, 48 E8
Woodpark NSW 6 G10, 8 G2
Woodridge Qld 133 J6, 135 E6
Woodroffe NT 113 J10
Woods Point SA 73 L10, 82 D4
Woods Point Vic. 47 P4, 48 H3
Woods Reef NSW 14 H7
Woods Well SA 73 L12, 82 D6
Woodsdale Tas. 161 L5
Woodside SA 70 E9, 71 H2, 73 K9, 82 C3
Woodside Vic. 49 J9
Woodside Beach Vic. 49 J9
Woodstock NSW 12 F6
Woodstock Qld 138 G2, 141 N12
Woodstock Tas. 158 G7, 161 J8
Woodstock Vic. 43 I1, 47 J3, 48 C3
Woodvale Vic. 50 A8, 55 O9
Woodvale WA 90 C5
Woodville NSW 15 J5
Woodville SA 68 B10, 70 B8, 71 E1
Woodville Gardens SA 68 C10
Woodville North SA 68 C10
Woodville Park SA 68 C10
Woodville South SA 68 C10, 69 C1
Woodville West SA 68 B10
Woody Point Qld 131 K7, 134 G9, 135 E2
Wool Bay SA 72 H9
Wool Wool Vic. 46 A8, 57 K7
Woolamai Vic. 47 L11, 48 E8
Woolaning NT 114 C7, 116 D5
Woolbrook NSW 15 I9
Woolgoolga NSW 15 N7
Wooli NSW 15 N6
Woollahra NSW 7 M12, 9 M4
Woolloomooloo NSW 5 G7, 7 M12, 9 M4
Woolloongabba Qld 129 F12, 131 I12, 133 I2
Woolner NT 111 H4, 112 C6
Woolomin NSW 15 I10
Woolooga Qld 137 M6
Woolooma NP NSW 13 L1, 15 I12
Woolooman Qld 132 A12
Woolooware NSW 9 J9, 11 L11
Wooloowin Qld 131 I10, 133 I1
Woolshed Vic. 51 J7
Woolshed Flat SA 73 I2, 74 G9
Woolsthorpe Vic. 56 G7
Woolwich NSW 7 L11, 9 L3
Woomargama NSW 12 B12, 17 O12, 51 M5
Woomargama NP NSW 12 B12, 17 P12, 51 M5
Woombye Qld 134 F4
Woomelang Vic. 16 E10, 55 I4
Woomera SA 74 E5
Woondum NP Qld 137 N6
Woongoolba Qld 133 O9, 135 F7
Wooragee Vic. 51 J7
Woorak Vic. 16 C12, 54 E7
Woorak West Vic. 54 E6
Wooramel Roadhouse WA 97 C8
Woorarra Vic. 48 H9
Wooreen Vic. 47 O11, 48 G8
Woori Yallock Vic. 47 M5, 48 E4

Woorim Qld 131 M1, 134 H8, 135 F1
Woorinen Vic. 16 G9, 53 L12, 55 L2
Woorinen North Vic. 53 L12, 55 L1
Woornack Vic. 16 E9, 52 H11, 54 H1
Woorndoo Vic. 57 I5
Wooroloo WA 93 E4, 96 C4
Wooroolin Qld 137 L6
Wooroonook Vic. 16 G12, 55 K7
Wooroonooran NP Qld 141 L7
Woosang Vic. 16 G12, 55 L7
Wootong Vale Vic. 56 E3
Wootton NSW 13 N2
Woowoonga NP Qld 137 M4
Worimi NP NSW 13 M4
Woronora NSW 8 H8, 9 I7, 11 K11
Woronora Dam NSW 8 E11
Woronora Heights NSW 8 H8
Woroon NP Qld 137 L6
Worsley WA 94 E3
Wowan Qld 139 L12
Woy Woy NSW 7 O1, 11 N3, 13 K6
Wrattens NP Qld 134 B1, 137 M6
Wrattonbully SA 54 B11, 56 B1, 82 G10
Wrightley Vic. 50 H10
Wroxham Vic. 20 D11, 58 F9
Wubin WA 98 C5
Wudinna SA 72 D3, 74 B11
Wujal Wujal Qld 141 L4
Wuk Wuk Vic. 49 M5
Wulagi NT 112 E3
Wulgulmerang Vic. 20 A10, 49 P1, 51 P12, 58 A7
Wulkuraka Qld 132 B5
Wundowie WA 93 F3
Wunghnu Vic. 17 K12, 50 E6
Wungong WA 91 G10
Wunkar SA 73 N8, 82 F2
Wurankuwu NT 116 C3
Wurdiboluc Vic. 46 D9, 57 M8
Wuthara Island NP (CYPAL) Qld 142 E6
Wutul Qld 137 L8
Wutunugurra NT 119 K11
Wy Yung Vic. 49 M5
Wyalkatchem WA 96 E3, 98 D6
Wyalong NSW 12 B6, 17 P6
Wyan NSW 15 N4
Wyandra Qld 136 B7, 147 O7
Wyangala NSW 12 F6
Wybalenna Tas. 160 A10
Wybong NSW 13 J2
Wycarbah Qld 139 L11
Wycheproof Vic. 16 G12, 55 K6
Wychitella Vic. 16 G12, 55 L7
Wycliffe Well Roadhouse NT 119 J11, 121 J1
Wye River Vic. 46 C11, 57 M10
Wyee NSW 13 L5
Wyeebo Vic. 51 M7
Wyelangta Vic. 46 A11
Wyena Tas. 163 L6
Wyening WA 96 C3, 98 C6
Wylie Creek NSW 15 L2, 137 L11
Wymah NSW 12 B12, 51 M6
Wymlet Vic. 16 D8, 52 G10
Wynarka SA 73 L10, 82 E3
Wynbring SA 81 M4
Wyndham NSW 20 D10, 58 G7
Wyndham WA 103 N4
Wyndham Vale Vic. 42 A8
Wynn Vale SA 68 F8

Wynnum Qld 131 L11, 133 L1, 134 G11, 135 E4, 137 N9
Wynnum West Qld 131 L11, 133 L1
Wynyard NSW 5 D6
Wynyard Tas. 162 E5
Wyomi SA 82 E9
Wyoming NSW 11 O2, 13 N1, 15 K12
Wyong NSW 11 P1, 13 L5
Wyong Creek NSW 11 O1
Wyperfeld NP Vic. 16 C10, 52 E12, 54 E2, 73 P11, 82 H5
Wyrra NSW 12 B5, 17 P5
Wyrrabalong NP NSW 11 P3, 13 L5
Wyuna Vic. 17 K12, 50 D6

Yaamba Qld 139 M10
Yaapeet Vic. 16 D10, 54 F4
Yabba Vic. 51 L7
Yabba North Vic. 50 F6
Yabbra NP NSW 15 M2, 137 L11
Yabmana SA 72 F5
Yacka SA 73 J5, 74 H12
Yackandandah Vic. 51 K7
Yagoona NSW 6 H12, 7 I12, 8 H4, 9 I4
Yahl SA 56 A5, 82 G12
Yalangur Qld 137 L9
Yalata SA 81 I6
Yalata Roadhouse SA 81 I6
Yalboroo Qld 139 J5
Yalbraith NSW 12 H8, 20 E2
Yalgoo WA 97 F11, 98 C2
Yalgorup NP WA 93 B11, 94 C1, 96 B7, 98 C9
Yallakool NSW 17 I10, 50 B2, 55 P3
Yallambie Vic. 43 J6
Yallaroi NSW 14 H3, 137 I12
Yalleroi Qld 138 D11
Yallingup WA 94 A6, 96 B9, 98 B10
Yallourn North Vic. 48 H7
Yallunda Flat SA 72 D7
Yaloak Vale Vic. 46 F4, 57 N5

Yalwal NSW 13 I10, 20 G4
Yamala Qld 139 I11
Yamanto Qld 132 B6, 134 C12, 135 B6
Yamba NSW 15 O5
Yamba Roadhouse SA 16 B6, 52 B6, 73 O7, 82 G1
Yambacoona Tas. 161 O10
Yambuk Vic. 56 F8
Yambuna Vic. 50 D5
Yan Yean Vic. 43 K1, 47 J4, 48 D3
Yanac Vic. 16 C12, 54 D6
Yanac South Vic. 54 D6
Yanakie Vic. 48 G10
Yanchep WA 93 A2, 96 B4, 98 B7
Yanchep NP WA 93 B2, 96 B4, 98 B7
Yanco NSW 17 N8
Yandaran Qld 137 M3
Yanderra NSW 13 J8, 20 G2
Yandeyarra WA 97 G1, 100 D3
Yandina Qld 134 F3, 137 N7
Yando Vic. 16 H12, 55 M6
Yandoit Vic. 55 N12, 57 N2
Yanerbie Beach SA 72 A3, 81 N10
Yanga NP NSW 16 H6, 53 N7
Yangan Qld 15 L1, 137 L10
Yangebup WA 91 B9
Yaninee SA 72 C3, 74 B10, 81 P10
Yanipy Vic. 16 B12, 54 C7, 82 H7
Yankalilla SA 71 D7, 73 J10, 82 B4
Yannathan Vic. 45 N10
Yantabulla NSW 19 K3, 147 M12
Yantanabie SA 72 B2, 81 O9
Yanununbeyan NP NSW 12 G11, 20 D5, 31 G8
Yapeen Vic. 55 N12, 57 N1
Yaraka Qld 147 L2
Yarck Vic. 50 F11
Yaringa Marine NP Vic. 44 G10, 47 K9, 48 D7
Yarloop WA 93 D12, 94 D1, 96 C7
Yaroomba Qld 134 G3
Yarra NSW 12 G9, 20 E3
Yarra Creek Tas. 161 P12

Yarra Glen Vic. 43 P3, 47 L4, 48 E4
Yarra Junction Vic. 47 M5, 48 F4
Yarra Ranges NP Vic. 47 N4, 48 F4
Yarrabandai NSW 12 C3
Yarrabilba Qld 133 I11
Yarrabin NSW 12 G2
Yarraby Vic. 16 G9, 53 K11, 55 K1
Yarragin NP NSW 14 D8
Yarragon Vic. 47 O9, 48 G7
Yarrahapinni Wetlands NP NSW 15 M9
Yarralin NT 116 D12, 118 D3
Yarralumla ACT 33 A9, 34 D5
Yarram Vic. 49 I9
Yarraman NSW 14 G4
Yarraman Qld 137 L7
Yarrambat Vic. 43 K3, 48 D3
Yarramony WA 93 G1
Yarramundi NSW 6 A2
Yarrangobilly NSW 12 E11, 20 B5
Yarrangobilly Caves NSW 12 E12, 20 B6
Yarrara Vic. 16 C6, 52 D7, 73 P8
Yarraville Vic. 42 F8
Yarrawalla South Vic. 55 N7
Yarrawarrah NSW 8 H9, 11 J11
Yarrawonga NT 113 K9
Yarrawonga Vic. 17 M12, 50 H5
Yarriabini NP NSW 15 M9
Yarrobil NP NSW 12 G1, 14 E12
Yarrock Vic. 16 B12, 54 C7, 82 H7
Yarrow NSW 34 H10
Yarroweyah Vic. 17 L12, 50 F4
Yarrowitch NSW 15 K10
Yarrowyck NSW 15 J8
Yarto Vic. 16 E10, 54 G2
Yarwun Qld 137 K1, 139 N12
Yass NSW 12 F9, 20 C3
Yatala Qld 133 L10
Yatala Vale SA 68 H7
Yatchaw Vic. 56 F5
Yatina SA 73 J3, 75 I11
Yatpool Vic. 16 E6, 52 G7
Yattalunga NSW 11 O3
Yatte Yattah NSW 13 I11, 20 G5

Yaugher Vic. 46 B10
Yea Vic. 47 L1, 48 E1, 50 E12
Yealering WA 96 F6, 98 D8
Yearinan NSW 14 E9
Yearinga Vic. 54 C7, 82 H7
Yednia Qld 134 B4, 137 M7
Yeelanna SA 72 D7
Yeerip Vic. 50 H6
Yeerongpilly Qld 132 H4, 133 I3
Yelarbon Qld 15 I2, 137 J11
Yellangip Vic. 54 G6
Yellingbo Vic. 45 N1, 47 L6
Yellow Rock NSW 6 A4, 10 G6
Yellowdine WA 98 F6
Yelta SA 72 H6
Yelta Vic. 52 G5
Yelverton WA 94 B6
Yelverton NP WA 94 A6, 96 B9, 98 B10
Yenda NSW 17 M7
Yendon Vic. 46 D4, 57 M4
Yengo NP NSW 11 L1, 13 K4
Yennora NSW 8 G2, 11 J8
Yeo Yeo NSW 12 D8, 20 A2
Yeodene Vic. 46 B10, 57 L8
Yeoval NSW 12 F3
Yeppoon Qld 139 M10
Yerecoin WA 96 C2, 98 C6
Yering Vic. 43 P4, 47 L5, 48 E4
Yerong Creek NSW 12 B10, 17 O10, 51 L2
Yeronga Qld 132 H3, 133 I3
Yerranderie NSW 10 B11, 13 I7, 20 F1
Yerrinbool NSW 13 I8, 20 G2
Yetholme NSW 12 H5
Yetman NSW 15 I3, 137 J12
Yeungroon Vic. 55 K8
Yimbun Qld 134 A6
Yin Barun Vic. 50 G9
Yinkanie SA 16 A6, 73 N7, 82 F1
Yinnar Vic. 47 P10, 48 H8
Yirrkala NT 117 N4
Yokine WA 90 E8, 91 C3
Yolla Tas. 162 E5

Yongala SA 73 K3, 75 I11
Yoogali NSW 17 M7
Yoongarillup WA 94 C6, 96 B9
York WA 93 H4, 96 D4, 98 C7
York Plains Tas. 161 L3
Yorke Valley SA 72 H7
Yorketown SA 72 H9
Yornaning WA 96 E6
Yoting WA 96 F4, 98 D7
Youanmite Vic. 17 L12, 50 F6
Youarang Vic. 50 G6
Youndegin WA 96 E4, 98 D7
Young NSW 12 E7, 20 B1
Younghusband SA 73 L9, 82 D3
Yowah Qld 147 M8
Yowie Bay NSW 9 J9
Yowrie NSW 20 E8, 58 H4
Yuelamu NT 120 G4
Yuendumu NT 120 F4
Yugar Qld 130 F8, 134 E10, 135 C3
Yulara NT 120 E10
Yuleba Qld 136 H6
Yulecart Vic. 56 E4
Yumali SA 73 L11, 82 E5
Yuna WA 97 D12, 98 A3
Yunderup WA 93 C9
Yundi SA 71 F6
Yundool Vic. 50 G6
Yungaburra Qld 141 L7
Yungaburra NP Qld 141 L7
Yungera Vic. 16 G8, 53 K9
Yunta SA 73 L2, 75 K10
Yurayir NP NSW 15 N6
Yurgo SA 73 M10, 82 F4
Yuroke Vic. 42 F1, 47 I4
Yuulong Vic. 57 J10

Zanthus WA 99 J5
Zeehan Tas. 162 D10
Zeerust Vic. 50 E6
Zetland NSW 9 L5
Zillmere Qld 131 I9, 134 F10, 135 D3
Zuccoli NT 113 L11

PRODUCED AND PUBLISHED IN AUSTRALIA BY UNIVERSAL PUBLISHERS PTY LTD

Universal Publishers is a division of Hardie Grant Publishing Pty Ltd
ABN 83 000 087 132

HEAD OFFICE
Level 7, 45 Jones Street, Ultimo NSW 2007
www.ubd.com.au
For trade orders, please contact Penguin Random House
customer service
Ph 1800 338 836 Fax +61 3 8537 4497
Email: orders@unitedbookdistributors.com.au

VICTORIA
Hardie Grant Publishing
Building 1, 658 Church Street, Richmond VIC 3121
Private Bag 1600, South Yarra VIC 3141
Ph (03) 8520 6444 Fax (03) 8520 6422
www.hardiegrant.com.au

Eighth edition. This edition published by Universal Publishers Pty Ltd, 2016
Copyright © Explore Australia Publishing, 2016

ISBN 9780731930623

10 9 8 7 6 5 4 3 2 1

All rights reserved. Explore Australia Publishing Pty Ltd and Sensis Pty Ltd are the owners of the copyright subsisting in this publication. Without limiting the rights under copyright reserved below, no part of this publication may be reproduced, copied or transmitted, in any form or by any means (electronic, mechanical, microcopying, photocopying, recording, storage in a retrieval system or otherwise), without the prior written consent of Universal Publishers Pty Ltd and Sensis Pty Ltd. Universal Publishers Pty Ltd and Sensis Pty Ltd will vigorously pursue any breach of its copyright.

The maps in this publication incorporate data copyright © Commonwealth of Australia (Geoscience Australia), 2006. Geoscience Australia has not evaluated the data as altered and incorporated within this publication, and therefore gives no warranty regarding accuracy, completeness, currency or suitability for any particular purpose.

Copyright Imprint and currency – VAR Product and PSMA Data
"Copyright. Based on data provided under licence from PSMA Australia Limited (www.psma.com.au)".
Hydrography Data (May 2006)
Transport Data (May 2015)

Disclaimer While every care is taken to ensure the accuracy of the data within this product, the owners of the data (including the state, territory and Commonwealth governments of Australia) do not make any representations or warranties about its accuracy, reliability, completeness or suitability for any particular purpose and, to the extent permitted by law, the owners of the data disclaim all responsibility and all liability (including, without limitation, liability in negligence) for all expenses, losses, damages (including indirect or consequential damages) and costs which might be incurred as a result of the data being inaccurate or incomplete in any way and for any reason.

Maps contain Aboriginal Land data (2010), which is owned by and copyright of the relevant Queensland, Northern Territory, South Australia and Western Australia state government authorities. The authorities give no warranty in relation to the data (including accuracy, reliability, completeness or suitability) and accept no liability (including, without limitation, liability in negligence) for any loss, damage or costs (including consequential damage) relating to any use of the data.

The publisher would like to thank the following organisations for assistance with data and information: *New South Wales:* Office of Environment & Heritage, NSW National Parks and Wildlife Service; *Australian Capital Territory:* ACT Planning & Land Authority, Australian Government Department of the Environment; *Victoria:* Department of Environment, Land, Water & Planning; *South Australia:* Department of Environment, Water and Natural Resources; *Western Australia:* Department of Indigenous Affairs Western Australia, Department of Environment and Conservation, Aboriginal Lands Trust; *Queensland:* Department of Environment & Resource Management, Queensland Parks and Wildlife Services; *Northern Territory:* Department of Land Resource Management, Northern and Central land councils; *Tasmania:* Department of Primary Industries, Parks, Water and Environment.

Publisher's disclaimer The publisher cannot accept responsibility for any errors or omissions. The representation on the maps of any road or track is not necessarily evidence of public right of way or safe travelling conditions.

Publisher's note Every effort has been made to ensure that the information in this book is accurate at the time of going to press. The publisher welcomes information and suggestions for correction or improvement. Write to the Publications Manager, Explore Australia Publishing, Ground Floor, Building 1, 658 Church Street, Richmond, VIC 3121, Australia, or email info@exploreaustralia.net.au

Acknowledgements
This edition produced by Universal Publishers Pty Ltd and Explore Australia Publishing Pty Ltd
Publications Manager: Jenny McEwan
Cartographers: Bruce McGurty, Emily Maffei, Robyn Hinchliffe
Project Manager: Alison Proietto
Editor: Anna Collett
Design: Leonie Stott
Layout: Megan Ellis
Pre-press: Megan Ellis, Splitting Image
Printed by 1010 Printing International Ltd

Abbreviations

SATC	South Australia Tourism Commission
TA	Tourism Australia
TEQ	Tourism and Events Queensland
TNT	Tourism NT
TT	Tourism Tasmania
TV	Tourism Victoria
TWA	Tourism Western Australia

Photography credits
Front cover The Great Ocean Road, Victoria (Australian Scenics/Getty Images)

Title page Karlu Karlu (Devils Marbles), Red Centre, Northern Territory (© YAY Media AS/Alamy Stock Photo)

Contents Yacca Lookout, Willow Springs Station, Flinders Ranges, South Australia (SATC)

Pages iv–v Peter Lik/TEQ; vi TWA; viii Andrew Smith/TA; xviii–1 courtesy Destination New South Wales; 2 Don Fuchs/courtesy Destination New South Wales; 4 Hamilton Lund/ courtesy Destination New South Wales; 30 & 32 © VisitCanberra; 35 Hamilton Lund/TA; 36–37 Mike Dunn/TV; 38 & 40 TV; 64, 66 & 83 SATC; 86 & 88 TWA; 108 & 110 TNT; 124–125 Darren Jew/TEQ; 126 Petet Lik/TEQ; 128 Paul Ewart/TEQ; 152, 154 & 168 TA; 169 SATC

Back cover (clockwise from main image) The Pentecost River and Cockburn Ranges, Kimberley, Western Australia (© Radius Images/Alamy Stock Photo); Cape Bruny Lighthouse (Rob Burnett/TT); Spotted-tail quoll (Rob Burnett/TT); Inverawe Native Gardens (Bill Chestnut/TT)

 This motoring atlas can be recycled through your normal council or workplace paper recycling service. If this publication has a plastic sleeve, simply remove before recycling.
For more information on recycling in your area, visit **www.RecyclingNearYou.com.au** or call your local council.